5—

8/23

Professional Cameraman's Handbook

Fourth Edition

Sylvia Carlson
Verne Carlson

Foreword by

David L. Quaid, ASC

FOCAL PRESS
An Imprint of Elsevier
Boston   London

Focal Press is an imprint of Elsevier

Permissions may be sought directly from Elsevier's Science and Technology Rights Department in Oxford, UK. Phone (44) 1865 843830, Fax: (44) 1865 853333, e-mail: permissions@elsevier.co.uk. You may also complete your request on-line via the Elsevier homepage: http://www.elsevier.com by selecting "Customer Support" and then "Obtaining Permissions".

Recognizing the importance of preserving what has been written, it is the policy of Elsevier to have the books it publishes printed on acid-free paper, and we exert our best efforts to that end.

Library of Congress Cataloging-in-Publication Data

Carlson, Sylvia.
    Professional cameraman's handbook / by Sylvia Carlson and Verne Carlson.
— 4th ed.
        p.   cm.
    Verne Carlson's name appears first on the earlier edition.
    ISBN-13: 978-0-240-80080-6   ISBN-10: 0-240-80080-X
    1. Cinematography—Handbooks, manuals, etc.   I. Carlson, Verne.   II.
Title.
TR850.C37   1993
778.5'3—dc20
                                                                    93-31799
                                                                    CIP

ISBN-13: 978-0-240-80080-6

British Library Cataloguing-in-Publication Data
A catalogue record for this book is available from the British Library.

For information, please contact:
Manager of Special Sales
Butterworth–Heinemann
225 Wildwood Avenue
Woburn, MA 01801–2041
Tel: 781-904-2500
Fax: 781-904-2620

Transferred to Digital Printing 2011

Contents

Foreword to the Fourth Edition

A special note to industry newcomers—students who have taken "The Art of Film," introductory cinema courses.

The following "Foreword to the Third Edition" was, with few changes, written 20 years ago. It opened Carlson's *Green Book* (second edition) and was later adapted for the *Red Book* (third edition), as the editions are fondly referred to by the industry. Sylvia Carlson now has asked me to write the foreword to her *Blue Book,* which, like its predecessors, is designed to help the professional and student cinematographer to function efficiently and survive in the sometime art form and sometime trade—the film business in the 1990s.

I believe that the original foreword largely still stands and reflects the daily problems that beset the Director of Photography and the Camera Assistant; however, one phase of the business that is not stressed is the *business* of the business. Although I haven't conducted a serious study, I don't know of any specific college courses that deal with this reality. All communication courses emphasize the art of film, which they should, to a degree. Unfortunately, students are rarely told that if they can't successfully handle the money, as well as the aesthetics, no one will let them play artist.

The obvious point is that books such as the *Professional Cameraman's Handbook* can help every member of the crew to better understand equipment and technique, and ultimately to achieve top efficiency.

A great production manager, George Justin, when faced with a shooting delay on his set, would loudly remind his company, "Tick, tock, nothing's moving but the clock!"

Thus, the Director of Photography is a money manager, who with the assistance of the crew, must deliver daily a product that is aesthetically exciting, technically exact, and *on budget.*

And—oh, yes—he or she must, in each expensive minute of every working day, contribute to the art of the film.

David L. Quaid, ASC

Foreword to the Third Edition

Ultracam, Arri 535, Panavision Platinum, Aaton-XTR, Arri 35-BL III, Arri 16SR, Panaflex, Crystalok, J-5 Zoom Control, XR 35, Steadicam. These outer-space names identify a sampling of the incredible array of exquisitely designed professional cameras and accessories developed by many companies for the filmmaker of the 1990s and even of the next century.

After a hiatus of some 25 years during which no really remarkable innovations took place, giants such as Arnold & Richter, Ed Di Guilio, Frank Leonetti, Robert Gottschalk, Anton Bauer, and Garrett Brown—to mention only a few—embarked on an engineering spree that finally provided modern tools for the Cinematographer. The game has not been the same since. New camera systems proliferate yearly. Each system has its adherents, and all filmmakers benefit from the engineering competition among the camera manufacturers. The modern camera will deliver the same photographic quality and will be as quiet as the venerable Mitchell BNC, but here the similarity ends. Today's professional motion picture camera is extremely light in weight, instantly portable, and infinitely sophisticated; this equipment—combined with the new films, the Ultra Superspeed lenses, and advanced lab techniques—enables the filmmaker to get on film almost anything the eyes can see . . . in color. The camera is no longer a passive observer—it has increasingly become a part of the action. Many Directors now use the camera as a lecturer would use a pointer, with the zoom lens continuously expanding or contracting the frame in order to underline or highlight an important action or to place emphasis on a key prop. The daily use of the total range of lenses from the "fisheye," through the normal complement of lenses (18mm–152mm), to giants of the 600mm, 1000mm, 2000mm magnitude is taken for granted. Lenses serve a greater purpose now than just recording action. The Director and Cinematographer choose a lens with a perspective that will permit the set or environmental elements to dominate the action; conversely, a lens with the opposite perspective is selected to permit the action to dominate the set elements or background. The flattening effect of the longer focal-length lenses and their attendant limited depth of field, combined with present-day zone-focusing techniques, has made it possible for the Director to shift dominance from element to element, from person to person, from foreground to background in one continuous take, through shifting focus from plane to plane as the action develops.

Today's Camera Assistant is expected to flawlessly perform the focus pulls while smoothly altering the focal length of the zoom lens, on take after take, setup after setup, as the day's work progresses. In a more perfect world, the Assistant would not be rushed by the production staff because a resultant inadvertent but invisible error could be disastrous. The Assistant must be aware that too much time spent at reloading, at doing paperwork, or at any one of the hundreds of separate functions performed daily, will hold up the progress of the entire company. It is the responsibility of the professional to develop a high degree of efficiency and briskness of manner, to avoid unnecessary delay.

Most errors "on the set" are visible almost immediately—when committed by crew members other than the Camera Assistant. For example, if an Electrician forgets to illuminate a "kicker" light, it is visible when the subject moves into position; if a Grip pushes the camera dolly at the wrong speed, the error is immediately visible; a Sound Mixer can "play back" the takes immediately. No real harm is done by any of these people. However, when the Assistant does not function properly, the result of his or her mistake is invisible . . . until the film is projected onto the screen.

Many Producers and Assistant Directors forget that the Assistant is the only person on the set who can "kill" the job. If magazines are loaded improperly, the job is dead. If follow-focus moves are bad, the job is dead. If out-of-focus shots aren't discovered until the screening room, the *Operator* is the one who gets fired. If the bookkeeping of camera reports or instructions to the lab are in error, a reshoot will probably have to be scheduled.

The Director of Photography is responsible for the photographic integrity of the film. The Camera Assistant and the Operator are responsible to the Director of Photography and for the proper care and maintenance of the equipment on the set. The camera must never be left unattended—for any reason. In the absence of the Camera Assistant, the Dolly Grip, or some other responsible person, must have the camera under constant observation so that if the camera is hit by a moving set piece or tampered with by some unauthorized person, measures can be taken to correct any problem.

Contemporary cinematography not only demands a much broader knowledge and greater skill from the Director and Cinematographer, but it also places an incredible burden on the Camera Assistant. He or she not only must be thoroughly familiar with the camera and the standard complement of lenses, but also must be an expert with a fantastic array of specialized equipment now in daily use and must know the many complicated procedures so important to his or her work.

Because more and more equipment is arriving on the market each year, it has become increasingly important for the working technician to keep abreast of the proper application, maintenance, adjustment, and field repair of the myriad of equipment used on even the most modest film project.

The overworked, harassed Camera Assistant, in-plant, or Documentary Cameraperson finally has, in the *Professional Cameraman's Handbook*, a "bible" in which can be found guidance in the distillate of Verne Carlson's professional experience as a Hollywood Assistant Cameraman, Camera Operator, and Director of Photography.

One of the union camera locals requires a test for the admission of Camera Assistant to membership. The candidate can be tested on his or her knowledge of many modern cameras and many of the standard "oldies" that are still in use worldwide. I cannot imagine how a candidate could attempt to take this examination without this manual.

In this volume, the Carlsons cover all phases of the Cinematographer's responsibility, from loading-room procedures to the most up-to-date information on the most advanced equipment and techniques.

For me, a working Director of Photography whose assignments are global, the specter of a lost or damaged camera is no longer as terrifying a prospect as it was in the past. In the event of such a problem, and after locating whatever equipment is available locally, with just a quick perusal of the *Professional Cameraman's Handbook* for proper loading and operating procedures for the particular and possibly peculiar camera, life and the job can go forward.

A most vitally needed book; I will never be without a copy in my meter case.

David L. Quaid, ASC

Preface

This book is for on-the-job use as a practical, how-to guide for assembling, threading, and troubleshooting the equipment involved. The range of material includes 35mm cameras and accessories, 16mm cameras and accessories, and procedural information to aid the user of motion picture equipment.

The material is designed to be valuable to both the professional and the student, to be consulted on the job for immediate assistance, and to be studied when more time is available.

It is not our intention to favor or "sell" any item mentioned. As with previous editions, hand-held cameras with less than a 400-ft capacity are not included. Many new cameras and accessories are covered, however. Furthermore, included in this edition are several items that might not normally have been included but which may be helpful to you, the readers.

In a greater sense, this is *your* book, professionals and prospective professionals who work day in and day out to create motion pictures. The comments and kind words we've heard from so many of you out there have been most gratifying! We especially appreciate the input we have received from our readers "in the trenches," describing their shortcuts, refined procedures, and time-savers. Obviously, procedures vary from country to country, coast to coast, and even production to production, but this book needs to represent the closest things we have to "standards."

As it has over the past 23 years, the *Professional Cameraman's Handbook* will continue to evolve, and that will include updates and the correction of any errors that may have crept in. We'll make appropriate changes as they are needed.

In the years since this book was originally conceived and written, times have—to say the least—changed. A change we welcome is the one that has brought increasing numbers of women into our industry. Bravo to the women and thanks to the men who have assisted in this process.

We have worked for gender-inclusiveness where possible, by using gender-neutral terms. In addition, when appropriate, we have used the more inclusive "camera professional" instead of the once-universal "cameraman." Please know that pronouns of either gender are inclusive and that no terms used are meant to be discriminatory in any way.

In the course of our years in the film industry, Verne and I have had the good fortune to work and talk with many talented camera professionals who generously shared their knowledge and expertise with us. We believe that the way to repay and thank them is to pass along that "hand-up" by sharing *our* experiences as well.

Thank you, and good shooting!

Sylvia Carlson

Acknowledgments

Many people have influenced and helped the authors over the years. Some are no longer with us, others have drifted away or retired from the industry, while a few are so busy filming we never see them anymore. To mention them individually would be a book in itself. Those who have contributed their time, expertise, and assistance in verifying and checking the technical data for this edition are: Pierre Michoud, AATON; Bill Herndon, Paul Bourque, *Agfa-Gevaert;* Volker Bahnemann, Bill Russell, Steve Chamberlain, *Arriflex Corporation;* Audrey Stern, *Birns and Sawyer;* Ed DeGuilio, David Bray, Chuck Jackson, *Cinema Products;* Denny Clairmont, Alan Albert, *Clairmont Camera;* Frank Reinking, Don Adams, *Eastman Kodak Co.;* Ken Kishimoto, Masaru (Mac) Jibiki, *Fuji Photo Film Ltd.;* Grant Loucks, Mike Kelly, *Alan Gordon Enterprises, Inc.;* Susan Lewis, *Lewis Communications;* Cary Clayton, *O'Connor Engineering, Inc.;* Tak Miyagishima, Dan Hammond, David Elkins, *Panavision, Inc.:* Erik Falkenberg, Florian Granderath, *Sachtler A.G.;* Frank Leonetti, Robin Lloyd-Davies, *Ultracam Camera Co.;* Carl Porcello, Richard Porcello, *Ultravision;* Marvin Stern, Steve Hubbert, Brian Putansu, and Mihail Sarbu.

A continuing note of thanks to the following people for their extensive assistance in this edition and prior editions of the book: Dr. Robert Richter, Victor James, Abbott Sydney, Peter Waldek, Kenji Saotome, John Jurgens, Jim Johnson, Albert Weber, Robert Gottschalk, Chadwell O'Connor, Eric Falkenberg, Mark Armistead, Alex Wengert, Shane Kelly, Robert Kaplan, Jack Goetz, Steve Safford, Ralph Westfall, Ray Grant, Stanley Clay, Dick Barlow, William Edwards, Maurice Schoenfeld, Ken Allen, Leo Diner, James B. Drought, Gerald Slick, Craig Haagensen, David Morenz, John Fante, and Rexford Metz, A.S.C.

Our special gratitude goes to two editors who never lost faith in the project, Phil Sutherland and Sharon Falter.

Manufacturers and United States Agents of Cameras and Related Equipment

Cameras and Support Gear:

AATON
2, Rue de la Paix
38001 Grenoble, France

AATON USA
4110 W. Magnolia Blvd.
Burbank, CA 91505

Arnold & Richter Cine Technik
Türkenstrasse 89
8000 München 40
Germany

Arriflex Corporation (USA East)
500 Route 303
Blauvelt, NY 10913

**Arriflex Corporation
   (USA West)**
600 No. Victory Blvd.
Burbank, CA 91502

Cinema Products
321 S. La Cienega Blvd.
Los Angeles, CA 90016

Eclair International
14, Rue Gaillon
75002 Paris, France

**Mitchell Camera Corp./Flight
   Research**
5210 Charles City Rd.
Richmond, VA 23231

**Moviecam F.G. Bauer Filmtechnik
   GmbH**
Auhofstrasse 254
A-1130 Vienna, Austria

O'Connor Engineering
100 Kalmus Dr.
Costa Mesa, CA 92626

Panavision (35mm)
18618 Oxnard St.
Tarzana, CA 91356

Panavision (16mm)
6799 Hawthorn Ave.
Hollywood, CA 90028

**Sachtler AG
   Kommunikationstechnik**
Gutenberstrasse 5
D-8044 Unterschleissheim bei München
Germany

Sachtler America (USA East)
55 No. Main St.
Freeport, NY 11520

Sachtler America (USA West)
3316 West Victory Blvd.
Burbank, CA 91505

Ultracam
5609 Sunset Blvd.
Hollywood, CA 90028

Film:

NOTE: Only corporate headquarters are listed. Agencies are international and too numerous to include here. Listings are available from the manufacturers.

AGFA-Gevaert, Ltd.
Seteststraat 27
Mortsel-Antwerpen 2640
Belgium

Eastman Kodak, Inc.
343 State St.
Rochester, NY 14650

Fuji Photo Film Company, Ltd.
26-30 Nishiazabu
2-Chome, Minato-ku
Tokyo 106, Japan

Lenses:

Angenieux (Ets Pierre)
St. Heand
Loire 4257, France

Canon, Ltd
7-1 Nishi-Shinjuku
2-Chome
Tokyo 163, Japan

Century Precision Optics
10713 Burbank Blvd.
No. Hollywood, CA 91601

Paillard, S.A.
(Kern Optical Products)
1450 Ste. Croix
V.D., Switzerland

Panavision
18618 Oxnard St.
Tarzana, CA 91356

Rank Taylor Hobson, Ltd
(Cooke)
2 New Star Rd.
Leicester, LE4 7JQ, England

Josef Schneider Optische Werk
Ringstrasse 132
Bad-Kreuznach
Reinhold-Pfalz 6500
Germany

Carl Zeiss GmbH
Tatzendpromenade 1
Jena, Bad-Wuert 6900
Germany

xiv

How to Use This Book

This book is divided into two sections. The first section covers functions, methods, and procedures important to the working Camera Professional. The second section covers 40 widely used production cameras and related equipment.

In the first section, each chapter is titled by general category; a numbered heading within the chapter refers to a certain aspect of the category. A numbered subheading with a letter added emphasizes a detail within the heading. Further particulars within the subheading are *italicized*. For example:

Category:	Chapter 6: On-the-Job Procedures
Heading:	**6.1 PRIOR TO SHOOTING**
Subheading:	**6.1a Preshooting Inventory**
	6.1b Setting Up
	6.1c Film Scratch Test
	6.1d "Hair Check"

In the second section, chapters are titled by camera manufacturer. A numbered heading within the chapter refers to a particular camera *model* fabricated by that manufacturer. A numbered subheading with a letter added emphasizes a *component* of that camera model. Further particulars of parts that comprise the components are *italicized* within the text. For example:

Manufacturer:	Chapter 14: Mitchell Cameras, Magazines, Blimps, and Accessories
Heading:	**14.1 MITCHELL 35mm STANDARD/HIGH-SPEED CAMERA**
Subheading:	**14.1a Base**
	14.1b Rackover
	14.1c Focusing tube
	14.1d Motors
	Eyepiece

Throughout the text, WARNINGS, CAUTIONS, and NOTES following the explanatory body provide safeguards relating to the preceding subject.

In using this handbook, it must be remembered that all mechanical instructions are given from the Operator's point of view—as he or she stands in back of the camera in the "shooting position." Therefore, some parts and components on cameras (especially turrets) might seem to be found in a position opposite from the written instruction in the text. For example:

Turret Release. At lower right.

When *facing* the turret (the obvious position to work on it), the release lever will be at the lower left. However, by mentally orienting oneself to the Operator's point of view (standing in *back* of the camera), the lever will be at the lower right, as per the instruction. It was necessary to base everything from the Operator's point of view to maintain consistency in instructions as to left, right, forward, and rear positions of the individual parts of the components.

Because the data and procedures presented here are the most efficient methods known to and tested by the authors on the sound stages in major production centers, the information may in some instances differ from manufacturers' engineering data and procedural recommendations; instructions have been included herein that cannot be found in any other manual.

chapter 1

The Camera Professional's Duties and Responsibilities

In the major film studios, the duties and responsibilities of each member of the camera crew are strictly defined.

The following contains the essentials of the "Division of Work and Duties" section of the agreement between Hollywood Film Producers and the International Photographers of the Motion Picture Industries, Local 659 (Cameramen), of the International Alliance of Theatrical Stage Employes and Moving Picture Machine Operators of the United States and Canada. The material has been modified somewhat and expanded to include job requirements based on experience in the field:

> At all times, Camera Professionals . . . shall be responsible for doing their work to the utmost of their ability, artistry, and efficiency, and strive to uphold the best traditions of the photographic profession. Bearing in mind that upon their efforts rests the ultimate responsibility of reproducing in artistic and visible form the results of the great expenditures undertaken by the Producer, they shall also strive to perform their work as efficiently, rapidly, and excellently as is possible, seeking to heighten their efficiency and that of the Production unit with which they work.
>
> The Director of Photography (First Cameraman) must be completely familiar with and able to light studio and location settings; compose scenes; take meter readings; select lenses; determine the use of filters, gauzes, mattes, and diffusion discs; call attention to and solve any photographic problems pertaining to the production that may arise.
>
> Whenever requested by the Producer, he or she shall help and advise the Producer, attend story conferences, give advice and suggestions in connection with the design and selection of sets, costumes, and locations as they relate to photography, and generally render assistance in simplifying production, in heightening production values, and effecting economies.
>
> The Camera Operator (Second Cameraman) must be completely familiar with and able to execute smooth and efficient camera movements; maintain the composition(s) prescribed by the Director of Photography; certify each "take" as it relates to the camera operation; set the groundglass focus; ascertain the parallax; regulate all shutter changes; note footage count; ensure the security of the mounted camera.
>
> The Camera Assistant must be completely familiar with and able to check out camera equipment and accessories to determine they are in working order and that no items are missing; inventory and record all assigned raw stock; load magazines; assemble and prepare the camera at the photographic site; make hand tests; run the tape; set marks; check

parallax; handle the slate; make camera reports; set lens aperture; regulate all focus changes; record meter readings; execute use of filters, gauzes, mattes, and diffusion discs; change lenses, check gate, change magazines; thread camera; disassemble and store camera equipment and accessories; charge camera batteries; unload and reload magazines; label, pack, and ship exposed stock to the laboratory; reinventory film supply; present duplicate camera, raw stock, and exposed stock reports to the Production Manager; any further necessary and incidental work that may be required.

Small production houses, in-plant industrial film units, and news and documentary film units may not always adhere closely to these definitions. Nevertheless, before a person can be considered a well-rounded Camera Professional, he or she must know and be able to perform the duties of each classification. This knowledge separates the professional from the amateur.

chapter 2

Camera-Film Identification

The physical properties and chemical composition of film stock are well covered in other books. In addition, detailed data sheets comprehensively covering such information as ASA indexes, D-log E curves, etc. are available from individual film manufacturers. Therefore, there is no attempt to duplicate much of this information here. Rather, this chapter reviews the major and some of the often-overlooked points with which the Camera Professional must be familiar.

The film-stock information provided is accurate at the time of publication. However, the major raw-stock manufacturers continue to develop new technologies and may change film types or code numbers or introduce new products. It is always best to consult with the manufacturers or suppliers when purchasing film.

Raw stock (i.e., unexposed film) is marked in various ways so that the Camera Professional with unidentified raw stock can follow a few simple procedures and consult some tables to correctly identify the product in question. In addition, knowledge of certain standards and specifications enables Camera Professionals to select raw stock for each job, based on the final intended use of the film. Also, efficient methods for ordering, handling, and safeguarding raw stock can save valuable time and needless trouble. This information is called *camera-film identification* and refers only to raw stock.

Camera-film identification consists of identifying (1) film type, (2) perforations and pitch, (3) winding, and (4) spool and core type.

2.1 FILM-TYPE IDENTIFICATION

Film cans and cartons are clearly labeled as to type, emulsion, and roll number (often erroneously called *slit* or *cut*) of a specific batch. To aid in further identification, each manufacturer incorporates characteristics on and/or in the raw-stock emulsion. Such identifications generally include the following (see Tables 2–1 through 2–3):

2.1a Punchmarks at Head or Tail of Rolls

Eastman Kodak Company punches tiny circular dots into the head and tail of each roll of rawstock. When the head-end of the roll extends from the feed side of a magazine, it is easy to read the dots as a three-letter code, e.g., PXN, ECN, etc. Often, the film's emulsion number and roll number are punchmarked at the head of the roll as well.

In the darkroom, film loaders soon learn to run their fingers across the perforations and "read" the code letters in the absence of light.

Agfa-Gevaert and Fuji Photo do not punchmark their film rolls.

Table 2–1 Film Type Identification (Agfa Corporation—Agfa-Gevaert N.V., Belgium)

Film Name	Type	Code	Latent Image Rapid I.D.
Agfacolor Negative	(35mm)	XT 100	N
(tungsten)	(16mm)	XT 100	N
Agfacolor Negative	(35mm)	XT 320	H or F
(tungsten)	(16mm)	XT 320	H or F
Agfacolor Negative	(35mm)	XTS 400	S
(tungsten)	(16mm)	XTS 400	S
Agfa Negative	(35mm)	PAN 250	H
B&W	(16mm)	PAN 250	H
Gevachrome* (Color Reversal Tung)	(16mm)	702	N
Gevachrome D* (Color Reversal Day)	(16mm)	722	D
Gevachrome II* (Color Reversal Tung)	(16mm)	732	H

Note Agfa-Gevaert 35mm and 16mm daylight spools contain approximately 4 additional meters (13-ft) for threading and unloading and is sufficient to allow complete light protection.
Agfa-Gevaert 35mm and 16mm darkroom loads contain approximately 3 additional meters (10-ft) for threading.
Agfa-Gevaert calls its machine-readable latent image: BARCODE.
*Gevachrome 16mm film, while not available in the United States, is in use worldwide.

2.1b Latent Image Rapid Identification

Manufacturers incorporate data which cannot be ascertained until the film is developed. With B&W rawstock, while it is often possible to run a light along the film edge and read either the footage number or a code letter or number/letter, with color rawstock, this procedure cannot be followed due to the opacity of the base.

Once the film is developed, however, letters and/or numbers enable an individual to make a rapid identification of the type of film that has been exposed, e.g., Agfa-Gevaert XTS 400 carries the letter S; Eastman Kodak 5293, carries the letter L, Fuji Photo F-500, the letter/number N70, etc.

However, while Agfa-Gevaert and Fuji Photo apply rapid i.d. data to all their film rolls, Eastman Kodak applies it only to a selected few.

2.1c Latent Image Data for Film Editors and Manufacturer's Use

All 65mm and 35mm negative camera films contain latent-image "human readable" and "machine-readable" information along the edge of the film. The human-readable portion of the edge data contains incremental edge numbers every 64 perforations (per foot), plus other information: the product name, manufacturer's name, zero reference marks, frame index markers, and randomly inserted symbols which enable editors to check workprint and negative against each other.

The machine-readable portion of the data, adjacent to the human readable key number, is also placed as a mid-foot key number (every 32 perforations), and contains the manufacturer's code, film type, incremental number and system information.

Table 2–2 Film Type Identification (Eastman Kodak Company, United States)

Film Name	Type	Code	Latent Image Rapid I.D.
Eastman Double-X	5222 (35mm)	DXN	
(B&W Negative)	7222 (16mm)	DXN	
Eastman Plus-X	5231 (35mm)	PXN	
(B&W Negative)	7231 (16mm)	PXN	
Eastman Ektachrome Reversal	5239 (35mm)	VND	
(Video News Film-Daylite)	7239 (16mm)	VND	
Kodak Ektachrome EF Reversal	5240 (35mm)	VNF	
(Video News Film-Tungsten)	7240 (16mm)	VNF	
Eastmancolor Negative	5245 (65mm)	EXS	K or N*
(tungsten)	5245 (35mm)	EXS	
	7245 (16mm)	EXS	
Eastmancolor Negative II	5247 (65mm)	ECN	B
(tungsten)	5247 (35mm)	ECN	
Eastmancolor Negative	5248 (65mm)	EXM	
(tungsten)	5248 (35mm)	EXM	
	7248 (16mm)	EXM	
Eastman Ektachrome Reversal	7250 (65mm)	VNX	
(Hi-speed Video News Tung)			
Eastman Ektachrome Reversal	7251 (16mm)	VXD	VXD
(Hi-speed Video News Day)			
Kodak Plus-X	7276 (16mm)	PXR	
(B&W Reversal)			
Kodak Tri-X	7278 (16mm)	TXR	
(B&W Reversal)			
Eastmancolor Negative	5293 (65mm)	EXT	L
(tungsten)	5293 (35mm)	EXT	
	5293 (16mm)	EXT	
Eastmancolor Negative	5296 (35mm)	EXH	J
(tungsten)	7296 (16mm)	EXH	
Eastmancolor Negative	5297 (65mm)	ECD	C
(daylite)	5297 (35mm)	ECD	
	7297 (16mm)	ECD	

Note Eastman 35mm and 16mm daylight spools contain approximately 4 additional meters (13-ft) for threading and unloading and is sufficient to allow complete light protection. Eastman 35mm and 16mm darkroom loads contain approximately 3 additional meters (10-ft) for threading.
    *Eastman calls its machine-readable latent image: KEYCODE.

16mm films, while currently lacking machine-readable data, are expected to contain the same information and identification as the 65mm and 35mm films in the near future.

2.2 EXPOSURE INDEXES

Table 2–4 lists the exposure settings recommended by manufacturers for their films. These exposure indexes are indirectly referenced to ASA film speeds and are simply guides for achieving the best exposure for a given situation.

Table 2–3 Film Type Identification (Fuji Photo Film, Ltd., Japan)

Film Name	Type #	Code	Latent Image I.D.
Fujicolor Negative	8510 (35mm)	F-64	N10
(tungsten)	8610 (16mm)	F-64	N10
Fujicolor Negative	8520 (35mm)	F-64D	N20
(daylite)	8620 (16mm)	F-64D	N20
Fujicolor Negative	8730 (65mm)	F-125	N30
(tungsten)	8530 (35mm)	F-125	N30
	8630 (16mm)	F-125	N30
Fujicolor Negative	8550 (35mm)	F-250	N50
(tungsten)	8650 (16mm)	F-250	N50
Fujicolor Negative	8560 (35mm)	F-250D	N60
(daylite)	8660 (16mm)	F-250D	N60
Fujicolor Negative	8770 (65mm)	F-500	N70
(tungsten)	8570 (35mm)	F-500	N70
	8670 (16mm)	F-500	N70
Fuji Panchromatic FN (B&W Neg)	71112 (35mm)	FG	FN
Fuji Panchromatic RP	72161 (16mm)	RP	1

Note Fuji Photo 35mm and 16mm daylight spools contain approximately 34 meters (112-ft) for threading and unloading and is sufficient to allow complete light protection. Fuji Photo 35mm and 16mm darkroom loads contain approximately 4 additional meters (10-ft) for threading.
  Fuji Photo calls its machine-readable latent image: M.R. CODE
  Fuji Photo does not manufacture color reversal.
  Fuji Photo B&W film is not available in the U.S.

2.3 PERFORATIONS AND PITCH

Perforations and pitch used in the United States conform to the "Cutting and Perforations Dimensions for Raw Stock," as set forth by the American National Standards Institute (ANSI). These standards and all other standards and recommended practices pertaining to motion-picture films and to their use in cameras and projectors were developed by the Society of Motion Picture & Television Engineers (SMPTE), who have the sole responsibility for their accuracy. Committees of the SMPTE periodically review these standards to ensure that they are kept up to date. The standards are released through ANSI. A complete list of motion-picture standards and nomenclature is available from ANSI; requests should be sent to 1430 Broadway, New York, NY 10018.

All 35mm camera film and 16mm *silent* camera film is double perforated with two precisely located rows of holes, one along each edge of the film. However, 16mm *sound* camera film is perforated with one row of holes only, to allow for a direct sound track or magnetic striping.

Variations for both 35mm and 16mm are in (a) perforation shape and (b) length of pitch (see Fig. 2–3).

2.3a Perforation Shapes (Figs. 2–1, 2–2)

It should be noted that "negative perforation" and "positive perforation" designate the size and shape of the *perforation* and not the type of film (i.e., negative [camera film] or positive [print stock]. As a rule, film with negative perforations is designed so that prints can be made from it, while film with positive perforations is designed for use as print stock. However,

6

Table 2–4 Manufacturer's Recommended Exposure Indexes

Film Name	Film Type/Number	Tungsten	Daylight
Agfacolor Negative	XT 100	100	64 (w/85 filter)
Agfacolor Negative	XT 320	320	200 (w/85 filter)
Agfacolor Negative	XTS 400	400	250 (w/85 filter)
Agfa B&W Negative	PAN 250	200	250
Agfa Gevachrome	702	80	40 (w/85B filter)
Agfa Gevachrome D	722	32 (w/80A filter)	125
Agfa Gevachrome II	732	400	250 (w/85 filter)
Eastman Double-X Neg.	5222/7222	200	250
Eastman Plus-X Neg.	5231/7231	64	80
Eastman VNF-Day	5239/7239	40 (w/80A filter)	160
Kodak VNF-Tung	5240/7240	125	80 (w/85B filter)
Eastmancolor Negative	5245/7245	12 (w/80A filter)	50
Eastmancolor Neg. II	5247/7247	125	80 (w/85 filter)
Eastmancolor Negative	5248/7248	100	64 (w/85 filter)
Eastman Hi-speed VNF-T	5250/7250	400	250 (w/85B filter)
Kodak Hi-speed VNF-Day	7251	100 (w/80A filter)	400
Kodak Plus-X	7276	40	50
Kodak Tri-X	7278	160	200
Eastmancolor Negative	5293/7293	200	125 (w/85 filter)
Eastmancolor Negative	5296/7296	500	320 (w/85 filter)
Eastmancolor Negative	5297/7297	64 (w/80A filter)	250
Fujicolor Negative	F-64	64	40 (w/85 filter)
Fujicolor Negative	F 64D	64	—
Fujicolor Negative	F-125	125	80 (w/85 filter)
Fujicolor Negative	F 250	250	160 (w/85 filter)
Fujicolor Negative	F-250D	64 (w/80 filter)	250
Fujicolor Negative	F-500	500	320 (w/85 filter)
Fuji Panchromatic FN	71112	64	80
Fuji Panchromatic RP	72161	64	80

high-speed camera film has positive perforations. The rounded Kodak Standard (KS) corners of high-speed film are stronger than the sharp Bell & Howell (BH) corners and so the film is better able to withstand the strain of the initial roll through a high-speed camera. (See Figs. 2–1 and 2–2.)

2.3b Pitch (Fig. 2–3)
In both 35mm and 16mm film, *pitch* is the distance from the leading edge of one perforation to the leading edge of the next perforation. Pitch is commonly referred to as *long* or *short,* depending on the distance for this dimension.

Most camera films are perforated "short" pitch because they will be printed on a continuous-contact printer on a circular printing drum. The negative is next to the drum, and the print stock is on the outside. Geometrically, the negative stock must have shorter pitch than the print stock, to produce rock-steady sharp prints.

2.3c Perforation and Pitch Selection
The selection of raw stock with a particular perforation shape and pitch dimension is predicated on the intended use of the film, as outlined in Table 2–5.

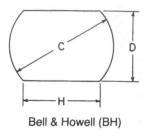
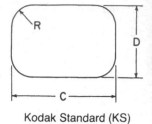

Bell & Howell (BH)   Kodak Standard (KS)

Figure 2–1 Raw-stock perforation shapes (35mm). The Bell & Howell (BH) perforation (left) has curved sides, a straight top and bottom, and sharp corners. This is called a *negative perforation,* ANSI PH 22.93, where C = 0.1100; D = 0.0730; and H = 0.082. The Kodak Standard (KS) perforation (right) has straight sides, a straight top and bottom, and a slight radius on the corners. This is called a *positive* or *high-speed perforation,* ANSI PH 22.139, where C = 0.1100; D = 0.0780; R = 0.020. *Note:* The letters C, D, H, and R conform to the dimension letters used by ANSI and are expressed in decimal inches. Many countries other than the U.S. use metric measurement, and thus may express these dimensions in millimeters. The letters BH and KS refer to those who developed the particular perforation. *Note:* Eastman Kodak has altered the BH perforation by "rounding" the sharp corners to conform to the slight radius on the corners of the KS perforation. Other manufacturers still maintain the sharp corners.

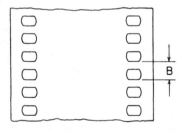

Figure 2–2 Raw-stock perforation shape (16mm). All 16mm perforations are rectangular, with a straight top and bottom, straight sides, and a slight radial curve on the corners. Per ANSI PH 22.12, C = 0.0720; D = 0.0500; R = 0.010. The letters C, D, and R conform to the dimension letters used by ANSI and are expressed in decimal inches.

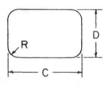

Figure 2–3 Pitch measurement: in 35mm, B = 0.1866 (short pitch) or 0.1870 (long pitch); in 16mm, B = 0.2994 (short pitch) or 0.3000 (long pitch). The letter B conforms to the dimension used by the SMPTE to denote pitch and is expressed in decimal inches.

2.3d 65mm Camera Film Perforation and Pitch

The 65mm motion-picture cameras use film perforated to the same standards and specifications as regular 35mm raw stock, with a short pitch of 0.1866, but they use only KS (never BH) perforations.

2.4 WINDINGS

2.4a EI and EO

The standard winding of film manufactured in the United States is *emulsion in* (EI). On special order, any American manufacturer will supply film wound *emulsion out* (EO). While many foreign cameras require film wound EO, the cameras designated in this manual use film

Table 2–5 Perforation and Pitch Selection

Film Type	Intended Use	Common Designation	ANSI Spec. No.	Pitch Designation[a]
35mm	For making release prints	Negative perforation, short pitch	PH 22.93	BH—1866
	Direct projection or high-speed up to 1000 frames per second	Negative perforation, long pitch	PH 22.34	BH—1870
	Ultra high-speed (1000 frames per second or more)	High-speed perforation	PH 22.36	KS—1870
16mm	For making release prints	Camera original, double perforation, short pitch	PH 22.110	2R—2994
	Direct projection and/or single-system cameras	Camera original, sound (or single) perforation, long pitch	PH 22.12	1R—3000
	Direct projection and/or high-speed	High-speed perforation, long pitch	PH 22.5	2R—3000

Note Speed of 1000 frames or more is considered ultra high-speed for the tensile strength of film but not motors. See 7.6g, "High-Speed (Slow Motion) Motors," for motor ratings.

[a]BH indicates negative type perforations; KS indicates positive type perforations. 1R indicates one row of perforations; 2R indicates two rows of perforations. The numbers following these abbreviations designate the pitch dimension.

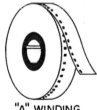

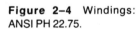

Figure 2–4 Windings: ANSI PH 22.75. "A" WINDING EMULSION SIDE IN "B" WINDING EMULSION SIDE IN

wound EI. Exceptions are the 35mm Eclair Cameflex and the 16mm Eclair NPR, which are designed to take either wind.

2.4b A-wind; B-wind (Fig. 2–4)
The 16mm single-perforated (sound) film is supplied in *A-wind* or *B-wind* (see Fig. 2–4). "A" and "B" refer to position of the perforations on an EI roll. A-wind is intended for making contact prints in the laboratory and is *not* for camera use. B-wind is intended for use as camera stock, and also for making optical prints in the laboratory. With the emulsion facing the camera aperture, only B-wind film will fit single-pulldown-claw cameras.

If in doubt as to whether film is A- or B-wind, a simple darkroom procedure will identify the winding immediately: With the emulsion side in, hold the roll in the left hand; then pull the film end with the right hand, making certain that the film leaves the roll clockwise at the top. B-wind

9

Table 2-6 Spool and Core Types

Film Type	Manufacturer	Spool (length)				Core (diameter)			
		15m (50')	30m (100')	60m (200')	120m (400')	25mm (1")	50mm Univ (2")	75mm (3")	100mm (4")
35mm	Agfa Corporation	CNU-30	CNU-30			CNP-1	CNP-2	CNP-3	CNP-2
	Eastman Kodak		S-83				U	K	
	Fuji Photo Film						U	K	
16mm	Agfa Corporation	CSU-30	CSU-30		CSU-61		CSP-3	CSP-33	CSP-32
	Eastman Kodak		R-90	R-190	R-153		T	Z	
	Fuji Photo Film		R-90	R-190	R-153		T	Z	

Table 2-7 Film Orders: Examples

Company	(1) Rolls	(2) Width	(3) Length per Roll	(4) Name	(5) Type No.	(6) Perforation and Pitch	(7) Wind[a]	(8) Spool or Core[b]
Agfa Corporation	10	35mm	305m (1000')	Agfacolor	XT 320	N[c]	EI	CNP-2
	12	16mm	120m (400')	Agfacolor	XT 125		EI	CSP-3
Eastman Kodak	8	35mm	120m (400')	Double-X Neg	5222	(BH 1866)		U
	7	16mm	360m (1200')	Plus-X Rev	7276	(1R 3000)	B-wind	Z
Fuji Photo Film	6	35mm	305m (1000')	Fujicolor	F500	(BH 1866)		U
	9	16mm	120m (400')	Fujicolor	F64	(2R 2994)		T

Note The numerals in the column headings refer to the listing in the text.
[a]Indicate B-wind for camera use when ordering single-perforation film.
[b]When no spool or core type is designated by the manufacturer, then the spool's metric/footage length or core diameter is noted.
[c]Agfa perforation codes for 16mm are A-wind = S-1, B-wind = S-2, double perforation = S-1.2. These codes are equivalent to ANSI specifications for 16mm. The 35mm perforation code is N (negative).

perforations will be farthest from the body; A-wind perforations will be closest to the body.

Some Camera Professionals use the expression, "A left clock is far better," to remind themselves that holding the roll in the *left* hand, with the film leaving the roll *clock*wise, the *far* perforation is *Better*.

2.5 SPOOL AND CORE TYPES

Each manufacturer designates its own metal spools and/or plastic cores, as indicated in Table 2–6.

2.6 ORDERING RAW STOCK

Each manufacturer uses a system for filling orders, to ensure the most expedient service. Confusion and delay in response to orders invariably can be traced to information omitted or improperly submitted.

Manufacturers recommend that orders contain the following information: (1) number of rolls; (2) width of film; (3) length of roll; (4) name of film; (5) type number; (6) perforation and pitch; (7) designation B-wind, to indicate in-camera use for single-perforated film; (8) core or spool type. (See Table 2–7.)

2.7 SHIPPING INSTRUCTIONS

Shipping instructions to the manufacturer should contain complete information, including (1) *when* the order is to be sent ("Ship"); (2) *conveyance* preferred ("Via"); (3) *address* of consumer ordering ("To"); (4) *return* address; (5) and any *other* pertinent data that would facilitate delivery ("SPECIAL INSTRUCTIONS"). (See Table 2–8.)

Table 2–8 Shipping Instructions: Examples

Ship	Via	To	Special Instructions
ASAP (i.e., as soon as possible) To arrive (specify date film will be required, at least 2 days before start of production)	AIREX (air express) AIRFRT (air freight) Your carrier (manufacturer's shipping agent, usually by truck) Specific delivery company (consumer's shipping agent)	Name of consumer Address of consumer City, state of consumer ATT: (name of person who is to receive film)	If consumer desires to pick up shipment, mark shipping label, "HOLD AT AIRPORT; CALL UPON ARRIVAL" (include phone number). When shipment leaves the manufacturer's establishment: "TELEGRAPH [OR PHONE] CARRIER, WAYBILL NUMBER, FLIGHT OR CARLOAD NUMBER." Communicate by phone or telegraph: "NOTIFY US OF ANY SHORTAGES OR DELAYS IN SHIPMENT."

It should be noted that although the supplier invariably places a warning label on the shipping carton, which reads, "PHOTOGRAPHIC FILM—KEEP AWAY FROM RADIOACTIVE MATERIALS," it is important to notify the supplier to label the carton as such. Because of the constant flow of radioactive isotopes for medical use on common carriers, there is a constant threat of contamination to all film shipments—raw stock and exposed. If a shipment is suspect or arrives without a warning label, *set it aside,* and send one roll to the manufacturer, with the notation, "RAW STOCK—CHECK FOR EXPOSURE TO RADIATION—NOTIFY RESULTS IMMEDIATELY BY PHONE," and be sure to attach a proper warning label to the wrapper of that roll. It is better to wait for a new, properly labeled shipment than risk a streaked or fogged negative and having to reshoot.

In some situations, added precaution may be wise. Lead-lined pouches and cases, which help to minimize radiation exposure, are available from most motion-picture equipment and supply houses.

chapter 3

Loading-Room Procedures

Loading-room procedures must be studied thoroughly; when they become "second nature," they will ensure maximum efficiency. A loader should never deviate from the routine: Consistency in placement of film, tools, and supplies enable the loader to complete work in darkness with the ease and familiarity of working in daylight.

3.1 TESTING THE LOADING ROOM

The most important step in loading is the first: guaranteeing an absolutely lighttight room. A loading room must be considered unsafe until tested, regardless of whether it is a permanent, temperature-controlled, air-filtered installation or a portable plywood "hotbox" on a sound stage. Ambient light filtering through wall punctures, air vents, or doorjamb cracks is not noticed until at least 5 minutes after the darkroom is entered. A rule of thumb for testing lighttight security is to hold the hand 12 in. from the face after being in the darkroom 5 minutes; if the hand is seen, light leakage exists and can be plugged up with black masking tape. In any case, every loading room *must* be made lighttight.

3.2 THE HOTBOX

The sound-stage portable loading room "hotbox" usually takes up no more than 4 × 4 ft of floor space, a sufficient area for the work to be done. It is generally constructed and used as follows (see Fig. 3–1): The door, with interior lock, is at the loader's back. Opposite the door is a workbench approximately 18 × 48 in. for loading the magazines. The bench surface is prepared by placing—to the *left*—the same number of cans of raw stock as the number of magazines to be loaded. The magazine to be loaded (or unloaded) is placed in the *center*. Canned, exposed film is placed to the *right*.

On the floor below the bench, the raw stock inventory is placed to the *left*. A small box or wastebasket is placed in the *center,* and, next to the basket, space is reserved for short-end cans. A carton containing empty unload cans and black bags is placed to the *right*.

Empty magazines, or *exposed magazines* to be unloaded, are placed on floor behind and to loader's left (as loader faces bench); loaded magazines are placed on floor behind and to loader's right.

Directly over the bench, hanging on nails, are (from left to right) one roll of camera tape, one pair of scissors, one magazine brush, one air syringe (more elaborate loading rooms are equipped with air hoses to clean magazines), one marking pen, and one film-inventory list.

On a shelf above the loading bench are a box of spare take-up cores,

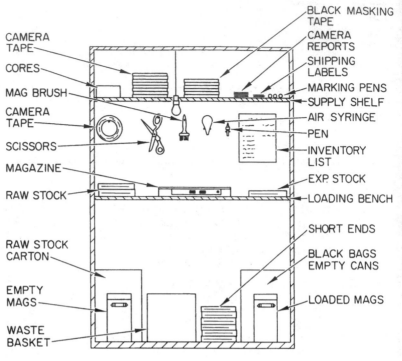

CAMERA TAPE
CORES
MAG BRUSH
CAMERA TAPE
SCISSORS
MAGAZINE
RAW STOCK
RAW STOCK CARTON
EMPTY MAGS
WASTE BASKET

BLACK MASKING TAPE
CAMERA REPORTS
SHIPPING LABELS
MARKING PENS
SUPPLY SHELF
AIR SYRINGE
PEN
INVENTORY LIST
EXP. STOCK
LOADING BENCH
SHORT ENDS
BLACK BAGS EMPTY CANS
LOADED MAGS

Figure 3–1 Hotbox elevation.

spare rolls of camera tape, spare rolls of black masking tape, extra camera reports, shipping labels, and additional marking pens.

An overhead light with a short pull-chain should be above and behind the loader. (Long pull-chains and wall switches are subject to accidental snagging in moments of haste—and there are many such moments!) The overhead light should be low enough so that the loader's shadow always covers the magazine being loaded. Should the light be turned on accidentally or the door opened when a magazine lid is off, the loader's shadow may protect the roll from exposure at least enough to confine fogging to the perforations only, thereby saving the frame area. Direct light would fog deep into the picture area and render the entire roll useless in the split second before the light could be extinguished. In either case, a "slop test" (see Sec. 3.11) would be mandatory.

CAUTION: *Regarding loading-room lightbulbs*—If a bulb does not illuminate in the room when the chain is pulled, or when seating the bulb in the socket, or when checking the plug-in connector, for safety's sake *completely remove the bulb from the socket!* Many a loader, after deciding that nothing electrical is in working order, has had the sad experience of a bulb suddenly lighting up the darkness with a full roll of raw stock (or worse, exposed stock!) uncovered. By then, the pounding on the wall and the Electrician's reassuring voice calling, "Hey, I got the juice to the line for you!" gives little comfort.

3.3 PREPARATION OF MATERIALS

Dirt is the prime enemy of all loaders: A loading room must be cleaned thoroughly prior to bringing in supplies, equipment, and/or magazines, and it should be cleaned again when the job is completed.

Upon *receipt of raw stock,* an inventory is taken, and the number of cases and/or cartons is noted. This inventory is kept separately from the camera-report inventory (see Chapter 5, "Camera Reports") and is posted above the bench.

NOTE: A *case* contains many cartons. A *carton* contains one can. A *can* contains a roll of film wound on a core, and wrapped in a black bag if it is a darkroom load, or wound on a spool if it is a daylight load. Some 16mm cans contain two rolls, each of which is wrapped in an individual black bag.

The contents of full cases of 35mm and 16mm film are indicated in Tables 3–1 and 3–2, respectively.

The *footage count on each carton label* must be checked. Occasionally a roll from the manufacturer will be less than standard footage length, in which case the footage amount must be circled prominently in ink on the carton label, as well as on the can label. This will serve to call attention to the irregular amount.

Later, *when loading the short roll,* a small piece of camera tape (a "reminder tape") is prepared, stating the footage amount and the word "only" (e.g., "975 ft ONLY") as though it were a short end. The tape is put next to the magazine ID (identification) tape (see Sec. 3.5). When the magazine is later mounted on the camera, this reminder tape is placed below the camera footage counter, as a constant notice to the Operator that there is not a full roll. Once the roll has been expended, of course, the reminder is removed.

Table 3–1 35mm Case Contents

Roll Length	Number of Cans	Approximate Shipping Weight (lbs/kilos)
1000′ (B&W)	5	30/13.6
1000′ (Color)	5	30/13.6
400′	20	52/23.6
200′	20	29/13.2
100′ (on S-83 Spool)	50	43/19.5

Table 3–2 16mm Case Contents

Roll Length	Number of Cartons	Approximate Shipping Weight (lbs/kilos)
1200′	20 singles	60/27.2
	10 doubles	60/27.2
400′	30	44/20
200′ spool	30	30/13.6
100′ spool	50	24/11

For noncamera films, two 16mm × 1200′ rolls (B&W or color) are packed in one 35mm × 1200′ film can. Each roll is individually wrapped in a black labpack bag.

3.4 LOADING

Cans of raw stock (equal to the number of magazines to be loaded) are placed to the *left* on the work bench. The magazine is placed in the *center* and cleaned thoroughly. (See Sec. 7.9, on magazines, Chapter 7.) The can of raw stock is unsealed by peeling a short section of tape from the circumference of the can and then affixing the tape end to the wall of the loading room. While the can is held firmly, to keep the lid from opening, the can is rotated downward so that the tape unrolls and sticks to the wall.

A *visual check of the bench* is essential before turning off the light, in order to determine the location of the magazine lid and other necessary items. *When the room is dark,* the can is opened, and the roll of raw stock is taken out of the black bag.

WARNING: Some manufacturers use a *sealing tape* on a roll of film, to prevent unraveling of the stock. This innocent-looking tape, approximately $1 \times \frac{1}{4}$ in., if not properly disposed of, can become a cause of grief, expense, damage to the camera, and loss of a crew's time. When this tape is removed from a roll, it must be *stuck immediately to the inside of an empty can* so that it will not accidentally fall into an open magazine and eventually do great damage to the camera mechanism.

The raw stock is loaded into the magazine, the feed lid replaced, and the black bag stored in the empty can.

NOTE: It is often difficult to insert the film end into the light trap roller. The film is thin, and when it meets resistance from the rollers, it buckles. To overcome this problem with nongear magazines, a diagonal (lengthwise) "fold" is made of the *first 8 in. of the film end;* the doubled thickness will feed in more easily. When loading gear-thread magazines, cut across a frame through the middle of both perforations. This permits the film end to mesh with the gear tooth, and threading can continue.

The take-up side of double-compartment and coaxial magazines (see Sec. 7.9, "Magazines," Chapter 7) may be worked on in the light. The feed and take-up sides of displacement-type magazines must be loaded in the dark.

The *take-up core* is placed on the core holder, with the slanted slot in the core angled away from the direction in which the film takes up. Approximately 3 in. of the film end is folded back upon itself, and the fold is inserted into the core slot. A few turns of the spindle wheel in the direction of take-up wraps enough film around the film end to prevent its slipping out of the core slot. By wetting a few inches of emulsion near the core with spit and giving it one more full turn, the film will adhere to itself and be prevented from unraveling in the magazine.

Magazines with permanent cores merely require insertion of the film end into the core slot and being locked into place.

3.5 MAGAZINE I.D.

After loading a magazine, a piece of identification tape is placed on the lid. (On double-compartment and coaxial magazines, the tape is placed on *the take-up lid, not the feed lid;* the tape goes over the magazine lock on displacement magazines.) The tape is always extended across the opening of the lid so that the lid can not be removed thoughtlessly; it also serves as a warning that exposed film is on the inside of the take-up lid. Each piece of camera (I.D.) tape is inscribed with the following information:

1. Total amount of footage in the raw stock roll—e.g., "400 ft"
2. Type, emulsion batch, roll (cut), and can number—e.g., "5247-786-18-35"

NOTE: The total amount of footage and type of film are important to the laboratory; the emulsion batch, roll (cut), and can number are important to a manufacturer in tracing defects in film stock.

3. Magazine serial number—e.g., "Mag. No. 683"

NOTE: The magazine number is essential should the negative have a scratch—the Camera Professional can then determine whether the malfunction is in the camera or in a particular magazine.

4. Roll number (numerical order of magazine when placed on the camera—e.g., Roll No. 1)

NOTE: The roll number is very important to the Editing Department.

5. Date the magazine was loaded—e.g., "7/8/1995"
6. The loader's initials—e.g., "G.S."

The information in the foregoing examples should thus appear on the I.D. tape as follows:

400 ft	5247-786-18-35
Mag. No. 683	Roll No. 1
7/8/1995	G.S.

In addition to the magazine I.D., which is affixed to the *take-up lid,* many loaders also stick a small piece of camera tape on the *feed* side of a magazine lid as another safety measure, on the premise that having to remove tapes gives someone (regardless of the "hurry up" pressure applied) second thoughts about opening lids in daylight and possibly exposing film. To be absolutely sure, open *all* magazines in the dark.

REMEMBER: *Anyone finding an unmarked magazine has the right to assume it to be empty.*

3.6 UNLOADING
3.6a Complete Rolls
When unloading an exposed magazine, change the total amount of footage on the I.D. tape, substituting for the original number the amount of footage to be sent to the laboratory and adding "EXP" (e.g., "380 ft EXP").

The I.D. tape is lifted and placed in the *center* of the take-up lid. The unload can, with lid removed, is placed to the *right* of the magazine. The black labpack bag is readied. (Placing the hand in the bag and spreading the fingers makes it easy to receive the exposed stock.)

NOTE: In an emergency, a double-folded page from a newspaper or heavy wrapping paper can be substituted for the black bag.

Before the light is extinguished, make a visual check of the placement of all items. With the light out, the take-up side of the lid is removed and the exposed film is put inside the black labpack bag.

CAUTION: Some magazines have reusable cores. Do *not* ship the core to the laboratory with the exposed stock.

Exposed film is *never* sealed to itself, as was the raw stock in the original packing; instead, the roll is rotated until the tail of the film is at the bottom of the black bag. The bag is then folded to conform to the roll size, the opening tucked under, and the package placed in the can. Replace the can lid, then squeeze it tightly between an arm and the ribs while taping it.

NOTE: Exposed-film cans are sealed with plain camera tape. If the original tape used to seal the raw stock can is needed to seal a can of exposed film, the tape should be inverted so that the identifying numbers (type number, roll number, etc.) on the tape are upside-down when the can is stacked with the *label up*. Plain tape or inverted numbers quickly identify exposed film or short ends.

The ID tape is removed from the magazine lid and used to affix the camera report (see Sec. 5.4, "Disposition of Reports," Chapter 5) to the lid of the can containing the exposed film. The label of the can is marked "Roll No. _____ EXP." This is necessary in the event the camera report is removed or lost.

3.6b Partially Exposed Rolls

When a magazine containing a partially exposed roll is to be emptied completely, *two* unload cans (one to the left for the raw stock, one to the right for the exposed film) are placed on the bench. The exposed film, regardless of length, is canned first, and the can is labeled with the ID tape from the magazine.

The can of raw stock is marked with a piece of tape across the label, with the words, "SHORT END," the emulsion number, footage amount, date canned, and loader's initials, as in the following example:

SHORT END
5247-786-18-35
170 ft only
7/8/1995
G.S.

NOTE: Some production companies require that all 35mm short ends of less than 100 ft and all 16mm short ends of less than 40 ft be wrapped, taped, and deposited in the silver-reclamation bin.

3.6c Unused Rolls

Before canning raw stock that has been loaded but not used, rather than breaking the film off and destroying the head ID, three or four frames of the piece of film protruding from the light traps are marked in ink with a large "XXX" to indicate the film ahead of it has been exposed while loading. The film is *not* retaped to itself to conform to the manufacturer's packing. When loaded but not used, and recanned, the can is marked as follows:

[Type of camera] loaded but not used
Emulsion No.
Run in and marked approx. _____ ft from head of roll
[Date canned]
[Loader's initials]

This marking permits the next loader to run down to the mark with the assurance that the film following the mark has not been exposed.

All film ends should be cut square across the film width (bisecting a perforation) before being canned. One attempt to thread the jagged end of a torn roll into a gear-driven magazine will make a loader appreciate the squared film end.

3.7 EXPOSED FILM

Ship exposed film to the laboratory as soon as possible, to avoid deterioration of the latent image. Until it is ready for shipment, exposed film is kept in a cool, dry place—separate from raw stock inventory so it will not be mistakenly loaded as raw stock (this *has* happened!)

3.8 ON LOCATION

When working out of a truck or station wagon, space may be limited. In that circumstance, the same case must be utilized for both raw and exposed stock. The following system should be used (see Fig. 3-2):

3.8a Cans in Cartons

All raw stock is to be placed in the case so that only one of the sealed flaps on each carton is up, unbroken, and visible to the loader. After loading magazines, empty cans (e.g., 400–1200 ft) are replaced in their original cartons; the cartons are to be set on their sides with the flap out of the carton (to indicate can is empty). On cartons with fold-in "ears" beneath the carton flap (e.g., 100-ft spools), one ear is allowed to protrude (to indicate can is empty) while the other ear is folded in and under the flap, which is then reinserted into the carton. Exposed stock is always to be marked "EXP." On large cartons, the flap is reinserted into the carton and sealed with tape. On cartons with fold-in "ears" beneath the carton flap,

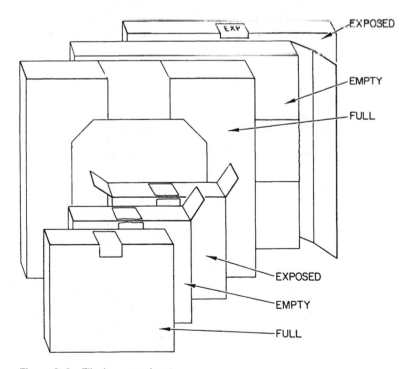

Figure 3–2 Film boxes and cartons.

both ears are allowed to protrude (to indicate exposed stock) and only the flap is reinserted into the carton.

3.8b Cans without Cartons

Quite often, cans of film in a case do not have cartons. Cans of raw stock always have manufacturer's tape on the circumference. Printed on the tape (and on the can label) will be the type, emulsion batch, and roll (cut) numbers.

When raw stock is taken out of a can, the manufacturer's printed tape should be removed and thrown away: A film can without tape is empty.

When exposed film is put back into a can, the circumference of the can should be wrapped with blank camera tape, and a camera report is attached to the lid. The label must now be marked, "Roll No. _____ EXP."

When these procedures are consistently followed, the one case will accommodate (a) raw stock with manufacturer's printed tape; (b) empty cans without tape (empties should always be placed between the raw stock and the exposed film); and (c) exposed film with blank tape. With this method, all can be distinguished at a glance.

3.8c Cans to Lab

When cans of exposed film are *taken* to the laboratory with the original camera reports attached, they are stacked (top one inverted, so as to present the bottom up) and wrapped with camera tape. When *shipped* (as from location), exposed-film cans are either placed in individual cartons, taped together, or packed tightly in a case. All empty spaces in the case are stuffed with paper to keep the cans from sliding or bumping.

All shipping cases are secured with camera or Gaffer's tape and are prominently marked, on *all* sides:

EXPOSED FILM—KEEP FROM RADIATION

The amount of insurance placed on shipped film is at the discretion of the production company (*rule of thumb:* Double the production cost required to film the rolls exposed—to pay for the original shoot and a reshoot). A waybill number, carrier name, and flight or route number are obtained and saved until a report either from the laboratory or the Production Manager) indicates that the shipment has reached its destination.

3.9 THE CHANGING BAG

The changing bag is a "portable loading room" (or "portable darkroom") used on location or whenever film must be handled in the dark and a darkroom is not available. The bags are manufactured in several sizes: the larger the bag, the greater the ease of working within it.

Fabricated of canvas (or rubber) enclosed in a black cloth cover, a changing bag is actually a bag within a bag, with its own zipper at the top for insertion and removal of magazines and film. Both layers of material are sewn together along their edges and along the perimeter of two elastic-cuffed sleeves. This arrangement permits insertion of the hands and arms into the sleeves. When the arms are in the sleeves above the loader's elbows (with zippers closed) a lighttight compartment is created for the safe loading and unloading of magazines.

The first rule for working in a changing bag is *don't* panic! Should something go wrong, the loader must *stop, think,* and *retrace procedural steps.* If necessary, start over from the beginning, but *never* come out of the bag unless the film is safely covered in the film can or the magazine. A loader never rushes no matter how much hurry-up pressure is applied.

3.9a Preparation

Remove the folded changing bag from its carrying container, unzip both zippers, and shake the bag vigorously to remove any foreign matter. Turn the bag inside-out before and after each job, and inspect for pinholes, rips, and debris. Although the bag is lightproof, avoid using it in direct light. Heat of the sun or light filtering through pinholes in the fabric may damage the film.

3.9b Loading

Spread the bag out flat. The magazine to be used must have a core on the take-up spindle and must have been cleaned thoroughly before placing it inside the bag. *Always* insert the magazine into the bag with the feed side to the left, the take-up side to the right, and the light traps toward the loader. The *lids* must be *on* to avoid the chance of dust, dirt, or debris dropping into the magazine.

Remove the sealing tape from the can of raw stock, and place the can in the bag to the *left* of the magazine. Close both zippers, tuck them under the bag, and insert hands and bar arms into the sleeves to a depth past the elbows. Remove the magazine lid and place it *under* the magazine to conserve the work area. Lift the cover of the raw stock can, invert the cover, and place it *under* the can. Remove the raw stock from the labpack bag, and hold the film in the left hand; remove any sealing tape the manufacturer may use to prevent unreeling of the raw stock, and apply that tape to the inside of the raw stock can. Load the raw stock into the magazine, then replace the magazine lid and check to make sure it is secure. Remove arms from the sleeves, unzip the bag, and remove the magazine. Tape and mark the magazine according to standard loading-room procedures (see Sec. 3.5). Put the labpack bag in the film can, and replace the cover on the can.

3.9c Unloading

Unzip the bag, and place the exposed magazine inside. Lift the ID tape, and place it in the center of the magazine lid. Place the unload can, nested in its cover and containing a labpack bag, to the right of the magazine. Ready the labpack bag. Zip the changing bag, tuck the zippered end under, and insert arms in sleeves to above the elbows. Remove the lid on the magazine take-up-side. Place the exposed stock in the labpack bag and can, and replace the can cover.

CAUTION: Some magazines have reusable cores. Do *not* ship them off to the laboratory!

Unzip the bag, tape the can around its circumference, and affix the ID tape and camera report to the can.

3.9d Folding the Bag

Changing bags packaged by the manufacturer are folded to fit a shipping box. Users invariably—and wrongly—fold the bag along the same creases. All zipper and sleeve openings require protection from dirt and snagging. To ensure a longer life, cleanliness, and minimum damage, store the changing bag as follows (see Fig. 3–3): (a) Lay flat, zippers at the top, closed. (b) Fold sleeves at the bottom inward. (c) Bring up bottom half of the bag's side toward the top. (d) Fold zipper end halfway down to meet the sleeve edge. (e) Fold right side inward halfway. (f) Fold left side in to

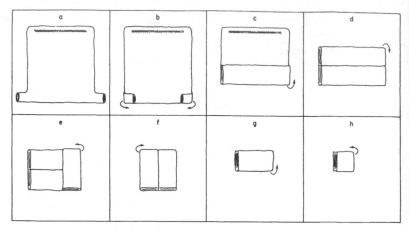

Figure 3-3 Folding the changing bag.

meet the right edge. (g) Bring up the bottom to meet the top. (h) Fold right side again to meet left side.

Store the properly folded bag in its zippered carrying container.

NOTE: After each use, the bag is shaken out, turned inside-out, and checked for dirt, debris, and damage before refolding.

3.9e Emergency Changing Bag

In extreme situations, a *lined* overcoat may be used as a changing bag as follows: Lay the coat out flat, open, buttons up, coattail nearest the loader. Place the can of film and magazine inside. Button the coat, fold it in half over the magazine, collar toward the loader. Tuck the coattail under, and the collar under the coattail. Place the arms in the coat sleeves and work on the magazine.

CAUTION: Use the emergency bag in a dark or heavily shaded area. Throw an extra blanket over the coat to add to its lighttight security.

3.9f The Changing Bag and Airline Security

Many assistants hand-carry all exposed footage when traveling, particularly overseas. Production coordinators should have made special arrangements for handling valuable footage and bypassing usually federally mandated x-ray searches, particularly in an era of heightened airline security. It is obviously an extreme risk to check exposed footage through normal airport luggage systems.

Some assistants travel with a changing bag just in case, security clearance or no, film tins need to be hand-checked. Understand that security officers may refuse to hand-check anything inside a black bag; the best and safest route is to have full and proper security clearance from the start.

3.10 HARRISON FILM-CHANGING TENT

The Harrison Film-Changing Tent is a portable tabletop darkroom, intended for loading motion picture film on location when a darkroom is not available. The unit uses two tent poles, and—when assembled—resembles a dome-shaped tent with arm sleeves in the door. It also can be used unassembled (without the poles), as a conventional changing bag.

The Harrison Tent accommodates every size and shape of 16mm, 35mm, and 65mm 1000' magazines. The tent comes with an 18-in. long by 6-in. diameter stuff sack for storage and traveling. The 12-in. shock-corded aluminum pole sections snap into two long pole sections.

3.10a Instructions

Unzip the two double zippers in the door panel, and turn the tent inside-out to remove any particles. With the silver side up, lay the tent on a flat surface, and insert one tent pole diagonally through the pole sleeves. The tip of each pole end fits into a corner pocket (made of black webbing), located at each of the tent's four corners. Securely hold the finger loop attached to the corner pocket; pull the loop toward you while pushing the pole upward and outward (away from you) so that the pole tip slides into the pocket. Repeat with the second pole.

CAUTION: Do not bend aluminum pole to make assembly easier, as this weakens the pole. Assemble the tent one pole at a time.

3.10b Storage

Remove tent poles and lay tent out flat with silver side up. Leave zippers slightly open to allow air to escape while rolling up. Fold tent in half, then roll tightly from one end. Once rolled up, tent will easily fit into its stuff sack. Put tent poles into stuff sack.

3.11 HAND TESTS

A *hand test* (sometimes called a "slop test") is an emergency procedure used when the services of a film-processing laboratory are not available, e.g., when on location. This procedure, common during the early days of filmmaking, is rarely used today but still may be necessary on occasion. Hand tests are not intended for exposure checks because the processing procedures and control obtained at a commercial laboratory cannot be duplicated by hand.

A hand test is conducted when (a) the accuracy of a camera shutter or the focus of a lens is in doubt; (b) an effects matte must be cut for insertion into a special effects camera's focusing tube to align an object in a previously filmed scene to an object yet to be photographed (e.g., artwork to live action, or vice versa); or (c) the identity of an unmarked roll of raw stock must be determined (see "Film-Type Identification," Sec. 2.1, Tables 2–1 through 2–5).

3.11a Chemicals and Equipment

The chemicals and implements necessary to conduct a hand test are as follows:

Slop-Test Kit

Chemicals		*Equipment*
High-contrast developer, e.g.,		Daylight-loading developing tank with
Agfa-Gevaert	Agitol	reel that accepts at least 5 ft of film
Fuji	Fujidol	Quart jars or cups for measuring
Ilford	I.D. Eleven	
	Plus	
Kodak	D-76	
Hypo (hyposulfite fixative)		
Water		

The slop-test kit is considered standard equipment. High-contrast print developer can be purchased as a prepared liquid or made up from a dry chemical. Commercially prepared liquid developers are mixed by the manufacturer at a ratio of approximately 1:10 (dry chemical to water). The prepared solution is then diluted by the loader at a ratio of 1:1 (solution to water) in a minimum quantity of 1 quart.

If prepared liquid is not available, the loader can use the dry chemical by preparing the solution according to the directions on the package. Generally, the mixture is 1:10 for stock solution; the *stock solution* is then diluted 1:1 to yield a minimum quantity of 1 quart of *working solution*. The daylight tank and bottles of prediluted solution or packages of dry chemical can be purchased at most camera stores. The expiration date on bottles or packages should be checked periodically for freshness.

3.11b Developing

Ten feet of test film is shot, although only a foot or two will be used for each test; unneeded excess footage is discarded.

In total darkness: The magazine and the developing tank are opened. A strip (approximately 1–3 ft) of exposed film is broken off the take-up roll and wound onto the developing tank reel. With the reel deposited inside the tank, *both* the tank lid and magazine lid are replaced.

In daylight: The diluted developer is poured into the tank, which is agitated by rotating the reel collar of the tank periodically until development is completed. Developing time varies in an uncontrolled situation such as on location; therefore, only a roughly approximate time factor can be given, and the loader should experiment to discover the best timing.

Approximate Development Time

Color neg.	7 min	Color rev.	7 min
Medium-speed b&w neg.	4	High-speed color rev.	10
High-speed b&w neg.	2	Medium-speed b&w rev.	5
		High-speed b&w rev.	3

After development: With development time completed, drain the tank and rinse it several times with water. Add the hypo, and allow the film to fix for a minimum of 5 minutes, agitating the tank often. Drain the tank, remove the lid, and rinse the film in water approximately 10 minutes (30 minutes if the film is to be used as an effects matte).

NOTE: Slopped color film (both negative and reversal) of *all* manufacturers exhibits an overall orange cast (color "masks") when removed from the tank or tray. Color values *cannot* be determined with a slop test.

When practical, it is far better to use a still-photographer's darkroom and trays instead of the daylight tank.

When all tests are completed, dispose of the excess exposed film, and thread the unused raw stock onto the magazine take-up core.

chapter 4

Slates

A *slate* is an identification board containing data pertinent to the production being filmed. There are two basic types of slates: (1) sync and (2) insert.

4.1 SYNC SLATE

The top of a sync slate consists of two halves of white plexiglass, heavy wood, or some similar material, painted with diagonal black and white lines (see Fig. 4–1). The upper half (*clapstick*) is hinged at one end to the lower half (*base*), which is nailed to the data board (*slate*).

The data on the slate consists of (a) information and (b) identification.

4.1a Information

NOTE: While the position of lines of information may vary from slate to slate, the basic data written on the board are as follows:

Scene Number. This corresponds to the scene number in the script or storyboard pertaining to the action. It is also the scene number written in the camera report. The number is obtained from the Script Supervisor or the Director.

Numerals must be written clearly and distinctly. The numeral one ("1") is always written as a straight vertical line (I)—no hook at the top or horizontal line at the base. The numeral four ("4") is always closed at the top. The numerals six ("6") and nine ("9") or any combination of digits with a "6" or "9" are always underlined to distinguish the proper base to the numeral. The numeral seven ("7") has a straight horizontal top with a vertical stem angled to the left—no hooks or base line. (A very short horizontal bar through the stem—thus: "7"—is optional in the United States but common practice in Europe and Asia.) A zero ("0") is elliptical and closed at the top. Drawing a line through the zero—thus "θ"—is not practiced in the United States but is common in Europe and Asia.

A *pick-up* (i.e., a short take of the action within the same scene number) or a variation of the scene for which no number has been established (i.e., different angle, intercut, etc., of the same action within the same scene number) is slated with the same scene number, and a letter of the alphabet added to it.

When shooting sound, the added letter is always spoken out by the Sound Mixer as a word (e.g., A—Apple; B—Baker; C—Charlie; D—Dog; E—Easy). Letters not used in slating are I—Item, O—Oboe, Q—Quebec, U—Uncle, Z—Zebra. These letters closely resemble numerals (especially when written hurriedly) and can cause confusion in the

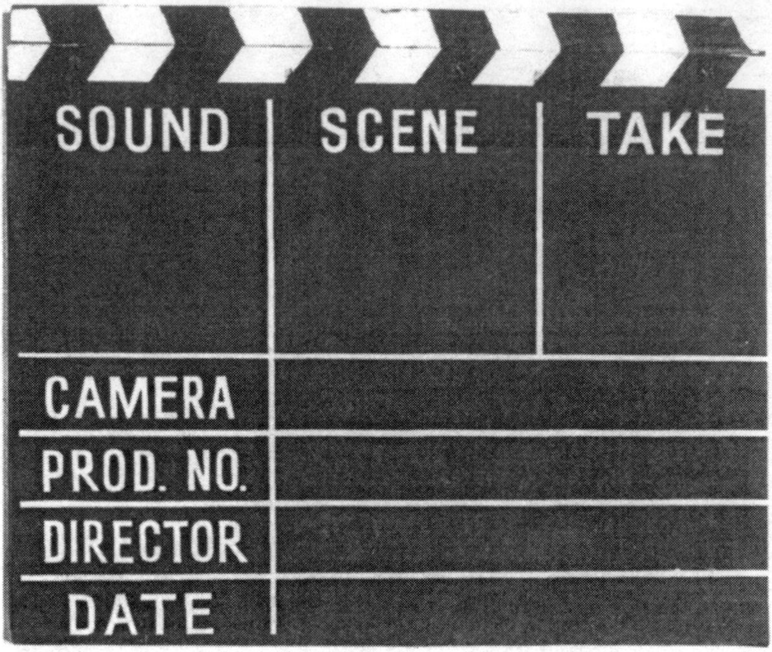

Figure 4–1 Sync slate.

Editorial Department; e.g., the letter "I" ("eye") looks like the numeral "1" ("one"); "O," "Q," and "U" resemble "0" ("zero") either closed, with an accidental mark in it, or unclosed at the top; and "Z" is too similar to the numeral "2" ("two").

If all the letters of the alphabet are used up, then a second letter is tacked onto the first letter (e.g., AA, AB, BA, BB, CA) and are spoken as Apple-Apple, Apple-Baker, Baker-Baker, etc.

Take Number. This corresponds to the number of times the scene is repeated, and it is numerically consecutive, until the Director and/or Camera Professional decides to change angle or scene. Only when the scene number changes, or when a pickup or variation of the scene occurs, does the take number revert back to numeral number one (1).

The scene, take, and roll numbers are written by using either a marker on plexiglass or chalk on painted wood. If using chalk, a powder puff discarded by the Makeup Department is a good eraser. The puff may be attached to the slate with string or tucked into a wide rubber band stretched around the slate.

Some Camera Assistants make "sets" of numerals with camera tape. Strips 1–2 in. long are numbered "1" through "0" with a felt marking pen, bent over at the top to form a little tab for ease of handling, stuck to the back of the slate, and brought from the back of the slate and applied to the front, as needed. Some commercially prepared slates come with such numeral sets, to be attached by velcro or some similar temporary adhesive.

4.1b Identification

NOTE: The following identification spaces on the slots are customarily covered with camera tape, on which the slateholder writes with a felt marking pen, to ensure that data will not be erased during production.

Production Number. The production number is the number assigned to that particular film. Picture title alone is inadequate. It is essential to keep the production number correct. If scenes from more than one production are being photographed, the production number must be changed accordingly each time, as it is the Editorial Department's only guide as to which production the scenes belong.

Director. The last name of the film's Creative Director.

Camera. The last name of the Director of Photography. On a multicamera film, the Camera Operator's name may appear beneath the Director of Photography's for identification purposes only, but this is not a rule.

Date. The month, day, and year when the scene and take were photographed.

Some sync slates may carry additional identification, such as "Ext/Int," "Day/Night," "Produced by." If so, then:

Ext/Int; Day/Night. A checkmark for one in each pair indicates to the Timer in the laboratory the lighting of the scene. The Timer refers to the camera report for more specific details. (See "Remarks" in Secs. 5.1b and 5.2b).

Produced by. The name of the *company* (not the individual) producing the film.

4.2 SLATING PROCEDURE

Most production companies prefer to have each roll slated with a roll number and, on multicamera films, the camera number as well.

The scene, take, and sound numbers are obtained from the Script Supervisor or the Director. The face of the slate is then held in such a position that the Sound Mixer can see and verify the numbers. Once these are acknowledged, the Camera Assistant then turns the slate toward the camera.

It is the Camera Operator's responsibility to frame the slate properly so that it may be read through the camera viewing system and thus on the developed film. Directions to the Assistant are "up," "down," "camera left" (to the Slateholder's right), "camera right" (to the Slateholder's left), "upstage" (away from camera), "downstage" (toward camera), "flare" (which calls for the top of the slate to be tipped forward to eliminate unreadable *bloom* [light striking the slate] across the data), and "clockwise" and "counterclockwise" (which refer to moving one corner of the slate toward the camera so as to place the slate more squarely to the Operator).

The hinged upper half of the slate painted with diagonal lines (*clapstick*) is utilized for synchronized-sound takes by raising it and bringing it down sharply against the lower half (*base*). The visual meeting of the two halves on film, when matched to the aural signal on tape, provide the Film Editor with synchronization marks for sound and picture. Because the Editor must determine the exact moment of impact visually, it is imperative that a proper slate be recorded on film.

Some newer camera systems offer electronic synchronization, in which, upon command, a small light flash is recorded on the film outside the field of view as, simultaneously, a distinctive tone is recorded on the tape.

A Camera Assistant new at slating invariably moves the slate downward as the clapstick is brought down to meet the base. The resultant blurred image causes unnecessary work ("syncing takes") in the Editorial Department. The proper way to execute a slate is to grasp the bottom of the slate in one hand, and the clapstick in the other. At the command to "roll film," the clapstick is raised to show the Editor it is a sound take, and also that it is prior to the sync marks. After the Sound Mixer has called the sound and/or the scene and take number(s), the clapstick is brought down sharply and positively and is not allowed to bounce open. The hand at the bottom of the board prevents the slate from moving downward and blurring the image. The slate, with clapstick closed, is held motionless for about 1 second, then swiftly swung down and out of frame.

The clapstick is never opened under any circumstances when shooting an MOS shot. Doing so will invariably institute a search by the Editorial Department for a sound take in spite of the "MOS" (for "Mit (With) Out Sound") written on the slate. It will be assumed that the Camera Assistant forgot to erase the "MOS" and that a sound take *was* rolled.

A Camera Assistant never hurries while slating, but once the information has been recorded on film, the Assistant moves fast to clear the scene.

Should the clapstick be either improperly photographed or missed by the Operator, the slate is reinserted into the scene and a loud command "Second Marker!" shouted before hitting the clapstick again. This tells the Editor that the first clapstick noise on the tape is unusable and that the correct sync mark is the second marker noise, as called by the Assistant (or Sound Mixer).

Tail Slate. In some instances, a slate cannot be photographed at the head of the scene. When the action for the picture has ended, the camera and recorder are kept running. The slate is presented to the camera *upside down*, the clapstick opened until the Sound Mixer calls "Tail slate!" and the scene and take numbers. The clapstick is then brought *up* sharply and positively and is not allowed to fall open.

4.3 INSERT SLATE

The insert slate is a small pocket-size identification board (see Fig. 4–2) without a clapstick. It is most often required when filming MOS, or, as the name implies, for inserts on a sound stage when long lenses are used and for which the large standard slate is impractical. The information and identification data are essentially the same as on a sync slate, with the following exceptions:

4.3a Unit

The number assigned to the group doing the photography, such as the various crews of Directors, Camera Professionals, Grips, and Electricians who may be assigned to filming certain segments of one film. A second unit is virtually standard on theatrical films, and it is quite common for third, fourth, fifth (and sometimes further) units to be shooting a TV documentary or special at the same time. The unit numbers identifies each group in such cases.

4.3b Camera

The type of camera and manufacturer's serial number—e.g., Arri 1254.

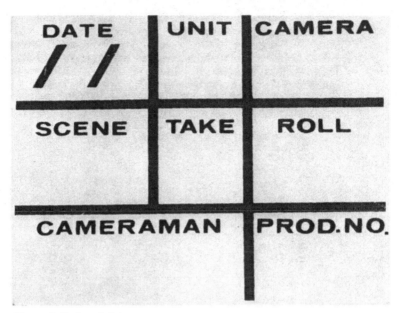

Figure 4–2 Insert slate.

4.3c Roll Number
The numerical order of the film roll as it is exposed during the course of production. Second or documentary units may place a short descriptive title rather than numbers in the scene- and take-number spaces. A series of scenes will be filmed under this short title and only changed when moving to a new location or sequence. Roll numbers on the film and corresponding "cap sheets" (see Sec. 5.3) containing all the information pertinent to the scenes and takes on that roll are the only clues the Editorial Department has to identify location and relevance to the film.

4.4 TIME CODE AND TIME-CODE SLATES
Time code is a system of identifying film or videotape by assigning each frame a chronological number based on a 24-hour clock. The incremental code numbers are continuously recorded on the film or videotape as it is shot and, simultaneously, on the separate sound track. The time code thus can be used to help synchronize picture and track. In addition, time code provides an extremely precise system of reference, facilitating efficient production and postproduction. As of this writing, most newer-model cameras offer some type of time-code capability.

Although time-code standards and systems for videotape have been clearly established, there are several different approaches to film time code. A common system uses a time-code generator in the camera, which is crystal-synchronized (often via a master clock) with the sound recorder, to optically print the code and other important information on the film edge. This other information may include the precise real time each film frame was exposed, the production number, film stock and type, and camera number. The code and other information may be printed in both computer-readable and human-readable code.

Time Code Slates. Slates are still necessary when using time-code systems, to ensure proper identification, and traditional slates may be used. However, a special time-code slate displays (through red, photographable L.E.D. number readouts) the time code as fed to it by a master clock. The assistant still uses chalk, a marker, or tape marks for scene and take numbers, etc., and works the clapstick to mark the start of a take. Such slates typically are used by multiple-camera television productions.

chapter 5

Camera Reports

A *camera report* is a sheet or card providing data pertinent to a particular roll of exposed film. Two or three copies are made of each report.

There are three basic types of camera reports:

1. *Clipboard-type or vertical format*—This report hangs on a clipboard, which is to be placed below the camera dolly or tripod or may be taped to the back of the slate.
2. *Magazine-type or horizontal format*—This report is inserted in a holder on, or is taped to, the magazine take-up side.
3. *Caption sheet* (often called "dope sheet")—This report is used for films with no script.

The data on a camera report is divided into three sections: (1) identity; (2) information; (3) inventory.

5.1 TYPICAL CLIPBOARD-TYPE CAMERA REPORT

Entries in the sections of the clipboard-type camera report (Fig. 5–1) are as follows:

5.1a Identity

Company. The name of the production company.

Address. The billing address of the production company. If the processed film and/or prints are to be shipped to any address other than the billing address (e.g., to the screening room, editorial services), the notation "SHIP [print only, negative only, or print and negative] TO: [fill in other address]," is written in the information section, in addition to a notation on the purchase order that accompanies the exposed film.

Production. The production number assigned to that particular film. Picture title alone is inadequate. During heavy scheduling of a TV series, or a group of commercials covering a given product, the Editorial Department has little time to figure out the film to which a scene or roll belongs. The production number leaves no doubt.

If more than one production number is slated on one roll, the *first* production number slated is placed in the identity section; thereafter any different production number precedes its scene number (e.g., 6844—scene no. 6, takes 1 and 2 in Fig. 5–1) and is placed in the *information* section (see "Scene No." in Sec. 5.1b). A scene number *not* preceded by a production number belongs to the production number placed in the *identity* section (Sec. 5.1a).

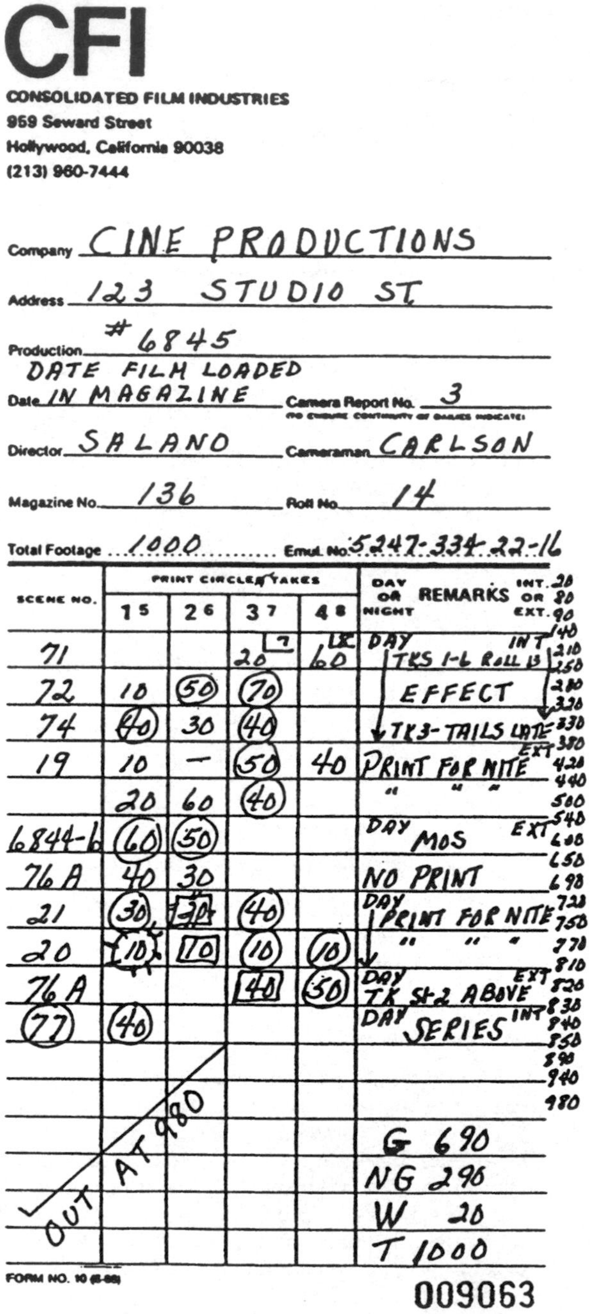

CFI

CONSOLIDATED FILM INDUSTRIES

959 Seward Street

Hollywood, California 90038

(213) 960-7444

Company _CINE PRODUCTIONS_

Address _123 STUDIO ST_

Production _#6845_

Date _IN MAGAZINE_ Camera Report No. _3_

DATE FILM LOADED

Director _SALANO_ Cameraman _CARLSON_

Magazine No. _136_ Roll No. _14_

Total Footage _1000_ Emul. No. _5-247-334-22-16_

SCENE NO.	PRINT CIRCLED TAKES				DAY OR NIGHT	REMARKS	INT. 20 or 80 EXT. 90
	1 5	2 6	3 7	4 8			
71			20 ⑦	LR 60	DAY	TKS 1-6 Roll 13	INT 140 210 250
72	10	㊿	⑦⓪			EFFECT	280 320
74	㊵	30	㊵			↓ TK3-TAILS LATE	330 380
19	10	—	㊿	40		PRINT FOR NITE	EXT 420 440
	20	60	㊵			" " "	500
6844-6	㊿	㊿			DAY	MOS EXT	540 600 650
76 A	40	30				NO PRINT	690
21	㉚, ㉚		㊵		DAY	PRINT FOR NITE	720 750
20	⑩,	⑩	⑩	⑩		" " "	770 810
76 A			㊵	㊿	DAY	TK St-2 ABOVE EXT	820 830
㊐	㊵				DAY	SERIES INT	940 850 890 940 980
						G 690	
	OUT AT 980					NG 290	
						W 20	
						T 1000	

FORM NO. 10 (8-88)

009063

Figure 5–1 Typical clipboard-type camera report. Courtesy of Consolidated Film Industries.

Date. The month, day, and year the film was loaded into the magazine. If, in an extreme situation, a partially exposed roll must remain in the magazine overnight (a bad practice—all exposed film should be canned and processed as soon as possible), a line is drawn in the information section, and the new date is written below the line.

Camera Report No. Each day, the numerical order of the camera reports starts anew—i.e., 1, 2, 3, etc. The laboratory will assemble and return the "dailies" according to the numerical order of the camera reports, so they can be screened in the same order in which they were filmed.

NOTE: "Dailies" are usually sent to the editor at the production company. The negative is usually held at the laboratory until the completion of filming and then sent to the negative cutter.

Director. The last name of the film's Creative Director.

Cameraman. The last name of the Director of Photography.

Magazine No. The serial number assigned the specific magazine by the manufacturer. Some manufacturers stamp a number on their emblem or close to the magazine throat. The inscribed serial number takes precedence over any stenciled or painted digits on the magazine because these numbers may be duplicated when two or more magazines are assigned to one camera. Knowing the manufacturer's serial number (which is never duplicated) aids in tracing any malfunction (scratches, edge fog, etc.) that may appear on the processed roll. Magazines with no manufacturer's number are, of course, assigned a number by the loader.

Roll No. The numerical order of the magazine as it is placed on the camera in the course of production.
 Whenever a roll is broken and the unexposed portion threaded into the take-up, a new roll number and camera report are assigned to that portion of film remaining, regardless of its length.

Total Footage. The total amount of raw stock loaded into the magazine.

Emul. No. The manufacturer's type of film, emulsion (batch), roll, and, in some instances, an i.d. number used for internal quality control, that is printed on the raw-stock can label (see Sec. 2.1).

5.1b Information

Scene No. Corresponds to the number on the slate and to the number or description in the script (or picture on a storyboard).

Takes. Only the *footage expended* on the take is entered, not the take number or dial (footage-counter) reading.
 When using a camera with an additive dial, the Operator rounds off the dial reading to the nearest 10 ft when using 35mm film (or nearest 5 ft when using 16mm) and gives the Assistant only the first two digits (e.g., 213 ft is called "21"; 379 ft is called "38"; 675 ft is called on the long side—"68").
 As the numbers on the dial increase, the Assistant must subtract the *previous* reading from the new reading in order to determine the footage expended on the take.
 Because a clipboard-type camera report has no provision for a dial entry, the dial reading given by the Operator must be either written along the right-hand edge of the report or calculated on a separate sheet of paper.

When using a camera with a subtractive magazine indicator, the amount of footage expended must be estimated because the indicator is not as accurate as a digital footage counter. As the indicator decreases, the Assistant must subtract the *new* reading from the previous reading in order to determine the footage expended on the take.

The footage expended on each take is placed in its appropriate space, and as each line of four takes is filled, the next line below is used for succeeding takes (e.g., scene no. 19, in Fig. 5–1).

A carryover of takes from a previous roll (e.g., scene no. 71, takes 7 and 8, in Fig. 5–1), while placed in their appropriate space, also have a take number in the upper right-hand corner to indicate to the Lab and the Editorial Department that they are a carryover and that there are no other takes ahead of those numbers on that particular roll.

Any time a take is less than 10 ft in length and is a "no print," or if the camera has not run but the Sound Mixer has voice-slated the sound tape, thereby requiring that the next take number be used on the slate, a straight line (—) rather than a footage count is inserted (e.g., scene no. 19, take 2 in Fig. 5–1). If less than 10 ft in length and a "print," it is given a minimum count of "10."

A circled take indicates to the laboratory that the particular length of film is to be printed for screening (e.g., scene no. 71, take 8 in Fig. 5–1).

All "holds" are indicated with a square ("squared"; e.g., scene no. 76A, take 3, in Fig. 5–1). The square indicates to the Editorial Department that the take is acceptable to the Director even though the circled take is preferred. Laboratories will print a "hold."

Takes and holds marked for printing and then later rejected after being circled or squared are canceled out by drawing short lines through the circumference of the circle (e.g., scene no. 20, take 1) or the sides of the square (e.g., scene no. 21, take 2 in Fig. 5–1).

Remarks. This section is important to the Laboratory Timer, as well as the Editorial Department.

The "DAY/NIGHT" and "EXT/INT" notations often make the difference between a mediocre print and the very essence of the Director of Photography's intent when timed dailies are desired. Without the proper information to the Timer, a day-for-night scene (e.g., scene nos. 19, 20, and 21 in Fig. 5–1) may appear underexposed, or the Timer may choose the wrong printing light in an attempt to save what is considered to be an incorrectly exposed scene. The print will be wrong, the recommended printing light will be wrong, the production company will have to have the scene reprinted (cost and delay), and the Director of Photography will be displeased with the treatment of an attempted effect.

Any special effect (focus change, lights on, lights off, etc.) is noted as "Effect" (e.g., scene no. 72, takes 1, 2, Fig. 5–1.)

Previous takes of a scene no. located on another roll are noted for the Editorial Department (e.g., scene no. 71, takes 1–6, Fig. 5–1).

All tail (or "end") slates are noted (e.g., scene no. 74, take 3, tail slate) so that the Laboratory Technician who reads the camera report will know which takes to "pull." He or she separates the circled and squared takes from the developed negative and makes prints from them. Because the Technician only uses the photograph of the slate as a guide to separate "good" from "no good" takes, the notation warns to look for a different picture or clear frame (which denotes a camera stop) instead of a slate.

The Editorial Department makes use of the notation also, when it is assembling the print.

All silent takes are noted MOS to indicate to the Laboratory and Editorial Department that no sound accompanies the picture.

When there are no prints of a particular scene (e.g., scene no. 76A, takes 1, 2, Fig. 5–1), a definite "No Print" notation is mandatory, since the Laboratory and Editorial Department have no way of knowing if it is a "no print" or if the Assistant forgot to circle a take. Telephone calls, searches, and delay in delivery of prints to the production company will thus be avoided.

A number of takes shot on one slate is noted as "Series" (e.g., scene no. 77, take 1, Fig. 5–1) so that the Editorial Department will know to expect more than one take of the same action.

At the end of the roll, or at the end of the day's shooting, the information section of the report is reviewed with the Script Clerk or Sound Recordist to verify all prints and holds.

5.1c Inventory

Good (G), no good (NG) and waste (W) footages and their totals (T) are written in the lower right corner of the report.

The totals of just the good and no good takes are written across the face of the report in an area clear of the information data.

5.2 TYPICAL MAGAZINE-TYPE CAMERA REPORT

Entries in the sections of the magazine-type camera report (Fig. 5–2) are as follows.

5.2a Identity

Company. The name of the production company.

Pic. Title. The working name of the picture while in production (may be released to the public under a different title).

Production No. The production number assigned to that particular picture. It is more important than the film's title. Once assigned to a production it never changes.

Director. The last name of the film's Creative Director.

Customer Order No. The production company's purchase order number. This only applies when submission of film is for the first time, or when a production company and laboratory have not signed an agreement covering an entire production.

Cameraman. The last name of the Director of Photography.

Cam. No. When more than one camera is used to film a scene (such as explosions or one-time stunts) this camera number refers to an assigned letter rather than a numeral. Camera A is always the main camera. Camera B is assigned to cover a secondary important angle, camera C, another angle, etc., etc. A quick glance at the lettered Cam. No. informs the film editor which angle, and camera, covered the shot.

Sheet No. / of /. Filled in only when more than one camera report is used to note data pertinent to that particular roll of exposed film. If, for example, three reports were used to record the data, the sequential reports would read: Sheet No. 1 of 3; Sheet No. 2 of 3; Sheet No. 3 of 3.

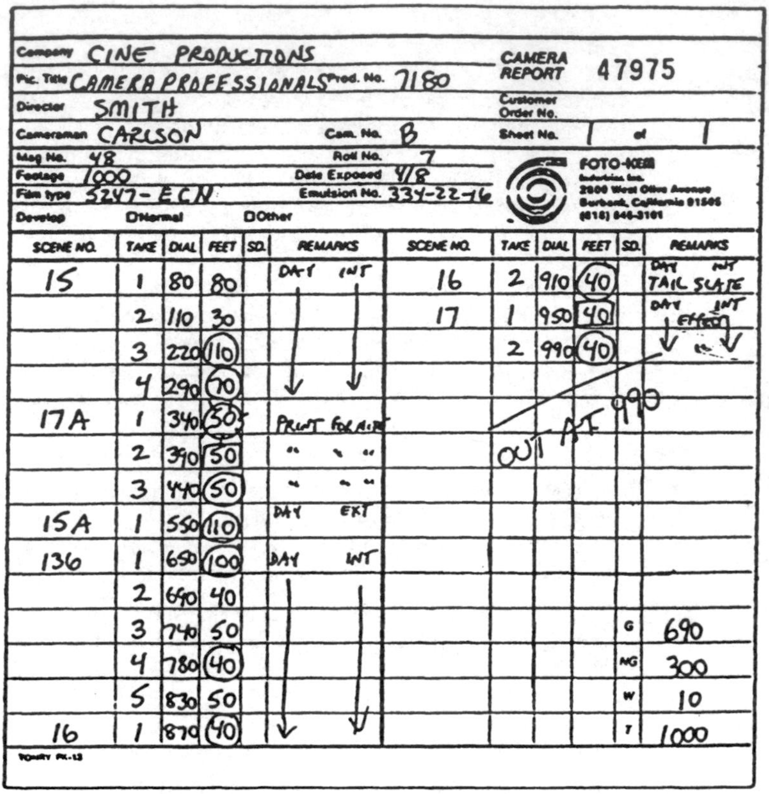

Company CINE PRODUCTIONS
Pic. Title CAMERA PROFESSIONALS Prod. No. 7180
CAMERA REPORT 47975
Director SMITH
Customer Order No.
Cameraman CARLSON Cam. No. B Sheet No. 1 of 1
Mag No. 48 Roll No. 7
Footage 1000 Date Exposed 4/8
Film type 5247-ECN Emulsion No. 334-22-16
Develop ☐Normal ☐Other
FOTO-KEM Industries, Inc. 2800 West Olive Avenue Burbank, California 91505 (818) 846-3101

SCENE NO.	TAKE	DIAL	FEET	SD.	REMARKS	SCENE NO.	TAKE	DIAL	FEET	SD.	REMARKS
15	1	80	80		DAY INT	16	2	910	(40)		DAY INT TAIL SLATE
	2	110	30		↓ ↓	17	1	950	[40]		DAY INT EFFECT
	3	220	(110)		↓ ↓		2	990	(40)		↓ " ↓
	4	290	(70)		↓ ↓						
17A	1	340	(50)		PRINT FOR AIR						
	2	390	[50]		" " "	OUT AT 990					
	3	440	(50)		" " "						
15A	1	550	(110)		DAY EXT						
136	1	650	(100)		DAY INT						
	2	690	40		↓ ↓						
	3	740	50		↓ ↓					G	690
	4	780	(40)		↓ ↓					NG	300
	5	830	50		↓ ↓					W	10
16	1	870	(40)		↓ ↓					T	1000

Figure 5–2 Magazine-type camera report. Courtesy of Foto-Kem Industries, Inc.

Mag No. The inscribed serial number assigned the specific magazine by the manufacturer.

Roll No. The numerical order of the magazine as it is placed on the camera in the course of production.

Footage. The total amount of raw stock loaded into the magazine.

Date Exposed. The date (month and day) the magazine was loaded.

Film Type. Both the type number and its common name (e.g., XTS 400-ACN; 5247-ECN; F250-FCN). The type number and common name serve as a double-check when canning the film, and also for the Laboratory Technician when preparing the film for development.

Emulsion No. The manufacturer's batch, roll, and I.D. number that is printed on the raw-stock can label (see Sec. 2.1).

5.2b Information

Scene No. Corresponds to the number on the slate and to the scene number or description in the script or storyboard.

Take. Same as "Takes" in the clipboard-type report (in Sec. 5.1b) but running vertically.

Dial. The cumulative footage as registered on the camera dial (footage Counter) rounded off to the nearest 10 feet.

Feet. The footage expended on the particular shot.

SD. On some (but not all) productions a check mark ($\checkmark$) mark is made to indicate it is a sound take. A silent take would normally be marked MOS in this space, but in practice, an MOS shot is noted in "Remarks."

Remarks. Same details apply as in "remarks" in the clipboard-type report (Sec. 5.1).

5.2c Inventory
The total (T) of the good (G), no good (NG) and waste (W) footages are noted in the lower right corner of the report.

5.3 TYPICAL CAPTION-SHEET-TYPE CAMERA REPORT

NOTE: The caption-sheet-type camera report (*cap sheet* or *dope sheet*) is used primarily when shooting without a script, as for news or documentary films.

Entries in the sections of caption-sheet-type camera report (Fig. 5–3) are as follows:

5.3a Identity

Date. Month, day, and year the film was exposed.

Crew. Either the name or number assigned to the unit or the last name of the Director of Photography.

Stock. Both the manufacturer's type number and the common name.

ASA. The exposure rating given the film by the Director of Photography (which may be double, triple, or quadruple the manufacturer's recommended rating).

Location. The city or area in which the filming is done.

Footage. The amount of exposed film being sent to the laboratory.

Subject. The particular person(s) or material the film is about.

Roll No. The numerical order of the roll of film exposed during the production. It is essential to film a roll number, to enable the Editorial Department to find, identify, and place the scenes in proper context in the film.

Lab. No. A control number assigned to the roll by the laboratory. This number is not filled out by the loader because the lab number is not assigned to the roll of film until the day it is developed by the laboratory—which might be days or weeks after it was exposed. The Camera Crew has no control over the laboratory or its particular numbering system.

5.3b Information

Shot Description. The contents of the scenes on the roll. This includes the type of shot (i.e., MS, CU, Zoom), names of the persons or materials in

DATE	TODAY'S DATE	**UPI NEWSFILM** ⊛ ⊕		LAB. No.	

CAMERAMAN'S DOPE SHEET

CREW: __UNIT # 4__ STOCK: __DXN 7222__ ASA: __500__

LOCATION: __SAN FRANCISCO__ FOOTAGE: __370'__

SUBJECT: __BRIDGE PAINTERS__

Roll No.	SHOT DESCRIPTION
6	L.S. BRIDGE FROM SEA, S.F. IN B.G.
	M.S. BRIDGE TOWER
	M.S. SUSPENSION CABLE — DECK LEVEL
	M.C.S. WORKMEN CLIMB CABLE
	C.U. WORKMEN IN + OUT OF FRAME TOWARD CAMERA
	M.S. FROM TOWER — WORKMEN CLIMB UP
	M.C.S. WORKMAN SLINGS BOS'N CHAIR — ZOOM IN
	M.S. PAINTER IN BOS'N CHAIR LOWERS SELF
	L.S. FROM DECK LEVEL — PAINTERS UP HIGH
	L.S. PAINTERS P.O.V. FROM UP HIGH
	CUTAWAY TRAFFIC ON BRIDGE
	" S.F. BUILDINGS IN B.G. PAN LEFT
	" TOLL GATE
	Out at 370'

FILL OUT ABOVE COMPLETELY AND ACCURATELY. ATTACH ALL AVAILABLE BACKGROUND MATERIAL.
SHIP WITH FILM IMMEDIATELY VIA AIR EXPRESS TO: UPI NEWSFILM, 448 W. 56th ST., N.Y. 19, N.Y.

Figure 5–3 Typical caption sheet report. Courtesy of UPITN.

the shot, the action taking place, and screen direction of subject (left to right, tailaway, right to left, etc.).

5.3c Inventory

The total of all the film *exposed that day* is written on the last sheet only.

5.4 DISPOSITION OF REPORTS

Every roll of film must be accompanied by a camera report, even though no slates are shot and the roll is a "print all." This is important should the negative turn up with a defect after processing. An investigator can more easily pinpoint the source of the defect when given the film, emulsion, can, magazine, and roll numbers.

NOTE: It is also standard procedure for a laboratory to "print all" when no camera report accompanies the can. (They assume that every frame is desired, having nothing to indicate otherwise.) An unnecessary printing expense may be incurred. For example, if only a 20-ft print on a 1000-ft exposed roll is desired, a report would indicate this. No report would result in 1000 ft of print, 980 ft of which would be unusable.

The original white sheet is folded in half and taped face up to the can of exposed film (so the laboratory can read at a glance the company name and type of film). All copies of the report are considered "hot" and should be presented to the Assistant Director (or the Camera Department Head) immediately after canning exposed film so that they may be distributed to the various departments that depend upon the data.

The Assistant Director sends the second sheet to the Editorial Department, and the third sheet is retained by the Assistant Director for the daily Production Report. Other copies (called "accounting sheets") are sent to other departments (accounting, camera, etc.).

NOTE: The reports herein are representative only. A given laboratory's or studio's reports may vary, requiring more or less data and copies, or in size or format, depending upon circumstances peculiar to its operations. No endorsement or criticism of any laboratory, studio, or format is here intended by inclusion or omission.

5.5 THE SCRIPT SUPERVISOR

It is extremely important to maintain good communication with the Script Supervisor. When shooting numerous or complicated takes, reshoots, scenes with inserts, reaction shots, over-the-shoulder shots, etc., reports to the lab indicating which shots should be processed or printed *must* match the Script Supervisor's notes.

chapter 6

On-the-job Procedures

Many in-plant units, television stations, small production houses, and similar groups require their Operative Camera personnel to perform what are, in the major film studios, the duties of the Camera Assistant. These are functions that all Camera professionals, regardless of status or place of employment, must know, and know well, if they are to work effectively on their own assignments.

Some of this chapter's information concerns older cameras with offset viewfinder or variable-speed "wild" motors. Camera Professionals are educated in time-tested procedures. Newer-model reflex cameras may relegate such tasks as parallax checking (Sec. 6.1f) to the history shelves, yet, in many countries these older technologies and procedures are often utilized on sound stages, especially in the filming of special effects. In spite of the razzle-dazzle of electronics, many effects must still be done, and can be done, on film. It will enhance your professional value if you are able to handle jobs regardless of the type or age of the camera.

The following is a detailed exposition of the procedures and responsibilities of the Camera Assistant.

6.1 PRIOR TO SHOOTING

6.1a Preshooting Inventory

The Camera Assistant is responsible for collecting and checking out the camera and related equipment. A checklist itemizing the equipment needed to build the camera unit from the ground up greatly facilitates the performance of this assignment. This, incidentally, is not a figure of speech. The photographic system is properly assembled from the ground up, with the spreader or tripod as starting point.

A basic *checklist* to guide the Assistant should cover the following items: spreader, tripod (or tripods), tripod head, camera, motor, power line, magazines, lenses, filters, accessories, raw stock, slate, camera reports, empty film cans, and labpack bags.

Location jobs require the following additional items: changing bag and shipping cartons and labels.

NOTE: It is the responsibility of the Producer to provide raw stock, camera tape, masking tape, camera reports, filters, shipping labels, black labpack bags, extra film cans, and packing cases, but their inclusion in the preshooting inventory is the responsibility of the Camera Assistant.

6.1b Setting Up

The camera is first set up without the magazine; the mechanism is oiled, power line connected, and the camera run unthreaded to warm up the motor and camera. On cold stages or exterior locations, a rule of thumb calls for starting the camera with the footage counter at zero and running it until the counter indicates at least the amount of footage equal to the magazine that will be on the camera. Temperature variations influence the amount of warm-up time, and call for judgment on the part of the Camera Assistant.

While the camera warms up, the *slate* and *camera reports* are prepared, with appropriate identification. Marking-tape strips for actors are also readied (see Sec. 6.2a).

The *lens case* for a dolly-mounted camera is always kept on the front running board, with the slate next to it. The Assistant's ditty bag (tool kit—see Sec. 6.4) is hung below the camera, with the magazine and accessory cases kept as close to the dolly as practical.

NOTE: On sound stages, a camera-equipment case with both latches closed indicates it is empty and not in use. With only one latch closed, it is "working," i.e., being entered for lenses, magazines, accessories, etc. (and therefore is to be kept close to the camera). No latches closed means a careless Assistant is on the job (the possibility of the contents of the case being spilled onto the stage floor is great, especially when a new setup is called for and everything must be moved.)

Unless the Director of Photography calls for a lens of a specific focal length, *the first lens mounted up* is a wide-angle so that the Director of Photography and the Director can observe as much of the set as possible to determine lighting, composition, placement of personnel (or product), or the lens required for the shot.

NOTE: *Whenever* a new lens is brought up, the aperture is set at its widest opening, and the *approximate* distance from camera to subject is set so that the Director of Photography and/or Director can view the scene in focus.

The courtesy of requesting the Director of Photography's permission to "load camera" is more to inform the Director of Photography that the camera will be unavailable for a short time, rather than the act of a subservient crew member. If the Director of Photography does not need the camera for checking composition and/or lighting arrangements, the Director of Photography will grant permission to load.

When a magazine containing less than a normal load of raw stock is placed on the camera, a *short-load reminder tape*—i.e., a short strip of white camera tape—is placed at the rear of the camera (below the footage counter), showing the amount of raw stock in the magazine so that the Operator is always aware of the short load.

6.1c Film-Scratch Test

Once the camera is threaded, a *film-scratch test* is made. With the camera door open, approximately 2 ft of film is run past the gate. On double-compartment-type and coaxial-type magazines, the take-up lid is removed and the film unwound from the core. (Displacement-type magazines require reversing the camera and running the film back out). The surface of the emulsion and base are examined by holding the film surface at a 90° angle to a light source and tilting the film (toward and away from the observer) so as to cause the light to "skip" along the surface. A scratch will be apparent immediately.

To determine where a camera scratch originates, the Assistant runs film through the threaded camera. The Assistant then stops the camera and with a felt pen marks the film at the following points: (1) where it exits the magazine feed rollers; (2) before it enters the gate; (3) after it exits the gate; and (4) where it enters the magazine take-up rollers. The Assistant then unthreads the camera very carefully and examines the film. The area causing the trouble is indicated by the origin of the scratch on the film. The suspect area is carefully checked for film chips, emulsion build-up, dirt, or burrs on the mechanism. Burrs are removed with crocus cloth, while other offenders are removed with an orangewood (not metal!) stick.

6.1d Hair Check

After a camera has been threaded and a few feet of film run-in, a *hair check* is made. Any lint, dust, and film chips in the camera aperture photograph as large ropes, therefore careful examination of the camera aperture at the first threading and subsequently after each print is mandatory.

NOTE: There are three schools of thought on hair checks: pull-the-plate advocates, pull-the-lens advocates, and sight-through-the-lens advocates.

Some Directors of Photography prefer the Assistant to *pull-the-plate*— i.e., open the camera door, clear the registration pins and pulldown claw, remove the film from the race, pull the removable plate, and check it. Theoretically, any hair or other debris will be caught in the recess of the plate, but this does not always work out in practice. It has been the sad experience of many Camera Professionals to print a supposedly "clean take," only to discover when screening rushes that a hair had left its indelible mark. When the film was removed from the race, the hair came out with it and had escaped detection. The plate came out "clean."

Pull-the-lens advocates prefer the Assistant to remove the "taking" lens, clear the shutter from the aperture, and shine a flashlight into the lens port. The film emulsion acts as a bright backing, clearly outlining any "hair" in the aperture. Also, on cameras with deep-set apertures, anything resting in the depth of the aperture (which would be missed by pulling the plate) can be seen clearly.

The *sight-through-the-lens* method is accomplished by clearing the shutter from the aperture, leaving the lens in the port, opening the lens to its widest aperture, placing a flashlight to the observer's cheekbone, and, sighting along the barrel of the flashlight, shining the beam into the lens. By moving the head and flashlight *together,* the magnified aperture is easily traced. While somewhat difficult to accomplish at first, once learned—sighting along the light and moving head and light together—this method is quicker and far more reliable than any other the author has used. If the area is clean, no lens removal is necessary. If a magnified hair or other debris is present, of course, the lens must be removed from the port. This method can only be used on 40mm lenses or longer. Anything shorter than 40mm requires pulling the lens, as magnification is poor.

6.1e Cleaning the Aperture

To *clean the aperture,* the tip of a bulb syringe is inserted into the port and gently squeezed to blow the area clean. Stubborn lint or chips will require the insertion of an orangewood stick (never metal) for their removal. With the obstruction removed, a short burst of film is rolled through the camera while observing the aperture, to be certain no more hairs drop in before the lens is replaced.

6.1f Parallax Check

On cameras fitted with off-set viewfinders, a *parallax check* is made, with the cooperation of the Camera Operator. The procedure is repeated each time a different lens is brought up. On cameras fitted with a follow-focus attachment, the lens and follow-focus cam gear are both first set at infinity. The cam, matching the focal length of the camera's taking lens, is placed on the viewfinder harness. The follow-focus and lens gears are then meshed and secured. The view-finder ribbon mattes are then conformed to match the lens "up."

With the lens set at infinity, the Camera Assistant hooks a measuring tape to the camera, then steps out to a distance of 15 ft, paying out the tape. The Assistant then pulls the measuring tape taut (parallel to the floor), places a finger on the 15-ft mark, lifts the tape vertically—approximately 18 in.—and holds it motionless. The Operator sights through the racked-over camera focusing tube, aligns the focus tube's vertical cross hair with the vertical measuring tape, then rotates the follow-focus knob to align the vertical cross hair of the offset viewfinder with the vertical tape. (With no follow-focus attachment on the camera, the lens focus would be set at 15 ft and the Operator would manually move the viewfinder to align the cross hair and lock it into position.) The Camera Assistant remains motionless until the Operator compares the focusing tube and viewfinder cross hairs once more. When the Operator says, "set," the Assistant walks to the camera and verifies the lens focus at 15 ft. Any large variation requires checking to see whether (a) the correct cam is mounted on the viewfinder; (b) the viewfinder reducing lens is on (or off), depending on which lens is up; (c) the viewfinder is properly riding the cam roller; or (d) one tooth of the lens gear needs to be shifted. Often, the *witness mark*—i.e., the white stripe on the lens gear that aligns to the stripe on the follow-focus gear, has been mis-set. A lens gear that has no witness mark should be set with its infinity mark matched to the lens-mount scribe. If the follow-focus gear does not mesh easily with the lens gear, the lens should be set with the infinity mark one tooth *beyond* the mount scribe (i.e, past infinity) to mesh the gears.

Very slight variations in parallax can be corrected if the Operator turns the parallax-adjustment screw located below the viewfinder. Even if "right on," the procedure is repeated at 10-ft and 5-ft intervals.

If the three measurements differ, then it is more important that the parallax-adjustment screw below the offset viewfinder be adjusted for the closest measurement (i.e., 5 ft). The Operator then sets the focusing-tube cross hair on a subject at 10 ft and 15 ft, checking the position of the viewfinder cross hair at those respective measurements, to know on which side of the viewfinder cross hair the subject will be centered on the film at those distances. (See Sec. 7.2c.)

6.1g Flare Check

A *flare check* determines whether any spill from backlights or kickerlights is shining into the lens. *Flare* is eliminated by either readjusting the barn door on the offending light or placing a flag on a stand between the camera and the offending light.

6.2 DURING SHOOTING

With film-scratch test, hair check, flare check, and, if needed, parallax check completed, the Director of Photography is informed in a loud and clear voice, "Camera ready!" This also serves notice to everyone in the crew that shooting is close to commencement. (Some production companies have a bell rigged to the camera as a "camera ready" signal.)

Once the rehearsal or scene is ready to be filmed, the Assistant always remembers the word "FAST":

> F—focus (distance of camera to subject)
> A—aperture (*f*/stop or T-stop setting)
> S —shutter (degree of opening)
> T—tachometer (speed of camera)

6.2a Focus Measurements

Focus measurements are always taken as unobtrusively as possible, without interfering with the Director and/or Actors.

Marking-Tape Strips. Lengths of black tape approximately 4 in. long, which have been torn off the roll when setting up earlier and applied to the camera magazine or housing until needed, are used to mark the position of the Actors and are placed on the studio floor in an "X"or a "V." Then, even if the subject leaves the mark, there is a reference for measurement.

Follow-Focus Marks. If there are numerous subject and/or camera moves in one take, many Assistants place a strip of white camera tape close to the follow-focus knob and mark it with position numbers and actual focus distances (e.g., 1 − 10 ft, 2 − 15 ft, 3 − 9 ft); then, setting the lens at the actual focus distances, mark the follow-focus dial with only the position numbers (e.g., 1, 2, 3). The camera tape is used for reference in the event that the count is forgotten while filming. A quick check of the footage mark on the lens against the focus distance marked on the tape gives the position. Also, if the camera is dollied out of sequence, a quick check of position against focus or vice versa will provide orientation.

The Dolly Grip invariably marks a position on the floor at the back end of the camera in chalk or with tape, and the smart Camera Assistant will mark the same position number on the floor in front of the camera, whenever possible, for quick reference as to his or her whereabouts in the sequence.

Estimating Focus. Another habit every Camera Professional develops is estimating the distance from camera to subject *before* checking it against the actual tape measurement. Constant practice then prepares the Assistant to make a quick focus adjustment with reasonable accuracy while filming, should the subject or camera (or both) miss the preset marks. On interiors, it is also helpful to predetermine the depth and width of the set, and then measure the $\frac{1}{4}, \frac{1}{2}$, and $\frac{3}{4}$ distances, using important props or set dressings as reference marks. In due time, the Assistant will reach the point of needing only one measurement per setup, and thereafter, no matter where the subject or camera moves, will adjust focus accordingly, being less than 6 in. off true distance. However, it takes considerable time and practice to achieve a proficiency of that caliber.

Other Problems. On a dolly shot involving long lenses, the Assistant will mark the floor every 12 in. and mark each corresponding foot on the follow-focus knob. As the dolly's front runningboard reaches each floor mark, the focus is conformed to that mark.

When a subject moves toward the camera and it is impossible to mark the floor, set dressings are used as reference points and their distances marked accordingly on the follow-focus knob; or, as noted elsewhere, if possible, a measuring tape is hooked into the subject's belt and reeled in or out by a Second Assistant, who calls off the footage for the First Assistant who is "pulling focus."

6.2b Lens-Aperture Stops

The general practice of the Camera Assistant is to ask the Director of Photography whether the readings will be in f/stops or in T stops. Thereafter, the lens stops are set to conform to this preference.

When given a stop, the Assistant *always* repeats the reading aloud to verify understanding of it. The Director of Photography (who is thinking about many things at one time) is thus reminded of her or his statement and is also provided the opportunity to affirm or correct the reading.

Directors of Photography usually try to maintain a constant foot-candle measurement (especially on interiors) so that exposure and density remain constant throughout the film. In the event the Director of Photography should forget to mention the stop, the Assistant can be fairly (but not always) safe by setting the diaphragm at the last reading given or asking the Director of Photography whether the reading is the same as the last one.

In the event the Assistant forgets to stop down, is not sure of having done so, or has set the wrong stop, it is the Assistant's responsibility to mention the error to the Director of Photography. The Assistant does not fear the consequences of failure (there isn't a person alive who hasn't made a mistake, or been the victim of one). The Director of Photography may not appreciate the loss of the shot, but professionalism will require the Director of Photography's recognition of the integrity of the Assistant in admitting the mistake. Unless the Director of Photography is a prima donna, he or she will quietly order a retake, giving the reason to the powers that be that the shot did not meet the "artistic standards" of the profession (the Director of Photography's prerogative). When the day's work is over, however, it is also the Director of Photography's prerogative to take the Assistant aside (far from the cast, crew, and clients), thank the Assistant for the integrity brought to the job, and *then* voice an opinion about the loss of the shot, in whatever manner the Director of Photography chooses. The professional Assistant admits the mistake, offers no excuses, and endeavors not to repeat the error.

Then they both forget it and start fresh the next day.

6.2c Shutter

On cameras equipped with *variable shutters,* whenever a shutter is changed from its normal opening, the *Operator* sets the shutter, and the Assistant makes *two* "reminder tapes," each of which should be marked with the exact shutter angle. One (marked "SHUTTER") is prominently taped to the Assistant's side of the camera. The other is taped to the shutter handle and extended down the back of the camera to cover the footage counter, so that the Operator is forced to lift the tape in order to give the footage count to the Assistant. This procedure in itself will remind the Operator that the shutter is set less than normal, and to check the degrees of opening each time the tape is lifted.

Thereafter, at each reading, the Assistant reminds the Director of Photography that the stop is being set at a specific aperture and degree of opening, so that the Director of Photography can be certain to compensate for it (e.g., "2.8 at 135°").

Once the shutter is returned to normal, both reminder tapes are discarded. The shutter handle is reset by the Operator and double-checked by the Assistant to verify that the shutter is open and locked into position.

6.2d Tachometer

Synchronous and constant-speed motors require no checking, provided the voltage necessary to run the motor is known to be constant. The voltage to the camera is checked periodically by the electricians. Any dimming or brightening of lights on the set, or variation of motor noise while filming, is of course an indication of a change in motor speed (and therefore a difference in exposure). Cameras not equipped with a tachometer need close checking; it is common practice, where voltage variation is suspected, to wire a voltmeter (which acts as a "tachometer") into the line that is feeding "juice" to the camera. This is especially helpful when filming in a strange location and using an AC line from an unknown power source.

Low voltage applied to a synchronous or constant-speed motor will run the camera more slowly than normal; suspect voltage can also be checked by observing the camera pulldown claw with a strobe light. Most often, however, it is discovered by hearing the slow motor speed.

Too high a voltage will either blow a fuse of cameras so equipped, heat an unfused synchronous motor, or heat a constant-speed motor abnormally and eventually burn it out.

Variable-speed motors require a tachometer. While the camera speed is set by the Operator, whose responsibility it is to make certain the speed is constant when the camera rolls, the Assistant always leans around the Operator to verify it.

6.2e Filters

It is essential to mark the *type* of filter in the camera, to avoid mistakes in exposure. Whenever a filter is inserted into the camera or lens, a "reminder tape" marked "FILTER IN" is prominently placed on the camera or lens, to avoid the possibility, for instance, of moving from an exterior location to an interior with a filter in place. (Even those with the best of memories can overlook this simple item in the haste of breaking down and setting up again.) This especially applies to zoom lenses with rear-mount filter holders.

When sliding a gelatine filter holder into a camera fitted with a filter slot, it is imperative that the Assistant open the camera door (or remove a lens) and verify that the holder is seated (i.e., clears the aperture) and that pressure has not pushed the filter out of place in the holder (which would result in a partially filtered frame). The filter will slide in its holder if the gelatine has not been cut evenly to conform to the perimeter of the holder or if it has not been seated deeply enough in the holder. To avoid sliding, of course, it should be taped in place *inside* the holder before insertion into the slot.

Filters are more sensitive than lenses to fingerprints, dust, scratches, etc.; therefore the Assistant exercises greater care when handling them. Care against filter "burn" is perhaps most important to guard against, although it is the least considered (and least known) precaution taken. *Burn* is caused by the delicate gelatine being rubbed as it is inserted into the filter slot. An almost imperceptible difference in the thickness of the gelatine results, which, depending on the lighting of a scene, may show up on the projected film as a diffused spot or streak, a lighter area within the frame, an opaque area, or halation. Many scenes have been reshot, lenses unnecessarily bench-checked, or cameras retired because of an unexplainable "smudge" on the negative. A careful check—at the time of insertion—of the filter holder would have avoided all the trouble.

A glass filter (which is usually a sheet of gelatine sandwiched between two pieces of optical flat glass) may not "burn," but wide scratches or abrasions on the optical flat have a similar effect.

Quite often, a gelatine neutral-density filter will be used to partially filter sky or brightly lit areas. Most Camera Assistants include a sheet of optical flat glass in their kit, which they insert into the matte box. Then, sighting through the camera focusing tube, they trace on the flat—with a grease pencil—the area to be filtered. It calls for considerable manual dexterity, as often the Assistant must sketch backward and left-handed, and orientation is difficult. Once traced, the optical flat is removed, the gelatine filter placed on the flat *opposite* the grease marks and cut to conform to the grease pencil mark. It is then taped to the flat and reinserted into the matte box to check whether the filter is properly cut and placed. If trimming is unnecessary, the grease pencil marks are removed with alcohol, the flat reinserted, and alignment rechecked before shooting.

WARNING: It is imperative that the filter be aligned with the lens stopped down to the aperture at which the scene will be photographed (never wide open). Even a slight variation of light values from one "take" to the next is sufficient cause for realignment of the filter in the matte box.

6.2f Film Jams

Film jams—i.e., pile-ups of film inside the camera movement area—are an accepted (albeit not too graciously) fact of life in film work. They halt production and must be cleared quickly and, most important, efficiently.

One of the most common causes of camera jams is improper loading of the magazine feed side. Many feed spindles are fitted with ball-type or spring-action-type spindle keys that retract into the spindle post whenever a core is slid over the feed spindle. It is imperative when loading the magazine to rotate the raw-stock core until the spindle key engages the core slot. Otherwise, when the magazine is mounted on the camera, the raw-stock (feed) core rotates at a slightly slower speed than the feed spindle until inevitably the ball-type or spring-action-type key on the spindle pops up into the core slot. At that moment an almost imperceptible halt in the rotation of the raw-stock core occurs. However infinitesimal the interruption of the film flow into the camera, it is enough to put the film perforation out of alignment with the pulldown claw and to cause a jam.

Other causes of film jams are improper sizes of loops, improper engagement of registration pins or sprockets in film perforations (misthreading), slippage of belt or gear (too loose or greasy), improper take-up winding, and lack of take-up on the magazine. Consistent jamming caused by some emulsion surfaces "sticking" in the gate (usually a characteristic of emulsions with high ASA ratings) can be eliminated in an emergency by applying a noncorrosive silicon spray to the gate or plate. (Usually, the cure is to send the camera or magazine to the factory to have the plate relieved a few thousandths of an inch or have the solid piece pressure plate segmented, i.e., divided into three parts.)

When *removing jammed film,* the Assistant should exercise *extreme care* so that the internal workings—especially registration pins, pulldown claws, sprockets, and plate—are not bent or scratched.

Jammed camera film is always broken at the magazine feed and take-up rollers and is removed from the camera interior *by hand*—never with pliers or screwdrivers. When film has doubled back or is so lodged in the mechanism that the sprocket-guide rollers or plate cannot be cleared easily, all excess film must first be removed and the remaining lodged film gently pulled *by hand* back and forth along the axis of the normal film flow to clear it. If needlenose pliers *must* be applied to remove the film, most Camera Professionals give serious consideration to retiring the camera, as it is almost certain that some part of the mechanism will be sprung out of alignment.

NOTE: It is the practice of some ignorant Camerapeople to clear a small jam and roll the excess film into the take-up side and continue shooting without taking into consideration that the tensile strength of film stock is weakened when pleated, and torn sprockets or nicked raw stock may pull apart when the film is *pulled* through the developing machine. (A 2-minute experience in a laboratory in the midst of clanging bells and frantic Technicians shoving people aside in an attempt to save film that has broken somewhere in the line will acquaint one with the location of the original panic button—it stops the developing machine!)

Once clear of jammed film, the camera must be blown out completely—especially checking the aperture for film chips—and reoiled before threading. Once rethreaded, the sound of the mechanism, the visual movement of raw stock as it travels from feed to take-up side, and the tachometer (for variation of speed) require careful checking. After a short burst of film and the first "take," inspection of the aperture *again* is mandatory to ensure that film chips—which might have lodged in the shutter mechanism at the time of the jam—have not been thrown into the aperture area.

Then filming resumes.

6.3 END OF SHOOTING DAY

At the end of the shooting day, the Camera Assistant makes a final "hair check," runs off an additional amount of footage (usually 5 ft in 16 mm, 10 ft in 35 mm) into the take-up to ensure that the last take will not be fogged when unthreaded or stapled to the laboratory leader when being developed.

The Assistant then checks with the Director of Photography and Operator to learn whether there is any special camera accessory desired for the next day. If so, the Assistant orders it from the Camera Department or the Assistant Director. The Assistant verifies the camera reports (prints and holds) with the Sound Mixer and the Script Supervisor. The Assistant then unthreads and disassembles the camera and packs it away in its proper cases.

In the darkroom, the Assistant unloads the magazines and cans and then prepares the exposed stock for shipment (in many cases, the

Assistant personally takes it) to the laboratory. The magazines are then reloaded for the next day's shooting, if necessary.

A fresh inventory of raw stock is taken (including what is in the freshly loaded magazines), and this report is submitted to the Assistant Director.

All camera cases are returned to the camera department and/or stored in the camera room.

Invariably, the Assistant is the last person to leave the job, and while crossing the darkened stage, the Assistant can look forward to being the first person there in the morning—and starting the procedure all over again.

6.4 TOOLS

The tools used by the Camera Assistant are worth mentioning here. The Assistant carries tools in a *ditty bag*—a canvas pouch (with pockets of various widths sewn to the sides to accommodate tools and accessories), which is affixed to a triwebbed bridle ending in a snap hook. The bag is hung below the tripod or camera dolly.

The tools a Camera Assistant carries in the ditty bag vary, based upon personal preference, but the basic kit generally consists of the following:

50-ft cloth measuring tape	$\frac{1}{4}$-in., $\frac{3}{16}$-in., $\frac{1}{8}$-in. blade-width screw-
lens brush	drivers
magazine brush	No. 1, No. 2 Phillips-head screw-
flashlight	drivers
scissors	4-in. diagonal cutters
tweezers	one sheet of crocus cloth (ferric-
rubber-bulb syringe	oxide coated)
two orangewood sticks	black cloth, 6 × 18 in.
magazine brake	white grease pencil
set of jeweler's screwdrivers	chalk
set of hex wrenches, $\frac{1}{32}$–$\frac{3}{16}$ in.	felt marking pen
6-in. combination pliers	pencils
6-in. needlenose pliers	lens tissue
6-in. crescent wrench	camera oil

The *50-ft cloth tape* is used for measuring the distance from subject to film plane.

The *lens brush,* of soft sable or camel's hair, is always capped to keep it dirt and grease free.

An inexpensive 2-in.-wide painter's *brush,* with bristles cut to a length of $1\frac{1}{2}$ in. (to give it stiffness) is excellent for cleaning magazine interiors and rollers.

The *flashlight* permits viewing the aperture, lens settings, etc., on a darkened sound stage.

Scissors are for cutting gelatine filters, tape, etc.

Tweezers are for handling cut filters, small screws, and small pieces of masking tape.

A *rubber-bulb syringe* provides sufficient air pressure to blow lint from the aperture, chips from the camera interior, and dust from filters and lenses.

Orangewood sticks, one large and one small, are the only instruments to use in the removal of emulsion buildup in the camera aperture or plate.

The *magazine brake* prevents the film from unraveling on the feed side of the magazine (see "Magazine Brake," under Sec. 7.9c for construction of a magazine brake).

The various *screwdrivers, pliers, wire cutters* and *hex wrenches* are necessary for camera assembly, teardown, and emergency camera repairs.

Crocus cloth is used for cleaning motor contacts, removing rust, etc.

The *black cloth* can be draped over the space between the matte box and the camera whenever there is the possibility of stray light striking the rear of the glass matte-box filter and "kicking back" into the lens, or if there exists the possibility of a sidelight directing a beam between matte box and camera and striking the face of the lens.

The *white grease pencil* is utilized to mark focus and focal-length positions directly on a zoom-lens barrel. The grease wipes away easily.

The *chalk, felt marking pen,* and *pencils* are for writing on the slate, camera tape, and follow-focus discs, respectively.

Lens tissue is the only item to use when cleaning a lens, besides a good lens brush.

Camera oil—**not** machine oil—should be used on the camera's interior movement.

There are many items not on the list that Camera Assistants consider indispensable; however, with the exception of those mentioned herein, no two Camera Professionals can agree on what they are, for everyone, it seems, has a favorite tool or item that "everybody should have in a kit."

chapter 7

Introduction to Equipment

A piece of equipment responds in its performance in direct proportion to the amount of thoughtful care and study it is given, and a motion-picture camera is no exception. Technically, a camera is a machine—a mechanical device. However, this is only part of the story; a camera is also a delicate creative tool that requires special attention and handling if it is to perform up to its maximum potential.

There are two types of production cameras: those equipped with a reflex viewing system and those equipped with an offset-viewfinder system. Almost all newer model cameras have reflex viewing systems. Some older cameras with offset-viewfinder systems are still in use. Many of these offer the option of being converted to reflex.

7.1 THE REFLEX VIEWING SYSTEM

Cameras equipped with reflex viewing systems use prisms and mirrors between the picture-taking lens and the viewing eyepiece so that a scene may be directly viewed through the taking lens during shooting.

No rackover or parallax correction is necessary, as it is in the offset-viewfinder system.

The eyepiece of most reflex systems views exactly the same area as the camera aperture. However, some systems permit the Operator to view a limited area *outside* the aperture field. The camera-aperture area is scribed on the groundglass and the Operator must keep the composition within the scribed limits in order to photograph only the desired area.

Any focus change is immediately apparent, and the Operator can directly correct the focus, if necessary, provided that the "pulling focus" coincides with the movement of the subject toward or away from the camera and given a thorough familiarity with the direction the focus ring rotates in order to follow focus.

A disadvantage of the reflex system is that the more the lens aperture is stopped down, and the more filters that are added to the matte box or lens, the less light is transmitted to the eyepiece. Heavy filtering in conjunction with small lens openings can make viewing difficult, as compared to the unobscured viewing through an offset viewfinder.

Some reflex cameras *do* have a filter slot behind the mirrored shutter, which eliminates the front-filter problem. On these cameras, the taking lens is stopped down less than normal because filter positioning reduces light only to the film, and not to the eye. However, many Camera Professionals are reluctant to place a gelatine into a filter slot because of its proximity to the focal plane. Any dirt or dust on the gelatine will register conspicuously on the negative when the lens is stopped down to an aperture that brings the debris into focus on the film.

7.2 VIDEO ASSIST

This recent and important capability provides film productions with increased flexibility and efficiency. Video-assist systems, usually an option available on newer-model cameras, use a *video tap* to literally tap into the image-laden light in the reflex viewing system. Special optics divert a portion of this light to a video camera mounted on the film camera. An image sensor (usually a charged couple device—CCD) within the video camera converts the light to electrical signals, thus processing images identical to those received by the film. These signals are transmitted to a video monitor for immediate viewing, to a video recorder for recording on videotape, or to both.

Video assist can provide any of the following benefits:

1. When the video image is displayed on a monitor while the film camera is running, people other than the camera operator can view the framed shot exactly as it is being recorded on film.
2. When recorded on tape while simultaneously filming, the video image can be played back on the set immediately after a take, allowing for instant analysis of artistic and technical results and for more informed retake decisions.
3. It allows the frame shot to be viewed when the camera is in a dangerous or difficult position. Mobile camera-stabilizing systems such as the Steadicam (see Chapter 22) use video assist in this way.
4. It enables the crew to preframe shots when superimposing one sequence or single-frame image over another.
5. Some systems produce video of quality sufficient to perform preliminary (offline) editing using only the video. Decisions can be made easily using the video and then implementing them on film. This process is easier if the camera also has time-code recording capabilities (see Sec. 4.4), which allows easier matching of video and film.

Video assist may or may not produce color video images. In addition, video created this way may have consistent flicker, due to the intermittent nature of light taken through a rotating mirror reflex shutter. However, such flicker can be eliminated by special "pellicle" reflex mirrors or by electronic processing.

The video-assist camera may have an independent power source or may need to be plugged into the camera's power system.

Video assist is increasingly becoming a standard part of film-camera systems; thus, good Camera Professionals should at least understand its principles of operation.

7.3 THE OFFSET-VIEWFINDER SYSTEM

7.3a Rackover

Cameras equipped with an offset-viewfinder system use a monitoring viewfinder attached to the side of the camera *and* a focusing tube. Direct viewing of a scene through the taking lens cannot be achieved *during shooting*. However, direct viewing of the scene through the taking lens can be achieved *before and after* each take by aligning the focusing tube with the taking lens. This alignment process is *rackover*.

On the majority of offset-viewfinder cameras covered in this volume, rackover is accomplished by the Operator's rotation of a handle and lateral shifting of the camera body. On other cameras, rackover is accomplished by the Operator's rotation of a handle, which causes a prism to be inserted between the taking lens and a focusing-tube eyepiece—the camera body is not moved.

Rackover is necessary so that the Operator can check focus, composition, and make corrections for parallax. Looking through the focusing tube, the Operator sees the scene as the camera will "see" it.

In any case, the camera aperture has been displaced, and the Operator must remember to "rack back" before filming begins, or images will not be recorded.

7.3b Conforming Viewfinder to Taking Lens

The field of the offset monitoring viewfinder must conform to the field of the taking lens, as seen through the focusing tube; this is accomplished by either of two methods:

1. When the viewfinder is equipped with a focal-length scale and adjustable ribbon mattes (within the viewfinder itself), the mattes are moved horizontally and/or vertically to the focal reference marked on the scale; 2. When a viewfinder is *not* equipped with adjustable mattes, a plastic matte is inserted into a slot in the viewfinder itself.

7.3c Correcting for Parallax

With viewfinder field conformed to the taking-lens field, the Camera Professional must then consider parallax.

For a motion-picture camera, a practical definition of *parallax* is the difference between the viewpoints of the offset viewfinder and the taking lens.

Manufacturers position the taking lens on the turret of offset-viewfinder cameras as close as possible to the viewfinder in order to minimize parallax. However, it cannot be entirely eliminated, and the Operator must compensate for it.

(A simple example of parallax is seen by fixing on an object and alternately closing and opening each eye. The apparent jump of the object results from the lateral difference between the "lens" of one eye and the "viewfinder" of the other. With both eyes open, the lines of sight are parallax-corrected because the lines of sight of the eyes intersect—i.e., converge—at a specific distance because of the automatic accommodation built into normal human vision.)

Parallax is compensated for by conforming both the *viewfinder cross hair* and the *focusing-tube cross hair* to the subject so that at a specific distance the lines of sight of both viewfinder and taking lens intersect. In other words, by matching the cross hairs, a simple mathematical triangulation is achieved (see Fig. 7–1). If (a) the lateral difference between the taking lens and the viewfinder is considered the base of a right triangle, and (b) the line of sight of the lens is considered the adjacent side of the triangle, then (c) the line of sight of the viewfinder forms the hypotenuse of the triangle.

To accomplish the intersection of lines of sight, the viewfinder must be pivoted (or its optics shifted) laterally. At infinity, the rear of the viewfinder is almost parallel to the camera body because the subject is far away and parallax is at a minimum. However, at an 18-in. distance from camera to subject, the rear of the viewfinder must be pivoted (or its optics shifted) away from the camera body as much as 6–12 in. (depending upon the camera model) in order to achieve intersection of the lines of sight.

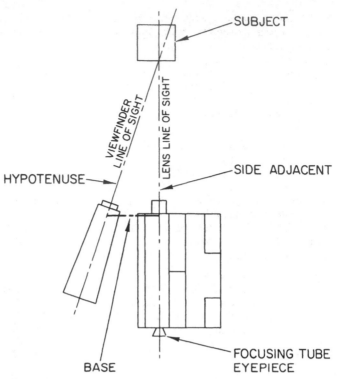

Figure 7–1 Parallax triangulation diagram.

The relationship of the camera to the subject must also be kept in mind. If the lens and viewfinder are locked-in for a specific distance, the lines of sight will converge only at that distance. If the distance between camera and subject increases or decreases appreciably and the Operator keeps the viewfinder cross hair on the subject, the line of sight of the lens will be off the subject.

Correcting with Follow-Focus Attachment. This problem can be eliminated by mounting an accessory follow-focus attachment on the camera, which utilizes a gear-and-cam system that regulates the viewfinder in conjunction with the focus (see the Mitchell follow-focus attachment, for example).

Use of the follow-focus attachment requires an Assistant to "pull focus." The Operator is fully dependent upon the Assistant for accuracy of composition because, if the lens focus is incorrect, the cam (which rides a worm-gear roller) will change the line of sight of the viewfinder to an incorrect setting, and the lens will not view what the viewfinder does. Therefore, the setting and correction for parallax is a vital cooperative effort.

Correcting without Follow-Focus Attachment. The follow-focus attachment cannot be used on some cameras. In these instances, the Operator and Assistant must determine the starting and ending positions of the move to be made by the camera (or subject). With the camera racked over, the cross hair of the focusing tube and viewfinder are aligned and locked-in for the shortest distance between camera and subject.

Once this setting has been made, the focusing-tube cross hair is then aligned to the subject at the longest distance between camera and subject. Then the position of the subject is noted through the viewfinder. Obviously, the subject will not be in the cross hair of the viewfinder but to one side of it. The Operator must remember, at that particular distance, to position the subject at that particular place in the viewfinder, so that the lens will view the subject correctly. As the distance shortens, the Operator gradually centers the subject, so that upon reaching the shortest distance, the cross hairs of the viewfinder and the lens are correctly aligned.

7.3d Racking Back

Before filming starts, the racked-over camera must be racked back, to place the camera aperture and film in alignment with the taking lens. Some cameras are not fitted with an automatic cutout switch and will run in the rackover position; there are many Operators on record who have executed the best camera movements and compositions of their careers on blank film. Most Operators develop the habit of sighting through the viewing tube and then "wiping out" the scene as they rack the camera back into shooting position, to be certain they have actually aligned the taking lens and the film. It also affords the Operator a last-minute comparison of the lens field with the field outlined by the ribbon mattes in the viewfinder.

7.4 MATTES

The basic definition of a *matte,* as applied to cameras, is worth mention here. A true *matte* is a sheet or plate inserted into a camera and/or viewfinder to obscure a selected area of a scene by shortening it.

7.4a Offset Viewfinder Mattes

Viewfinder mattes are metal ribbons or plastic sheets.

Ribbon Matte. This is a set of very thin metal bands that can be adjusted within an offset viewfinder, so as to match the field of the particular lens in use (the taking lens). When adjusted, the ribbon mattes form a tic-tac-toe crosshatch, thus: ⊞ . The rectangular field formed within the crosshatch is known as the *aperture field,* because it delineates the area viewed by the actual camera aperture. The rest of the area within the viewfinder surrounding the rectangular aperture field is not obscured in any way. However, the Operator must keep the composition within the aperture field or the lens will not photograph the desired areas.

Plastic Matte. This is a semiopaque sheet with a precut aperture field appropriate for a particular focal length. When inserted into the viewfinder, it limits the viewing field to that appropriate for the focal length of the taking lens. The area surrounding the cutout aperture field is semiobscured, and the Operator must keep the composition within the cutout field.

Unobscured or semiobscured surrounding fields permit the Operator to see microphone booms, off-screen movements, or other objects that may interfere with the composition, thus warning the Operator in time to make proper adjustments before the taking lens views the unwanted object.

7.4b Hard Mattes

Hard mattes are opaque and made of thin metal. These include aperture mattes and focusing-tube mattes.

Aperture Matte. This shim is inserted into the aperture plate within the camera body to make certain that a portion of the film is not exposed when shooting. Most common is the Academy Matte, which covers what is ordinarily the area reserved on a print for the soundtrack.

Focusing-Tube Matte. This shim is inserted into the focusing tube, forward of the groundglass. This matte is necessary whenever an aperture matte is inserted into the aperture so that the focusing-tube field of the composition conforms to the aperture field.

NOTE: Frequently (especially when filming TV commercials), a matte is inserted into the focusing tube only, and not the aperture plate. This permits exposure of the full aperture. Later, the framing of the scene can be adjusted or reduced in the optical printer to achieve a better composition for the titles, product, etc.

7.4c Effects Mattes

An *effects matte* is a special-purpose cutout of metal, gauze, or film, and may be inserted into the aperture, the focusing tube, or the *matte box*—a holder in front of a lens that accepts filters, opaque or cutout mattes, gauzes, etc.

Most common of all effects mattes in studio production is the film-frame matte, used whenever match dissolves are desired. A frame of processed film (either negative or print) is punched out on a special matte cutter (to ensure perfect registration) and inserted into the focusing tube for alignment with another object.

Other special-purpose effects mattes, such as keyhole, binocular, and gunsight, are opaque shims or gauze inserted into the aperture-plate slot or matte box. However, these effects are more often left up to the optical department of a special-effects house. The time and cost necessary for the shooting of these aperture effects on a sound stage, with a full crew in attendance, often far exceeds the expense of having it done in an effects house.

7.4d Camera Mattes

A *camera matte* is an adjustable blade built into the camera body which enables the Camera Professionals to split any portion (horizontal, vertical, or both) of the aperture desired. Again, while this convenience is available to the camera crew, most effects of this nature are turned over to a special-effects department because of the time and cost involved.

NOTE: An erroneous use of the terms "TV mattes," "ratio mattes," etc., is often applied to the area scribed on the camera groundglass. This scribe indicates the Operator's "safe-action area," or "composition aspect ratio"; the action must be kept within this area because of the limitations of the screen imposed by TV-receiver "cutoff" or the intended release form of a film for theaters. The distinction should be clearly understood and proper nomenclature used.

7.5 FILTERS

A filter is one of the cinematographer's tools used to set the look of the film. Filters can create a variety of effects, such as changing the overall color of the scene, diffusing the image, correcting for different types of film stock, etc. A Director of Photography has a wide range of filters at his disposal during shooting. There are many different sizes and types of filters available for use on today's professional cameras. These filters are manufactured by many different companies, including Tiffen, Harrison & Harrison, Eastman, Fuji, and Agfa-Gevaert, to name a few of the most important ones.

7.5a Filter Sizes

Because of the various sizes of cameras, matte boxes, and lenses in use, filters also come in many different sizes. Table 7–1 lists some of the most common sizes of filters in use today.

7.5b Filter Types

The kind of effect that the Director of Photography wants to achieve will determine which filter to place on the camera. Most of the filters in use today are optically correct pieces of glass that have been tinted or altered in some way to create the specific filter. In addition to these glass filters, which are almost always placed in front of the lens, some cameras have the capability of accepting a gelatine filter in a slot behind the lens, on the lens itself, or in a slot in the aperture plate. Table 7–2 lists the most common filters used for color film, what they are used for, and the exposure compensation. Table 7–3 lists the most common filters for black-and-white (B&W) film. Many of the filters come in varying densities, the lower numbers being the lightest and the higher numbers being the heaviest.

7.5c Cleaning

Filters should only be cleaned if they contain smudges or fingerprints or are coated with dust or dirt. First remove dirt or dust by using a blower-bulb syringe or compressed air. Use lens tissue to clean smudges or fingerprints, but *only* after first moistening the filter surface. *Never* put a dry tissue to a filter. The most widely used and safest cleaner is the moisture from the human breath. Liquid lens cleaner should be used sparingly. Refer to Section 19.3a, "Lenses," for an effective way to clean using liquid cleaner.

CAUTION: Never use silicone-impregnated lens tissue to clean a filter. Never use dry lens tissue to clean a filter.

7.5d Mounting

Because of the various sizes of filters, lenses, and matte boxes, there are also many different ways to mount these filters onto the lens or camera. Some of the round filters will screw onto the front or rear element of the

Table 7–1   Filter Sizes

Round	Square	Rectangular
40.5mm	2″ × 2″	4″ × 5.65″
48mm	3″ × 3″	5″ × 6″
4½″	4″ × 4″	
138mm (5½″)	6.6″ × 6.6″	
6″		

Table 7–2 Filters for Color Film

Filter	Exposure Increase	Suggested Use
Black Dot	1	Diffusion filter; softens image, reduces wrinkles and facial blemishes
CC 30R		Correct color (absorbs blue and green) in underwater cinematography
Clear	0	Optical flat used to protect lens
Color	Varies	Enhances particular colors in scene, depending on color filter used
Coral	Varies	Warms up the overall image
Diffusion	0	Smooths out facial blemishes and wrinkles, softens the overall image
Double Fog	0	Create natural-looking fog effects
80A	2	Converts daylight type film for use with 3200K tungsten lamps
80B	$1\frac{2}{3}$	Converts daylight type film for use with 3400K tungsten lamps
812	$\frac{1}{3}$	Removes excess blue and improves skin tones
81EF	$\frac{2}{3}$	Used by many cinematographers instead of 85A (imparts less amber tone to whites)
82A	$\frac{1}{3}$	Reduces excess red in sunrise/sunset scenes when using daylight film, and/or when using 3400K film under 3200K tungsten lamps
85A	$\frac{2}{3}$	Converts tungsten film to 3400K for use in daylight
85B	$\frac{2}{3}$	Converts tungsten film to 3200K for use in daylight
85C	$\frac{1}{3}$	"Warms" scenes when using daylight film. "Cools" scene when using tungsten film
85N3	$1\frac{2}{3}$	85 combined with Neutral Density ND3
85N6	$2\frac{2}{3}$	85 combined with Neutral Density ND6
85N9	$3\frac{1}{3}$	85 combined with ND9
85N1.0	$3\frac{2}{3}$	85 combined with ND 1.0
85Pola	$2\frac{2}{3}$	85 combined with a Polarizer

Table 7–2 Filters for Color Film *(cont.)*

Filter	Exposure Increase	Suggested Use
Enhancer	$1\frac{1}{2}$–2	Increase saturation of red or reddish-orange objects
FLB	1	Color-correction fluorescent-light filter when using indoor type B film
FLD	1	Color-correction fluorescent-light filter when using daylight film
Fog	0	Creates a soft glow from highlights, produces a misty haze on the overall scene
Grad	Varies	One half contains the particular filter and the other half is clear
Haze 1	0	Reduces excess blue caused by haze. Used for aerials, mountain scenes, seashores
Haze 2	0	Greater UV correction than Haze 1, "Warms" hazy scenery
LLD	0	Allows use of tungsten film in low-light daylight with no exposure compensation
Low Contrast	0	Lowers contrast, causes colors to become muted, spreads light from highlights to shadows
Mitchell A & B	0	Diffusion filters; ("A" has less diffusion, "B" more). Softens overall image, reduces wrinkles and facial blemishes
Neutral Density	Varies	Causes a uniform reduction of light entering the lens
Polarizer	$1\frac{2}{3}$–2	Eliminates surface reflections, darkens a blue sky
Pro Mist	0	Diffusion filter; softens overall image, reduces wrinkles and facial blemishes
Sepia	Varies	Adds warm brown look, gives "old time," turn-of-century look to image
Sky 1A	0	Reduces blue, especially in shade
Soft Contrast	0	Softens harsh contrast, darkens highlight areas
Soft Net	$\frac{1}{3}$–$\frac{2}{3}$	Softens the image, smooths wrinkles and facial blemishes without image appearing out of focus
Split Diopter	0	Allows close focusing on object on one side of the scene
Star	0	Creates bursts of light from any light source in scene
Supafrost	0	Diffusion filter; softens image, smooths out facial blemishes and wrinkles
Ultra Contrast	0	Similar to Low Contrast and Soft Contrast
UV15	0	Reduces UV and haze
UV17	0	Greater haze correction than UV15

Table 7–3 Filters for Black-and-White Film

Filter	Exposure Increase: Ortho Day	Ortho Tung	Pan Day	Pan Tung	Suggested Use
6 Yellow 1	1	$\frac{2}{3}$	$\frac{2}{3}$	$\frac{2}{3}$	Darken sky, emphasize clouds
8 Yellow 2	$1\frac{1}{3}$	1	1	$\frac{2}{3}$	Greater contrast of clouds and foliage
9 Yellow 3	$1\frac{1}{3}$	1	1	$\frac{2}{3}$	Stronger cloud contrast
11 Green 1	—	—	2	$1\frac{2}{3}$	Pan film only. Flesh tones, flowers, landscapes
12 Yellow	$1\frac{2}{3}$	$1\frac{1}{3}$	1	$\frac{2}{3}$	Cuts haze in aerial photos
13 Green 2	—	—	$2\frac{1}{3}$	2	For pan film only; gives deep flesh tones, lightens foliage
15 Deep Yellow	$2\frac{1}{3}$	$1\frac{2}{3}$	$1\frac{2}{3}$	1	Dramatic sky and marine scenes
16 Orange	—	—	$1\frac{2}{3}$	$1\frac{2}{3}$	For pan film only; deeper than 15 Deep Yellow
21 Orange	—	—	$2\frac{1}{3}$	2	For pan film only; absorbs blue and blue-green; gives darker blue tones
23A Light Red	—	—	$2\frac{2}{3}$	$1\frac{2}{3}$	For pan film only; darkens sky and water; not for flesh tones
25A Red 1	—	—	3	$2\frac{2}{3}$	For pan film only; creates dramatic sky effects; use with infrared film for extreme sky contrast
29 Dark Red	—	—	$4\frac{1}{3}$	2	For pan film only; strong contrasts
47 Dark Blue	—	—	$2\frac{1}{3}$	3	For pan film only; accentuates haze and fog
47B Dark Blue	$2\frac{2}{3}$	3	3	4	Lightens same color for detail
56 Light Green	—	—	$2\frac{2}{3}$	$2\frac{2}{3}$	Darkens sky, good for flesh tones
58 Dark Green	3	$2\frac{1}{3}$	3	3	Produces very light foliage
61 Dark Green	—	—	$3\frac{1}{3}$	$3\frac{1}{3}$	Extreme lightening of foliage
87	Depends on use and processing				Infrared only
87C	Depends on use, and processing				Infrared only

Note The following filters may also be used for B&W film, with the same effects as when they are used with color film: Diffusion (all types), Diopter, Double Fog, Fog, Grad, Low Contrast, Neutral Density, Polarizer, Soft Contrast, Soft Net, Split Diopter, Star Filter.

lens. Other round filters may also be mounted to some type of lens hood or lens shade, which is then clamped onto the front of the lens, or screwed onto the lens. These round filters may also be mounted to a filter-retaining ring, which attaches to the back of the matte box of the camera. The ring usually snaps into the back of the matte box. Square or rectangular filters are usually mounted to the matte box by means of a sliding tray: Remove the tray from the matte box, insert the filter into the tray, and then replace the tray into the matte box.

7.5e Filter Cases

One of the best containers for storing filters is a case that contains cutouts corresponding to the size of the filters. The filters slide into these cutouts when not in use. The case is usually lined on the bottom and in the lid with foam, which acts as a shock absorber for the filters while they are being transported. The cutouts for the filter may be slots cut into the foam of the case, or they may be plastic tray slots of the correct size. Many filters come in some type of protective pouch when purchased. This pouch is a very good way to protect the filter when it is not in use. An empty, foam padded case, which allows you to place many of these filter pouches into it, is also a good way to protect and transport filters.

NOTE: Whenever a filter is not being used, it should be placed in a pouch, in a protective case, or in the slots of a custom filter case.

7.6 CAMERA MOTORS

Early cameras were hand-cranked, and some modern cameras, although motor driven, still incorporate the hand-cranking capability. When motors were first introduced to the industry, the sound stages reverberated with the alarming cry of, "What are they trying to do, eliminate the Operator" (Early Camera Professionals weren't called "cranks" without reason.) Today, the skill required to hand-crank a camera at the proper speed is a lost art and—for the most part—academic.

The nearest a modern-day Camera Professional gets to hand cranking is when the shutter obscures viewing optics. Most motors are equipped with a knob, which, when turned manually, moves the *intermittent*—i.e., pulldown claw, sprocket, shutter, and registration pins (often referred to as "the movement")—and clears the shutter from the viewing optics. On most offset-viewfinder cameras, this knob is called a "manual-motor-turning knob," while on most reflex cameras, it is called an "inching knob." Some cameras have a knob or plunger built into the camera body to clear the shutter from the viewing optics.

Motors built for cameras fall into eight general categories: (1) variable-speed motors, (2) constant-speed motors, (3) synchronous (sync) motors, (4) animation (stop-motion) motors, (5) interlock (self-synchronous [selsyn]) motors, (6) time-lapse motors, (7) high-speed (slow-motion) motors, and (8) crystal-sync motors.

7.6a Variable-Speed Motors

Often called "wild" motors, these are rheostat-controlled so that the frame-per-second rate can be adjusted. They are most often used when filming "silent," or when variation of speeds (within certain limitations) is required to speed up or slow down the action.

7.6b Constant-Speed Motors

Constant-speed motors are governor controlled to operate the shutter at a constant 24 frames per second (fps). Powered by direct current, they are most often used when filming "silent" and no variation of speed is desired, or when filming sound in conjunction with a sync-pulse recorder. To achieve synchronization, the camera or motor must be fitted with a sync-signal generator to provide a frequency signal to the recorder so that any variation in the motor speed (fast or slow) will be electronically recorded on the signal portion of the ¼-in. tape and the resolver will electronically control the speed of the transfer machine.

7.6c Synchronous (Sync) Motors

Sync motors have a definite speed strictly proportional to the frequency of the operating current (60 Hz in the United States, 50 Hz in Europe).

NOTE: The international unit of frequency measurement is the hertz (Hz), which is equal to 1 cycle per second.

Sync motors are most frequently used when filming sync sound (dialogue, etc.) in studios or areas where AC is available, in conjunction with sound recorders. To achieve synchronization, the camera motor and recorder must be connected to the *same AC power source* so that any variation in the frequency of the source will be transmitted to both units. In many studios, the Sound Department will *run camera*—i.e., the camera line will be connected to the recorder, and the camera will not run until the recorder is turned on. The recorder in turn is connected to one AC source, which supplies power and the same frequency to both units.

7.6d Animation (Stop-Motion) Motors

The stop-motion motor registers a single frame each time the motor switch is activated. They are most frequently used to give apparent movement to artwork or inanimate objects.

7.6e Interlock (Selsyn—Self-synchronous) Motors

In a selsyn system, two motors are electrically phase-connected so that one (the *drive*) provides the same rate of power, speed, and rotor position to another (the *slave*) so that the camera intermittent and a projector intermittent are in sync. They are most frequently used when filming rear-projection and front-projection process shots so that the camera photographing the live action in the foreground is synchronized with the rear- or front-projected background.

7.6f Time-Lapse Motors

The time-lapse motor is activated at long intervals by a preset timing device, to expose one frame at a time so that when the film is projected, the subject moves rapidly. While the time-lapse motor is similar to an animation motor, the timing device places the time-lapse motor in a separate classification. It is most frequently used in nature studies (such as when recording the blooming or growth of a flower) and in industrial research.

7.6g High-Speed (Slow-Motion) Motors

When the motor is operated at accelerated speed, the fps rate causes the camera to expose a greater-than-normal number of frames, so that when the film is projected at standard speed, the subject appears to move slowly. These motors are most frequently used for a time-extension effect, or for scientific study.

It should be noted that many manufacturers will call a slow-motion motor "high-speed" (and many Camera Professionals will mistakenly do the same), but the technical difference is important to remember, especially when renting equipment.

Motion-picture engineers agree that the frame-per-second (fps) speed of a motor determines certain classifications. For example:

Animation—1 frame per motor-switch activation
Time-lapse motor—below 10fps
Intermittent motor—10 to 30fps (variable or sync)
Slow-motion motor—30 to 300fps
High-speed motor—300 to 10,000fps
Very-high-speed motor—10,000 to 300,000fps
Ultra-high-speed motor—300,000-plus fps

Therefore, a camera motor must conform to the frame-per-second rate of the type photography desired.

7.6h Crystal-Sync Motors

Crystal-sync motors have overtaken the industry, replacing many of the aforementioned motors, and are now available for almost all required operating speeds. Their accuracy is based on the precise and predetermined vibrational rate of a quartz crystal (similar to those in quartz wristwatches and in internal computer clocks.) Because modern sound recorders use a crystal-sync time base, there is no need for cable or sync cord between camera and recorder. Most modern self-blimped cameras are fitted with integral crystal-sync motors powered by a battery pack or belt.

The action of the motor and the intermittent of a "non-self-blimped" camera creates noise; this noise is controlled by the use of either a Barney or a blimp.

7.7 BARNEYS

A Barney is a sound muffler for a camera and is used to minimize camera noise when absolute quiet is not essential, such as an outdoor location where the ambient noise level is equivalent to or slightly higher than the camera noise.

There are three types of Barneys: (1) A *sound Barney* is usually constructed of layers of insulating materials encased in a canvas or plastic cover, and lined with a nonabrasive wool–nylon fabric. (2) A *heater Barney* is of similar construction to the sound Barney but is wired electrically and serves to keep the camera warm in cold weather. A heater Barney is invariably covered with a reflective material so that the unit can also be used to insulate against the heat of the sun in desert or jungle locations. (3) A *magazine Barney* fits only the magazine and does not cover the camera. It is intended to muffle the noise of a nonsoundproofed magazine being used on a self-blimped camera (such as a 16mm Mitchell 1200-ft magazine on an Auricon Pro-600 camera).

Sound and heater Barneys are fabricated for use with a particular manufacturer's camera, and therefore will vary in size and shape, with opening and/or viewing ports suited for the camera.

Basically, however, a Barney is open at the bottom so that the unit can be draped over the camera. A front port allows the camera matte box to extend beyond the covering. Various flaps and latches provide access to the camera itself, while openings in the Barney permit various components (viewing systems, follow-focus units, etc.) to extend beyond the confines of the fabric.

Unlike a blimp, a Barney cannot be used as a noise suppressor when shooting on a sound stage.

The term "Barney" originated in the early days of sound filming when heavy horse blankets were used at exterior locations to cover the cameras and minimize the noise. At that time, a popular comic-strip character named "Barney Google" had a never-winning racehorse named "Sparkplug" who wore an old patched blanket. Cameramen would often call for a "Barney Google horse blanket." The term was then shortened to a "Barney Google," and eventually evolved into the present-day term.

7.8 BLIMPS

7.8a Description

A *blimp* is an acoustical housing designed to eliminate virtually all camera noise. Like a Barney, it varies in size and shape and has ports peculiar to the camera for which it is built. Unlike a Barney, it has no permanent openings, so that the camera is completely enclosed within it. Access doors permit camera adjustments.

Blimps are constructed of fiberglass, aluminum, magnesium, or a combination of these, and they are filled with layers of sound-absorbing materials and lined with velvet, corduroy, or similar fabric.

Blimp interiors are either fitted with a support similar to a tripod head plate or a special adapter for positioning the camera securely within it. Through a gear-and-cam system, the blimp's follow-focus unit permits the focusing of the camera lens from outside the blimp.

NOTE: On a blimp, the gear-and-cam system that is an integral part of the blimp is a follow-focus *unit,* but a detachable accessory, which can be mounted on a camera, is a follow-focus *attachment* (see "Correcting with Follow-Focus Attachment," in Sec. 7.3c).

On some models, a similar gear-and-cam arrangement also controls the lens-aperture setting. All have "spring-action" knobs or levers that must be depressed in order to engage camera components to change their positions.

A sunshade, either fixed or variable (bellows), mounts at the front of the lens-access door. The front optical flat must be constantly checked for cleanliness because any dirt, dust, or streaks on the glass will be readily photographed.

7.8b Insertion of Camera

Use of a blimp requires that most, but not all, cameras be adapted to the blimp, either by changing the eyepiece, motor, door, or by fitting the lenses with gears.

Insertion of the camera into the blimp and alignment of gears, fittings, couplings, etc., must be conducted with extreme care. If any part of the unit binds or doesn't fit easily, it is best to remove the camera from the blimp and reset the couplings, gears, fittings, etc., in their *throw-out position*—i.e., where they will not interfere with the camera components they serve.

The smoothness and ease of the blimp follow-focus unit is important. A stiff unit can frequently be freed by adjusting the pressure knob that creates drag for smoothness of operation. Stiffness may also be caused by the lens-ring gear (which meshes with the follow-focus gear) being improperly mounted on the lens. If canted, the lens gear will bind and interfere with the smoothness of a focus change. The lens-gear coupling should also be checked for a too-tight fit with the follow-focus.

7.8c Light Kickback

Most blimps are equipped with ports and internal work lights to provide easy viewing of the camera components. The internal lights must be extinguished prior to rolling the film, to avoid possible internal light rays "kicking back" into the lens and ruining the scene. Any external light, such as sunlight or a sound stage luminaire shining into a port can also cause kickback. The problem is easily cured by cutting flaps out of thin cardboard or film cartons and taping them, at the top only, over a port.

7.8d Noise Problems

Noise from a blimp can usually be traced to a poor fit of a blimp–camera component. Lens and follow-focus gears that are too tightly meshed will transmit camera noise through the shaft of the follow-focus handle. Conversely, if the gears are too loose, vibration chatter will be transmitted. Properly meshed gears have an infinitesimal air space between them.

On reflex cameras, the blimp eyepiece is separate from the camera-door viewing system. A *light trap sleeve*—a short tubular unit attached to the blimp eyepiece extension—slides over the prismatic assembly of the camera door. If this sleeve touches the assembly, noise will transmit through the eyepiece. Most Camera Professionals keep the eyepiece approximately $\frac{1}{8}$ in. away from the assembly to avoid any contact with it.

Sometimes an access-door gasket will be damaged, or the door will not seat properly, and camera noise will emanate from it. By walking around the blimp while the camera is running, it is often easy to discover the location of the noise leak. A piece of masking tape placed across the area of the leak will usually silence it.

Then too, the vibration of the camera inside the blimp will often trigger a component on the tripod head to vibrate "in sympathy." Such components should be looked for and tightened or taped.

WARNING: Perhaps the most important thing to remember about a front-hinged blimp is the magazine-access hood. Although many are balanced to remain open when changing a magazine or checking a scene through a viewing tube, with use, the balance weakens. The danger of the hood dropping suddenly and breaking a finger or inflicting a scalp wound is very real. Many Camera Assistants insert a wooden wedge between the blimp housing and hood at the hinges, to prevent such an occurrence.

While blimps are cumbersome and impede production schedules because of the added components and access doors, they are a far cry from the early days of sound shooting when small glass-walled camera huts were built to enclose the camera and crew, so as to avoid picking up the camera noise. These "ice-boxes," as they were called (because the ambient heat from the luminaires warmed the stage but never the interior of the hut), were not only soundproof, but also to a great extent "airproof." Directors who believed in long takes became favorite targets for disrespectful opinions expressed with obvious futility by the camera crew members inside the huts. The only benefit the long takes provided was running out of film and a chance to open the doors to let the warm air inside while changing magazines.

7.9 MAGAZINES

A magazine is a light-tight chamber that attaches to the camera and houses film stock before and after exposure at the camera aperture.

7.9a Capacities

35mm magazines accommodate 200-, 400-, 500-, 1000-, or 2000-ft darkroom loads; 16mm magazines accommodate 200-, 400-, 600-, or 1200-ft darkroom loads.

7.9b Nomenclature

All magazines, regardless of size or type, contain the following components:

Feed Spindle. The interior unit on which the core of the raw-stock roll or the core adapter fits.

Take-up Spindle. The interior unit on which the core of the exposed roll or the core adapter fits.

Feed Light Trap. The light-tight rollers, or passageway, through which the raw stock exits the feed compartment on the way to the camera aperture.

Take-up Light Trap. The light-tight rollers, or passageway, through which the exposed film enters the take-up compartment after passing the camera aperture.

Magazine Throat. That section of the magazine containing both the feed and take-up rollers and that fits into the opening in the camera body.

Lid. The removable part of the magazine, which permits access to the interior. Lids may be threaded, lip- and dog-locked, or key-locked and hinged.

Some, but not all magazines (depending upon manufacturer) also contain the following:

Feed-Spindle Wheel. The exterior wheel that is attached to the same shaft (through the magazine wall) as the interior feed spindle.

Take-up-Spindle Wheel. The exterior wheel that is attached to the same shaft (through the magazine wall) as the interior take-up spindle. On some magazines, the take-up spindle wheel accommodates the camera take-up belt.

Spindle-Wheel Guard. A raised (usually semicircular) piece of metal above the spindle wheel, which protects the wheel from contact with the bench (and possible damage) when the magazine is being loaded.

Feed-Guide Roller. The roller at the end of a metal arm inside the feed compartment. The roller rides the film edge to (a) keep the film edges straight and prevent the film from *dishing*—i.e., becoming concave (the outer edge of the roll being higher, or lower, than the core when laid flat), and/or (b) serve as a footage-counter indicator.

Take-up-Guide Roller. Same purpose as the feed-guide roller but located in the take-up compartment.

Footage Counter. An indicator on the arm of a roller that rides either the feed or take-up film roll so that the amount of unexposed film left in the magazine (*subtractive counter*) or amount of film exposed (*additive counter*) may be determined.

Some footage counters work off a sprocket.

Film-Tensioner Knob. A knob that, when depressed and rotated, engages the core and removes any slack in either the feed or take-up rolls.

7.9c Magazine Types

Camera magazines fall into four categories: (1) double-compartment type, (2) displacement type, (3) coaxial type, and (4) single-compartment type.

Double-Compartment-Type Magazine (Auricon, Panavision, Bell & Howell, Mitchell). This type of magazine has two separate lighttight chambers in tandem. The left, or front, chamber (feed side) accommodates the raw stock. The raw stock exits the left chamber through a light trap, then reenters (through a second light trap) the right, or back, chamber (take-up side).

The double-compartment-type has the advantage that the take-up side can be checked in daylight when loading the camera, before any exposed film is taken up into the back chamber.

Film is taken up in the Auricon and Mitchell magazines by means of a belt (neoprene or leather) that fits the magazine take-up spindle wheel and is driven by the camera driveshaft mechanism. The circumference of the exterior spindle wheels is grooved to accommodate the take-up belt. Finger holes or spokes in the wheel diameter are utilized to take up film slack in the magazine by hand.

Some double-compartment-type magazines are provided with adjustable felt pads, which brake against the feed-spindle wheel. This serves the purpose of preventing the film from unrolling in the feed compartment when the camera mechanism comes to a stop. (If film does unroll in the feed compartment, it may break when the camera is started up again; the weight of the roll itself is sufficient to snap the film when it is pulled taut.)

Magazine Brake. Because many magazines are not fitted with felt pads, a magazine brake is necessary to provide tension on the spindle wheel. A brake is especially important when filming at high speed.

A magazine brake (Fig. 7–2) consists of
(a) a leather thong, 6 1/2″ long by 1/8″ diameter; (b) 3/16″ by 0.20-gauge spring wire, 2 1/2″ long. A very small hole is punched about 1/8″ in from each end of the thong, and a piece of wire is inserted into each hole to form a hook. Each spring end is then attached to both hooks (forming a circle). The hooks are closed with pliers.

An emergency brake is made by knotting both ends of a short length of sash cord and then looping a rubber band around the knots. The brake spring (or rubber band) fits over the wheel guard while the leather thong (or sash cord) rides in the spindle-wheel groove. The slight tension against the spindle wheel prevents the unrolling of raw stock and thereby precludes the possibility of snapping the film when the camera is started again. This portable brake can be removed and placed on a new magazine at every reload.

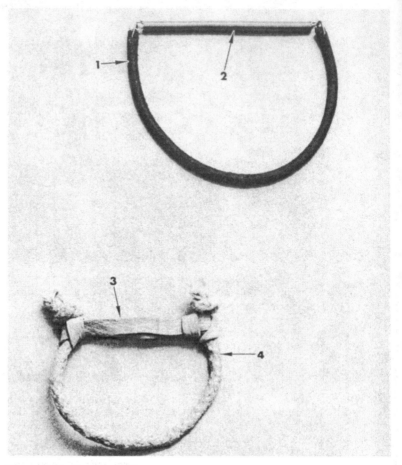

Figure 7–2 Magazine brakes.

1. $\frac{1}{8}''$ diameter leather thong
2. $\frac{3}{16}'' \times$ 0.20-gauge-springwire

3. Rubber band
4. Sash cord

NOTE: On magazines that have *no* spindle-wheel guards, a special ⊔-shaped bracket (inside dimension slightly larger than the width of the magazine) with a looped thong (or spring) attached to one arm of the "⊔" is inverted and slipped over the feed side of the magazine. The thong (or spring) is placed in the spindle-wheel groove.

Displacement-Type Magazine (Arriflex, Cameflex, etc.). This type of magazine has a single light-tight chamber. It is much more compact than the tandem magazine. As the raw-stock roll diminishes, the take-up roll increases in size, thereby displacing almost the same area occupied by the raw-stock roll.

While most displacement-type magazines are gear-driven, some magazines require an additional torque motor to take up the film into the chamber.

These magazines are usually fitted with an exterior subtractive footage counter. One or more interior guide rollers ride the film edge and prevent the film from dishing in the magazine and scraping the interior magazine wall. One roller serves as the footage-counter indicator.

Exterior spindle wheels are usually knurled knobs. Some displacement-type magazines may have film-tensioner knobs in place of spindle wheels to take up film slack in the magazine by hand. Because they are gear-driven, unrolling is minimized but not necessarily eliminated. Magazine brakes can be applied as with the gear-driven double-compartment-type magazine.

Coaxial-Type Magazine (Arriflex 1200, Eclair NPR, Cinema Products GSMO). This type of magazine is a double-compartment magazine with the feed and take-up chambers placed side-by-side instead of in tandem, with a concentric shaft accommodating both the feed and take-up rolls.

Coaxial-type magazines are gear-driven. Most (but not necessarily all) are fitted with an exterior footage counter and two interior guide rollers. One roller serves as a footage counter.

Single-Compartment-Type Magazine. This type of magazine is constructed for special cameras. A single chamber may be used for either a feed roll or a take-up roll; i.e., a compartment containing raw stock is placed on one side of the camera, the film threaded into the camera, and then the film end is wound on a core in another (take-up) compartment. In this way, a certain amount of film can be exposed, the take-up magazine removed from the camera without removing the raw stock and unthreading, a new take-up compartment placed on the camera, and filming continued.

7.9d Maintenance

As with other camera components, it is important that magazines be kept free of lint, dirt, and other debris. Interiors of magazines should be cleaned with an airhose. Where compressed air is not available, a bulb syringe may suffice.

Felt-lined magazines, however, often require cleaning with a short-bristled brush. Stubborn lint or film chips can be removed by wrapping a few turns of camera tape *inside-out* (i.e., sticky side facing out) around one hand, then pressing the sticky side gently against the interior surface to be cleaned. All magazines are *always* cleaned before loading and after unloading.

Light traps must be kept free of dust and film chips. They should be checked and cleaned often. Although light traps are supposed to be lightproof, it is always good practice to carry a magazine with one hand placed over the lighttrap when transporting it from case to camera.

When possible, the magazine throat should be opened periodically to properly clean the felt rollers. This is the area that produces most of the debris particles in the camera gate; thus, its cleanliness is very important, particularly in 35mm Techniscope and in 16mm, where the entire frame will be projected.

7.9e Miscellaneous

When *transporting loaded magazines* to a location, it is important to
(1) maintain the magazine in a vertical position with the light traps up, and of course, keep the magazine away from heat; (2) place a labpack bag over the light traps and secure it with tape; and (3) tape the feed and take-up spindle wheels to prevent the film from unrolling inside the magazine.

When *working in extreme heat or direct rays of the sun,* wrap and tape aluminum foil around the magazine, being certain that an air space is maintained between the magazine and the foil. The foil will reflect most of the sun's heat rays, and the air space will act as an insulator.

To *eliminate film scrape* against the interior walls of a magazine, relieve a threaded lid $\frac{1}{4}$ to $\frac{1}{2}$ turn; a lip- and dog-locked lid requires removing the magazine from the camera and jiggling the gears while tilting the magazine opposite to the side the film is scraping. An occasional *tap* on the scraping side may also help seat the film in the guide roller.

CAUTION: A sharp or heavy slap against a magazine in which there is a dished roll can cause lateral cinch marks in the emulsion; therefore, treat the magazine gently. If need be, return it to the loading room for reloading.

7.9f Lost Cores

When a magazine lacks a core and no other cores are available, the following procedures will usually suffice:

35mm.

On a magazine fitted with a plastic core spindle, load the feed side and thread the film end as usual into the take-up side. Fold the film back 6 in. from the film end, and tape the film fold to the spindle. Tuck the film end into the taped fold, and crease the film again; tuck the new film end into the creased film, and crease again; repeat until the film can no longer be tucked into itself. Rotate the take-up spindle and wrap the raw stock around the film pile just created. The film will take up with a hump in the roll. When unloading the exposed roll in darkness, the pile can be pulled out with needlenose pliers to loosen the roll around the spindle.

On a magazine fitted with a removable metal core spindle, purchase a bottle cork from any hardware store. If tapered, shave the cork into a cylindrical shape, making certain the diameter is at least 1 in. when finished. Cut the cork length slightly less than the depth of the magazine, and use a screwdriver smaller than the diameter of the spindle to fashion a guide hole in the cork. The guide hole should only be as deep as the spindle *shank* (i.e., *less* the length of the "horns" of the metal groove). Push the cork onto the shank, and anchor the horns into the cork. Tape the film to the cork, and form a core by folding as in the previous description for making a film pile.

An alternative is to pressure-fit (wedge) a plastic core onto the cork and then wedge a sliver of wood into the cork and core keyway.

16mm.

If fitted with a removable core holder, remove the holder, insert the film end into a 100-ft camera spool. Place the spool on the square driver pins of the take-up spindle. Let the take-up roller-guide arm ride against the spool on displacement-type magazines; as the roll increases in size, it will pick up the exposed film and guide it.

Make a note to the laboratory that a spool has been used as a take-up core.

If fitted with a nonremovable plastic core spindle, use the same procedure as with the 35mm magazine.

7.9g Core-Differential Compensation

When loading a short end from a 16mm $\times$ 1200-ft roll into a 400-ft magazine, the difference in core diameter must be taken into account

(1200-ft rolls are factory-wound on 3-in. cores: 400-ft rolls are factory-wound on 2-in. cores). Therefore, on a 3-in. core loaded into the feed side of a magazine, the total footage as registered on a subtractive magazine counter will read 60 ft higher than normal. All footage computations will have to be minus 60 ft.

A note should be placed below the magazine footage counter, stating, "3-in. core—deduct 60 ft."

chapter 8

Tripods

A *tripod* is a telescoping three-legged stand that is used to support a movable platform (tripod head), to which a camera is secured.

8.1 TRIPOD TYPES
There are several basic types of tripods, including the following (see Figs. 8–1 and 8–2):

1. *standard legs*—approximately 4 ft (1.22 m) when closed, approximately 6 ft (1.83 m) when extended
2. *sawed-off legs*—approximately 3 ft (0.91 m) when closed, approximately 5 ft (1.52 m) when extended
3. *baby (low) legs*—approximately 2 ft (0.6 m) when closed, approximately 3 ft (0.91 m) when extended

   NOTE: The length of each unit has a ± factor of 6 in. (152 mm).

4. *hi-hat*—approximately 4–6 in. (102–152 mm) high, nontelescopic

   NOTE: Each leg of this low mount has a flange (instead of shoes). Each flange is fitted with a drilled hole so that the unit may be mounted with nails or screws where a tripod cannot be used.

8.2 BASIC PARTS OF A TRIPOD
8.2a Top Casting
This is the round metal plate with a center hole, which accepts the tripod-head lockdown screw. A keyway at the top of the casting matches the key on the tripod head. Three hinges at the bottom of the casting accept the bolts (which are inserted through metal straps attached to the top of the tripod legs), which secure the legs to the top casting.

Most top castings are fitted with three *tie-down eyes* (drilled holes in the casting, or metal loops) next to or below the hinges.

Some top castings are bowl-shaped to accommodate a ball-type (adjustable) tripod head.

8.2b Legs
Legs are generally made of wood, or of various metals, particularly aluminum, carbon fiber, and other synthetic materials. Each leg has an outside and inside assembly. The hinge nut and bolt that secures each leg to the top casting may be adjusted. Proper tension is set by tightening the hinge nut until the leg can be (1) swung *easily* up and away from the top casting, (2) released, and (3) remain at the angle to which it was lifted. Insufficient tension (*slop*) allows the legs to drop away from the casting

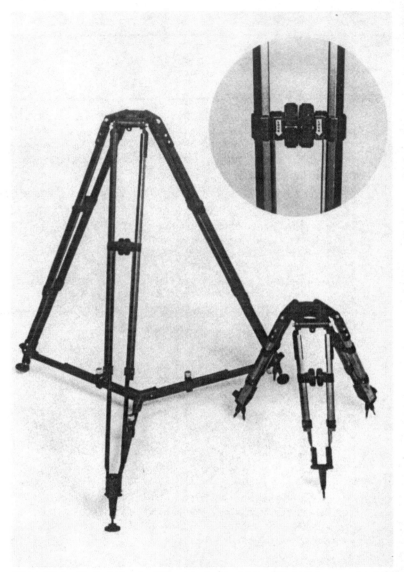

Figure 8–1 Typical tripods: O'Connor standard legs with built-in spreader (left) and rubber/spike feet, O'Connor baby legs (right). Courtesy of O'Connor Engineering Laboratories, Inc.

Figure 8–2 Various sizes of tripods. Courtesy of Sachtler Corporation of America.

1. 100mm ball casting baby legs
2. 150mm ball casting baby legs
3. 150mm ball casting medium legs
4. 100mm ball casting medium legs
5. Long legs with fluid head
6. Video 20 HD long legs tripods with fluid heads
7. Video 10 HD long legs
8. Video 25 HD long legs

when carrying the tripod; too much tension (*drag*) requires undue exertion in opening the legs when setting up the tripod.

8.2c Adjusting Knobs
These are circular units (single or double) placed between the leg assemblies. They loosen to raise or lower the inside leg assembly; they tighten to secure the leg against the outside assembly. Some baby tripods use thumbscrews instead of knobs.

8.2d Shoe
Each of these metal units at the foot of each leg has at least one of the three following parts:

1. *Point*—A sharp tapered metal unit at the toe of the shoe, which digs into the ground, floor, or spreader, to prevent the leg from sliding.
2. *Spur*—A sharp tapered metal unit similar to a point, but positioned on the inside of the shoe at an angle to the point. It may be close to the point or approximately one third higher on the shoe. The spur acts as a point when the tripod leg is swung outward on its hinge to an angle beyond which the point can safely secure the tripod leg.
3. *Kickplate*—A protruding piece of metal on the outside of the shoe; the kickplate is used as a step to sink the point into the ground or to anchor the shoe when elevating the tripod leg.

An important accessory is a rubber pad, encased in a suitable leather (or fabric) envelope, attached by a cord to the top casting. The pad cushions the weight of the camera when the tripod is carried from one setup to another.

NOTE: A 35mm tripod is heavier and larger in component size than a 16mm tripod. A 16mm camera may be safely used on a 35mm tripod; however the balance of a "spring-tension" tripod head (which is intended for a heavier instrument) may work against the Operator. The use of a 35mm camera on a 16mm tripod is not recommended, as the entire unit becomes top-heavy and can easily tip over.

8.3 SETTING TRIPOD FOR SHOOTING
In the past, most tripods were equipped with heads such as the Mitchell or Pro Jr., which required the user to adjust all three tripod legs to level the head. Such tripods are still used, although some now incorporate the more current and more common bowl-top and ball-bottom head configuration that allows easier and safer leveling of the head.

8.3a Uniform Leg Length
Bring the tripod legs together into the folded position as though to place them in a shipping case. Extend one leg to the desired length and tighten. Keep the legs in the folded position, loosen the other two legs, and allow their points to drop to the ground; tighten adjusting knobs. When the legs are spread out equidistant, the tripod head will be very close to level.
The camera lens is always aligned to one leg, which becomes the vertex of the triangle formed by the spread legs. The vertex of the triangle (always called "the forward leg") is pointed at the scene. The left-rear and right-rear legs at the back of the camera are far enough apart to permit the Operator to move around the tripod with minimal interference.

8.3b Leveling
Place the horizontal bar of the tripod head T-level in line between any two legs. Step on the kickplate; level with one of the three legs. Adjust the

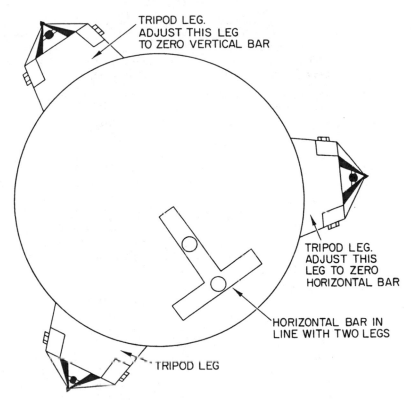

TRIPOD LEG.
ADJUST THIS LEG
TO ZERO VERTICAL BAR

TRIPOD LEG.
ADJUST THIS
LEG TO ZERO
HORIZONTAL BAR

HORIZONTAL BAR IN
LINE WITH TWO LEGS

TRIPOD LEG

Figure 8–3 T-level.

third leg up or down to center the bubble of the vertical bar of the T-level. The tripod head is now level (see Fig. 8–3).

This method is the fastest procedure with any tripod and is particularly effective when leveling a heavy camera.

Often, the tripod head can be leveled by simply rotating one leg in an arc.

Many tripods have numbers imprinted on at least two of the leg assemblies. Theoretically, when two legs are locked off at the same number, only one leg needs adjusting to level the camera. This is true only if all three points are *equidistant* from each other (form an equilateral triangle).

8.4 MOVING A TRIPOD

To minimize strain and inefficiency, there are three basic steps to moving a tripod from one setup to another: (1) lift, (2) balance, (3) placement.

8.4a Lift

Place the camera at eye level. Raise the tripod-head handle to approximately a 45° angle. Align the camera lens to the forward leg. Step *between* the two rear legs. Place the shoulder pad against the back of the tripod head, below the camera. Bend knees slightly and place right shoulder against the pad. Lengthen the forward leg approximately 4 in. and tighten.

(This tilts the camera back against the right shoulder.) Grasp the adjustable knobs of both rear legs with each hand. Push forward with right shoulder, and lift up on the rear tripod legs so as to pivot on the forward tripod leg only. Fold in the two rear legs to meet the forward leg. Straighten knees and lift the camera off the ground.

CAUTION: Always make certain that the tripod-head pan and tilt locks are secured before lifting the tripod!

8.4b Balance
Once the camera is lifted, place right arm around all three tripod legs, or through the right-rear-leg and forward-leg assemblies. Use shoulder as a fulcrum, and raise or lower the points to maintain fore-and-aft balance. Lean from the waist toward the left, to maintain side-to-side balance.

8.4c Placement
Make certain the tripod's forward leg is extended 4–6 in. Grasp the adjustable knobs of the two rear legs. Bend knees slightly, and set the point of the forward leg into the ground. Spread the two rear legs out and back from the forward leg, and plant them into the ground. Lower the extended forward leg to level the camera.

8.5 CARE AND MAINTENANCE
8.5a Shipping
Tripods should be shipped in cases for protection against damage. At a minimum, a *boot* (i.e., a two-piece unit that protects the shoes and top casting, but not the legs) should be used. In an emergency, cardboard boxes are fitted over the shoes and top casting and secured with camera tape. For some unfathomable reason, more care often is given to protecting the shoes than for the top casting. A tripod with a shoe completely broken off can still be leveled, but a cracked or broken top casting will render the entire unit useless.

8.5b Lubrication
Commercial paste or liquid waxes are not recommended for use with tripods because of their propensity to retain grit and dirt. A light application of hard beeswax cake or silicon spray (from a pressurized can)—to the outside of the inner-leg assembly *only*—is sufficient. Allow the lubricant to dry before "pumping" the assembly up and down, so that the wax will rub off the lubricate the outside-assembly highspots.

A sticky tripod can result from too much lubricant applied to both sides of the leg assemblies, as well as from not enough lubricant. (Two waxed surfaces collect dirt and grit faster than one waxed surface sliding over a smooth surface.)

8.5c Moisture and Rust
Any tripod wood that has been wet should be dried out *slowly*. Acceleration of the drying process produces warp and checking. Lubricate only when thoroughly dry. Metal parts, of course, may be dried immediately, checked for rust, and oiled lightly.

8.6 MISCELLANEOUS ACCESSORIES
8.6a Spreader
A *spreader* is used whenever setting a tripod on a hard surface (cement, metal, etc.). Three arms extending from a centerblock are fitted with receptacles to accommodate the tripod points. Constructed of wood or

metal, the arms are often adjustable. More elaborate spreaders have lockdown clamps that secure to the kickplate and anchor the tripod to the spreader. The unit is often mistermed a *triangle,* perhaps because the point receptacles, when placed equidistant, form the three points of an equilateral triangle.

Sometimes, rubber *feet* (semisuction-cup rubber pads on a balljoint) fasten to the points as a substitute for a spreader. While satisfactory for most purposes, the pads tend to come off the balljoint and are easily lost.

The most common spreader in use, of course, is a piece of rug that measures 4 × 4 ft.

When a spreader is not available, a length of chain, rope, or camera tape is tied around the outside of the equidistantly spread legs; this will prevent the legs from sliding out.

8.6b Tie-Down

The *tie-down,* used on raised platforms, camera cars, and other areas where the camera is in danger of tipping over, consists of a piece of chain 6–8 ft long, attached at one end to the *bridle*—three short (7–9-in.) lengths of chain. Each short length terminates in an S-hook. Each S-hook inserts into a tie-down eye located at the bottom of the top casting. The 6–8-ft length of chain dangles from the center of the bridle to the floor. A stage screw is secured to the floor directly below the center of the tripod head. A double-hooked turnbuckle is then attached to the chain and stage screw and is tightened sufficiently to apply tension to the chain and keep the tripod from tipping over.

CAUTION: There is a tendency to overtighten the turnbuckle. This can cause one of the adjusting knobs to slip, slowly lean the camera off level, or worse, cause the adjusting knob to suddenly give way and tip the camera over. Once the length of chain is taut, one or two additional turns will suffice to maintain its rigidity and tie-down capability.

chapter 9

Tripod Heads and Accessories

9.1 TYPES OF TRIPOD HEADS

There are many types and makes of tripod heads available to camera professionals. This chapter considers the friction, fluid, and geared heads—the three primary types found today—and describes the use of several common units representative of models generally available. Inclusion of specific manufacturers' equipment, listed alphabetically, does not signify endorsement, nor does omission of other tripod heads or models connote discredit.

Most newer heads are made of alloys of aluminum, some are magnesium, while older heads were often of cast steel. The three basic types are distinguished by the means by which resistance within the head, and therefore the head's movement, is created and varied:

1. The *friction head* employs the principle of surface resistance. The friction of fiber discs against metal washers creates drag on the lateral and vertical movements of the head.
2. The *fluid head* employs the principle of fluid resistance. The restricted flow of a high-viscocity liquid forced through grooves machined inside a metal drum creates drag on the lateral and vertical movements of the head.
3. The *geared head* employs the principle of mechanical advantage. The ratio of the angular speed of driving members to driven members of a gear train, linkage, or cable creates force on the lateral and vertical movements of the head.

A friction or fluid tripod head that has the handle placement at its left side only is constructed for use with an offset-viewfinder camera; a head that has the handle placement at its right side only is constructed for use with a reflex (through-the-lens-viewing) camera. A tripod head that allows for placement of a handle on either side is constructed for use with either type camera.

With a left-handled tripod head, the Operator takes a stance behind the offset viewfinder and grasps the handle with the right hand. This places the Operator away from the tripod legs and provides greater freedom of movement as well as better balance of the camera.

With a right-handled tripod head, the Operator embraces the camera in order to place an eye to the viewing system. The placement of the handle compensates for the Operator's closeness to the camera and will not interfere with his or her movements. Its position will also provide the camera better balance.

The geared head, originally constructed for use with an offset-viewfinder camera, is used with reflex cameras that are fitted with extended eyepieces. When using a geared tripod head, the Operator stands behind the offset viewfinder (or the extended eyepiece), takes a three-fourth stance toward the camera, reaches forward with the left hand for the pan handle, and reaches out with the right hand for the tilt wheel located at the rear of the geared head. In this position, the Operator's body is clear of the tripod legs, allowing ease of movement and balance and enabling the Operator to see easily into the offset viewfinder or to lean forward slightly to place the eye against the extended eyepiece.

Proper selection of a tripod head, predicated on the camera viewing system, will eliminate the need to struggle with the head and allow the Operator to concentrate more on the creative aspects of composition and camera movement.

In addition, the Operator must be so familiar with the components of the tripod head being used that its handling does not require conscious thought and—like the handling of a camera—is automatic.

9.2 ARRIFLEX GEARED HEAD

The three basic components of the Arriflex Geared Head (Arrihead) are: (a) tilt plate, (b) cradle, and (c) base (Figs. 9–1*a* and 9–1*b*).

NOTE: All directions are from the Operator's point of view.

9.2a Tilt Plate

The dovetailed top of the *tilt plate* (1) accepts a *sliding base* (2) into which a *quick-release plate* (3) is fitted. The quick-release plate is attached to the bottom of the camera by a standard 3/8″-16 tripod screw.

To Install Sliding Base on Dovetailed Tilt Plate. Remove one of two *5 mm stop screws* (4) at the left rear/right front of tilt plate with a flat-blade screwdriver.

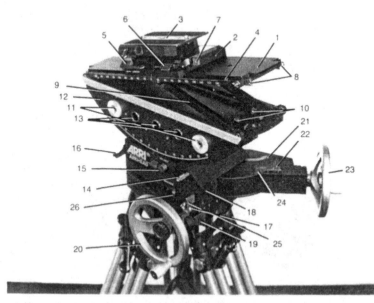

Figure 9–1a. Arriflex Geared Head (Arrihead), left rear view. Courtesy of Arriflex Corp.

CAUTION: Manufacturers and/or rental houses include up to three spare screws inserted in the stress rib underneath the tilt plate. Be sure that they are there *before* leaving for the location.

Depress the *locking lever* (5) on the base, align to the dovetail, and slide the unit onto the dovetail; release the locking lever to secure the base in the desired position; replace the 5mm stop screw.

To Insert Camera into Sliding Base with Quick-Release Plate Attached. Depress the *safety button* (6) and swing the *release lever* (7) from right to left until it clicks into position. Remove the quick-release plate and attach it to the camera. Insert the attached front toe of the quick-release plate into the dovetail on sliding base; lower the rear of plate until the release lever automatically snaps into the locked position.

To remove camera with attached plate, reverse this procedure.

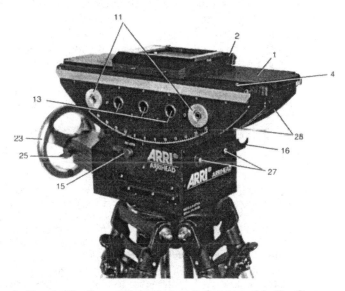

Figure 9–1b. Arriflex Geared Head (Arrihead). Courtesy of Arriflex Corp.

1. Tilt plate
2. Sliding base
3. Quick-release plate
4. 5mm stop screw
5. Locking lever
6. Sliding base safety button
7. Sliding base release lever
8. Outer release tabs
9. Wedge support arm
10. Inner release tabs
11. Pan-handle rosettes
12. Cradle
13. Carry rod bushings
14. Finder leveling-rod bushing
15. Tilt locks
16. Finder leveling-rod rest
17. Bubble level
18. Pan gearbox
19. Pan gear-shifting lever
20. Pan wheel
21. Tilt gearbox
22. Tilt gear-shifting lever
23. Tilt wheel
24. Tilt gearbox position lock
25. Friction brake
26. Pan lock
27. Slotted screws
28. Cradle rails

Lifting of Tilt Plate (Front or Rear). Squeeze the two blue *outer release tabs* (8) at the front or rear. Lift until the *wedge support arm* (9) clicks into the first stop. To move to the next stop, squeeze the blue *inner release tabs* (10) and lift. Stops are at 13°, 20°, 25°, 30°, 40°, 50°, and 60°.

WARNING: Obtain help in lifting the camera's weight to safely tilt the plate.

Reversing of Tilt Plate. Slide the wedge support arm past the last possible stop and release the two outer blue tabs so that the plate folds flat. Release the two blue outer release tabs at the opposite end of the plate and follow the foregoing instructions.

Pan-handle rosettes (11) are located in each corner of the *cradle* (12) and accept standard Sachtler pan handles.

NOTE: When using handles for fast panning or tilting, it is essential that the pan and/or tilt gears be disengaged (in neutral position). If desiring to use the unit as a gyro head, unlock the friction brakes but leave the pan and tilt in gear.

9.2b Cradle

The top surface of the cradle accepts the tilt plate. A tilt gear (not shown) engages a chain (not shown) to accomplish elevation/depression of the cradle.

Three 19mm (3/4″) diameter *bushings* (13) on each side of the cradle are for insertion of carry rods whenever simultaneously moving the Arrihead and camera together.

A *finder leveling-rod bushing* (14) is located at rear left of cradle. Blue *tilt locks* (15) are located on each side of the cradle. A *finder leveling-rod rest* (16) is located on the left front.

9.2c Base

A tritium (glow-in-the-dark) *bubble level* (17) is at the top left on the *pan gearbox* (18), which houses a five-position *pan gear-shifting-lever* (19). For first gear, slide the lever to the left of center. Gear positions are 1 (65 turns for 360° pan); neutral, 2 (35.5 turns for 360° pan); neutral; 3 (19 turns for 360° pan). To pan left, rotate the *pan wheel* (20) clockwise; to pan right, rotate the pan wheel counterclockwise.

The *tilt gearbox* (21) houses a five-position *tilt gear-shifting lever* (22). For the first gear, slide the lever to rear. Gear positions are 1 (17.5 turns for full 60° tilt), neutral; 2 (9.25 turns for full 60° tilt), neutral; 3 (4.75 turns for full 60° tilt). To tilt up, rotate the *tilt wheel* (23) clockwise; to tilt down, rotate the tilt wheel counterclockwise.

NOTE: Gearboxes with 5:1 reduction (not shown) are available for both pan and tilt.

The tilt wheel swings out laterally as much as 38° to the right and can be locked into any position throughout its travel, which allows the Operator either to select an optimal position for the tilt wheel when operating in close quarters or to clear a 304.8 meter (1,000 ft) 35BL magazine when tilting up. To position the wheel, unlock the blue *tilt gearbox position lock* (24).

Directly next to each tilt and pan wheel is a *friction brake* (25), which turns counterclockwise to loosen, and a *pan lock* (26), located above the pan gearbox on the left side of the cradle.

Two *slotted screws* (27) on the front of the head accept a bracket to which is attached a small Camera Assistant's "goodie box"—i.e., a container to hold small tools, a lens (while changing only), a tape measure, etc.

The bottom of the base accepts a 3/8"-16 steel tripod-locking screw (not shown) approximately 3.81cm (1 1/2") in length, which inserts through a 7.9cm (3 1/8") diameter plate (not shown) and clamps the head to the tripod. A 9.5mm (3/8") circular key (not shown) at the base inserts into a mating slot on a tripod or dolly.

9.2d Maintenance
Wipe down the *cradle rails* (28) after each shoot.

CAUTION: Do not lubricate the Arrihead.

9.2e Weight
19.5 kg (43 lbs).

9.3 MINI-WORRALL SUPER GEARED HEAD (CINEMA PRODUCTS)
The three basic components of the Mini-Worrall Geared Head are: (a) tilt plate, (b) cradle, and (c) base (Fig. 9–2).

NOTE: All directions are from the Operator's point of view.

9.3a Tilt Plate
The top of the *dovetailed tilt plate* (1) accepts a matching dovetailed *sliding base plate* (2) into which a standard 3/8"-16 *camera-lockdown screw* (3) is fitted.

NOTE: The dovetailed tilt plate will accept the CP-type, Arri-type, or Moviecam-type sliding base, or a Sachtler-type base with a quick-release plate.

To Mount Camera. CP-/Arri-/Moviecam-Type. Push the *base-plate-release lever* (4) forward, depress one of two *rail safety pins* (5) at the left front or right rear of the dovetailed rails, remove the sliding base plate and affix to camera with the lockdown screw. Align the camera and its base plate to the dovetails, depress the safety stop, and slide the base plate onto the rails. Push the base-plate-release lever toward yourself.
Sachtler-Type (Not Shown). Leave the sliding base on the dovetails. Rotate clockwise the base-plate-release lever at the rear of the sliding base. The spring-activated quick-release plate located in the sliding base will pop up. Leave the plate-release lever in clockwise position and remove the quick-release plate and attach it to the camera. When you place the camera, with the plate attached, on the sliding base, the lever will snap into place and secure the camera, with its plate, to the sliding base.

NOTE: See Section 9.7, Sachtler Fluid Head Studio II for further details regarding the sliding base.

To Remove a Camera from the Base Plate. Reverse the above procedure.

Lifting of Tilt Plate (Front or Rear). Squeeze the two *outer spring-loaded pivot pins* (6) at the front or rear. Lift the plate until the *tilt support arm* (7) clicks into the first of the *pivot-pin bushings* (8) in the cradle assembly. To move to the next stop, squeeze the two *inner spring-loaded pivot pins* (9) and lift the tilt plate. The pivot-pin bushings are set so that the tilt plate, when raised from level, locks in at 20°, 30°, 35°, 40°, 50°, 56°, 76°, 77° and 53°, whether lifted from the front or rear.

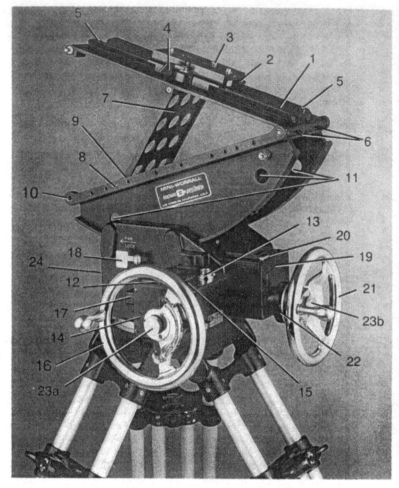

Figure 9–2. Mini-Worral Super Geared Head. Courtesy of Cinema Products Corp.

1. Dovetailed tilt plate	9. Inner spring-loaded	16. Pan wheel
2. Sliding base plate	pivot pins	17. Pan-wheel brake
3. Camera-lockdown	10. Pivot-pin bushing	18. Pan-wheel lock
screw	flanges	19. Tilt gearbox
4. Base-plate-release	11. Carry rod bushings	20. Tilt gear-shifting
lever	12. Eyepiece leveling-	lever
5. Rail safety pins	rod	21. Tilt wheel
6. Outer spring-loaded	13. Bubble level	22. Tilt-wheel brake
pivot pins	14. Pan gearbox	23a. Wheel lock nut
7. Tilt support arm	15. Pan gear-shifting	23b. Wheel lock nut
8. Pivot-pin bushings	lever	24. Slotted screws

WARNING: Obtain help in lifting the camera's weight to safely tilt the plate.

9.3b Cradle

The top surface of the cradle accepts the tilt plate and dual *pivot-pin bushing flanges* (10).

Two 19mm (3/4") diameter *carry rod bushings* (11) on each side of the cradle are for the insertion of carry rods whenever simultaneously moving the Mini-Worrall head and the camera together.

An *eyepiece leveling-rod* (12) is located at the left side of the cradle. A tilt lock (not shown) is at the right side of the cradle.

9.3c Base

A *bubble level* (13) is at the top left on the *pan gearbox* (14) which houses a five-position *pan gear-shifting lever* (15). For first gear, slide the lever to the left of center. Gear positions are 1 (51 turns for 360° pan); neutral; 2 (37 turns for 360° pan); and neutral; 3 (20 turns for 360° pan). To pan left, rotate the *pan wheel* (16) clockwise; to pan right, rotate the pan wheel counterclockwise. Internal pan gears (not shown) engage a cable (not shown) to accomplish lateral movement of the cradle. A *pan-wheel brake* (17) is located forward of the pan wheel.

A *pan-wheel lock* (18) is forward of the pan gearbox.

NOTE: On some Mini-Worral gear heads, the pan-wheel lock has been modified* so that it is now a continuously adjustable drag control for smoother pans.

A *tilt gearbox* (19) houses a five position *tilt gear shifting lever* (20). For first gear, slide the lever to the rear. Gear positions are 1 (7 turns from level to maximum 30° tilt); neutral; 2 (4 1/2 turns from level to maximum full 30° tilt); neutral; 3 (2 3/4 turns from level to maximum 30° tilt).

To tilt up, rotate the *tilt wheel* (21) clockwise; to tilt down, rotate the tilt wheel counterclockwise. A *tilt-wheel brake* (22) is located forward of the tilt wheel. Internal tilt gears (not shown) engage cables (not shown) to accomplish elevation/depression of the cradle.

NOTE: Geared heads up to serial number 154 were built with nonremovable handles. Units with serial numbers 155 and higher have removable and interchangeable handles attained by rotating the *wheel lock nuts* (23a and 23b) in the center of the wheels counterclockwise to loosen, clockwise to tighten.

Two *slotted screws* (24) at the front of the head accept a bracket to which is attached a small Camera Assistant's "goodie box"—i.e., a container to hold small tools, a lens (while changing only), a tape measure, etc.

Attached to the bottom of the base is a steel tripod-locking screw (not shown). The screw measures 6.7 cm (2 5/8") in diameter by 2.54cm (1") in length, with 8 threads per inch. The lock nut (not shown) that fits the screw and clamps the head to the tripod is constructed with slightly extended "bayonets" to aid in loosening the nut, which has a 9.8cm (3 7/8") outside diameter. The 9.5 × 19mm (3/8" 3/4") key (not shown) at the base inserts into a mating slot on a tripod or dolly.

---

*By Clairmont Camera, Studio City, California.

9.3d Weight

17.5 kg (39 lbs).

9.4 MITCHELL FRICTION HEAD

The two basic components of the Mitchell Friction Head are the camera mounting plate and the base (Fig. 9–3).

NOTE: All directions are from the Operator's point of view.

9.4a Plate

The spring-loaded 3/8"-16 *camera-lockdown-screw* (1) is connected by a pair of helical gears (not shown) to a knurled lockdown-screw knob on a shaft (not shown) at the front of the head. The lockdown-screw knob is also fitted with a steel taper pin, to which a keyed hand crank (not shown) is matched to secure the lockdown screw tightly. Rotating the lockdown screw clockwise tightens the screw, turning it counterclockwise loosens it.

The top surface of the cast steel *plate* (2) measures 18cm (7") wide by 20cm (8") long.

Elevation/depression drag is controlled by turning the scalloped *tilt tension knob* (3) counterclockwise to decrease, clockwise to increase.

The plate brake release is actuated by turning the *tilt-lock lever* (4) counterclockwise to loosen, clockwise to lock.

NOTE: The plate elevates/depresses ± 45°.

The *handle bracket* (12) at the left side travels in a restricted slot and secures at a desired angle (from 45° high to 45° low) by turning the

Figure 9–3. Mitchell Friction Head. Courtesy of Mitchell Camera Corp.

1. Camera-lockdown screw	5. Base	9. Bubble level
2. Plate	6. Pan-tension-knob collar	10. Pan-lock lever
3. Tilt tension knob	7. Pan-tension knob	11. Handle lock
4. Tilt-lock lever	8. Telescoping handle	12. Handle bracket
		13. Bracket-lock lever

90

bracket-lock lever (13) counterclockwise to mesh the bracket-lock teeth with the matching teeth on the head.

The stud and threads of the rudder on the *telescoping handle* (8) insert into the bracket 6.6cm (2 1/2″) deep. The handle measures 48.26cm (19″) overall when closed and can be extended to 67.5 cm (26 1/2″) overall when the *handle lock* (11) is loosened counterclockwise.

9.4b Base

The *base* (5) brake release is actuated by turning the *pan-lock lever* (10)—at the top of the base and forward of the two-way (horizontal/vertical) *bubble level* (9)—counterclockwise to loosen, clockwise to tighten.

Horizontal drag is controlled by turning the scalloped *pan-tension knob* (7)—below the bottom of the base—clockwise to increase, counterclockwise to decrease.

NOTE: The base can be panned 360°.

Attached to the bottom of the 18cm (7″)-diameter base is a steel tripod-locking screw (not shown). The screw measures 6.7cm (2 5/8″) in diameter by 2.54cm (1″) in length, with eight threads per inch. The lock nut (not shown) that fits the screw and clamps the head to the tripod is constructed with slightly extended "bayonets" to aid in loosening the nut, which has a 9.8cm (3 7/8″) outside diameter, from the screw. The 9.5 × 19mm (3/8 × 3/4″) key (not shown) at the base inserts into a mating slot on the tripod.

9.4c Maintenance

The manufacturer recommends wiping the entire head occasionally with an oily rag containing a rust-inhibiting agent, then wiping it clean with a dry rag. Surface rust should be removed with crocus cloth. Worn bushings or locks require factory replacement.

9.4d Miscellaneous

Selecting the Pan Tension Spring. The *pan-tension-knob collar* (6) may contain a standard tension spring (intended for use with either the Standard/Hi-Speed, NC, or S35R camera) or a heavy-duty spring (intended for use with the BNC, Blimped Mitchel 16, or other blimped non-Mitchell manufacture cameras). The type of spring required is determined by the camera to be used.

Reinforcing Camera Lockdown. If the length of the camera-lockdown screw fails to secure the camera tightly to the plate, a few strips of camera tape placed across the top of the plate will act as an anchor and eliminate any slippage of the camera.

9.4e Weight

35mm standard head: 8.4kg (18 1/2 lb); heavy duty BB (ball bearing) head: 12.25 kg (27 lb); 16mm head: 5.9 kg (13 lb).

9.5 O'CONNOR ULTIMATE FLUID HEAD MODEL 25–75

The three basic components of the O'Connor Ultimate Fluid Head Model 25–75 are the camera mounting plate, fluid head, and the base (Figs. 9–4a and 9–4b).

NOTE: All directions are from the Operator's point of view.

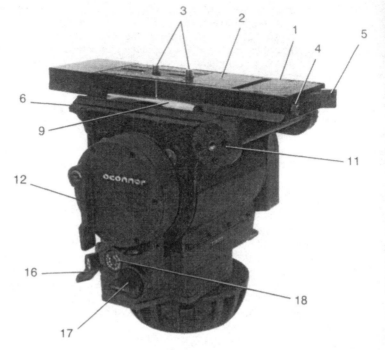

Figure 9–4a. O'Connor Ultimate Fluid Head Model 25-75, left rear view. Courtesy of O'Connor Engineering Laboratories.

1. Camera mounting plate
2. Quick-release plate
3. Camera-lockdown screws
4. Quick-release-plate lock button
5. Quick-release lock lever
6. Platform plate support
7. Platform release safety lock
8. Platform release lever
9. Platform hook

9.5a Camera Mounting Plate

There are three types of camera mounting plates manufactured for the Ultimate Model 25–75:

a. a European style *camera mounting plate* (1) measuring 2.54 × 9.5 × 30.48cm (1 × 3 3/4 × 12″) and fitted with a 120mm (4 3/4″) *quick-release plate* (2) containing two 3/8″-16 *camera-lockdown screws* (3)
b. an O'Connor dovetailed .95 × 9.5 × 30.48cm (3/8 × 3-3/4 × 12″) flat plate (not shown) with two 3/8″-16 camera lockdown screws
c. a Special Panavision dovetailed plate (not shown) that accepts a Panavision base. (See Chapter 16, Panaflex Cameras, Fig. 16–5) for details regarding mounting a Panavision base.

To Mount a Camera on a European Style Plate. Remove only the 120mm quick-release plate from the camera mounting plate by pushing up and to the right on the red *quick-release-plate lock button* (4). Hold the button in up position. Pull the red *quick-release lock lever* (5) toward the button. The lever will lock in place and the quick-release plate will pop up. Remove the quick-release plate and attach it to the camera base with

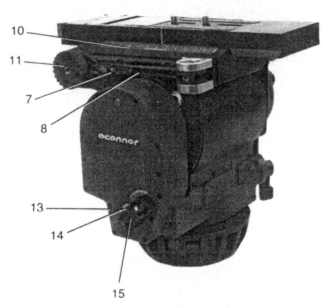

Figure 9–4b. O'Connor Ultimate Fluid Head Model 25-75, right front view. Courtesy of O'Connor Engineering Laboratories.

10. Scale
11. Pan-handle rosette
12. Tilt-lock lever
13. Tilt fluid knob
14. Tilt counterbalance indicator

15. Counterbalance lever
16. Pan-lock lever
17. Pan fluid adjustment knob
18. Bullseye bubble level

lockdown screws. Place the camera, with its attached plate, into the quick-release plate receptacle, its weight will depress the spring-loaded locking mechanism struts and snap the quick-release lock lever into a semi-locked position. Push the red quick-release lock lever further to the right and secure it in the fully locked position.

To Mount a Camera on an O'Connor Flat Plate. Attach the plate to the camera base with lockdown screws.

To Mount a Camera on a Special Panavision Dovetailed Plate. Depress the spring-loaded red lock-release button (not shown) at the left back side of Special Panavision dovetailed plate. Insert the Panavision camera mounting plate and slide it over and past until the lock release button pops up. Lock mount with the Panavision lock lever. Place the Panavision camera on a Panavision base as outlined in Panaflex Cameras, Section 16.1a, Base.

NOTE: All three camera mounting plates fit into the head's dovetailed *platform plate support* (6).

To Place Any of the Camera Mounting Plates on the Head. Pull the red *platform release safety lock* (7) toward the Operator. Swing the *platform release lever* (8) away from the head as far as it will go (approximately 150° arc). Place the camera mounting plate into the dovetail of the platform plate support (at Operator's left) and on top of the *platform hook* (9), allowing its weight to depress the hook, slide the plate *sideways* into the dovetail on the platform support until the hook snaps up and engages the dovetail of the plate. Swing the platform release lever back into the red platform release safety lock and secure it in place.

NOTE: The European plate (shown) is placed on the head with its red button and lever facing the Operator. The O'Connor flat plate (not shown) can be placed on the head facing either way. The Panavision plate (not shown) is placed on the head with its red button facing the Operator's left.

To Remove a Camera Mounting Plate from the Head. Pull the red platform release safety lock toward the operator. Swing the platform release lever away from the head as far as it will go. Depress the platform hook lever to retract the hook and lift the camera mounting plate away.

With the camera mounting plate already placed on the head, remove it from the head. Place the Special dovetail on the head, allowing its weight to depress the hook; side the unit *sideways* into the dovetail on the platform plate support until the hook snaps up and engages the dovetail. Swing the platform release lever back into the red platform release safety lock and secure in place.

NOTE: All three camera mounting plates can be moved forward or back through a 152.4mm (6″) range. The Panavision Special camera mounting plate has an additional 100mm (3.9″) of movement.

9.5b Fluid Head

A *scale* (10) at the right side of the platform plate support, marked in increments of 3.175mm (1/8″), is used for reference only, to mark the shift of a camera's balance. For example, when exchanging prime lenses with a zoom lens (and back again), note the scale number. Thereafter, at each change, shift the camera forward or backward to reference numbers known to compensate for the difference of weight on the camera front. You should also use the scale when the weight of film in the feed-side of a magazine moves into the take-up side, noting the reference numbers for full feed load, half-load, and full take-up load. Thus, once you have determined the camera balance, by shifting the camera along the scale reference marks, the head remains balanced at all times.

To Balance a Camera. Attach the handle to the *pan-handle rosette* (11).

NOTE: A standard handle is 42.5cm (16 3/4″) in length and fits to either the left or right side of the head. Handles are available with 30° or 45° bends. An O'Connor 48cm (19″) handle (with the same degrees of bend) is also available.

Rotate the *tilt-lock lever* (12) down (clockwise) to loosen; rotate it up (counterclockwise) to lock, at the left side of the tilt drum. Turn the *tilt fluid knob* (13) below the right tilt drum until the *tilt counterbalance indicator* (14), reference numbered 0–9, is at 0 (zero) drag setting. Pull the red platform release safety lock toward the Operator. Swing the platform release lever away from the head as far as it will go. Slide the camera and plate forward or back until the camera remains level when you grasp the handle loosely. Swing the platform release lever back into the red platform release safety lock and secure it in place.

To Counterbalance a Camera. Hold the pan handle and turn the tilt fluid knob at the right side of the tilt drum until the counterbalance indicator numbered 0–9, is at 0 (zero) drag setting. Tilt the camera up 30°. Flip out counterbalance lever (15) forward of the indicator and crank it clockwise to increase resistance, counterclockwise to decrease resistance. Tilt the camera down 30°; crank the counterbalance lever if the camera does not remain in place. Tilt the camera up or down 45°, then 60°. When the camera stays at any angle when tilted up or down, you have achieved proper counterbalance.

WARNING: If the lever does not turn, it has reached its mechanical stops. Trying to crank it beyond its limits will damage the head.

Elevation/depression drag is controlled by turning the tilt fluid adjustment knob—reference numbered 0 (minimum) to 9 (maximum)—clockwise to increase, counterclockwise to decrease.

NOTE: The O'Connor head tilts ±90°.

The horizontal brake is actuated by turning the *pan-lock lever* (16) down (counterclockwise) to loosen, up (clockwise) to tighten.
Horizontal drag is controlled by turning the *pan fluid adjustment knob* (17) reference numbered 0–9, clockwise to increase, counterclockwise to decrease.

NOTE: The O'Connor head pans 360°.

A phosphorescent *bullseye bubble level* (18) is above and behind the pan drag indicator.

9.5c Base
The O'Connor head is fitted with either a 150mm claw ball base or a Mitchell-type (flat) base. A 3/8"-16 steel tripod-locking screw (not shown), approximately 76mm (3") in length for the ball base and 29mm (1 1/8") in length for the Mitchell base, inserts through an 80mm (3 1/8") diameter washer (not shown) and clamps the head to the tripod. On the Mitchell base, a 9.5 mm (3/8") diameter key at the base (not shown) inserts into a retaining slot on a tripod.

9.5d Maintenance

If the Tilt Lock Lever Rotates Counterclockwise (Lock) More than 90°. Loosen the 10–32 set screw in tilt lock lever. Pull the lever away from the head and off the hexagonal shaft. Rotate the lever clockwise and fit it to the next flat on the hexagonal shaft. Be sure that the lever does not rotate more then 90°. (If it does, remove it and set it on the next flat surface of the hexagonal shaft.) Tighten the set screw.

If the Platform Release Lever Does Not Lock the Camera Platform Plate Tightly in Position. With the plate in the dovetail, pull the red platform release safety lock toward the Operator. Swing the platform release lever away from the head as far as it will go. Reach under the front of the platform and insert a 4.75mm (3/16") hex allen wrench into the 1/4"-20 hex socket head cap screw in the stainless steel block at the end of the release lever shaft; rotate it clockwise 1/2 of a turn. Close the platform release lever and ascertain the pressure on the plate.

WARNING: Do NOT overtighten! Spring washers can be damaged, rendering the unit inoperable.

If the Quick-Release Plate on a European Style Plate Does Not Lock Tightly in Position. Remove the quick-release plate from the platform plate. Insert a 4.75mm (3/16") hex allen wrench between the spring-loaded locking mechanism struts and rotate it counterclockwise to tighten.

WARNING: Do not turn the screw more than 1/6 of a turn at a time. Too many turns will prevent the unit from closing at all!

Replace the quick-release plate and ascertain the pressure against it. Adjust, if necessary, until the quick-release plate is secure in the platform plate.

The manufacturer states that the fluid head requires no maintenance in the field other than the adjustments noted above. Do not disassemble it.

9.5e Miscellaneous

Some 25–75 heads are fitted with two slotted screws (not shown) at the front, to which a bracket (not shown) can be attached to hold a Camera Assistant's "goodie box"—i.e., a container to hold small tools, a lens (while changing only), a tape measure, etc.

Some 25–75 heads are fitted with a bracket (not shown)—located behind the bullseye level—that accepts an eyepiece leveler extension (not shown).

9.5f Weight
11.4kg (25 lbs).

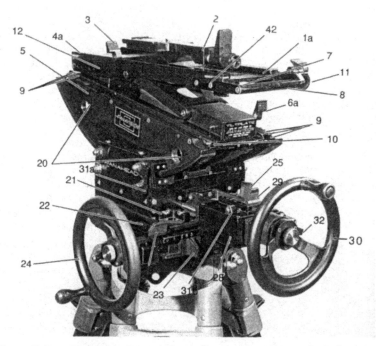

Figure 9–5a. Panavision Geared Head (Panahead), with standard tilt plate. Courtesy of Panavision, Inc.

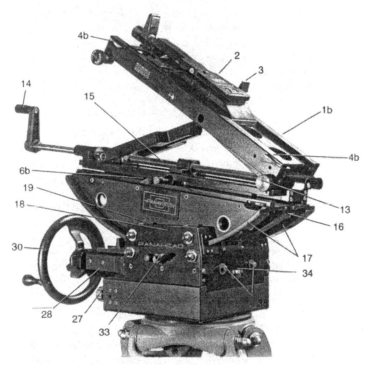

Figure 9–5b. Panavision Geared Head (Panahead), with dual tilt plate. Courtesy of Panavision, Inc.

1a. Standard tilt plate	12. Pilot-pin holes	25. Pan-tension lever
1b. Dual tilt plate	13. Tilt-plate locks	26. Pan brake
2. Sliding base	14. Hand crank	27. Worm-gear pres-
3. Base Lock	15. Worm gear	sure screw knob
4a. Stoplatch	16. Belt	28. Tilt gearbox
4b. Stoplatch	17. Rails	29. Tilt gear-shifting
4b. Stoplatch	18. Housing	knob
5. Cradle	19. Roller-housing	30. Tilt wheel
6a. Tilt-plate lock	cover	31. Eyepiece-leveler
6b. Tilt-plate lock	20. Bushings	a. bracket, b. rest
7. Lock release	21. Bubble level	32. Tilt brake
8. Grab handle	22. Pan gearbox	33. Tilt-tension lever
9. Safety shafts	23. Pan gear-shifting	34. Tilt-gear tension-
10. Stoplatch	knob	adjustment knob
11. Pan handle spline	24. Pan wheel	35. Slotted screws

9.6 PANAVISION GEARED HEAD

Three basic components of the Panavision Geared Head (Panahead) are the tilt plate, cradle, and base (Figs. 9–5a and 9–5b).

NOTE: All directions are from the Operator's point of view.

9.6a Tilt Plate

The dovetailed top of a *standard tilt plate* (1a) or a *dual tilt plate* (1b) accepts a *sliding base* (2) necessary to mount any Panavision camera to the Panahead. (See Section 16.1a, Base, for details.)

To Insert a Sliding Base into a Standard Tilt Plate. Loosen the *base lock* (3). Push in the *stoplatch* (4a) at the left front dovetail, slide the base toward the rear while depressing the stoplatch.

Alternative Method. Push in the stoplatch at the left rear dovetail of the plate, slide the base forward while depressing. Release the stoplatch and lock the base into the desired position in the dovetail of the tilt plate.

NOTE: The base slides into the dovetailed top of a tilt plate a distance of 23.5cm (9 1/4").

The dovetailed bottom of a standard tilt plate fits into the dovetailed top of the *cradle* (5) (see Section 9.6b, Cradle) and slides a distance of 38.1mm (1 1/2"). Lock it into the desired position in the cradle by rotating the two *tilt-plate locks* (6a) at the right side of the plate.

To Insert A Sliding Base into A Dual Tilt Plate. Loosen the base lock. Push in the *stoplatch* (4b) at the right front dovetail of the plate, slide the base toward the rear while depressing the stoplatch.

Alternative Method. Push in the stoplatch at the right rear dovetail of plate, slide the base forward while depressing. Release the stoplatch and lock the base into the desired position in the dovetail of the tilt plate.

NOTE: The base slides in the dovetailed top of a tilt plate a distance of 23.5cm (9 1/4").

The dovetailed bottom of a dual tilt plate fits into the dovetailed top of the *cradle* (see Section 9.6b, Cradle) and slides a distance of 38.1mm (1 1/2"). Lock it into the desired position in the cradle by rotating the single *tilt-plate locks* (6b) at the right side of the plate.

Lifting of Standard Tilt Plate. Loosen the front and rear tilt-plate locks at right of plate, push the tilt plate forward until it stops, then secure the front lock; depress the spring-loaded *lock release* (7) just forward of the *grab handle* (8) at the rear of the plate and lift up. Secure the rear tilt-plate lock at the desired angle of tilt. The tilt plate will lift and lock at any angle from level to 60°.

NOTE: When the tilt plate is placed at an angle of 5°, 15°, or 20° elevation, or if it is level but at the extreme rear of the cradle, it is necessary to use one of three *safety shafts* (9) at the left front or right rear of the cradle to hold the weight of the tilt plate and camera. Each shaft must be pushed in manually, with the tilt-plate base against it, to hold the shaft in position. Once the weight is relieved, the shaft will automatically spring back into place.

Reversing of Tilt Plate. Loosen the front and rear tilt-plate locks; push in on the tilt-plate *stoplatch* (10) at the right front or left rear of the dovetail of the cradle and push the tilt plate either forward or backward while depressing the appropriate stoplatch.

NOTE: There are two separate dovetail sections at the base of each tilt plate, so the stoplatch must be kept depressed in order to clear each section.

Accessory Pan Handle and Grip. A *pan handle spline* (11) at the right rear of the standard tilt plate accepts a removable tripod handle. A removable left-hand pan grip (not shown) fits into the *pilot-pin holes* (12) at the left front of the tilt plate.

To Attach Pan Grip. Align the pilot pins on the pan-grip bracket to the matching holes in the tilt plate; secure the two knurled-headed screws in the bracket to the plate.

NOTE: When using handles for fast panning, it is essential that the internal worm gear be disengaged from the central pan gear in the base (see worm-gear pressure screw knob, Sec. 9.6c, Base).

Lifting of Dual Tilt Plate. Rotate counterclockwise the front or rear spring-loaded *dual tilt-plate locks* (13) at both sides of the plate (the rear plate locks tilt down; the front plate locks tilt up); insert the grooved *hand crank* (14) into the receptacle on the shaft, rotate it slowly until the keys in the shaft and the grooves on the handle mesh; crank and rotate the *worm gear* (15) clockwise to raise the plate to the desired angle. The tilt plate will lift and lock at any angle from level to 60° and remain in place. Remove the handle.

NOTE: Safety shafts are not necessary to hold the weight of the tilt plate and camera when using the dual tilt plate.

NOTE: There is *no* handle spline on the dual tilt plate.

To Level Dual Tilt Plate. Insert the hand crank into the shaft; rotate the worm gear counterclockwise until level; push in the spring-loaded dual tilt locks and rotate clockwise to secure.

9.6b Cradle

The dovetailed top surface of the cradle measures 10.16 × 40 cm (4 × 15 3/4"). The dovetail accepts either the matching base of the tilt plate or just the sliding base alone, if you prefer. An internal tilt gear (not shown) engages a *belt* (16). The tension of the belt against the gear achieves a smooth action of the tilt. (See tilt-gear tension-adjustment knob, Section 9.6c, Base.)

The cradle is held to the base by rollers (not shown) that ride the *rails* (17) in a *housing* (18) at each side. Access to the two rollers in each housing is obtained by removing the *roller-housing cover* (19). The front and rear 19mm (3/4") diameter *bushings* (20) at each side of the cradle are for insertion of carry rods whenever moving both camera and Panahead together from a tripod to a dolly, or vice-versa.

9.6c Base

A two-way *bubble level* (21) is at the top left on the *pan gearbox* (22), which houses a four-position *pan gear-shifting knob* (23). For low gear, slide the knob to position 1; for standard gear, slide the knob to position 2; for neutral (gears disengaged) slide the knob to N; for fast gear, slide the knob to 3. To pan left, rotate the *pan wheel* (24) clockwise; to pan right, rotate the pan wheel counterclockwise.

Panning 360°. Low gear (position 1) requires 75 turns of the wheel; standard gear (position 2) requires 40 turns of the wheel; high gear (position 3) requires 22 turns of the wheel.

A *pan-tension lever* (25), above the lower base, applies additional drag to the pan gear. Turn the *pan brake* (26), at the left rear of the base on the pan shaft, toward the Operator to tighten, away from the Operator to loosen.

A knurled *worm-gear pressure screw knob* (27) at the right rear of the base applies additional pressure on the internal worm gear (not shown) that engages the central pan gear (not shown) and takes the "play" out of the pan gear.

NOTE: Loosen this knob completely so as to disengage the worm gear from the central gear when panning the head manually.

If "play" in the pan gear remains after tightening the worm-gear pressure screw knob, insert a 1.6mm (1/16") hex wrench into the side of the base below the knob and loosen the hex set-screw; loosen the worm-gear pressure screw knob and pull the base door toward you to expose the slotted pan gear-lock adjusting screw bushing (not shown); insert a screwdriver into the slotted bushing and turn it clockwise two to three turns, then retighten the hex set-screw at the side to secure the bushing; close the doors and tighten the knurled knob; check gear for "play"; repeat this procedure if necessary.

The *tilt gearbox* (28) houses a four-position *tilt gear-shifting knob* (29). For low gear, slide the knob to position 1; for standard gear, slide the knob to position 2; for neutral (gears disengaged) slide the knob to N; for fast gear, slide the knob to 3. To tilt up, rotate the *tilt wheel* (30) clockwise; to tilt down, rotate the tilt wheel counterclockwise.

Tilting 30° from Level. Low gear (position 1) requires 7 turns of the wheel; standard gear (position 2) requires 3 3/4 turns of the wheel; high gear (position 3) requires 2 turns of the wheel.

The top of the tilt gearbox has an *eyepiece-leveler bracket* (31) that accepts the base of an eyepiece leveler (not shown), which is then attached to the extension tube on a Panaflex camera in the studio mode. The tilt drive shaft extends from the upper part of the base in order to clear the tilt wheel from the cradle. Directly forward of the tilt wheel on the tilt drive shaft is a *tilt brake* (32), which is turned clockwise to lock, counterclockwise to loosen. A *tilt-tension lever* (33), located at the right side of the base, is used to apply additional drag to the selected speed, if so desired.

The *tilt-gear tension-adjustment knob* (34) at the front of the base should always be rotated downward as far as it will go to take the "play" out of the tilt gear.

Pan and Tilt Wheels. The pan and tilt wheels measure 16.19cm (6 3/8") in diameter and are detachable and interchangeable. Although either one fits into a tapered keyway within each driveshaft and is secured to the driveshaft by a center knurled-headed screw, one of the wheels has a detachable handle. It is usually used as the tilt wheel. The detachable handle can be reversed in the wheel or removed completely if the operator has to hug the camera closely for a shot. Thumb-depress the end of the detachable handle, so as to withdraw its internal pins, and then pull it away to remove it from the wheel.

Two *slotted screws* (35) above the tilt-gear tension-adjustment knob accept a bracket to which is attached a small Camera Assistant's "goodie box"—i.e., a container to hold small tools, a lens (while changing only), a tape measure, etc.

The bottom of the base accepts a 3/8"-16 steel tripod-locking screw (not shown) approximately 2.54cm (1 1/2") in length, which inserts through a 3.81cm (3 1/4") diameter plate (not shown) and clamps the head to the tripod. A 9.5 × 19mm (3/8 × 3/4") key (not shown) at the base inserts into a mating slot on a tripod or dolly.

9.6d Maintenance

Loosen captured screws in the roller housing cover, remove the cover, clean the rails and rollers.

WARNING: Clean all parts of the Panahead with naphtha only! Lubricate rails and dovetails with silicone only.

Apply light grease (low-temperature type) on pan and tilt selector-knob guides.

9.6e Weight

17.5 kg (38.5 lbs).

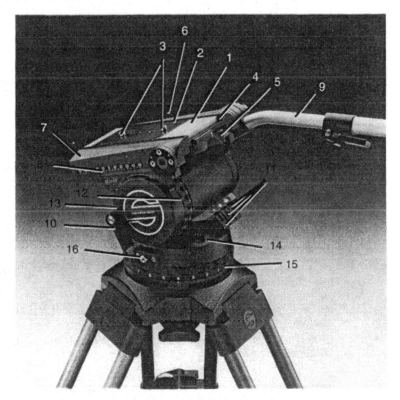

Figure 9–6. Sachtler Fluid Head Studio II Model. Courtesy of Sachtler Corp.

1. Balance plate
2. Quick-release camera-mounting plate
3. Camera-lockdown screws
4. Release lever safety catch
5. Camera mounting plate release lever
6. Balance plate lock lever
7. Dovetailed platform
8. Scale
9. Pan handle
10. Tilt lever
11. Counterbalance levers
12. Tilt adjustment knob
13. Pan-lock knob
14. Bullseye bubble lever
15. Pan-fluid adjustment knob
16. Viewfinder extension support bracket

9.7 SACHTLER FLUID HEAD STUDIO II

The three basic components of the Sachtler Fluid Head Model Studio II are the balance plate, the fluid head, and the base (Fig. 9–6).

NOTE: All directions are from the Operator's point of view.

9.7a Balance Plate

The *balance plate* (1) contains a *quick-release camera mounting plate* (2), fitted with two 3/8"-16 *camera-lockdown screws* (3) (which the manufacturer calls a "touch and go" plate) recessed in the balance plate.

To Mount a Camera on the Balance Plate. Depress the *release lever safety catch* (4) and rotate the *camera mounting plate release lever* (5) clockwise as far as it will go. The quick-release plate will pop up from its receptacle.

NOTE: Leave the release lever in the clockwise position. If closed, it will be impossible to place the camera on the head.

Attach the quick-release plate to the bottom of the camera with screws in the "touch and go" plate. Place the camera, with its attached plate, into the quick-release plate receptacle; its weight will depress the spring-loaded locking struts, release the safety catch, and snap the release lever into a locked position in the balance plate. Push the lever further to the right to ascertain that the mounting plate is firmly secured.

To Place a Balance Plate on the Head. Loosen the *balance plate lock lever* (6) at the right side of the plate. Insert the balance plate into the *dovetailed platform* (7) on the fluid head. Balance the camera, as explained in the next section.

9.7b Fluid Head

A *scale* (8) at the left side of the camera mounting plate, marked in increments of 5mm (3/16"), is used as a reference to balance the shift of the camera's weight, e.g., when adding a zoom lens, or when film moves into the take-up side of the camera magazine.

To Balance a Camera on the Head. Hold the *pan handle* (9), loosen the *tilt lever* (10), and ascertain that the balance plate lock lever is disengaged. Slide the camera and plate forward or back in the dovetailed platform until the camera remains level (centered) when the handle is grasped loosely. Tighten the balance plate lock lever.

NOTE: The balance plate can be moved forward or back through a 100mm (3.9") range.

To Counterbalance a Camera. Three *counterbalance levers* (11) compensate for different weights of cameras and their placement on the head. Icons of various thicknesses imprinted on the levers indicate the amount of spring-weight that can be applied to the head to maintain and keep the camera in any position set from level. These are, from right-to-left, a heavy-spring icon, a middle-spring icon, and a light-spring icon.

To Determine the Proper Counterbalance of Camera and Head. Ascertain that the camera is properly balanced (see above). Hold the pan handle firmly and rotate the 0–7 scaled *tilt adjustment knob* (12) clockwise to 0 (zero). Depress the heavy-spring imprinted icon lever.

NOTE: The head must be level in order for a counterbalance spring to engage.

Loosen the tilt lever and tilt the head up or down (at least 30°). Gently release the tripod handle to see if the camera will stay in position.

If the camera stays in position it is properly balanced. Adjust the 0–7 tilt drag (see below) to desired resistance.

If the camera tilts up and comes back to the center, depress and release the heavy-spring lever. Depress the center lever and/or the far left lever. Tilt the camera and gently release the tripod handle to see if the camera will stay in position.

If the camera continues to tilt down, leave the heavy-spring lever depressed. Depress the center lever and/or the far left lever. Tilt the camera and gently release the tripod handle to see if the camera will now stay in position.

If the camera "creeps" (slowly moves up or down) while tilted, simply add elevation/depression drag. Control elevation/depression drag by rotating the tilt adjustment knob counterclockwise to increase, clockwise to decrease. As the numbers increase, the 0–7 scale ranges from loose (0), to extreme resistance (7).

If the camera holds in one position but not another, check to see if it is balanced (centered) on the fluid head as explained at the beginning of this section.

NOTE: The Sachtler head will tilt ±60°.

A pan handle is extendable from 35cm (13 3/8″) to 52cm (20.5″) and fits to either the left or right side of the head.

The pan brake release is actuated by turning the *pan-lock knob* (13)—at the front of the unit and forward of the phosphorescent *bullseye bubble lever* (14)—counterclockwise to loosen, clockwise to tighten.

Horizontal drag is controlled by turning the scalloped *pan-fluid adjustment knob* (15) clockwise to increase, counterclockwise to decrease.

Most fluid heads are fitted with a *viewfinder extension support bracket* (16).

NOTE: The unit can be panned 360°.

9.7c Base

The Sachtler head is fitted with either a 150mm ball base or a Mitchell-type (flat) base. A 3/8″-16 steel tripod-locking screw (not shown), approximately 76mm (3″) long for the ball base or 3.81cm (1 1/2″) long for the Mitchell base, inserts through a 7.9 cm (3 1/4″) diameter washer (not shown) and clamps the head to the tripod. A 9.5mm (3/8″) diameter key (not shown) at the base inserts into a mating slot on a tripod or dolly.

9.7d Maintenance

The manufacturer states that the fluid head requires no maintenance in the field other than the adjustments noted above. Do not disassemble.

9.7e Weight

8.7 kg (19.2 lbs).

9.8 WORRALL GEARED HEAD

The three basic components of the Worrall Geared Head are the cradle, carriage, and base (Figs. 9–7a and 9–7b).

All directions are from the Operator's point of view.

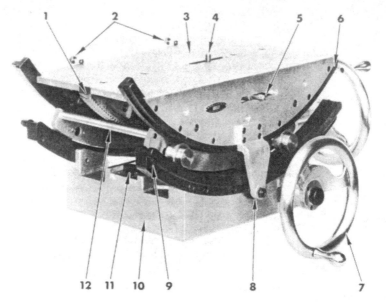

Figure 9.7a. Worrall Geared Head. Courtesy of Worrall Camera Company and Cinema Products.

1. Tilt gear	5. Lockdown-screw	9. Bracket stops
2. Adjustable side stops	shaft	10. Base
3. Cradle	6. Upper rails	11. Tilt worm-lock cap
4. Camera-lockdown	7. Pan handle	12. Carriage rods
screw	8. Side brackets	

9.8a Cradle

The top surface of the cast aluminum *cradle* (3) measures 40 × 23.5cm (15 3/4 × 9 1/4″). Before a camera can be placed on the cradle, the *adjustable side stops* (2) must be relieved to permit side movement of the camera while securing the 3/8″-16″ *camera-lockdown screw* (4) into the tapped hole in the camera base. The camera-lockdown screw can slide a distance of 63.5 mm (2 1/2″) in a restricted slot in the top of the cradle to facilitate engaging the tapped hole in the camera base. Also, when the camera-lockdown screw is loosened a few turns, the camera can be moved forward or backward to balance it on the cradle.

A pair of helical gears (not shown) connects the camera lockdown screw to the *lockdown-screw shaft* (5). The milled surfaces of the shaft accept a hand crank (not shown); on some models, the shaft may be fitted with a permanent knob. Rotate this shaft clockwise to tighten the screw, counterclockwise to loosen it.

Once you have secured the camera to the cradle, screw in the adjustable side stops to engage the side of the camera base and prevent it from swiveling on the cradle surface.

The cast bronze *tilt gear* (1) engages an internal worm gear (not shown) which, when activated, elevates/depresses the cradle.

The *upper rails* (6) ride on the *carriage* (16) and are stepped to prevent the cradle from moving sideways.

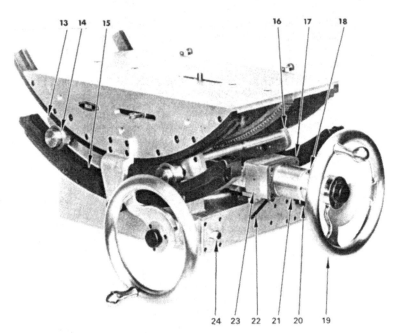

Figure 9.7b. Worrall Geared Head. Courtesy of Worrall Camera Company and Cinema Products.

13. Carriage rails	18. Pan brake (not visible)	21. Tilt-drive shaft
14. Differential rollers	19. Tilt handle	22. Tilt brake
15. Lower rails	20. Pan gear access knob	23. Tilt gearbox
16. Carriage		24. Pan-speed selector
17. Tilt-speed selector		

NOTE: All three components (cradle, carriage, and base) are held together as a unit by two *side brackets* (8), which are prevented from rocking off the base by four *bracket stops* (9), located at the extreme ends of both *lower rails* (15) in the *base* (10). (See Sec. 9.8c, Base.)

9.8b Carriage

The *carriage* (16) consists of four *differential rollers* (14), mounted on ball-bearing shafts screwed to two *carriage rails* (13), which are connected by two *carriage rods* (12). The differential rollers ride in the groove of the lower rail and the step of the upper rail. The carriage supports the cradle in its travel forward (tilt up) or back (tilt down).

9.8c Base

A pattern of nine holes in the lower rails allows for a three-position adjustment of the rails (forward, center, or back) to obtain a maximum elevation or depression of the cradle (42° from level). The rails are held in position (forward, center, or back) by 1/4"-20 × 7/8" socket-head cap screws, which require a 3/16" hex wrench to remove. Normally, the rails are in the center position.

Adjustment of the Lower Rail with the Camera on the Cradle. Remove the socket-head cap screws (two to three in each rail) with a 3/16" hex wrench.

105

Lift up on the cradle at the side bracket to support the weight of the camera. Slide each lower rail to its new position (back to obtain maximum depression, center for normal position, and forward to obtain maximum elevation) until a combination of three screwholes in the rail matches a combination of three tapped holes in the base. Reinsert the screws into the matching tapped holes. If a third screw is available, insert it into the center tapped hole.

Disengagement of the Tilt Gear at the Front of Base. Turn the *tilt worm-lock cap* (11) counterclockwise, slide the wedge forward, then push the worm gear (not shown) down. Slide the wedge back to its original position and tighten the tilt worm-gear lock. When disengaged, the geared head is set for free tilting.

Selection of Tilt Speed. The *tilt gearbox* (23) houses the two-speed *tilt-speed selector* (17). For low gear, move the selector forward; for high gear, move the selector back; to disengage the gears, center the selector.

The *tilt-drive shaft* (21) extends from the back of the base in order to clear the handle from the cradle. Directly below is the *tilt brake* (22), which is turned clockwise to lock and counterclockwise to release.

Selection of Pan Speed. The two-speed *pan-speed selector* (24) is located at the left back of the base. For high speed, move the selector left; for low speed, push the selector right; to disengage gears, center the selector.

Use of Pan and Tilt Handles. The *pan handle* (7) and *tilt handle* (19) are detachable and interchangeable. Either one fits into a tapered keyway within each drive shaft and is secured to the drive shaft by a center knurled-head screw. Both handles measure 16.66cm (6 9/16″) outside diameter. A smaller handle, 8.9cm (3 1/2″) outside diameter, is also manufactured.

Panning 360°. High speed requires 22 turns of the handle while low speed requires 60 turns of the handle to complete a full circle. To pan right, turn the handle counterclockwise (away from the Operator); to pan left, turn the handle clockwise (toward the Operator). A *pan brake* (18) is to the right of the tilt gearbox.

Tilting 42° from Center. From center to maximum elevation/depression, high speed requires 2 1/4 turns of the handle while low speed requires 15 turns. To tilt down, turn the handle counterclockwise; to tilt up, turn it clockwise.

Free Panning. Turning the *pan gear access knob* (20) opens the rear base door approximately 9.5mm (3/8″) and disengages the pan worm gear (not shown) from the pan gear (not shown) located in the base casting. When disengaged, the geared head is set for free panning.

NOTE: On some units, the factory-installed stop has been removed, permitting the door to be opened all the way.

Placement on a Tripod or Dolly. Attached to the bottom of the base is a steel tripod-locking screw (not shown). The screw measures 6.7cm (2 5/8″) in diameter by 2.54cm (1″) in length, with eight threads per inch. The lock nut (not shown) that fits the screw and clamps the head to the tripod is constructed with slightly extended "bayonets" to aid in loosening the nut, which has a 9.8cm (3 7/8″) outside diameter.

A 9.5 × 19mm (3/8 × 3/4″) key (not shown) at the base inserts into a mating slot on the tripod.

9.8d Maintenance

The manufacturer recommends the following:

1. All gears (pan, tilt, worm, helical) should be treated with an EP 90 (extreme pressure, 90 weight) grease that has a sticky additive in it.
2. The steel rails (upper and lower) should be wiped with oil containing a rust-inhibiting agent.
3. All threaded parts (screws, nuts, locks) should be coated with a light grease.
4. Surface rust should be removed with crocus cloth.

9.8e Miscellaneous

History. The Worrall Geared Head was originally designed for use with the BNC Mitchell camera but can be used with any camera and/or blimp.

Use of Risers. Most camera blimps require a riser (see Section 9.9) in order to clear the blimp lens-access door from the geared head's upper rails. Most nonblimped cameras require a riser in order to accommodate the matte-box rods and/or a Mitchell follow-focus attachment (see Section 14.11, Fig. 14–36), which extends below a camera's base.

Reinforcing Camera Lockdown. If the camera lockdown screw fails to secure the camera tightly to the plate, a few strips of camera tape placed across the top of the cradle will anchor and eliminate any swiveling of the camera on the cradle.

9.8f Weight

30.5 kg (67 lb).

9.9 RISER

A *riser* (Fig. 9–8) is available specifically for the Worrall Geared Head. Because it is made of two metal plates separated by four 3-in. spacers, the unit is often called a "bridge plate." It is required either when a follow-focus attachment (which extends below the camera base) is mounted to the camera or a blimped camera is mounted on the geared head (in order to clear the lens door from the upper rails). (See Section 9.8e.)

Bottom Plate. The bottom plate is fitted with a series of 3/8"-16 tapped holes to allow for placement choice on a geared head.

Figure 9–8. Riser.

1. Camera-lockdown screw   2. Knurled lockdown knob   3. Taper pin

Figure 9–9. Tilt plate.

1. Camera lockdown screw   2. Pressure lockdown knobs   3. Taper pin

Top Plate.   The top plate is fitted with a 3/8″-16 *camera-lockdown screw* (1) connected by a pair of helical gears to a *knurled lockdown knob* (2) on a shaft. The shaft is also fitted with a *taper pin* (3) to accommodate a keyed hand crank (not shown) to secure the lockdown screw tightly. The pin and knob always face forward when the riser is mounted on a geared or tripod head.

9.10 TILT PLATE

A tilt plate (Fig. 9–9), built specifically for the Worrall Geared Head, is necessary when a greater degree of tilt is desired than the geared head and/or the adjustment of the lower rails (see Section 9.8c, Worrall Geared Head, Base) can provide. It is the same as a riser (see Section 9.9), except that the top plate is hinged at the front and the back can be elevated up to 90°.

Bottom Plate.   The bottom plate is fitted with a series of 3/8″-16 tapped holes to allow for placement choice on a geared head, and tapped brackets to accommodate *pressure lockdown knobs* (2).

Top Plate.   The top plate is fitted with a 3/8″-16 *camera-lockdown screw* (1) connected by a pair of helical gears to a shaft fitted with a *taper pin* (3), which accommodates a keyed hand crank (not shown) to secure the lockdown screw tightly. The shaft and its pin always face forward when the riser is mounted on a geared or tripod head.

A vertical, adjustable screw (not shown) in the bottom plate is used to level the top plate when the unit is in the horizontal position. (Absolute level ensures greater accuracy of degree of tilt when the wedge is lifted.)

Tilt-Plate Designs.   Most tilt plates are fitted with slotted arms attached to the top plate at both sides (shown). Two pressure lockdown knobs insert through the restricted slots into brackets. The knobs are loosened to free the plate, secured when the rear of the top plate is manually lifted up and forward to the desired tilt position.

Some tilt plates use a worm gear and hand crank (not shown) to lift the rear of the top plate up and forward.

chapter 10

AATON 16mm Cameras

10.1 AATON XTR (AND LTR) 16mm CAMERA (Figs. 10–1a, 10–1b)

The XTR succeeded the earlier LTR model. Operation is fundamentally the same for both models except as noted. The basic LTR lacks some of the XTR features.

NOTE: All directions are from Operator's point of view.

10.1a Base

Bottom is fitted with 3/8"-16 tapped hole to accommodate tripod-lockdown screw.

WARNING: Do not use a tripod-lockdown screw longer than 12mm (½"). Longer screws can damage cameras's electronic circuits.

10.1b MOTOR

Removable crystal-sync 12-volt motor.

To Preset Camera Speed Insert coin in slot of *speed control knob* (27) and rotate. Speed settings are viewable in window at right of knob.

NOTE: Speed can also be set using the LCD below eyepiece if camera is running (see Section 10.1n, Liquid Crystal Display).

To Set Synchronous Speeds Rotate until 24, 25, or 30fps (29.97 if installed in camera) are set on speed control knob in blue detents.

To Set Nonsync Speeds Rotate until 6, 12, 16, 18, 20, 40fps, are set on knob in white detents.

To Set High-Speed Rotate until 54fps is set on knob in red detent.

NOTE: The camera requires 16 volts of power to achieve the Hi-speed setting of 54fps.

To Preset Camera Speed. Insert coin into slot of speed-control knob and rotate. Speed settings are viewable in window at right of knob and also on liquid crystal display (LCD) below eyepiece when camera is running. (See Section 10.1n, Liquid Crystal Display.)

To Change the Motor. Remove base-release *3mm Allen screw* (45) located between magazine guide rail and motor bracket.

WARNING: Keep *all* screws separated. Inserting wrong screws when reassembling will result in camera damage!

Invert camera and remove two base-release *4mm Allen screws* at bottom of camera (25). Lift base *slowly,* and place next to camera. Turn camera on its side, motor *up;* remove three 2.5mm Allen screws from motor retaining ring. Lift motor *carefully* to avoid damage to motor wiring and its

109

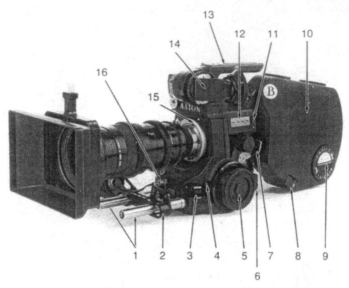

Figure 10–1a. AATON XTR 16mm camera (left front view). Courtesy of AATON Camera Company.

1. Matte-box/handgrip support rods
2. Follow-focus and handgrip bracket
3. On/Off/Test rocker switch
4. Photometer
5. Motor
6. ASA setting dial
7. Magazine release lever
8. Magazine lid catch
9. Magazine mechanical counter
10. Magazine feed side lid
11. Counter buttons
12. Liquid crystal display (LCD)
13. Carry handle
14. Viewfinder
15. Lens-mount locking ring
16. LEMO 2-pin on/off receptacle

connector; *gently* disconnect six-pin Socapex motor plug from camera receptacle. Remove motor, and replace with new unit. Reverse this procedure to reassemble.

10.1c Powerline (Fig. 10–2)

Outlets at back of camera, next to magazine mount.

Input to Camera. *XLR4 4-pin* (recessed male plug) *connector* (29). Clockwise (from lower left), pin 1 is ground; pins 2 and 3 are blank; pin 4 is plus 12-volts battery input.

12-Volt Nickel Cadmium (NiCd) Rechargeable Battery. Protruding four-pin receptacle and battery lug slides into matching XLR4 recessed plug and retainer slot.

CAUTION: High-speed (54fps) requires a battery of 16 volts, which is the same size as the 12-volt battery.

To secure battery to camera, tighten the knurled battery retainer screw.

NOTE: An accessory cable fitted with XLR4 connectors is available for use with an XLR4-fitted 12-volt, 4-ampere-hour (AH) battery belt.

Figure 10–1b. AATON XTR 16mm camera (right rear view). Courtesy of AATON Camera Company.

17. NiCd battery
18. Texo (time-code connector) housing
19. Handgrip connector cable
20. Handgrip

21. Handgrip lock
22. Sunshade/matte-box
23. Video tap cover
24. Magazine take-up lid

NOTE: AATON NiCd batteries require an AATON charger, or a micro-processor-controlled charger.

Lithium Battery. A non-rechargeable 12-volt, 8 AH battery is available from the manufacturer. When voltage drops to 10.8 volts, the lithium battery is discarded. It is *not* rechargeable.

NOTE: Manufacturer claims that a lithium battery can run 50–60 of the 122m (400 ft) magazines at 25°C (77°F), can be transported as nonvolatile cargo, and has a shelf life of 5–10 years, ± 2 months.

Accessories Jaeger 4-Pin Female Connector (30). Clockwise from top, pin 1 is ground; pin 2 is TV sync; pin 3 is the 2400Hz signal; pin 4 is plus 12-volts battery input.

NOTE: Pins 2 and 3 are for external speed controllers.

NOTE: The Jaeger 4-pin connector is not present on some models (e.g., XTR-j). On those models, a different input arrangement handles battery, video, and other hookups, and the speed controllers are connected on the Amphenol nine-pin connector.

5-Ampere Bussman Fuse (31). Blows out if power to camera exceeds 17 volts and/or if power to the camera is polarity-inverted. *To change* the fuse, turn camera *off.* Unscrew fuse cover counterclockwise. With tweezers, pull old fuse from camera body, insert new fuse, and screw fuse cover clockwise to secure.

CAUTION: *Always* have a spare 5-amp fuse available.

Video-Tap Connector (33). Amphenol 9-pin-recessed male receptacle— upper five pins: pin 1 is ground, pin 2 is TV sync, pin 3 is 2400 Hz, pin 4 is

Figure 10–2. AATON XTR 16mm camera (rear view, power panel). Courtesy of AATON Camera Company.

25. Base-release 4mm screws (not visible)
26. Electronic base
27. Speed control knob
28. Time-code 5-pin Lemo connector
29. Power XLR 4-pin connector
30. Accessories Jaeger 4-pin female connector
31. 5-amp Bussman fuse cap
32. Battery retainer screw
33. Video-tap 9-pin Amphenol connector
34. Video relay lens
35. Video-cap locking screw
36. Beam splitter access cap
37. On/off yellow LED
38. Nonsync red LED
39. Frame-line eccentric nut
40. Timecode recording head
41. Film guide rails
42. Camera magnetic drive wheel
43. Pulldown claw
44. Magazine guide rail
45. Base-release 3mm screw (not visible)

RX/TX microprocessor communication port, pin 5 is power (battery) input. Lower four pins: pin 6 is ground, pin 7 is strobe light to check the claw/timecode phase, pin 8 is start, pin 9 is power (battery).

Camera-Speed Indicator Diodes. At the top of power panel, the *red* (inboard) *LED* (38) does the following: (a) *illuminates* when camera is running in nonsync—variable speed (6, 12, 16, 18, 20, 40, and 54fps)—mode; (b) *slowly flashes* when battery power is below 10.5 volts; (c) *quickly flashes* when camera is not running at the fps (sync or variable) rate set on the speed-control knob, and/or when coming up to the speed that *is* set.

NOTE: The *red LED* is *extinguished* when camera is running at the set crystal sync (24, 25, 30fps [29.97fps if set on camera]) speed. The *yellow (outboard) LED* (37) is illuminated when camera is running regardless of the speed (sync or nonsync) set on camera.

Time Code LEMO 5-Pin Female Connector (28). Located in the base at the right side of camera. Pin 1 is ground; pin 2 is blank, pin 3 is ASCII code; pins 4 and 5 are blank.

WARNING: If the camera has not been run for at least 2 weeks, mount a 12-volt battery to the camera for a minimum of 3 hours before filming. The attached battery will charge the internal buffer battery, which will allow the camera's clock to keep time for 2 minutes during battery changes.

3-Position On/Off/Test Rocker Switch (3). Located at camera left front.

NOTE: On some cameras, the switch is horizontal; on other cameras, the switch is vertical. The manufacturer states that the positioning is by customer preference; however, if it is a rental, you take what you get.

NOTE: A similar switch is located in the handgrip accessory (see Handgrip Accessory, this section)

To start camera, depress horizontal rocker *down,* or vertical rocker *away* from motor.
To stop camera, center rocker switch.
To single-frame the camera, push horizontal rocker *up,* or vertical rocker *toward* motor, to the *test* position.

WARNING: To single-frame either by hand or by intervalometer, or to run the camera with a remote control, a magazine *must* be on the camera.

To clear mirror/shutter from gate:
1) Do *not* remove magazine from camera!

NOTE: On older models, motors had an inching knob. It was possible to insert a coin and rotate the mirror counterclockwise out of viewing position without removing the magazine. Due to forgetfulness of camera users to return the mirror before starting the camera again, which caused undue strain on the mirror gears and the risk of breakdown in the field, the manufacturer has eliminated the manual inching knob on the motors and replaced it with an electronic inching knob.

2) Depress horizontal rocker *up* or vertical rocker *away* from motor.
Viewfinder Test Mode. See Section 10.1f, "Viewfinder."
ASA Test Mode. See Section 10.1h, "ASA Setting Dial."

Handgrip Accessory. A *handgrip* (20) fits to the right-front of the *matte-box/ handgrip rod* (1). The adjustable handgrip is fitted with a three-position on/off/test rocker switch and a cable with a 2-pin LEMO plug.

To Mount Handgrip Remove the matte-box, slide the handgrip onto the right rod, adjust for the Operator's reach. Secure with the *handgrip lock* (21). Insert the plug on the cable into the matching *2-pin LEMO connector* (16) at lower front of camera. Replace matte-box.

NOTE: The 2-pin LEMO receptacle can also be used for an intervalometer (single-frame unit), or a camera remote-control On/Off switch and its cable.

To start camera, depress horizontal switch away from camera.
To stop camera, center rocker switch.
To single-frame the camera, depress horizontal switch toward camera.

WARNING: To single-frame the camera by hand or by intervalometer, or to run camera with a remote control, a magazine *must* be on the camera.

To clear the mirror/shutter from the aperture:
1) Do *not* remove magazine from camera! 2) depress horizontal switch toward camera.

10.1d Turret
None. Single lens mount. *Lens-mount locking ring* (15) only accepts lenses fitted with AATON mount or lenses fitted with AATON lens-mount adapter.

NOTE: Adapters are available for the Arriflex, Eclair, Panavision, Mitchell, Nikon, Leica R, and Olympus lenses.

WARNING: To match focal distance of port, *any* lens (especially a zoom lens) fitted with an AATON mount or adapter must have a flange focal distance of 40mm $\pm$ 5 microns.

CAUTION: To avoid damage to port's flange focal distance, *always* remove a zoom lens from the camera when in its case, especially during shipment.

To convert lens-mount locking ring to Super-16, see Section 10.1g, "To Convert Camera to/from Super 16."

10.1e Lenses
To fit lens to camera: 1) Rotate lens-mount locking ring clockwise. 2) Hold lens firmly with infinity scribe *up.* 3) Fit the three bayonets on the lens (or its adapter) to matching insets on the locking ring. Snug lens into mount *gently.*

WARNING: Unless locking ring slides easily over the lens bayonets, the lens is *not* properly seated. Do *not* use locking ring to force lens into mount!

To remove lens: 1) Grasp lens firmly. 2) Rotate lens-mount locking ring counterclockwise. 3) Pull lens *slowly* away from camera.

10.1f Viewfinder (Fig. 10–3)
Reflex. Adjustable. Image magnified 10×. Views more than full aperture. Groundglass carries both Standard 16mm and Super 16mm engravings.

NOTE: Viewfinder and groundglass (as well as lens-mount locking ring) must be realigned to change from one format to the other (see Sec. 10.1g, "To Convert Camera to/from Super 16").

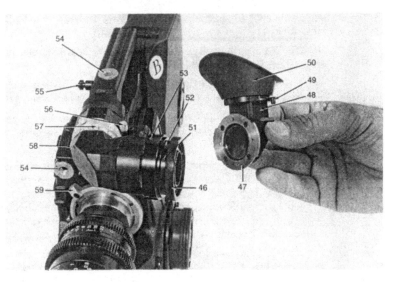

Figure 10–3. AATON XTR 16mm camera (eyepiece detail). Courtesy of AATON Camera Company.

46. Eyepiece lock
47. Eyepiece bayonet flange
48. Eyepiece
49. Eyepiece closer knob
50. Eyecup
51. Eyepiece-tension Allen screw
52. Eyepiece-lock holder ring
53. Gear-space screw

54. 3/8-16" threaded eyelight rod receptacle
55. Tape hook
56. Diopter-setting lock screw
57. Diopter-setting knob
58. Spacer (Super-16 mode)
59. Lens-lock lever (Super-16 mode)

NOTE: If a dark spot appears on the viewing screen, manufacturer warns against trying to remove it, stating that the spot is a broken fiber in the fiber optics.

To view through lens, place eye to eyecup (50). Eyecup is rotatable 360°.

NOTE: For left-eyed people, a bayonet-mounted eyepiece is available.

To lock eyepiece diaphragm open, push eyepiece-closer knob (49) *up.*
To lock eyepiece diaphragm closed, push eyepiece-closer knob *down.*
To align reflex mirror for viewing, automatic shutter stops in viewing position when camera is shut *off.* If closed, or partially closed, for any reason then start and stop camera.
To focus eyepiece (48), remove the lens. Loosen the *lock screw* (56) on ± 5 *diopter-setting knob* (57). Rotate the dioptric knob and focus on scribe of groundglass aperture. Tighten the diopter-setting knob.
To detach eyepiece, grasp eyepiece. Loosen the *eyepiece lock* knurled ring (46) and pull eyepiece away from housing.
To attach eyepiece extension: 1) Remove eyepiece. 2) Hold elbowed extension piece parallel to the taking lens (pointing forward) and insert into eyepiece lock. 3) Snug eyepiece lock onto extension. 4) Rotate

extension 180° to shooting position (toward Operator). 5) Tighten eyepiece lock. 6) Place eyepiece onto extension.

NOTE: The length of the extension eyepiece might require higher torque on eyepiece lock to hold it in place.

To hold extension in position, with a 3mm Allen wrench, loosen *eyepiece-tension Allen screw* (51) on the *eyepiece-lock holder ring* (52).

NOTE: On some models, the Allen-screw type of holder ring has been replaced by a knurled ring, eliminating the Allen screw when tightening or loosening.

If fitted with holder ring: With right hand, hold the extension parallel (eyepiece toward Operator). With left hand, rotate the eyepiece holder ring toward Operator a quarter turn to increase tension; tighten Allen screw if fitted with one. Remove hand from extension, check that it stays in place. If not, repeat in quarter-turn adjustments on eyepiece holder ring until extension remains parallel.

WARNING: Do not loosen any other screws on the viewfinder! If the *gear-space screw* (53) [inboard of eyepiece-lock holder ring] is loosened, it is a factory repair!

NOTE: When using an extension, a support rod or eye leveler is recommended.

10.1g To Convert Camera to/from Standard 16mm/Super 16

Requires 1) conversion tools, 2) two-piece centering tool, used for resetting the lens-port mount, 3) repositioning of the groundglass viewing screen 4) shifting of the viewfinder
Conversion Tools

- one 2.5mm Allen wrench
- one 3 mm Allen wrench
- one flat-blade screwdriver, 4mm ($\frac{1}{8}$″) wide by 0.05mm (0.02″) thickness

NOTE: When converting the camera, it is wise to use an empty film can lid as a depository for screws and parts.

Two-Piece Centering Tool for Resetting the Lens-Port Mount. The centering tool consists of a lens-port block and an aperture rod.

The *lens-port block* is a circular unit with a raised 50mm (2″) hub that inserts into the lens port. Around the perimeter of the lens-port block, and clear of the hub, are three lens-lock-ring screw-centering-holes and two lens-lock-ring pin depressions. These holes are used when aligning the lens-lock ring to the camera. A circular center hole in the block and its hub contains an aperture-rod registration pin.

The 90mm (3.5″) *aperture rod* inserts into the center hole of the block and hub. One end is shaped to form a plug that fits a standard 16mm aperture; its other end is shaped to fit into the camera's Super 16mm aperture. Grooves in the rod above each plug are strategically milled so that the rod cannot waiver in the hub. Although the camera aperture is milled for Super 16 and measures 7.4mm H × 12.4mm W, diagonally 14.5mm (0.292″ H × .493 W, diagonally 9/16″), which end of the rod goes into the camera's aperture depends on whether the camera is to be used for standard 16 or Super 16.

Aperture, Guide Rails, and Pulldown Claw. The milled *aperture* in the camera extends into the area normally used for the perforation in standard 16mm double-perforated film or the soundtrack in standard 16mm single-perforated film.

Film guide rails (41) on each side of the widened aperture prevent the film from "weaving."

WARNING: Never loosen or remove the factory-set guide rails. To realign them is a factory job.

CAUTION: Above the left guide rail is a circular *frameline eccentric nut* (39). The "nub" in its center is the end of a screw. It is often mistaken for a spring-loaded oil hole. Poking or trying to lift this nut can severely damage the camera and throw the frameline off-center, requiring a major repair job.

A single *pulldown claw* (43) transports the film through the camera.

Determining Present Centering Position. To determine whether the lens is centered for standard 16mm or Super 16mm, simply look at the lens lock (the metallic tab) on the lens-mount locking ring: If the lens lock is on the motor side of the camera (Operator's left), the lens is centered for standard 16mm; if the lens lock is on the battery side of the camera (Operator's right), the lens is centered for Super 16mm.

Repositioning of the Groundglass Viewing Screen *To determine whether the groundglass is set for standard 16mm or Super 16mm,* clear the mirror/shutter from the aperture (see Sec. 10.1c, "Powerline"). *To clear mirror/shutter from aperture* only: loosen (do *not* remove) the screw in the block (above the aperture) that holds the groundglass. Slide the groundglass block until it stops: (a) *For standard 16,* slide toward battery (Operator's right); *for Super 16,* slide toward motor (Operator's left).

CAUTION, WARNING, NOTE: Retighten screw to secure the block!

Shifting of the Viewfinder *To determine whether the viewfinder is positioned for standard 16mm or Super 16mm,* look down at the viewfinder base. Four screws hold the base to the camera. Two of the screws also hold down an L-shaped (1mm H × 8mm W × 29mm L) *spacer* (58) of which only the width and length is visible, its height being inserted downward. For *Standard 16,* the spacer should be on the motor side (Operator's left). For *Super 16,* the spacer should be on the battery side (Operator's right).

CAUTION, WARNING, NOTE: It is essential to determine all three (lens centering, position of groundglass, and viewfinder positioning) before filming starts. Checking only one or two modes can be disastrous! *Don't assume!*

To Convert Camera to Standard 16mm Mode: To center the lens lock ring; 1) Ascertain that camera is in Super 16 mode. 2) Unscrew stubby lock lever from the lens-mount locking ring. 3) Unscrew lens-mount locking ring. 4) Remove the three 2.5mm screws holding the lens-port inner ring. 5) Rotate inner ring until its two projecting pins are at upper left (motor side/approximately Operator's 10 o'clock). 6) Insert hub of lens-port block into camera, making certain the two lens-mount locking ring depressions on the centering tool mate with the pins on the inner ring. 7) *Carefully* insert the standard 16 end of the aperture rod into the block and hub, making certain to match the milled groove in the rod to the pin in the center hole. 8) Rotate the block and hub gently until the aperture-rod plug inserts into the aperture.

NOTE: With magazine removed, verify that the standard 16 plug has 2mm of space toward the motor side (Operator's left).

9) Align the three holes on the perimeter of the block to the screw holes on the camera body. 10) Insert the three 2.5mm screws through the lens-lock centering holes in the block, and secure the lens-port inner ring to the camera. 11) Remove block, thread lens-lock-ring onto port's inner ring, then screw lens lock to the lens-lock ring.

NOTE: Some lens-lock rings are engraved with the inscription "16" facing the motor side.

To set the groundglass block to standard 16mm mode, 1) Remove lens. Reach into the lens port and only *loosen* (do *not* remove) the screw in the block (above the aperture) that holds the groundglass. 2) Slide the groundglass block in its captive groove toward the battery (Operator's right) until it stops. 3) Tighten screw to secure the block.

CAUTION, WARNING, NOTE: Tighten the screw, but don't jam it!

To position the viewfinder to standard 16mm mode: 1) Remove the four 3mm × 6mm Allen-head screws in the viewfinder base. 2) Lift the viewfinder by its handle. 3) Grasp and lift the 1mm × 8mm × 29mm L-shaped spacer from the viewfinder base.

CAUTION: The spacer can be easily lost if dropped.

4) Slide viewfinder base toward battery (Operator's right), and insert spacer on motor side (Operator's left), making certain the 1mm lip is *down.* 5) Replace screws, and secure viewfinder to camera body.

WARNING: Use only the screws that were removed previously. Use of longer screws will damage the photometer inside the camera.

To Convert Camera to Super 16mm Mode: *To center the lens lock ring:* 1) Ascertain that camera is in standard 16mm mode. 2) Unscrew stubby lock lever from the lens-mount locking ring. 3. Unscrew lens-lock ring. 4) Remove the three 2.5mm screws holding the lens-port inner ring. 5) Rotate inner ring until its two projecting pins are at lower left (battery side/ approximately Operator's 5 o'clock). 6) Insert hub of lens-port block into camera, making certain the two lens-lock ring depressions on the centering tool mate with the pins on the inner ring. 7) *Carefully* insert the Super 16 end of the aperture rod into the block and hub, making certain to match the milled groove in the rod to the pin in the center hole. 8) Rotate the block and hub gently until the aperture-rod plug inserts into the aperture,

NOTE: With magazine removed, verify that the Super 16 plug fills the entire aperture.

9) Align the three holes on the perimeter of the block to the screw holes on the camera body. 10) Insert the three 2.5mm screws through the lens-lock centering holes in the block, and secure the lens-port inner ring to the camera. 11) Remove block, thread lens-lock ring onto port's inner ring, and screw lens lock to lens-lock ring.

NOTE: Some lens-lock rings are engraved with the inscription "S16" facing the motor side.

To set the groundglass block to Super 16mm mode: 1) Remove lens. Reach into the lens port and only *loosen* (do *not* remove) the screw in the block (above the aperture) that holds the groundglass. 2) Slide the groundglass block in its captive groove toward the motor (Operator's left) until it stops. 3) Tighten the screw to secure the block.

CAUTION, WARNING, NOTE: Tighten the screw, but don't jam it!

To position the viewfinder to Super 16mm mode: 1) Remove the four 3mm × 6mm Allen-head screws in viewfinder base. 2) Lift viewfinder by its handle. 3) Grasp and lift the 1mm × 8mm × 29mm L-shaped spacer from viewfinder base.

CAUTION: The spacer can be easily lost if dropped.

4) Slide viewfinder base toward motor (Operator's left), and insert spacer on battery side (Operator's right), making certain the 1mm lip is *down.* 5) Replace screws, and secure viewfinder to camera body.

WARNING: Use only the screws that were previously removed. Use of longer screws will damage the photometer inside the camera.

CAUTION: When filming in Super 16, always use single-perforated raw stock!

10.1h ASA Setting Dial *(6)*
Located at left side of camera behind motor. Reads in 12 increments: ASA 64, ASA 80, ASA 100, ASA 125, ASA 160, ASA 200, ASA 250, ASA 320, ASA 400, ASA 500, ASA 640, ASA 800, then reverts to ASA 64.

NOTE: An optional 12 increments from ASA 50 to 640 are available in some models.

To change ASA setting on dial, insert coin in slot of dial, and rotate counterclockwise. ASA speed is viewable in cutout at top of dial.

NOTE: When ASA is changed, it increases or decreases the intensity of the diode for the time code and the built-in photometer (see Sec. 10.1i).

To verify ASA set on dial, remove magazine from camera. Depress the three-position On/Off/Test camera switch (either on camera or on handgrip) to the *test* position. ASA will appear on LCD display (see Sec. 10.1n).

10.1i Photometer

Photometer On/Off Toggle. Switch for *photometer* (4) is located forward of motor and behind camera's On/Off/Test switch. Push toggle toward matte box to turn internal viewfinder LED display on or toward Operator to turn display off.
To use built-in photometer: 1) Place magazine (with film) on camera (see Sec. 10.1m); 2) Ascertain that ASA setting (see Sec. 10.1h) matches ASA of film in magazine.

WARNING: Photocells measure the light reflected from the film. Failure to have film in the magazine and the correct ASA on the dial will result in a false reading.

Press camera 3) On/Off/Test switch (see Sec. 10.1c above) to *test* position, and rotate mirror/shutter away from aperture; 4) Aim camera at object to be photographed; 5) Sight through viewfinder (see Sec. 10.1f, "Viewfinder"); 6) Push photometer On/Off toggle forward. Red, green and yellow photometer display diodes will appear above aperture.

Photometer Red/Green/Yellow Display LEDs: Reading from left to right, the far left diode is *red,* and it (a) *illuminates* when camera is running in nonsync (variable speeds 6, 12, 16, 18, 20, 40, and 54fps) mode,

NOTE: The red LED is *extinguished* when camera is running at set 24, 25, 30fps (29.97fps if camera is fitted for it) crystal-sync speeds.

(b) *slowly flashes* when battery power is below 10.5 volts, or (c) *quickly flashes* when camera is not running at fps (sync or variable) set on the speed-control knob, and/or when coming up to speed that *is* set.

NOTE: If the meter counter setting was in error (see Sec. 10.1n, "Liquid Crystal Display") and film still remains in the magazine, stop and start the camera. The red diode will be reactivated to its proper operational mode.

There are three *green* LEDs: 1) The *far-left green diode* indicates the most extreme underexposure of two stops; 2) the *far-right green diode* indicates the most extreme overexposure of two stops; and 3) the *center green diode* in the middle of the display indicates proper exposure (only if the index on the ASA setting dial matches the film in the magazine).

The *yellow (inboard) LED is illuminated when* the camera is running, regardless of the speed (sync or nonsync) set on the camera. Each *yellow diode* (five to the left of the center green diode, and five to the right of the center green diode) represents one third of a stop. Therefore, with the proper index on the ASA setting dial matching the ASA of the film in the magazine, proper exposure will be indicated by the center green diode in the middle of the display turning darker than normal. If a yellow diode darkens to the left or right of the center green diode, then—by counting the diodes—the Operator can ascertain (in one-third stops) how far the film is either over- or underexposed and can compensate either by adjusting the lens aperture or by adding/subtracting light

NOTE: Because two photocells measure the quantity of light reaching the film, the diodes provide the aforementioned exposure data whenever the camera runs, and regardless of the set fps. However,

WARNING: The camera does *not* automatically adjust the iris! The iris must be set by hand.

CAUTION: In extreme low-light conditions, the glow from the diodes can interfere with viewing. Diodes can be extinguished if desired by turning the toggle On/Off photometer switch off.

The *entire display* blinks (a) across all diodes when only 5m (15 ft) of film remains in the magazine, and (b) alternately (left half, then right half of diodes) when all film is expended.

10.1j Sunshade/Matte Box
A standard matte-box (22) is used with fixed focal-length lenses and/or a zoom, providing that the front lens does *not* exceed 86mm (3 7/16") in diameter. It fits onto and slides in and out on the handgrip support rod at the right front of camera and is lockable on the handgrip support rod.

Three mattes (for 32mm, 75mm, and 150mm lenses) slide into grooves in the front of the sunshade.

To mount: Loosen the lock nut (not visible) at the lower right front of the camera. Slide the handgrip rod into the camera body, then secure the lock nut.

NOTE: When using a handgrip and matte box together, the matte box *always* mounts *forward* of the handgrip.

NOTE: A four-stage swing-away matte box is also available for studio work.

10.1k Filters

Two filter stages on the standard matte box accept 75mm × 75mm (3″ × 3″) filters. Rear stage is rotatable. There are *no* internal filter slots. Four filter stages on a studio matte-box accept one 138mm circular, two 101.5mm × 142.24mm (4 × 5.6″) fixed, and one 152.4mm × 152.4mm (6 × 6″) rotating filters.

10.1l Door

None.

10.1m Magazine

120m (400 ft). Coaxial.

NOTE: There are no outer gears on the AATON magazine. Each magazine is fitted with a magnetic drive wheel that interfaces a *camera magnetic drive wheel* (42). In addition to transporting the film through the camera and magazine, the magnets drive electronic sensors and provide data about the LCD footage counter and memory. (See also Section 10.2d, Magazine, Magnetic Drive System.)

To mount: 1) Ascertain that film loop is properly set; 2) Hold camera base at front with left hand; 3) Hold magazine at back with right hand; 4) Rest magazine front in camera guide rail, then slide forward until it seats with an audible click; 5) Set LCD footage counter to 122m (see Sec. 10.1n).

To remove: 1) Grasp the back of the magazine firmly; 2) Push the *magazine release lever* (7) forward and slide the magazine away from the camera.

10.1n Liquid Crystal Display (LCD) (12)

Located at left front of camera below the eyepiece. When one or more of three adjacent vertical *counter buttons* (11) are selected, the LCD displays data as described in the following lists:

With Magazine Mounted and Camera not Running,

Depressing button(s)	*Results in*
1	Shows amount of film (in meters or feet) in magazine and its drive system index (see Sec. 10.2d, "Magnetic Drive System").
	NOTE: While the manufacturer claims that feet measurements are systematically installed on every U.K. and U.S. camera, the metric system is used on cameras for the rest of the world. Camerapersons have encountered both—and still make films.
1 + 3	Sets counter to 122m (400′) or shows amount of film (in meters) still available in magazine.

| 1 + 2 | Numbers decline from 122 to 0 in increments of 1 meter when magazine is mounted with a short end. |

NOTE: When countdown reaches the amount of film (in meters) in the short end, release button 2. If numbers are inadvertently set at less than the amount of short end, press 1 + 3 again, to display 122m; then depress 1 + 2 to reset counter.

With Magazine Removed and Camera Not Running,

Depressing button	*Results in*
1	Shows minutes and seconds if time code (which reads in minutes and seconds) is being used. Requires camera to be initialized (see Sec. 10.3c Time Code, Initializing camera). Noninitialized camera will display last input fed into LCD.
3	Voltage status of battery (if below 10.8 volts, replace).
Camera On/Off Test switch to *test* mode	Displays ASA setting for photometer and time-code exposure (see Sec. 10.1i, "Photometer")

With Magazine Removed and Camera Running,

Depressing button	*Results in*
2	Rate of motor speed (tachometer) in frames per second

10.1o Buckle-trip
None.

NOTE: Camera is fitted with a 5-ampere Bussman fuse that will burn out if electronics are overloaded (see Sec. 10.1c, Power line, 5-Ampere Bussman Fuse).

10.1p Tachometer
On LCD display (see Section 10.1n), with Magazine Removed and Camera Running.

10.1q Shutter
Nonadjustable. 180°.

NOTE: Mirror shutters of 180° are used in nations that film with 60-Hz HMI lighting at 24fps and 50-Hz HMI lighting at 25fps. Mirror shutters of 172.8° are used in nations that film with 50-Hz HMI lighting at 24fps.*

10.1r Lubrication
None. Manufacturer recommends that camera be checked annually.

10.1s Cleaning
Optics: Clean with bulb syringe or camel's-hair brush.
   Manufacturer recommends the following maintenance each time the film is changed: 1) Use an orangewood stick to remove emulsion buildup around aperture and in film race. 2) Clean single pulldown claw with soft brush. 3) Clean surface of mirror shutter with soft lens tissue or soft cotton tip.

---

*See *Professional Lighting Handbook* by Carlson and Carlson, Focal Press, for more details about filming with HMI lighting.

WARNING: Do *not* use lens cleaning fluid or alcohol on mirror!

4) Wipe groundglass with soft lens tissue.

10.1t Weight
With 120m (400 ft) load: 6 kg (13.2 lb).

10.1u Troubleshooting

Trouble	Probable Cause
Camera will not start	Dead battery; buss camera fuse (5 amps) blown; battery not seated on camera properly
Camera stops while filming	Film jam
Trigger on handgrip does not start camera or is intermittant.	LEMO plug not seated properly; dead battery; fuse blown, cable broken
Viewing system closed	Shutter closed; cap on lens
Soft focus on lens	Adapter not seated in port
Perforation tear; accordion pleat in film	Dirty side-pressure rail

10.2 AATON XTR (and LTR) 16mm MAGAZINE (FIGS. 10–4 and 10–5)

10.2a Type
Coaxial.

10.2b Capacity
120m (400 ft).

10.2c Lids
Two. Located at each side of magazine, which is divided longitudinally. Both lids are hinged at top. *Lid lock* (7) for each side located at bottom of magazine.

To open, turn lid-lock lever down and counterclockwise; raise lid *up.*

10.2d Magnetic Drive System
Magazine contains *no* outward drive gears. Instead, a circular magnetic wheel on the camera body interfaces with a similar *magnetic drive wheel* (11) on the feed side of magazine.

10.2e Magazine Sensors and I.D.
Not visible to the eye, sensors at top of each magazine identify an arbitrary recognition number, designated by the manufacturer as "A," "B," or "C," thereby making it possible to determine on the LCD (see Sec. 10.1n) which magazine is on the camera.

Magazine in use (A, B, or C) is also visually identified by placement of magnetic posts (9 *x* and *y*) inserted into one or both of two tapped holes located above the magnetic wheel on the feed side.

For identification purposes, this text labels the forward tapped hole "F" and labels the tapped rear hole "R." If "O" (open) represents the absence of a post and "P" (plugged) the presence of a post, then the following identification symbols permit a recognition of the magazine in use on the camera:

Posts in X and Y Holes	Magazine type I.D.
FO + RP	A
FP + RO	B
FP + RP	C

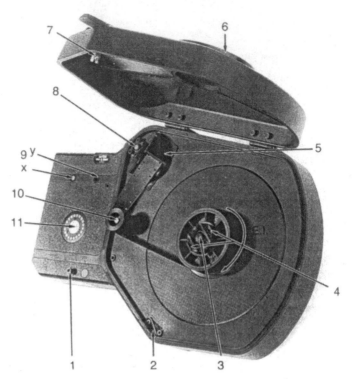

Figure 10–4. AATON XTR 16mm magazine (feed side). Courtesy of AATON Camera Company.

1. Magazine catch post
2. Internal lid-lock catch
3. Feed-side spindle
4. Feed-side core locks
5. Feed film passage
6. Magazine mechanical counter
7. Lid lock
8. Spare identification post
9. X/Y identification posts (B magazine shown)
10. Idler roller
11. Magazine magnetic drive wheel

NOTE: If using other than a "C" magazine, simply place unused post in hole at top forward point in feed compartment between the four Allen-head screws holding the guide roller.

10.2f Feed

Left half. (Magazine pressure plate should be at loader's left, the magnetic wheel facing up.) Film wound emulsion in (EI) pulls off *feed-side spindle* (3) clockwise. Film wound emulsion out (EO) pulls off spindle counterclockwise.

NOTE: Film wound EI should be loaded as pictured.

10.2g Take-up

Right half. (Magazine pressure plate should be at loader's right, the magnetic wheel facing *down*.) Film winds onto spindle counterclockwise, always EI.

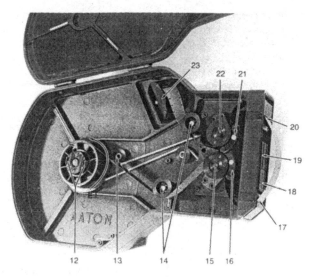

Figure 10–5. AATON XTR 16mm magazine (take-up side). Courtesy of AATON Camera Company.

12. Take-up spindle core locks
13. Belt tension roller
14. (a) Upper and 14(b) lower film rollers
15. Lower sprocket
16. Lower sprocket guide button
17. Lower film slot

18. Pulldown claw pressure plate
19. Image pressure plate
20. Upper film slot
21. Upper sprocket guide button
22. Upper sprocket
23. Take-up film passage

10.2h Loading

Feed Side: 1) Turn mechanical metric/footage counter (6) on feed lid counterclockwise. 2) Push lid-lock lever down and counterclockwise; raise hinged lid. 3) Depress core locks into feed-core spindle with thumb and forefinger. 4) In darkness, remove film from can and bag. Pull film off roll clockwise. 5) Place film roll on core spindle (3), and depress center of spindle to secure roll to spindle. 6) Place film to *left* of the *idler roller* (10). Insert film end into *film passage* (5) and push approximately 10cm (4") into the take-up side.

CAUTION: When loading single-perforated (B-wind) film, perforations must be away from lid on feed side, toward lid on take-up side.

Close hinged lid, rotate lid-lock lever clockwise to secure lid. Check lock by attempting to lift lid with fingernails. In light, reset the mechanical metric/footage counter on lid by turning it clockwise.

Take-up Side. Flip magazine over, push lid-lock lever down and counterclockwise; raise hinged lid.

NOTE: Take-up loading may be done in light.

10) Depress the white spring-loaded buttons on the *lower* and *upper sprocket guides* (16 and 21, respectively), and move the guides away from the *sprockets* (15 and 22, respectively). 11) Pull film end through *film passage*

(23), looping it below the *upper film roller* (14a), between the upper sprocket and upper sprocket guide, and through the *upper film slot* (20) until approximately 45cm (18″) exits the take-up side above the *image pressure plate* (19). 12) Engage film perforations on upper sprocket teeth and press the upper guide roller toward the upper sprocket until an audible click indicates proper closure. Push excess film back into feed side to upper film roller.

WARNING: Magazine is fitted with antibacklash sprockets. Do *not* rotate clockwise to take out excess raw stock in film path. To do so will damage the magazine—a factory repair job.

13) Place forefinger against *image pressure plate,* (19) and slide forefinger toward top of magazine. 14) Loop excess film over forefinger, and reinsert the film end into the *lower film slot* (17) below the *pulldown-claw pressure plate* (18).

NOTE: Manufacturer recommends a 15-frame loop outside the magazine. Forming the loop as outlined previously usually results in 15 frames (see "Setting the Loops," below).

15) Insert film between the lower sprocket and its guide rail, and under the *lower film roller* (14b). Engage film perforations on lower sprocket teeth and press the lower guide roller toward the *lower sprocket* (15) until an audible click indicates proper closure. *Manually* wind any excess film that may be inside magazine counterclockwise onto take-up core.

WARNING: Magazine is fitted with antibacklash sprockets. Do *not* rotate clockwise to take out excess raw stock in film path. To do so will damage the magazine—a factory repair job.

18) Place film roll on take-up spindle, allowing no slack, and depress center to spread core locks and secure roll to spindle. 19) Close hinged lid, rotate lid-lock lever clockwise to secure lid. Check lock by attempting to lift lid with fingernails.

To Set Loops Manufacturer recommends that before Loader places magazine on camera, Loader should pull film outside the magazine, away from the pressure plate, then press forefinger in center of arc to form two equal halves, which—when pushed into the camera body—will form the upper and lower internal loops.

Daylight Spools. XTR magazines do *not* accept daylight spools.

10.2i Unloading
In darkness, push take-up lid-lock lever down and counterclockwise; raise hinged lid. Depress core locks into take-up core spindle with thumb and forefinger. Place index finger on edge of film roll, thumb on core. Turn magazine over, remove film roll, and place exposed roll in black bag and can.

10.2j Metric/Footage Counter
On feed side of magazine; inscribed in meters and feet.
The metric counter indicates the first 5 meters of film exposed, then reads in increments of 10 meters thereafter (5, 10, 20, 30, etc.).
The footage counter indicates the first 15 feet of film exposed, then reads in increments of 50 feet thereafter (15, 50, 100, 150, etc.).

10.3 XTR OPTIONS AND ACCESSORIES
10.3a Video Relay

Requirements: (a) Insertion of camera's built-in beam splitter into view-finder system (b) placing an AATON video-relay head onto camera (c) attachment of special cable from video head, (d) use of a control unit (see Sec. 10.3b).

To Insert a Beam Splitter into Viewfinder System: 1) Unscrew the beam-splitter access cap at right top of camera, then remove it: 2) Insert a 1mm Allen wrench into screwhead located inside access port, and turn it counterclockwise 30 turns or until it locks. Rotate the screw 3 turns clockwise. 3) Replace access cap.

To Remove the Beam Splitter from Viewfinder System: 1) Unscrew beam-splitter access cap at right top of camera, then remove it. 2) Insert a 1mm Allen wrench into screwhead inside the access port, and turn it clockwise 30 turns or until resistance is felt, which indicates that pellicle is out of light path. 3) Replace access cap.

To Place Video Relay onto Camera: 1) Loosen video-cap locking screw above video cap; pull cap toward Operator to reveal video-relay lens.

CAUTION: Don't lose the cap! It *must* be placed back on the camera!

2) *Carefully* insert the video-relay (VR) camera with its protruding nine-pin Amphenol plug into the relay lens and matching Amphenol receptacle below the lens. 3) Tighten video-cap locking screw to secure unit in place.

To Attach Relay Cable. Cable (fitted with Socapex plugs) attaches to bottom plug on VR camera and to matching receptacle located on lower rear panel of control unit.

10.3b Control Unit

Unit must be powered by a 12-volt 4-AH battery, which plugs into the four-pin Cannon receptacle at the unit's base.

WARNING/CAUTION/NOTE: Do *not*—repeat—do *not* plug a battery into the camera body when using the control unit. To do so will destroy the cable and inflict damage on the electronics of the video relay.

Front of the Control Unit. Unit is fitted with three plugs. Starting from the top: Plug 1) Four-pin Jaeger plug connects, through a cable, to a TV control monitor.

NOTE: The TV control monitor is utilized to set black level, white level, lens diaphragm, sync information, brightness and contrast on the video camera.

Plug 2) Video out BNC plug connects, through a cable, to a larger, exterior, TV viewing monitor.

Plug 3) Ten-pin Honda plug connects, through a cable, to a videotape recorder.

Rear of Control Unit. Unit is fitted with an array of toggle switches and receptacles that serve two separate functions: 1) The left vertical row, flush to the control unit's casing, is the *video time-code inserter;* 2) the two rows on the raised panel are the *scanning head and control-unit function selectors.*

Video Time-Code Inserter Row. Starting at the top,

Circular Knob Rotates so that time reading (i.e., production number, year, month, day, hour, minute, second, and frame numbers) can be placed anywhere in the top two thirds of the video screen.

Stop Toggle   Deletes numbers from the video screen.

Time Toggle   Starts time code at zero.

LEMO Receptacle   Used when synchronizing with a coder (e.g., Nagra IV TC, Walkman Recorder, AATON Origin C, or AATON XTR).

SMPTE   BNC plug with a permanent SMPTE output signal.

Scanning-Head and Control-Unit Function Selectors.

NOTE: In order to change most control-unit power toggle switches to up, center, or down, their handles must be grasped between thumb and forefinger and *pulled* away from their sockets before moving.

Starting at the top left,

Sync-Mode Toggle Switch: Pushed *left* (slave), the control unit can receive an external sync signal; *centered,* off (no signal); *Pushed right* (master), the control unit delivers its own sync signal.

On/Off Toggle Switch: *On,* starts videotape recorder; *off,* puts recorder into pause position.

Battery/VTR Toggle Switch: *Pushed left* provides power to the camera *only* from the camera battery; *Pushed right* provides power to the camera, and video comes from the videotape recorder.

Rotatable Toggle Switch: Rotates the image on the control unit video by 90°.

Power Toggle: Up,   power is fed to the camera from the video tape recorder; *centered,* power is off; *down,* power is from the battery attached to the control unit.

Scan Inverters: Two side-by-side toggle switches are used to electronically reverse the highs and lows of the scanned image on the video monitor.

Fuse Access Knob: Covers a 5-ampere fuse.

3.5mm Headphone Outlet: Can be used by the Camera Operator.

Camera Head (Socapex 19-Pin Camera Cable Connector):   Requires SPX 19 cable with plugs that match same type of connector on the Video Relay.

Control-Unit Panel.   The side of the control unit is fitted with slotted fine-tuning adjustment screws located beneath plastic covers; screws are used by technicians in adjustments of the unit's electronics. A video monitor is required in order to use them.

NOTE: Side is marked with callouts to denote outlets and switches at front and rear of control unit and should not be confused with callouts of the adjustment screws.

Facing the control-unit panel, the controls are as follows, starting at the top, and reading left to right:

White Level: Adjusts full peak above or below the sync level.

Neg/Post: Changes the video image positive or negative.

Focus Adjustment: Focuses the video camera from center to edges.

Black: Adjusts for zero illumination.

Details: Fine adjustments of image.

Horizontal Setting: Moves monitor image left or right

Horizontal Amplitude: Equalizes side edges of video image.

Vertical Amplitude: Equalizes top and bottom of video image.

Vertical Centering: Fine adjustments to sides, top, and bottom amplitude corrections.

VTR: Utilized to match the technical television standard being used:

- 525 lines/60 Hz, for 24fps in NTSC countries
- 625 lines/50 Hz, for 25fps in PAL/SECAM countries
- 625 lines/48 Hz, for 24fps in PAL/SECAM countries

10.3c Origin CX Masterclock

Used to initialize camera and/or audio recorder time code as to local time and date by direct entry. The battery-operated Masterclock provides a time code on the film edge and provides a signal to the audiotape (see also Sec. 4.4, "Time Code and Time Code Slates").

To Initialize Camera: 1) Insert LEMO plug on Masterclock into SMPTE receptacle at rear of camera base. 2) Turn On/Off switch on Masterclock to *On.*

NOTE: Although the camera must *not* be running, it is essential that an AATON battery be connected to camera when initializing it.

WARNING: The ASA setting (see Sec. 10.1h, "ASA Setting Dial") on the camera must be set to match the film in use so that edge numbers on film will be crisp and readable.

3) When the question "Production Number?" appears on the Masterclock display, use the 10 keys (numbered 1 through 0) to enter the information, then depress the shift key marked " = ." Other questions (i.e., "Year?", "Month?" "Date?" "Hour" "Minutes" "Seconds" and frame rate, i.e., "Frames") will appear on display. Use the numbered keys to enter data and the shift key " = " to change to another category.

NOTE: If an error occurs that exceeds its programmed data (e.g., month, 1–12; date, 1–31; hour, 1–24; minutes or seconds, 0–60), the display will show a continuously flashing "ERR." Simply reinsert the correct data.

WARNING: Errors within the programmed data (e.g., entering numeral 8, when 9 was intended) will *not* cause the display to flash "ERR."

4) Start clock by depressing the "*" key. A flashing bar in the display indicates that the clock is keeping time and will continue to do so for 5 minutes. Then it turns off.

NOTE: To display the data before the clock turns off, depress the shift key " = ."

To Verify Whether Camera or Recorder Has Time Code Already Running: Insert LEMO plug of Masterclock into matching LEMO on camera or recorder. Depress the "*" key, and read the display. If no data appears, depress the shift key " = ."

NOTE: The display will only read hours, minutes, and seconds. To read other data, continue to depress the shift key marked " = ."

If Camera or Recorder Is *Not* Time-Coded, display will not read. By depressing the "*" key, the Masterclock will transfer its data to the camera or recorder. The display will read "GOOD."

WARNING: If the camera or recorder is not connected to a battery, or the LEMO plug is not properly connected, the display will read "VOID."

If Camera or Recorder Is Already Time-Coded, but Masterclock Is Not. By depressing the key "*," data from camera or recorder will transfer to the

Masterclock. Display will show a flashing bar for 5 minutes, to indicate it is counting. This is ample time to transfer data from camera to recorder (or vice-versa) or to another camera/recorder so that all are in sync for later editing purposes.

If Masterclock *and* Camera and/or Recorder Each Contain Time-Code Data. Depress key "*." Masterclock will compare its data with those of the camera or recorder. Then, 1) If time codes are the same (i.e, less than one-half a frame difference), display will read "GOOD." 2) If time codes differ within 1/2 to 1-1/2 frames, display will read "FAIR." This indicates that the equipment will need to be reinitialized soon (see *"To Initialize Camera,"* above). Display will thereafter flash, "RELOAD."

NOTE: When "RELOAD" appears on the display, depress the key "*" for at least 5 seconds to reload the camera and or recorder. Release, repeat depressing key "*" until the display reads, "GOOD."

3) If time code differs more than 1-1/2 frames, display reads "BAD." This indicates that the equipment needs to be reinitialized immediately (see *"To Initialize Camera,"* above). Display will thereafter flash, "RE-LOAD."

NOTE: When "RELOAD" appears on the display, depress the key "*" for at least 5 seconds to reinitialize the camera and or recorder. Release. Repeat depressing key "*" until the display reads, "GOOD."

4) If a battery is not on the camera or recorder, display reads, "VOID." 5) If the Masterclock's internal 9-volt NiCad battery needs charging, display reads, "BATT."

NOTE: Connecting the Masterclock to a 12-volt battery will recharge it immediately. There is also a small separate battery charger just for that purpose, but it requires 14 hours to recharge the unit.

chapter 11

Arriflex Cameras, Magazines, Blimps, and Accessories

11.1 ARRIFLEX 535 35mm CAMERA (Fig. 11.1)

NOTE: All directions are from operator's point of view.

11.1a Base

Fitted with two 3/8″ × 16- thread tapped holes and one pilot hole to accommodate a tripod lockdown screw, riser, or bridge plate.

11.1b Motor

Built-in 24V, crystal controlled, disk-type, DC. *A manual frame rate selector switch* is located on the right side of the camera body. It can be set for quartz-controlled speeds of 24, 25, 29.97 and 30 fps.

To Set Desired Speed. Insert a coin or screwdriver in slot of selector switch and rotate.

NOTE: Each selected frame rate falls into a detent and can be read through a *plexiglass window* to the right of the switch.

NOTE: The frame rate can also be selected by using either a Camera Control Unit (CCU) (see Sec. 11.3a), or a Variable Speed Unit (VSU) (see Sec. 11.3e). Both are separate electronic accessories.

To Reverse Camera. Requires attachment of the Camera Control Unit (CCU) [see Sec. 11.3a].

11.1c Powerline

Input to Camera. *Two-pin Fischer plug* provides 24 volts of power to camera body.

NOTE: With crescent of plug at left, top pin is +24v; bottom pin is ground.

Outlets. Three nine-pin Fischer plugs. Lowest nine-pin is *CCU plug* (see Section 11.3a). Center nine-pin is ESU/MCL/SCU plug (see Sec. 11.3g, 11.3b, and 11.3f, respectively). Top 8-pin is VSU/RU plug (see Sec. 11.3e and 11.3d, respectively).

Power Sources. (not shown): Batteries are: switchable 12v/24V (code NC 24/7R) for use with 304.8m (1,000-ft) magazines; and an on-board (code NC 24/2) for use with 122m (400-ft) magazines. A 24v AC power supply (code AC NG 24 R) is also available.

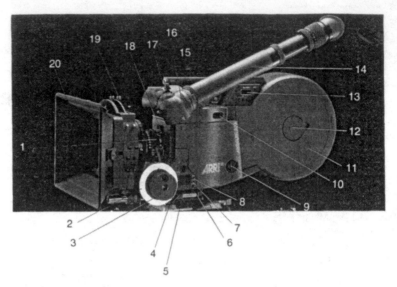

Figure 11–1a Arriflex 535 camera (left side). Courtesy of Arnold & Richter K.G.

1. Lens
2. Marking disc
3. Follow Focus Knob
4. On/Off (RUN) button
5. LCD
6. Phase button
7. Reset button
8. Mode button
9. Door latch
10. Arriglow switch

11. Magazine
12. Magazine lid lock
13. Magazine electronic ftge indicator
14. Eyepiece extension
15. Carry handle
16. Aspect ratio lock release
17. Viewfinder
18. Lens lock
19. Filter holders
20. Matte-box

Main Power Switch (ON/OFF). *A recessed toggle* is located on lower right bottom of electronic housing cover.

NOTE: The main power switch does not start the camera but only supplies the camera electronics and motor with standby power.

Power ON Position (Forward). Camera is ready to operate (standby). *LCD window* shows "0000."

NOTE: When the Power ON switch is first pushed forward, the *running light* illuminates (red) and conducts a three-second circuitry test. The red running light extinguishes if no error condition is detected. If an error condition *is* detected or "0000" is *not* displayed, the LCD will show diagnostic information (see Sec. 11.1m, Liquid Crystal Displays, and 11.1t, Troubleshooting).

NOTE: If a gel filter is installed in the behind-the-lens gel holder (see Sec. 11.1i) then the LCD will also display the word FIL (filter).

Power OFF position. Cuts power to the camera electronics and motor completely.

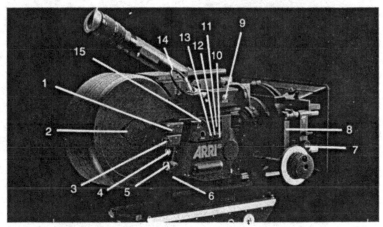

Figure 11–1b Arriflex 535 camera (right rear). Courtesy of Arnold & Richter K.G.

1. VSU/RU Connector (VSU in place)
2. Magazine lid lock
3. SCU/MCL/ESC connector (SCU in place)
4. CCU-1 connector
5. Power cable connector
6. Camera main power switch
7. Lower iris rod bracket knob
8. L-bracket
9. CCD-1
10. LCD
11. Program button
12. Reset button
13. Mode button
14. Magazine mechanical indicator
15. On/Off (RUN) button

Camera Stop/Start. Two *Run buttons* are located on each side the camera body (above the LCD on the left side, behind the LCD on camera right side).

To start camera. Press either button once.

NOTE: During run-up to the preselected frame rate the running light will be momentarily red, then turn green once selected speed is reached.

CAUTION: Out-of-sync running, as well as possible errors (e.g., film jam, low battery (BAT), and film end (END) will turn the light red. During out-of-sync running the LCD will show ASY, an indication also visible to the operator in the viewfinder.

To stop camera. Press either RUN button again.

NOTE: When the camera is stopped, the running light will momentarily turn red, then extinguish.

Fuses. Two. Located on right camera bottom under the *slotted fuse cover* (not visible).

To replace. With coin or screwdriver, remove cover to remove pico fuses.

Figure 11–1c Arriflex 535 camera (handheld mode). Courtesy of Arnold & Richter K.G.

1. On/Off switch
2. Left handle
3. Wing nut

4. Dovetailed top plate
5. Shoulder rest

NOTE: Forward pico is motor fuse rated at 15 amps. Pico closest to Operator is electronics fuse rated at 2.5 amps.

Remove the defective fuse with a pair of tweezers or special tool Arriflex calls a *Hirschmann clip*.

NOTE: Spare pico fuses are stored under the clear plastic retainer in the base of the fuse cover. Unscrew plastic retainer to gain access to fuses.

WARNING: Before setting up camera or taking it on location always ascertain that spare fuses are under the retainer!

Replace defective fuse and cover.

11.1d Turret
None. Single lens mount.

11.1e Lenses
Standard on the 535 are PL (positive lock) 35 mm zoom and prime lenses with a mount diameter of 54mm and flange focal distance of 51.98 ± 0.01 mm.

WARNING: Lenses with 41mm (bayonet) diameter standard mounts or with bayonet to PL adapters can*not* be used.

NOTE: Heavy zoom, telephoto, or anamorphic lenses require a special support (see Sec. 11.3h) to prevent an uneven load on the lens mount.

NOTE: Before mounting a lens, ascertain that the lens mount is in the normal or Super 35mm format position (see Sec. 11.1g).

To fit lens to Camera. Rotate the *lens locking ring* clockwise to its end position to reveal lens locator pin (not shown). Hold lens.

NOTE: Most lens barrels are referenced in meters on one side and feet on the other side. Preferred reference should be in UP position.

Align proper guide-groove (there are four, located every 90 degrees around the perimeter of the lens mount) to the lens locator pin and guide lens straight into the lens port. Rotate lens locking ring counterclockwise to secure.

To Remove Lens. Grasp lens firmly; rotate lens locking ring clockwise; pull lens slowly away from camera.

11.1f Viewfinder (Fig. 11–2)
Reflex; orientable; rotates 360°. Image magnified 6.5 ×. Views more than full aperture.

NOTE: There are two interchangeable viewfinders: *standard* (also referred to as a "swingover"), with an accessory *extension,* used when in studio mode, and the *hand-held,* used when in hand-held mode.

Standard (Swingover) Viewfinder. Can be pivoted in a 270° arc from left to right over the top of the camera body. Viewfinder locks at 0°, 90° (but only if the carry handle is fitted with a stop bracket), and 180°.

To Swing Over Standard Viewfinder 180°. Pull the *slide lock* and rotate the viewfinder arm until it locks into 180° detent.

To Adjust the Eyepiece Eccentric for Different Viewing Positions (or Rotate 360°). Press *eyepiece safety lock button* and turn eyepiece to desired position. Release button to lock in position.

To Remove Eyepiece. Hold the eyepiece firmly and turn the *eyepiece lock ring* counterclockwise to the OPEN position. Press the eyepiece lock button, and turn eyepiece lock ring further. Pull eyepiece away.

To Attach Eyepiece. Align eyepiece so that keys and keyways engage. Turn the lock ring clockwise until safety lock clicks.

To View through Lens. Place eye to viewfinder eyecup.

To Close Eyecup. Rotate *eyecup closure latch* forward of eyecup counterclockwise.

NOTE: The eyecup closed position is only recommended when filming locked-down shots in bright sunlight or in an intense illumination situation where light might strike the eyepiece and expose film through the viewfinder. See also: *To De-anamorphosize and/or Close Eyepiece Diaphragm* (page 138).

Optional Heated Eyecup (Not Shown). Prevents eyepiece from misting in varying temperatures and humidity. The heated eyecup is available in two versions: HE-3A (oval) and HE-3F (concentric). It is attached in place of the standard eyecup and connected to the camera electrical system via a removable cable.

To Activate Heated Eyecup. Plug the cable into the camera's *eyecup heater plug,* located below *bubble level.* Two heat levels (HI/LO) can be

Figure 11-2 Arriflex 535 viewfinder detail. Courtesy of Arnold & Richter K.G.

1. Eyecup
2. Eyecup closure latch
3. Focus knob
4. Eyepiece lock button
5. Eyepiece lock ring
6. Aspect ratio lock button (not visible)
7. Aspect ratio button
8. Magnification lock button

9. Magnification ring
10. Slide lock
11. Viewfinder arm
12. Viewfinder friction knob
13. Bullseye level
14. Beamsplitter knob
15. Contrast filter knob
16. Video tap on/off toggle

selected via a toggle switch on the eyecup. A green *Heat On LED* next to the connector illuminates when the eyecup begins heating and extinguishes when proper temperature is reached.

CAUTION: If camera and electrical accessories are powered by batteries, eyecup heating should be shut off between set-ups in order to save power.

Standard Viewfinder Extension (Not Shown). Recommended when using 304.8m (1000 ft) magazines.

NOTE: Due to optical design, viewfinder extension inverts the image when installed.

To Make Certain Image Is Upright when Extension Is Installed. Loosen *viewfinder friction knob,* depress *prism release button,* and turn viewfinder approximately 30° clockwise. Release prism button and continue to rotate the viewfinder clockwise to its initial viewing position. Prism button locks automatically. The image now appears in viewfinder upside down.

To Attach Extension. Remove eyepiece by pressing the eyepiece lock button, turning the eyepiece lock ring counterclockwise to the OPEN position, and pulling the eyepiece away. Align keys and keyways of viewfinder eccentric and extension and insert. Turn release ring to the CLOSED position to lock.

CAUTION: Be sure the swingout extension support arm faces the camera.

Attach the eyepiece to the viewfinder extension as above.

Lengthening Viewfinder Extension. If required, the viewfinder extension can be lengthened up to approximately 100mm. Rotate locking ring located at the rear of extender counterclockwise and extend tube to the desired length. Rotate locking ring clockwise to secure.

Leveling Rod for Viewfinder Extension (Not Shown). Holds eyepiece of viewfinder extension level with the Operator's eye. Fastens to the extension with a slide bracket. Bottom part of rod attaches to either an Arrilex geared head (see Chapter 9, Sec. 9.2) or a tripod with a special mount. Rod adjusts to any length by unlocking two knurled tension screws located along the rod and sliding the telescoping segments up or down.

Hand-Held Viewfinder. Shorter than standard viewfinder so as to bring Operator's eye forward and place camera's center of gravity on user's shoulder. Its eyepiece is permanently attached and can*not* be detached. Therefore, entire viewfinder system must be changed when changing from studio mode to hand-held mode and vice-versa.

NOTE: The offset viewfinder is designed for operation from camera left side only, and can only be attached in this position (does not have swing-over capabilities).

To Change Either Viewfinder. *To remove,* hold viewfinder firmly and turn *bayonet ring* toward Operator's right (direction of arrow on ring). Move slide lock toward eyepiece (Operator's left). Pull viewfinder away from camera.

To Attach Either Viewfinder. Hold viewfinder firmly and align to camera. Move slide lock toward Operator's left. Insert viewfinder into camera. Release slide lock. Turn bayonet ring toward Operator's left (opposite direction of arrow on ring) and finger tighten.

To Clear Reflex Mirror so as to View Camera Aperture for a "Haircheck." Lightly depress *phase button* located back of left front LCD.

NOTE: Acting as an inching knob to move the mirror aside is only one function of the phase button (see Sec. 11.3b for others).

To Return Mirror for Viewing through Eyepiece. Lightly depress phase button again.

To Focus Eyepiece. Rotate *focus knob* on barrel of eyepiece.

To Deanamorphosize Eyepiece and/or Close Eyepiece Diaphragm. Press the *aspect ratio locking button* and turn the *aspect ratio rotary knob* to the corresponding symbol noted below. Lock in position by releasing the button.

Symbol: □   Standard format
Symbol: ▭   Anamorphic position
Symbol: ⊠   Eyepiece closed

NOTE: The eyepeice closed position is only recommended when filming in bright sunlight or when using any intense scene illumination, as it prevents stray light from exposing film through the viewfinder.

To Magnify Viewfinder Image (from 6.5X to 13X). Depress *magnification lock button.* Rotate *magnification ring* so that the witness mark points to the large dot [13 × magnification] on the ring.

To Demagnify Viewfinder Image. Depress magnification lock button. Rotate magnification ring so that the witness mark points to the small dot [6.5 ×] for normal viewing.

Visible Framelines (Illuminated "Arriglow"). As many as three stored aspect ratio format outlines can be made visible in the viewfinder by flipping the *frameline toggle switch.* Flipped DOWN, format ratio labels appear above the illuminated framelines; flipped UP, viewfinder shows framelines with *no* format labels visible. CENTERED, the toggle switch turns the framelines off.

NOTE: Format framelines must be preselected by using the Camera Control Unit (CCU) (see Sec. 11.3a).

To Adjust Frameline Brightness. Turn *Arriglow intensity knob* located at top left of camera body in the (+) or (-) direction.

NOTE: The *Arriglow green LED* located to the right of the intensity knob illuminates when the Arriglow function is switched on.

NOTE: Operational warnings (e.g., ASY, BAT, END, etc.) (see Sec. 11.1m, Liquid Crystal Display [LCD]) when seen in the viewfinder are shown outside the area marked by framelines.

Groundglass. Located inside camera at top of lens mount above the mirror shutter. Accessible only through the lens port.

NOTE: The groundglass can be replaced with either a fiber optic focusing screen or a combination groundglass/matte holder for composite photography.

To Remove Groundglass. Remove lens, open camera door, rotate *movement inching knob* until *mirror shutter* clears aperture. Place Arri tool (manufacturer calls it a "Hirschmann clip") into catch on the groundglass frame, then carefully pull the groundglass out through the lens port.

To Insert Groundglass. Be sure dull side of groundglass is DOWN and clean. Use the Hirschmann clip on the groundglass frame and gently slide groundglass into its holder. Correctly placed, the groundglass snaps into the holder in a horizontal position.

11.1g Super 35mm Conversion

The 535 camera can be converted to Super 35mm, but it is an Arri Service Center job and requires an experienced technician to avoid critical changes in the flange focal distance.

11.1h Matte-Boxes (MB-14, MB-14W, MB-15, MB-16, LMB-3 and LMB-4)

The 535 accepts five basic matte-boxes: (see Sec. 11.12 Matte-Boxes and Filter Holders).

11.1i Filters.

Internal Filter Slot. Located within the film gate mechanism.

To Insert. Open camera door, swing the movement block back (see Sec. 11.1l, Threading) and remove the film gate (see Sec. 11.1r, Cleaning). Hold the filter holder at its edge and pull it straight out from the film gate. Carefully open the filter holder, insert the required gel filter, and trim off the exposed edge. Be sure the gel is visible through the small pinhole punched through the holder. Slide the filter holder back into the film gate and reinstall the film gate.

CAUTION: The camera LCD (see Sec. 11.1m) showing "FILTER" indicates a gel has been inserted, but not that the gel has been correctly positioned in the holder. It is essential that the correct positioning of the gel filter be verified by removing the lens and seeing that the filter covers the aperture.

Selectable Contrast Filter. Two built-in, with rated densities of ND.3 and ND.6, which can be inserted into the finder by a selector lever, located on the top of the camera body. For viewing without contrast filters, return the lever to its (0) position.

Filters that fit in matte-boxes vary in size, depending on the matte-box. (See Sec. 11.12, Matte-Boxes and Filter Holders.)

11.1j Door

Located on left side of camera body, hinged at front.

To Open. Pull out door lock tab and rotate counterclockwise. Swing door in a horizontal plane away from camera.

To Close. Swing door shut. Press in gently on right (camera rear) side of door. Rotate door lock clockwise to secure. Push door lock tab back in, flush with surface of door.

11.1k Magazines

304.8m (1000 ft) and 122m (400 ft).

To Mount. Prepare camera for threading (see Sec. 11.1l). Open camera door; draw a film loop from the magazine's supply side (just enough to slide four fingers between film base and magazine). Align dovetails of the magazine to dovetails in camera and, while guiding the film loop into the camera body, slide the magazine toward operator's right until the lock closes with a strong, audible click.

To Remove. If film short ends are still threaded through the camera, pivot the block backwards, open the keepers, and release the magazine (see Sec. 11.1l for details). Slide the magazine partway out of the camera housing while unthreading the film loop from the movement and sprockets. Once clear, slide the magazine away from the camera.

If the film is entirely in the magazine's take-up compartment, unlock and slide the magazine out of the camera housing.

WARNING: Upon removal of a magazine, if transporting the camera (in or out of its case) is necessary ALWAYS make certain the movement block is forward and in the locked position. Factory overhaul.

11.1l Threading (Fig. 11–3)

If throat cover or an empty magazine (neither shown) is on camera, press the *magazine release lever* toward operator and pull throat cover/magazine away. Rotate knurled *inching knob* until its witness mark aligns to "LOADING POSITION" indicator. Rotate the *movement locking lever* counterclockwise and pivot top of the movement block backwards. Turn the *film retainer lever* counterclockwise to OPEN and release the keepers from the upper and lower sprockets. Remove and clean the film gate (see Sec. 11.1r, Cleaning). Reinsert.

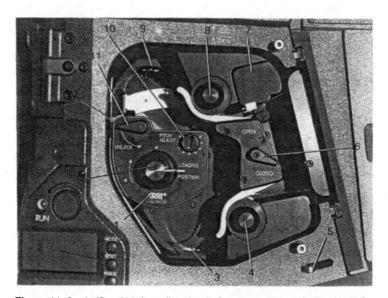

Figure 11–3 Arriflex 535 threading detail. Courtesy of Arnold & Richter K.G.

1. Movement block
2. Phase button
3. Lower white film path marking
4. Lower loop knob
5. Magazine release lever
6. Film retainer lever
7. TimeCode module

8. Upper loop knob
9. Upper white film path marking
10. Pitch adjustment knob
11. Movement block locking lever
12. Film gate
13. Inching knob

To Thread. Guide the film loop first between the *upper sprocket* and keeper and then between the *lower sprocket* and keeper. Insert film between the film gate and the movement block.

NOTE: Draw any extra needed film from the magazine supply side.

Turn the *film retainer lever* to CLOSED, making certain perforations engage the teeth on the sprockets. Rotate the *movement locking lever* clockwise and *gently* move the block to its forward position making certain the registration pins engage the film perforations. Rotate the knurled *inching knob* slightly back and forth to make sure the gate pulldown claws properly engage the film perforations. Align the inching knob's witness mark with the white dot located at the 12 o'clock position on the movement block. Depress and turn the *upper loop knob* to align the film loop with the upper loop line; depress and turn the *lower loop knob* to align the film with the lower loop line.

NOTE: If the film protrudes *slightly* beyond the upper and lower white film path markings, the threading is still OK.

Rotate the knurled inching knob manually in the direction of the arrow (clockwise) to ascertain that film is in gate and on sprockets correctly. Press Phasebutton to check film movement. Close door.

NOTE: The 12 o'clock dot on the movement block mark serves as a timing check (the film gate must be completely covered by the mirror shutter during the pulldown phase). When the witness mark on the knurled inching knob aligns with the white dot on the movement block, the leading edge of a properly timed mirror shutter is positioned at the Operator's 1–2 o'clock position.

Pitch Adjustment. Slotted *pitch adjustment knob* is located on movement block, upper right of inching knob. Built-in to minimize noise of movement.

NOTE: While manufacturer recommends that prior to filming a noise test be conducted with film of the same emulsion batch as that which will be used during production, correct setting of pitch may differ on each roll because of slight variations of rawstock perforation pitch and/or film shrinkage.

Optimum setting of control is determined by ear while threaded film stock is run through camera with door open and by adjusting the claw pivot point.

To Adjust Claw Pivot Point. Grasp pitch adjustment knob in thumb and forefinger and rotate from neutral (6 o'clock) either four points toward lens or four points toward Operator until the movement runs at its quietest.

NOTE: The adjustment range is limited by fixed mechanical stops in order to prevent film damage.

11.1m Liquid Crystal Displays (LCDs)

Two; located at lower left front of camera body and upper middle right of camera body.

Three vertical buttons alongside the left front LCD are marked from top to bottom: MODE, RESET, and PHASE.

Three horizontal buttons beneath the upper right LCD are marked from left to right: MODE, RESET, and PROGRAM.

The two Mode and Reset displays show identical information, and each contains two lines of information.

Modes. There are three basic Modes except when a Time Code (TC) Module (see below and Sec. 11.3b) is used. With a TC module attached, the camera is provided with two additional modes for a total of five modes. Modes are successively activated by pressing the "MODE" button next to each display. The activated mode is displayed for approximately 30 seconds, then the display automatically returns to the standard MODE 1.

Mode 1. When power is first applied, the camera is considered to be in Mode 1, Standby Status (no button pressed), and, if the magazine is properly mounted, film loop correctly set, and movement block locked in position, both LCDs will display the numerals "0000" on an upper line (or cumulative exposed footage previously shot, if the camera has been in use), and 00.00 on the lower line. If they do not, the camera is not correctly assembled and the display will so indicate (see Sec. 11.1t, Troubleshooting).

Mode 1 (Button Not Pressed). *Upper line displays:* Footage exposed during current take in feet or meters (resets automatically when camera is restarted). Standard unit is feet; this can be changed to meters using the optional Camera Control Unit (see Sec. 11.3a).

Lower line displays: Frame rate (fps).

NOTE: When the camera is started by pressing either RUN button, the display is continuously in MODE 1 (exposed footage/frame rate).

When the Variable Speed Unit (VSU) and Remote Unit (RU) are attached to the camera, the respective label "SU" or "RU" is displayed on the lower line of MODE 1.

Mode 2 (Button Pressed Once). *Upper line displays:* Angle of shutter opening.

NOTE: Shutter angle can be changed directly on the camera (see Sec. 11.1p), or by using a Shutter Control Unit (see Sec. 11.1p), or a Camera Control Unit (see Sec. 11.3a), or a Remote Unit (Sec. 11.3d).

Lower line displays: Preset frame rate (fps).

Mode 3 (Button Pressed Twice). *Upper line displays:* Total film exposed on the last take and always reverts to 0 when camera starts.

NOTE: With CCU attached (see Sec. 11.3a), the Mode selection can be varied.

Lower line displays: Current battery voltage.

Mode 4 (Button Pressed Three Times). Operates only with Time Code module attached.

Upper line display: Time code reading in hours and minutes.

Lower line: Time code reading in seconds and frames.

Mode 5 (Button Pressed Four Times). Operates only with Time code module attached.

Upper and lower lines display: Eight selectable user bits, i.e., personalized information (numbers) the user wishes to put on the film to identify a scene or sequence.

Reset Button. With camera in MODE 1 (standby) status, depress button to clear and/or correct error in the display. Camera will not operate until all error numbers are cleared.

With Camera in MODE 2 status, depress button to set a shutter angle (see Sec. 11.1p, Shutter LCD display control.)

With camera in MODE 3 status, depress to reset total film exposed counter.

Phase Button (Left Hand Display Only). This has two basic functions:

1. Camera in MODE 1 (standby) status: As an electronic inching knob, i.e., rotates the mirror shutter and the movement one slow turn when depressed.

2. Camera in MODE 2 status: Serves as a phase shifter (eliminates raster bar from picture) when filming video monitors. To clear raster bar, depress button while camera is running at 24 fps until raster bar is clear of the frame. The phase shifting may be verified by checking the fps display.

Program Button (Right Hand Display Only). Activates and retrieves programs stored in the camera by the Camera Control Unit (see Sec. 11.3a).

NOTE: The right hand display also contains a knurled disc that controls the ASY (asynchronous) warning tone. If the disc is rotated to the end of the (-) direction, the ASY sound is completely shut off.

11.1n Buckle-Trip
Two microswitches. One above upper sprocket, one below lower sprocket. LCD reads JAM when film pile-up occurs in camera.

11.1o Tachometer
Frame rate may be read in three places:

Frame Rate Selector Switch (manual): Located on right side of camera body. The selected frame rate can be read through a small plexiglass window just to the right of the switch (see Sec. 11.1b Motor).

LCD Displays: Frame rate shown in lower lines of MODES 1 and 2. (See Sec. 11.1m, Liquid Crystal Displays).

11.1p Shutter
Variable. 180 degrees.

To Change Shutter Angle Electronically. Use the following separate units:

• *LCD display control* (see also Sec. 11.1m). 180°, 172.8°, and 144° angles can be set directly on the camera. In display MODE 2, press the RESET button until one of the three desired shutter angles is shown on the LCDs; then release the button.
• *Camera Control Unit (CCU)* (see Sec. 11.3b): From 11-180° in increments of .01°. This unit is the most precise of all.
• *Remote Unit (RU)* (see Sec. 11.3d): Adjusts from 11.2° to 180°.
• *Shutter Control Unit (SCU)* (see Sec. 11.3g): Adjusts shutter from 11.25° to 180°.
• *Mechanical (manual) adjustment of shutter:* From 11–180 degrees, predominantly in 15-degree preset steps, i.e., 11°, 15°, 30°, 45°, 60°, 75°, 90°, 105°, 120°, 135°, 144°, 172.8°, and 180°.

CAUTION: Mechanical adjustment of the shutter is recommended in an emergency situation only, i.e., when the electronic shutter adjustment(s) fail (E4 appears in LCD).

To Adjust Shutter Mechanically. Remove lens. While looking into lens port, open camera door, rotate inching knob until the two recessed hex screws (locking and adjustment) located in the center of the shutter are accessible through the lens port. With a 2mm hex wrench, turn the locking hex screw nearest lower LCD display in the LOOSE direction until it stops.

CAUTION: The locking device must be released before every manual shutter adjustment. Never turn any adjustment forcibly!

Insert the 2mm hex wrench in the adjustment hex screw nearest the crystal frame rate selector switch; simultaneously press lightly on the wrench and turn the adjustment screw until only a few degrees from the desired angle marked on the shutter. Stop. Turn the locking hex screw to the LOCKED position. Continue to rotate the adjustment hex screw until the shutter snaps into the detente of the selected angle.

Lubrication. None in the field. A factory service.

11.1r Cleaning.
Optics. Clean with bulb syringe or camel's-hair brush.

Manufacturer recommends the following maintenance each time the film is changed: (1) Remove emulsion build-up around aperture and in film race with orangewood stick or similar soft skewer. The entire film gate may be removed for cleaning (see below). (2) Clean pulldown claw and mechanism with soft brush. (3) Clean surface or mirror-shutter with soft lens tissue or soft cotton tips (foam tipped, surgical quality are good). (4) Use bulb syringe on camera interior to remove dust, dirt, etc.

Removing/Replacing Film Gate. Remove for cleaning or changing format masks.

To remove: With camera door open, (1) Turn witness mark inching knob to LOADING position on movement block. (2) Pull down the film gate release lever located at the top left of camera compartment. The gate will gently spring away from the camera housing. (3) Take the film gate out of its holder by pulling it upwards with a slight pressure. It is not necessary to remove film from the camera to do this.

CAUTION: Keep fingers out of the film gate opening to prevent damaging the mirror shutter.

To reinstall. (1) Place film gate into its holder in the camera housing. Be sure the bottom of the gate seats properly in the housing. (2) Pull the film gate release lever down. (3) Press gently on the top of the gate until it snaps into position.

WARNING: DO NOT use acetone, nitro-diluent, alcohol, or other cleaning fluid for maintenance!

11.1s Weight
17.5 kg (38.6 lbs), with standard viewfinder, 120m (400') load, and without film and lens.

11.1t Troubleshooting
Error indications are displayed either on LCD displays or in the viewfinder. An acoustic signal indicates a possible asynchronous condition (see Sec. 11.1m). In case of under or over power voltage the camera cannot be switched on and the running light will illuminate red.

Error indications on the camera displays:

FILTER		Internal gel filter in film gate
JAM		Film jam
ASY		Out of sync
END (flashes)		Film runout warning
END		Out of film
BAT		Low Battery (less than 22v)
TC		Time Code activated
TC (flashing)		Time Code not recording/TC batteries dead
fps (flashing)		No external frequency being picked up by ESU
Upper line:	0000	Movement block not locked in position
Lower line:	_000	
Upper line:	0000	Film jam in upper film loop area
Lower line:	0_00	
Upper line:	0000	Film keepers not locked in position
Lower line:	00_0	
Upper line:	0000	Film jam in the lower film loop area
Lower line:	000_	
Upper line:	_000	Magazine not properly attached
Lower line:	0000	
Upper line:	0_00	Magazine not ready for operation
Lower line:	0000	(this indication disappears after approximately two seconds if no error exists)

11.2 ARRIFLEX 535 MAGAZINE (FIG. 11–4a and 11.4b)

11.2a Type
Co-axial.

11.2b Capacity
304.8m (1000 ft), 122m (400 ft).

11.2c Lids
Two. Located at each side of magazine, which is divided longitudinally. Lids are not hinged, but rather are fully removable. Lids locks are located in center of lids.

To Open. Press the safety release button in center of lid lock and lift the magazine lid lock tab. Turn the lid lock tab counterclockwise until it stops and then lift off the magazine cover.

11.2d Drive System
Electronic interface, torque-controlled.

11.2e Feed
Right half. Magazine throat should be at loader's right, magazine counter, magazine catch, and film-loading gear UP. Film (would emulsion in) pulls off spindle counterclockwise.

11.2f Take-up
Left half. Magazine throat should be at loader's left, magazine lock UP. Film winds on to collapsible core clockwise, emulsion always in.

11.2g Loading
Feed Side. (1) Place magazine on flat surface, remove magazine cover, and move footage-counter roller-guide arm arm down and to the right until it locks in recessed guide. (2) Lift the manual inching knob and the

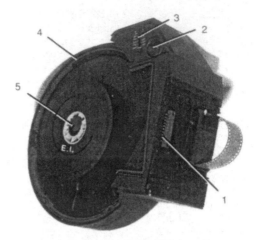

Figure 11–4a Arriflex 535 magazine (feed side). Courtesy of Arnold & Richter K.G.

1. Electronics connector
2. Inching knob
3. Mechanical counter
4. Footage-counter roller-guide arm
5. Hinged locking knob

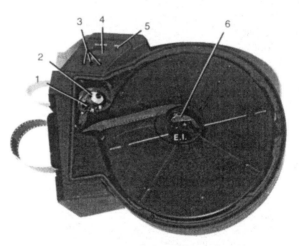

Figure 11–4b Arriflex 535 magazine (take-up side). Courtesy of Arnold & Richter K.G.

1. Channel release button
2. Film channel
3. Footage counter buttons
4. LCD footage counter
5. Mode button
6. Collapsible take-up core

hinged locking clip in the center of the feed core. (3) In darkness, remove film roll from can and bag and place beside magazine.

NOTE: To expedite engagement of film in magazine gears, cut the film to bisect a perforation.

NOTE: Manufacturer recommends that magazine lid be used as a height-compensation base for the film roll. Be sure that the film roll is flush and even.

(4) Insert film end into feed throat, slowly rotating knurled manual inching knob counterclockwise until the gear sprockets engage the film perforation. (5) Place the film roll on the feed shaft, making certain spindle key engages the core keyway. Flip down the hinged locking clip. (6) Continue rotating inching knob until film emerges from the magazine throat. (7) Close and lock the magazine lid. Be certain the rim of cover fits snugly into magazine guide grooves. Pull on cover to be certain cover is secure.

CAUTION: Fold the magazine manual inching knob down.

Take-up Side. (8) Flip magazine over and remove take-up cover.

NOTE: Take-up loading may be done in light.

(9) Gently pull the head of the film out of the upper slot of the magazine throat and feed it into the lower slot of the throat. (10) Gently push the film until it emerges inside the take-up compartment of the magazine. (11) Insert the head of the film into the collapsible film core. Move clamp on core outward to secure film. Wind the film roll approximately one turn. Be sure the film is locked at a right angle to the take-up shaft to prevent dishing of the film roll.

NOTE: In contrast to other Arriflex magazines, loop size is not important when loading. The loops can be adjusted when threading.

(12) Replace magazine take-up cover. Be certain the rim of cover fits snugly into magazine guide grooves. Pull on cover to be certain cover is secure.

11.2h Unloading
(1) In darkness, place magazine on flat surface with take-up side facing up. (2) Remove magazine take-up cover. (3) Disengage clamp on core by pushing inward. (4) Place index finger in core space, thumb on edge of roll. Slide the other hand under the roll to prevent sagging. (5) Lift the roll out and place on a flat surface. (6) Insert a plastic film core in the roll's center.

NOTE: The plastic core sits loosely in the film roll, but provides sufficient stability.

(7) Place exposed roll in bag and can.

11.2i Footage Counters
LCD Footage/Meter Counter. Located on upper front left (take-up) side of magazine. Next to the display are a MODE button and three SET buttons. The display has two MODES:

- *MODE 1 (button not pressed).* Loader can set the quantity of film stock loaded in the magazine by pressing any combination of the three set buttons. In this mode, when the camera is running, the unexposed film stock remaining in the magazine is continuously displayed in meters or feet. During reverse camera run, the quantity of film transported back into the magazine is automatically added to the remaining film stock. The display can be set and read while the magazine is not attached to the camera.

• *MODE 2 (button pressed).* With time code operation, the identification of the film sensitivity (TCS) must be set on the display. (See Sec. 11.3b and page 160.)

Manual Footage/Meter Counter. Located on upper front right (feed) side of magazine. This counter uses a spring-loaded manual counter arm to measure the remaining footage. This is not a continuous display.

To measure remaining stock, push down the slide bar in the middle of the display; resistance indicates the level of stock remaining. When the slide bar is released, the counter arm resets automatically.

NOTE: A loop protector, which also functions as a magazine carrying handle, should be installed before transport or storage of empty or loaded magazines. This helps to prevent film and magazine throat damage.

11.3 ARRIFLEX 535 ACCESSORIES

11.3a Camera Control Unit (CCU-1) (Fig.11-5)

The CCU-1 is a computer accessory that can electronically program the 535 camera with the most common camera functions.

The CCU-1 consists of a case with (a) a power cable, (b) a battery compartment, (c) an ON/OFF button, (d) a keyboard, and (e) a display window.

Power Cable. Connects to the camera with a 1.83m (6-ft) length cable that inserts into the lowest 8-pin Fischer plug at the back of the camera (see Chapter 11.1, 535 35mm Camera and Sec. 11.1c, Powerline).

Figure 11-5 Camera control unit (CCU). Courtesy of Arnold & Richter K.G.

1. Camera cable connector
2. Neckstrap hook
3. On/Off switch
4. Display window
5. Keyboard
6. Battery compartment

ON/OFF Button. At right side of the computer case. Depress to start/stop unit, but only works if the camera *main power* is on (see Chapter 11.1, 535 35 mm Camera and Sec. 11.1c, Powerline).

Battery Compartment. The unit is either powered by 24 volts from the camera battery or by 8 AA size internal batteries.

NOTE: Internal batteries are only good for approximately 5 hours steady running. When on internal battery power alone, the unit is automatically switched off 5 minutes after the last keyboard key is depressed.

Keyboard. Displays symbols, letters and numbers and functions as follows:

- *Top row:* Light bulb symbol, 7, 8, 9, A, D, EXIT, HELP, RUN
- *Middle row:* .(decimal point) 4, 5, 6, B, E, F3, F4, SEND
- *Bottom row:* 0 (zero) 1, 2, 3, C, F, F1, F2, ENTER

Most keys (0–9, ENTER, SEND, EXIT, HELP, RUN) are employed in all eight menus to select a specific function; some lettered-numbered keys (F-1, F-2, F-3, F-4) are only utilized in three functions; the lettered keys (A, B, C, D, E, F) are utilized in two menus.

- The *light bulb symbol* illuminates/extinguishes the display window.
- *0–9* numerals correspond to numbered selections featured on each main menu and submenu screen.
- *ENTER* accepts selected data input and stores it in the computer where it remains until transmitted to the camera or deleted.
- *SEND* transmits the selected data that is entered into the computer, to the camera.
- *EXIT* terminates the function on any selected menu and returns the computer screen to the main menu.
- *HELP* brings up textual information relating to the current menu on display.
- *RUN* activates/deactivates the camera.

Display Window. Before the CCU-1 is connected to the camera and it is turned ON (not connected to the camera), the right side of the display window will read OFFLINE and will show the Main Menu.

When the CCU is connected to the camera and the camera's main power is OFF, the display window will read OFFLINE and will show the Main Menu.

When the CCU is connected to the camera, and the camera's main power is turned ON, the display window will show the Main Menu and show the camera status report.

Main Menu. A Main Menu displays 8 submenus with the following functions:

1. Speed (sets frame rates)
2. Shutter (determines shutter angles)
3. Remote (duplicates LCDs at a distance from the camera)
4. Format (sets Arriglow aperture markings in viewfinder)
5. Time Code (enters time code and user bits)
6. Options (sync tone, metric/footage setting, film end warning, counters)
7. Program (for preselected speed and shutter angle changes)
8. Info (regarding camera status, counters, E-numbers, sound mode)

Error messages appear in the upper right of the window until corrected.

Error messages displayed in the lower right of the window remain until the next key is depressed.

NOTE: Error messages are those letters/numbers E2 through E13 that indicate a malfunction in the camera (see Subsection 8, Info Menu, below).

Duplicate camera status (e.g., SPEED and SHUTTER) are also visible.

To Select a Desired Submenu. Press corresponding Main Menu number 1 through 8. Main Menu will be replaced with selected submenu (1 through 8).

Speed Menu. Key 1 deletes the Main Menu, brings up the SPEED menu and displays the fps speed set on the CCU-1 and the fps speed set on the camera, as well as nine camera speed selections: 1: 24 fps; 2: 25 fps; 3: 29.97 fps; 4: 30 fps; 5: 50 fps; 6: -24 fps (reverse); 7: -25 fps (reverse); 8: VAR (variable); 9: ADJUST (adjustable).

Keys 1 through 5 set forward camera fps in the speeds displayed.

Keys 6 and 7 set reverse camera fps in either of the two - (minus) speeds displayed. Key 8 (VAR) permits a variable fps rate setting after pressing 8, followed by keying numerically, the frame rate desired.

NOTE: The VAR can input frame rates from 3 to 50 fps in increments of 0.01 (100ths) fps.

NOTE: The frame rate will show on the CCU-1 window in increments of 0.001 (1/1000ths) fps; the camera LCD will only display the frame rate in increments of 0.01 (100ths) fps.

Key 9 (ADJUST) in conjunction with F-1 and F-2 keys, permits the variation of the frame rate up or down in 1/1000ths of a frame increments. Therefore:

After keying the desired fps (either numerically 1 through 7, or VAR), and then keying 9, followed by pressing the F-1 key, the camera speed can be increased in + 0.001 fps increments.

After keying the desired fps (either numerically 1 through 7, or VAR), and then keying 9, followed by pressing the F-2 key, the camera speed can be slowed in -0.001 fps increments.

To Select a Desired fps Function.

1. Press corresponding menu number frame rates 1 through 9 (and F-1 or F-2, if part of the input process).
2. Press ENTER (stores into the computer).
3. Press SEND (relays data to the camera).
4. Press RUN (starts camera).

To Return to the Main Menu. Press EXIT.

To Return to 24 fps (or Any Other Frame Rate Displayed in main menu). While camera is running,

1. Press 1 (or other desired frame rate number).
2. Press ENTER (stores data into the computer).
3. Press SEND (sends data to the camera).

To Return to the Main Menu. Press EXIT.

Shutter Menu. Key 2 deletes the Main Menu, brings up the SHUTTER menu and displays the shutter angle in degrees set on the CCU-1 and the shutter angle in degrees set on the camera, as well as 8 pre-set shutter degree selections: 1: 180° 2: 172°, 3: 144°, 4: 135°, 5: 90°, 6: 45°, 7: 22.5°, 9: VARIABLE.

NOTE: The numeral 8 does NOT appear in the shutter menu. Keys 1 through 7 select shutter angles in the pre-set degrees shown.

To Select a Desired Preset Function:

1. Press corresponding menu number 1 through 7.
2. Press ENTER (stores data into the computer).
3. Press SEND (sends data to the camera).
4. Press RUN (starts camera). Data appears in LCDs.

To Return to the Main Menu. Press EXIT.

Key 9 (VAR): permits the setting of a) a shutter angle other than those listed 1–7,

To Set a Shutter Angle Other than That Showing on the Submenu.

1. Press VAR menu number 9.

NOTE: CCU window and the camera LCD's flash intermittently.

2. Type in desired shutter angle using numerical keys.

NOTE: Once data is entered, CCU and camera LCDs stop flashing. Selected shutter angle appears in the CCU display window and on the camera LCDs.

3. Press ENTER (stores data into the computer).
4. Press SEND (relays data to the camera).
5. Press RUN (starts the camera).

To Return to the Main Menu. Press EXIT.

3. Remote Menu. Key 3 deletes the Main Menu, brings up the Remote Menu and displays the amount of exposed film in the camera magazine (either in meters or feet depending on the selected input), the frame rate of the camera, and four F-selections:

F1—PHASE; F2—MODE; F3—RESET; F-4—PROG

The F1, F2, F3, F4 buttons on the keyboard perform the same functions of the three vertical buttons alongside the camera's left front LCD marked MODE, RESET, and PHASE, as well as the three horizontal buttons beneath the camera's upper right LCD marked MODE, RESET, and PROGRAM. (See Sec. 11.1, 535 35mm Camera and 11.1m Liquid Crystal Displays (LCDs), for details regarding these buttons.)

NOTE: Camera LCDs have an additional Mode 4 and Mode 5 which operate only when a Time Code module is attached to the camera. The CCU has a separate TIME CODE menu (see Menu 5, below). Therefore, the REMOTE Menu is not used to access Modes 4 and 5.

To Select a Desired Remote Function.

1. Press corresponding menu number F-1, F-2, F-3, or F-4.
2. Press RUN (starts camera).

To Return to the Main Menu. Press EXIT.

4. Format Menu. Key 4 deletes the Main Menu, brings up the Format Arriglow menu, and displays a selection of nine Arriglow framelines that can be set in the viewfinder. (See also Sec. 11.1, 535 35mm Camera and 11.1f, Viewfinder, Visible Framelines.)

The space following the title CAMERA is reserved for identification of the frameline(s) set in the viewfinder; otherwise, the area is blank. As each frameline is entered, the input data is noted in the space.

Arriglow framelines are:

1. SUPER 35/1A (anamorphic 2.35:1 centered on a Super 35 frame)
2. SUPER 35/2 (1.85:1 centered on a Super 35 frame)
3. SUPER 35/3 (combination 1.85:1 and 2.35:1 centered on a Super 35 frame)
4. ANAMORPH (2.35:1)
5. ACADEMY
6. BROAD 1 1:185
7. BROAD 2 1:66
8. SILENT
9. TV

NOTE: As many as three formats can be entered and seen in the viewfinder.

To Select a Desired Pre-Set Function.

1. Press corresponding menu number(s) 1 through 9.
2. Press ENTER (stores data into the computer).
3. Press SEND (sends data to the camera viewfinder).

To Delete a Pre-Set Function.

1. Press corresponding menu number(s) 1 through 9.
2. Press ENTER (stores data into the computer).
3. Press SEND (deletes Arriglow format in the camera viewfinder).

To Return to the Main Menu. Press EXIT.

5. Time Code Menu. Key 5 deletes the Main Menu, brings up the Time Code/User bits menu and displays two preset selections: (1) TIMECODE in hours:minutes:seconds:frames that are set on both the CCU-1 and the camera, and (2) USERBITS that are entered into the CCU-1 and camera. Time Code and User bits are independent of each other.

About Time Code. Time Code (TC) data identifies each film frame with a number consisting of hours, minutes, seconds, and frames, and requires the insertion of a TC module in the camera in order to optically record on film between the perforations and the exposed frame (see Sec. 11.3b, Time Code Module).

To Select a Desired Preset Function.

1. Press corresponding menu number 1 or 2.
2. Press ENTER (stores data into the computer).

CAUTION: Forgetting to press ENTER after selecting 1 or 2 will result in that function not "locking in."

To Set the Time Code.

1. Press numerical keys 0–9 to establish a desired time to be encoded on the film. Most Time Codes are started at 00:00:00, but any combination

of numbers can be used. The maximum time that can be entered is 23 hours, 59 minutes, 59 seconds.

2. Press ENTER (stores data into the computer).
3. Press SEND (sends data to the camera). Data appears in LCDs.
4. Press RUN if starting camera is desired.

About User Bits. User Bits (UB) permit the insertion of up to eight numbers or letters (or a combination of both) for specific coded information relevant to the camera user (e.g., to identify the second camera, an area filmed, a sequence in which the scene belongs, etc, etc. See Sec. 11.3b, Time Code Module.) Settings are at the user's discretion.

To Set the Userbits:

1. Press Menu selection #2 to access Userbit menu.
2. Press ENTER (stores data into the computer).

NOTE: Square in Userbit flashes.

3. Press numerical keys 0–9 and/or letters A–F to establish a desired entry to be encoded on the film. Any combination of numbers/letters can be used. User bits, once entered, unlike Time Code, do not change.
4. Press SEND (sends data to the camera).
5. Press RUN if starting camera is desired.

To Return to the main menu. Press EXIT.

NOTE: Refer to Section 11.3b and/or the Arriflex Time Code Manual if more detailed data is required.

6. Options Menu. Key 6 deletes the Main Menu and brings up the Options Menu with a display of four preset selections: (1) ASYNC - MODE; (2) LENGTH - UNIT; (3) END WARNING; and (4) COUNTER DISPLAY MODE. Each of these preset selections breaks down into further sub-menus.

To Select a Desired Preset Menu.
1. Press corresponding menu number 1 through 4.

1. ASYNC - MODE (asynchronous, or out-of-sync tone) controls the placement or elimination of the acoustic tone heard whenever the CCU-1 and/or camera is started or stopped. When selected, the async-mode shows a sub-menu with 4 sub-set selections: 1: - END; 2: BEGIN - ; 3: BEGIN - END; 4: - -.

To Select a Desired ASYNC Function.
(1) Press corresponding numeral key 1 through 4.

NOTE: No. 1 places the audible tone at the end of a take.
No. 2 Places the audible tone at the beginning of a take.
No. 3 Places the audible tone at the beginning *and* end of a take.
No. 4 There is no tone.

(2) Press ENTER (stores data into the computer); (3) Press SEND (sends data to the camera).

To Return to the Options Menu. Press EXIT.
To Return to the Main Menu. Press EXIT twice.

2. LENGTH - UNIT sets the camera counter to meters or feet. When selected, the length - unit shows a sub-menu with 2 sub-set selections: 1: METER; 2: FEET.

To Select a Desired Meter/Feet Function.
(1). Press corresponding numeral key 1 or 2; (2) Press SEND (sends data to the camera counter).
To Return to the Options Menu.   Press EXIT.
To Return to the Main Menu.   Press EXIT twice.

3. END WARNING sets the film end warning length in both the camera viewfinder and on the camera LCDs. Warning shows in meters or feet, depending on the input of the length- unit (see above). Meter/footage length can be set anywhere from 0–99.

NOTE: 0 = NO end warning.

To Select a Desired Meter/feet Length Function.
(1) Press ENTER key (clears computer for entry of new data); (2) Press numerical keys to set desired length.

NOTE: Input is automatically stored after two digits have been entered. Entry of less than two digits requires pressing the ENTER key again.

To Return to the Options Menu.   Press EXIT.
To Return to the Main Menu.   Press EXIT twice.

4. COUNTER DISPLAY MODE changes the method the LCD footage counters show the exposed and remaining footage in Mode 1 and Mode 3 screens (see also Chapter 11.1, 535 35mm Camera, Sec. 11.1m Liquid Crystal Displays (LCDs), for details regarding these modes). When selected, the Counter Display Mode transmits a submenu with three Mode 1 and Mode 3 subset selections for the CCU-1 and one Mode 1 and Mode 3 for the Camera.

The display reads:

CCU		*CAMERA*	
MODE 1	MODE 3	MODE 1	MODE 3
1. TOTAL	TAKE	TOTAL	MAGAZIN
2. TAKE	TOTAL		
3. TOTAL	MAGAZIN		

TOTAL is the total footage exposed since the last RESET Button was pressed (see Chapter 11.1, 535 35mm Camera, Sec. 11.1m Liquid Crystal Displays (LCDs), for details concerning the RESET button). TAKE is the total footage exposed during the previous take. MAGAZIN is the amount of footage remaining in the magazine.
To Select a Desired Mode Function.   (1) Press corresponding numeral key 1 through 3; (2) Press ENTER (stores data into the computer); (3) Press SEND (sends data to the camera).
To Return to the Options Menu.   Press EXIT.
To Return to the Main Menu.   Press EXIT twice.

7. Program Menu. Key 7 deletes the Main Menu and brings up the Program Menu. Press desired keys 1–6 to enter or modify a program. Each selected submenu displays two preset lines in which to input and manage changes in SPEED and/or SHUTTER as well as the TIME desired in which to execute the maneuver.

Line 1 beneath the titles SPEED, SHUTTER and TIME is used to input the *start* of the program.

Line 2 beneath the titles SPEED, SHUTTER and TIME is used to input the *end* of the program.

Beneath lines 1 and 2, are the letters E: EDIT; A: AUTO; F: FETCH; and D: DELETE.

• EDIT is used to input and change any of six programs that can be stored in the computer.
• AUTO is used to calculate shutter angles that correspond with camera speeds for uniform exposure.
• FETCH is used to retrieve data stored in the camera and file it.
• DELETE cancels the selected program.

To Program a Camera for Change of Speed, Change of Shutter Angle, and Length of Time during a Take.

NOTE: Camera speeds can be set between 3 and 50 fps. The maximum change from one speed to another cannot exceed 30 fps of speed (e.g., 20 fps to 50 fps, but not 10 fps to 50 fps, etc.).

Shutter speeds can be set from 11 to 180°. The maximum change from one shutter angle to another shutter angle is 80° (e.g., 45° to 125° but not 45° to 180°).

Time can be set from 1 to 100 seconds (e.g., 1–100 seconds but not 1–105 seconds).

1. Press no. 1 key to establish first program.

NOTE: By pressing keys 1–6 it is possible to set up as many as six separate programs (change of speed, shutter and time) in the computer.

2. Press EDIT key. Flashing appears on line one beneath SPEED.
3. With numeral key(s) insert fps desired.

NOTE: Speeds can be entered in 100ths of a frame (e.g., 29.97, or 32.50, etc.).

4. Press ENTER (stores data into the computer). Selected fps speed appears in the CCU display window on line 1. Flashing appears on line one beneath SHUTTER.
5. With numeral key(s) insert starting shutter angle desired.

NOTE: Shutter angles can be entered in 10ths of a degree (e.g., 90.5, or 34.7, etc.).

6. Press ENTER (stores data into the computer). Selected shutter angle appears in the CCU display window on line 1. Flashing appears on line two beneath SPEED.
7. With numeral key(s) insert fps desired.

NOTE: Speeds can be entered in 100ths of a frame (e.g., 29.97, or 32.50, etc.).

8. Press ENTER (stores data into the computer). Selected ending fps appears in the CCU display window on line 2. Flashing appears on line two beneath SHUTTER.
9. With numeral key(s) insert ending shutter angle desired.

NOTE: Shutter angles can be entered in 10ths of a degree (e.g., 90.5, or 34.7, etc.).

10. Press ENTER (stores data into the computer). Selected ending shutter angle appears in the CCU display window on line 2. Flashing appears on line two beneath TIME.
11. With numeral key(s) insert time desired (in seconds) to go from start to end on change of speed and shutter angles.

NOTE: Time can be set from 1 to 100 seconds.

12. Press ENTER (stores data into the computer).

> *To Store Program in Camera.* Press SEND.
> *To Return to the Program Menu.* Press EXIT.
> *To Return to the Main Menu.* Press EXIT twice.
> *To Add More Programs.* Press no. 2 key to establish second program;

input steps 2–12 outlined above. Press no. 3 key to establish third program; input steps 2–12 outlined above, etc. (up to 6 programs). After entering desired program number:

> *To Store Program in Camera.* Press SEND.
> *To Return to the Program Menu.* Press EXIT.
> *To Return to the Main Menu.* Press EXIT twice.
> *To Bring up Any Program at Any Time.*

1. Press key no. 7 on Main Menu to bring up Program Menu.
2. Select Program Number 1 through 6.
3. Press F (FETCH) key.
4. Press numerical keys 1–6 to bring up desired program.
5. Press ENTER

> *To Store Program in Camera.* Press SEND.
> *To Return to the Program Menu.* Press EXIT.
> *To Return to the Main Menu.* Press EXIT twice.
> *To change fps and/or degree of shutter angle from one setting to another once they have been programmed:*

1. Press numerical key (1–6) of program to be changed.
2. Press DELETE to cancel the entire program, or
3. Press EDIT, to start flashing under SPEED, line one. Continue to press EDIT until line or space to be changed is reached, then:
4. Press numerical keys to enter data.
5. Press ENTER.
6. Press EDIT to move to next selection, or

> *To Store Program in Camera.* Press SEND.
> *To Return to the Program Menu.* Press EXIT.
> *To Return to the Main Menu.* Press EXIT twice.
> *To compute the shutter angles required on the camera when changing from one fps rate to another fps rate, and the time (in seconds) required to go from one setting to another, during a take:*

1. Press key no. 7 on Main Menu to bring up Program Menu.
2. Press numbered program to be changed.
3. Press A (AUTO).
4. Press C (CALCULATE).

NOTE: CCU will display correct shutter angles to maintain constant exposure based on maximum shutter opening and will display the minimum time required to do so.

To Store Program in Camera.   Press SEND.
To Return to the Program Menu.   Press EXIT.
To Return to the Main Menu.   Press EXIT twice.
To clear all *data stored in CCU Program Menu:*

1. Press numerical key (1–6) to bring up program to be cleared.
2. Press DELETE.
3. Press ENTER.

To Clear Program from Camera.   Press SEND.
To Return to the Program Menu.   Press EXIT.
To Return to the Main Menu.   Press EXIT twice.

NOTE: Data intended to design a program can be entered in the CCU without it being connected to the camera. To send or retrieve a program, however, the CCU *must* be connected to the camera.

8. Info Menu.   Key 8 deletes the Main Menu and brings up the Info Menu with a display of four preset selections: (1) STATUS; (2) COUNTER; (3) E-NUMBERS; and (4) SOUND CCU ON/OFF. Each of these preset selections breaks down into further submenus.

To Select a Desired Preset Menu.   (1) Press corresponding menu number 1 through 4.

1. STATUS submenu shows the condition of the camera, its fps speed, Time Code (on or off) shutter angle, length unit (feet or meters), when the async signal is heard (beginning, end, beginning *and* end, or off), if a filter is in the camera, and the Arriglow format(s) visible in the viewfinder.

NOTE: There are no selections, or changes that can be made in this mode. Strictly for information.

To Return to the Info Menu.   Press EXIT.
To Return to the Main Menu.   Press EXIT twice.

2. COUNTERS submenu shows the status of the camera counters in feet or meters (depending on the length-unit selected in the Options menu). TOTAL shows the film exposed since the Reset button *on the camera* was pressed. TAKE shows the amount of film exposed on the last take. MAGAZIN shows the amount of film left in the magazine. U-BAT shows the amount of voltage left in the battery.

NOTE: There are no selections or changes that can be made in this mode. Strictly for information.

To Return to the Info Menu.   Press EXIT.
To Return to the Main Menu.   Press EXIT twice.

3. E-NUMBERS submenu shows information regarding problems when the camera fails to operate and when certain E (error) numbers (E-2 through E-13) appear on the camera CCDs. There are no selections or changes that can be made in this mode. Strictly for information.

E-2 Camera out-of sync	E-8 Film runout
E-3 Shutter opening incorrect	E-9 No TV scan signal from shutter
E-4 Shutter angles incorrect	E-10 Camera program wrong
E-5 Magazine film count wrong	E-11 Time Code program error
E-6 Magazine status wrong	E-12 No motor scan signal
E-7 Time Code generator error	E-13 55 fps limitation exceeded

NOTE: Not all errors mean the camera is nonfunctional since the camera is constantly "checking itself" and the E-number might just be a glitch. It is possible in many instances to continue filming. If error numbers appear, shut off main power to camera. When you switch power back on, if error still appears, contact the nearest Arriflex Service Center for camera status information.

To Return to the Info Menu.   Press EXIT.
To Return to the Main Menu.   Press EXIT twice.

4. CCU SOUND ON/OFF in Info menu shows the status of the warning tone on the CCU-1.

To Turn CCU Sound On or Off.   While in Info menu, Press key no. 4 to darken desired status (ON or OFF).
To Select Other Data in the Info Menu.   Press EXIT.
To Return to the Main Menu.   Press EXIT twice.

11.3b   535 Time Code/User Bits Module (Fig. 11–6)

About the 535 Time Code.   Time Code (TC) optically exposes each film frame with a number consisting of hours, minutes, seconds, and frames. It requires the insertion of a TC module in the camera in order to optically record on film between the perforations and the exposed frame. Most Time Codes start at 00:00:00:00, and progressively increase from there; but any combination of numbers can be used to start the identification. The maximum time that can be entered is 23 hours, 59 minutes, 59 seconds.

Time Code can be used at four speeds: 24 fps, 25 fps, 29.97 fps, and 30 fps. TC will not record any variation of frame rate from those speeds.

Figure 11–6   Time Code/User Bit Module. Courtesy of Arnold & Richter K.G.

1. Finger grip

About the 535 User Bits. User Bits (UB) optically expose up to eight numbers or letters (or combination of both) for specific coded information relevant to the camera user (e.g., to identify a second camera, an area filmed, a sequence in which the scene belongs, etc.). Settings are at the user's discretion and unique in that the recorded information only has meaning to the user.

NOTE: Time Code and User bits are independent of each other. User bits, unlike Time Code, do not change as they are recorded.

On the 535, a Time CODE (TC)/User Bits (UB) Module replaces the Film Counter Module located in the upper right camera interior.

To Install TC/UB Module. With the camera main switch OFF (no power), (1) Remove magazine; (2) pull Film Counter Module straight out from camera interior in direction of arrow on counter (toward Operator's left); and (3) insert TC/UB Module and push in until it stops.

NOTE: Once installed, the camera's built-in TC generator begins to count. The numbers are visible on the camera's LCD only in Mode 4 (see 11.1m Liquid Crystal Displays LCDs). The MODE 4 numbers are NOT the TC recorded on film but are a means of affirming that the generator is working.

To Prepare Camera for TC and UB Data Input.

1. Install Time Code memory batteries.

To Install. Loosen screw and remove accessory screw at top-front of camera carry-handle. Press the tiny recessed button release with a paper clip, slide lid forward. Lift insulator up and pivot forward. Insert two Type N 1.5v batteries with proper polarity (indicated in holders).

NOTE: With the camera unplugged, batteries retain Time Code memory approximately 8 hours.

2. Place loaded magazine on camera (see Sec. 11.1k, Magazines). Set inching knob on movement block to LOADING POSITION. Thread camera (see Sec. 11.1l, Threading). Ascertain that the top and bottom of the film loops are precisely set at internal loop marks above and below the movement block. Advance film one frame (to LOADING POSITION again) and check if loops align to top and bottom loop marks. If not, adjust.

WARNING: Setting loops incorrectly could offset the exposed film frame by one or more perforations!

3. Verify that the film is threaded *between* the TC module and the "finger" below it.

CAUTION: Failure to insert film between the module and its finger will result in improper recording on the film.

4. Set intensity of film stock on magazine (see also Sec. 11.2 Magazines, Footage Counters, LCD Footage/Meter Counter, Mode 2 [button pressed], and the Time Code Sensitivity (TCS) Table that follows).

TCS Table

Mfr:	Type	Stock	TCS Value
AGFA	XT 125	Color Neg	6
	XT 320	Color Neg	7
	30/166	B&W Rev	8
	30/195	B&W Rev	7
EASTMAN	5247	Color Neg	6
	5294	Color Neg	5
	5295	Color Neg	6
	5296	Color Neg	4
	5297	Color Neg	5
	5239	Color Rev	6
	5240	Color Rev	5
	5222	B&W Rev	8
	5224	B&W Rev	8
	5231	B&W Rev	8
FUJI	8510	Color Neg	7
	8514	Color Neg	5
	8520	Color Neg	5
	8530	Color Neg	6
	8550	Color Neg	4

5. Connect the Camera Control Unit (see Sec. 11.3a, CCU-1, Power Cable) into the lowest 8-pin Fischer plug (labeled CCU) at the back of the camera, or connect a Master Clock into the plug second from the bottom (labeled MCL).

NOTE: A Master Clock (MCL) is NOT an Arriflex product. The most used MCL on the 535 is a Nagra IV-S TC 1/4" audio tape recorder, or Nagra R-DAT.

6. Program the CCU (see Sec. 11.3a CCU-1, Time Code Menu).

NOTE: Time Code and User Bits can only be programmed from the CCU.

Camera LCD Information with Time Code Module in Camera.
With Camera in Standby Mode (Power on, Camera Not Running). (1) If the initials TC are NOT displayed in the LCD, check if Time Code has been entered in the CCU, or MCL; or if camera fps is set at other than 24, 25, 29.97, or 30 fps. (2) If TC is flashing, Time Code will NOT be recorded when camera runs; eight hours time has elapsed between time code settings on CCU. (3) TC is displayed continuously, Time Code properly set.
With Camera in Run Mode (Power on, Camera Running). (1) If the initials TC are NOT displayed in the LCD, check battery voltage; or main switch was on when TC module was installed; or if camera fps is set at other than 24, 25, 29.97, or 30 fps; or a magazine is not on the camera. (2) If TC is flashing, Time Code is NOT recording onto film; film improperly threaded through Time Code Module and its finger.

To Visually Verify if Time Code Is Optically Recording on Film. (1) Prepare camera (install batteries, place magazine on camera with short end, thread film, set loops, etc.). (2) Set camera speed to 24, 25, 29.97 or 30 fps. (3) Set TCS on magazine to 9 (highest sensitivity). (4) Transmit TC data from CCU and check that TC appears in the camera LCD. (5) In dim light, run camera. As film travels between the TC Module and its finger, firmly hold an orange stick (not metal) and insert it just above the film as it rolls over the finger.

CAUTION: Holding the stick loosely could whip it into the camera body.

(6) Press the stick against the TC Module and gently angle the film down so as to see the inside top surface of the film as it travels through the camera interior. A thin unreadable red line appearing on the far side of the film will verify that the TC is recording. If the line is not visible, the TC Module is NOT recording and should be changed.

11.3c 535 Video Assist Systems (Fig. 11–7)
The Video Assist Systems consist of B&W or color plug-in video modules (Video Optic Module [VOM-1 B&W or VOM-2 color]). The VOM-1 is limited in controls. The VOM-2 has a built-in flicker reduction ON/OFF switch, a BNC connector for a video monitor, a flange connector for a mini-monitor, blinking LED to indicate the operation of flicker reduction on the monitor, and automatic flicker reduction cut-out when frame rate drops below 15 fps (PAL) or 17 fps (NTSC).

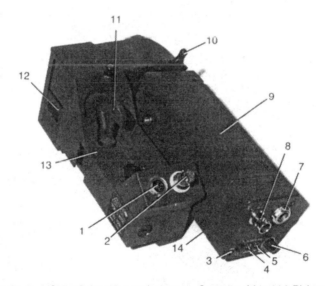

Figure 11–7 VOM-2 Color video assist system. Courtesy of Arnold & Richter K.G.

1. Power plug
2. VOM BNC plug
3. Auto white balance
4. Outdoor/Indoor Toggle
5. Auto/Manual gain control toggle
6. Flicker reduction switch
7. 7-pin video camera connector
8. Monitor BNC plug
9. CCD-2 camera
10. Positive lock mount
11. VOM lock lever
12. Optics door
13. VOM
14. Video camera iris (not visible)

NOTE: With the advancement of video cameras, newer units reach the market every day and may vary slightly from this text in placement of controls, switches, outlets, etc. The principles outlined here will be the same, however.

A bayonet-mount video camera with 2/3″ pick-up area and frequency reduction, available in B&W (CCD-1) or color 1/2″ pick-up area and frequency reduction, (CCD-2). The CCD-2 is available in 50 or 60 Hz, PAL or NTSC versions, has white balance switches, Automatic Gain Control (AGC), Manual Gain Control (AGC), a 3-digit display on the video image, and a blinking bar on the video image to indicate film camera is ON.

To Mount VOM on 535 Camera. (1) Make certain the camera main power is OFF. (2) Lift lock lever on the port cover located at top right front of camera, rotate it counterclockwise and lift cover away.

NOTE: On the VOM-2, the CCD is attached. It can only be removed with tools. Once the VOM-2 is attached to the film camera, the VOM and CCD are ready to operate. It is (3) Slide optics door on the left of the VOM open. (4) Lower VOM to the camera, rotate the lock clockwise and secure it.

To mount 12v DC video camera to VOM-1. (1) Rotate the small PL mount on the VOM counterclockwise. Insert camera into VOM and rotate PL-mount clockwise to secure.

To Use Either/or VOM and CCD Camera. Rotate 3-position Beamsplitter Selector Knob at top of 535 camera to desired transmission value (VIEWFINDER; 50/50; VIDEO)

NOTE: When there is NO video assist system on the camera, the Beamsplitter Knob should *always* be turned to VIEWFINDER (80% light transmitted to the viewfinder). With a video assist on the camera, position 50/50 splits the light evenly between the video assist and viewfinder; position VIDEO transmits 90% of the light to the video assist and 10% of the light to the viewfinder.

Turn main camera power ON.

CCD-1 Controls.

To Activate Video Tap. Connect VOM power cable to video camera plug. Flip up power on/off toggle switch lower left of camera carrying-handle. A green LED on the handle will light to indicate video tap is on.

To Connect VOM to a Monitor. Attach monitor cable to the BNC plug located next to the VOM power cable at the rear of the camera.

NOTE: A mini-monitor can be mounted in the bracket at the upper rear of the carry handle.

To Connect Camera to a Mini-Monitor. Attach mini-monitor cable to the plug above the carry handle toggle switch.

VOM-1. *Rotary Coding Switch:* Reach *under* the video camera and, with a screwdriver, rotate the Rotary Coding Switch.

NOTE: Manufacturer recommends for best results to set Rotary Coding Switch (that reads ABCDEF0123456789) on the B&W CCD-1 camera to 9. Other letters/numbers can be selected at the user's discretion if those recommendations are not satisfactory.

VOM-2 *Control Panel:* At rear of unit. Consists of BNC plug for outlet to a monitor, a 7-pin Power Cable plug, and a 4-position rotary Flicker Reduction (FR) switch.

To Activate Video Tap. Connect VOM power cable to 7-pin video camera plug.

To Connect VOM to a Monitor. Attach monitor cable to the BNC plug located next to the 7-pin VOM power cable at the rear of the VOM.

NOTE: A mini-monitor can be mounted in the bracket at the upper rear of the carry handle.

To Connect Camera to a Mini-Monitor. Attach mini-monitor cable to the plug above the carry handle toggle switch.

Flicker Reduction Rotary Switch. Rotates to 4 positions: FR OFF; FR ON; STORE; COMPARE.

About Flicker Reduction (FR). Differences between the video signal and the film camera's frame rate (fps) causes variations in brightness on the video image. The VOM retains the image being viewed (subimage) and blends it with the image the camera sees, thus reducing any variations in brightness (flicker) to a minimum.

NOTE: Flicker Reduction does not work at less than 17 fps NTSC (525 lines, 60 Hz), or 15 fps PAL (625 lines, 50 Hz).

With the FR switch set at:

• FR OFF—Video image will flicker.
• FR ON—Video flicker will be reduced.

NOTE: When film camera is in ON position, a blinking bar appears in the monitor to indicate FR is in operation.

• STORE—Monitor shows a one-field-image that has been placed in memory.
• COMPARE—Monitor alternatively shows one image from memory and one picture of the video camera.

NOTE: COMPARE Mode is often used when an image has been stored and then later recalled for line-up purposes.

Video Camera Iris. Knurled wheel located at the bottom of the camera.

To Adjust. Rotate knurled wheel until monitor image is of desired quality.

11.3d Remote Unit (RU-1) (Fig 11–8)

Unit is designed to control the main 535 camera functions: RUN (see Sec. 11.1 Powerline), VSU (see Sec. 11.3e, Variable Speed Unit), SCU (see Sec. 11.3f, Shutter Control Unit) and PROG (see Sec. 11.3a, Program Menu) from a distance of up to 25m (75 ft).

The RU-1 has a Variable Speed Unit (VSU) dial next to a Shutter Control Unit (SCU) dial. Between the two, at the top, is a Program Button (PROG) and below, a Camera ON/OFF Button (RUN). Two toggle switches are located lower left and right.

Left Toggle Position. When set to the left, the VSU and SCU are electronically coupled. Set to the center, the toggle is neutral. Set to the right, the VSU is placed in Variable Speed Control.

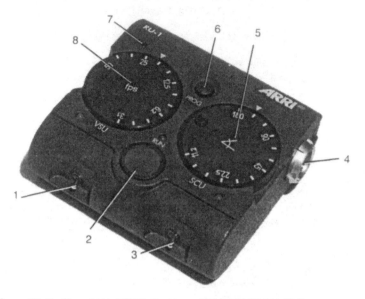

Figure 11–8 Remote Unit (RU). Courtesy of Arnold & Richter K.G.

1. Left toggle (In Variable Speed Control Mode)
2. Run button
3. Right toggle (in shutter control position)
4. Camera cable plug
5. Shutter control unit (SCU) dial
6. Program button
7. VSU/SCU coupled indicator light
8. Variable speed unit (VSU) dial

Right Toggle Position. When set to the left, the toggle is neutral. Centered, the toggle is neutral. Set to the right, the shutter can be varied (providing the left toggle is centered and not in the left position). SCU light, at lower right, illuminates with toggle set to the right.

To the left, above the VSU, is a red AUTO LED that illuminates when the VSU and SCU are electronically coupled.

The RU control cable socket plugs into the unit's right side. Its other end is plugged into the top connector socket at the upper rear right of the camera body.

The RU is activated when plugged into the camera.

The VSU dial allows the operator to set frame rates from 3 to 50 fps.

NOTE: When the RU is switched on, the frame rate set on the RU dial overrides the frame rate stored in the normal camera operation program. The new frame rate and the symbol RU are then visible on the LCD display.

The SCU dial allows the Operator to set shutter angles from 11.2° to 180°.

NOTE: When the right toggle is switched on, the shutter angle set on the RU dial overrides the shutter angle stored in the normal camera operation program and the angle selected with the SCU dial becomes active and visible on the two LCD displays.

To Install Remote Unit (RU-1).   Remove the Variable Speed Unit (VSU) (see Section 11.3e) from the camera. Connect the RU-1 cable to the camera.

To Use Remote Unit (RU-1).   (1) Set VSU dial to desired fps frame rate. (2) Set SCU dial to desired shutter angle. (3) Press RUN to start/stop camera.

To Change Camera Speed and Compensate for Shutter Angle.   (1) Set lower left toggle switch to the left.

NOTE: Red AUTO LED will illuminate.

(2) Press RUN to start camera. With thumb, rotate VSU dial to alter fps speed. Shutter will automatically compensate for correct exposure.

NOTE: 50fps = 180°
25fps = 90°
12.5fps = 45°
6.25fps = 22.5°, etc.

NOTE: Program Mode set on the CCU (see Sec. 11.3a, Menu no. 7, Program Menu) can be activated by pressing the PROG button prior to running the camera.

11.3e Variable Speed Unit (VSU) (Fig 11–9*a*)
Frame Rate Selection Using VSU. The VSU is a separate unit that is plugged into the topmost connector socket on the back right side of the camera body. The VSU is activated by a simple toggle switch. It enables the operator to set frame rates from 3 to 50 fps.

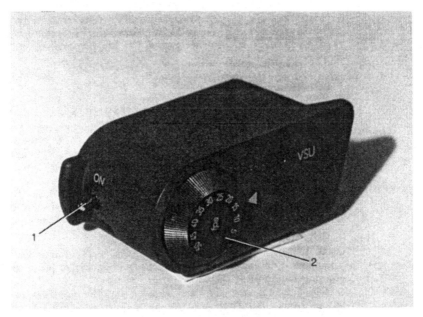

Figure 11–9a   Variable Speed Unit (VSU). Courtesy of Arnold & Richter K.G.

1. On/Off toggle   2. Fps setting dial

Figure 11–9b Shutter Control Unit (SCU). Courtesy of Arnold & Richter K.G.

1. On/Off toggle   2. Shutter angle setting dial

NOTE: When the VSU is switched on, the frame rate set by the VSU overrides the frame rate stored in the normal camera operation program. The new frame rate and the symbol VU are then visible on the LCD display (see Sec. 11.1m).

11.3f Shutter Control Unit (SCU) (Fig. 11–9b)

Shutter Control Unit (SCU). A separate unit that permits electronic adjustment of mirror shutter, from 11 to 180 degrees, during filming. The SCU is plugged into the connector socket at the upper rear right of the camera body, the second plug from the top. The SCU is turned on with a simple toggle switch. When the SCU is switched on, the shutter angle stored in the normal camera operation program (via the Camera Control Unit (CCU) [see Sec. 11.3a]) is suppressed, and the angle selected with the SCU becomes active and visible on the two LCD displays. The shutter angle is selected by the dial on the SCU. Changing the shutter angle from 11 to 180 degrees while the camera is running takes less than one second.

11.3g External Sync Unit (ESU-1) (Fig. 11–10)
Used to synchronize the 535 camera with a 75 ohm video signal, a computer, or a video monitor. It also functions as a phase shifter and Pilotone generator.

The ESU has an Audio dial with fps and Hertz indicators next to a Phase Adjust dial (with a safety cover marked LOCKED and OPEN covering the dial). Between the two, below, is a Camera On/Off Button (RUN) with an LED that lights when the camera runs. Two toggle

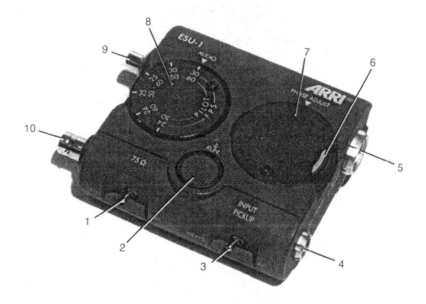

Figure 11-10 External Sync Unit (ESU). Courtesy of Arnold & Richter K.G.

1. Left (75 ohm) On/Off toggle
2. Camera On/Off button
3. Right (input pickup) On/Off toggle
4. External computer or video source plug
5. Camera cable plug
6. Phase shift dial
7. Phase adjuster cover
8. Fps/Hz setting dial
9. External tape recorder plug
10. 75 ohm sync cable plug

switches are located lower left and right. The right toggle turns the input pickup to On when set to the left, Off when set to the right. The left toggle turns the 75 ohm switch to On when set to the left, Off when set to the right.

The unit's upper right socket accepts the ESU cable. The cable's other end is plugged into the connector socket second from the top at the upper rear right of the camera body.

The lower right cable socket accepts a cable plug to an external computer or video source.

The upper left cable socket accepts the plug of an external tape recorder.

The lower left cable socket accepts the plug of a 75 ohm sync cable to an external NTSC or PAL video signal.

The rear of the unit has a switch that sets the pulse to frame ratio.

To Install External Synchronization Unit (ESU). (1) Remove the Variable Speed Unit (VSU) (see Section 11.3e). (2) Connect the ESU-1 cable to the camera and upper right plug on the ESU unit.

NOTE: ESU should appear on the camera LCDs when the camera main switch is turned ON (standby). If improperly connected the *fps* on the LCDs will blink. Reconnect.

To Use External Sync Unit (ESU-1).

To Start/Stop Camera.   Press RUN.

To Sync an External Computer or Video Source.   Connect a special (Arri # KC32) cable to the computer or video, and to the lower right cable socket.

NOTE: The LED on the ESU-1 will illuminate if signal is being received. If LED does not light, "sync-lock" the camera.

To "Sync-Lock" the Camera.   Connect a 75 ohm cable to the external computer or video source and the lower left cable socket.

To Supply a Pilotone Signal to an Audio Tape Recorder.   Connect a cable to the recorder and the upper left cable socket. Set left toggle switch to On.

CAUTION: The signal fps and Hertz generated must be the same as that set on the back of the unit.

To Set Matching Camera Signal and Hertz on ESU.   Rotate left dial and match fps/Hz to Audio pointer: 24 fps 50 Hz; 24 fps 60 Hz; 25 fps 50 HZ; 25 fps 60 Hz, 30 fps 50 Hz; 30 fps 60 Hz.

To Use as a Phase Shifter to Eliminate Horizontal Roll Bar on a Video Monitor.   Rotate Phase Adjuster cover counterclockwise to the OPEN position. Press RUN and start camera. Observe the monitor and rotate the phase shift dial until the rollbar is off the monitor screen. Rotate Phase Adjuster cover clockwise to close.

To Sync to AC mains, a Projector, or to "Slave" to Another Camera.   Connect a cable to the source and the lower right cable socket. Set right toggle switch to *input*.

To Set the Audio Signal Pulse to fps Frame Ratio at Back of the Unit.   Slide switch at rear of unit to correspond to data below:

	1 to 1 Ratio	
Number of Pulses		*Per Frames*
50		50
24		24
	2 to 1 Ratio	
60		30
50		25
	5 to 2 Ratio	
60		24

11.3h Lens Support (not shown)

Used with heavy zoom, telephoto or anamorphic lenses. Support system consists of two parts: snap-on lens support and a clamp ring. Requires use of the top plate and rods from the BP-5 bridgeplate (see Sec. 11.11, 35mm Bridgeplates).

To Mount Lens Support.   (1) With locking lever of unit at operator's left, align and pressure-snap semicircular cutouts at base of lens support onto top of 19mm bridge plate support rods. Unit will click into place. Turn Locking Lever clockwise.

To Mount Clamp Ring.   Insert shaft of the clamp ring support shaft on screw located at the bottom of the lens support and tighten.

To Loosen Lens Support on Rods. Rotate the locking lever at the left side of the support counterclockwise.

To Secure Lens Support on Rods. Tighten the locking lever at the left side of the support clockwise.

To Remove Lens Support from Rods. Loosen the locking lever at the left side of the support and slide the unit forward and off the rods.

11.3i Servo Zoom Drive (not shown)

Consists of: (a) a motor bracket, (b) a drive motor, and (c) a zoom control.

NOTE: It is necessary to use a zoom lens with an affixed gear ring.

To Prepare Camera. a) Install lens support and clamp ring on support rods of bridgeplate (see Sec. 11.11b Bridgeplates). Insert zoom lens with affixed gear ring into camera lens port (see Sec. 11.1c Lenses) and secure in clamp ring. c) Install drive motor into motor bracket.

To Install Motor. Loosen thumbscrew, open bracket and insert the motor; close bracket and tighten thumbscrew.

NOTE: When inserting motor, the drive-teeth face the gear ring on the lens and the power connector points away from the camera.

To Mount Bracket. Loosen clamp at base of bracket and fit unit to the right support rod.

To Engage Motor with Lens. Align and push motor toward lens until motor teeth mesh with lens gear ring. Tighten motor thumbscrew. Tighten clamp at base of bracket.

To Engage Zoom Control Unit. Insert one cable into the remote switch outlet at the lower right front of the camera, and the second cable into the outlet on the motor.

11.3j Two-Speed Follow-Focus System (FF-3) (not shown)

To Mount FF-3. (1) With focus knob and gear swing arm at Operator's left, align and pressure-snap semicircular cutouts at base of unit onto top of 19mm bridgeplate support rods. Unit will click into place. Secure in place by locking the lever at the unit's base. (2) Mount corresponding gear for selected lens by pulling swing arm away from unit and inserting gear in holder.

NOTE: There are two gears available. Narrow gear is for Cooke zoom lenses; wide gear is for all other lenses.

(3) Align swing arm gear with gear ring on lens and secure with the lock lever at the top left of the unit.

Focusing Knob. Rotates 360°. Knurled knob is fitted with an inset and button. Inset accepts either the shaft of a focusing lever or shaft of a flexible focus extension with knob. Button is depressed in order to change focus knob gear ratio.

Gear Ratios. Two: Standard (1:1) and High (1:66).

To Change to High Gear Ratio. Depress and hold button on focus knob and pull the knob away from camera until unit clicks in detente.

To Change to Standard Gear Ratio. Depress and hold button on focus knob and push the knob toward camera until unit clicks in detente.

Circular Marking Disc. Behind the knob; used to scribe focus changes.

NOTE: A focusing index can be rotated 360° around the perimeter of the marking disc and locked in any position.

Follow-Focus Extensions. To operate from camera-right with a 167.66mm × 167.6mm (6.6 × 6.6) production matte-box on the camera, an extender must be fitted to the right side of the FF-3 unit before attaching a right-hand knob.

NOTE: With NO matte-box on the camera, an extender is not necessary. A knob can be fitted to the right-side of the FF-3. A right side knob accepts a focus lever as well as a flexible focus driver.

11.3k Shoulder Support (See Fig. 11.1c.)

Used when hand-holding camera. Top of dual-handled support is fitted with a dovetailed baseplate and a curved shoulder rest.

To Mount Camera to Shoulder Support. (1) Remove dovetailed top plate from a BP-5 bridgeplate (see Sec. 11.11, 35mm Bridgeplate) and attach to bottom of camera. (2) Slide the top plate into the dovetailed base plate of the shoulder support until it stops. (3) Tighten the slide lever to secure. (4) Insert battery cable into front remote switch/zoom motor control connector.

NOTE: Manufacturer recommends using a hand-held battery (NCØ24/2) when shooting with the shoulder support. The battery also serves as a counterweight.

To Remove Camera from Shoulder Support. (1) Loosen slide lever in top plate. Slide top plate forward and away from camera.

Dual handles are adjustable by loosening/tightening wing nuts on handle bracket. An *ON/OFF Switch* is in the right handle. To connect, insert cable from switch to front Remote/Zoom Motor Connector. There is NO remote switch on the left handle. *Curved shoulder rest* is placed at camera's center of gravity (with 122m (400 ft) load) for better distribution of weight.

11.3l Bridgeplate

See also Sec. 11.11. The 535 BP-5 bridgeplate uses 17-in. length × 19mm support rods, although shorter lengths are available.

11.4 ARRIFLEX 35 III CAMERA (Figs. 11–11a, 11–11b, 11–11c)

NOTE: All directions are from the Operator's point of view.

11.4a Base

Fitted with 3/8″-16 tapped hole to accommodate tripod lockdown screw, riser, or bridgeplate (see Sec. 11.11) and two pilot holes.

NOTE: A special *riser* is required in order to hand-hold camera with dual grips, or to use accessories that mount to *bridgeplate*. A *support bracket* must be fitted to *bridgeplate support rods* (see Sec. 11.11) to support a zoom lens.

Base of riser has a single 3/8″-16 thread tapped hole and one pilot hole and is fitted with a 3/8″-16 thread thumbscrew to attach riser to camera. At each side of riser are *mounting rosettes* that accommodate handgrips.

An accessory *shoulder pod* can be fitted to the base of camera.

Figure 11–11a   Arriflex III—Studio mode (left side). Courtesy of Arnold & Richter K.G.

1. Follow-focus knob
2. Marking disc
3. Limiter
4. Matte-box
5. Follow-focus lens gear
6. Footage read button
7. Meter/footage selector switch
8. Tachometer
9. Meter/footage counter
10. Counter reset button
11. Viewfinder
12. Magazine cover lock
13. Eyepiece focus ring
14. Eyecup
15. Eyepiece open/close knob
16. Camera door latch
17. On/Off toggle
18. Lens lock

11.4b Motor

12-volt built-in crystal control.

NOTE: The III motor is NOT interchangeable with other Arriflex 35mm cameras.

Frame rate selector switch: located forward of *bubble level.*

To Set to 24 fps or 25 fps.   Remove plastic window by unscrewing. Slide switch to 24 fps or 25 fps. Be sure that the *CONSTANT/VARIABLE switch* located below four-pin Cannon power plug is set to "CONST" (constant).

To Set Variable Speed.   Set CONSTANT/VARIABLE switch to "VAR" (variable). Rotate *variable-speed knob* at lower right side of camera (forward of 11-pin Fischer plug). Visually check fps counter to determine speed.

Figure 11–11b Arriflex III with 304.8m (400 ft) magazine (right rear). Courtesy of Arnold & Richter K.G.

1. Meter/footage counter
2. Take-up spindle wheel
3. Eyecup
4. Power plug
5. Mode selector toggle switch
6. Battery cable dovetail bracket
7. 304.8m (400-ft) magazine
8. Feed spindle wheel
9. Bubble level
10. Magazine release catch
11. Constant speed selector switch and fuses (not visible)
12. Handgrip bracket
13. Bridge plug cover
14. Handgrip 4-pin socket
15. Accessory plug
16. Speed Adjustment knob
17. Inching knob

NOTE: Camera will run 5–50 fps with 12-volt battery.

To Run Camera above 50 fps. Requires 24 volts and a *variable-speed control* (see Sec. 11.30, which contains wiring that connects to two 12-volt batteries. Unit contains a rheostat that varies speed. Cable from rheostat connects to six-pin *bridge plug.*

To Reverse Camera. Insert a Reverse Bridge Plug (not shown) in place of the Forward Bridge Plug located at upper right-side of camera.

NOTE: The Forward Bridge Plug completes the 35 III camera circuitry. The Reverse Bridge Plug enables the flow of electronics (and all the camera's gearing) to travel in an opposite direction.

CAUTION: A reversing magazine is necessary on the camera when a Reverse Bridge Plug is used (see Sec. 11.4j, Note: re a reversing magazine).

WARNING: Camera counter counts *forward* when camera is in *reverse.* *This must be understood when calculating footage!*

Figure 11–11c Arriflex III—Hand-held mode. Courtesy of Arnold & Richter K.G.

1. Liteweight matte-box

11.4c Powerline

Input to Camera. Cannon female end of battery cable fits to recessed four-pin plug located at top rear of camera. Insert five-pin male end of cable into battery.

NOTE: The dovetail located below CONST/VAR switch accommodates a dovetail bracket that encircles the battery cable approximately 6 in. from female end.

ON/OFF Switch. Located at left front of camera. Push *up* to start; push *down* to stop camera.

To Mount/Adjust Accessory Handgrip. Align wingscrew on handgrip bracket to tapped hole at right front of camera body; tighten in desired position; insert attached 4-pin handgrip into flat socket at right side of camera.

Fuses.

Electronics. 0.75 ampere pico. Located next to frame rate selector switch forward of the *bubble level*. To change, unscrew plastic cover, pull fuse with Hirschman clip or needlenose pliers; insert a new fuse. Fuse is available at most electronic parts stores.

NOTE: A spare fuse is usually stored in a slot marked "RES" (Reserve) under the clear cap.

Motor. 15 ampere pico. To change, remove right side cover of camera. The 15 amp pico fuse is located toward rear of camera.

11.4e Lenses
Newer cameras are fitted with a PL (Positive Lock) mount. Many models accept bayonet mount lenses. A few cameras accept standard mounts.

PL (Positive Lock) Mount.
To mount. Align notch lens mount flange with locator pin on the upper left of the port. Insert lens in port and turn the locking ring on the camera counterclockwise to secure.
To remove. Turn locking ring clockwise, grasp lens firmly and gently pull it from the port.

Bayonet Mount.
To Mount. Rotate lens barrel until channel in the mount aligns with the infinity mark on the lens; squeeze the lens locking levers at each side of the port; with follow-focus grips up, slide mount into port. Rotate lens counterclockwise until it locks.
To Remove. Rotate follow-focus grips up. Squeeze locking levers at each side of the port. Grasp lens firmly and gently pull it from the port.

Standard Mount.
To Mount. Depress lens lock button forward of optic tube; align keyway on rear of lens with index key in lens port; slide lens into mount; release lens lock.
To Remove. Depress lens lock button forward of optic tube; pull gently from port.

NOTE: 16mm and 35mm bayonet mount and standard mount Arriflex lenses are interchangeable, with the following exceptions: 5.7mm, 11.5mm, and 25mm. These will not "cover" a 35mm aperture. The only wide-angle lenses that cover a 35mm aperture are the 9.8mm, 14.5mm, 18.5mm retrofocus, and the 28mm *made for 35mm cameras.*

WARNING: To avoid damage to the mirror shutter, remove lens guard from the following bayonet mount lenses: First Series Superspeed Distagon 25mm; First Series Superspeed Distagon 35mm; Zeiss Planar 50mm.

WARNING: The Arriflex-III will *NOT* accept a Tega Kinoptik 9.8mm lens unless the lens barrel has been rotated so that its bevel clears the mirror shutter!

11.4f Viewfinder
Reflex with magnified 6.5 × image.

Five Types. Fixed, offset, pivoting, fixed with video, and pivoting with video.
Fixed. Viewfinder is an integral part of door and nonadjustable. Optic tube is fitted with a plate so that an anamorphic attachment lever can be added when using anamorphic lenses.

NOTE: When anamorphic lever is attached to camera, it is essential that spacer be inserted between eyepiece flange and optic tube.

Offset. Viewfinder is raised above door to accommodate hand-holding.

Pivoting Rotating. Viewfinder position can be pivoted 270° for convenience of viewing.

Fixed with Video and Pivoting with Video. Same features above but with video tap ports added.

NOTE: Each time camera is started or stopped, a red LED *out-of-sync indicator* illuminates briefly at bottom of view finder.

Blinking red light indicates battery is low.

When in variable mode, a green LED illuminates in viewfinder.

To Align Reflex Mirror for Viewing. Depress inching knob at right rear of camera and turn.

CAUTION: DO NOT depress inching knob while camera is running.

NOTE: Camera always stops with shutter in viewing position.

To Focus Eyepiece. Rotate scalloped knob on barrel of eyepiece.

NOTE: Barrel is numbered $+5$ to -5 as a reference for individual's eye setting.

To Change or Clean Groundglass. Remove lens. Depress and rotate inching knob to open shutter and avoid scratching mirror. Insert 3.175 mm (1/8-in)- wide screwdriver through lens port; turn lock screw DOWN to clear groundglass holder. Insert groundglass tool or paper clip into eyelet of groundglass holder and pull toward lens opening.

To Replace Groundglass. Be certain dull flat side of groundglass faces mirror. Insert groundglass into its holder with clip; push toward aperture. Insert 3.175mm (1/8-in.) wide screwdriver and turn lock screw UP.

To Detach Eyepiece. Rotate clockwise the knurled ring forward of eyepiece lock on viewfinder and pull eyepiece from keyed slots.

11.4g Matte Box

The III will accept six basic matte-boxes: the MB-14, MB-14W, MB-15, MB-16, LMB-3, LMB-4, and Standard (see Sec. 11.12 Matte-boxes and Filter Holders).

11.4h Filters

There is NO internal filter slot. All filters must be placed on the lens or in a matte box. Filters that fit into matte-boxes vary in size, depending on the unit (see Sec. 11.12 Matte-Boxes and Filter Holders).

11.4i Door

Hinged at front.

To Open. Rotate clockwise the door lock located on camera body behind door. Swing door away from camera.

To Close. Swing door to camera, rotate door lock counterclockwise to secure.

To Remove Door. Open door; pull latch located inside door at lower hinge; lift UP; pull door away.

To Replace. Align door to hinges, pull latch inside door, and lower door; release latch.

11.4j Magazines

122m (400-ft.), 304.8m (1000-ft), and 61m (200-ft)

To Mount. Pull *magazine release latch* at right top of camera to release magazine retaining lip. Pull film loop into camera cavity. Seat rear magazine dovetail into camera body, then lower front magazine dovetail to camera. Release magazine-release lock.

To Remove. Unthread camera. Pull magazine-release latch at right top of camera to release magazine retaining lip; lift magazine away.

NOTE: A 122m (400 ft) magazine with steel gearing reverses only when used with a Reverse Bridge Plug in the camera (see Sec. 11.4b, Motor, To Reverse Camera). 304.8m (1000 ft) and 61m (200 ft) magazines do NOT have a reverse capability.

A *reversing magazine* can be distinguished from other magazines by noting that its take-up collapsible core can be interchanged with the feed-side core holder. To exchange cores, loosen with a screwdriver and lift. Load film on take-up side.

NOTE: Arriflex III camera will accept IIC and 3C magazines (see Sec. 11.14).

11.4k Threading (Fig. 11–12)

Open door wide. Pull steel pin on film gate, open gate as far as it will go. Check film guide for emulsion and/or dirt. Rotate internal knurled disc until its arrow aligns to dot on claw plate.

NOTE: Alignment of arrow and dot clears the pulldown claw and registration-pin from the gate.

Figure 11–12 Arriflex III threading. Courtesy of Arnold & Richter K.G.

1. Thumbnail slot
2. Aperture plate
3. Steel pin
4. White dot

5. Alignment dot
6. Internal knurled disc
7. 4.05V "memory" battery cap

Insert film into gate. With middle finger and index finger conform the film so that the top loop bisects the white dot above the gate. Rotate knurled disc in camera body until the single registration pin or the pulldown claw engages a perforation.

WARNING: If top loop is too large, the film will be scratched down the middle. Ascertain that the top loop ALWAYS bisects—or is slightly lower than—the white dot above the gate!

Close the gate. Make certain gate closes with an audible click. Rotate inching knob to check engagement of the pulldown claw.

11.4l Buckle-Trip
None.

11.4m Footage and Frame Counters
Located at left front of camera. Top LED reads in single increments 0–9999 in meters or feet (switchable on newer cameras). Counters illuminate when camera runs.

NOTE: Older models do not have a frame counter.

> *To Read Counter When Camera Is Off.*   Depress READ button.
> *To Reset Counter.*   Depress READ and RESET buttons *at the same time.*

NOTE: Having to depress both buttons prevents accidental zeroing if RESET button alone is hit.

Coin-Slotted Cap. In camera body. Visible only when camera door is open. Contains a 4.05-volt battery for internal memory of footage counter. With battery in camera, counter retains footage count for up to 12 hours before erasing information from display. Permits overnight storage of camera, location moves, etc.

NOTE: Red light below tachometer glows when battery is low.

CAUTION: If footage counter loses display because of dead battery or storage longer than 12 hours, it cannot be reset mechanically. Requires removing magazine from camera and running camera until display reads previous footage/metric and frame totals.

> *To Change 4.05-Volt Battery.*   Unscrew coin-slotted cap, *pull* battery.

NOTE: Prior to discarding battery, clean positive and negative ends, reinsert, and check. If red light still glows, replace battery.

Insert new battery with negative side facing *outward.*

WARNING: Newer cameras are fitted with a 5-year lithium battery (for memory), located inside the counter assembly and changeable only by a service shop.

11.4n Tachometer
Below footage counter. Registers speeds in single increments up to 130 fps.

11.4o Shutter
180°. Nonadjustable on older cameras.
Many cameras are fitted with limited-shutter adjustments of 135°, 144°, 172.8°, and 180°.

Newer cameras are fitted with shutters adjustable predominantly in 15-degree preset steps (i.e., 15°, 30°, 45°, 60°, 75°, 90°, 105°, 120°, 135°, 144°, 172.8°, and 180°).

To Adjust Shutter. Remove lens to reveal mirror shutter. Rotate inching knob until a 2mm locknut on the shutter becomes visible. Insert 2mm Allen wrench into locknut. Hold shutter with finger (avoid touching mirror) and press wrench in *gently.* Slowly turn the wrench until the shutter numbers rotate out from behind the shutter mirror. (Turn to operator's left to reduce shutter; turn to operator's right to open shutter.) When desired shutter angle is nearly reached, release pressure on the Allen wrench, continue rotating, and allow the shutter to enter detente of desired shutter angle.

11.4p Lubrication

Manufacturer states that camera needs NO oiling or greasing except for annual checkout (a service center job).

Occasionally, in the field, lightly smear a dip of ARRI grease on the pulldown claw with the forefinger.

11.4q Cleaning

Optics. Clean with a bulb syringe.

It is recommended that the following maintenance be done *each time film is changed:* (1) Check aperture plate and pressure plate. (2) Remove emulsion build-up with orangewood stock. (3) Wipe plates with soft cotton handkerchief (not linen). (4) Use bulb syringe on camera interior to remove dust, dirt, etc.

To Check Aperture Plate. Open camera door. Rotate internal knurled disc until the arrow on the movement block is at 2 o'clock. (This differs from threading—i.e., the arrow and dot are NOT aligned. STOP!)

WARNING: Before opening or removing the aperture plate, ALWAYS make certain shutter is open. Confirm by looking through lens port; shutter is open if the mirror *cannot* be seen but the pressure plate can. Doublecheck by looking through the viewfinder. Optics are obscured if shutter is open.

REPEAT: *It is important* to make certain the shutter is open *before* removing the aperture plate. This avoids accidental chipping, cracking, or scratching of the mirror, which will result in a major camera overhaul.

Pull steel pin of film gate and open. Open latches (if any) above and below the aperture plate. Ascertain that pulldown claw and registration pin are clear of the gate. Insert thumbnail into slot at side of aperture plate. Depress plate toward camera wall and pry toward back. Pull plate out.

To Replace Aperture Plate. Align aperture plate to guide-grooves. Tilt back slightly and slide aperture plate into grooves. Push forward; release.

NOTE: The preceding instruction also applies when changing an aperture plate for one with a different aspect ratio (e.g., 1.85 to full aperture, etc.) A variety of aperture plates are available from manufacturer, with matching groundglasses.

11.4v Weight

With 304.8m (1000 ft) load: 9.2 kg (20.25 lb)
With 122m (400 ft) load: 7.5 kg (16.5 lb)
With 61m (200 ft) load: 6.6 kg (14.5 lb)

Trouble	*Probable Cause*
Camera will not start	Powerline connection faulty; battery dead.
Intermittent start and stop	Battery connections loose; broken connection in powerline.
Torn perforations; ripped film	Improper threading.
Door will not close	Dirt or film chip(s) in door.
Lens will not focus	Lens not seated; camera too close for minimal distance of lens; elements damaged.
Cut-in on groundglass	Lens not seated; sunshade extended.

11.5 ARRIFLEX 35 III MAGAZINES (Fig 11.13)

11.5a Type
Displacement

11.5b Capacity
304.8m (1000 ft) (not shown), 122m (400-ft), and 61m (200-ft) (not shown).

NOTE: A 122m (400 ft) magazine is capable of holding a 152.4 (500 ft) roll of film.

11.5c Lid
One. Lug-and-dog locked.

To Open 304.8m (1000 ft). Depress and turn three latches counterclockwise. Lift.

To Open 152.4m (500 ft) and 61m (200 ft). Depress safety spring in lid recess; rotate single lock bar counterclockwise (from "C" to "O"). Lift.

11.5d Feed
Left side. Film (wound emulsion in) pulls off spindle clockwise.

11.5e Take-up
Right side. Film winds on spindle clockwise, emulsion always in.

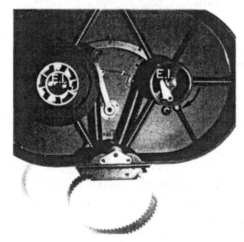

Figure 11–13 Arriflex 35 III 122m (400-ft) magazine. Courtesy of Arnold & Richter K.G.

1. Remove lid
2. Reposition footage-counter roller-guide arm. For 304.8m (1000 ft.) *magazine:* Push footage counter roller guide arm UP, and lock arm in pressure catch, top of magazine. *For* 122m (400-ft) *and* 61m (200-ft) *magazine:* Swing footage-counter roller-guide arm to right, and lock arm in pressure catch next to take-up spindle.
3. In darkness, remove film roll from can and bag. Pull film off roll clockwise. Insert film into left side of magazine throat, slowly rotating gear at bottom counterclockwise with thumb until gear in throat engages film perforation; continue to thread through at least 6 inches of film.

NOTE: To expedite engagement of film and magazine gear, cut film to bisect perforations.

4. Place film roll on feed spindle. Rotate knurled feed-spindle wheel until spindle key spring engages core keyway. Release footage-counter roller-guide arm, make sure that flanges ride the film perforations.

NOTE: In 304.8m (1000 ft) magazine, the counter arm drops automatically when the cover is replaced.

5. Pull film end around front of magazine until cut perforations touch marking rib (raised metal bar) on outside of magazine. Hold gear; bring film end back, and insert end into right-hand channel of magazine throat. Rotate gear until perforation engages gear and film moves into magazine.

WARNING: Do not allow excess film to exit feed side while trying to engage perforation and take-up gear.

NOTE: It is important to maintain proper loop size: 54 perforations regardless of capacity.

6. Insert film end into collapsible take-up core; move clamp inward to secure film.
7. To replace lid, hold lid at 45° angle, insert lugs (at bottom) into mating slots in magazine; lower lid to a secure fit. *304.8 (1000 ft) magazine:* Rotate 3 cover latches clockwise *122m (400 ft) or 61m (200 ft) magazine:* Rotate lockbar clockwise until safety spring pops up. Pull up on lid and run fingernails around its edge to determine that lid is secure.

To Take Out Film Slack. Rotate spindle wheels at back of magazine; take-up rotates counterclockwise; feed rotates clockwise.

Film-Loop Guard. Depress film loop against magazine mouth. Slide loop guard (with notch inward) over film and under retaining plate.

11.5g **Unloading**
In darkness, remove lid. Disengage take-up clamp (push outward) on collapsible core; turn magazine over and remove film. Place exposed roll in bag and can.

11.5h **Footage Counter**
At back of magazine. Subtractive in increments of 20 ft/5m.

11.6 ARRIFLEX 35 BL III, 35 BL 4 AND 35 BL 4s CAMERAS (FIG. 11–14)

NOTE: All directions are from the Operator's point of view.

The Arriflex 35 BL III, Arriflex 35 BL 4, and Arriflex 35 BL 4s, are essentially the same camera. They differ in their motors (see Sec. 11.6c),

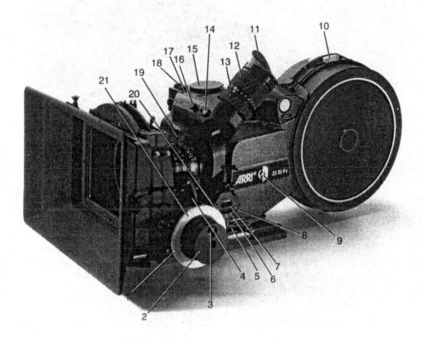

Figure 11–14a Arriflex BL 4s (left side). Courtesy of Arnold & Richter K.G.

1. Follow-focus marking disc
2. Follow-focus knob
3. Follow-focus gear-ratio knob
4. Follow-focus swing-arm gear
5. Camera On/Off button
6. Fps display
7. Footage/meter counter display
8. Reset button
9. Door latch
10. Magazine latch
11. Eyecup
12. Viewfinder focus barrel
13. Diopter scale
14. Prism release button
15. Video tap cover
16. Eyepiece lock
17. Bubble level
18. Arriglow On/Off switch
19. Inching button
20. Read button
21. Meter/footage switch (behind follow-focus knob)

viewing systems (see Sec. 11.6f), pitch adjustments (see Sec. 11.6k), lubrication (see Sec. 11.6p) and the type of magazines they use (see Sec. 11.7, 35 BL III Magazines and 35 BL 4 and 4s Magazines). Except where specifically noted, information herein applies to all three cameras.

11.6a Base
Bottom fitted with one 3/8″-16 tapped hole to accommodate tripod lockdown screw.

11.11b Motors
12-volt built-in crystal control is standard.

Figure 11–14b Arriflex BL 4s (right rear). Courtesy of Arnold & Richter K.G.

1. Main power connector
2. 11-pin Fischer accessory connector
3. Plastic fps/Hz selector switch cover
4. Magazine counter
5. Tape hook
6. Inching button (not visible)
7. 11-pin Fischer accessory connector
8. Time Code accessory connector
9. Carry handle
10. Magazine latch

Motor-Speed Selector Switch. Located at rear of camera. Permits the following crystal frame rates and frequencies:
BL III and BL 4:   24 fps 60 Hz; 25 fps 50 Hz.

WARNING: *BL 4 only:* Some rental houses have configured the 25 fps 50 Hz switch to 30 fps 60 HZ. ALWAYS verify fps speed on a rental by observing the tachometer!

BL 4s: 24 fps 60 Hz; 30 fps 60 Hz.

To Set Selector Switch to Desired fps/Hz Mode. Unscrew plastic cover at rear of camera. Slide switch to desired speed/Hz.

NOTE: There is NO reverse capability to any of the cameras.

Fuse. Under same window as fps/Hz switch.
  To Replace. Unscrew cover, pull fuse with ARRI clip or paperclip, and insert new fuse. Special fuse, available only from manufacturer, is rated at 0.75 amps. A spare 0.75 amp fuse is stored in slot marked "RES" (reserve) under the clear cap.

Volume Control Potentiometer. Below fuse window. Controls volume of audible signal of out-of-sync warning system.
  To Adjust Volume. Start camera, and flip-buckle-trip. With a screwdriver, rotate potentiometer to decrease or increase level.

Variable-Speed Motor. Requires variable-speed control accessory (see Sec. 11.30), which plugs into 11-pin Fischer plug at back of camera (see Sec. 11.6c Powerline). Accessory bypasses crystal control of camera.

To Vary Speed. Rotate rheostat on variable-speed control until tachometer on camera registers desired fps.

WARNING: Manufacturer recommends that 35 BL III be operated between 6 and 42 fps, and 35 BL 4 and 35 BL 4s between 6 and 40 fps in variable mode. *Faster speeds will damage camera!*

11.6c Powerline

Input to Camera: Four-pin Cannon female end of battery cable fits to recessed four-pin Cannon plug located at bottom rear of camera. Insert male end of cable into battery.

NOTE: Clockwise from keyway pin 1 is (−), pins 2 and 3 are unused, and pin 4 is + 12V.

ON/OFF Switch. Located in handgrip at right front of camera. Depress to start; depress to stop. Additional ON/OFF switch is at left front of camera below footage and fps counters.

CAUTION: Either ON/OFF switch can be used to start/stop camera, but if *both* switches are ON, camera continues *to run if only one switch is turned OFF.*

Handgrip. *To mount or adjust handgrip:* Align wingscrew on handgrip bracket to tapped hole in camera body; tighten in desired position; insert attached six-pin LEMO plug into right front receptacle on camera.

NOTE: Counterclockwise, with female half-moon portion of receptacle *up:* female pin 1 is + 12v, 2 is ground (−), pin 3 is continuation of circuit, male pins 4, 5, and 6 are blank.

11-pin Fischer Accessory Plug. Located above power plug. A second plug, located on top front of electronics housing. Both plugs serve numerous functions: variable-speed unit plug (see Sec. 11.30); remote ON/OFF switch that attaches to tripod handle, power out zoom motor, external sync control, rear-screen projection (master/slave camera and projector sync), or as a technician's monitor plug for various camera checkouts.

Red Blinking Indicator. At back of camera, indicates camera is running.

Fuses—BL III.
Electronics. 0.75 ampere pico, under the same window as the fps/Hz switch.
   To change. Unscrew cover, pull fuse with Hirschman clip or needlenose pliers; insert new fuse. Fuse is available at most electronic parts stores.

NOTE: A spare fuse is usually stored in a slot marked "RES" (Reserve) under the clear cap.

Motor. 15 ampere pico. *To change:* Remove right side cover of camera. The 15 amp pico fuse is located toward rear of camera.

CAUTION: Although right-side cover is secured with captive screws (which can't be lost), the thin gasket between cover and camera (for noise and dirt isolation) is extremely fragile. Remove, handle, and replace cover carefully!

BL 4 and BL 4s.
Electronics. 1 ampere pico, under the same window as the fps/Hz switch.

To change. Unscrew cover, pull fuse with Hirschman clip or needlenose pliers; insert new fuse. Fuse is available at most electronic parts stores.

NOTE: A spare fuse is usually stored in a slot marked "RES" (Reserve) under the clear cap.

Motor. 15 ampere pico.
To change. Remove right side cover of camera. The 15 amp pico fuse is located toward rear of camera.

CAUTION: Although right-side cover is secured with captive screws (which can't be lost), the thin gasket between cover and camera (for noise and dirt isolation) is extremely fragile. Remove, handle, and replace cover carefully!

Arriglow. 0.50 ampere pico located in Arriglow module.

CAUTION: Arriglow fuses are NOT field replaceable.

BL 4s Only.
Accessories. 3 ampere pico. *To change:* Remove right side cover of camera. Located near 15 amp fuse toward rear of camera. Loosen two screws at each end of the fuse wires, remove, and replace.

CAUTION: Although right-side cover is secured with captive screws (which can't be lost), the thin gasket between cover and camera (for noise and dirt isolation) is extremely fragile. Remove, handle, and replace cover carefully!

Volume-Control Rheostat. Forward of 0.75 amp fuse cover. Controls degree of loudness of out-of-sync warning system. *To adjust volume:* Turn motor-speed selector switch to "L", and rotate rheostat counterclockwise to decrease, clockwise to increase.

11.6e Lenses
To Mount Lens. Align notch in lens-mount flange with locator pin on upper left of camera port. Insert lens into camera, and turn lens locking ring counterclockwise.
To Remove. Grasp lens firmly; rotate lens locking ring clockwise, withdraw lens from lens port.

NOTE: The BL III, BL 4, and BL 4s do NOT require a lens housing.

11.6f Viewfinder
Reflex. Image magnified 6.5X.
To View through Lens. Push two round buttons inside eyecup clockwise to open.

NOTE: There is NO start-marking lamp module or flash in the viewfinder as in the 35 BL I and 35 BL II cameras.

To Align Reflex Mirror for Viewing. **BL III:** Open camera door, turn inching knob clockwise to align indicator mark on knob with the line on the movement block.

NOTE: Some BL III cameras may have been modified and fitted with an electronic inching button.

BL 4, BL 4s: Depress electronic inching button at front of electronics housing.

NOTE: Camera stops with shutter in viewing position except when shutter has been inched by hand (e.g., when threading).

To Focus Eyepiece. Rotate scalloped ring to focus on grain of groundglass.

To Replace. Be certain dull side of groundglass is DOWN. Insert goundglass holder into top of lens opening, slide toward aperture, and push UP.

To Alter Viewfinder Position for Viewing. **BL III:** Grasp viewfinder and rotate it perpendicular to the camera (viewfinder has an Abbey-Prism that automatically turns the image over).

BL 4, BL 4s: Depress the prism-release button on top of the viewfinder's elbow, and rotate the finder forward a minimum of 10°. Release the button, continue rotating viewfinder through 180° until the prism audibly clicks into position. Rotate viewfinder back to viewing position.

To Detach Eyepiece. Rotate clockwise the knurled ring forward of the eyepiece lock on the viewfinder and pull eyepiece from the keyed slots.

Arriglow. **BL 4 and BL 4s only:** Allows Operator to illuminate aperture framelines in the viewfinder when shooting in low-light-level situations.

To Illuminate/Extinguish Framelines. Rotate Arriglow potentiometer at top right of viewfinder assembly to turn on/off and/or increase/decrease intensity.

To Replace. Be sure dull side of groundglass is down. Insert groundglass holder into top of lens opening, slide toward aperture, and push up.

11.6g Matte Box

Six basic matte-boxes are available: the MB-14, MB-14W, MB-15, MB-16, LMB-3, LMB-4, and Standard (see Sec. 11.12, Matte-boxes and Filter Holders).

11.6h Filters

There is NO internal filter slot. All filters must be placed on the lens or in a matte-box. Filters that fit into matte-boxes vary in size, depending on the unit (see Sec. 11.12, Matte-boxes and Filter Holders).

11.6i Door

Hinged at front.

To Open. Rotate door lock counterclockwise. Swing door away from camera.

To Close. Swing door toward camera. Press in on upper right side of door. Rotate door lock clockwise to secure.

11.6j Magazines

122m (400 ft) and 304.8m (1000 ft).

To Mount. Slide movement block to first locking point (see Sec. 11.6k). Be certain that magazine lock is rotated counterclockwise *up* toward "AO" (aus-open). Align top steel guides and dovetails of magazine to dovetails on camera. Slide magazine toward power plugs until magazine reaches limit. Rotate magazine lock clockwise down to ZC (zu-close).

To Remove. Retract movement block (see Sec. 11.6k). Rotate magazine lock counterclockwise *up* toward "AO" (aus-open). Slide magazine toward loader until clear of camera.

WARNING: Upon removal of magazine, if transporting camera (in or out of its case), ALWAYS make certain that movement block is forward and the dust cover is on the camera. This prevents the movement block from being jarred from its forward position and breaking the reflex mirror. *NEVER transport a camera without its dust cover!*

11.6k Threading (Fig 11–15)

Before Mounting Magazine   (see Section 11.6j, Magazine).

1. Rotate knurled internal inching knob until scribe on knob aligns to scribe on movement block to retract dual registration pins and set the pulldown claws in position to engage perforations.
2. Depress movement-block-release lever located at left front inside camera opening toward loader.
3. Grasp top and bottom of movement block and slide toward rear.

NOTE: There are two distinct locking points in moving the block back. The first locking point is the threading position; the second locking point (all the way back) is for cleaning and access to the aperture plate and start-marking module.

Figure 11–15   BL 4s threading. Courtesy of Arnold & Richter K.G.

1. Upper loop scribe
2. Upper camera dovetail
3. Upper magazine dovetail
4. Magazine lock (closed)
5. Movement block cover
6. Movement block in forward position
7. Lower magazine dovetail
8. Lower camera dovetail
9. Buckle trip
10. Lower film loop
11. Movement-block release lever (not visible)
12. Perforation-alignment pin (depressed)
13. Internal inching knob

4. Remove the aperture plate and pressure plate (see Sec. 11.6q, To Remove Aperture Plate, WARNING) and clean. Slide movement block to first locking point for threading and mount magazine (see Sec. 11.6j, Magazine). Conform upper loop to indicator in interior of camera and place film perforation on perforation alignment pin to prevent film from slipping. Slide movement block forward (block will automatically depress perforation alignment pin and release film). Rotate internal inching knob to be certain that registration pins and pulldown claws have engaged film perforations properly. Depress ON/OFF switch in handgrip. Observe action of film. If satisfactory, close door and reset footage counter.

Pitch Control. **BL 4s only:** Built-in to minimize noise of movement. Correct setting of the pitch control might differ on each roll because of variations in rawstock perforation pitch and/or film shrinkage. Optimum setting of control is determined by ear while threaded filmstock is run through camera with door open and by adjusting the claw pivot point until the eccentric (movement) runs at its quietest.

To Adjust Pitch Control. Start camera. With film running, insert a 2mm Allen wrench into matching hex screw in movement block. Rotate wrench toward + or − for minimum noise.

11.6l Buckle-trip

Located below movement block. Roller on buckle-trip arm cuts out power when pulled up by a short lower loop or when film jams in camera. *To reset,* depress roller on buckle-trip arm down and toward rear.

11.6m Footage Counter

Additive LED (Light Emitting Diode) footage counter located at left front of camera displays 0–9999 in increments of 1 ft, then reverts to 0.

To Read. Depress button marked "READ" to view LED display.

To Reset. Depress READ and RESET buttons simultaneously.

NOTE: Having to depress both buttons prohibits accidental zeroing if reset button alone is hit.

NOTE: If footage counter loses display, it *cannot* be reset mechanically. Requires removing magazine from camera and running the camera until display reads previous footage total.

There is NO frame counter.

Slotted cap forward of counter contains a 4.05 volt battery for internal memory of footage counter. With battery in camera, counter will retain footage count for up to 12 hours before erasing information from display. Permits overnight storage of threaded camera, or long location moves, etc.

WARNING: *Red light* below tachometer glows when memory battery is low.

To Change 4.05-volt Battery. Unscrew coin-slotted cap, then *pull* battery.

NOTE: Prior to discarding battery, remove from camera, clean positive and negative ends, reinsert, and check. If red light still glows, replace battery.

Insert new battery with negative side facing *outward.*

WARNING: Newer cameras are fitted with a 5-year lithium battery (for memory), located inside the counter assembly and changeable only by a service shop.

11.6n Tachometer
LED display below footage counter registers fps only when camera runs.

11.6o Shutter
Variable. The 180° shutter can be adjusted to 135°, 144°, or 172.8°.

To Adjust Shutter Angle. Remove lens. While looking into lens port, open camera door, rotate inching knob until the adjustment hex screw located in the shutter is accessible through the lens port. Insert 2mm Allen wrench into the hex screw. Hold shutter with finger (avoid touching the mirror). Press lightly on the wrench and turn the adjustment screw gently until the shutter numbers rotate out from behind the mirror. Continue to rotate the adjustment hex screw until only a few degrees from the desired shutter angle. Release pressure on the Allen wrench, continue rotating, and allow the shutter to click into detente.

11.6p Lubrication (Fig. 11–16).
Manufacturer recommends two to three drops of oil on wicks in cam shaft reservoirs every 60,000 ft (every 6,000 ft, filming at high speed).

CAUTION: Manufacturer warns: Oiling too frequently and/or excessive oil can damage the movement.

35 BL 4s

WARNING: 35 BL 4s is NOT to be lubricated in the field. Its movement has oil-impregnated bearings and does not lubricate in same way as other 35BL models.

11.6q Cleaning
Optics. Clean with bulb syringe or soft camel's-hair brush. Manufacturer recommends the following maintenance *each time film is changed:* (1) Remove aperture and pressure plates.

WARNING: Before removing aperture and/or pressure plate, ALWAYS make sure that shutter is open (i.e., mirror on shutter is horizontal), by looking through the lens port (mirror cannot be seen, but pressure plate can), and/or by looking through the viewfinder and noting that the optics are obscured.

REPEAT: It is IMPORTANT to be sure the shutter is open *before removing the aperture plate!* This will avoid accidental chipping, cracking, or scratching of the mirror.

To Remove Aperture Plate. Slide movement block to its second position. (see Sec. 11.6k, Threading, NOTE regarding two distinct locking points.) Insert forefinger under aperture plate, lift, and pull toward rear.

To Replace. Insert top of aperture plate in guide-grooves, slide plate up, and push bottom toward lens until it clicks into place.

NOTE: The foregoing also applies when changing the camera's aperture plate for one with a different aspect ratio (e.g., 1.85 to a full aperture). A variety of aperture plates are available from the manufacturer, with matching groundglasses.

Figure 11–16 BL III and BL 4 lubrication. Courtesy of Arnold & Richter K.G.

1. Pressure plate
2. Pressure-plate reservoir
3. Camshaft reservoir
4. Camera steel guide
5. Upper dust-cover pilot hole
6. Camera dovetail
7. Magazine-catch coupling
8. Lower dust-cover pilot hole
9. Movement block (cover removed to illustrate use) in back position
10. Movement-block release lever
11. Perforation-alignment pin
12. Start-marking-lamp module
13. Aperture plate

To Remove Pressure Plate Lift pressure-plate spring (located above movement block) UP, and push pressure plate back.

To Replace. Be sure shoulder of pressure plate slides *under* pressure plate spring and seats into register plate before bringing spring down to secure pressure plate in place.

(To Continue Cleaning.) (2) Remove emulsion build-up with orange-wood stick. (3) Wipe plates with soft cotton handkerchief (not linen). (4) Use bulb syringe on camera interior to remove dust, dirt, etc.

11.6r Weight.
(With 122m (400 ft) load) 14.5 kilos (319 lb).

11.6s Troubleshooting

Trouble	*Probable Cause*
Camera will not start	Powerline connection faulty; buckle-trip not reset; battery dead; motor fuse blown.
Intermittent start and stop	Battery connections loose; broken connection in powerline.
Torn perforations; ripped film	Improper threading.

Door will not close	Dirt or film chip(s) in door; movement block not seated forward.
Viewing system blacked out	Shutter closed; eyepiece cap closed; lens cap on.
Lens will not focus	Lens not seated; camera too close for minimal distance of lens; elements damaged.
Cut-in on groundglass	Lens not seated; matte box extended.
Warning tone	Camera speed out of crystal sync; buckle-trip not reset.
Camera will not stop when switched to OFF	Other ON/OFF Switch in ON position.
LED footage counter erratic; gives false footage	Memory battery low; footage counter defective.

11.7 ARRIFLEX BL III, BL4, AND BL4s MAGAZINES (FIG. 11–17)

NOTE: Except where noted, the BL III, BL4, and BL4s Magazines are essentially the same.

11.7a Type
Co-axial.

11.7b Capacity
122m (400-ft) and 304.8m (1000-ft).

11.7c Lids
Two. Dog-locked.

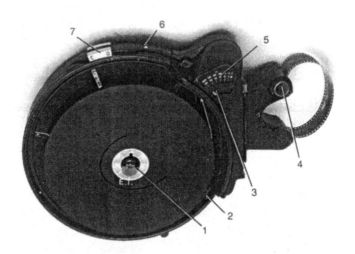

Figure 11–17a Arriflex BL4s magazine (feed side). Courtesy of Arnold & Richter K.G.

1. Core latch
2. Counter roller guide
3. Roller guide lever
4. Film-loading gear

5. Footage/meter counter
6. Loop marking notch
7. Feed side magazine lock

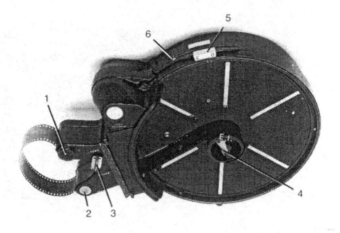

Figure 11–17b Arriflex BL4s magazine (take-up side). Courtesy of Arnold & Richter K.G.

1. Plastic disc (upper loop timing adjustment)
2. Lower loop timing adjustment
3. Magazine lock
4. Collapsible core
5. Cover lock
6. Loop marking notch

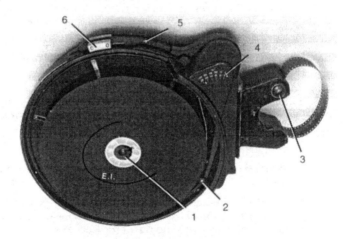

Figure 11–17c Arriflex BL III magazine (feed side). Courtesy of Arnold & Richter K.G.

1. Core
2. Counter roller-guide arm
3. Film-loading gear
4. Footage/meter counter
5. Loop marking notch
6. Cover lock

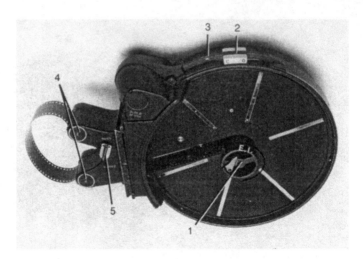

Figure 11–17d Arriflex BL III magazine (take-up side). Courtesy of Arnold & Richter K.G.

1. Collapsible core
2. Cover lock
3. Film-loading gear
4. Tapped thumb screw holes
5. Loop marking notch
6. Cover lock

To Remove. Lift magazine cover lock away from magazine rim and push to left; lift cover straight up.

11.7d Feed
Right half. (Magazine throat should be at the Loader's right, with magazine counter, magazine catch, and film-loading gear UP. Film wound emulsion in.) Pulls off spindle counterclockwise.

11.7e Take-up
Left half. (Magazine throat should be at Loader's left, magazine lock UP.) Film winds onto collapsible core clockwise, emulsion always in.

11.7f Loading
(1) Remove magazine cover.

BL III and BL4. (2) Move footage-counter roller-guide arm down and to the right until it locks into recessed guide.

BL4s. Does NOT have a footage-counter roller-guide arm that automatically lowers as film is expended (see Footage Counter, Sec. 11.7h). Counter arm remains up and out of the Loader's way.

(3) In darkness, remove film roll from can and bag. Insert film end into feed throat, slowly rotating knurled film-loading gear counterclockwise until gear in throat engages perforation. Continue rotating film-loading gear until film exits magazine.

NOTE: To expedite engagement of film in the magazine gears, cut the film so as to bisect a perforation.

(4) Place film on feed spindle making certain spindle key engages core keyway. (5) Replace feed cover.

BL III and BL4. Footage-counter roller-guide will automatically drop to edge of roll. (6) Be sure that rim of cover fits snugly into magazine guide grooves. Push magazine cover lock to right. Pull on cover to be certain cover is secure. (7) Flip magazine over, remove take-up cover.

NOTE: Take-up loading can be done in daylight.

(8) Bring film end back from magazine throat until film end extends to marking notch on top of magazine. Hold film-loading gear. Bring film end down and insert end into lower channel of magazine take-up throat. Rotate film-loading gear until perforation engages take-up gear and film moves into magazine.

CAUTION: It is important to maintain proper loop size. Do not allow excess film to exit feed side while trying to engage perforation into take-up gear.

(9) Insert film end into collapsible take-up core. Move clamp on core outward to secure film. (10) Replace take-up cover. Make sure that rim of cover fits snugly into magazine guide grooves. Push magazine cover lock to right. Pull on cover to be certain cover is secure.

BL4s. The BL4s is fitted with knurled inset *upper and lower loop timing gears* in the left side of the feed and take-up throats. The gears adjust the sprocket and quiet the magazine even more. (The BL III and BL4 magazines do not have this feature.)

Upper Loop Timing Adjustment. *Made with the magazine removed from the camera, and just before loading:* Rotate the clear plastic disc at the top magazine throat clockwise. Remove it for access to two half-moon gears divided by a perpendicular knurled thumbwheel in the center. Depress either gray half-circle gear to free the thumbwheel. Turn the thumbwheel toward − (minus) until resistance lessens, then turn it toward + (plus) until a slight resistance is felt. Inch the magazine by hand. As film moves forward, listen for a slight crinkling noise indicating that magazine is not properly adjusted for its quietest travel. If film moves forward silently, replace the plastic disc cover. If noise persists, turn the thumbwheel slightly in the opposite direction while inching the magazine until film travel is quietest. Replace plastic disc cover over upper-throat half-moon gears.

Lower Loop Timing Adjustment. *Made with the magazine on the camera and film threaded:* If an incorrect lower loop size is formed, make certain the camera is turned off; depress and rotate the lower full-circular gear in the bottom of the magazine throat to raise or lower the loop size.

11.7g Unloading

In darkness, remove take-up cover. Disengage clamp on core (push inward). Place index finger in core space, thumb on edge of roll. Turn magazine over and let film drop into the hand. Place exposed roll in bag and can.

11.7h Footage Counter

At right side of magazine. Subtractive dual counters: top counters registers footage; lower counter registers meters.

BL III and BL4. Magazines have a counter-arm wheel that rides the edge of the film and automatically registers the amount of film remaining in the magazine.

BL4s. Magazine has no film-riding wheel. To verify amount of footage in the magazine requires rotating a lever (near the counter) and bringing the wheel to meet the film. Upon release of lever, spring-action clears wheel from film roll.

NOTE: Some rental houses have removed the counter-arm wheel from BLIII and BL4 magazines and installed a lever similar to the BL4s for quieter operation.

11.7i Miscellaneous

BL4 and BL4s. *High-speed guide rollers:* When filming from 60 to 100 fps, a 35 BL 4 and 35 BL 4s magazine requires the attachment of high-speed guide rollers where the film loop exits and re-enters the magazine. *To mount rollers:* insert appropriately marked (top/bottom) high-speed roller-guide-locating-pin into pilothole and fasten screws on roller bracket into tapped thumbscrew hole.

NOTE: When magazine is threaded in camera, ALWAYS loop film *below* the top roller and *above* the lower roller.

11.8 ARRIFLEX 35 BL I AND 35 BL II CAMERAS* (FIGS. 11–18a and 11–18b)

NOTE: All directions are from the Operator's point of view.

The Arriflex 35 BL had many changes after serial number 35327. Earlier models are designated 35 BL I, later models 35 BL II. The internal casting in the 35 BL I had to be supplied with additional shock mountings; all 35 BL IIs are shock-mounted. Motors on the 35 BL II have about three times the torque of 35 BL I motors. The BL II has all new electronics. The BL I has a four-pulldown claw movement; the BL II has a two-pulldown claw movement (and is quieter as a result).

Differences will be noted under each model heading; except where specifically noted, information herein applies to both cameras.

11.8a Base

Bottom fitted with one 3/8"-16 tapped hole to accommodate tripod lockdown screw.

11.8b Motors

35 BL I. 14-volt built-in crystal control is standard.

35 BL II. 12-volt built-in crystal control is standard.

NOTE: Neither the 35BL I nor the 35BL II motor is interchangeable with other 35mm Arriflex camera models.

Motor-Speed Selector Switch. Located at right side of camera. Permits use of built-in motor in the following modes: 24 fps/60 Hz, 24fps/50 Hz, and 25fps/50 Hz.

NOTE: Switch is set to "L" (lights) only to test frame and edge-marking lamps visible in viewfinder (see Sec. 11.8g), and to test audible warning signal. In this mode, lights and signal remain constant. If lamps are extinguished or signal is inaudible, bulbs or circuitry of motor may have to be replaced.

To Set Selector Switch to Desired fps/Hz Mode. Insert screwdriver or coin into slot in switch, and move to desired fps/Hz mode.

---

*Manufacturer states that the designation "BL" stands for "blimped."

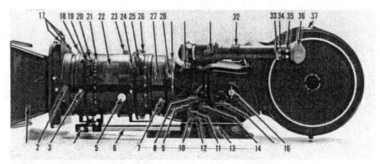

Figure 11–18a Left side 35BL I with 1000-ft magazine, zoom lens housing, and finder extension. Courtesy of Arnold & Richter K.G.

1. Sunshade
2. Optical ring
3. Lockdown screw
4. Housing-support bracket
5. Lens-support wing
6. Support rods
7. External housing lockdown screw
8. Reset button
9. Read button
10. Additional On/Off switch
11. 4.05 battery cap
12. fps counter
13. Cam lock
14. Footage counter
15. Inching lever
16. Door lock
17. Filter holders
18. Focus stops
19. Focus handle
20. Plug
21. Focus strip
22. Focus viewing window
23. Roof plug
24. Focal length strip
25. Zoom handle
26. Plug
27. Iris viewing window
28. Iris gear pin
29. Iris gear
30. Lens housing catch
31. Viewfinder extender
32. Retaining collar
33. Knurled ring
34. Eyepiece focus lock
35. Eyepiece focus ring
36. Eyecup
37. Take-up cover lock

NOTE: Neither camera has reverse capability.

WARNING: When using the accessory, the 35 BL I can be run at a speed of up to 100 fps; the BL II can only be run at speeds up to 50 fps.

11.8c Powerline

Input to Camera. Four-pin Cannon female end of battery cable fits to recessed four-pin Cannon plug located at bottom rear of camera. Insert male end of cable into battery.

NOTE: **35BL I**—Clockwise from the keyway, pin no. 1 is ground ($-$), pins no. 2 and 3 are blank; pin no. 4 is $+14$v.

35 BL II—Clockwise from keyway, pin no. 1 is ground ($-$), pins 2 and 3 are blank, pin no. 4 is $+12$v.

ON/OFF Switch.
35BL I and 35 BL II Located in handgrip at right front of camera. Depress to start; depress to stop.

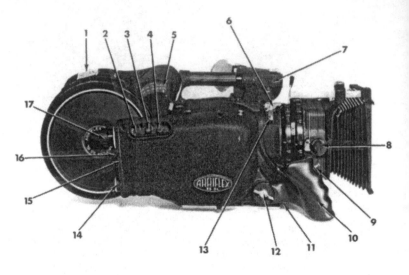

Figure 11–18b   Arriflex 35BL II (right side). Courtesy of Arnold & Richter K.G.

1. Feed-side magazine cover lock
2. Motor-speed selector switch
3. Fuse
4. Volume-control rheostat
5. Magazine footage counter
6. Lens-housing catch pin
7. Auxiliary boom accessory
8. Knurled knob
9. ON/OFF switch
10. Handgrip
11. Handgrip plug (not visible)
12. Wingscrew
13. Lens-lock release
14. Power plug
15. Technician's monitor plug (not visible)
16. Pilotone plug
17. Variable-speed accessory plug

35BL II only.   Additional ON/OFF switch is at left front of camera below footage and fps counters.

CAUTION: Either ON/OFF switch can be used to start/stop 35 BL II but if *both* switches are ON, camera will continue to run if only one switch is turned to OFF.

To Mount or Adjust Handgrip.   Align wingscrew on handgrip bracket to tapped hole in camera body; tighten in desired position; insert attached six-pin LEMO plug into right front receptacle on camera.

NOTE: Counterclockwise with female half-moon portion of receptacle *up:* female pin 1 is + 12v, pin 3 is continuation of circuit, male pins 4, 5, and 6 are unused.

Zoom-Lens Handgrip Bracket.   Required when using a varifocal lens. Lens housing (see Sec. 18.e) and handgrip must be removed from camera. Zoom lens bracket is mounted in tapped hole that normally accommodates the handgrip. The handgrip in turn is attached to the zoom-lens bracket as an aid to proper balance.

   Outlets (at back of camera): Five-pin capped military plug located at top rear is utilized on the 35 BL I and 35 BL II as an emergency direct connector to the motor, bypassing the electronic crystal circuitry.

NOTE: A special cable, fitted with five-pin outlet, fits to an Arriflex hi-speed 35 IIC Variable Speed Control Accessory (see Sec. 11.30, Fig. 11–53) when bypassing the circuitry.

CAUTION: On direct connection, the camera will run at a speed that depends on the voltage of the battery (there is NO governor in the camera).

WARNING: The 35BL I is designed to run 0–100 fps; the 35BL II is NOT designed to run faster than 50 fps.

WARNING: The five-pin capped military plug is a bridging plate and *must* be left in place at all other times. Removal of the cap will disengage the electronics and the camera will NOT run.

NOTE: Clockwise from keyway at 12 o'clock, pin 1 is ground (−), pins 2, 3, and 5 are unused, and pin 4 is (+).

Pilotone (5-pin Tuchel) Plug. For noncrystal-sync tape recorders, is located below military plug.

NOTE: Clockwise from keyway at 12 o'clock, pin 1 is sync pulse, pin 2 is common, pin 3 is + 12v bloop signal, pins 4 and 5 are bridged in male cable plug to activate the system.

11-Pin Fischer Accessory Plug. Located above input to camera plug. Serves four basic functions: (1) Variable-Speed Control Unit plug (see Sec. 11.30); (2) Remote ON/OFF switch, that attaches to tripod handle; (3) External Sync Control (for use with a TV camera or another 35BL, or for Rear-Screen Projection with camera and projector sync, etc.); (4) Technicians monitor plug for various camera checkouts.

Blinking Light. At back of camera (most models), indicates camera is running.

Start-Marking Lamps (Full-Frame and Edge-Marking). Mounted in a plug-in module located below camera aperture.

To Remove Module. Remove aperture plate (see Sec. 11.8q regarding aperture plate removal). Insert ARRI clip into hook on module. Pull toward rear.

NOTE: Invert module so that register pins are *up* and plug is toward Operator. Bulb at left is edge fogging lamp. Center bulb is full-frame fogging lamp. Bulb at right is "out-of-sync" monitor lamp (flashes red).

To Change Lamp in Module. Use tweezers to remove and insert.

To Insert. Align module register pins and plug to receptacle; push toward lens. Be sure that module is tight.

Fuses: BL I and BL II.

Electronics. 0.75 ampere pico, forward of Motor-speed Selector Switch.

To change. Unscrew cover, pull fuse with Hirschman clip or needlenose pliers; insert new fuse. Fuse in available at most electronic parts stores.

Motor. 15 ampere pico.

To change. Remove right side cover of camera. The 15 amp pico fuse is located toward rear of camera.

CAUTION: Although right-side cover is secured with captive screws (which can't be lost), the thin gasket between cover and camera (for noise and dirt isolation) is extremely fragile. Remove, handle, and replace cover carefully!

Volume-Control Rheostat. Forward of 0.75 amp fuse cover. Controls degree of loudness of out-of-sync warning system. To adjust volume, turn motor-speed selector switch to "L" and rotate rheostat counterclockwise to decrease, clockwise to increase.

11.8d Turret

None. Single lens port accepts Arriflex (standard and bayonet mount) lenses only.

11.8e Lens Housing

Fits to front of camera to cover lens. Unit has lens-viewing window, both focus and T-stop marking strip rings and holders, external lens-lock release, internal focus bracket, and internal T-stop bracket.

To Mount. (1) Be sure that lens is removed from camera. (2) Align dual register pins at base of housing to matching dual pilot holes at front of camera. (3) Tilt top of housing toward lens-housing catch.

CAUTION: Make certain that catch pin on housing is properly secured in catch before releasing.

To Remove. (1) Hold housing securely! (2) Depress catch pin lever at top of housing and remove.

Viewing window. At left side of camera; permits viewing of footage and T-stop scales on lens.

NOTE: Older housings may not have a window.

Focus and T-stop Marking Strips. Imprinted to match specific lenses.

To Insert Focus Strip. (1) Select strip that matches lens mounted on camera. (2) Place infinity end of strip into keyway (nearest viewfinder) at indicator arrow on keyway. (3) Slide strip into keyway until strip reaches its limit.

To Insert T-stop Strip. (1) Select strip that matches lens mounted on camera. (2) Place widest-aperture end of strip into keyway (nearest optical flat) at indicator arrow on keyway. (3) Slide strip into keyway until strip reaches its limit.

Coupling Alignment (Fig 11–19). To engage lens with focus and T-stop rings, (1) rotate knurled knob at right side of housing marked "Auf–Zu" (open–closed) to "Auf," and swing filter holder and sunshade away. (2) Make sure that witness mark on internal focus bracket aligns to matching witness mark on inside of housing. (3) Rotate internal T-stop bracket to 6 o'clock. (This will align T-stop strip widest-aperture mark to witness mark on left side of T-stop ring.) Make certain that bracket is flipped forward and down. (4) Set lens at infinity and at widest aperture. Insert lens into camera. (See Sec. 11.8f, Lenses, To Mount Lens, for detail of this.)

NOTE: Configuration of lens housing limits focal length of lens within housing to an 85 mm. Lenses longer than 85mm can be used on camera, but housing must be removed, so sound-deadening property of housing is lost.

(5) Close filter holder and rotate knurled knob to "Zu" (closed).

Adapter for Zeiss Super-Speed Lenses. When Zeiss Super-Speed lenses are used on the camera, a special adapter is necessary. Adapter is like a

Figure 11–19 Arriflex 35BL coupling detail of lens housing. Courtesy of Arnold & Richter K.G.

1. Witness mark
2. Internal-focus-bracket witness mark
3. Internal-focus-bracket pads
4. Spring-loaded hinge pins
5. Groundglass
6. Pressure plate
7. Internal T-stop bracket (partly raised to illustrate)
8. Lens bayonet lock
9. Lens lock (one of two)
10. "AUF-ZU" knurled knob catch
11. Internal lens-lock lever arms
12. External lens-lock levers (not visible)

standard housing, with the following exceptions: (1) Focus and T-stop strips are universal-type—i.e., it is not necessary to change strip at each lens change (just re-mark). (2) The focus is the front ring (nearest the optical flat). (3) The T-stop is the rear ring (nearest viewfinder).

Zoom-Lens Housing.

NOTE: When using a zoom-lens housing on 35BL I or 35BL II, it is essential that a bridgeplate (see Sec. 11.11 Bridgeplates) be used to support the camera and housing.

20–120 mm Lens Preparation. To use a zoom lens in a housing, an iris ring, a focal ring, a support ring, and a focus ring must be fitted to the lens.

CAUTION: The two halves of each adapter ring and the supporting ring must be installed with equal tension on each side (i.e., the space between the rings must be equidistant).

Iris Ring. Scribed with "T." Matched to T on lens when adapter is fitted to iris barrel. Catch-plate on ring faces forward.

Focal Ring. Scribed with "120." Aligned to 120 on lens barrel.

NOTE: Inside of ring is stepped and fits to lens barrel.

At infinity, catch-plate on ring is at 9 o'clock and faces forward.

Support Ring. Placed just short of touching the focal barrel. Female support receptacles are at 6 o'clock when lens is inserted into camera.

NOTE: *Always* rotate focal-length barrel to longest focal length before placing support ring on lens, to ensure full rotation of barrel.

NOTE: A 25–250mm lens has no support ring.

Focus Ring. Aligns to scribe on lens so that travel of focus is from 3 o'clock to 9 o'clock.

Catch-plate on ring is at infinity and faces toward Operator.

NOTE: Bevel inside ring snugs to focus barrel.

WARNING: Alignment of rings to scribed markings on the lens may vary, especially on the focus barrel, where the lens might have been collimated for a particular camera. Readjustment of rings is quite common.

Housing-to-Camera Adapter. Replaces standard lens housing. Adapter fits to front of camera *before* insertion of zoom lens. Unit has rotatable iris ring, one spring-loaded iris-engagement screw, two external housing lockdown screws (one at 2 o'clock, other at 7 o'clock), a viewing window cutout, and two rabbit ears that engage lens-release ears on lens mount.

To mount. (1) Make certain that lens is removed from camera. (2) Align dual register pins at base of adapter to matching dual pilot holes at front of camera. (3) Tilt top of adapter toward lens housing catch. (4) Insert zoom lens in port (see Sec. 11.8f To Mount Lens).

To remove. (1) Hold housing-to-camera adapter securely! (2) Depress levers at top of adapter, and remove.

20–120mm Lens Housing. Mounts to adapter *after* lens has been inserted into camera.

Viewing Windows. At left side of housing and adapter. Permits viewing of metric/footage scale, focal-length scale, and T-top scale of lens.

Housing Preparation. (1) Ascertain that the two housing-mounting screws on adapter (at 2 o'clock and 7 o'clock) are backed off counterclockwise approximately four revolutions. (2) Unscrew two bottom support wings from barrel, and remove roof support plug (to clear support ring on lens). (3) Back off all spring-loaded screws (two in housing, one in adapter) counterclockwise approximately four revolutions to clear focus, focal length, and iris ring on lens.

NOTE: The three threaded screws have internal spring-loaded pins that seat in the catch-plate on the rings.

To Mount Housing on Adapter. (1) Make certain that cap is on lens, to avoid accidental contact with front element. (2) Face front of adapter, place thumbs between support wings and housing; slide barrel over lens.

CAUTION: Make certain that wings are above support rods!

(3) Align and slide slots on housing (at 2 o'clock and 7 o'clock) to screws on adapter; tighten screws. (4) Push up on front of zoom lens. Push wings into housing, and tighten screws.

WARNING: Have each wing seated to support ring before tightening screws. Do **NOT** use the screw to draw the ring into the barrel! Doing so will strip the threads, rendering the housing useless.

(5) Release front of zoom lens after seating wings. (6) Insert roof plug, and tighten. (7) Tighten spring-loaded screw on adapter; rotate iris gear on adapter until spring-loaded pin engages catch-plate on T-stop ring of lens.

CAUTION: Check through viewing window to ascertain that iris settings rotate through complete range of T-stops.

(8) Tighten spring-loaded screw on focal gear; rotate focal-length gear on housing until spring-loaded pin engages plate on focal ring (audible click indicates engagement).

CAUTION: Check through viewing window to be sure that lens barrel rotates through full focal-length range. If not, remove housing, readjust focal ring on lens.

(9) Tighten spring-loaded screw on focus gear. Rotate focus gear on housing until spring-loaded pin engages catch-plate on focus ring (audible click indicates engagement).

CAUTION: Check through viewing window to ascertain that focus on lens rotates from 1 meter to infinity.

(10) Remove lens cap; insert 152mm (6″) round optical ring with glass toward subject until unit is seated on three spring-loaded ball bearings. Tighten lockdown screw (at 9 o'clock) to secure ring. (11) Slide housing-support bracket on rods until flush to the rear of the forward support. Place matte-box bracket and matte box on rods (see Sec. 11.12, Matte-Boxes).

Strips for Focal Length and Focus. Located forward of gears on housing.

NOTE: Manufacturer recommends grease-pencil or lead pencil for marking rings; ink stains strips, making them unusable.

Focus Point Stops. Two screws located forward of geared ring and strip.
To Use. Loosen screws, set focus at desired far/near (or both) focal point. Bring screw to stop on lens; tighten screw.

Focal-Length Stops. Two screws forward of geared ring and strip.
To Use. Loosen screws, set focal length wide/telephoto (or both). Bring screw to stop on lens; tighten screw.

Geared Rings. Here tapped holes to accommodate a wand for changing focal length (zooming) and/or focus.

11.8f Lenses

All standard lenses for the 35BL must be fitted with an adapter ring for diaphragm control, in order to adjust the lens diaphragm from exterior of lens housing.

Adapter Ring for Diaphragm Control. Special ring fits to barrel of lens. Projecting piece on ring engages adapter bracket in lens housing.

NOTE: Manufacturer states that 35 IIC lenses can be used but recommends factory installation of rings and calibration to a particular camera.

To Mount Lens. (1) Align maximum-aperture and infinity scribes to witness mark on lens. (2) Make sure that T-stop bracket inside housing is flipped forward and down. (3) Squeeze lens lock on housing, and slide lens into camera. (4) Release lens lock.

NOTE: Single ear of "wings" on lens slides *between* focus bracket pads.

(5) Flip T-stop bracket *up* to engage projection on diaphragm adapter ring.

11.8g Viewfinder
Reflex Image 6.5 × magnified.

To View through Lens. Press eye against eyecup to open automatic-closure device.

NOTE: Each time camera is started, start-marking lamp (see Sec. 11.8c) flashes in viewfinder.

To Lock Autoclosure Device Open. Pull eyecup from finder, rotate inner knurled locknut clockwise. Lock eyecup.

To Align Reflex Mirror for Viewing. Depress inching lever (in door) marked "SHUTTER."

NOTE: Camera stops with shutter in viewing position except when using variable-speed mode or when shutter has been inched by hand (e.g., when threading).

CAUTION: Do not depress lever while camera is running.

To Focus Eyepiece. Rotate narrow scalloped ring on eyepiece clockwise to "LOOSE." Rotate large scalloped ring nearest eyecup to focus on grain of groundglass. When focus is set, turn narrow ring counterclockwise to "FIX."

Groundglass. Located inside camera at top of lens mount (visible with lens removed and mirror shutter in viewing position).

To Change. (1) Remove lens. (2) Depress inching lever in door to rotate mirror shutter (to avoid possibility of scratching mirror). (3) Insert tweezers or paper-clip into hook of groundglass holder; push down and pull toward lens opening.

To Replace. (1) Make sure that dull side of groundglass is *up*. (2) Insert groundglass holder into top of lens opening, slide toward aperture and push up.

To Alter Finder Position for Viewing. 35 BL I: grasp finder, and rotate perpendicular to camera (up 90° or down 30° from normal viewing position). Viewfinder clicks into detent at normal viewing position but not into a detent in any other position; however, viewfinder will remain at angle selected.

35 BL II. Same as 35BL I except that viewfinder is tighter. Requires good grip on finder barrel.

WARNING: When viewfinder is fitted with an eyepiece extension, do *NOT* use the tube as a lever to change the eyepiece position or as a carrying handle! To do so will ruin the internal gearing and alter the position of the internal rotating prism, resulting in a false level reference! *DO* alter the eyepiece by turning it at a position close to its pivot point (at camera-prism box).

NOTE: Four screws in cap atop prism box can be removed so that a video tap can be mounted on the 35BL II (a factory conversion).

To Detach Eyepiece. Rotate clockwise the knurled ring forward of eyepiece lock on viewfinder, and pull eyepiece from keyed slots.

11.8h Sunshade

Fits to front of filter holders (see Sec. 11.8i). Sunshade/bellows slides forward and back on square boom that attaches to filter holders (see Sec. 11.8i) forward of lens housing.

To Mount. Slide lips at bottom of sunshade bracket under filter holder, tip toward camera until sunshade snap catch engages catch on filter holders.

Auxiliary Boom Accessory. At top of camera, forward of carrying handle; accepts sunshade boom when using lenses longer than 85mm.

11.8i Filters

Removable filter holders accommodate two 101.6×101.6mm (4in $\times$ 4in) filters and one 76.2×76.2mm (3in $\times$ 3in) optical flat. (Earlier models only accommodate one filter.)

WARNING: Always use an optical flat to block camera noise that may travel through lens into shooting area. Optical flat for 35BL is approximately 1/4″ thick. Manufacturer states that filters of same size and thicknesses as optical flat are available for exterior filming.

To Insert or Remove Optical Flat. Rotate knurled knob at right side of lens housing marked "Auf–Zu" (open–closed) to "Auf." Swing filter holders away. Grasp optical flat holder, depress locking pin, and lower it *gently* 90°. Insert or remove optical flat. Lift holder 90° to lock into place.

To Remove Dual-Filter Holder Unit. Squeeze spring-loaded hinge pins at left front of lens housing until pins clear bracket mounts on lens housing. Slide away.

NOTE: Removal of filter holders will also remove sunshade (see Sec. 11.8h).

The 35BL I and 35BL II has *NO* internal filter slot.

11.8j Door

Hinged at front.

To Open. Rotate door lock counterclockwise toward "AO" (aus–open). Swing door in a horizontal plane away from camera.

To Close. Swing door toward camera. Press in on upper right side of door. Rotate door lock clockwise toward "ZC" (zu–close) to secure.

11.8k Magazines

122m (400 ft) and 304.8m (1000 ft)

To Mount. (1) Slide movement block to first locking point (see Sec 11.8l). (2) Make sure that magazine lock is rotated counterclockwise *up* toward "AO" (aus–open). (3) Align top steel guides and dovetails of magazines to dovetails on camera. (4) Slide magazine toward power plugs until magazine reaches limit. (5) Rotate magazine lock clockwise down to "ZC" (zu–close).

To Remove. (1) Retract movement block (see Sec. 11.8l). (2) Rotate magazine lock counterclockwise *up* toward "AO" (aus–open). (3) Slide magazine toward loader until clear of camera.

WARNING: If magazine is not mounted on camera and camera is being transported (in *or* out of its case), *ALWAYS* be sure movement block is forward and dust cover is on the camera to prevent the movement block from being jarred from its forward position and thereby breaking the reflex mirror a major factory overhaul. NEVER transport the camera without its cover.

11.8l Threading (Fig 11–20)

Before Mounting Magazine *(See Sec. 11.8k, Magazines):*

   1. Rotate knurled internal inching knob until scribe on knob aligns to scribe on movement block to retract dual registration pins and set the pulldown claws in position to engage perforations.
   2. Depress movement-block-release lever located at left front inside camera opening toward loader.
   3. Grasp top and bottom of movement block and slide toward rear.

NOTE: There are two distinct locking points in moving the block back. The first locking point is the threading position; the second locking point (all the way back) is for cleaning and access to the aperture plate and start-marking module.

   4. Remove the aperture plate and pressure plate (see Sec. 11.8r, To Remove Aperture Plate, WARNING) and clean. Reinsert both. (5) Slide

Figure 11–20   Arriflex 35BL threading. Courtesy of Arnold & Richter K.G.

1. Upper loop scribe	9. Buckle trip
2. Upper camera dovetail	10. Lower film loop
3. Upper magazine dovetail	11. Movement-block release lever
4. Magazine lock (closed)	(not visible)
5. Movement block cover	12. Perforation-alignment pin
6. Movement block in forward position	(depressed)
7. Lower magazine dovetail	13. Internal inching knob
8. Lower camera dovetail	

movement block to first locking point for threading and mount magazine (see Sec. 11.8k, Magazines). (6) Conform upper loop to indicator in interior of camera and place film perforation on perforation alignment pin to prevent film from slipping. (7) Slide movement block forward (block will automatically depress perforation alignment pin and release film). (8) Rotate internal inching knob to be certain that registration pins and pulldown claws have engaged film perforations properly. (9) Depress ON/OFF switch in handgrip. Observe action of film. If satisfactory, close door and reset footage counter.

11.8m Buckle-trip

Located below movement block. Roller on the buckle-trip arm cuts out power when pulled up by a short lower loop or when film piles up in camera. *To reset,* depress roller on buckle-trip arm down and toward rear.

11.8n Footage Counter

35BL-I. Located at left front of camera above tachometer. Additive Counter registers 0–9999, in increments of 1 ft, then reverts to 0.

To Reset. Depress reset button (at left of counter) continuously until counter reverts to 0.

NOTE: There is *no* frame counter.

35BL-II. Additive LED footage counter located at left front of camera displays 0–9999 in increments of one foot, then reverts to zero.

To Read. Depress button marked READ to view LED display.

To Reset. Depress READ and RESET buttons simultaneously.

NOTE: Having to depress both buttons prohibits accidental zeroing if reset button alone is hit.

NOTE: If footage counter loses display, it cannot be reset mechanically. Requires removing magazine from camera and running camera until display reads previous footage total.

There is *no* frame counter.

Slotted cap forward of counter contains a 4.05-volt memory battery for footage counter. With battery in camera, counter will retain footage display up to 12 hours before erasing information. Permits overnight storage of camera with film in it or long locations moves, etc.

To change 4.05-volt battery, unscrew coin-slotted cap, and pull battery. Insert new battery, with negative side facing outward.

NOTE: Prior to discarding battery, clean positive and negative ends, reinsert, and check. If red light still glows, replace battery.

NOTE: Some cameras are fitted with a tiny red light below the fps display that will glow when memory battery is low.

11.8o Tachometer

35BL I. At left front of footage counter. Registers speed from 0 to 100 fps in increments of two frames.

35BL II. Below footage counter. LED display registers only when camera runs. Registers speeds from 6–50 fps in increments of one frame.

11.8p Shutter

Nonadjustable. Equivalent to 180°.

11.8q Lubrication (Fig. 11–21)

Manufacturer recommends two to three drops of oil on wicks in cam shaft reservoirs every 60,000 ft (every 6,000 ft when filming at high speed).

CAUTION: Manufacturer warns that oiling too frequently and/or excessive oiling can damage the movement.

11.8r Cleaning

Optics. Clean with bulb syringe or soft camel's-hair brush. Manufacturer recommends the following maintenance *each time film is changed:* (1) Remove aperture and pressure plates.

WARNING: Before removing aperture and/or pressure plate, ALWAYS make sure that shutter is open (i.e., mirror on shutter is horizontal), by looking through the lens port (mirror cannot be seen, but pressure plate can), and/or by looking through the viewfinder and noting that the optics are obscured.

REPEAT: It is IMPORTANT to be sure the shutter is open *before removing the aperture plate!* This will avoid accidental chipping, cracking, or scratching of the mirror.

To Remove Aperture Plate. Slide movement block to its second position (see Sec. 11.8r Threading, NOTE, re two distinct locking points). Insert forefinger under aperture plate, lift, and pull toward rear.

Figure 11–21 Arriflex 35BL lubrication and cleaning detail. Courtesy of Arnold & Richter K.G.

1. Pressure plate
2. Pressure-plate spring
3. Camshaft reservoir
4. Camera steel guide
5. Upper dust-cover pilot hole
6. Camera dovetail
7. Magazine-catch coupling
8. Lower dust-cover pilot hole
9. Movement block (cover removed to illustrate use) in back position
10. Movement-block release lever
11. Perforation-alignment pin
12. Start-marking-lamp module
13. Aperture plate

To Replace. Insert top of aperture plate in guide-grooves, slide plate up, and push bottom toward lens until it clicks into place.

NOTE: The foregoing also applies when changing the camera's aperture plate for one with a different aspect ratio (e.g., 1.85 to a full aperture etc.). A variety of aperture plates are available from the manufacturer, with matching groundglasses.

To Remove Pressure Plate. Lift pressure-plate spring (located above movement block) UP, and push pressure plate back.

To Replace. Be sure shoulder of pressure plate slides *under* pressure-plate spring and seats into register plate before bringing spring down to secure pressure plate in place.

(To Continue Cleaning): (2) Remove emulsion build-up with orange-wood stick. (3) Wipe plates with soft cotton handkerchief (not linen). (4) Use bulb syringe on camera interior to remove dust, dirt, etc.

To Replace. Make certain that shoulder of pressure plate slides *under* pressure-plate spring and seats tightly into register plate before bringing spring down to secure pressure plate in place.

11.8s Weight

with 122mm (400 ft) load: 11.34 kg (25 lbs); with 304.8m (1000 ft) load: 12.7 kg (28 lbs).

11.8t Troubleshooting

Trouble	*Probable Cause*
Camera will not start	Powerline connection faulty; buckle-trip not reset; battery dead; motor fuse blown.
Intermittent start and stop	Battery connections loose; broken connection in powerline.
Torn perforations; ripped film	Improper threading.
Door will not close	Dirt or film chip(s) in door; movement block not seated forward.
Viewing system blacked out	Shutter closed; eyepiece cap closed; lens cap on.
Lens will not focus	Lens not seated; camera too close for minimal distance of lens; elements damaged.
Cut-in on groundglass	Lens not seated; sunshade bellows extended.
Lens will not enter port	Guide-key in camera mount bent.
Flashing light in viewfinder and warning buzzer	Camera speed out of crystal sync; buckle-trip not reset.
Camera will not stop when switched to OFF	Other ON/OFF Switch in ON position.
LED footage counter erratic; gives false footage	Memory battery low.

11.0 ARRIFLEX 35 BL I AND BL II MAGAZINES (FIGS. 11–22a and 11.22b)

NOTE: Except where otherwise indicated, operation, specifications, and care for Arriflex 35BL I and BL II magazines are identical.

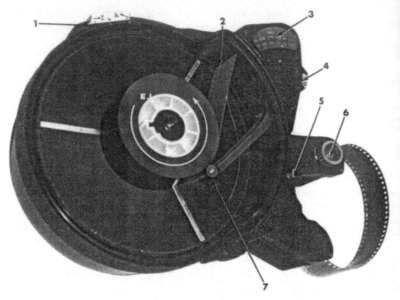

Figure 11–22a Arriflex 35BL magazine (feed side). Courtesy of Arnold & Richter K.G.

1. Feed-magazine cover lock
2. Feed throat
3. Footage counter
4. Magazine steel guide
5. Magazine catch
6. Film loading gear
7. Footage-counter roller-guide-arm

11.9a Type
Coaxial.

11.9b Capacity
122m (400 ft) (shown) and 304.8m (1000 ft).

11.9c Lids
Two. Dog-locked.
   To remove. Lift magazine cover lock *away* from magazine rim, and push to left; lift cover straight up.

11.9d Feed
Right half. (Magazine throat should be at Loader's right, with magazine counter, magazine catch, and film-loading gear *up*.) Film (wound emulsion in) pulls off spindle counterclockwise.

11.9e Take-up
Left half. (Magazine throat should be at Loader's left, magazine lock *up*.) Film winds onto collapsible core clockwise, emulsion always in.

11.9f Loading
(1) Remove magazine cover, and move *footage-counter roller-guide arm* down and to right until it locks into recessed guide. (2) In darkness, remove film roll from can and bag. Insert film end into feed throat, slowly rotating knurled film-loading gear counterclockwise until gear in throat engages perforation. Continue rotating film-loading gear until film exits magazine.

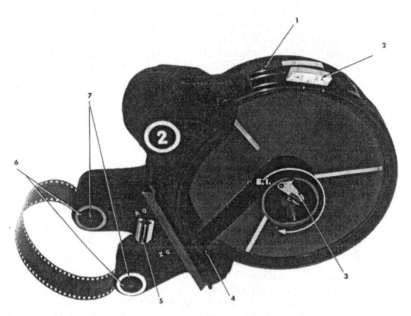

Figure 11–22b Arriflex 35BL magazine (take-up side). Courtesy of Arnold & Richter K.G.

1. Loop-marking notch
2. Take-up magazine cover lock
3. Collapsible core
4. Take-up throat
5. Magazine lock (open)
6. Pilot holes
7. Tapped thumb-screw holes

NOTE: To expedite engagement of film in magazine gears, cut film to bisect a perforation.

(3) Place film roll on *feed spindle,* make sure that *spindle key* engages *core keyway.* (4) Replace feed cover. Footage-counter roller-guide arm will automatically drop to edge of roll. Make sure that rim of cover fits snugly into magazine guide grooves. Push *magazine-cover lock* to right. Pull on cover to be sure that cover is secure. (5) Flip magazine over, and remove take-up cover.

NOTE: Take-up loading may be done in light.

(6) Bring film end back from magazine throat until film end extends to marking notch on top of magazine. Hold *film-loading gear.* Bring film end down, and insert end into lower channel of magazine take-up gear, as film moves into magazine.

CAUTION: It is important to maintain proper loop size. Do not allow excess film to exit feed side while trying to engage perforation in take-up gear.

(7) Insert film end into collapsible take-up core. Move clamp on core outward to secure film. (8) Replace take-up cover. Make sure that rim of cover fits snugly into magazine guide grooves. Push magazine-cover lock to right. Pull on cover to be sure that cover is secure.

High-Speed Guide Rollers. When filming from 60 to 100 fps, a 35BL I/35BL II magazine requires attachment of high-speed guide rollers where film loop exits and reenters magazine. *To mount rollers,* insert appropriately marked (top/bottom) high-speed roller-guide locating pin into pilot hole, and fasten screws on roller bracket into tapped thumbscrew hole.

NOTE: When magazine is threaded in camera, *ALWAYS* loop film below top roller and above lower roller.

Film-Loop Guard. 35BL has no film-loop guard but does have a magazine-throat protector.

11.9g Unloading
In darkness, remove take-up cover. Disengage clamp on core (push inward). Place index finger in core space, thumb on edge of roll. Turn magazine over, and let film drop into hand. Place in bag and can.

11.9h Footage Counter
Subtractive dual counters at right side of magazine. Top counter registers footage of polyester (thin base) film; lower counter registers acetate (standard base) film.

11.10 ARRIFLEX 35mm VIEWFINDER EXTENDER (FIG. 11–23)
The 22.86cm (9″) Arriflex 35mm viewfinder extender inserts between viewfinder and eyepiece to extend the eyepiece behind the camera to allow ease of operation when camera is mounted on tripod or geared head.

Two types of 35mm viewfinder extenders are available: *Straight* and *Anamorphic.*

Straight Viewfinder Extender. Does not have a housing with a 3-position lever. It cannot be used with anamorphic lenses, nor can it be closed off to prevent stray light from entering the eyepiece and "kicking back" onto the film.

Figure 11–23 35BL viewfinder extender. Courtesy of Arnold & Richter K.G.

1. Camera attachment threads
2. Magnifier ring
3. Barrel
4. Leveler-rod support

Anamorphic Viewfinder Extender. Contains a housing with internal optics controlled by a 3-position lever that, depending on the lens in use (spherical or anamorphic), permits in position 1 (lever up): viewing of a standard full aperture, or position 2 (lever parallel): viewing of an unsqueezed anamorphic aperture. Position 3 (lever down) closes the entire viewing system so that stray light will not enter the eyepiece and "kickback" onto the film.

11.10a Retaining Collar
Older finders have a *filter holder,* in which a circular contrast filter may be inserted while checking the lighting of a scene and then filter is retained or withdrawn when filming begins.

NOTE: On an anamorphic extender, the holder is inserted or removed at bottom; on standard extender, the holder is inserted or removed at the top.

Access to Filter Holder. Rotate retaining collar until holder is exposed. Remove. When holder is reinserted, retaining collar must be rotated to close over it.

CAUTION: Failure to close retaining collar can result in loss of filter holder and in stray light entering extender, and "kicking back" onto film.

11.10b Mounting

Anamorphic Extender. (1) Remove eyepiece from camera by rotating knurled locknut on viewfinder. (2) Align pins and threads on *small barrel* to viewfinder. Secure with knurled locknut. (3) Align pins and threads on eyepiece to large barrel on extender. Secure with knurled locknut.
Straight Extender.
NOTE: Straight extender is mounted opposite of the anamorphic extender.

(1) Remove eyepiece from camera by rotating knurled locknut on viewfinder. (2) Align pins and threads on *large barrel* of extension tube to viewfinder. Secure with knurled locknut. (3) Align pins and threads on eyepiece to small barrel on extender. Secure with knurled locking nut.

NOTE: With either finder extender in place, all adjustments noted in Section 11.6f and 11.8g Viewfinder, apply.

11.11 ARRIFLEX 35mm BRIDGEPLATES

11.11a BP-5 Bridgeplate (Fig. 11–24a)
The BP-5 bridgeplate accommodates all flat base cameras. It is not exclusive to the 535 as many Cinematographers assume.
Unit consists of (a) a sliding top plate; (b) a base plate; (c) support rods.

Sliding Top Plate. Fitted with two 38″-16 captive screws, a Cam-action Locking Lever at its left side, and two channels that accommodate support rods at its front. Attaches to base of 535 camera with the two captive screws.

NOTE: To use the Sliding Top Plate when filming Super 35, the engraved inset plate in the unit must be reversed. (See Section 11.1g, Super 35mm Conversion).

To Reverse Inset Plate. Remove the three screws and rotate the engraved top plate 180°; reinstall the screws.

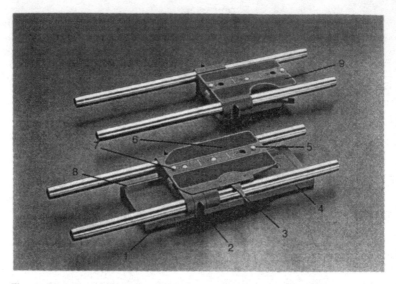

Figure 11–24a Arriflex 35mm bridgeplates. Courtesy of Arnold & Richter K.G.

1. Model BP5 Base plate
2. Support rod locking lever
3. Locking lever
4. Spring-loaded safety pin (not visible)
5. ⅜"-16 lockdown screw
6. Sliding top plate
7. Camera base pilot pin
8. Fixed stop screw (not visible)
9. Model BP6 Bridgeplate

Dovetailed bottom of top plate slides into matching dovetail of base plate.

Base Plate. Attaches to either a 3/8"-16 lockdown screw on a quick-release plate, on a tripod, or on a geared head tilt plate (see Chapter 9 for details of mounting).

A fixed stopscrew in the right front of the base always points forward; a spring-loaded safety-pin is always placed at the rear of the plate and to the Operator's left.

Dovetailed top of base plate accepts matching dovetailed bottom of top plate.

Support Rods. Insert into channels in the base plate and are secured in place with Support Rod Locking Levers. BP-15 rods are 43.18cm (17") in length × 19mm in diameter, although shorter lengths are available.

WARNING: BP-5 Bridgeplates have 15mm diameter rods. It is important to check rod diameter so that matte-boxes and other accessories will fit properly!

To Assemble BP-3 Bridgeplate. Depress safety-pin at left rear of base-plate. Align dovetails of both plates and slide the top plate forward onto the base plate until the spring-loaded pin pops up again.

CAUTION: Always ascertain that spring-loaded pin pops up after sliding top plate is forward.

Top plate can now be moved back and forth (slide) on the base plate.

To Secure Sliding Top Plate on Base Plate. Tighten Cam-action Locking Lever at left side of top plate.

To Remove Top Plate from Base. Loosen the Cam-action Locking Lever, depress the spring-loaded pin, and pull the top plate toward the Operator and away.

11.11b Old-Style Bridgeplate (Fig. 11–24*b*)

The Old-Style Bridgeplate accommodates any flat-base camera. Unit consists of (a) a sliding top plate, (b) a base plate, and (c) support rods.

Sliding Top Plate. Fitted with a 3/8"-16 wingnut camera lockdown screw in its center, a spring-loaded location pin that inserts into matching hole in camera base at the top-front, a Cam-action Locking Lever at its left side, and two channels that accommodate support rods at its front. Attaches to base of camera with the location pin and camera lockdown screw.

Dovetailed bottom of top plate slides into matching dovetailed top of base plate.

Figure 11–24*b* Arriflex old-style bridgeplate. Courtesy of Arnold & Richter K.G.

1. Sliding top plate
2. Camera lock-down screw
3. $\frac{3}{8}$"-16 tapped holes
4. Support rod screw
5. Spring-loaded location pin
6. Support rods
7. Cam-action locking lever
8. Support rod screw
9. Spring-loaded pin
10. $\frac{3}{8}$"-16 tapped holes
11. Base plate
12. Stop screw
13. Mfr's name always points forward.

Base Plate. Has three 3/8″-16 tapped holes at its bottom to accommodate a tripod/tiltplate lockdown screw (see Chapter 9 for details of mounting).

A fixed stopscrew in the right front of the base always points forward; a spring-loaded safety pin is always placed at the rear of the plate and to the Operator's left.

Dovetailed top of base plate accepts matching dovetailed bottom of top plate.

Support Rods. Insert into channels in the base plate and secured with Support Rod Screws. Old-Style rods are 25.4cm (10-in) in length × 15mm in diameter, although shorter lengths are available.

To Assemble Old-Style Bridgeplate. Depress safety pin at left rear of baseplate. Align dovetails of both plates and slide the top plate forward onto the base plate until the spring-loaded pin pops up again.

CAUTION: Always ascertain that spring-loaded pin pops up after top plate is forward.

Top plate can now be moved back and forth on the base plate.

To Secure Sliding Top Plate on Base Plate. Tighten Cam-action Locking Lever at left side of base plate.

To Remove Sliding Top Plate from Base Plate. Loosen the Cam-action Locking Lever in base plate, depress the spring-loaded pin, and pull the top plate toward the Operator and away.

11.12 MATTE-BOXES (MB-14W, MB-14, MB-15, MB-16, LMB-3, LMB-4, AND 35-BL PRODUCTION TYPE) AND FILTER HOLDERS (Figs. 11–25a and 11–25b)

The following matte-boxes are used with the 535, 535B, 35-III, 35BL-3, 35BL-4, 35BL-4s, and 16SR-2 cameras.

11.12a MB-14W

The MB-14W (wide angle) (not shown) is especially made for use with a 10mm Zeiss lens. It has two independently rotating 167.6mm × 167.6mm (6.6 × 6.6 in.) filter stages. Each stage holds two filter frames. The stages can be separated and are removable.

NOTE: The MB-14W has only one geared filter frame, which allows for a graduated filter to be raised or lowered during a shot.

A 101.6mm × 101.6mm (4 × 4 in.) filter stage can be used in place of the 167.6mm × 167.6mm (6.6 × 6.6 in.) stage.

11.12b MB-14 (Fig. 11–25a)

The MB-14 is used with lenses 12mm and longer. It accepts three, four, or six independently rotating 167.6mm × 167.6mm (6.6 × 6.6 in.) filter stages. Each stage holds two filter frames. The stages can be separated and are removable.

NOTE: The MB-14 has one geared frame in each stage so that numerous graduated filters can be raised or lowered during a shot.

A 101.6mm × 101.6mm (4 × 4 in.) filter stage can be used in place of the 167.6mm × 167.6mm (6.6 × 6.6 in.) stage.

The rear of both the MB-14W/MB-14 matte boxes holds either a 152mm (6 in.), 138mm (5.4 in.), or 114mm (4.5 in.) filter ring, and/or an item the manufacturer calls a reflex prevention ring (a circular piece of metal intended to prevent light rays from striking the back of a filter and reflecting into the lens).

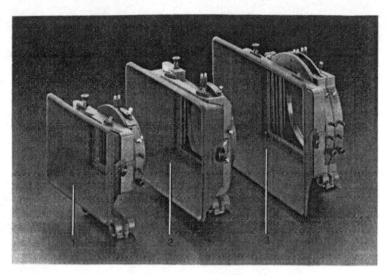

Figure 11–25a 535 Matte-boxes. Courtesy of Arnold & Richter K.G.

1. MB16   3. MB14
2. MB15

11.12c MB-15

The MB-15 is used with lenses 14mm and longer. It has two 127mm ×
152mm (5 × 6 in.) filter stages. The rear of the matte box will hold a
152mm (6 in.), 138mm (5.4 in.) or 114mm (4.5 in.) filter ring and/or a
reflex prevention ring and has essentially the same appropriate gears and
levers on the insertion/adjustment of the stages as the MB-14W.

11.12d MB-16

The MB-16 is used with lenses 16mm and longer. It has two 101.6 ×
101.6mm (4 × 4 in.) filter stages. The rear of the matte box will hold a
114mm (4.5 in.) filter ring and/or a reflex prevention ring and has
essentially the same appropriate gears and levers on the insertion/
adjustment of the stages of the MB-14.

NOTE: The MB-14W, MB-14, and MB-16 matte-boxes are hinged on the
camera right side and open laterally for access to lenses, etc. The MB-15
matte-box is NOT hinged.

The top of each sunshade is fitted with *lockdown knobs* to hold an
accessory bracket (not shown).

To Mount Either Matte-Box Cited Above.   Insert two long *43cm (17 in.) rods*
into a Bridgeplate (see Sec. 11.3a) and secure with set screws. Slide
L-bracket onto long rods. Insert short 15.24cm (6 in.) *eccentric (rotatable
off-center) rod* into top channel of bracket, and short 15.24cm (6 in.) *geared
(serrated) rod* into lower channel and secure. Align lower matte-box channel
to geared rod, rotate upper eccentric rod, and align to fit to upper matte-box
channel. Rotate bracket knob SLOWLY; allow internal teeth in bracket to
grasp ridges of lower rod and bring matte-box onto rods. Adjust matte-box
to lens; rotate *sunshade lock* to secure.

To Insert Filter Holder into Matte-Box.   Loosen appropriate knurled *holder
lock* (one of four) at side of *filter stage*. Insert *filter holder* from top.
Snug—do not tighten—the holder lock screw.

To Remove Either Stage from Sunshade. Slide *stage lock lever* forward, slide stage horizontally toward Operator's left.

To Rotate Either Stage. Unscrew *rotating stage lock* (top knurled knob) in desired stage, rotate.

To Rotate Round Filter in Matte-Box. Unscrew knurled *round filter lock,* rotate.

To Raise/Lower Graduated Filter. Rotate *filter gear knob.*

NOTE: Each filter gear knob accepts a "follow-focus whip" which inserts into the knob for ease of movement of the graduated filter.

11.12e LMB-3

The LMB-3 matte box is attached directly to a lens (having an 80mm diameter) by snugging the unit's clamp-ring screw. It has two 101.6mm × 101.6mm (4 × 4 in.) filter stages. The unit is attached directly to a lens having an 80mm diameter by snugging the unit's clamp ring screw. The LMB-3's most prevalent use is when the camera is in the hand-held mode.

11.12f LMB-4

The LMB-4 (not shown) matte-box is attached directly to a 10mm Zeiss lens by snugging the unit's clamp-ring screw. It has two 101.5mm × 101.5mm (4 × 4 in.) filter stages.

The following matte-box is used with the 35 BL I, and 35 BL II.

11.12g 35 BL Production Type Matte-Box (Fig. 11–25b)

Manufactured prior to the above-mentioned units and is often encountered when using the older Bridgeplate (See Sec. 11.11). Consists of: (a) 38.1 cm (15 in.) length rods, (b) a bracket, (c) 15.24cm (6 in.) length rods, and (d) filter holders with sunshade.

a. *38.1cm (15 in.) rods:* Used in place of 25.4cm (10 in.) length rods that are standard with the old Bridgeplate. Rear of the rods are placed flush to the rear of the rod channel openings in the Bridgeplate base.

NOTE: Early Bridgeplates have closed-end channels which restrict the depth of seating of the rods.

b. *Bracket:* Fitted with four rod channels. Two side channels accept 15.24cm (6 in.) rods; lower two channels slide on to 38.1cm (15 in.) rods in the Bridgeplate base.

c. *15.24cm (6 in.) rods:* Insert into side channels of bracket. Rear of rods fit flush to rear of channel openings in the bracket.

d. *Filter holders:* Side channels on bracket slide on to 15.24 (6 in.) rods.

Unit accepts two 165mm × 165mm (6.5 × 6.5 in.) square filters and one 152mm (6 in.) round filter. Square filter stages rotate. Slots in square filter stages accommodate filter holders. Filter-retaining screws secure holders in place.

WARNING: If filter slots in the square stages are vertical and the retaining screws loosen, the filter will drop out of the stage. Always rotate stages so that the filter holders slide into the stage from the side, and the filter-retaining screws are at the top.

Rotatable 152mm (6 in.) round filter is held in place by pressure-springs.

11.13 ARRIFLEX 35 IIC AND 35 3C CAMERAS (FIGS. 11–26a and 11–26b)

NOTE: All directions are from the Operator's point of view.

Figure 11–25b Arriflex production matte box. Courtesy of Arnold & Richter K.G.

1. Sunshade
2. 165mm square filter holders (rotatable)
3. 152mm round filter holder (rotatable)
4. Filter locks
5. 15cm (6-in) rods
6. Bracket
7. 38cm (15-in) rods

The Arriflex 35 IIC and Arriflex 35 3C are basically the same camera. They differ only in their motors (see Sec. 11.13c), turret (see Sec. 11.13e), and viewing systems (see Sec. 11.13g). Except where specifically noted, information herein applies to both cameras.

11.13a Base

Bottom rear is fitted with $\frac{3}{8}$"-16 thread tapped hole to accommodate tripod lockdown screw. Bottom front is fitted with a guide stud, which extends 9.5 (3/8") below the base.

11.13b. Hi-hat

Required when using camera on a flat tripod head.

To mount camera.   Insert camera motor through top of hi-hat. Insert forward guide stud into groove at hi-hat front. Secure 3/8"-16 thread lockdown screw to camera.

11.13c Motors

Mount vertically to base of camera; motor also serves as a handgrip.

Motor housings differ:

• IIC V/R (forward/reverse) toggle switch; short-burst button; ON/OFF switch; two-pin battery plug; rheostat on a "wild" (variable-speed); motor/fuse on a governor-controlled (constant-speed) motor.
• 3C A 24/25 frame-rate switch; out-of-sync (red) LED indicator; battery status (green) LED indicator; sync/variable toggle switch; short burst button; ON/OFF switch; disc rheostat.

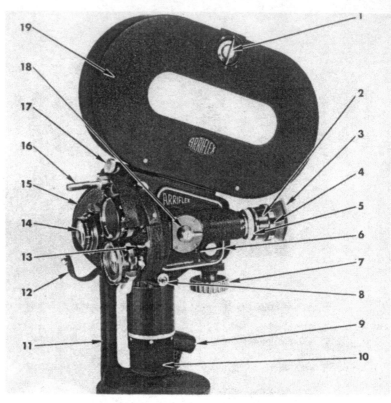

Figure 11–26a Arriflex IIC (left front view with matte box removed). Governor-controlled (constant-speed) motor. Courtesy of Arnold & Richter K.G.

1. Magazine cover latch
2. Eyepiece
3. Eyecup
4. Eyepiece focusing ring
5. Eyepiece coupling nut
6. Door lock
7. Camera lockdown screw of adapter
8. ON/OFF toggle switch
9. Power-cable socket
10. Governor-controlled (constant-speed) motor
11. Hi-hat adapter
12. Sunshade bracket
13. Turret grip
14. Taking lens
15. Contour grip
16. Sunshade mount
17. Magazine-lock knob
18. Viewfinder closing lever
19. 122 (400-ft) magazine

NOTE: A 3C motor is capable of constant speed (24 fps or 25 fps), and variable speed.

Mounting/Removing Motors

To Mount. Invert camera. Place motor ON/OFF toggle switch on same side as camera door. Align center transfer gear with motor-drive gear and lower onto base of camera. Secure to base with screws.

NOTE: Secure motor with four screws on the IIC; with three screws and a threaded holding stud at the left side of the 3C.

Figure 11–26b Arriflex IIC (right-rear view with matte box). Variable-speed motor. Courtesy of Arnold & Richter K.G.

1. Footage counter
2. Bellows boom locking screw
3. Sunshade pressure clamp
4. Contour grip
5. Bellows/matte box
6. Filter adjust knob
7. Adjustable filter holder
8. Inching knob
9. Variable-speed motor
10. Rheostat cap
11. Power-cable socket
12. FWD/REV switch
13. Short-burst button
14. Tachometer
15. 400-ft magazine

To Remove. Invert motor, loosen screws and threaded stud. Lift motor up slowly until clear of internal gears.

CAUTION: The center fiber transfer gear might light with the motor. If it does, replace the gear, and position it so that the teeth of the transfer gear work against the teeth of the camera-drive gear.

The following motors are available for the Arriflex IIC.

Variable Speed Motor. 16v DC, 24-28v DC. Slow motion; (maximum 80 fps) 32v DC.

NOTE: A minimum of 12 volts is required to run a camera with a 400-ft load at 24 fps, but requires 16 volts or more to run a camera 25 fps to 48 fps.

To Adjust Variable/Slow Motion Motor Speed. Rotate rheostat cap (at bottom of motor below the power-cable socket) clockwise for fast, counterclockwise for slow. Motor speed marks are for reference only.

Correct fps speed is obtained by observing tachometer (at right rear of camera). (See also section 11.13o, Tachometer, CAUTION).

To Reverse. Turn small toggle switch (located above powercable socket) from V to R.

Governor-Controlled (Constant-Speed). 16v DC (24 fps); 16v DC (25 fps); 24v DC (24 fps); 24v DC (25 fps).

Synchronous. 10v AC 60 Hz (24 fps); 110v AC 50 Hz (25 fps); 220v AC 50 Hz (25 fps, single- or 3-phase).

Animation/Time Lapse. 110v AC 60 Hz (stepped down and rectified to 24v DC); 110v 50 Hz (stepped down and rectified to 24v DC).

11.13d Powerline

IIC *Input to Camera.*
Variable Speed Motor. Power-cable socket is located at base of motor above the rheostat. The split recessed socket pins can be separated slightly to ensure the female cable plug fits snugly onto the pins.

WARNING: The left pin of the socket is + 16v and must be aligned with the + (positive) mark on the female plug on the battery cable. The right pin is − (negative).

CAUTION: The metal pins are fragile and will break if handled roughly. If one side of a split pin *is* broken off, a matchstick inserted into the female plug, in the space the broken pin would ordinarily occupy, will act as a wedge and provide a good electrical contact.

Governor-Controlled (Constant-Speed) Motor. Power-cable socket is located above the fuse cap. To prevent incorrect polarity insertion of the power plug into the motor, which can damage the electronics, the socket is fitted with one large-diameter (positive) pin and one small-diameter (negative) pin.

3C *Input to Camera.*
Four-pin power-cable socket is located above the base cap. Clockwise, pin no. 1 is − (negative); pins no. 2 and 3 are blank; pin no. 4 is + (positive).

Cable.

- IIC Insert the male end of the cable into the battery (" + " on plug aligns with red " + " on battery). On some cables, a pressure catch near the male end can be attached to a clip on the battery to hold the male plug securely to the power source.
- 3C The four-pin female plug inserts into the motor; the five-pin plug attaches to the battery.

ON/OFF Toggle Switch.

- IIC At top left side of motor. Push forward for ON, rearward for OFF.
- 3C At top left side of motor. Push rearward for ON, forward for OFF.

Short Burst Button.

- IIC At top-rear of motor. Allows Operator to depress button with thumb while holding the camera.
- 3C At top-front of motor. Allows Operator to depress button with forefinger while holding the camera.

Fuses.

IIC *Motor:* 4 amp, 5 × 20mm (3/4") located beneath the motor base cap. *To change:* unscrew cap at base of motor.

3C Electronics: 0.75 amp pico. *Motor:* 10 amp pico.

CAUTION: 3C fuses are NOT field replaceable.

11.13e Turret

IIC Three-position. Accepts equal number of lenses.

NOTE: NO divergence of ports as with 16mm "S" and 16mm "M".

To Rotate Turret. Grasp turret grip opposite taking lens. Depress (or lift), until desired lens rotates into position nearest the contour grip at the right side. Turret snaps into place.

NOTE: Turret grips have indented data marks to help Operator determine which lens is in "taking" position, i.e., the widest-angle lens, one dot; normal lens, two dots; and telephoto lens, three dots. Each lens should be mounted *opposite* the data mark to which it corresponds.

CAUTION: When using less than three lenses on a turret, always plug the empty port(s) to avoid a light leak to the aperture.

3C Fitted with a PL (Positive Lock) plate (a hard front, nonturreted, fixed mount).

11.13f Lenses

IIC Accepts bayonet and standard mount lenses unless specially retrofitted with a PL (positive lock) plate (see 3C, below).

To Mount Bayonet/Standard Lens on Turret. Rotate lens barrel until its infinity mark aligns to the channel in the lens. Grasp lens by its knurled footage ring. Squeeze locking levers at each side of the lens port on the turret and insert the lens into the port with the follow-focus grips ("wings") *up*. Release locking levers. Gently tug at lens to make certain the levers have gripped the channel at the rear of the lens mount.

NOTE: Lenses should correspond as closely as possible to the data marks on the turret grips.

To Remove. Rotate follow-focus grips up. Grasp knurled footage ring on lens. Squeeze locking levers at each side of lens port and gently pull lens away.

NOTE: 16mm and 35mm bayonet mount and standard mount Arriflex lenses are interchangeable with the following exceptions: 5.7mm, 11.5mm, and 25mm. These will not "cover" a 35mm aperture. The only wide-angle lenses that cover a 35mm aperture are the 9.8mm, 14.5mm, 18.5mm retrofocus, and the 28mm *made for 35mm cameras.*

3C

To Mount PL Lens on PL Plate. Align notch in lens flange with locator pin on upper left of mount. Insert lens into mount and turn the locking ring counterclockwise to secure.

To Remove. Turn locking ring clockwise, grasp lens firmly and gently pull it from the port.

11.13g Viewfinder

Reflex. Image magnified 6 1/2 × .

To Align Reflex Mirror for Viewing. Rotate knurled inching knob at right side of camera (located rear of contour thumb grip) until shutter is cleared.

NOTE: Cut two pieces of camera tape into "pointers"; place one on inching knob, and the other on camera. Alignment of these two points indicates shutter is cleared from mirror. Assistant can align points immediately upon completion of a shot. Operator can see the scene without groping for inching knob.

Eyepiece. To Detach. Rotate knurled eyepiece coupling nut on finder clockwise, and pull eyepiece from keyed slots.

Hinged Metal Cap (IIC only). Located inside eyecup; closes viewing system. Cap must be closed when Operator's eye is not covering eyepiece, so that stray light cannot strike mirror and kick back onto film.
Light Trap.
IIC. Another means of closing viewfinder and avoiding light "kick back" into lens. , push two-position *viewfinder* closing lever on front side of viewfinder *down* to close; push *up* to open. ("Z" (zu) = closed; "A" (auf) = open).

NOTE: Older models have a lever at the bottom of the viewfinder that pushes forward to close; back to open.

To focus: rotate narrow scalloped ring (nearest eyecup) to the word "lose" (loose). Rotate large scalloped ring (nearest eye cup) to focus on the groundglass. When focus is set, turn the narrow ring counterclockwise to "fest" (tight).

NOTE: On older IIC models, loosen small lever on the eyepiece. Rotate barrel to scribe numbered with " + " or " – " diopter settings. Focus on groundglass. When focus is set, lock small lever.
Groundglass. To Remove. (1) Remove taking lens. (2) Reach into lens port and turn locking screw (on groundglass frame) counterclockwise. With fingers or paper clip hook, pull groundglass straight out.

NOTE: The groundglass inserts only one way—with the smooth surface of the groundglass toward the eyepiece.

CAUTION: On older IIC models, the internal groundglass is fixed, and removal of the gate is necessary for access. The smooth surface is toward the eyepiece. The manufacturer recommends that only a competent technician change the groundglass on older IIC models, as replacement of the gate requires accurate adjustments.

11.13h Sunshade/Matte Box
Two types available for the IIC: fixed and bellows. Both are detachable from camera.
To Mount Either Type. Fit sunshade pressure clamp over sunshade mount (above and to right of turret), making sure that registration hole at bottom of sunshade fits over lower sunshade bracket, which is below and forward of handgrip. Secure knurled screw of pressure clamp clockwise.

Bellows Type (shown). Adjustable. Bellows slide in/out on boom. To extend matte box, loosen knurled locking screw on boom above matte box (fully extended bellows protects a 50mm lens).

Masks. Both fixed and bellows types of matte boxes accept sliding masks (for lenses longer than 50mm) in slot in front of sunshade.

11.13i Filters

Fixed Matte Box/Sunshade Type of Filter Holder (not shown). Accepts one 76.2mm × 76.2mm (3 × 3″) filter.

To Insert. Pull retaining spring pin at left of filter housing. Flip (hinged) top door of filter holder open, push filter down until seated. Close door, release retaining spring.

To Remove. Pull retaining spring pin at left of filter housing; open top door; push filter up from bottom.

Bellows Type of Adjustable Filter Holder. Accepts one 76.2mm × 76.2mm (3 × 3″) glass filter, or one 76.2mm × 101.6mm (3 × 4″) glass filter.

To Insert. Pull retaining spring pin at left of filter housing, open top door, push filter down until it rests on bottom of holder bracket. Rotate knurled filter-adjust-knob below filter holder counterclockwise to lower holder into matte box. Close top door, and release retaining spring. Adjust filter to desired position.

11.13j Door

IIC. Dog-locked.

To Remove. Rotate recessed door lock (below finder) counterclockwise, from "Z" (zu = closed) to "A" (auf = open).

CAUTION: Door is not hinged.

To Close. Turn door lock to "A." Insert back of door into camera door recess; swing front of door flush with camera. Rotate lock to "Z." Grasp finder and pull gently, to be sure door is properly secured to camera.

3C. Hinged.

To Remove. Push locking slide forward and swing door open. Pull back hinge release (located below optics on inside of door); lift door up off its hinges.

To Replace. Gently lower door part way on its hinges. Pull back hinge release and lower door to its stops. Release hinge release. Close and secure by sliding lock toward Operator.

Viewfinder optics in door is brighter than optics in IIC viewfinder.

Two-styles available: Pivoting (270°) or Offset (fixed).

11.13k Magazines

122m (400 ft) and 61m (200 ft.)

To Mount. 1) Rotate knurled magazine lock knob above turret clockwise until spring action frees lock knob. 2) Remove cover plate from top of camera. Make sure that gears of magazine are at same side as camera gears. Insert film into camera cavity. 3) Seat rear male dovetail into rear female dovetail on camera housing, then lower front male dovetail into housing. Rotate inching knob to mesh gears properly. 4) Depress knurled magazine lock knob, and rotate counterclockwise to lock.

To Remove. Unthread camera. Rotate magazine lock knob clockwise, and lift magazine away.

11.13l Threading (Fig. 11–27)

Rotate inching knob until single pulldown claw is in center of pressure-pad slot and withdrawn from the gate. With pressure plate *closed,* mount

Figure 11–27 Arriflex IIC and 3C threading detail. Courtesy of Arnold & Richter K.G.

1. 15-perforation loop
2. Plate catch
3. Pressure plate
4. Pulldown claw
5. Gear cover

magazine, allowing loop to fill camera interior. Pull plate catch with forefinger, swing plate open with thumb. (3) Pull film around pressure plate, and insert it into gate. With middle and index fingers, conform film to upper loop guideline. (4) Rotate inching knob clockwise until pulldown claw moves up and engages a perforation. Proper size of loop contains 15 perforations between the mouth of magazine and the claw. (5) Close pressure plate, and rotate inching knob to check engagement of claw. If satisfactory, depress short-burst button, and observe action of film. If satisfactory, close camera door.

11.13m Buckle-Trip
Installed on some IIC and on all 3C models. Located above lower guide track. A rubber covered switch arm cuts off power when pulled up by a short lower loop.

To Reset. Push arm down gently.

11.13n Footage and Frame Counter
None on camera (see Sec. 11.4h).

11.13o Tachometer
At back of camera. Registers speeds from 0 to 50 fps, in increments of one frame per second (1 fps).

CAUTION: A variable-speed motor *can* and *will* run faster than 50 fps. Do not assume that by turning the motor rheostat so that the tachometer needle registers 50, the camera is running at 50 fps. Incorrect exposure can result if camera speed is not slowly and *deliberately* set by Operator.

11.13p Shutter
Depends on model.

IIC.   Has a fixed 180° shutter.

3C.   Has a variable 165° shutter, adjustable in increments of 15 degrees.

NOTE: Models I and IIA have a 120° shutter. Models IIB and IIC have a 180° fixed shutter. Models IIBV and IICV (Variable shutter models) have a 165° shutter adjustable in increments of 15 degrees and are adjusted same as on the 3C.

To Read Variable Shutter. Align color at edge of mirror-reflex shutter with its corresponding scale: Black edge = inner scale (closest to the handgrip). Red edge = outer scale (closest to turret center knob).

To Change Shutter Opening. Remove taking lens to view shutter increments. Turn knurled shutter-adjusting knob (on camera's right side—not found on the II), in direction of arrow, to limit of its rotation. Then *press in,* to arrest shutter blade. Rotate knurled knob (rear of contour thumb grip) until shutter clicks into desired opening. Release inching knob and spring-loaded shutter-adjusting knob.

CAUTION: Shutter must be set into a scribed increment. If it is set *between* increments, it will drift while running, thereby rendering an incorrect exposure.

WARNING: Shutter should be checked before and after mounting each magazine. If the end of a roll goes through the gate, the crimped tail-end of film can pull shutter edge down and/or closed. It has happened.

11.13q   Lubrication (Fig. 11–28)
Manufacturer recommends lubricating the following parts every 15,000–20,000 ft. Unscrew knurled knob and remove gear cover marked "Fett (grease)" from interior of camera.

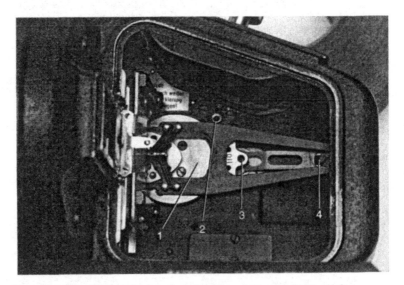

Figure 11–28   Arriflex IIC lubrication. Courtesy of Arnold & Richter K.G.

1. Claw cam (grease)   3. Trunnion (oil)
2. Intermediate gear stud (grease)   4. Pivot block (oil)

Grease. Claw cam: intermediate gear stud (hole at right of loop indicator plate).

Oil. Trunnion (two holes): Pivot block. (Six to eight drops each.)

CAUTION: Do not oil the gears! Manufacturer warns, *oiling too frequently and/or excessive oil can damage camera mechanism.*

11.13r Cleaning
Optics: Clean with bulb syringe or camel's-hair brush.
Manufacturer recommends the following *each time film is changed:*

1. Open plate catch, and check plate and pad for emulsion buildup.
2. Remove emulsion buildup with orangewood stick.
3. Wipe plates with chamois or soft cotton handkerchief (not linen).
4. Use bulb syringe on camera interior to remove dust, dirt, etc.

11.13s Weight
(With 122m [400 ft] load) 7.5kg (16 $\frac{1}{2}$ lb)

11.13t Troubleshooting

Trouble	Probable Cause
Camera will not start	Battery connections loose; battery dead; buckle-trip not reset; fuse burned out.
Intermittent starting	Slotted powerline prongs (in battery or camera) squeezed together, making poor contact; lugs on battery cell loose; broken connection in powerline.
Torn perforations; ripped film	Improper threading.
Door will not close	Dirt or film chip in door recess.
Viewing system blacked	Shutter closed; eyepiece cap closed; lens stopped down past $f/22$; lens elements damaged.
Lens will not focus	Lens not seated; camera too close for minimum distance of lens; elements damaged.
Cut-in on groundglass	Viewing mirror "sees" aperture (wide-angle lens) of lens, but camera aperture does not—no problem if turret is seated properly. Turret not seated; matte box (normal lens) extended.
Lens will not enter port	Guide key inside turret bent up or down.
Film does not take up	Magazine take-up spindle loose; in magazine, film is loose on take-up core.

11.14 ARRIFLEX 35 IIC AND 35 3C MAGAZINES (FIG. 11–29)

11.14a Type
Displacement.

11.14b Capacity
61m (200 ft) and 122m (400 ft) (both shown)

11.14c Lid
One Lug-and-dog locked.
To open. depress safety spring in lid recess, rotate lock bar counter-clockwise (from "C" to "O"). Lift.

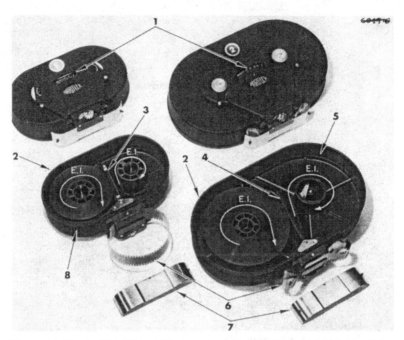

Figure 11–29 Arriflex IIC and 3C magazines. Courtesy of Arnold & Richter K.G.

1. Subtractive footage counter
2. Marking rib
3. Footage counter/roller-guide arm 200 ft
4. Footage counter/roller-guide arm 400 ft
5. 400-ft magazine
6. 54-perforation loop
7. Loop guards
8. 61m (200-ft) magazine

11.14d Feed

Left side. Film (wound emulsion in) pulls off spindle clockwise.

11.14e Take-up

Right side. Film winds on spindle clockwise, emulsion in.

11.14f Loading

(1) Remove lid; swing footage-counter/roller-guide arm to right, and lock arm in pressure catch next to take-up spindle. (2) In darkness, remove film roll from can and bag. Pull film clockwise off roll. Insert film end into left side of magazine throat, slowly rotating gear at bottom counterclockwise with right thumb until gear in throat engages film perforation; thread at least 6 in. of film through.

NOTE: To expedite engagement of film and magazine gear, cut film to bisect the perforations.

(3) Place film roll on feed spindle. Rotate knurled feed-spindle wheel until spindle key spring engages core keyway. (4) Release footage-counter roller-guide arm, making sure that flanges ride film perforations. (5) Pull film end around front of magazine until cut perforations touch raised film-length indicator on outside of magazine. Hold gear; bring film end

back, and insert end into right-hand channel of magazine throat. Rotate gear until perforation engages gear and film moves into magazine.

WARNING: Do not allow excess film to exit feed side while trying to engage perforation and take-up gear.

NOTE: It is important to maintain proper loop size: 54 perforations for both 122m (400 ft) and 61m (200 ft) magazines.

122m (400 ft) Magazine. Insert film end into collapsible take-up core; move clamp inward to secure film.

61m (200 ft) Magazine. Fold back 3–4 in. of film onto itself, and insert the double thickness into core slot; wind film on core clockwise, and fit core onto spindle. Rotate knurled take-up spindle wheel until spindle-key spring engages core keyway.

To Replace Lid. While holding lid at 45° angle, insert lugs (at bottom) into slots in magazine; lower lid to a secure fit; rotate lock bar clockwise from "O" to "C" until safety spring snaps up. Pull up on lid, and run fingernails around edge to be sure that lid is secure.

To Take Out Film Slack. Rotate spindle wheels at back of magazine; take-up rotates counterclockwise; feed rotates clockwise.

Film-Loop Guard. Slide loop guard (with notch inward) over film and under retaining plate.

11.14g Unloading
In darkness, remove lid.

122m (400 ft) Magazine. Disengage take-up clamp (push outward) on magazine that has a collapsible core; place index finger in core space, thumb on edge of roll; turn magazine over, and remove film. Place exposed roll in bag and can.

61m (200 ft) Magazine. Place index finger in center of core, thumb on edge of roll; turn magazine over, and remove film. Place exposed roll in bag and can.

11.14h Footage Counter
At back of magazine. 122m (400 ft) magazine is subtractive 500–0 ft, in increments of 20 ft. The 61m (200 ft) magazine is subtractive 220–0 ft, in increments of 20 ft.

11.15 ARRIFLEX 35mm MODEL 400 BLIMP (FIG. 11–30)

NOTE: All directions are from the Operator's point of view.

The Model 400 Blimp accepts the Arriflex 35mm IIC, and 35mm 3C (see Sec. 11.13, Figs. 11–26a and 11–26b). The cameras must first be mounted to a 110v AC Sync Motor on Plate (see Sec. 11.17, Fig. 11–32).

11.15a Base
Bottom is fitted with two 3/8″-16 tapped holes to accommodate tripod-lockdown screw.

11.15b Camera Preparation

Eyepiece. Remove from camera. Attach viewfinder extension tube to eyepiece, and insert unit into blimp extension-tube access hole. Rotate lock lever on blimp clockwise to secure tube.

Figure 11–30a Arriflex 35mm Model 400 blimp (front view). Courtesy of Arnold & Richter K.G.

1. Magazine access hood
2. Magazine access clamp
3. Camera access clamp
4. Running light
5. Blimp door
6. Internal light button
7. Marking strip port
8. Focus knob
9. Lens access lever
10. Sunshade locknuts

Doom. Remove regular camera door with its viewfinder (see Fig. 11–26a), and replace it with straight-tube door—a camera-blimp accessory (not shown).

Motor. Remove either the variable-speed or the governor-controlled (constant-speed) motor, and replace with AC-synchronous-motor plate (see Sec. 11.17).

11.15c Access

To Camera. Raise the lower-camera-access clamp on left side door, then lower the door 90°.

To Lenses. Rotate lens-access lever clockwise at left front of matte-box glass door; swing door open.

To Magazine. Lower the upper-magazine-access clamp at left side of blimp, then lift magazine access hood *up*.

11.15d Camera Insertion

1. Push out pin in rear focus knob at back of blimp (below eyepiece), then pull knob toward Operator. 2. Reach inside blimp, and slide rear-focus extension rod toward back of blimp. Remove rod. 3. Loosen the two knurled screws, and remove the two base lockdown nuts from internal triangle camera-mounting plate accessory. 4. Insert the camera mounted on the plate (see Fig. 11.32) without magazine into blimp. The locating stud on the right side of the base is inserted into a mating hole of the camera-mounting plate. 5. Reinsert the two base lockdown nuts, and

Figure 11–30b Arriflex 35mm Model 400 blimp (rear view). Courtesy of Arnold & Richter K.G.

1. Extension tube
2. Access hole
3. Rear focus knob
4. Tachometer port
5. Footage counter port

6. Telephone-dial inching knob
7. ON/OFF switch
8. Sync-pulse outlet (optional)
9. Power-supply plug

secure the synchronous-motor plate to the camera-mounting plate. 6. Replace the focus-extension rod: (a) insert rod pin into mating focus-knob groove first, then (b) fit flange on rod to the three studs in the front gear. 7. Push rear focus knob forward. Insert pin into rear focus knob to secure. 8. Mount camera magazine through magazine-access hood.

11.15e Powerline

External

Power-Supply Plug. Recessed six-pin male Tuchel plug is inserted into female receptacle at right rear of blimp.

ON/OFF Switch. Single-pole switch at right rear of blimp.

To Operate Internal Lights. Depress button at left front (above aperture and footage viewing port).

NOTE: Early models do not have this feature.

Internal

Coupling for Adapter Cable. Three-pin plug inside blimp (above tachometer port) inserts into extension plug on camera motor. There is *no* sync-pulse outlet on the Model 400 unless it has been customized.

Running Light. Red light located above eyepiece glows when camera runs.

11.15f Sunshade

To mount. Raise the upper knurled lock nut at front of lens door. Lower the bottom lock nut. Align slots at rear of sunshade housing with lock-nut brackets. Lower the upper lock nut, raise the bottom lock nut, and secure sunshade to the lens door. Bellows moves in/out on two rods. Tighten knurled lock screw on each rod to secure.

11.15g Coupling Alignment

Focus Marking-Strip Indicator. On lens gear housing.

To Insert strip. 1. Open lens access door; place long hole of marking strip over lower catch on lens gear housing. 2. Wrap marking strip around lens-gear housing; push the upper spring-loaded catch *up.* Place small hole of strip over spring-loaded catch; release.

To Scribe Footage Marks on Marking Strips. Open camera-access door, and insert a pencil into notch inside blimp at left of lens gear ring.

To Mark Blank Strips. Couple lens to focus knob (see "Standard Lenses," below.) Set lens at infinity. Make infinity pencil mark (∞) on strip. Set focus at each footage indication on lens barrel, and transcribe each setting to marking strip. At bottom, write focal length of lens for which strip has been marked. There is *no* f/stop scale on marking strip. All *f/* stops are set manually.

Standard Lenses.

1. Open lens-access door, and set taking lens at infinity. Rotate lens gear in lens-access door, and align the two dots (one on gear, one in door).

CAUTION: Be sure that the rubber end of the spring-tension focus bracket arm on the lens gear is *up.*

2. Close and lock the lens-access door. Reach through the side door, and depress the rubber end of the focus bracket arm into the "wings" of the lens.

f/Stop Drive. None; *f/* stops must be set manually.

Focus Knob. Scalloped knob at left front of blimp is coupled to the rear focus knob so that the Operator can focus.

11.15h Filters

A 76.2mm × 76.2mm (3 × 3″) glass filter inserts into a holder in the gear-ring housing. The rotating spring latches secure the filter in the holder.

11.15i Viewfinder/Focus Tube

To Align Reflex Mirror for Viewing. Place fingertips into recess of "telephone-dial" knob at back of blimp. Depress and rotate to engage motor.

To Use Eyepiece. Rotate narrow scalloped ring on eyepiece clockwise to the word "lose." Rotate large scalloped ring nearest eyecup to focus on groundglass; turn narrow ring counterclockwise to "fest."

To Use Light Trap. Hinged metal cap in eyepiece snaps closed to prevent stray light from striking the mirror and kicking back onto the film.

11.15j Ports

Vertical window at left side above focus knob permits viewing of marking strip. Tachometer and footage-counter ports are at back of blimp.

11.15k Weight

(Less Camera) 17.7kg (39 lb)

Figure 11–31   Arriflex flat base. Courtesy of Arnold & Richter K.G.

1. Motor-mounting screw holes
2. Motor-drive gear hole
3. Camera-lockdown screw
4. Camera mounting screws

5. Locating stud receptacle
6. Base fiber transfer gear
7. Camera-gear receptacle

11.16   ARRIFLEX FLAT BASE (FIG. 11–31)

The flat base permits the use of the 35mm Arriflex IIC and 3C on a standard tripod head without the Arriflex Adapter Plate. It may be used with a variable- or constant-speed motor.

Bottom of flat base is fitted with one 3/8″-16 tapped hole to accommodate a tripod lockdown screw. (Some bases may also be fitted with a 1/4″-20 tapped hole.)

11.16a   Mounting Camera onto Plate

1. Invert camera; remove the motor and the fiber transfer gear (see Sec. 11.3C, Motors, *To remove*). (Older-model bases also require removal of front locating stud at camera base; never bases are fitted with a locating-stud receptacle). 2. Insert camera transfer-gear shaft into base of fiber transfer gear. Secure front of camera to base through bottom of plate with three mounting screws; secure rear of camera through bottom of plate with 3/8″-16 lockdown screw. 3. Turn camera right side up; invert motor; insert motor-drive gear into hole to mesh with timing-belt gear. (Short-burst button faces Operator, and ON/OFF switch faces right side of base.) Secure motor to base with motor-mounting screws.

11.17   ARRIFLEX 110V AC SYNC MOTOR ON PLATE (FIG. 11–32)

The synchronous motor on a plate permits the use of the 35mm Arriflex with a 110V AC power source. It may be used on a standard tripod and/or within a blimp.

Bottom of Plate.   Fitted with 3/8″-16 tapped hole to accommodate tripod lockdown screw. Synchronous motor is permanently affixed to plate.

Gear Box in Plate.   Contains double-height transfer gear that meshes with camera-drive gear.

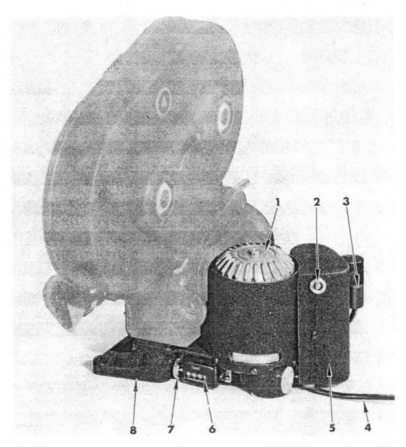

Figure 11–32 Arriflex 110V synchronous motor on plate. Courtesy of Arnold & Richter K.G.

1. Synchronous motor
2. ON/OFF switch
3. Three-prong plug
4. Line to AC outlet

5. Switch box
6. Footage counter
7. Counter reset knob
8. Camera-mounting plate

11.17a Mounting Camera onto Plate

1. Remove camera motor, transfer gear, and locating stud from camera (some cameras also require removal of projecting inching-knob guard). 2. Loosen two long screws, and remove gear box cover from plate. 3. Secure camera onto plate with two long screws (which insert from plate bottom and into two forward tapped holes of camera). 4. Secure spring-loaded 3/8″-16 camera lockdown screw into bottom rear of camera from plate bottom. 5. Zero the footage counter. 6. Insert three-prong male extension cord from motor into three-prong female plug on front of switch box.

NOTE: (a) Switch box containing condensor ON/OFF toggle switch slides into pressure catches on motor housing. Long extension on switch box inserts into AC outlet. (b) With unit in blimp, switch box is not used; instead,

Figure 11–33a Arriflex 16SR, left side. Courtesy of Arnold & Richter K.G.

1. SR APEC
2. Auto-iris control ring
3. Focal length ring handle
4. Focus ring
5. 10–100mm Zeiss zoom lens
6. Matte-box boom shoe
7. Release/locking lens lever (1 of 2)
8. Auxiliary handgrip mount
9. Test button
10. Restricted slot
11. Main camera switch
12. Door lock
13. Eyecup
14. Eyepiece focus ring
15. Eyepiece focus lock
16. Rotatable viewfinder
17. Carrying handle
18. Auxiliary ON/OFF switch
19. Knurled ring

the three-prong male extension plug on motor is inserted in mating plug in blimp. Six-prong female plug (with condensor in the line) is inserted into recessed six-prong female plug on blimp. (c) Single-jack extension is for sync-pulse cord.

11.18 ARRIFLEX 16SR-1 AND 16SR-2(16 mm) CAMERAS* (FIGS. 11–33a and 11–33b)

NOTE: All directions are from the Operator's point of view.

Unless otherwise noted, the operation, features, and maintenance of both 16SR-1 and 16SR-2 model cameras are identical. For additional specific 16SR accessories, see Sections 11.30, "Variable Speed Control," and 11.12, "Matte Boxes."

11.18a Base
3/8″-16 tapped hole accommodates tripod-lockdown screw.

---

*Manufacturer states that "SR" stands for "Silent Reflex."

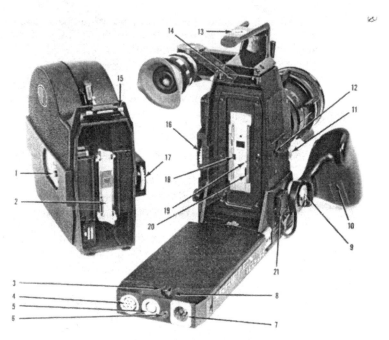

Figure 11–33b Arriflex 16SR (right rear) magazine removed. Courtesy of Arnold & Richter K.G.

1. Feed side door lock
2. Pressure plate
3. Magazine guide
4. 5-pin Pilotone plug
5. 11-pin Fischer plug
6. Battery adapter tapped hole
7. 4-pin battery receptacle
8. Running light
9. Handgrip wingnut
10. Standard handgrip
11. Lens release/locking lever (1 of 2)
12. Filter slot
13. Auxiliary ⅜"-16 tapped hole
14. Magazine guide
15. Hinge pin
16. Camera drive gear
17. Magazine drive gear
18. Time-code slot
19. Register pin
20. Pulldown claw slot
21. 4-pin flat receptacle

NOTE: Tapped hole will not accept screw longer than 7 mm (17/64 in.).

CAUTION: Use of longer screws may damage camera electronics!

11.18b Motor

Built-in crystal 24 fps 60 Hz, 25 fps 50 Hz, 30 fps 60/72 Hz

To Set Motor Speed/Frequency. Remove magazine from camera. Use coin to remove plastic cover in top of flat base.

16SR-1: use tweezers to lift out the wire jumpers and insert into either 24 or 25 fps receptacles (center receptacle is neutral) and 50 or 60 Hz receptacles (center receptacle is neutral).

WARNING: Some rental houses have configured the SR-1 25 fps 50 Hz switch to 30 fps 60 Hz. ALWAYS verify fps speed on a rental by observing the tachometer!

16SR-2: has labeled switches in place of jumpers. The newest models are equipped with a 30 fps 60 Hz in place of 25 fps 50 Hz switch to enable one to shoot for direct transfer to videotape.

WARNING: Do *not* insert jumpers between fps and Hz receptacles.

Variable-Speed Mode. Requires variable-speed control (see Sec. 11.30) and inserts into 11-pin Fischer plug at back of camera (see Sec. 11.8c).

11.18c Powerline

Outlets. At rear of camera base.

Input to camera. Recessed four-pin power-cable receptacle is located at far-right rear. Accepts male Cannon plug or battery adapter. From Operator's point of view and counterclockwise from key, pin 1 is − (minus); pins 2 and 3 are unused; pin 4 is + (plus) 12 volts.

Battery Adapter. Inserts into four-pin receptacle; secured by slotted screw to tapped hole at rear of base; 12-volt battery is slid over square post of hinged battery adapter plug, and assembly is swung forward to contact magazine.

NOTE: Square matching slot in battery fits tightly. Battery must be slid down post until flush with hinge before pushing battery toward magazine. Magnet secures battery to magazine.

11-Pin Fischer Accessory Connector. Accepts the following accessories: (1) variable-speed unit (see Sec. 11.30); (2) remote ON/OFF switch that clips to tripod handle; (3) external sync control (for use with a TV camera or another 16SR), or rear-screen projection (camera and projector sync); (4) phase-control unit (eliminates video roll bar when filming TV monitor at 25 fps; a 24 fps camera needs a 144° shutter); (5) Multiple remote control unit (an accessory that does all the aforementioned).

5-Pin Plug. Pilotone outlet for noncrystal tape recorders.

NOTE: As Operator faces plug with keyway at 3 o'clock, pin 1 is 60 Hz Pilotone signal; pin 2 is common ground (−); pin 3 is 12-volt bloop signal; pins 4 and 5 are bridged in the Pilotone cable to activate the system.

Red Running Light. Above the outlets base; flashes when camera is running.

Main Camera Switch. Three-position lever left side of camera. Three pilot holes show red marker when switch is in any of the three positions. In "zero" position (*up*), camera is *off.* Just below center is "standby" position.

NOTE: Camera switch must be in "standby" position to operate Start/ Stop buttons on standard handgrip (described later herein) or remote ON/OFF switch.

In "start" position (*down*), camera is activated and overrides any accessory.

When ON/OFF switch is positioned at "start" or "standby,":

SR-1: A restricted slot (forward of "start" or "standby" position) contains a pin that is pushed up to prevent switch from swinging *up* to "zero" position (OFF).

NOTE: This is important, especially if an auto-iris type of lens is on the camera—it prevents the lens from opening automatically (see Sec. 11.18e "Lenses").

16SR-2: Pin is located below the ON/OFF switch.

Test button. Located above ON/OFF switch; runs camera at 2 fps. Used to check threading when magazine is first installed.

4-Pin Flat Receptacle. On right side of camera; accepts plug from standard handgrip. Spring-clip secures plug to the receptacle. Pin 1 (closest to Operator) is − (minus) pins 2 and 3 are unused; pin 4 is " + (plus)."

Handgrips. Two are built for the camera: Standard and Auxiliary.
Standard Handgrip. Fastens to rosette at forward right side of camera. *To mount,* (1) align screw in handgrip to tapped hole in center of rosette. Tighten wingnut clockwise to engage. Adjust handgrip for comfort, then secure tightly. (2) Insert four-pin flat plug into flat-pin receptacle. Secure plug with spring-clip retainer.
ON/OFF Plunger in Handle. *To start,* set camera ON/OFF switch to center position. Depress plunger in handgrip. Plunger remains depressed and camera continues to run. *To stop,* depress and release plunger in handgrip.

NOTE: Grip Extender available is 75 mm (3 in.) bar; can be adjusted for length and height so that handle is in better position for balance.

Auxiliary Handgrip. Mounts either left or right side. Does *not* contain an ON/OFF switch or lens controls. Used as handle for Operator who prefers two handgrips. Mounting is same as standard handgrip (on rosette at left front side of camera).

Fuses.
Electronics. 0.75 ampere pico.
Motor. 10 ampere pico.
     Both fuses are located in the base and are visible beneath a slotted circular plexiglass cover.

NOTE: The older SR-1 might not have a plexiglass cover. To change a fuse requires removing six (6) screws in the top base cover.

11.18d Turret
None. Single lens mount accepts Arriflex steel bayonet or standard mount lenses.

Auto-Iris Control Ring: Surrounds lens mount. Purpose is to engage and automatically open aperture (when camera stops) or close aperture (when camera starts) on Auto-Iris zoom lens (see Sec. 11.18e, "Lenses").

NOTE: (a) Only the SR2 Auto model has a match-needle exposure unit built-in with servo-motors that will drive an appropriately equipped Auto-Iris zoom lens (see Section 11.18e, Lenses)
(b)The SR-2 model (without a control ring) has a match-needle exposure unit built-in.
(c)The SR-2 SE model has NO exposure system.

     Red and black arrows on turret flange are alignment marks for lens (red mark on lens to red mark on flange; white mark on lens to black mark on flange).

11.18e Lenses
Standard equipment is either a Zeiss 10–100 mm "Auto-Iris" Vario Sonner zoom lens or an Angenieux 10–150 mm "Auto-Iris" zoom lens. Standard lenses also may be used.

Auto-Iris Zoom Lens.

NOTE: Automatic exposure control in lens requires camera to have automatic exposure control motor (not all units do).

Zoom lens has two control pins on end of bayonet mount that fit into two slots within camera body (visible through lens port). In each slot is a sliding wedge that takes data from Arriflex Precision Exposure Control (APEC; see Sec. 11.19f "Exposure Meter") and presses against each pin. One sliding wedge moves to compensate for overexposure, while other sliding wedge moves to compensate for underexposure. With "over" and "under" wedges working against each other, information is transmitted through the aperture drive ring to the iris on the lens. When camera stops, aperture automatically opens to wide position.

To Set Auto-Iris Mode on Zoom Lens. Depress pin on iris barrel, rotate T-stop dot on lens beyond T-16 to "A"; release pin.

To Take Lens Out of Auto-Iris Mode. Rotate aperture barrel to T-22. Pin will pop out. Lens will stay on manual until reset to "A."

To Use Auto-Iris Zoom as Macro-lens. Zoom lens to 150mm. Rotate pin on lens barrel to interfere with focal-length barrel. Lens will not zoom wider than 40mm.

CAUTION: When zoomed wider than 40mm for macroshots, the lens will vignette.

To Mount Lenses:

Auto-Iris Lens: (1) Align ears on lens base with grooves in camera mount so that index mark on lens is facing left (toward exposure meter). (2) Rotate Auto-Iris driver-ring coupling until aligned with ear of iris ring. Slide lens into mount (ear of ring slides into coupling of driver ring). (3) Rotate lens counterclockwise until engaged.

Standard Arriflex Lens. (1) Rotate lens barrel until channel in mount aligns with witness mark on lens. Grasp lens by its knurled footage ring. (2) Depress locking levers at each side of lens port, and insert lens into port with black infinity mark at the left side. Slide channel at rear of mount over guide key inside port. Release locking levers. (3) Gently tug at lens to make sure that levers have gripped channel at rear of lens mount.

To Remove Lenses:

Auto-Iris Lens: Depress lens-release lever at right side of camera and hold lens firmly and rotate clockwise. Gently slide from mount.

Standard Arriflex Mount Lens: Depress both lens-release levers (one on each side of mount), and gently slide lens from mount.

11.18f Viewfinder

Reflex. Image magnified 10×. Orientable.

To View through Lens. Place eye to eyecup, and press in slightly to open light trap.

NOTE: To avoid automatic closure of eyecup, remove rubber eyecup assembly (pull off), and rotate knurled ring around eyepiece rear element clockwise until resistance is felt.

To Alter Finder Position for Viewing. Grasp viewfinder, and rotate to desired position. Viewfinder rotates through three axes: 360° perpendicular to camera, 190° arc from left to right side of camera (swing over), and 25° away from viewing tube.

NOTE: Viewfinder is pressure-activated. Does not require locks. Image is constant left to right, top to bottom.

To Align Reflex Mirror for Viewing. Shutter automatically stops in viewing position when camera is shut *off.* If closed, or partially closed, rotate inching knob above ON/OFF switch, and rotate counterclockwise.

To Focus Eyepiece. Rotate narrow scalloped ring on eyepiece clockwise to "LOOSE." Rotate large scalloped ring nearest eyecup until frameline and crosshair on fiber screen are sharp. Tighten narrow ring counterclockwise to "FIX."

Fiber Optic. Views more than full aperture. Outer lines denote TV projection aperture. Inner line (TV pumpkin) denotes TV safe-action area. Also views Exposure Meter, below

To change fiber optic: Remove lens; rotate mirror shutter clear of fiber screen. Insert groundglass tool or paperclip into "T" of groundglass-assembly holder, and pull gently. Reinsert with frame markings down.

CAUTION: Make sure that fiber screen is slid completely in, to avoid framing error in viewfinder.

Full-Frame Start Mark. Only activated when Pilotone is plugged into camera. *To replace start mark bulb,* swing viewfinder above carrying handle. Lay camera on left side, with ON/OFF switch *up.* Remove two screws holding cover plate to camera.

CAUTION: Do not lose dark slide and spring on rear of cover plate!
Use Hirschman tool or paperclip to hook and remove start-mark assembly; pull out; replace bulb. Re-insert and replace cover.

NOTE: Newer cameras are SMPTE Time-Code compatible. Camera requires that time-code generator and optical LED block be inserted in gate area. A service technician's job. It canNOT be done in the field!

Out-of-Sync Warning Light. Red LED illuminates in viewfinder.

To Detach Eyepiece. Rotate silver knurled ring forward of eyepiece lock on viewfinder clockwise, and pull eyepiece from keyed slots.

Exposure Meter. At upper left of camera, above inching knob. Measures light behind lens. *Automatic meter* is necessary when using Auto-Iris lenses. Automatically opens diaphragm when camera stops; automatically closes diaphragm to proper exposure when camera starts. May be overridden manually.

WARNING: Meter does *not* alter diaphragm on a non-Auto-Iris lens!

Non-Auto-Iris. Set lens diaphragm manually to match needle in viewfinder with black center dot. Does not open or close automatically.

WARNING: If ON/OFF switch (see Sec. 11.18c) is in "O"-position, indicator needle in viewfinder will rest on black dot at all *times* and *can be misconstrued as a correct measurement on meter.*

To prevent false measurement in viewfinder when using built-in exposure meter, move ON/OFF switch to Standby (measuring) position. Slide cover in locking slot (forward of Start and Standby position) *up.* Move internal pin *up* to locked position, to prevent main camera-switch lever from moving forward to OFF and rendering a false reading in viewfinder.

NOTE: In order to use exposure meter, ON/OFF switch must be in center (measuring) position or moved to start position.

To Set ASA/DIN Index on Meter. Apply thumb to center of knurled disc on APEC, and rotate to correspond to ASA/DIN of film in camera. Can be set at ASA/DIN of 16/13, 20/14, 25/15, 32/16, 40/17, 50/18, 64/19, 80/20, 100/21, 125/22, 160/23, 200/24, 250/25, 320/26, 400/27, 500/28.

NOTE: Horizontal arrows on dial are spaces left blank for future ASA/DIN numbers. With arrows visible on dial exposure meter is not active!

To set fps and corresponding exposure time. Apply thumb to upper forward knurled disc on APEC and rotate to change fps/exposure time. Can be set at 24–25 fps/48–50 sec.; 32fps/64 sec.; 40fps/80 sec.; 48fps/96 sec.; 64fps/128 sec.; 80fps/160 sec.

WARNING: Setting fps and exposure time does *not* alter speed of camera. It does alter information to servo motor controlling aperture on lens. To alter camera speed (except for sync speed 24/25/30fps), an external variable speed unit (see Sec. 11.30) is necessary.

11.18g Sunshade/Matte Box

Used with fixed-focal-length lenses. Sunshade/bellows slides in and out on short square boom, which attaches to filter stages, which in turn slide onto a lightweight support that mounts in accessory shoe beneath taking lens.

To Mount, Insert plate at rear of boom into shoe on camera. Rotate knurled knob, and secure.

11.18h Filters

Two filter stages (not shown) accept 76.2 × 76.2mm (3 × 3-in) square filters. Rear round stage holds 94mm-diameter filter and is rotatable.

Gelatine. Not standard. Some early SR-1 cameras might be found that have a filter slot (manufacturer calls it an "effects mask slot") located at the right side of the camera above the four-pin flat receptacle behind the spring-loaded cover.

To insert the SR-1 Gelatine Filter Holder. Press pin on light trap door toward Operator; insert filter until it stops.

To Verify Position of Filter. Remove magazine, determine visually that filter "covers" aperture.

11.19i Door

None.

11.18j Magazine

122m (400 ft)

To Mount. Make sure that film loops are of equal size; safety latch on magazine is open (toward rear); depress magazine lock, tip nose of magazine forward (about 45°) (Fig. 11–34*a*), and insert hinge pin into camera magazine guide until it snaps in. Swing magazine downward until it seats and audibly clicks. Flip safety lock forward. (Fig. 11–34*b*) Depress red "test" button above main camera switch to engage film perforations.

To Remove. Move safety lock on magazine to rear. Depress magazine-release lever, and lift magazine. Slide magazine out of camera-magazine guide, and lift.

11.18k Buckle-Trip

None.

NOTE: Camera is fitted with a safety circuit breaker that stops camera when electronics become overloaded or a short occurs. Resets automatically in 10 seconds or less if problem is a brief overload.

1. Safety lock open
2. Magazine lock depressed

Figure 11–34a Arriflex SR mounting of magazine on camera, battery laid back. Courtesy of Arnold & Richter K.G.

1. Manual footage counter
2. Magazine release lock lever
3. Magazine release lever
4. Battery
5. Battery adapter
6. Battery adapter locking screw

Figure 11–34b Arriflex magazine in place and battery forward. Courtesy of Arnold & Richter K.G.

NOTE: Some newer magazines have an optical film-runout "detector" to sense an end-of-film condition.

To Determine if Camera Is Equipped with an End-of-Film Detector. Remove magazine from camera and check for two round clear plexiglass windows at the lower left of the aperture.

To Determine if Magazine Is Equipped with an End-of-Film Detector. Remove magazine from camera and check to see if face of magazine is equipped with a tiny built-in reflecting mirror.

NOTE: When film is traveling through a magazine equipped with an end-of-film detector, an infrared beam is blocked by the film stock. When the film runs out, the beam is reflected and an automatic shut-off of the camera occurs.

241

11.18l Footage Counter
None.

11.18m Tachometer
None.

11.18n Shutter
Nonadjustable; 180° standard; 144° and 172.8° optional.

11.18o Lubrication
None.
Manufacturer recommends annual check of camera.

11.18p Cleaning
Optics: Clean with bulb syringe or camel's-hair brush.
Manufacturer recommends the following maintenance (*each time film is changed*) (1) Remove emulsion buildup from gate area with orangewood stick; (2) wipe plates on camera and magazine with chamois or soft cotton (not linen) handkerchief; (3) Clean single pulldown claw and registration pin with soft brush.

11.18q Weight
With 122m (400 ft) load and zoom lens: 5.6 kg (12.5lb).

11.18r Troubleshooting

Trouble	Probable Cause
Camera will not start	Circuit breaker tripped; dead battery; battery connection loose; main power fuse (10 amps), located in upper board in camera base, blown.
Trigger on handgrip does not start camera	ON/OFF switch set to "O" (OFF); dead battery; circuit breaker tripped.
Torn perforations; ripped film	"Test" button not pressed when camera first loaded; film in magazine not slid under retaining hooks on plate.
Viewing system closed	Shutter closed; cap on lens.
Standard lens will not enter port	Guide key inside lens port is bent and will not enter channel.
Bayonet-type mount wobbles in port	Lens not given 1/4 turn to "lock it in."
Red LED remains on in viewfinder at all times	Camera out of sync.

11.19 ARRIFLEX 16MM SR-1 AND SR-2 MAGAZINE (FIGS. 11–35a, 11–35b, 11–35c, 11–35d)

11.19a Type
Coaxial

11.19b Capacity
122m (400 ft)

11.19c Lids
Two. Located at each side of magazine, which is divided longitudinally. Both lids are lug-and-dog locked. Hinged at rear.
To open. Depress red button behind door lock; rotate lock counterclockwise toward A/O (Auf/open); lift.

Figure 11–35a   Arriflex 16SR magazine feed side. Courtesy of Arnold & Richter K.G.

1. Subtractive footage counter   3. Feed throat slot
2. Footage counter roller guide

11.19d Feed

Right side. (Magazine throat should be at Loader's right, with magazine catch *up*.) Film (wound emulsion in) pulls off spindle counterclockwise.

11.19e Take-up (Fig. 11–35a)

Left side. (Magazine throat should be at Loader's left with magazine catch *up*.) Film winds on collapsible core clockwise, emulsion always in.

11.19f Loading (Fig. 11–35a)

(1) Open magazine cover, move footage-counter roller-guide arm down and to left until it locks in recessed guide. (2) In darkness, remove film roll from can and bag. Insert film end into feed throat; push through until film end emerges from top of magazine throat.

NOTE: Gently turning the magazine drive gear will ease the film end through the magazine throat.

CAUTION: When loading single-perforated (B-wind) film, perforations must be toward lid on feed side, away from lid on take-up side.

NOTE: To expedite engagement of film with film gears, cut film to bisect a perforation.

(3) Place film roll on feed spindle, and make sure that spindle key has engaged core keyway. (4) Release footage-counter guide arm (must be done manually), and make sure that roller rides film roll properly. (5) Close lid; rotate door lock clockwise. Pull on lid, to check that cover is secure. (6) Flip magazine over, open take-up lid, and push film-guide arm down (Fig. 11–35b).

NOTE: Take-up loading may be done in light.

(7) Bring film end out of throat and down to white threading mark near center of magazine base (Fig. 11–35c). Use magazine drive gear to keep film taut from exit of feed throat to marking notch, to maintain correct

Figure 11–35b Arriflex 16SR magazine take-up side. Courtesy of Arnold & Richter K.G.

1. Additive footage counter
2. Take-up throat slot
3. Magazine drive gear
4. Take-up roller guide

length of film (approximately 32 perforations from feed exit to notch). (8) Insert film end into take-up throat until perforation engages magazine drive gear. Turn drive gear until film end enters magazine take-up side.

CAUTION: It is important to maintain proper loop size. Do not allow excess film to exit feed side while trying to engage perforation in take-up gear.

To Secure Film End in Magazine with Collapsible Core. Insert film end into collapsible core. Move clamp inward to secure film.

To Secure Film End in Magazine with Plastic Core. Place core on take-up spindle. Insert film end into core slot, and wind film onto take-up core clockwise (emulsion in). (9) Release film-guide arm, and make sure that roller rides film properly. (10) Close door; rotate door lock clockwise. Pull on lid to check that cover is secure. Slide film loop under four retaining hooks on magazine film-pressure plate (Fig. 11–35d). Slide film on plate until upper and lower loops are equal. Put loop protector on front of magazine.

To Load 30.48m (100 ft) Daylight Spools. Depress center of core spindles, and remove core holders and/or collapsible core. Push film-guide arms down, and secure in catches. Place spools on square driver pins of spindles.

NOTE: 122m (400 ft) daylight spools are 3.17mm 1/8″ too large to fit into the magazine.

11.19g Unloading

In darkness, open take-up side magazine lid. Move counter-arm roller down until it locks.

1. Preset loop (approx. 32 perfs)
2. Film retaining hooks
3. Magazine drive gear
4. Lower magazine throat
5. White marking notch (not visible)

Figure 11–35c Arriflex SR magazine preset loop detail. Courtesy of Arnold & Richter K.G.

1. Upper magazine throat
2. Film retaining hooks
3. Magazine lock
4. Safety lock
5. Hinge pin
6. Magazine drive gear
7. White marking notch (not visible)

Figure 11–35d Arriflex SR magazine loop detail. Courtesy of Arnold & Richter K.G.

Magazine with Collapsible Core. Disengage clamp on core (push out-ward). Place index finger in core space, thumb on edge of roll. Turn magazine over, and let film drop into hand. Place exposed roll into bag and can.

Magazine with Plastic Core. Place index finger on core, thumb on edge of roll. Turn magazine over, and let film drop into hand. Place exposed roll into bag and can.

11.19h Footage Counters

Two. Counter at back of magazine is *subtractive* in increments of 12.19m (40 ft). Counter at side is *additive* in increments of 12.19m (40 ft).

NOTE: When using daylight spools, side counter is the only indicator of footage expended.

11.20 ARRIFLEX 16SR VIEWFINDER EXTENDER (FIG. 11–36)

The extender tube assembly is a 178mm (7-in.) unit that inserts between a prism box and eyepiece. Unit is added when camera is mounted on a tripod or geared head.

11.20a Mounting

1. Remove eyepiece from camera by rotating knurled nut on viewfinder. 2. Align pins and threads on large barrel of extension tube to viewfinder. Secure with knurled nut. 3. Align pins and threads on eyepiece to viewfinder tube; secure with knurled nut on extender.

11.20b Stability Hook

Located in extender barrel. As barrel is rotated, a metal hook with rubberized shaft extends from barrel. Hook inserts into eyelet below cameras carrying handle. Barrel is then rotated until rubberized shaft becomes taut and stabilizes extension tube.

CAUTION: When altering position of viewfinder, disengage hook. When position is reached, re-engage hook.

NOTE: With extender in place, all adjustments noted in Sec. 11.8f "viewfinder," apply.

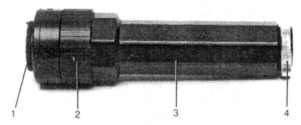

Figure 11–36   SR viewfinder extender tube. Courtesy of Arnold & Richter K.G.

1. Viewfinder attachment threads
2. Extender barrel
3. Extender tube
4. Eyepiece locking ring

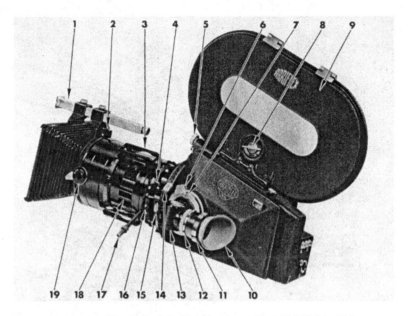

Figure 11–37a Arriflex 16BL (left side). Courtesy of Arnold & Richter K.G.

1. Sunshade boom
2. Sunshade snap catch
3. Focus grips
4. T stop grip
5. Magazine lockdown knob
6. Door lock
7. Viewfinder lock nut
8. Magazine lock
9. 12mm (400-ft) magazine
10. Eyecup

11. Focusing ring
12. Focus locking ring
13. Rotating viewfinder
14. Lens release
15. Lens lock
16. Zoom ring
17. Zoom stick
18. Center scalloped ring
19. Filter holder access knob

11.21 ARRIFLEX 16BL CAMERA* (FIGS. 11–37a and 11–37b)

NOTE: All directions are from Operator's point of view.

11.21a Base

Bottom fitted with two ⅜"-16 tapped holes, to accommodate tripod-lockdown screw.

WARNING: Inserting a long tripod-lockdown screw in either hole can accidentally activate the bypass (pistol-grip) ON/OFF switch and cause the camera to run. A thin strip of cardboard placed between camera base and tripod head plate will eliminate the problem.

11.21b Motors

To Mount

1. Remove the four exterior screws, and detach motor-housing cover (see "10" on Fig. 11–37b) at right side of the camera. 2. Open camera door,

---

*Manufacturer states the designation "BL" is for "Blimped."

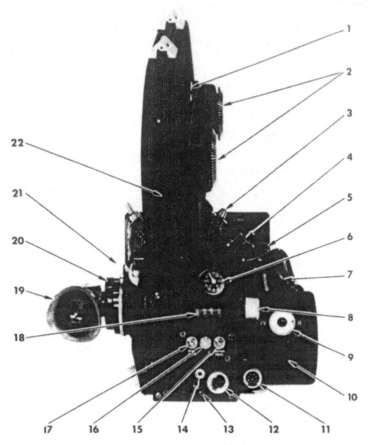

Figure 11–37b Arriflex 16BL (rear). Courtesy of Arnold & Richter K.G.

1. Magazine footage counter
2. Spindle wheels
3. Inching knob
4. Sound connection to amplifier
5. ON/OFF button
6. Tachometer
7. Contour grip
8. Counter reset knob
9. FWD/REV access cap
10. Motor housing cover
11. Power plug
12. Sync-pulse plug
13. Manual perforation scene marker
14. Phone jack
15. Edge-marker signal
16. Camera running signal
17. Full-frame exposure bloop bulb
18. Footage counter
19. Eyecup
20. Viewfinder lock nut
21. Door lock
22. 122m (400-ft) magazine

and remove the two internal screws and plastic-housing cover from transfer gear (see "3" on Fig. 11–39). 3. Remove motor pinion from motor-drive shaft. Insert motor into motor socket, aligning multipin connector. Press in until motor is firmly seated. Secure motor with three internal motor-mounting screws by inserting them into motor from *inside* the camera. 4. Secure the motor pinion to center of drive shaft. Replace plastic housing inside camera. Replace motor housing cover at right side of camera.

NOTE: BL motors are not interchangeable with S- or M-type motors.

To Set FWD/REV Switch on Constant-Speed Motor. Unscrew plastic cap at rear of motor-housing cover, and slide switch to left for FWD, to right for REV. Position of switch can be checked through the window in plastic cap.

NOTE: A minimum of 12 volts is required to run the camera with a 122 m (400-ft) load.

A 110V AC line requires a step-down transformer/rectifier.

Motors available for Arriflex 16BL.

Variable Speed Motor. 12V DC.

Governor-Controlled (Constant-Speed) Motor. 12V DC (24 fps); 12V DC (25 fps).

Synchronous Motor. 110V AC 60 Hz (24 fps); 110V AC 50 Hz (24 or 25 fps via gear change).

Quartz-Crystal Motor (for cordless double system recording). 12V DC 24 fps (60 Hz signal to tape recorder); 12V DC 25 fps (50 Hz signal to tape recorder).

NOTE: When fitted with an Arriflex Quartz-Crystal motor, type A-16, the camera is referred to as a 16 BLEQ.

11.21o Powerline

Input to Camera. Tuchel female end of cable fits to recessed Tuchel male plug located below counter-reset knob. Insert male end of cable into battery.

ON/OFF Button(s) (earlier models, not shown, have two buttons). Located in handgrip at right of camera. On *two-button models,* depress front button for continuous run, rear button for OFF or for short bursts. To start camera silently (to eliminate front button click) depress rear button first, then depress front button and release rear button.

Two-Pin Plug (not visible). At bottom of contour grip; for an accessory remote ON/OFF switch, which clamps to tripod handle.

Pistol-Grip Accessory. Inserts into one of the two ⅜"-16 tapped holes in base. When using a pistol grip fitted with a plunger, the trigger on the grip acts as an ON/OFF switch, bypassing the switch on the hand grip.

Outlets (at back of camera).
1. Main power plug (nine-pin Tuchel) is located below counter-reset knob.
2. Synchronous-pulse (five-pin Tuchel) plug is located below lamps.

NOTE: As Operator faces plug, with keyway at 6 o'clock, pins 1 (at 7 o'clock) and 2 (at 10 o'clock) are the AC pulse for the sound recorder: pin 3 (at 12 o'clock) is the scene-marking oscillator (pulse for "beep" on recorder); pins 4 (at 2 o'clock) and 5 (at 5 o'clock) are connected in cable and provide power for the full-frame and edge-marking bulbs. Lights will *not* work until cable is plugged into camera.
3. Upper female jack accommodates single-system monitoring phones.
4. Lower center-pin jack accommodates manual-perforation scene marker.

Bulbs (left to right):

1. The interior *full-frame exposure bulb* is in series with an exterior (left-side) bulb: exterior bulb lights up when interior signal registers on film frame.
2. The center *blinking-signal bulb* indicates the camera is running.
3. The interior *edge-marking bulb* is in series with an exterior (right-side) bulb. Exterior bulb lights up when interior signal registers on film edge.

    To Replace Bulbs.   Remove covers at back of camera.
1. *Full-frame exposure:* Unscrew exterior bulb and replace. Open camera door, depress leaf spring above gate, and swing it forward. Gently lift interior bulb up and out. Replace. Depress and turn leaf spring to lock. 2. *Blinking signal:* Unscrew bulb and replace. 3. *Edge-marker:* Unscrew exterior bulb, and replace. Open camera door, and depress leaf spring below gate. Tilt unit forward, and draw socket downward. Replace interior bulb. Push leaf spring up and back to secure.

NOTE: With regard to full-frame and edge-marking bulbs, *always* replace *both* bulbs in series. Because life expectancy of each bulb is approximately the same duration, two fresh bulbs will eliminate alternate burnouts.

Fuses.

Electronics.   1 ampere pico. Located in electronic module. *To change,* loosen four screws, remove back of camera to expose fuse in module.
Motor.   15 ampere pico. Located behind motor drive gear.

CAUTION: The 15 amp fuse is soldered in-line and is NOT field replaceable.

11.21d Turret

None. Single floating mount and locking rings accept blimped varifocal lens or standard lenses. (See Sec. 11.21e for exceptions.)

11.21e Lenses

Standard equipment is a blimped Angenieux or Zeiss varifocal lens. Focus marks are inscribed on exterior of lens housing (meters in white, feet in red). The focus reference mark is at left side. Plastic window at top of housing permits viewing of corresponding footage and lens focal-length setting. A small window at top of mount allows viewing of lens diaphragm setting (in T stops on an Angenieux 12–120 mm lens; in *f*-stops on a Zeiss 12.5–75 mm lens).

    An inscribed "T" mark at left side of mount is used for the diaphragm-setting reference.

    To Mount Lens.   Grasp lens housing by the center scalloped ring only. With plastic window *up,* align bayonet prongs with grooves in camera mount. Slide lens in until the three tabs on the lens housing are seated into locking-ring notches on camera. Rotate lens mount counterclockwise until it clicks. Rotate large lens lock counterclockwise (toward "FIX") to secure. Hand-tighten only.

    Insert zoom handle into single tapped hole, then back off one-half turn to allow positioning of handle at desired location on mount. Tighten handle, and lock it by rotating the lower (larger) knurled knob of handle clockwise.

    To Zoom.   Use either the handle or the scalloped zoom ring to change focal length.

To Focus. Rotate one of the three double-bracketed focus grips on lens barrel.

To Remove Lens. Rotate large lens lock clockwise in direction of arrow (toward "LOOSE"). Depress lens release (near the door lock). Rotate lens mount clockwise, and slide the lens from bayonet mount.

To Mount Standard Lenses.

1. Depress the lens release to retract lens lock at bottom of socket. 2. Align lens-guide slot with dot in mount (dot indicates position of guide key), and insert the lens. 3. Let up on the lens release. Tug the lens *gently* to make sure that lock has engaged lens.

NOTE: 28mm or shorter lenses cannot be used on the BL mount because their rear elements will touch the rotating mirror. *Exceptions:* 10mm Cinegon (Schneider), serial nos. 9861975 and higher; 8mm Distagon (Zeiss); 5.7mm Tegea (Kinoptic).

11.21f Viewfinder

Reflex. Image magnified 10X.

To View through Lens. Press eye against eyecup to open automatic closure device.

To Lock Autoclosure Device Open. Pull eyecup from finder. Rotate inner knurled locknut clockwise. Replace eyecup.

To Align Reflex Mirror for Viewing. Depress and rotate inching knob (shaped like a witch's hat) above contour handgrip.

CAUTION: Do not depress inching knob while camera is running.

To Focus Eyepiece. Rotate narrow scalloped ring on eyepiece clockwise to the word "LOOSE." Rotate large scalloped ring nearest eyecup to focus on grain of groundglass. When focus is set, turn narrow ring counterclockwise to "FIX."

Groundglass. On side of movement block. For access, open camera door. Views more than full aperture. Outer scribe denotes full aperture; inner scribe denotes TV aperture.

To Change. Loosen two small screws; lift holder out. Always replace with smooth surface toward eyepiece.

To Alter Finder Position for Viewing. Rotate viewfinder locknut counterclockwise toward "A." Rotate eyepiece in desired direction (it rotates 360°), perpendicular to camera. Set eyepiece at desired position. Rotate viewfinder locknut clockwise to "Z" to secure. Unit also swings out 25° horizontally from camera door.

To Remove Viewfinder from Camera. Rotate viewfinder locknut counterclockwise toward "A." Rotate viewfinder to vertical position, eyecup up. Pull viewfinder away from camera's internal bayonet lock (not shown).

To Detach Eyepiece. Rotate clockwise the knurled ring forward of eyepiece lock on viewfinder and pull eyepiece from keyed slots.

11.21g Sunshade

Sunshade/bellows slides in and out on square boom, which attaches to zoom lens.

To Remove from Zoom Lens. Lift sunshade snap catch (at top of rear sunshade plate). Pull sunshade down and forward.

To Mount on Zoom Lens. Rest the projecting piece (at rear of sunshade) between the two lugs at front of lens. Push top of shade toward lens until sunshade snap catch engages rear sunshade plate.

To Use with Conventional Lens. Requires an Arriflex Universal Lens Housing Unit (now shown). The sunshade mounts onto the Lens Housing the same as onto zoom lens.

Sunshade Boom. Scribed with various extension limitations. Set the forward knurled boom lock between the two scribed arrows for desired focal length.

NOTE: Camera shoe located below magazine lock knob is intended for use with a quick-detach carrying handle and *not* with sunshade boom, as on other Arriflex cameras.

11.21h Filters

To Remove Filter Holder from Lens. Rotate knurled knob at left side of lens housing marked "Auf-Zu" (open–closed). Swing sunshade away. Grasp circular filter holder by its knurled ring, and pull it out.

To Insert Filter into Holder. Rotate the filter notch toward nearest corner until both square cutouts match. Insert a 76.2 × 76.2mm (3 × 3) in. filter, and rotate filter lock to secure.

NOTE: Rotation direction is determined by thickness of filter. Less than 5mm (Arriflex manufacture)—rotate lock counterclockwise. More than 5mm (Wratten manufacture)—rotate lock clockwise.

WARNING: When no filter is used, an optical flat must always be inserted into filter holder, to block camera noise that may travel through lens and into shooting area.

To Insert Holder into Lens. Grasp holder by knurled edges. Align pin on holder with any one of the four holes in the mount. Insert into lens. Close and lock sunshade.

11.21i Single-System Sound Module

To Insert Sound Module into Camera. (see Fig. 11–38). Remove internal transparent plastic gear cover, which is secured by two screws. Remove the three green screws, which protect the threaded screw holes for mounting the module. These screws are located: 1. In upper left-hand section near connector plug. 2. In lower left-hand section. 3. In lower right-hand section.

The single-system module is inserted by aligning and plugging it into the miniature electrical connector, then securing the module with the three green screws.

11.21j Door

Hinged at back.

To Open. Rotate door lock counterclockwise (toward "A"). Swing eyepiece in a horizontal plane away from camera.

To Close. Swing eyepiece toward camera. Rotate door lock clockwise (toward "Z") to secure.

11.21k Magazines

122m (400 ft) and 61m (200 ft)

To Mount.

1. Rotate clockwise the knurled lock knob (above lens) until spring action frees lock. 2. Remove dust cover from camera housing, and insert film loop into camera cavity. 3. Seat rear male dovetail of magazine into rear

female dovetail on camera housing. Lower the front male dovetail into the camera housing. Rotate inching knob to engage gears. Thread camera (see Sec. 11.21l). 4. Depress magazine lock knob and rotate it counterclockwise to lock.

To Remove. Remove film from gate. Rotate magazine lock clockwise until lock is free. Lift magazine away.

11.21l   Threading (Fig. 11–38)
1. Push pressure-pad catch toward interior wall, and swing hinged pressure pad open. 2. Rotate inching knob until single registration pin enters gate and single pulldown claw is withdrawn from gate. 3a. Insert film into gate. Conform upper and lower loops to scribed lines in interior. Rotate inching knob until registration pin enters gate and engages perforation. Close pressure pad.

CAUTION: Pressure-pad lock must be engaged, and film must lie *inside* the side guide springs. Double check after each loading.

3b. *For single system,* after threading film through gate, thread film according to white guideline scribed on sound module. Open pressure

Figure 11–38   Arriflex 16BL threading detail. Courtesy of Arnold & Richter K.G.

1. Pressure plate	9. Magazine roller
2. Full-frame exposure bulb leaf spring	10. Flywheel brake
3. Lower pivot arm	11. Guide rail
4. Pressure roller	12. Sound drum
5. Idler roller	13. Tension roller
6. Thumb lever	14. Lower roller
7. Upper roller	15. Edge-marking bulb leaf spring
8. Recording heads	

roller by pressing, to right, the thumb lever protruding from the idler roller on the lower pivot arm. 4. Insert film between the pressure roller and the large upper roller. 5. Insert film between the recording heads and the guide rail. 6. Guide film around sound drum and over lower roller. 7. Guide film under tension roller and to right of magazine roller, into magazine.

NOTE: When camera is started, the tension roller will adjust upward automatically, pulling tension arm upward and releasing flywheel brake.

8. Depress ON/OFF switch in contour grip. Observe action of film. If satisfactory, close door, and reset footage counter.

11.21m Buckle-trip
None.

11.21n Footage Counter
Located at back of camera below tachometer. Additive. Counter registers 0–999 ft in increment of 1 ft, then reverts to 0. Additional *red digit* in counter registers 0–1 ft in increments of 1/10 ft.

To reset. depress large knurled knob at right of counter, and rotate counterclockwise.

NOTE: There is *no* frame counter.

11.21o Tachometer
At back of camera. Registers speeds from 0 to 50 fps, in increments of 1 fps.

CAUTION: Camera is not governor-controlled. A variable-speed motor *can and will* run faster than 50 fps. It cannot be assumed that by arbitrarily turning the rheostat so that the needle registers 50, the camera is running at 50 fps. Incorrect exposure can result if the camera speed is not deliberately and conscientiously set.

11.21p Shutter
Nonadjustable. Equivalent to 180°.

11.21q Lubrication (Fig. 11–39)
Manufacturer recommends two to three drops of oil every 10,000 ft. Depress ball-bearing oil valve behind film gate to lubricate the intermediate counter gear.

CAUTION: Manufacturer warns that oiling too frequently and/or excessive oiling can damage camera mechanism.

11.21r Cleaning
Optics: Clean with bulb syringe or camelhair brush.
Manufacturer recommends the following maintenance *each time film is changed:*
1. Open pressure pad, and check plate and pad for emulsion buildup. 2. Remove emulsion buildup with orangewood stick. 3. Wipe plates with chamois or soft cotton (not linen) handkerchief. 4. Use bulb syringe on interior of camera, to remove dust, dirt, etc.

11.21s Weight
(with 122m (400-ft) load) 9 kg (20 lb).

Figure 11–39 Arriflex 16BL lubrication (sound module removed). Courtesy of Arnold & Richter K.G.

1. Intermediate-counter-gear lube hole
2. Plastic gear cover
3. Transfer gear
4. Motor gear
5. Motor pinion
6. Interior edge-marking bulb holder
7. Module-mounting screw holes
8. Motor mounting screws
9. Module-mounting screw hole
10. Interior full-frame exposure bulb holder
11. Sound-module electrical connector

11.21t Troubleshooting

Trouble	Probable Cause
Camera will not start	Battery connections loose; battery dead; motor not making contact
Intermittent starting and stopping	Lugs in battery loose; broken connection in powerline; motor governor has carbon buildup
Torn perforations; ripped film	Improper threading
Door will not close	Dirt or film chip(s) in door; film not seated in gate
Viewing system blacked out	Shutter closed; eyepiece cap closed; lens stopped down past $f/22$; lens cap on
Lens will not focus	Lens not seated; camera too close for minimum distance of lens; elements damaged

Cut-in on groundglass (wide-angle lens)	Viewing mirror "sees" aperture of lens, but camera aperture does not—no problem if lens is seated properly
Cut-in on groundglass (normal lens)	Lens not seated; matte box extended
Lens will not enter port	Guide key inside turret bent so that it will not enter lens channel; lens not suited for BL (shorter than 28mm)—see "Note" at end of Sec. 11.21e
Film does not take up in magazine	Magazine take-up spindle loose; film loose on take-up core; incorrect magazine friction

11.22 ARRIFLEX 16BL MAGAZINE (Fig. 11–40)

11.22a Type
Displacement.

11.22b Capacity
122m (400 ft) (Fig. 11–40) and 61m (200 ft) (not shown).

11.22c Lid
One. Lug- and dog-locked. Hinged at top.

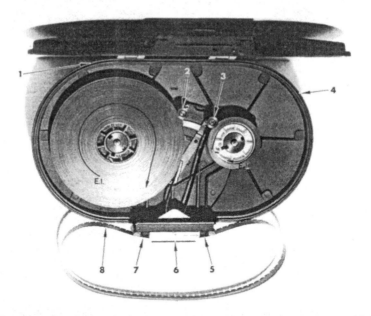

Figure 11–40 Arriflex 16BL 122m (400-ft) magazine. Courtesy of Arnold & Richter K.G.

1. Marking notch for silent loop(40–41 perforations)
2. Footage counter/feed roller guide
3. Take-up roller guide
4. Marking notch for sound loop (72–75 perforations)

5. Take-up light trap
6. Loop retaining plate
7. Feed light trap
8. 72-perforation loop

To open. Depress safety spring in lid recess. Rotate lock bar counter-clockwise (from "C" to "O"). Lift.

11.22d Feed
Left side. Film (wound emulsion in) pulls off spindle clockwise.

11.22e Take-up
Right side. Film winds onto spindle clockwise, emulsion always in.

11.22f Loading
1. Raise lid. Swing footage-counter/roller-guide arm to right, and lock it into pressure catch of take-up roller-guide arm. 2. In darkness, remove film roll from can and bag. Insert film end into left side of magazine throat, slowly rotating gear at bottom of magazine clockwise with thumb, until gear in throat engages film perforation. Thread at least 6 in. through.

NOTE: To expedite engagement of film in the magazine gears, cut the film to bisect a perforation.

3. Place film roll on the feed spindle. Rotate knurled feed-spindle wheel until spindle key engages the core keyway. 4. Release footage-counter/roller-guide arm, making sure that film rides between flanges of roller guide. 5a. *For BLs fitted with double (silent) system.* Rotate gear until film end extends clockwise around left outer edge of magazine to the notch at left of left hinge. 5b. *For BLs fitted with a single-system sound module:* Rotate gear until the film end extends clockwise around the left outer edge of magazine to the notch at the right of the right hinge. 6. Hold gear. Bring film end back counterclockwise, forming a loop, and then insert end into right-hand channel of magazine throat. Rotate gear until perforation engages gear and film moves into magazine.

CAUTION: It is important to maintain the proper loop size: 40–41 *visible* perforations for double system; 72–75 *visible* perforations for single system. Do not allow excess film to exit feed side while trying to engage perforation onto take-up gear.

7a. *When magazine has a collapsible core:* Insert film end into collapsible take-up core. Move clamp inward to secure film. 7b. *When magazine has a plastic core:* Place core on take-up spindle. Rotate knurled take-up spindle wheel until spindle key engages the core keyway. Insert film end into core slot, and wind film onto take-up core clockwise (emulsion in). 8. Close hinged lid. Rotate recessed lock clockwise to "C."
    To Take up Film Slack. Depress and rotate knurled spindle wheels at back of magazine. Take-up rotates counterclockwise. Feed rotates clockwise.
    To Load Daylight Spools. Depress center of core spindles, and remove core holders and/or collapsible core. Squeeze film-tension arms together, and snap into catch in center of magazine. Place spools on square driver pins of spindles.

Film-Loop Guard. Depress film loop against magazine mouth. Slide loop guard (with notch inward) over film and under retaining plate.

11.22g Unloading
In darkness, open magazine lid.

When Magazine Has a Collapsible Core. Disengage clamp on core (push outward). Place index finger in core space, thumb on edge of roll. Turn magazine over, and let film drop into hand. Place exposed roll into bag and can.

When Magazine Has a Plastic Core. Place index finger on core, thumb on edge of roll. Turn magazine over, and let film drop into hand. Place exposed roll into bag and can.

11.22h Footage Counter
At back of magazine. Subtractive 152.4m (500–0 ft) in increment of 15.24m (50 ft).

11.23 CINEMA PRODUCTS "CRYSTALOK" CRYSTAL MOTOR ATTACHMENT for Arriflex 16BL (Fig. 11–41)
A crystal control/variable speed unit manufactured by Cinema Products; attaches to an Arriflex 16BL and provides a camera with a crystal-sync speed control at either 24 or 25 fps (depending upon gearing of camera), as well as a variety of sync speeds.

NOTE: The CMA will not operate unless camera is fitted with an Arriflex standard universal motor. Motor attachment only provides crystal sync control in *forward* mode. A universal motor will not run in reverse.

To Mount. (1) Loosen three thumbscrews on motor-attachment collar, and slide unit over end of camera motor housing. Tighten thumbscrews. (2) Insert Amphenol female end of pigtail extending from motor attachment into recessed male Amphenol plug on camera body (located below counter reset knob).

WARNING: Do not insert Amphenol plug on pigtail back into motor. (It *has* been done!)

(3) Insert power cable from battery into Amphenol plug on motor attachment. (4) Ascertain that speed-selector knob on motor attachment is set at desired fps. Verify by comparing tachometer on camera.

Speed-Selector Knob. Located at top of motor attachment. With witness mark on knob at SYNC, camera will run at either 24 fps or 25 fps (depending on gearing). Camera speed can be varied from 14 fps to 48 fps

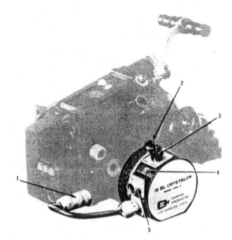

1. Pigtail Amphenol plug
2. Thumbscrew (one of three)
3. Speed selector knob
4. Warning light
5. Power cable plug

Figure 11–41 Cinema Products "Crystalok" for 16BL. Courtesy of Cinema Products.

by turning speed-selector knob off SYNC mark clockwise and visually monitoring camera tachometer.

To Return Motor to SYNC Mode. Rotate speed-selector knob counterclockwise to SYNC.

Warning Light. Atop motor attachment. Blinks if camera runs out of sync or is off of selected speed in variable-speed mode.

11.24 ARRIFLEX 16 16S CAMERA* (Figs. 11–42*a* and 11–42*b*)

NOTE: All directions are from the Operator's point of view.

11.24a Base

Bottom fitted with ⅜"-16 and ¼"-20 tapped holes to accommodate tripod-lockdown screws.

11.24b Motors

Governor-Controlled (Constant-Speed) Motor (not shown).   Inching knob is at back of motor. Motor does *not* reverse.

Variable-Speed Motor. (Fig. 11–42*b*)   Small knurled knob at rear is inching knob. Larger knurled knob at rear is FWD/REV switch, which must be rotated clockwise for forward, counterclockwise for reverse.

To Adjust Variable-Speed Motor.   Rotate entire ribbed motor shell (which is a rheostat) clockwise for fast, counterclockwise for slow. Motor-speed scribe marks on rheostat are for reference only. Correct fps speed is obtained by observing fps tachometer.

To Mount Either Motor.   Loosen motor-lock lever counterclockwise. Rotate motor until cylinder-locating pin aligns with keyway (approximately "7 o'clock"). Insert motor into motor cavity firmly until cylinder shoulder abuts camera box housing. Rotate locking lever clockwise.

To Remove Motor.   Loosen motor-locking lever counterclockwise. Pull motor straight back.

NOTE: A minimum of 8 volts is required to run a camera with a 122m (400-ft) load. An 110V AC line requires a stepdown transformer/rectifier.

Magazine Torque Motor (Fig. 11–42*b*).   Fits to back side of magazine. Unit is essential when using 61m (200-ft) or 122m (400-ft) magazines on camera.

To Mount Torque Motor on Magazine.   Place magazine with lid *down* and subtractive footage counter *up*. Rotate torque motor lock-levers (at each side of motor drum) *up*. Insert lock-lever catches of motor into magazine keyways. Rotate lock levers out and down (follow arrows) to secure. Set direction lever on "F" (forward) or "R" (reverse), to coincide with direction set on camera motor. After each take, rotate knurled magazine take-up wheel to remove film slack.

Groundwire receptacle is at base of motor drum.

To "Ground" the Torque Motor.   Insert one end of groundwire into motor groundwire receptacle and other end into groundwire receptacle on female end of powerline plug (see Sec. 11.24c).

To Reverse Motor with 122m (400-ft) Magazine Attached.   Set large knurled knob (at rear of camera motor) counterclockwise to "R." Set magazine torque motor to "R." Cover lens when running film back to beginning of scene intended for double exposure.

---

*Manufacturer states that designation "S" is for "Standard."

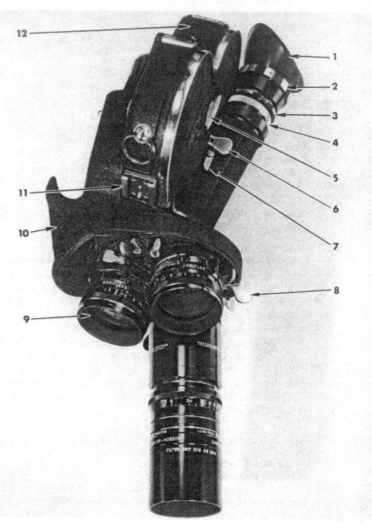

Figure 11–42a Arriflex 16S 30m (100-ft) spool configuration (without matte box, top view). Courtesy of Arnold & Richter K.G.

1. Eyecup
2. Focusing ring
3. Focus locking ring
4. Eyepiece coupling nut
5. Door lock
6. ON/OFF switch
7. Lock release
8. Turret grip
9. Taking lens
10. Contour grip
11. Matte-box boom shoe
12. Cavity cover

Figure 11–42b Arriflex 16S with matte box and 400-ft magazine. Courtesy of Arnold & Richter K.G.

1. Magazine footage counter
2. Knurled magazine feed wheel
3. Torque motor lock levers
4. Torque motor
5. Tachometer
6. Footage reset disc
7. Frame reset disc
8. Filter holder
9. Inching knob
10. Power-cable socket (not visible)
11. Motor FWD/REV switch
12. Variable-speed motor
13. Motor locking lever
14. Frame counter
15. Footage counter
16. Groundwire receptacle (not visible)
17. Knurled magazine take-up wheel
18. Torque motor FWD/REV switch
19. 122m (400-ft) magazine

261

Motors Available for Arriflex 16S:
Variable-Speed Motor. 8V DC.
Governor-Controlled (Constant-Speed) Motor: 8V DC (16 fps), 8V DC (24 fps), 8V DC (25 fps).
Synchronous Motor. 110V AC 60 Hz (24 fps) with step-down transformer/rectifier for 8V DC to torque motor; 110V AC 50 Hz (25 fps) with step-down transformer/rectifier for 8V DC to torque motor.
Animation/Time-Lapse Motor. 110V AC 60 Hz, 110V AC 50 Hz.

NOTE: Animation motors require intervalometer for time-lapse photography.

11.24c Powerline

Input to Camera. Power-cable socket is located at rear of camera base (left of motor). Split recessed socket pins may be separated slightly, to secure female cable plug snugly on pins.

CAUTION: Metal pins are very fragile and will break if separated roughly.

A latch above socket (see Fig. 11–43 for detail) engages a rubber catch on female plug and holds it in proper polarity. Plus (+) is left pin, closest to the door.
    The female plug may have a groundwire receptacle (below rubber catch), which accommodates other end of groundwire that should be inserted into torque-motor groundwire receptacle (see Sec. 11.24b).
    Male-end of cable should be inserted into battery. Plus (+) on plug aligns with red plus (+) on battery. Male split pins may be wedged apart slightly to obtain a snug fit.
    If there is a pressure catch on the cable, attach it to a battery holddown lock, to hold male plug securely to power source.

ON/OFF Switch in door.   Push lever down to turn power on; lever locks into place. Depress lock release (forward of the lever) to turn power off.

NOTE: When using a pistol-grip accessory fitted with a plunger, the trigger acts an an ON/OFF camera switch, bypassing the ON/OFF switch in camera door. Insert pistol-grip into the ⅜"-16 tapped hole in the camera base.

Fuses. None.

11.24d Turret
Three-position. 21° divergent ports.
    To Rotate. Grasp turret grip opposite taking lens. Depress (or lift) until desired lens rotates into position nearest contour grip at right side. Turret snaps into place.

NOTE: Turret grips have indented data marks, which are visible to Operator and help in determining which lens is in *taking position*—i.e., the widest-angle lens, one dot; the normal lens, two dots; and the telephoto lens, three dots. Each lens should be mounted opposite data mark to which it corresponds.

11.24e Lenses
    To Mount on Turret. Rotate lens barrel until channel in mount aligns with infinity mark on lens. Grasp lens by its knurled footage ring. Squeeze

locking levers at each side of lens port on turret, and insert lens into port with follow-focus grips ("wings") *up*. Slide channel at rear of mount over the guide key inside the lens port. Release the locking levers. Gently tug at lens to make certain that levers have gripped the channel at rear of lens mount.

NOTE: Lenses should correspond as closely as possible to data marks on turret grips.

To Remove Lens. Rotate follow-focus grips *up*. Grasp knurled footage ring. Squeeze locking levers at each side of lens port, and gently pull lens away.

CAUTION: When using fewer than three lenses, always plug empty port(s), to avoid a light leak to the aperture.

NOTE: 16mm and 35mm Arriflex lenses are interchangeable, with the following *exceptions:* 5.7mm, 10mm, 11.5mm, 16mm, and 25mm. These will *not* cover a 35mm aperture. The only wide-angle lenses that *will* cover a 35mm aperture are 9.8mm, 14.5mm, 18.5mm retrofocus, and the 28mm *made for 35mm cameras.*

11.24f Viewfinder
Reflex. Image magnified $10 \times$.
To Align Reflex Mirror for Viewing. Rotate inching knob at rear of motor.
To Detach Eyepiece. Rotate knurled eyepiece coupling nut on viewfinder clockwise, and pull eyepiece from keyed slots.

Hinged Metal Cap (not shown): Closes viewing system. This cap must be closed when Operator's eye is not covering eyepiece, so that stray light cannot strike mirror and kick back onto film.
To Focus **Newer Models** (Fig. 11–42*a*) Rotate narrow scalloped ring on eyepiece clockwise to the word "lose" (loose). Rotate large scalloped ring nearest eyecup to focus on groundglass. When focus is set, turn narrow ring counterclockwise to "fest" (tight).

Older Models (not shown): Loosen small lever on eyepiece. Rotate barrel to scribes numbered with "+" or "−" diopter settings. Focus on groundglass. When focus is set, lock small lever.

Groundglass. Behind eyepiece. Views full aperture. Cannot be changed on the job.
To Clean. Remove eyepiece to expose smooth surface of groundglass.

11.24g Sunshade/Matte Box
Either end of sunshade/matte box slides in and out on square boom.
To mount. Insert notched plate at rear of boom into shoe on camera housing above turret. Rotate knurled knob at front of boom until locking pin engages centering hole of shoe.

11.24h Filters
Holders (with retaining springs) house two 50.8×50.8mm ($2 \times 2''$) glass filters, or two 50.8×50.8mm ($2 \times 2''$ gelatines, which slide into a separate gel frame. Gel frame clips into holder.

NOTE: Rear filter housing rotates. Threaded opening at rear housing accepts an adapter to hold a Series 8 glass filter.

To Insert Filter. Slide two "keyed" filter holders into left side of matte box. Spring catch of housing must engage notch in holder.

To Disengage Filter Holders. Depress catch at bottom right of matte box, and slide holder out.

11.24i Door

Dog-locked.

To Remove. Rotate recessed door lock counterclockwise to "O."

CAUTION: Door is not hinged.

To Close. Turn door lock to "O." Align door with contour of camera, and secure lock clockwise to "C." Grasp finder, and pull gently to check that door is properly secured to the camera.

11.24j Magazines

61m (200-ft) and 122m (400-ft).

To Mount.

1. Rotate FWD/REV switch on *torque motor* counterclockwise to "F" (FWD). Rotate large knurled knob on *camera motor* clockwise to "F." 2. Lift up lock lip (on nose of magazine. Pull pressure-locked cavity cover from top of camera housing. 3. Pull loop of film from feed side, and insert it into camera cavity. 4. Seat rear male dovetail that is on magazine nose into rear female dovetail of camera housing; then lower front male dovetail into camera housing. 5. Press lock lip down until magazine locks into camera housing.

CAUTION: Hand-tighten only! Lock lip does not necessarily seat flush with magazine. Do *not* force it down!

6. Hook spring-loaded lock-lip catch into lock lip. Thread camera (Sec. 11.24k, below)

To Remove Magazine. Unthread camera. Remove lock-lip spring; lift lock-lip *up*. Raise magazine. Replace cavity cover on camera.

11.24k Threading (Fig. 11–43)

1. Depress pressure-pad catch, and swing hinged pressure pad open. 2. Depress pivot-pin button on sprocket-guide roller assembly (located below and to left of sprockets), and move springloaded rollers away from sprockets. 3. Rotate inching knob either way until single registration pin enters gate and single pulldown claw is withdrawn from gate. 4. Insert film into gate, and engage a perforation on the registration pin. Hold film with thumb and forefinger, and rotate the inching knob until pulldown claw engages a perforation. Close pressure pad with thumb pressure.

CAUTION: It is extremely important to double-check that pressure-pad catch is engaged!

5. Conform upper film loop to scribed line in camera. Insert film to left of central roller, then between upper sprocket-guide roller and sprocket. Engage perforations on sprocket; swing upper sprocket-guide roller toward sprocket to hold film in place. 6. Conform lower loop to scribed line in camera. Insert film between lower sprocket-guide roller and sprocket, then to right of central roller. 7. Push sprocket-guide roller assembly *gently* toward sprockets. Rotate take-up wheel counterclockwise on torque motor to pull up slack.

Figure 11–43 Arriflex 16S threading detail (magazine cover removed to show film path). Courtesy of Arnold & Richter K.G.

1. Door guide pin
2. 30.48m (100-ft) spool feed spindle
3. Pivot-pin button
4. Central roller
5. Magazine lock lip
6. 30.48m (100-ft) spool take-up spindle
7. Power-cable latch
8. Power-cable to power cable socket
9. Door guide pin
10. Internal ON/OFF switch
11. Buckle-trip
12. Spring-loaded sprocket-guide rollers
13. Pressure-pad catch

CAUTION: Slack film on take-up side can loop under the 30.48m (100-ft) spool take-up spindle inside camera while it is being pulled up into magazine. This could result in a full roll of scratched film.

8. Depress internal ON/OFF switch, and observe action of the film. If satisfactory, turn off camera and close door.

NOTE: 30.48m (100-ft) daylight spools are threaded as just described, except that spools are placed on spindles within camera housing.

11.24l Buckle-trip
Located below the lower spring-loaded sprocket-guide roller (Fig. 43). The roller on the buckle-trip arm cuts out power when pulled up by a short lower loop. It also prevents film end from running through gate, or film from piling up in camera.

NOTE: Earlier models (not shown) may not have a buckle-trip.

To Reset. Depress pivot-pin button on the sprocket-guide roller assembly. When assembly opens, the buckle-trip is automatically reset.

To Override. If buckle-trip microswitch fails to reset, push plunger in door below eyepiece. Narrow base of toggle lever (located back of internal ON/OFF switch on most models, missing on others) will pivot forward when plunger strikes heavy side of lever. Buckle-trip will not function thereafter.

To Cut Out Override. Place forefinger on narrow base of toggle lever, and push base toward rear of camera.

11.24m Footage and Frame Counters
Located at back of camera above motor. Additive.

Footage Counter. Registers 0–36m (0–118 ft) in increments of .61m (2 ft), then reverts to 0 (zero). Applies to daylight spools or 61m (200-ft) magazines. When 122m (400-ft) magazines are used, magazine counter is utilized.

Frame Counter. Registers 0–39 frames in increments of 1 frame, then reverts to 0 (zero).

To Reset Either Counter. Rotate separate reset discs located at right of counters.

11.24n Tachometer
Located at rear of camera above footage counter. Registers speeds from 0 to 50 fps, in increments of 1 fps.

CAUTION: Camera is not governor-controlled. A variable-speed motor *can and will* run faster than 50 fps. It cannot be assumed that by arbitrarily turning the rheostat so that the needle registers 50, the camera is running at 50 fps. Incorrect exposure can result if the camera speed is not deliberately and conscientiously set by the Operator.

11.24o Shutter
Nonadjustable. Equivalent to 180°.

11.24p Lubrication (Fig. 11–44)
Manufacturer recommends six to eight drops of oil on the following parts every 9144m (30,000 ft): 1. Depress top ball-bearing oil valve above sprockets to lube intermediate counter gear. 2. Depress ball-bearing oil valve near film gate to lube intermediate shutter gear.

CAUTION: Manufacturer warns that oiling too frequently and/or excessive oiling can damage camera mechanism.

3. Rollers—one drop of oil.

NOTE: After oiling, run camera to eliminate excess oil, and wipe clean.

11.24q Cleaning
Optics: Clean with bulb syringe or camel's-hair brush.

Figure 11–44 Arriflex 16S lubrication. Courtesy of Arnold & Richter K.G.

1. Intermediate counter gear   3. Intermediate shutter gear
2. Rollers

     Manufacturer recommends the following maintenance *each time film is changed:* 1. Open pressure pad, and check plate and pad for emulsion buildup. 2. Remove emulsion buildup with orangewood stick. 3. Wipe plates with chamois or soft cotton (not linen) handkerchief. 4. Use bulb syringe on camera interior to remove dust, dirt, etc.

11.24r Weight
(With 122m (400-ft) load) 66kg

11.24s Troubleshooting

Trouble	*Probable Cause*
Camera will not start	Battery connections loose; roller guides not closed against sprockets; battery dead; motor not making contact; buckle-trip not reset
Intermittent starting and stopping	Slotted power-line prongs (either in battery or camera) squeezed together, making poor contact; lugs in battery loose, broken connection in power line
Torn sprockets; ripped film	Improper threading
Loops pull taut each time camera starts	Camera motor switch is forward while torque motor switch is in reverse (or vice versa)

Door will not close	Camera "ON" switch in door is depressed; dirt of film chip in door recess
Viewing system blacked out	Shutter closed; eyepiece cap closed; lens stopped down past $f/22$; lens cap on
Lens will not focus	Lens not seated; camera too close for minimum distance of lens; elements damaged
Cut-in on groundglass (wide-angle lens)	Viewing mirror "sees" aperture of lens, but camera aperture does not—no problem if turret is seated properly
Cut-in on groundglass (normal lens)	Turret not seated, matte box extended
Lens will not enter port	Guide key inside turret bent up or down, therefore will not enter lens channel
Torque motor does not take up	Contact pins on magazine and/or motor not touching (or dirty); contact spring on magazine is loose or dirty; FWD/ REV switch in neutral position
Film does not take up in magazine	Magazine take-up spindle loose; film loose on take-up core; torque motor FWD/ REV switch in neutral position

11.25 ARRIFLEX 16S MAGAZINE (Fig. 11–45)

11.25a Type
Displacement.

11.25b Capacity
122m (400 ft) (shown) and 61m (200 ft) (not shown).

11.25c Lid
One. Lug- and dog-locked. To open, depress safety spring in lid recess; rotate lock bar counterclockwise (from "C" to "O") lift.

11.25d Feed
Left side. Film (wound emulsion in) pulls off spindle clockwise.

11.25e Take-up
Right side. Film winds onto spindle clockwise, emulsion always in.

11.25f Loading
1. Remove lid. Swing footage-counter/roller-guide arm *up,* and lock into catch near top of magazine. Swing take-up roller-guide arm *up,* and lock into catch below the counter arm. 2. In darkness, remove film roll from can and bag. Pull film off roll clockwise. Insert film end through feed side and past the light-trap rollers. 3. Place roll on feed spindle. Rotate knurled feed-spindle wheel until spindle key engages core keyway. 4. Insert film through take-up side light-trap rollers, and into magazine interior. 5. Hold core. Rotate knurled spindle wheel until spindle key engages core keyway. Insert film end into core slot, and wind up on take-up spindle clockwise (emulsion in). 6. Lower take-up roller-guide arm and feed (footage-counter) roller-guide arm, making certain that film rides between flanges of roller guides of both arms.

To Replace Lid. While holding magazine lid at a 45° angle, insert lid lugs (at bottom) into mating slots in magazine, then lower lid to a secure fit. Rotate lid lock bar clockwise from "O" to "C" until safety spring snaps up. Pull on lid, and run fingernails around its edge to make certain that lid is locked properly.

Figure 11–45 Arriflex 16S 400-ft. magazine. Courtesy of Arnold & Richter K.G.

1. Feed roller guide	3. Take-up light trap	5. Feed light trap
2. Take-up roller guide	4. Magazine nose	6. Magazine lock lip

To Take Out Film Slack. Rotate knurled spindle wheels at back of magazine. Take-up rotates counterclockwise. Feed rotates clockwise.

To Load Daylight Spools. Depress center of core spindles. Remove core holders. Place spools on square driver pins of spindles. Swing take-up roller-guide arm and feed (footage-counter) roller-guide arm *up,* and lock into their catches.

Film-Loop Guard. The 16S has *no* film-loop guide. Guards are only manufactured for the 35IIC, 16M, and 16BL.

11.25g Unloading

In darkness, open lid, and swing *up* take-up roller-guide arm, and lock into its catch. Place middle finger on core and thumb on edge of film roll. Turn magazine over, remove film, and place roll into bag and can.

11.25h Footage Counter

At back of magazine above torque motor. Subtractive: 152.4–0m (500–0 ft) in increments of 6.10m (20 ft).

11.25i Torque Motor

See "Magazine Torque Motor" in Sec. 11.24b.

11.26 ARRIFLEX 16M CAMERA* (Fig. 11–46)

NOTE: All directions are from the Operator's point of view.

---

*Manufacturer states that designation "M" is for "magazine."

Figure 11–46a Arriflex 16M with Zeiss 12.5–75mm Vario Somnar zoom lens (left front). Courtesy of Arnold & Richter K.G.

1. 122m (400-ft) magazine
2. Magazine lock
3. Sunshade boom shoe
4. Taking lens position

5. Turret grip
6. Door latch
7. Lock release
8. ON/OFF switch

11.26a Base

Bottom fitted with ⅜″-16 tapped hole to accommodate tripod-lockdown screw.

To align camera correctly on tripod. "square" the right side of base with the tripod head.

11.26b Motor

Constant-Speed Motor (not shown). Has an inching knob at back of motor.

Variable-Speed Motor (Fig. 11–46b). Small knurled knob at rear is inching knob. Larger knurled knob at rear is FWD/REV switch; knob must be rotated clockwise for forward, counterclockwise for reverse.

To Adjust Variable-Speed Motor. Rotate entire ribbed motor shell (which is a rheostat) clockwise for fast, counterclockwise for slow. The motor-

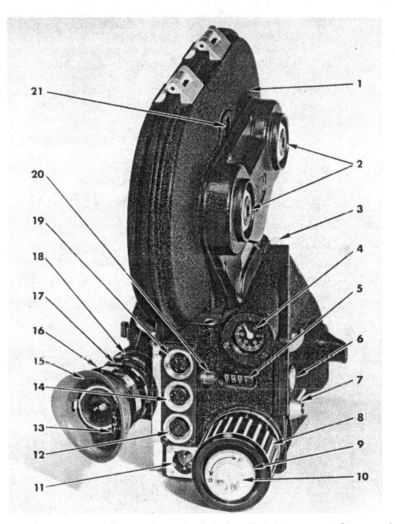

Figure 11–46b Arriflex 16M with 61m (200-ft) magazine (rear view). Courtesy of Arnold & Richter K.G.

1. 61m (200-ft) magazine
2. Spindle wheels
3. Exterior full-frame exposure bulb
4. Tachometer
5. Footage and frame counters
6. Counter reset knob
7. Motor lock
8. Variable-speed motor
9. FWD/REV switch
10. Manual inching knob
11. Power plug
12. Spare power plug
13. Hinged metal cap
14. Sync-pulse plug
15. Eyecup
16. Focus knob
17. Focus lock
18. Eyepiece coupling nut
19. Blank plug
20. Exterior edge-marking bulb
21. Magazine footage counter

speed scribe marks on the rheostat are for reference only. Correct fps speed is obtained by observing tachometer.

To Mount Either Motor. Loosen motor-lock lever counterclockwise. Rotate motor until cylinder-locating pin aligns with keyway (approximately 7 o'clock). Firmly insert motor into motor cavity until cylinder shoulder abuts camera-box housing. Rotate locking lever clockwise.

To Remove Motor. Loosen motor-lock lever counterclockwise. Pull motor straight back.

NOTE: An AC line to a variable or governor-controlled 8-volt motor requires a step-down transformer/rectifier.

Motors Available for Arriflex 16M.
Variable-Speed Motor. 8V DC.
Governor-Controlled (Constant-Speed) Motor. 8V DC (16 fps), 8V DC (24 fps), 8V DC (25 fps).
Synchronous Motor. 110V AC 60 Hz (24 fps), 110V AC 50 Hz (25 fps).

NOTE: 16M sync motor has no need for step-down transformer/rectifier as does the 16S (no 8V DC torque motor on 16M).

Animation/Time-Lapse Motor. 110V AC 60 Hz, 110V AC 50 Hz.

NOTE: Animation motors require intervalometer for timelapse photography.

11.26c Powerline

Input to Camera. Cannon female end of cable fits to lowest Cannon male plug on panel at back of camera. Male end of power line is inserted into battery. Plus (+) on cable fits to red plus (+) on battery. Split pins may be separated to obtain a snug fit.

CAUTION: Pins are very fragile and will break if separated roughly.

ON/OFF Lever Switch. Located in door. Push lever down to turn power on; the lever locks into place. Depress lock lever (forward of the switch) to turn power off.

NOTE: When using a pistol-grip accessory fitted with a plunger, the trigger acts as ON/OFF camera switch, bypassing ON switch in camera door. Pistol-grip is inserted into ⅜"-16 tapped hole in camera base.

Panel of Four Outlets at Back of Camera (Fig. 11–46*b*). One Cannon plug and three Tuchel plugs (starting from bottom and working up):
Plug 1. Three-pin Cannon plug for battery power.

NOTE: As Operator faces plug with keyway at 9 o'clock pin 1 (at 6 o'clock) is battery plus; pin 2 (at 12 o'clock) is blank; pin 3 (at 3 o'clock) is ground (minus).

Plug 2. Three-pin Tuchel plug is a parallel battery-power outlet. It can be tapped to run auxiliary equipment off of battery power. If either lug 1 or the Cannon input are unusable, plug 2 can be used, to supply power to the camera.

NOTE: As Operator faces plug with keyway at 9 o'clock, pin 1 (at 6 o'clock) is battery plus; pin 2 (at 12 o'clock) is blank; pin 3 (at 3 o'clock) is ground (minus).

Plug 2. Three-pin Tuchel pin is a parallel battery-power outlet. It can be tapped to run auxiliary equipment off of battery power. If either plug 1 or the Cannon input are unusable, plug 2 can be used, to supply power to the camera.

NOTE: As Operator faces plug with keyway at 9 o'clock, pin 1 (at 12 o'clock) is blank; pin 2 (at 3 o'clock) is ground (minus); pin 3 (at 6 o'clock) is battery + (plus).

Plug 3. Five-pin Tuchel for sync pulse.

NOTE: As Operator faces plug with keyway at 9 o'clock, pin 1 (at 11 o'clock) is ground (minus); pin 2 (at 1 o'clock) is AC pulse for sound recorder; pin 3 (at 3 o'clock) is scene-marking oscillator (pulse for beep on recorder); pins 4 (at 5 o'clock) and 5 (at 7 o'clock) are connected in cable and provide power for camera lights. Lights will *not* work until cable is plugged into camera.

Plug 4. The top four-pin Tuchel plug is a blank on most cameras. It can be wired for special applications. If plug is custom wired, specific instructions must be obtained for its use.

Interior Full-Frame Exposure Bulbs. In series with exterior bulb located near matte box; lights up as signal is registered on film.

To Change Full-Frame Exposure Bulbs. Rotate exterior plastic bulb housing counterclockwise to remove housing (use a rubber band as a grip on the plastic), pull bulb out with tweezers (a black tube with bulb at other end will emerge). Replace *both* bulbs, and reinsert into camera. Rotate plastic housing clockwise.

CAUTION: If bulb rod (the black tube) is removed from camera, cover bulb socket with black tape to prevent a light leak into camera.

Interior Edge-Marking Bulb. In series with exterior bulb; located at rear of camera.

To Change Edge-Marking Bulbs. (a) *Interior bulb:* Remove slotted screw at base of camera, and remove bulb with tweezers. Insert new bulb, and replace screw. (b) *Exterior bulb:* Rotate plastic housing counterclockwise (use a rubber band as a grip on the plastic), unscrew bulb, and insert new one. Replace cap.

NOTE: In regard to full-frame and edge-marker bulbs, *always* replace *both* bulbs in series. Because life expectancy of each bulb is approximately the same duration, two fresh bulbs will eliminate alternate burnouts.

Fuses. None.

11.26d Turret

Three-position; 21° divergent ports.

To Rotate. Grasp turret grip opposite taking lens. Depress (or lift) until desired lens rotates into position nearest the contour grip at right side. Turret snaps into place.

NOTE: Turret grips have indented data marks, which are visible to the Operator and help in determining which lens is in the taking position— i.e., widest-angle lens, one dot; normal lens, two dots; and telephoto lens, three dots. Each lens should be mounted opposite data mark to which it corresponds.

11.26c Lenses

To Mount on Turret. Rotate lens barrel until channel in mount aligns with infinity mark on lens. Grasp lens by its knurled footage ring. Squeeze locking levers at each side of lens port on turret, and insert lens into port, with the follow-focus grips (wings) *up.* Slide the channel at rear of mount over guide key inside lens port. Release the locking levers. Gently tug at lens to make certain that levers have gripped the channel at rear of lens mount.

NOTE: Lenses should correspond as closely as possible to data marks on turret grips.

To Remove Lens. Rotate follow-focus grips *up.* Grasp knurled footage ring. Squeeze locking levers at each side of lens port, and gently pull lens away.

CAUTION: When using fewer than three lenses, always plug empty port(s) to avoid a light leak to aperture.

NOTE: 16mm and 35mm Arriflex lenses are interchangeable, with the following *exceptions:* 5.7mm, 10mm, 11.5mm, 16mm, and 25mm. These will *not* cover a 35mm aperture. The only wide-angle lenses that *will* cover a 35mm aperture are 9.8mm, 14.5mm, 18.5mm retrofocus, and the 28mm *made for the 35mm cameras.*

11.26f Viewfinder

Reflex. Image magnified 10×.

To Align Reflex Mirror for Viewing. Rotate inching knob at rear of motor.

To Detach Eyepiece. Rotate clockwise the knurled eyepiece coupling nut on finder, and pull eyepiece from keyed slots.

Hinged Metal Cap. Closes viewing system. Cap must be closed when Operator's eye is not covering the eyepiece, so that stray light cannot strike mirror and kick back onto film.

To Focus. Rotate narrow scalloped ring on eyepiece clockwise to the word "lose" (loose). Rotate large scalloped ring nearest the eyecup to focus on groundglass. When focus is set, turn narrow ring counterclockwise to "fest" (tight).

Groundglass. Behind eyepiece. Views full aperture. Cannot be changed on the job.

To Clean. Remove eyepiece to expose smooth surface of groundglass.

11.26g Sunshade/Matte Box

Either end of sunshade/matte box slides in and out on square boom.

To mount, insert notched plate at rear of boom into shoe on camera housing above turret. Rotate knurled knob at front of boom until locking pin engages centering hole of shoe.

11.26h Filters

Holders (with retaining springs) house two 50.8 × 50.8mm (2 × 2″) glass filters, or two 50.8 × 50.8mm (2 × 2″) gelatines (which slide into a separate gel frame). The gel frame clips into the holder.

NOTE: Rear filter housing rotates. Threaded opening at rear housing accepts an adapter to hold a Series 8 glass filter.

To Insert Filter. Slide two keyed filter holders into left side of matte box. Spring catch of housing must engage notch in holder.

To Disengage Filter Holders. Depress catch at bottom right of matte box, and slide the holder out.

11.26i Door
Hinged at front.
To Open. Slide knurled latch (below viewfinder tube) forward. Swing eyepiece in a horizontal plane away from camera.
To Close. Swing eyepiece toward camera. Slide knurled latch toward rear.

11.26j Magazines
61m (200 ft), 122m (400 ft), 366m (1200 ft).

To Mount.
1. Depress spring-lock lever at side of magazine lock. Rotate lock (at front left) counterclockwise until it clicks open. Remove dust cover. 2. Insert film loop into camera cavity. Seat rear male dovetail of magazine into rear female dovetail on camera housing. Lower the front male dovetail into the camera housing.

NOTE: Gears of camera are spring-loaded and automatically engage gears of magazine.

3. Rotate magazine lock clockwise.

CAUTION: Hand-tighten only.

4. Thread camera (Sec. 11.26k).
To Remove Magazine. Remove film from gate, and depress spring-lock lever. Rotate magazine lock-set counterclockwise until it clicks open. Remove magazine.

11.26k Threading (Fig. 11–47)
1. Push pressure-pad catch toward camera interior wall, and swing the hinged pressure pad open. 2. Rotate inching knob until single registration pin retracts from gate and single pulldown claw is withdrawn from gate. 3. Insert film into gate. Hold film with thumb and forefinger so as to adjust film up or down in gate. Clear lower loop from guide track at bottom of film chamber (this should clear when pulldown claw is at its lower point of travel). Upper loop will form automatically. 4. Rotate inching knob until registration pin enters gate and engages perforation. Close pressure pad with forefinger.

CAUTION: It is extremely important to engage the pressure pad catch. Double check after each closing.

5. Rotate the inching knob, and check that lower loop clears guide track. Adjust if necessary by repeating steps 3 and 4. Transport a few inches of film through the gate manually. If satisfactory, proceed to step 6.
6. Depress internal ON/OFF switch in camera. Observe action of film. If satisfactory, close door and zero the footage counter.

11.26l Buckle-trip
Located above lower guide track (Fig. 11–47). Roller on the arm cuts out power when pulled up by a short lower loop. It also prevents film end from running through gate.
To Reset. open or close camera door. Buckle-trip resets automatically. 16M has *no* override such as the 16S has.

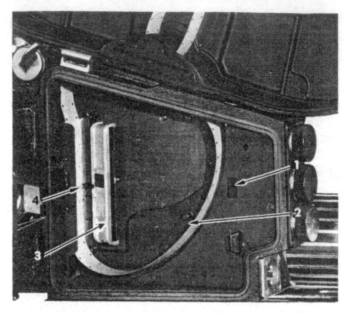

Figure 11–47 Arriflex 16M threading detail. Courtesy of Arnold & Richter K.G.

1. Internal ON/OFF switch
2. Buckle-trip

3. Pressure pad (open)
4. Pulldown claw

11.26m Footage and Frame Counters
Located at back of camera above motor. Additive.

Footage Counter. Registers 0–30.17m (0–99 ft) in increments of .3048 (1 ft), then reverts to 0 (zero).

Frame Counter. Registers 0–39 frames in increments of 1 frame, then reverts to 0 (zero).
To Reset. Rotate single disc at right of counter.

11.26n Tachometer
At back of camera above footage and frame counters. Registers speeds from 0 to 50 fps, in increments of 1 frame per second.

CAUTION: Camera is not governor controlled. A variable-speed motor *can and will* run faster than 50 fps. It cannot be assumed that by arbitrarily turning the rheostat so that the needle registers 50, the camera is running at 50 fps. Incorrect exposure can result if camera speed is not deliberately and conscientiously set by Operator.

11.26o Shutter
Nonadjustable. Equivalent to 180°.

11.26p Lubrication (Fig. 11–48)
Manufacturer recommends six to eight drops of oil on the following parts every 9144m (30,000 ft):
1. Depress top ball-bearing oil valve near center of camera interior to lubricate intermediate counter gear. 2. Depress ball-bearing oil valve near film gate to lubricate intermediate shutter gear.

Figure 11–48   Arriflex 16M lubrication. Courtesy of Arnold & Richter K.G.

1. Intermediate counter gear   2. Intermediate shutter gear

CAUTION: Manufacturer warns that oiling too frequently and/or excessive oil can damage the camera mechanism.

11.26q Cleaning

Optics: Clean with bulb syringe or camel's hair brush.

Manufacturer recommends the following maintenance *each time film is changed:*

1. Open pressure pad, and check plate and pad for emulsion buildup. 2. Remove emulsion buildup with orangewood stick. 3. Wipe plates with chamois or soft cotton (not linen) handkerchief. 4. Use bulb syringe on camera interior to remove dust, dirt, etc.

11.26r Weight

(with 122m (400-ft) load) 6.5 kg (14 ½ lb)

11.26s Troubleshooting

Trouble	*Probable Cause*
Camera will not start	Battery connections loose; battery dead; motor not making contact; buckle-trip not reset
Intermittent starting and stopping	Slotted power-line prongs in battery squeezed together, making poor contact; lugs in battery loose; broken connection in power line
Torn perforations; ripped film	Improper threading

Door will not close	Camera ON switch depressed; dirt or film chip in door recess
Viewing system blacked out	Shutter closed; eyepiece cap closed; lens stopped down past f/22; lens cap on
Lens will not focus	Lens not seated; camera too close for minimum distance of lens; elements damaged
Cut-in on groundglass (wide-angle lens)	Viewing mirror "sees" aperture of lens, but camera aperture does not—no problem if turret is seated properly
Cut-in on groundglass (normal lens)	Turret not seated; matte box extended
Lens will not enter port	Guide key inside turret bent up or down; therefore will not enter lens channel
Film does not take up in magazine	Magazine take-up spindle loose; film loose on take-up core

11.27 ARRIFLEX 16M MAGAZINE (Fig. 11–49)

11.27a Type
Displacement.

11.27b Capacity
122m (400 ft) (shown) and 61m (200 ft) (not shown).

Figure 11–49 Arriflex 16M 400-ft magazine. Courtesy of Arnold & Richter K.G.

1. Marking rib
2. Footage counter/roller-guide arm
3. Take-up roller arm
4. Collapsible take-up core
5. 36-perforation loop

11.27c Lid

One. 122m (400-ft) lid is lug- and dog-locked. 61m (200-ft) lid is hinged at top.

To Remove. Depress safety spring in lid recess. Rotate lock bar counterclockwise (from "C" to "O"). Lift.

11.27d Feed

Left side. Film (wound emulsion in) pulls off spindle clockwise.

11.27e Take-up

Right side. Film winds on spindle clockwise, emulsion always in.

11.27f Loading

(1a) *122m (400-ft) magazine:* Remove lid. Swing feed footage-counter/ roller-guide arm *up,* and lock into catch near top of magazine. Swing take-up roller-guide arm up, and lock into catch below counter arm roller.
(1b) *61m (200-ft) magazine:* Raise lid. Swing both footage-counter and take-up roller-guide arms toward center of magazine, and lock into catches.
(2) In darkness, remove film roll from can and bag. Insert film end into left side of magazine throat, slowly rotating gear at bottom clockwise with thumb until gear in throat engages film perforation. Thread at least 6 in. through.

NOTE: To expedite engagement of film in magazine gears, cut film so as to bisect a perforation.

(3) Place film roll on feed spindle. Rotate knurled feed-spindle wheel until spindle key engages core keyway. (4) Rotate gear until film end extends clockwise around left outer edge of magazine to marking rib (a raised bar on outside of magazine). (5) Hold gear. Bring film end back counterclockwise, and then insert end into right-hand channel of magazine throat. Rotate gear until perforation engages gear and film moves into magazine.

CAUTION: It is important to maintain the proper loop size: 36 *visible* perforations. Do not allow excess film to exit feed side while trying to engage perforation of film end into take-up gear!

(6a) *When magazine has a collapsible take-up core:* Insert film end into slot of collapsible take-up core. Move clamp inward to secure film.
(6b) *When magazine has a plastic core:* Place core on take-up spindle. Rotate knurled take-up-spindle wheel until spindle key engages core keyway. Insert film end into core slot, and wind film onto take-up core clockwise (emulsion in). (7) Release take-up roller-guide arm and then feed footage-counter/roller-guide arm, making certain that film rides between flanges of roller guides.

To Replace 122m (400-ft) Lid. While holding lid at a 45° angle, insert bottom lugs into mating slots in magazine, then lower lid to a secure fit. Rotate lid-lock bar clockwise from "O" to "C" until safety spring snaps up. Pull on lid, and run fingernails around edge slit, to ascertain that lid is locked tight.

To Take Out Film Slack. Rotate knurled spindle wheels at back of magazine. Feed rotates clockwise, take-up rotates counterclockwise.

To Load Daylight Spools. Depress center of core spindles. Remove core holder and collapsible core. Place spools on square driver pins of spindles. Swing take-up and feed roller-guide arms *up,* and lock into catches.

Film-Loop Guard. Depress film loop against magazine mouth. Slide loop guard (with notch inward) over film and under retaining plate.

11.27g Unloading

In darkness, remove magazine take-up lid.

When Magazine Has a Collapsible Core. Disengage clamp on core (push outward). Place index finger in core space, thumb on edge of roll. Turn magazine over, and let film drop into hand. Place exposed roll into bag and can.

When Magazine Has a Plastic Core. Place index finger on core, thumb on edge of roll. Turn magazine over, and let film drop into hand. Place exposed roll into bag and can.

11.27h Footage Counter

At back of magazine. Subtractive; 152–0m (500–0 ft.) in increments of 6.10m (20 ft.)

NOTE: The 122m (400-ft) magazine will run forward and reverse. The 61m (200-ft) magazine will run forward only.

11.28 ARRIFLEX 16M 366m (1200-ft) MAGAZINE (Figs. 11–50a and 11–50b)

11.28a Type
Coaxial.

11.28b Capacity
366m (1200 ft.)

Figure 11–50a Arriflex 16M 1200-ft magazine feed side. Courtesy of Arnold & Richter K.G.

1. Crossover chamber (closed)
2. Chamber latch
3. Gears (not visible)
4. Feed throat
5. Extend film end to marking rib
6. Marking rib

Figure 11–50b Arriflex 16M 1200-ft magazine: crossover loop and take-up side. Courtesy of Arnold & Richter K.G.

1. Crossover chamber (open)
2. Approximately 19 perforations visible
3. Crossover chamber sprocket
4. Take-up throat
5. Take-up gear
6. Feed gear
7. 36-perforation loop

11.28c Lids

Two. Threaded.
To remove, unscrew counterclockwise; lift.

11.28d Feed

Left side. Film (wound emulsion in) pulls off spindle clockwise.

11.28e Take-up

Right side. Film winds on spindle counterclockwise, emulsion always in.

11.28f Loading

NOTE: Feed compartment is *up* when crossover chamber is at Loader's right.

1. Unscrew feed lid. 2. In darkness, remove film roll from can and bag. Insert film end into feed throat, slowly rotating gear at bottom counterclockwise with thumb until gear in throat engages perforation. Thread 15.24 cm (6″) through.

NOTE: To expedite engagement of film in magazine gears, cut film so as to bisect a perforation.

3. Place film roll on feed spindle, making certain that spindle key engages core keyway. 4. Replace feed lid. 5. In light, rotate gear until film end extends to marking rib (raised bar on the outside of magazine). 6. Hold gear. Bring film end back counterclockwise, then insert end into right-hand (take-up) channel of magazine throat. Rotate gear until perforation engages gear and film moves into magazine.

CAUTION: It is important to maintain proper loop size: 36 *visible* perforations. Do not allow excess film to exit feed side while trying to engage perforation of film end into take-up gear!

7. Push back on crossover chamber latch and open crossover chamber. Rotate gear until film end enters crossover chamber and touches its open cover (approximately 19 perforatjons will be visible). 8. Turn magazine over so that crossover chamber is at Loader's left. Unscrew take-up lid. Insert film end into crossover chamber sprocket, and rotate gears until a sufficient amount of film enters take-up chamber to be wound on take-up core. 9. Close crossover chamber, and secure cover firmly.

CAUTION: *Do not reopen* crossover chamber cover in light *after* film has been *exposed and taken up* into magazine. Passageway between chamber and take-up compartment is *not lighttight* when cover is open.

10. Replace take-up lid.
Film-loop guard: Depress film loop against magazine mouth. Slide loop guard (with notch inward) over film and under retaining plate.

11.28g Unloading
In darkness, unscrew take-up lid. Place index finger in core space, thumb on edge of roll. Turn magazine over, remove film. Place exposed film into bag and can.

11.28h Footage Counter
None.

11.29 ARRIFLEX 16 BLIMP (for 16S and 16M Cameras) (Figs. 11–51*a* and 11–51*b*)

NOTE: All directions are from the Operator's point of view.

NOTE: Most of this section pertains to fiberglass blimps, however, many aluminum blimps are in use. Thus, while information in this section applies to both models, specific differences are noted under sections entitled "Aluminum Blimp." Most notable exceptions are listed under Secs. 11.29e ("Power Line"), 11.29f ("Sunshade"), 11.29g ("Coupling Alignment"), and 11.29h ("Filters"). The aluminum blimp accepts only the 16S camera; the fiber glass blimp accepts either 16S or 16M cameras and features other mechanical and electrical improvements.

11.29a Base
Bottom fitted with two ⅜"-16 tapped holes, to accommodate tripod-lockdown screw.

11.29b Camera Preparation

Eyepiece. Remove from camera. Place prismatic double-elbow assembly (periscope) on camera. Attach camera eyepiece to viewfinder extension tube, and insert unit into blimp extension-tube access hole. To secure, rotate clockwise the knurled locknut on pressure lock.

Motor. Remove variable-speed motor, and replace with AC synchronous motor or DC governor-controlled (constant-speed) motor.

NOTE: Depending on type of motor in use—AC synchronous or DC governor-controlled (constant-speed) motor—the internal inching-knob *coupling* inside blimp must be changed to fit motor knob. A 3mm (⅛ in.) hex wrench is necessary to change coupling.

Figure 11–51a Arriflex fiberglass blimp with 16M camera and zoom lens extension. Courtesy of Arnold & Richter K.G.

1. Matte box
2. Zoom-lens door extension
3. Periscope
4. f/stop-focus-marking strip
5. Strip knurled ring

Detachable Base Plate. Remove from blimp, and attach to bottom of camera.

CAUTION: Edge of a 16S base plate is straight; edge of a 16M base plate is contoured: They are *not* interchangeable.

To Mount Base Plating. Invert camera. Align base-plate screw with tapped hole in camera base making sure that the two locating studs on plate are on same side as contour handgrip and motor. On cameras with a clockwise thread, rotate the inner flat-screw head with the two-finger cutout. On cameras with a counterclockwise thread, rotate the outer knurled screwhead. Secure plate to camera base; make certain that the left front of the camera is flush with the alignment block of the base plate.

11.29c Access

Fiberglass Blimp:

To Camera. Raise clamp on left side door, and lower the door 90°.

To Lenses. Rotate clockwise the lever at left front of matte box glass door, and swing open.

To Magazine. Raise clamp at rear of blimp, lift top forward.

To Change Magazine Access Hood. Insert 5mm 3/16" rod or hex wrench into heads of hinge pins at front of door, and unscrew. Replace with 1200-ft hood.

Aluminum Blimp

Access to Magazine. Lower the clamp at side of blimp to release; raise hinged top.

Figure 11–51b Arriflex 16 fiberglass blimp (rear view). Courtesy of Arnold & Richter K.G.

1. Magazine footage counter window
2. Tachometer and counter window
3. Inching knob dial
4. ON/OFF toggle switch extension
5. ON/OFF toggle switch
6. Sync-pulse plug
7. Power plug
8. Focus knob

9. f/stop control
10. Bubble level
11. Light trap
12. Eyepiece
13. Locknut
14. Camera access latch
15. Magazine access latch

Figure 11-52 Arriflex 16 fiberglass blimp (detail). Courtesy of Arnold & Richter K.G.

1. Marking-strip knurled ring
2. Focus bracket arm
3. Forward catch
4. f/stop-focus-marking strip
5. Periscope
6. Light-trap sleeve
7. Focus-knob coupling

11.29d Camera Insertion

1. Turn the two pressure locks (at front and back of inner frame) 90° to the frame. 2. Insert camera, mounted on its base plate, *without a magazine,* into the blimp, keeping camera tipped at a slight angle, to clear the two *vertical* locating studs in blimp frame (unit the camera rests on). 3. Align and insert the two *horizontal* locating studs *of the base plate* (attached to camera) into mating retaining blocks above right side of blimp frame. 4. Lower the camera, and engage base-plate sockets onto vertical locating studs in blimp frame. 5. Rotate the two pressure locks (front one clockwise, rear one counterclockwise) to secure the base plate.

NOTE: The clamp screw (located between the two horizontal base plate studs) must be adjusted so that release button for blimp-frame lock maintains base plate rigid laterally.

6. Slide viewfinder-extension tube (with camera eyepiece attached) into the extension-tube access hole. Place light-trap sleeve over extension tube (inside blimp).

CAUTION: Extension tube should not touch the double-prismatic assembly. Slide light-trap sleeve forward to cover the space between extension tube and elbow assembly.

7. Rotate clockwise the knurled lock nut on pressure lock (outside blimp), to secure the extension tube. 8. Mount the magazine on camera through magazine access hood.

Fiberglass Blimp-External (shown): Four-pin Tuchel plug inserts into female receptacle at back of blimp below inching wheel. Extension of plug has an ON/OFF toggle switch in box that clamps to tripod handle.

NOTE: Depress ON/OFF switch on camera to ON position to run camera from blimp switch.

Power Panel.   At right side of blimp.
Synchronous-Pulse Plug.   Recessed male five-pin Tuchel plug.
Power-Supply Plug.   AC or DC; recessed male eight-pin Tuchel plug. AC cable is fitted with a Tuchel plug at power-source end and requires a step-down transformer in the line, with its indicator set to FWD-110V. DC cable is fitted with a standard two-prong battery connector plug.
Two Fuses.   In vertical alignment, top fuse is for power, bottom fuse for lights.

Aluminum Blimp-External (not shown).   One single-pole ON/OFF switch is at right rear of blimp.

NOTE: Camera ON/OFF switch must be depressed to ON position in order to run camera from the blimp switch.

Power-Supply Plug.   Recessed eight-pin Tuchel (AC or DC) below ON/OFF switch. AC cable requires a step-down transformer in the line, with its indicator set to FWD-110V. DC cable is fitted with a standard two-prong battery connector. Red light above viewfinder glows when camera is running.

Fiberglass Blimp—Internal (not shown).
Internal Lights.   Located above focus strip, lens aperture and focus, magazine footage counter, tachometer, and camera footage counter.
Synchronous Pulse.   Five-pin Tuchel plug inside rear of blimp is inserted into back of 16M camera.
Coupling for Adapter Cable.   Six-pin plug inside front of blimp inserts into adapter cable.

NOTE: Depending on camera being used, adapter cable that is inserted into six-pin plug coupling is fitted with either a 16M Cannon plug at camera end or a standard two-prong 16S female plug at camera end.

Aluminum Blimp—Internal (not shown).
To Operate Internal Lights.   Depress button above focus-strip port (left front of blimp). Internal lights are located above focus strip, lens aperture and focus, tachometer, and camera footage counter.
Adapter Cable.   Fitted with a standard two-prong 16S female plug at camera end.

NOTE: No synchronous-pulse connection, unless customized.

Fiberglass Blimp   (shown).
To mount.   insert boom into bracket at front of lens-access door. Bottom of bellows slides into two holders on lens-access door, to secure bottom. At top of bellows, two hooks insert into lip of lens-access door, to secure the top. Bellows moves in and out by loosening the knurled knob in bracket that holds the boom.

Aluminum Blimp (not shown).

To mount. raise the upper knurled locknut at front of lens door. Lower the bottom locknut. Align slots at rear of sunshade housing with locknut brackets. Lower the upper locknut, raise bottom locknut, and secure sunshade to lens door. Bellows moves in and out on two rods. Tighten knurled lock screw on each rod, to secure.

11.29g Coupling alignment

Fiberglass Blimp (shown).

Focus and *f*/Stop Marking-Strip Indicators: At base of inner frame. Indicators are visible through left-door port.

Focus indicator is at top and should be rotated to rear to set for infinity.

The *f*/stop indicator is at bottom and should be rotated forward to set for widest opening of lens.

To Insert Strip.
1. Open camera-access door. Place small hole of marking strip over rear catch. 2. Push the forward catch (at front of strip recess) toward the rear. Place large hole of strip over forward catch; release.

Knurled Ring. Located forward of scale strips. Unit rotates counterclockwise to bring one of three scale strips into viewing position (one strip for each lens on turret).

NOTE: Strips may be calibrated in ink (by manufacturer) with *f*/stops (or T stops) and distance scales for individual lenses, or they may be blank.

To Mark Blank Strips for f/Stop. Couple lens to *f*/stop knob (see following description, "*f*/Stop Scale"). Set lens at widest opening. Make pencil mark on strip above *f*/stop-scale indicator. Set stop at each aperture setting on lens barrel, and transcribe each setting to marking strip.

At right side of strip, write focal length of lens for which the strip has been marked.

To Mark Blank Strips for Focus. Couple lens to focus knob (see following description, "Standard Lenses"). Set lens at infinity. Make infinity pencil mark (∞) on strip below footage indicator. Set focus at each footage indication on lens barrel, and transcribe each mark to marking strip. At right side of strip, write focal length of lens for which the strip has been marked.

To Couple Lens and *f*/Stop.

Marked Strips. Be certain the focal length of lens, indications on lens, and marking indicator agree. (An indicator that is out of alignment can be adjusted by sliding it on support wire.)

f/Stop Scale. Rotate *f*/stop control (knurled knob at back of blimp, below bubble level) until *f*/stop indicator (lower one on marking strip) is at extreme *front.*

f/stop drive arm. Rotate *f*/stop indicator forward (as just described). Set lens to its widest opening. Lower *f*/stop drive arm so that spring tension of arm causes its lip to engage diaphragm ring of lens.

CAUTION: Diaphragm of lens must agree with setting on scale when coupled.

Standard Lenses.
1. Rotate focus knob (in door below eyepiece-extension tube) counterclockwise until the upper footage indicator is at extreme rear (infinity). 2. Open lens access door. Set lens at infinity (wings aligned to lens channel—i.e., *up.* 3. Insert rubber end of focus bracket arm between

wings of lens. Secure bracket arm to pilot pins on outer focusing ring. Rotate knurled lockdown screw to secure.

Zoom Lens. Use of zoom lens necessitates mounting of a door extension and using a lens-installation kit (an accessory of blimp).

To Add Zoom-Lens Door Extension (see Fig. 11–51a)

1. Insert 5mm (3/16″) rod or hex wrench into heads of hinge pins on lens-access door, and unscrew. 2. Insert zoom-door extension into hinges of blimp, and secure with hinge pins. Rotate slotted knob to lock left side to blimp. 3. Insert lens-access door into hinges of zoom-extension unit. Secure with hinge pins. Rotate lever counterclockwise to lock left side to extension unit.

Installation kit

To Mount Lens-Support Frame. Squeeze spring-loaded catch on frame, and insert it into filter-holder bracket (forward of focus ring).

Support Flap. Insert four retaining screws through flaps into holes in support frame to secure flap in place.

To Mount Focus-Control Slip-on Ring.

NOTE: This unit is installed before inserting lens into camera turret.

Set lens at infinity. Place focus-control ring on lens-focus barrel (forward of lens focus mark) with female bracket facing *toward the camera.* Secure with two set screws.

To Mount Focus-Coupling Arm.

NOTE: Unit is installed before inserting lens into camera turret.

Secure focus-coupling arm on inner *f*/stop ring inside blimp, *toward* lens-access door. Insert arm into focus-control slip-on ring.

To Mount Zoom-Control Slip-on Ring.

NOTE: Unit is installed before inserting lens into camera turret.

Set lens to longest focal length. Place ring on lens focal-length barrel (to rear of focal-length marks) with wings facing *toward the lens-access door.* Secure with two set screws.

To Mount Zoom Coupling Arm.

NOTE: This unit is installed *after* inserting lens into camera turret.

Place rubber end of arm between wings of zoom-control slip-on ring. Secure arm to outer focusing ring in blimp, *toward camera.*

f/Stop Scale.

CAUTION: Stops must be set manually.

Aluminum Blimp (not shown).

Focus Marking-Strip Indicator. A straight line in marking-strip viewing window at left front of blimp.

To Insert Marking Strip.

1. Open lens-access door, and place long hole of marking strip over catch on lens-gear housing. 2. Wrap strip around lens-gear housing. Push spring-loaded catch *up.* Place small hole of strip over spring-loaded catch. Release.

To Scribe Footage Marks on Marking Strip: Open camera-access door, and insert a pencil into notch inside blimp, at left of lens-gear ring.

To Mark Blank Strips. Couple the lens to the focus knob (see following description, "Standard Lenses"). Set lens at infinity. Scribe infinity pencil mark (∞) on strip. Set focus at each footage indication on lens barrel, and transcribe each setting to marking strip. At bottom of strip, write focal length for which strip has been marked.

f/Stop Scale. None. The f/stops must be set manually. A mirror on a bracket is inserted into camera matte-box shoe, which permits viewing of f/stop.

Standard Lenses.

1. Open lens-access door, and set taking lens at infinity. Rotate lens gear in lens-access door, and align the two dots (one in door, one on gear).

CAUTION: Make sure that rubber end of spring-tension focus-bracket arm (on lens gear) is *up* before aligning the dots.

2. Close and lock the lens access. Reach through the side door, and depress rubber end of focus bracket arm into wings of lens.

Focus Knob. Scalloped knob at left front of blimp is automatically coupled to rear focus knob, so that Operator can focus.

f/Stop Drive. None.

Zoom Lens. *No* zoom lens can be installed unless blimp has been customized, in which case zoom lens is usually a permanent installation.

11.29h Filters

Fiberglass Blimp (shown) Uses a filter holder. The holder swivels; a pressure snap keeps holder in place. A single glass 7.62 × 76.2mm (3 × 3″) filter slides into holder from left side.

To mount. open lens-access door. Depress spring-loaded catch on holder, and slide filter into bracket.

Aluminum Blimp (not shown): The 76.2 × 76.2mm (3 × 3″) filter mounts against glass of lens-access door and is held in place by four swivel locks.

11.29i Viewfinder/Focus-Tube

To Align Reflex Mirror for Viewing. Place fingertips into recesses of telephone dial inching knob at back of blimp below tachometer viewing port. Depress and rotate to engage motor's inching knob.

Eyepiece. Rotate narrow scalloped ring on eyepiece clockwise, to the word "loose." Rotate large scalloped ring nearest eyecup to focus on groundglass. Turn narrow ring counterclockwise toward the word "fix" to secure.

Light Trap. Hinged metal cap in eyepiece snaps closed to prevent stray light from striking mirror and kicking back onto film.

11.29j Ports

Fiberglass Blimp (shown). Horizontal window at left side permits viewing of focus (distance) and f/stop scales. Tachometer and counter windows are at back of blimp. Magazine footage-counter window is at right side of blimp hood.

Aluminum Blimp (not shown). Vertical window at left side permits viewing of focus (distance) scale. Tachometer window is at back of blimp above telephone-type dial. Second window at left of telephone-type dial permits viewing of footage counter. *No* window in magazine hood.

11.29k Weight

(Without camera.) Fiberglass blimp: 12.8kg (28 1/4 lb) aluminum blimp; 25.5 kg (56 1/4 lb).

11.30 ARRIFLEX VARIABLE SPEED CONTROL ACCESSORY for 35 BL-1, 35 BL-2, 16SR-1, 16SR-2, and 16BLEQ Cameras (FIG. 11–53)

The variable-speed-control accessory is used when other than sync speed is desired on the 35BL-1, 35BL-2, the 16SR-, 16SR-2, or a 16BLEQ (a 16BL equipped with an Arriflex crystal-controlled motor). Plug-on unit inserts into 11-pin Fischer receptacle on camera (see 35BL, 16SR) and overrides the cameras built-in sync-speed control circuits. The variable-speed-control accessory contains a sync/variable switch; a camera-selector knob; an fps indicator with speed-selector knob; and an ON/OFF button.

11.30a Sync/Variable Switch

Recessed toggle switch at end of control box. When set to *Sync*, camera will run at 24 or 25 fps (depending on gearing of camera). When set to *Variable*, camera will run at speed selected on the fps indicator.

11.30b Camera-Type Selector

Three-position knob located at end of box next to cable. Knot can be set for use with either 35BL, 16SR, or 16BLEQ cameras.

CAUTION: Setting the knob to the type of camera other than the one in use will result in damage to the camera.

WARNING: *Never* run the 35 BL II in excess of 50 fps.

11.30c FPS Indicator

Reversible disc is marked on the one side with a scale from 5 to 50 fps in increments of 5 fps for use with either the 35BL, and a scale from 6 to 48 fps in stages of 6, 12, 24, 48 fps only for the BLEQ; marked with a scale from 5 to 75 fps in increments of 5 fps for use with either 16SR on the other side.

To set scale for either 35BL/16BLEQ, or 16SR. remove circular retaining spring located below speed-selector knob; lift scale with fingernails;

Figure 11–53 Arriflex variable-speed-control accessory. Courtesy of Arnold & Richter K.G.

1. To 11-pin plug on camera
2. Camera-type selector knob (not visible)
3. Speed-selector switch
4. Circular retaining spring
5. fps indicator
6. ON/OFF button
7. Sync/variable selector switch
8. Pan handle clamp

reverse scale, making certain to re-engage hole of disc on its pilot pin; replace circular retaining spring.

NOTE: Desired fps on scale can be visually matched to reference dot on control box; speed of 35BL can be verified by comparing the indicator with the LED tachometer; speed of BLEQ can be verified by observation of tachometer; only on 16SR must speed of camera be taken at face value on indicator.

NOTE: When using speed-control accessory with either type of camera, align reference dot on the disc to 5 fps at camera start, then rotate knob and disc *slowly* to desired fps. Otherwise, damage to camera may result.

11.30d ON/OFF Button

Thumb-actuated. Next to Sync/Variable Switch. *To start,* depress button, which locks in place. *To stop,* depress button, then release.

11.31 ARRIFLEX PERISCOPE FINDER ATTACHMENT (Fig. 11–54)

The periscope finder attachment (PFA) is an optical unit placed between

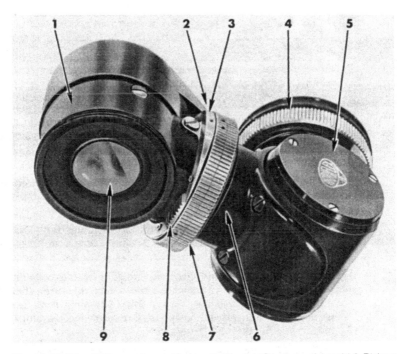

Figure 11–54 Arriflex periscope finder attachment. Courtesy of Arnold & Richter K.G.

1. 180° rotation
2. Connecting-shank release button (not visible)
3. Index ring
4. Eyepiece coupling unit
5. 25° movement
6. 360° rotation
7. Milled ring (unlocked position)
8. Small knurled shim of index ring
9. Front lens (fits to camera)

camera groundglass and eyepiece. It permits left-eye viewing and/or placement of camera at a desired angle for special or trick shots.

The PFA is provided with three movements: 1. 180° rotation of the front lens around the center of the groundglass in a plane perpendicular to camera body. 2. 360° rotation of the connecting shank between groundglass and eyepiece in a plane parallel to camera body. 3. 25° movement of eyepiece around its own fulcrum in a plane at right angles to camera body.

The threads at the front lens accommodate the camera eyepiece coupling nut (see Fig. 11–54). Front lens does not have mating lugs (such as are found on eyepiece) to insert into mating slots on camera. This is to allow for 180° rotation feature of the PFA.

Index ring (secured to front lens by two screws) is marked by a single red dot. Index ring also has small knurled shim located on its side. Shim engages camera eyepiece coupling nut and secures the PFA in position on camera.

Milled ring on connecting shank is marked with (a) two red dots, which, when aligned opposite single dot on index ring, indicates the *unlocked* position of knurled shim on side of index ring, and (b) a single dot which, when aligned opposite single dot on index ring, indicates the *locked* position of knurled shim.

Triangular-shaped back cover of front lens is fitted with a button (not shown). When this button is depressed, the connecting shank is released and may be rotated 360°.

NOTE: Rotation of connecting shank causes image seen in viewfinder, as well as aperture outline, to rotate. Although image seen in the viewfinder may be at a 45° angle, 90° angle, or even upside-down, image seen by camera is upright. A simple method to overcome possible disorientation when using this attachment is to align sides of viewfinder aperture lines with a vertical object, or to align a horizontal object with top and bottom lines. With a minimum of practice, this turns out to be not as complicated as it seems, and Operator does *not* have to rotate his/her own head to "level out" the picture.

Rear of PFA is fitted with two slots to accommodate eyepiece lugs. PFA coupling nut secures eyepiece to the unit.

11.31a Mounting

(1) Remove eyepiece from camera by rotating the knurled camera eyepiece coupling nut clockwise. (2) Make certain *all* lens surfaces are clean. Align PFA front lens with camera groundglass, and secure.

CAUTION: Camera and eyepiece coupling nuts are double threaded. Unless units are flush with each other when mounted, they will cross-thread (requiring a factory repair job). Coupling nuts must screw on easily. When difficulty is encountered, unscrew the coupling nut, rotate it at least one full turn, and try again.

(3) Place PFA in desired position, and tighten the camera coupling nut. Turn milled ring until its single red dot aligns with indexing dot. This causes the small knurled shim on the index ring to engage the camera coupling nut and hold the PFA in position.

NOTE: If knurled shim fails to hold PFA in position, (a) rotate milled ring until the two red dots align opposite the index dot, (b) tighten camera coupling nut even more, so that next tooth of coupling nut will be engaged when the single red dot on milled ring is aligned with index ring.

(4) Insert the two guide pins of eyepiece into the two guide keys at rear of PFA; rotate the knurled PFA coupling nut counterclockwise to secure it to the unit.

11.32 ARRIFLEX PRECISION EXPOSURE CONTROL (APEC) (Fig. 11–55)

The *APEC* is a *through-the-lens (TTL)* exposure-control system is used on many Arriflex cameras. It provides information to the Operator on the amount of light reflected from the subject. It does *not* automatically compensate the diaphragm on the lens except on certain 16SR models. (Such models are identified by removing the lens and looking into top of the port on the camera. A *red or yellow plastic ramp* indicates the automatic feature. Some cameras have "AUTO" engraved near the ON/OFF switch housing.) On nonautomatic cameras, the Operator must adjust the lens iris until the needle indicator visible in the viewfinder aligns to the center dot. All APEC optics and electronics are part of the viewfinder system and operate on information relayed by the mirror shutter. A beam splitter divides the light between the meter and viewfinder optics. An APEC does *NOT* interfere with the lens-to-film path.

To check exposure through lens. read scene at center of frame, regardless of image size.

NOTE: As with most TTL systems, APEC is often used as a *spot meter* when a camera is equipped with a zoom lens. Scene is read with lens in telephoto position. In *macrocinematography,* where image area is too small to use a standard light meter, APEC can be utilized.

CAUTION: The mirror-shutter must cover lens fully in stopped position, or a false reading will result.

An APEC-equipped camera has an *exterior control knob* and an *internal exposure indicator* (in the viewfinder).

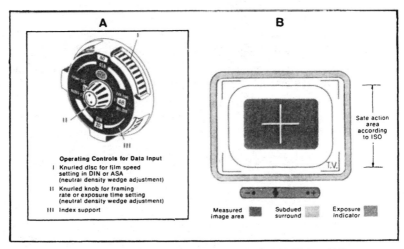

Figure 11–55 Arriflex APEC control. Courtesy of Arnold & Richter K.G.

1. Interior control knob   2. Internal exposure indicator

To set fps rate and exposure time. rotate center knob to desired speed. Exposure can be set to 24 fps 1/48 sec, 25 fps 1/53 seconds, 32 fps 1/64 seconds, 40 fps 1/80 seconds, 48 fps 1/96 seconds, or 50 fps 1/100 seconds.

NOTE: Setting the speed on the exterior control knob does *not* alter camera speed (determined by the fps speed set on the motor).

WARNING: *ALWAYS* make sure that the ASA/DIN setting corresponds to motor speed, or a false reading will result!

To set ASA/DIN. rotate knurled disc to desired ASA/DIN of 16/13, 20/14, 25/15, 32/16, 40/17, 50/18, 64/19, 80/20, 100/21, 125/22, 160/23, 200/24, 250/25, 320/26, 400/27, or 500/28.

CAUTION: When setting ASA/DIN for a film with two indexes (interior/ exterior), always set ASA/DIN for the higher rating.

WARNING: The correction factor of a polarizing filter must be added *AFTER* an APEC TTL reading is measured without the polarizer, or a false reading will result!

11.32b **Internal Exposure Indicator**

Needle-Type Indicator. Works in conjunction with the internal exposure meter and is located in different areas of the viewfinder, depending on the camera.

- 16SR—At the left side of the groundglass. The upper dot (+) indicates scene is two stops overexposed; lower dot (−) indicates scene is two stops underexposed.
- 16BL—At the bottom of the groundglass. The right dot (+) indicates scene is one stop overexposed; left dot (−) indicates scene is one stop underexposed.
- 16S—At the top of the groundglass. The right dot (+) indicates scene is two stops overexposed; left dot (−) indicates scene is two stops under-exposed.

Correct exposure is indicated when the needle is aligned to the center dot by *manually* altering the diaphragm setting *on the lens.*

NOTE: After alignment to center dot, it is normal for needle to deflect when camera starts, then realign to center dot.

CAUTION: If camera has been stored in low light or with lens cap on, open lens to its widest aperture, allow photoresistors to respond (about 1 minute) before using APEC.

chapter 12

Cinema Products, Cameras, Magazines, and Accessories

12.1 CINEMA PRODUCTS 35mm XR 35* CAMERA (Fig. 12–1a and 12–1b)

NOTE: All directions are from the Operator's point of view.

12.1a Outer Case

Consists of two sound-insulated sections: (1) main housing in which magazine housing is an integral part, (2) motor housing.

Figure 12–1a. XR 35 (left front). Courtesy of Cinema Products.

1. LED counter
2. Bayonet-type lens lock
3. Follow-focus bracket lock knob
4. Readout button
5. Camera access knob
6. Contrast knobs
7. Eyepiece

8. Eyepiece-focus knob
9. Focus-lock grip
10. Magnification/light-trap knob
11. Ratio-selector knob
12. Follow-focus knob
13. Marking disc

---

*Manufacturer states that the designation "XR 35" stands for "Crystal (X) Reflex 35mm gauge".

Main Housing. Fitted with two ⅜″–16 tapped holes on bottom. A modified Mitchell NC is permanently installed within the main housing.

Access to camera. Rotate access knob in door clockwise; pull out and down.

Access to magazine. Pull latch at rear of magazine housing. "Clamshell" access doors open outward. Small circular recessed knob in right-hand door is to hold magazine belt.

Viewing port. At right side; provide visual check of magazine belt and spindles; port does *not* open.

Motor Housing. Attaches to right side of main housing; covers motor.

To Install. Slide bottom lip of motor housing into recessed support at base of main housing. Push until latches in top of motor housing engage catches in main housing.

To Remove. Depress button at top rear of motor housing to disengage internal latches.

12.1b Base

Inside main housing. Has *no* turret. Instead, a simple bayonet base lens is mounted through the main housing and locked into place by rotating the lens lock counterclockwise.

Filter slots are in upright section of base.

12.1c Viewfinder/Focusing Tube

Reflex image magnified 5 ×. Located in main-housing door.

To Change or Clean Groundglass. (1) Remove lens. (2) Insert eraser end of pencil into lens opening (or wrap handkerchief around finger); slide groundglass toward front of camera. Grasp glass by edges, and remove; clean and reinsert.

CAUTION: A separate matte is forward of the groundglass. Grooves that hold it are very narrow, and care should be taken that the matte is not crimped in any way.

NOTE: Groundglass is constructed to fit just one way (smooth surface toward rear of tube) and has a projection to ensure this. The projection should always be in a *down* position. If up, the cross hair will be off center.

Effects Matte. A frame of film cut with the Mitchell Matte Cutter (see Sec. 14.11d).

To insert effects matte. Slide frame upside-down into matte slot (the space between groundglass and separate matte, forward of groundglass), perforations toward access door.

Ratio Selector. For use with anamorphic or standard lenses. Align dot on knob with *2:1* to set optics for anamorphic unsqueezed viewing. Align dot on knob to *STD* for standard ratios (1.85, 1.66, etc.).

Magnification. To magnify 10 ×, rotate dot on HI-CLOSED-LOW knob to HI. For normal viewing, align dot to LOW. To prevent stray light from entering eyepiece and striking film when Operator is not looking through eyepiece, align dot to CLOSED.

Contrast filters. Two. Filter 1 is 0.90 ND. Filter 2 is 0.40 ND. Rotate dot to vertical position to view through either filer.

CAUTION: Knobs are spring-loaded and must be held in place to check contrast values.

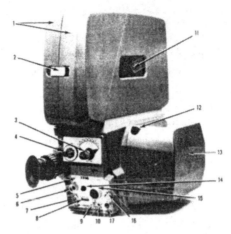

Figure 12–1b. XR 35 (right rear). Courtesy of Cinema Products.

1. Clam-shell access doors
2. Magazine-access knob
3. Shutter knob
4. Filter-selector knob
5. Green light
6. Start button
7. Stop button
8. Power-level motor
9. Sync/volume knob

10. Red light
11. Magazine-viewing part
12. Motor-housing disengage button
13. Motor housing
14. 15-amp circuit breaker
15. Sync-signal speaker
16. Power switch
17. Powerline receptacle

Eyepiece. Large knurled knob nearest eyecup rotates to achieve focus on groundglass. Circular grip forward of knurled knob rotates clockwise to lock eyepiece at desired focus.

12.1d Motor

30–volt synchronous/variable motor.

To Change Crystal Motor. Remove outer housing to reveal motor. Loosen four 10/24 fillister head screws, pull motor *gently* away from housing.

Inside Motor. The lower 5-pin plastic plug is for *LED* counter. The filter-wheel interlock connection is a four-stepped LEMO (self-locking) plug. The main power connector is a Bendix 12-pin cable grommet in the motor recess. The red dot to red dot on couplings aligns viewing mirror.

WARNING: If dots are not aligned, shutter mirror will not come into viewing position when camera is stopped. If coupling comes off, put mirror in viewing position (see Sec. 12.1p, *"To clear shutter from lens"*), and make certain that red dot is up.

To Change the Crystal Frame-Rate Speed. Remove two screws on indicator plate; flip switch to desired frame rate (24 fps or 25 fps). Retighten screws to lock.

To Run Motor in Crystal Sync. Push red button (forward of fps rate meter located on outside of motor) *in*. Motor will run at speed set on inside indicator plate (24 fps or 25 fps).

To Run Motor at Variable Speed. Push red button forward of fps rate meter and let it pop *out.* Start camera. Rotate knurled knob surrounding red button to desired speed: 1–32 fps.

WARNING: *Always* leave motor-housing cover off blimp when filming variable speed, to avoid possibility of shooting sound takes out of sync.

12.1e Power Panel

Powerline. Insert elbowed three-pin Bendix plus extension of powerline into receptacle at lower right rear of camera.

Power Switch. Above powerline receptacle; provides electricity to camera.

WARNING: Turning camera off with this switch will cause loss of synchronization, and shutter may stop closed, or partially closed, obscuring the viewing system.

CAUTION: With this switch in OFF position, camera will not run!

STOP/START Buttons. Located at left rear of camera; used to turn camera on and off. *Green light* above *Start* button indicates when camera is running. When camera starts, a sync signal sounds. *Red Light* at right of sync volume knob lights when signal sounds.

Sync Volume Knob. Controls loudness of signal. Turn counterclockwise to diminish, clockwise to increase.

CAUTION: Turning sync volume all the way to left will eliminate signal completely.

Power Level Meter. Indicates condition of 30volt battery. With indicator needle in green, battery is good; with needle in yellow, battery is low and camera is subject to variation in speed; with needle in red, battery is in need of charge.

15-Amp Circuit Breaker. Pops out of housing if heavy surge of power hits camera. *To reset,* push gently until breaker clicks into place.

12.1f Turret

None. Single lens mount. Accepts BNCR mount lenses, standard or anamorphic.

12.1g Lenses

To fit lens to camera through main housing. (1) Lower and lock the follow-focus knob bracket (see Sec. 12.1h). (2) Rotate lens lock on main housing clockwise as far as it will go. (3) Align hole in lens flange with the positioning stud located in upper left of lens port. Insert the lens flange flush with camera; make sure that stud engages the lens-flange hole. (4) Rotate lens lock counterclockwise to secure. (5) Align phenolic gear to lens gear, and engage.

12.1h Focus Controls

On main housing.

To Change Focus. Rotate either of two follow-focus knobs located at both sides of bracket (at front of camera). Circular and notched marking discs at both sides are magnetic, removable, and rotatable. They can be marked with grease or lead pencil for focus marks. Insert a fingernail under disc, and pry away from housing to remove and clean.

To Lock Focus Handle. Rotate lower knob at front of bracket.

To Align Phenolic and Lens Gears. (1) Loosen follow-focus bracket lock knob (upper knob at front of bracket). Depress right-side follow-focus knob, and secure it by rotating bracket lock knob counterclockwise. (2) Insert lens into camera (see Sec. 12.1g). (3) Release follow-focus bracket lock knob, and engage lens gear. Secure follow-focus bracket lock knob.

12.1i Sunshade/Matte Box (not shown)

Mounts on two rods (one above the other), which fit into a vertical bracket. Knob tightens rods in place. *To release vertical bracket* and move *matte box aside,* depress lever at front of vertical bracket, swing matte box aside. Sunshade will accommodate all lenses down to 18mm.

12.1j Filters

Matte box holds two circular 114.3mm (4 1/2-in.) filters. Single screw on each ring holder keeps filter in place on rear of sunshade.

Gelatine.   Camera is fitted with wheel that accommodates six filters. Each filter can be brought up singly by Operator. Filter comes to rest forward of the film plane but back of the viewing system. Operator does not have to view through filter.

Access to Filter Slots.   At right front of camera body (not shown).

To Insert Filters, remove outer case motor housing cover. Grasp knurled knob of filter block, and pull, revealing filter slot. Insert filter holder with bent portion of holder (used as a finger grip) pointed *away from* Operator. Replace filter block. Replace motor-housing cover.

CAUTION: Exercise care that gelatine does not rub or scratch as it is being slid into place.

WARNING: Inserting a series of filters is of no value unless their respective positions are marked at back of camera on disc of knob marked "Filter."

Filter Knob.   Black dots marked on scale at 12, 2, 4, 6, 8, and 10 o'clock indicate filter positions. Value of desired filter must be marked on scale 180° from white dot, i.e., with *white dot* on the knurled knob at 12 o'clock, the value (or type) of gelatine inserted into filter slot at right front of camera should be marked on the scale at 6 o'clock. With white dot at 2 o'clock and filter inserted, scale should be marked at 8 o'clock; with white dot at 4 o'clock, filter scale marked at 10 o'clock; white dot at 6 o'clock, filter scale marked at 12 o'clock; white dot at 8 o'clock, scale marked at 2 o'clock; white dot at 10 o'clock, scale marked at 4 o'clock.

To change filter, depress filter knob, and rotate until white dot aligns with desired filter marked on scale.

NOTE: A warning signal sounds when filter wheel is being turned to indicate that filter is obstructing the aperture. When clear, knob will pop out, and signal will stop.

WARNING: If signal continues, filter is *not* clear of aperture. An interlock prevents camera from running if filter wheel is out of position.

To Check Filter after Insertion.   Remove lens, open camera door. Rotate inching knob on movement to clear reflex mirror from aperture. Check position of filter through lens port.

12.1k Magazine 304.8m (1000 ft)

To Mount.   (1) Open "clamshell" doors of outer case. Attach camera belt to hook on right door. (2) Pull a loop of film from the magazine feed side. (3) Insert the magazine toe in the magazine guide groove (at top of camera). Draw film loop into camera body. (4) Slide magazine forward and down until snap-latch on camera catches stud on magazine. (5) Thread camera (see Sec. 12.1l).

To Remove Magazine. (1) Unthread film, and break it. (2) Place two fingers under belt, pull laterally away from magazine, rotate fingers clockwise, and lift belt from spindle-wheel grooves. Attach belt to hook in door. (3) Disengage magazine by depressing magazine snap latch, to release stud holding magazine. (4) Lift magazine back and clear of camera and out of housing.

12.1l Threading (Fig. 12–2)

(1) Press buckle-trip apron toward rear of camera to avoid accidental starting of camera during threading procedures (see Sec. 12.2m). Warning signal will sound; turn toggle power switch at rear of camera to *OFF.* Rotate upper and lower sprocket-guide rollers counterclockwise away from the sprocket.

(2) Rotate inching knob on movement until pulldown claw retracts from register plate (a back and upward stroke). Pull registration-pin throw-out knob, and move it toward rear of camera.

Figure 12–2. XR 35 threading detail. Courtesy of Cinema Products.

1. Aperture plate
2. Upper aperture-plate lock
3. Register plate
4. Roller
5. Matte slot
6. Pressure plate
7. Lower aperture plate lock
8. Pulldown claw
9. Inching knob
10. Rollers
11. Registration-pin throw-out knob
12. Upper sprocket-guide rollers
13. Take-up roller
14. Buckle-trip roller
15. Buckle-trip apron
16. Lower sprocket-guide rollers
17. Buckle-trip reset knob

(3) Raise upper and lower aperture-plate locks, and remove aperture plate by pulling *gently*. If plate does not slide easily, check to see that pulldown claw and/or registration pins are clear of plate.

(4) Clean plate. Make a special check of pulldown claw and registration-pin holes for emulsion buildup or film chips; replace plate. Depress aperture-plate locks to secure.

(5) Swing pressure-plate spring arm clockwise. Remove pressure plate from register plate. Clean, making sure rollers revolve freely. Replace pressure plate and spring arm.

(6) Pull film from magazine feed side. Extend loop to lower front corner of camera (a rough guide for amount of film needed for threading).

Starting clockwise from magazine take-up side, insert film (a) under large take-up film roller nearest to magazine take-up rollers, then to right of buckle-trip roller; (b) then to left of smaller roller, and between lower sprocket-guide rollers, and sprocket; (c) *under* small lower roller at left of sprocket-guide rollers, and *over* small roller below pulldown-claw eccentric.

Starting counterclockwise from magazine feed side, insert film (a) between upper sprocket-guide rollers, and *under* smaller roller above registration-pin throw-out knob; (b) then in groove (the race) between removable aperture plate and stationary register plate.

(7) Align film to perforation register pin. Hold film in race, pull registration-pin throw-out knob, and move it toward aperture plate *gently,* to determine whether registration pins are entering film perforations. If pin touches film, raise or lower the film in the race while moving the throw-out knob back and forth until pins engage perforations.

(8) (a) *Adjust lower loop* so that when lower sprocket-guide roller closes, loop will clear bottom of camera interior by 3–6mm (1/8–1/4 in) at lowest arc of loop. (8) (b) *Adjust upper loop* so that when upper sprocket-guide roller closes, top of loop aligns with top of movement plate.

(9) Rotate magazine take-up spindle wheel, and, in a clockwise direction, slip belt into wheel groove (this follows rotation of take-up wheel and subjects the belt to a minimum of stretching).

(10) Rotate the inching knob on the movement, and observe film being transported in camera. If satisfactory, proceed to next step.

(11) Pull buckle-trip reset knob (inside camera below buckle-trip apron), and turn toggle power switch at back of camera to *ON;* hold pins on upper and lower sprocket-guide rollers with thumb and forefinger.

CAUTION: Keep the knuckles of the hand clear of the movement!

Apply power in short bursts, and observe action of film. If satisfactory, stop camera, close door, and reset footage counter.

"Two-axis" Stroke and Position Adjustment. Built in, to minimize noise of movement. The correct setting of stroke and position adjustment may differ on each roll because of variations in raw stock perforation pitch and/or film shrinkage. Optimum setting of each axis is determined by ear—i.e., by listening while threaded film stock is run through camera with door open and adjusting each eccentric until movement runs at its quietest.

Adjustment of top eccentric shifts the claw pivot point in relation to pulldown claw.

Adjustment of lower eccentric shifts the claw pivot point in relation to registration pins.

To Make Adjustments. (1) Thread camera as described. (2) Loosen the two 6/32 × 3/8 in. lock screws (heads take a 7/16 Allen ball-head screwdriver), and then return screws and *snug them only* (do not tighten). (3) Run camera.

Manufacturer recommends.

Stroke Adjustment. While camera is running: (1) Grasp registration throwout knob and pull registration-pins back. (2) Insert flat screwdriver blade into top eccentric slot and rotate clockwise or counterclockwise until camera runs its most quiet. (3) Stop camera. Reengage registration pins, checking to see that pins do not touch film or nick perforation. If pins are touching film, then retract registration pins, and back off on adjustment screw slightly. Test and continue to adjust until clear.

Position Adjustment. (1) With registration pins engaged, run camera. (2) Insert flat screwdriver blade into lower eccentric slot and rotate clockwise or counterclockwise until camera runs most quietly. (3) Repeat stroke and position adjustments with registration pins still engaged until quietest operating settings are achieved. (4) Tighten lock screws.

Field Experience Recommendation. Everything just described *except* that registration pins are not withdrawn when making stroke adjustment. While the intent of withdrawing the registration pins is to bring about optimum pulldown of claw, often the registration pins will nick perforation edge (in some instances, piercing the film) when engaged and camera is turned on. Also the following:

WARNING: Tighten lock screws after adjustments are completed.

REPEAT: Tighten lock screws! Failure to do so will result in loss of adjustment due to vibration, torn and damaged film, and possible damage to movement. Tighten the lock screws!

12.1m Buckle-trip

Apron (a curved metal plate) is located behind take-up side of sprocket (see Fig. 12–2). The apron cuts out power automatically if film fails to take up when camera is running, and SYNC signal sounds. Power should be deliberately cut out prior to threading (by tripping apron toward rear of camera) to prevent accidental starting of camera, and then toggle power switch turned to OFF to silence the sync signal.

To reset. Pull buckle-trip reset knob below apron until unit snaps forward.

12.1n Footage Counter

LED counter at left front side of camera. Additive; displays footage expended when power switch is in ON position. To read footage with power switch in OFF position, depress tiny readout button located at right of counter.

NOTE: Until and unless the digital-counter reset button is depressed and counter zeroed, the LED footage counter will "remember" the footage used and will continue to add even though power has been disconnected and camera stored overnight, a week, a month, etc. It is imperative to zero the footage counter after each magazine change.

To Reset. Depress digital counter reset button back of door.

NOTE: Cameras 1–7 have mechanical counter at rear of camera. Additive. Registers each foot of film transported through camera up to 9999 ft, then reverts to zero. *To reset mechanical counter:* Depress button at right of counter.

12.1o Tachometer

On motor. (See Sec. 12.1d)

12.1p Shutter

Variable: 5–180 degrees. Calibration and pointer located at rear of camera.

To Change Shutter Opening. Depress knurled shutter knob, turn to desired shutter opening, and release knob. Knurled ring behind shutter knob rotates clockwise to lock the shutter setting.

To Clear Shutter from Lens. Open door to camera, rotate manual motor-turning knob on movement.

12.1q Lubrication (Fig. 12–3)

Manufacturer recommends lubrication of the following parts every 610 m (2,000 ft) with one or two drops of camera oil:

Eccentric (movement). Registration-pin pads; plunger arm and bracket (both sides); sliding block, rear bearing, sliding-block bearing of pulldown claw; eccentric-arm bearing, timing block unit.

Rollers. Every 3048m (10,000 ft) except for large take-up roller and buckle-trip roller, which should be lubricated every 914 m (3,000 ft).

NOTE: After oiling, run camera to eliminate excess oil, then wipe interior.

Pressure-Plate Rollers. Every 3048m (10,000 ft).

12.1r Cleaning

Optics. Clean with bulb syringe or soft camel's hair brush. Manufacturer recommends the following maintenance *each time film is changed:* (1)

Figure 12–3. XR 35 lubrication detail. Courtesy of Cinema Products.

1. Pressure-plate rollers (not visible)
2. Top eccentric lockscrew
3. Registration-pin rods
4. Eccentric arm bearing
5. Eccentric arm bearing
6. Pulldown claw rear bearing
7. Swivel block
8. Plunger arm bracket
9. Toggle-arm rear bearing
10. Toggle-arm rear bearing
11. Lower eccentric lockscrew
12. Sliding-block

Remove aperture and pressure plates. (2) Remove emulsion buildup with orangewood stick. (3) Wipe plates with soft cotton handkerchief (not linen). (4) Use bulb syringe on camera interior to remove dust, dirt, etc.

12.1s Weight
With 304.8m (1000-ft) load: 43 kg (95 lb)

12.1t Troubleshooting

Trouble	Probable Cause
Camera will not start	Powerline faulty, power switch OFF, low temperature
Camera "hunts"	Camera not warmed up; voltage variation in powerline
Camera door will not close	Sprocket-guide rollers not seated properly; registration-pin throw-out knob not forward; film chip or dirt in door
Film jam	Improper threading; take-up belt not on spindle wheel
Lens will not focus	Mount not seated properly; lens damaged
Viewfinder not clear	Shutter closed; magnification knob in CLOSED position; red dots on motor not aligned; camera out of time.
Cut-in on viewing tube	Internal filter holder not seated; matte in tube not seated; matte box is extended
Torn or punctured film	Improper threading
Film will not slide into race	Registration pin or pulldown claw not retracted; emulsion or film chip in race
Film scratches	Dirt or emulsion buildup on: aperture plate, sprocket-guide rollers, pressure plate, registration pins, or magazine rollers
No take-up or sporadic take-up	Belt slipping, or belt too loose
Continuous warning signal	Buckle-trip not reset; filter not in proper position
No warning signal when camera starts	Motor not in sync mode; sync volume turned off

12.2 CINEMA PRODUCTS XR 35 MAGAZINE (Fig. 12–4)

12.2a Type
Displacement.

12.2b Capacity
304.8m (1000 ft)

12.2c Lid
One. Lip and screw-lock.
  To Remove. Rotate knurled knob at top of lid and unscrew. Lift top and slide up to clear lips from bottom of magazine.

12.2d Feed
Left side. Film (wound emulsion in) pulls off spindle clockwise.

Figure 12–4. XR 35 304.8m (1000-ft) magazine. Courtesy of Cinema Products.

1. Manual footage counter arm
2. Magazine toe
3. Magazine throat (not visible) and light traps
4. Manual footage counter knob (not visible)
5. Magazine heel

12.2e Take-up

Right side. Film winds on spindle counterclockwise, emulsion always out.

12.2f Loading

(1) Remove lid. (2) In darkness, remove film from can and bag. (3) Insert film end between the left feed-idler rollers, and push through the feed-side light-trap rollers. (4) Place film roll on feed spindle. Rotate feed spindle until spindle pin engages the core keyway. (5) Insert film end through the take-up-side light-trap rollers: push film through the take-up rollers. (6) Insert film end into core slot, and wind film onto take-up spindle counterclockwise (emulsion side out). Replace lid.

12.2g Unloading

(1) In darkness, remove lid. (2) Place index finger on core, thumb on edge of film roll. (3) Turn magazine over, remove film roll, and place exposed roll into black bag and can.

12.2h Footage Counter

Counter is *not* automatic. It is intended to be used by Operator when clamshell is opened and take-up knob is *manually* turned to get an estimate of the amount of unexposed film left in magazine. It must be rotated clockwise to touch film perforations before it registers footage, and it only registers footage remaining.

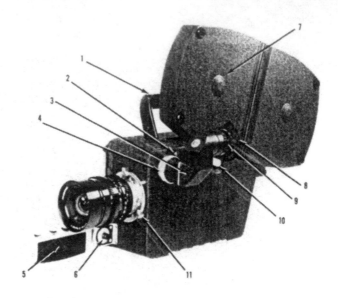

Figure 12–5a. CP-16R (left front). Courtesy of Cinema Products.

1. Carrying handle
2. "Out-of-sync" light
3. Viewfinder
4. Knurled nut

5. Standard handle
6. Start/stop button
7. 122m (400 ft.) maga-
   zine

8. Eyepiece
9. Eyepiece locknut
10. Oblong door knob
11. Lens lock

12.3 CINEMA PRODUCTS CP-16R* CAMERA (Fig. 12.5a and 12.5b)

NOTE: All directions are from the Operator's point of view.

12.3a Base

Fitted with one 3/8"–16, and one 1/4"–20 tapped hole to accommodate tripod-lockdown screw, or an accessory dovetailed camera plate (see Sec. 12.9, Studio Rig. Accessory)

12.3b Motor

Built-in crystal sync/variable. Runs at 24 fps or 25 fps depending on internal sync pulley installed in camera. With 24 fps sync pulley, variable speeds can be set at 12, 16, 20, 28, 32, or 36 fps. With 25 fps sync pulley, variable speeds can be set at 12.5, 16.5, 21, 29, 33.5, or 37.5 fps.

---

*The manufacturer has produced numerous models of the CP camera, all of which share a basic design and operation. Variations in the models are identified as follows:

"R" designates a model that uses lenses fitted with a CP mount, and has a built-in reflex viewfinder.

"16" and "16A" designates a model that uses "C"-type lens mounts, and uses lenses fitted with off-set viewfinders—particularly the Angenieux reflex zoom.

"/A" designates a model that has a built-in magnetic recording module (includes recording heads, amplifier, dual low-impedance microphone inputs, auxiliary mixer input, etc).

"/DS" indicates a double-system sound mechanism.

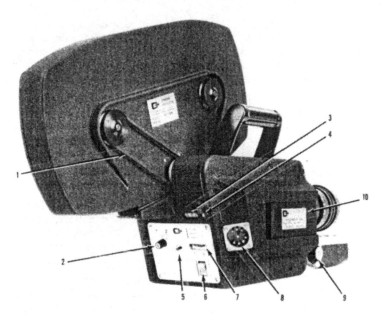

Figure 12–5b. CP-16R (right rear). Courtesy of Cinema Products.

1. Take-up belt
2. Speed-selector knob
3. Footage counter
4. Reset button
5. Battery-test button

6. Run/start switch
7. Battery-level meter
8. 8-pin receptacle
   (some models)

9. Standard handle
   lock knob
10. 20V battery

12.3c Power Panel

At back of camera.

Input to Camera. Automatic when 20 volt battery is slid into battery channel located in right-side auxiliary camera cover.

To Insert or Remove Battery. Depress button at front of channel, slide battery.

NOTE: Pins located in channel will accept battery in only one position. When not in use, manufacturer recommends battery be reversed in channel so as not to drain power from battery.

Run/Stop Switch. At lower right. Additional ON/OFF switch (depress ON, Dress OFF) located in forward handgrip. Handgrip mounts to front of camera with four 3/8″–6/32″ fillister head screws.

Power Level Meter. Indicates condition of 20 volt battery. With indicator needle in green, battery is good; with needle in yellow, battery is low and camera is subject to variation in speed; with needle in red, battery is in need of charge. Indicator needle only operates when camera is on.

To Check Condition of Battery when Camera Is Off. *Gently* depress the pin marked "Battery Test", observe power level meter.

To Alter Film Speed. Depress *speed selector knob,* and rotate to desired fps rate; release knob.

8-pin Receptacle. At rear of auxiliary camera cover. Accepts female Cannon plug for sound cable. Clockwise, from the keyway as Operator faces receptacle: Pin 1 is record head; pin 2 is blank; pin 3 is blank; pin 4 is shield (ground); pin 5 is blank; pins 6 and 7 are monitor heads; pin 8 is record head.

AC Power Supply/Battery Charger (not shown). Unit is used to supply AC power from wall outlet to camera through an extension cable fitted with a 3-pin Cannon plug that fits to an AC/DC power adapter (see subsequent description).

Selector Switch. Permits use of 115V or 230V AC, 60 or 50 Hz. Unit is also fitted with a single receptacle that accepts a battery charger cable so that a standard 20-volt battery can be charged at the same time.

AC/DC Power Adapter (dummy battery) (not shown). Inserts into battery channel on camera in place of standard battery. Unit contains (1) a three-pin receptacle that accepts a Cannon plug from AC power supply/ battery charger, and (2) a single receptacle that accepts a battery-charger cable so that a standard 20-volt battery can be charged at the same time.

WARNING: To prevent possible damage to the camera, (1) insert dummy battery in channel *first.* Ascertain that it is seated. (2) Attach Cannon plug on extension to receptacle on dummy battery *second.* (3) Insert Edison plug on AC power supply/battery charger into wall outlet *last.*   .

12.3d Turret
None. Single lens-lock accepts CP mount lenses only.

12.3e Lenses
Lenses must be fitted with CP lens-mounts, or lens-mount adapters.
   To Fit Lens to Camera.   1. Rotate lens lock clockwise as far as it will go. 2. Align hole in lens flange with the positioning stud located at top of lens port. Insert lens-flange flush with camera body, making certain that the positioning stud engages the lens-flange hole. 3. Rotate lens lock counterclockwise to secure.

12.3f Viewfinder
Reflex. Image magnified 12 × .

NOTE: On older models (before serial no. 2100), viewfinder image is only magnified 8 × .

Views more than full aperture. Area within outer outline denotes full aperture; also has TV outline (pumpkin) and markings of 1.85:1 ratio for blow-up to 35mm (1.66 markings are also available). Markings are plated on fiber optics.

NOTE: Groundglass is available if preferred (from manufacturer or dealer).

   To View through Lens.   Press eye against eyepiece.
   To Open/Close Eyepiece.   Rotate scalloped ring forward of eyecup.
   To Align Reflex Mirror for Viewing.   Open camera door; rotate inching knob forward until reflex mirror comes into position.

NOTE: Camera stops with shutter in viewing position except when utilizing variable-speed mode, or when shutter has been inched by hand (e.g., when threading).

To Focus Eyepiece. Loosen locknut forward of eyepiece; rotate knurled knob until frame lines on fiber optics are sharp.

NOTE: On older models, loosen thumb screw, and rotate barrel until frame lines on fiber optics are sharp; retighten thumb screw.

To Detach Eyepiece. Loosen knurled nut next to camera body. Pull eyepiece away from housing.

Information Display (Fig. 12–6). Visible at top and bottom of viewfinder. At top, reading from left to right, the letters "VU," "S," "B," or "F" appear when activated.

VU. Only appears when camera is fitted with a right-side camera cover that contains a Cinema Products Crystasound Amplifier. VU monitor the record level and appears very bright when distortion of sound occurs, or very dim when sound level is low.

S. Appears when camera is "out of sync,"—i.e., not operating at speed indicated on speed-selector knob. Also appears briefly each time camera starts and/or stops at the same time external "out of sync" light (located upper left of camera door) blinks.

B. Appears when battery is low at the same time needle in power level meter reaches the yellow/green dividing line, or lower. Indicates that camera is subject to variation in speed.

F. Appears when film is low. Indicates that only 10% of film remains in feed side of magazine. Works only on 61m (200 ft) or 122m (400 ft) loads. Requires prior setting of *low-film warning switch* (located inside camera body) to match footage capacity of magazine placed on camera. When magazine capacity is greater than 122m, turn switch to OFF.

At bottom, reading from left to right, the *symbols and digits* $-$, -1, $-.5$, 0 $+.5$, $+1$ or $+$ appear *only* when camera is fitted with either a *semi-automatic exposure control* or *full automatic exposure control*.

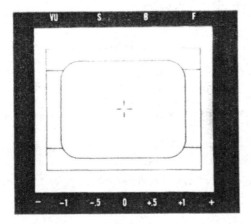

Bottom row: exposure information

Top row: audio modulation level indicator; out-of-sync warning; low battery warning; and end-of-film warning

Figure 12–6. CP-16R reflex viewfinder information display. Courtesy of Cinema Products.

NOTE: The fitting of either exposure control to the camera is a factory installation and cannot be done on the job.

Both exposure units use a silicon sensor (located above fiber optics in lens port). When the number 0 appears in viewfinder, exposure is correct (within 1/8-stop). If either 0 *and* − .5 or 0 *and* + .5 illuminate *at the same time,* then exposure is either underexposed (−) 1/8-stop, or overexposed (+) 1/8-stop. If either − .5, − 1, or − illuminates only, then exposure is 1/2, 1, or 1 1/2 stops underexposed, respectively. If + .5, + 1, or + illuminates only, then exposure is 1/2, 1 or 1 1/2 stops overexposed, respectively.

WARNING: Unless eyepiece is closed, or Operator has eye to eyecup, stray light can strike sensor and affect exposure readings.

Semiautomatic Exposure Control. (Fig. 12–9)   Control panel located at front of camera to right of lens port. Panel contains the following:
ON/OFF switch.   Activates sensor.

NOTE: After switch is turned *on,* the unit requires about 1 minute to stabilize and be ready for use.

ASA Selector Knob.   Settings range from ASA 12 to ASA 400.
FPS Selector Knob.   Settings of 12, 16, 20, 24, 28, 32, 36 fps (or 12.5, 16.5, 21, 25, 29, 33.5, 37.5 fps, depending on sync pulley inside camera).

NOTE: FPS selector knob located on front of camera does *not* change camera speed; it merely alters the exposure reading. However, it *must* match FPS rate on the *speed-selector knob,* located at back of camera in order to provide correct exposure to film.

WARNING: *Always* ascertain that FPS selector knob and speed selector knob match!

Fully Automatic Exposure Control.   In addition to control panel containing ON/OFF switch, ASA selector knob, and FPS selector knob, camera must be fitted with an additional panel located below lens port. Panel has mode select control and outlet plug.
Mode Select Control.   Three modes possible:
Auto-view Mode: Automatically adjusts exposure while ON/OFF switch located on control panel is *on* and camera is running. When camera is stopped, exposure control motor drives lens aperture to fully open, and then becomes inactive.
Auto Mode.   Automatically adjusts exposure while ON/OFF switch located on control panel is *on* and running. When camera is stopped, exposure control motor does not open lens, but remains stopped down.
Manual Mode.   Operates as a semi automatic exposure control (see previous description).

Exposure Control Motor.   Must be attached to lens by special brackets, including a gear fitted to iris control of lens.

NOTE: A small length of cable on the motor plugs into a receptacle next to mode-selector switch.

Slating Lamp.   Only on cameras that have been *modified* at factory. A lamp in aperture area illuminates and either exposes 3 to 5 frame edges, or 3 to 5 full frames, depending on modification.

NOTE: In addition to a start-frame marking lamp, a stop-frame marking capability is possible, but it is not found on all modified cameras. A bloop tone signal, sync pulse output signal (60 or 50 Hz), and 20 volts power for use with a wireless system are also part of the modification. Manufacturer states that modified cameras are designated CP-16RP.

A modified camera is recognizable by an eight-pin *pilotone cable connector* added to back power panel, below speed-selector knob.

To Clean or Replace Fiber Optic Plate or Groundglass. Located inside camera at top of lens mount (visible with lens removed and mirror shutter in viewing position). (1) Rotate inching knob, and move mirror out of way. (2) Reach finger into lens port; press spring clip holding fiber optic in place toward camera body and then down. Swivel spring clip out of way. (3) Place adhesive side of masking tape onto fiber optic, and pull straight out. A spring clip holder will come with it. (4) Clean fiber optic with alcohol or acetone. (5) Reinsert with plating (or scribe) *down* (facing mirror) and the spring clip holder *on top of* the fiber optic or groundglass.

NOTE: The image plated on the fiber optic and/or groundglass is *offset*, i.e., not exactly centered top to bottom. Proper placement of the fiber optic calls for the shortest distance from image to edge of optic to be placed *facing the aperture.*

(6) Replace spring clip by pushing in and up.

12.3g Sunshade
See Sec. 12.9 on the studio rig.

12.3h Filters
External filters must be fitted to individual lenses. No matte box, *except* on studio rig (see Sec. 12.9g).

Gelatine. Filter slot located in aperture plate assembly. When inserting filter, the bent portion of holder (used as a finger grip) *always* points toward Operator.

NOTE: A built-in rubber extender in camera door presses against bent portion of holder when door is closed, ensuring proper seating of filter.

Filter Holder Receptacles. Two. Located behind the movement.

12.3i Door
Hinged at bottom.
To Open. (1) Move viewfinder up and forward. (2) Push front of oblong door knob down, then pull door.
To Close. Lift door until flush with camera and latch closes with an audible snap.

12.3j Magazines
122m (400 ft)
To Mount Magazine. (1) Pull a loop from feed side. (2) Insert magazine toe into magazine guide groove (at top of camera). Draw film loop into camera body. (3) Slide magazine forward and down hard until Stud on magazine inserts into magazine latch. Thread camera (see Sec. 12.3k).
To Remove Magazine. Unthread film, and break it. Place two fingers under take-up belt, pull laterally away from magazine, rotate fingers clockwise, and lift belt from spindle-wheel grooves. Disengage magazine

by pressing magazine latch handle away from Operator. Lift magazine, and remove.

12.3k Threading (Fig. 12–7)

NOTE: Cameras are usually fitted with a "dummy" soundhead that is replaced with a magnetic recording head when recording single-system sound.

To Replace "Dummy" Head with Magnetic Head. (1) Unscrew scalloped nut on dummy support post; pull unit straight out. (2) Align matching color codes, and insert male plug of magnetic connector into camera body plug. (3) Slide magnetic head onto support post as far as it will go. Place rectangular hole of clip onto matching key of post. Rotate clip clockwise until it secures the magnetic head. Engage scalloped nut on support post.

To Thread Camera. (1) Lift pressure-plate retaining spring. Remove pressure plate, and place on bottom of camera interior below gate.

NOTE: Manufacturer states that it is not necessary to remove the pressure plate when threading. This is true. However, field experience substantiates the belief that removal of the unit allows more thorough checking of plate and aperture cleanliness and quicker pulldown-claw engagement of film.

(2) Slide pulldown-claw protector toward rear of camera to expose single pulldown claw. Rotate inching knob until claw retracts from gate. Release claw protector. (3) Pull film from magazine side. Extend loop to right-front of camera (a rough guide for amount of film needed for threading). *Insert film* (a) to right of rear feed roller (directly below magazine feed rollers); (b) left of forward feed roller; (c) *between* upper-left sprocket-guide roller and

1. Forward feed roller
2. Pressure-plate retaining spring
3. Pressure plate
4. Filter slot
5. Pressure-plate finger grip
6. Pulldown claw protector
7. Scalloped nut
8. Retaining clip
9. Small triple roller
10. Center triple roller
11. Large triple roller
12. Loop control roller
13. Upper left sprocket-guide roller
14. Upper right sprocket-guide roller
15. Sprocket
16. Inching knob
17. "Dummy" recording roller
18. Spare filter holders
19. Magnetic head roller

Figure 12–7. CP-16R threading detail. Courtesy of Cinema Products.

loop-control sprocket. (4) Bring film up to form upper loop. Pull pressure-plate retaining spring back and insert film into gate. Drop pressure-plate retaining spring, making certain the curvature of top loop is not too short. (5) Pull back claw protector. Rotate inching knob until pulldown claw enters gate and engages film perforation. Release pulldown-claw protector. Raise pressure-plate retaining spring. Insert pressure plate (small pin up), and lower retaining spring so that notch in spring engages the finger grip of pressure plate. (6) Loop film to right of small triple roller, over center triple roller, then under the large triple roller. Depress hub on magnetic head roller. Insert film *between* record and playback heads and recording roller, then to right of loop-control sprocket. Adjust film so that lower loop clears bottom of camera by 0.31cm (1/8 in.). (7) Thread film *between* the upper-right sprocket-guide roller and the loop-control sprocket. Finally, loop film to right of lower take-up roller. (8) Remove slack on take-up core. Engage belt on magazine take-up spindle wheel. Rotate inching knob, and observe film being transported in camera. If satisfactory, (9) Apply power in short bursts and observe action of film. If satisfactory, stop camera, reset footage counter, and close door.

12.3l Buckle-trip
None.

12.3m Footage Counter
At back of camera. Additive. Registers each foot of film transported through camera. 0–9999, then reverts to 0 and counts forward again. There is *no* frame counter.

NOTE: Some cameras are manufactured with a metric counter. Window of metric counter is yellow. Reading is in meters and decimeters.

To Reset Counter. Depress button at right of footage counter.

12.3n Tachometer
None.

12.3o Shutter
Nonadjustable: 170 degrees.

12.3p Lubrication
None. Manufacturer recommends that annual lubrication of camera be done by authorized factory representatives.

12.3q Cleaning
Optics: Clean with bulb syringe or camel's hair brush.

CAUTION: Use *only* the bulb syringe on the reflex mirror, as the silver is delicate and lifts easily. Alcohol or acetone may be used on fiber optics only when necessary.

Manufacturer recommends the following maintenance *each time film is changed:* (1) Remove and clean pressure plate. (2) Remove emulsion buildup with orangewood stick. (3) Wipe grate with chamois or soft cotton handkerchief (not linen). (4) Use bulb syringe on interior of camera to remove dust, dirt, etc.

12.3r Weight
With 122m (400 Ft) load: 7.7 kg (16 lb. 14 oz)

NOTE: With amplifier add .4 kg (1 lb, 1 oz)

12.3s Troubleshooting

Trouble	*Probable Cause*
Camera will not start	Battery dead; battery not secure in cover: fuse in camera cover burned out; camera jam; motor circuitry damaged
Camera stops while filming	Film jam
Film jam	Improper threading; perforations incorrectly placed on sprockets
Torn or punctured film	Improper threading; loop uneven
Film scratches	Dirt or emulsion buildup in aperture plate, sprocket-guide rollers, pressure plate, or magazine rollers
No take-up, or sporadic take-up	Film loose on take-up core; belt too loose; belt slipping; camera circuitry faulty
Door will not close	Film chip or dirt in door recess
Camera runs overspeed	Crystal n.g., transistor n.g., LED shorted
Camera runs slowly, sync light remains on	Low battery; motor n.g.

12.4 CINEMA PRODUCTS PLC-4A MAGAZINE* (Fig. 12–8)

12.4a Type
Double compartment.

12.4b Capacity
122m (400 ft)

12.4c Lids
Two. Hinged at center of magazine. Clip-on locked.
   To open: Depress two thumb-activated latches on lid. Rotate counter-clockwise one-quarter turn until latches pop up. Bright band on latch indicates that magazine lid is open.

12.4d Feed
Left side. Film (wound emulsion in) pulls off spindle clockwise.

12.4e Take-up
Right side. Film winds on spindle counterclockwise, emulsion always out.

12.4f Loading
(1) Unlatch feed lid. (2) In darkness, remove film roll from can and bag. Pull film off roll clockwise. (3) Insert film end between feed-idler roller and magazine-compartment wall (emulsion faces idler roller). Push film through the feed light-trap rollers (4) Place roll on feed spindle. Rotate feed-spindle wheel until spindle pin engages core keyway. (5) Lower the feed lid; depress two thumb latches, and rotate clockwise one-quarter turn until latches remain *down*. Check lid in light to see whether bright band on each latch can be seen. If band is visible, latch is *not* secure, so tighten. (6) In light, insert film end into take-up light trap. Push film between

---

*NOTE: Manufacturer states that the designation PLC-4A stands for "Plastic Lightweight Compartment 400-ft Model A".

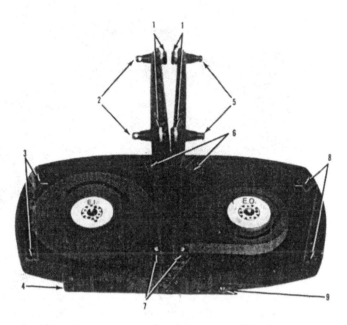

Figure 12–8. PLC-4A magazine. Courtesy of Cinema Products.

1. Thumb-activated latches
2. Latch studs
3. Latch catches
4. Magazine toe
5. Latch studs

6. Core storage pins
7. Light-trap rollers
8. Latch catches
9. Lock mount stud

magazine-compartment wall and take-up idler roller (emulsion faces the roller). (7) Hold core. Rotate take-up spindle wheel until spindle-pin engages core keyway. (8) Insert film into core slot, and wind on take-up spindle counterclockwise (emulsion side out). (9) Lower the lid, depress two thumb latches, and rotate clockwise one-quarter turn until latches remain *down*. Check to see whether bright band on each latch can be seen. If band is visible, latch is *not* secure; so tighten!

NOTE: Mitchell-type magazines, 122m (400 ft) and 366m (1200 ft), *will* fit all models of CP-16 cameras but require insertion of a Cinema Products lock mount stud in the tapped hole in the Mitchell magazine, to secure it to magazine latch.

Also, the 360m (1200 ft) magazine requires that a longer belt be installed on camera.

12.4g Footage Counter
None on magazine.

12.5 CINEMA PRODUCTS J-5 ZOOM CONTROL ACCESSORY (Fig. 12–9)
The J-5 zoom-control accessory is built exclusively for the CP-16R camera. Unit consists of three basic components: (1) motor, (2) handgrip, (3) bracketry.

Figure 12–9. CP-16R J-5 zoom control. Courtesy of Cinema Products.

1. Semiautomatic exposure control plate
2. 4-pin plug
3. Handgrip lock
4. 3-pin LEMO plugs
5. 4-pin LEMO plug
6. Motor collar
7. 4-pin LEMO plug
8. Motor
9. Bracketry
10. Toothed ring
11. Handgrip

12.5a Motor

Silent servo-torque. Gear on motor meshes with gear on lens.

NOTE: J-5 motors are available in two models:
Slow speed (full zoom in 4 1/2 seconds)
Fast speed (full zoom in 2 1/2 seconds)

Collar on motor permits the sliding of unit after it has been mounted in its bracketry (see Sec. 12.5c) so that motor can be adjusted to match focal-length gear on lens.

12.5b Handgrip

Replaces standard handgrip at front of camera. Adjustable.

To Mount. (1) Remove four 3/8 × 6/32″ fillister-head screws holding standard handgrip mount to camera. (2) Pull standard handgrip and mount away from camera body to expose four-pin receptacle. (3) Align four-pin plug in J-5 handgrip mount to four-pin receptacle, and secure J-5 mount to camera with the four fillister-head screws. (4) Insert four-pin LEMO plug on cable into receptacle on end of motor and the other end into the lower matching receptacle on end J-5 handgrip. (5) Insert three-pin LEMO plug on cable into upper three-pin receptacle of J-5 handgrip and other end into receptacle on handgrip mount.

NOTE: Older J-5 handgrips have a permanent wire between handle mount and handgrip. Newer models permit an easy change should one cable break, a feature the older models lacked.

To Adjust J-5 Handgrip. Loosen handgrip lock, adjust handle to most comfortable holding position, tighten handgrip lock.

ON/OFF Switch. In handgrip; thumb-actuated; overrides Start-Stop switch at back of camera. Push *down* for ON: push *up* for OFF.

Zoom Control. Sliding knob located on angle of handgrip behind ON/OFF switch. *To widen lens:* Slide knob toward Operator. *To zoom in:* Push knob away from Operator.

NOTE: Speed of zooms are regulated by the distance that sliding knob is moved from center to its extreme limit, up to maximum speed of motor (slow speed: $4\frac{1}{2}$ seconds; fast speed: $2\frac{1}{2}$ seconds).

12.5c Bracketry
Varies in size, depending on zoom lens. A figure-8 bracket holds motor to lens. A toothed ring must be fitted to lens focal-length barrel.

NOTE: It is essential to know type of zoom lens to be used before selecting bracketry.

CAUTION: If a CP-16R is fitted with a fully automatic exposure control (see Sec. 12.3f), then a special bracket and lens ring are necessary.

12.5d Assembly Procedure
(1) Replace standard handgrip with J-5 handgrip. (2) Attach toothed ring to focal-length barrel. (3) Attach bracketry and motor to lens; adjust to match teeth on motor ring. (4) Attach cable with four-pin LEMO plug; attach cable with three-pin LEMO plug.

12.6 CINEMA PRODUCTS ORIENTABLE VIEWFINDER (Fig. 12–10)
Orientable Viewfinder is a foldable-optical-unit that is an option to the standard viewfinder. With a magnification of 12X, it permits (1) viewing with left eye, and/or (2) erect image when eyepiece is rotated to any position.

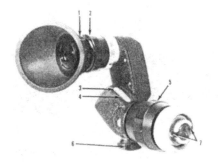

1. Eyepiece "dowser"
2. Eyepiece focus ring
3. Red button
4. Serrated thumb catch
5. Erect image lock
6. Image orientation lock
7. Keyways

Figure 12–10. CP-16R orientable viewfinder. Courtesy of Cinema Products.

Orientable viewfinder is provided with four controls: (1) erect image lock; (2) image orientation lock; (3) eyepiece focus ring; (4) eyepiece "dowser."

Erect Image Lock. Permits 360° rotation of viewfinder in a plane parallel to camera body while viewed image remains constant.

To Release, rotate image lock knob *away* from Operator. *To secure viewfinder in place,* rotate image lock knob *toward* Operator.

Image Orientation Lock. Permits image to "tumble" when viewfinder is rotated so that image can be oriented to Operator's viewing position (sideways, angled, etc.). *To release image,* rotate knurled orientation lock knob counterclockwise. *To secure the image,* rotate orientation lock knob clockwise.

NOTE: *To clean internal optics,* depress red button on prism box, and slide serrated thumb catch over red button to keep it depressed. Pull prism box away from camera. *To replace,* align key on prism box to keyway on optical barrel. Depress red button; *gently* push prism box over optical barrel until thumb catch engages with an audible click. Release red button. Tug prism box *gently* to ascertain that it is engaged.

Eyepiece Focus Ring. Adjusts + or − 5 diopters. *To focus,* rotate focus ring until frame lines on fiber optics are sharp.

Eyepiece "Dowser". Controls open/close diaphragm on eyepiece. *To open/close,* rotate ring located forward of eyecup.

To mount orientable viewfinder to camera. Align keyways on viewfinder to keys on camera body. Slide viewfinder toward camera body, and rotate locking ring toward Operator.

12.7 CINEMA PRODUCTS EXTENSION-TUBE ASSEMBLY (Fig 12–11)

Extension tube assembly is a 178mm (7-in) unit that inserts between orientable viewfinder prism box and the eyepiece. Extension-tube assembly is used when camera is mounted on studio rig (see Sec. 12.9) tripod, or dolly.

12.7a Mounting

(1) Remove eyepiece from orientable viewfinder by rotating eyepiece coupling nut counterclockwise. (2) Attach threaded coupling nut of extension tube to threaded end of viewfinder prism box. (3) Attach

Figure 12–11. CP-16R extension-tube assembly. Courtesy of Cinema Products.

1. Eyepiece end

2. Prism box end

coupling nut of eyepiece to threaded end of extension tube; tighten clockwise.

NOTE: When extension tube is attached, optical image is inverted 180° top to bottom.

To Orient Image. (1) Release image orientation lock; rotate eyepiece 180° *away* from Operator; secure lock. (2) Loosen erect image lock; rotate eyepiece 180° *toward* Operator; secure lock.

NOTE: With extension-tube assembly in place, all adjustments noted in Section 12.6, "Orientable Viewfinder," apply.

12.8 CINEMA PRODUCTS J-4 ZOOM CONTROL ACCESSORY (Fig. 12–12)

The J-4 zoom control accessory can be used on 35mm and 16mm cameras and zoom lenses. Unit consists of four basic components: (1) motor; (2) control box; (3) joy stick handle; (4) bracketry.

12.8a Motor

Silent servo-torque. Gear on cylindrical-shaped motor meshes with gear on lens. Collar on motor permits sliding so that it can be adjusted to match the focal-length gear on the lens. Collar on motor fits to variety of brackets.

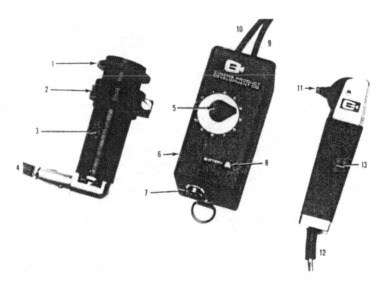

Figure 12–12. J-4 zoom-control accessory. Courtesy of Cinema Products.

1. Gear
2. Collar
3. Motor
4. To control box
5. Speed-selector knob
6. Control box (16V battery inside)
7. Trickle charger receptacle
8. Meter
9. To joystick
10. To meter
11. FWD/REV control
12. To control box
13. Joystick handle

WARNING: Gear on motor must be changed to accommodate a belt when motor is used on CP-16R Studio Rig (see Sec. 12.9) or Arriflex 16BL.

To Change Gear. (1) Push down on retaining cap (nearest toothed gear), and slide horseshoe-shaped spring-loaded retaining ring from groove on J-4 motor shaft. (2) Pull retaining cap from motor. (3) Remove flat washer and spring-washer. (4) Remove fine-toothed gear. (5) Install wide-toothed belt drive pulley. (6) Replace spring-washer and flat washer. (7) Replace retaining cap. (8) Push down on cap, slide horseshoe-shaped retaining ring (with part number showing) onto the motor shaft groove.

NOTE: Use of the J-4 motor with large lenses (e.g., Angenieux 25–250, Canon Macro 25–120mm) may require an additional shim placed on other side of spring-washer–i.e., flat washer, spring-washer, flat washer.

12.8b Control Box

Unit contains (1) 16-volt nickel cadmium (chargeable) battery; (2) speed-selector knob that provides a speed range from 1 1/2 seconds through 4 1/2 seconds on a fully charged battery; (3) meter that indicates condition of battery.

NOTE: A separate *battery trickle charger* fits to two-pin receptacle at end of control box. Trickle charger is available in 120V AC 50/60 Hz model, or 240V AC 50 Hz model. To fully charge battery requires 14 hours on trickle charger.

Speed Selector Knob. Numbers 1–10 on control box are for reference only. 1 is slowest speed, 10 fastest speed. Motor speed must be verified against stopwatch for precise timing of zoom.

Auxiliary Power Cable. While not considered a basic component, an auxiliary cable is available for use when battery in control box is weak or dead. One end of cable plugs into an **Arriflex** (two-prong) 16-volt standard battery. Other end plugs into receptacle at end of control box that normally accepts trickle-charger plug.

12.8c Joystick Handle

Length of unit fits firmly in hand with thumb on FWD/REV control or can be taped to pan-handle with FWD/REV control up.

With thumb-actuated FWD/REV control at center position, unit is *off*. When pushed *up/down* to its extreme limit, zoom motor will run at speed set on control box. By pushing FWD/REV control *between* center and extreme limit, operator can control zoom speed more *slowly* than the speed set on control box.

12.8d Bracketry

Bracketry will vary with type of zoom lens and camera to be used. Bracketry *must* fit configuration of both. Brackets and toothed gear are available for the following cameras and lenses.

NOTE: Any listed lens can be used with any listed camera, *providing* that proper bracket is selected.

35mm Cameras	*35mm Zoom Lenses*
Cinema Products XR 35	Angenieux 25–250mm
Arriflex	Angenieux 20–120mm
Mitchell NC/BNC	Canon K-35 25–120mm
Mitchell S35R/Mark II	Cooke-Varotal 20–100mm
Eclair CM-3B	

1. Extension tube assembly
2. Matte-box rod
3. J-4 bracket locknut
4. Matte-box rod locknut
5. J-4 zoom control
6. Start/stop switch
7. Tripod mounting block
8. Riser block
9. Quick-release latch

Figure 12–13. CP-16R reflex shown equipped with *studio rig,* J-4 zoom control, orientable viewfinder (with 7-in. extension-tube assembly). Courtesy of Cinema Products.

16mm Cameras	*16mm Zoom Lenses*
Arriflex (S, M, BL SR)	Angenieux 12–120mm
Cinema Products CP-16	Angenieux 9.5–95mm
(reflex and nonreflex)	Canon 12–120mm
Eclair (NPR, ACL)	Zeiss 10–100mm

12.9 CINEMA PRODUCTS STUDIO RIG ACCESSORY FOR CP-16R CAMERA (Figs. 12–13, 12–14)

Studio rig accessory for CP-16R camera consists of (1) dovetailed camera plate, (2) tripod mounting block, (3) riser block, (4) matte box rods, (5) lens support bracket, (6) follow-focus mechanism, (7) matte box.

Lens and camera must be prepared before studio rig can be utilized; once mounted on studio rig, further adjustments must be made to rig, camera, and lens before filming commences.

12.9a Dovetailed Camera Plate

Mounts to camera base. Fitted with one 3/8″-16 and one 1/4″-20 screw for proper alignment to corresponding tapped holes in camera base.

NOTE: Some plates may have a pin instead of a 1/4″-20 screw.

12.9b Tripod Mounting Block

Necessary in order to mount studio rig on tripod or geared head. Fitted with eight 3/8″-16 tapped holes, lengthwise, to accommodate tripod or geared head lockdown screw. Number of tapped holes permits adjustment for balance.

12.9c Riser Block

Fits to tripod mounting block to accommodate matte-box rods. Four 1/4″-20 × 19.1mm (3/4″) screws (heads take 4/8 (3/16″) Allen wrench) secure unit to mounting block.

Quick-release latch: At back of block; accepts dovetailed plate that is mounted to camera base. *To release plate,* pull latch handle toward Operator. *To lock plate in riser block,* push handle away from Operator. Ascertain that camera is securely held.

Figure 12–14. CP-16R studio rig detail. Courtesy of Cinema Products.

1. Zoom pulley
2. Start/stop switch connector
3. Motor/accessory mounting bracket
4. To J-4 control box
5. J-4 motor
6. Lens-support bracket

7. Follow-focus knob
8. Marking disc
9. Follow-focus bracket
10. Stainless steel plunger
11. Matte box
12. Foam "doughnut"

NOTE: As a rule, the tripod mounting block and riser block are joined as a unit and never disassembled.

12.9d   Matte-Box Rods

Insert into front of riser block. One knurled matte-box screw holds two 27.94cm (11-in.) rods in place. *To mount rods,* insert first rod into right accommodation cavity until it reaches stop. Insert second rod into left accommodation cavity and align front of rod to first rod. Secure knurled matte-box rod locknut clockwise.

12.9e   Lens Support Bracket

Slides onto mattebox rods. Two types available:
   (1) *J-4 motor mounting type,* with raised lateral bar.

NOTE: J-4 motor bracket that accommodates the cylindrical J-4 motor contains a lateral channel that slides onto the lateral bar of the lens-support bracket and is secured in place with a single screw.

CAUTION: *Always* fit J-4 motor bracket to lens-support bracket with bracket ring *down.* Rig will *not* work if ring is up. Collar on J-4 motor then slides into bracket ring with powerline receptacle *toward* Operator, the gear *away* from Operator.

Top of bracket has ⅜″-16 tapped hole to accommodate a threaded post with an adjustable "V"-block, which cradles a zoom lens. A motor *cannot* be attached to this bracket.

(2) *Smooth-sided type,* lacking a raised lateral bar with only a ⅜″-16 tapped hole at top of bracket to accommodate a threaded post with adjustable "V"-block, which cradles a zoom lens. A motor *cannot* be attached to this bracket.

A locknut at left side secures either unit to the matte-box rod.

12.9f Follow-Focus Mechanism

Slides onto matte-box rods. Unit has two follow-focus knobs (one at each side of mechanism).

NOTE: Phenolic gear on mechanism (that engages focus gear on lens) faces the Operator.

Circular and notched marking discs—at both sides—are magnetic and removable and can be marked with grease or lead pencil for focus marks.

To remove and clean, insert a fingernail under disc, and pry away from housing.

To adjust follow-focus mechanism to lens gear: (1) Set zoom-lens focus to its shortest distance. (2) Loosen knurled nut at front of mechanism, depress phenolic gear, tighten knurled nut. (3) Slide mechanism toward lens until front of phenolic gear (above the knurled nut) aligns to gear on lens. (4) Loosen knurled nut, ascertain that phenolic gear meshes with lens gear, tighten knurled nut. (5) Tighten locknut at left side to secure mechanism to matte box. (6) Rotate follow focus knob and set lens to infinity.

12.9g Matte Box

In two stages (Fig. 12–15)

First Stage. Slots at top and bottom and slots at sides accept rectangular filters of any length × 101.6mm (4 in.) vertically or horizontally, or a single 101.6 × 101.6mm (4 × 4 in.) filter holder.

To Insert Rectangular Filter Vertically. (1) Depress button at left top of matte box, and rotate until short segment of bent line scribed on button is vertical. (2) Slide rectangular filter into matte box from top.

NOTE: With *short* segment of scribed line vertical, filter will slide in slot freely from slight hand pressure.

To Lock Filter in Place. (1) Depress button at left top, rotate until long segment of scribed line is vertical. (2) Hold button, slide rectangular filter into matte box from top to desired position, release button.

NOTE: With long segment of scribed line vertical, knob *must be depressed* in order to slide filter.

To Insert Rectangular Filter Horizontally. (1) Depress button at left top of matte box, rotate until short scribed line is vertical.

NOTE: With short scribed line vertical, filter slides freely.

(2) Pull stainless steel plunger on filter adapter at right top of matte box from its circular counterbore. (3) Grasp filter adapter tab (in center of vertical matte box opening), lift adapter. (4) Depress button at left top of matte box, and rotate until short scribed line is horizontal and *pointing*

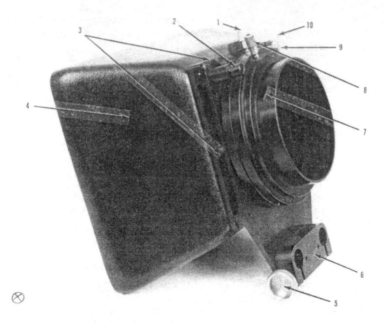

Figure 12–15. CP-16 studio rig matte box. Courtesy of Cinema Products.

1. First round filter screw
2. Filter button
3. Rectangular filter slots
4. Sunshade
5. Matte-box rods lockdown screw

6. Matte-box support plate
7. Lightshield
8. Lightshield screw
9. Stainless steel plunger
10. Second round filter screw

toward lens. (5) Pull stainless steel plunger on filter adapter, and insert adapter into left side of matte box slot. (6) Release plunger, and ascertain that it seats in circular counterbore below scribed button. (7) Slide rectangular filter into matte box from left side.

NOTE: With short segment of scribed line pointing toward lens, filter will slide in slot freely.

To Lock Filter in Place. (1) Depress button, and rotate until long segment of scribed line faces lens. (2) Hold button, slide rectangular filter into matte box from left side to desired position, release button.

NOTE: With long segment of scribed line pointing toward lens, button must be depressed in order to slide filter into matte box.

To Use Square Filter. (1) Rotate button until short scribed line is horizontal and points toward lens. (2) Pull plunger on filter adapter, grasp adapter tab, remove adapter, and store it in filter case. (3) Rotate button until short segment of scribed line is vertical. (4) Place square filter into filter holder; insert holder into matte box from top.

Second Stage. Accepts two round filters 114.3mm (4 1/2 in.) in diameter.

NOTE: Some matte boxes are made to accept 138mm (5.43 in.) diameter filters.

WARNING: Ascertain the diameter of holders *before* ordering filters!

To Position Circular Filters in Round Holders. (1) Remove matte box from rods. (2) Loosen thumb screw on light shield (stage nearest front of lens) until holder can be tilted back. Disengage internal pin from bottom of groove of holder that is forward of light shield. (3) Hold shield *up;* push filter past three wire springs inside ring.

NOTE: Forward filter holder is removed the same way. Filter is retained in forward holder by a threaded ring instead of springs.

To Replace Round Holders. (1) Align holder to rear of matte box, and tilt top of holder back. (2) Insert internal pin in bottom of holder into external groove of filter holder ahead of it. Tilt top of holder forward; tighten thumb screw into top of external groove of filter holder ahead of it.

CAUTION: Ascertain that bottom pin is engaged in groove of holder in front of it!

12.9h   Camera and Lens Preparation

Camera. (1) Place dovetailed camera plate on camera base. (2) Remove the four 6/32 × 3/8" fillister-head screws holding standard handgrip mount to camera. (3) Insert four-pin camera cover plate into receptacle, and secure with same four fillister-head screws. (4) Plug connector of start/stop switch into cover plate receptacle.

Lens. (1) Remove from camera. (2) Slide focus-gear ring over rear element of lens with hub facing the *front* element; push onto focus barrel as far as it will go. (3) Tighten Allen screws on focus gear uniformly.

NOTE: Lens Allen wrench: 4/40 × 1/8" oval head set-screw.

(4) Slide zoom pulley over rear element of lens with hub facing the *rear* element as far as it will go—but do *not* tighten screws. (5) Mount lens to camera.

12.9i   Final Adjustment

(1) Place tripod mounting block with riser block (see Secs. 12.9b and 12.9c) on tripod or geared head. (2) Open quick-release lever on riser block; place camera with its dovetailed plate (see Sec. 12.9a) in riser block and secure. (3) Insert matte box rods (see Sec. 12.9d), and secure. (4) Slide accessory mounting bracket with motor, and then follow-focus mechanism, onto rods. Adjust follow-focus mechanism to lens focus gear (see Sec. 12.9f); secure. (5) Adjust the accessory mounting bracket (see Sec. 12.9e) so that motor gear is in line with drive belt on focal-length barrel; secure. (6) Place drive belt with slack on motor gear, and make fine alignment of motor gear to drive belt by moving the J-4 motor longitudinally in its collar; secure motor. (7) Attach connector to J-4 zoom motor, and *slowly* run drive belt through full focal range a few times to make certain that belt and motor gear are aligned; secure the three set-screws in zoom pulley uniformly.

NOTE: Set screws on pulley are 0.0050 (fifty thousandths) in. in length and take a 4–40 Allen wrench.

(8) Slide motor bracket laterally in accessory mounting bracket slot, and adjust tension on focal-drive belt.

WARNING: Use just enough tension to eliminate slack! Too much tension will cause lens misalignment!

(9) Place foam "doughnut" on hub of zoom focus gear. (10) Mount matte box (see Sec. 12.9g) on rods, and align support plate to end of rods; secure.

CAUTION: Ascertain that focus gear on lens does not strike matte box when focus barrel is "racked out" all the way.

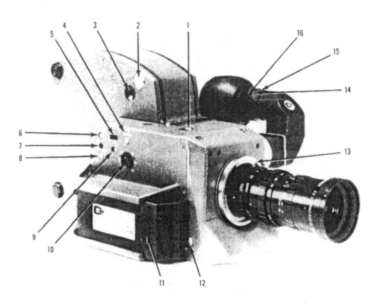

Figure 12–16a. Cinema Products GSMO camera (right front). Courtesy of Cinema Products.

1. Drive-gear release
2. Subtractive-indicator knob
3. Subtractive indicator
4. Display button
5. Metric/footage counter
6. Reset button
7. "Low battery" light
8. Battery-test button
9. Metric/footage slide switch
10. Speed-selector switch
11. Battery
12. Battery-release button
13. Lens lock
14. Eyepiece-focus knob
15. Focus locknut (not visible)
16. Dowser

12.10 CINEMA PRODUCTS GSMO CAMERA* (Figs. 12–16a and 12–16b)

NOTE: All directions are from the Operator's point of view.

12.10a Base

Fitted with one $\frac{3}{8}$"-16 and one $\frac{1}{4}$"-20 tapped hole to accommodate tripod-lockdown screw, or a standard handgrip with plate, or a J-5 zoom control accessory (see Sec. 12.5) attached to plate.

---

*Manufacturer states that the designation "GSMO" stands for "Gun Sight Man Operated" and pronounces it "Gismo".

Figure 12–16b. Cinema Products GSMO camera (left rear) magazine removed. Courtesy of Cinema Products.

1. Magazine lock
2. Filter slot
3. Drive-gear release
4. Camera-drive gear
5. Pulldown claw

6. Pulldown-claw cam and shaft-guide
7. 6-pin LEMO pluq
8. Camera-guide groove
9. Run/stop switch

Four-pin receptacle in base accepts plug on base plate that is used with either standard handle or J-5 accessory.

NOTE: Six 3/8″-11/32″ tapped holes in camera (two in base, two in front, two in top) are for mounting accessories.

12.10b Motor

Built-in crystal sync/variable.

Speed selector switch: At camera right side. Arrow on switch aligns to desired speed. Camera runs in sync mode at 24fps or 25fps. Variable speeds can be set at 12fps, 16fps, 32fps, 48fps or 64fps.

12.10c Powerline

Input to camera: Automatic when battery is slid into the battery channel at right side of camera. *To remove battery:* Depress button at front of channel; slide battery forward.

NOTE: Pins in battery channel will accept battery in only one position. When not in use, manufacturer recommends that battery be reversed in channel, to avoid draining power from battery.

Battery Test. Red light at back of speed-selector switch illuminates when 20-volt battery is low.

Run/Stop Switch. Rocker-type at back. Additional ON/OFF switch (depress ON, depress OFF) located in standard and J-5 handgrip when mounted to camera.

Six-pin LEMO Plug: Located above rocker ON/OFF switch; accepts plug for sync pulse to tape recorder. Also accepts extension plug for remote speed control.

There is no receptacle for cable to sound recorder.

12.10d Turret

None. Single lens lock accepts CP mount lenses only.

NOTE: Manufacturer offers Arriflex-to-Cinema Products adapters to enable use of Arriflex mount lenses on camera.

12.10e Lenses

Lenses must be fitted with CP lens mount, or lens-mount adapters.

To Fit Lens to Camera. (1) Rotate lens lock clockwise as far as it will go. (2) Align hole in lens flange with the positioning stud located at top of lens port. Insert lens flange into the camera body, making certain that positioning stud engages lens-flange hole. (3) Rotate lens lock counter-clockwise to secure.

12.10f Viewfinder

Reflex. Image magnified 12x.

Views more than full aperture. Area within outer line denotes projector aperture; also has TV outline (pumpkin) and markings of 1.85:1 for blow-up to 35mm. Markings are plated on fiber optics, *not* a groundglass.

To View through Lens. Press eye against eyepiece.

To Open/Close Eyepiece. Rotate ring forward of eyecup.

To Focus Eyepiece. Loosen locknut forward of eyepiece; rotate knurled knob until frame lines on fiber optics are sharp.

To Detach Eyepiece. Loosen knurled nut next to camera body. Pull eyepiece away from housing.

To View Aperture.

NOTE: Camera *always* stops with shutter in viewing position. In order to view *aperture* to see film, make a hair check, etc., the following is necessary:

Remove lens. Place finger on serrated rubber ring below mirror (*NOT* on the mirror!), and rotate shutter clockwise until aperture is in view. After viewing the aperture, replace lens. Shutter will automatically stop in viewing position when camera is run for a few frames.

Information Display. Visible at top of viewfinder.

S. (red light on early models) appears when camera is *out of sync,* i.e., not operating at speed indicated on speed-selector knob. Also appears briefly each time camera starts.

B. Appears when battery is low. Indicates camera is subject to variations in speed.

Exposure Control. None in early models. Subsequent models may have this feature.

Slating Lamp. None. Subsequent models may have this feature.

To Clean or Replace Fiber-optic Plate: Located inside camera at top of lens mount (visible with lens removed and mirror-shutter in viewing position). (1) Rotate mirror until aperture is visible (see "To View Aperture" above). (2) Place adhesive side of masking tape on the fiber optic, and pull straight out. (3) Clean fiber optic with alcohol or acetone. (4) Reinsert with etching optic (apply pressure) *down* (facing the mirror) until seated.

NOTE: The image plated on the fiber optic is *offset*—i.e., not exactly centered top to bottom. Proper placement of fiber optic calls for the shortest distance from image to edge of optic to be placed *facing the aperture.*

12.10g Sunshade/Matte Box
None.

12.10h Filters
External filters must be fitted to individual lenses.

Gelatine: Filter slot located in aperture plate assembly. *To insert,* remove magazine; insert filter holder *from bottom.*

NOTE: The GSMO filter holder is *not* interchangeable with other Cinema Products filter holders.

CAUTION: The filter holder is placed *behind* the viewing system. Check position each time magazine is changed!

12.10i Magazines
122m (400 ft), 61m (200 ft), 30.48m (100 ft)

To Mount. (1) Rotate magazine lock at left front of camera clockwise to open. (2) Hold front of camera at base. Align front of magazine to camera-body opening; slide magazine forward. (3) Push drive-gear release at top front of camera toward battery to facilitate seating the magazine.

WARNING: Make sure that guide latch at right side engages camera guide groove in camera! Seat magazine.

(4) Rotate magazine lock counterclockwise to lock.

NOTE: Final engagement of lock requires extra effort to seat it.

CAUTION: Camera will *NOT* run if magazine lock is not closed.

To Remove Magazine. (1) Grasp magazine at rear, rotate magazine lock to *open,* hold camera. (2) Push drive-gear release at top front of camera toward battery to retract camera drive gear from magazine. (3) Slide magazine *straight back* until clear of camera body.

12.10j Buckle-trip
None.

NOTE: Camera is fitted with an automatic circuit breaker that will stop camera if film jams, a circuit overloads, etc. *To reset automatic circuit breaker:* (1) Turn camera off. (2) Remove magazine from camera, and check magazine threading. (3) Slide battery forward until clear of contact pins in camera body, then reinsert battery. (4) Turn camera on, and check.

12.10k Footage Counter
LED (light-emitting diode) counter is displayed when camera runs. Slide-switch at right rear permits reading in meters ("M") or feet ("F"). Additive. Registers 0–9999 in increments of 0.1 meters or 0.1 foot.

WARNING: Once the slide-switch has been set to either meters or feet, it must remain in that mode. Switching from one scale to another in midcount will result in erroneous readings (even when switched back to its original mode).

To Read Counter when Camera Is Stopped. Depress button forward of LED counter marked *"Display."*

To Reset Counter. Depress *both* reset button at right-rear side of camera *and* display button at each side of counter *at the same time.*

NOTE: Having to depress both display and reset buttons prohibits accidental zeroing if reset button alone is hit.

There is *no* frame counter.

NOTE: Memory of LED counter is automatically recharged by the camera battery. There is *no* separate memory battery.

12.10l Tachometer
None.

12.10m Shutter
Nonadjustable; 180°.

12.10n Lubrication
Manufacturer recommends one small drop of oil on the following parts every 720m (2400 ft): pulldown-claw cam, pulldown shaftguide.

CAUTION: Manufacturer warns that oiling too frequently and/or excessive oil can damage the camera mechanism.

NOTE: After oiling, run camera to eliminate excess oil, and wipe clean.

12.10o Cleaning
Optics: Clean with bulb syringe or camel's hair brush.

Manufacturer recommends the following maintenance *each time the magazine is changed:* (1) Remove emulsion buildup with orangewood stick. (2) Wipe plates on magazines with chamois or soft cotton handkerchief (not linen). (3) Clean tip of pulldown claw with soft brush. (4) Clean engagement pins and matching receptacles on camera and magazine with brush or chamois.

12.10p Weight
With 122m (400-ft) load; 4.5 kg (10 lb)
With 61m (200-ft) load: 3.9 kg (8.75 lb)
With 30.48m (100-ft) load: 3.4 kg (7.5 lb)

12.10q Troubleshooting

Trouble	Probable Cause
Camera will not start	Battery dead: magazine lock not closed; battery not making contact; improper threading
Noise when camera runs	Improper threading; engagement pins dirty
Camera suddenly stops when running	Improper threading; circuit breaker activated (see Sec. 12.10j); film jam
Film jam	Improper threading; perforations incorrectly placed on sprockets
Camera runs slowly, sync light remains on	Low battery; electronic failure

12.11 CINEMA PRODUCTS GSMO 122m MAGAZINE (Figs. 12–17a, 12–17b and 12–17c)

12.11a Type
Coaxial

Figure 12–17a. Cinema Products GSMO 122m (400-ft) magazine feed side. Courtesy of Cinema Products.

1. Feed roller
2. Light trap

3. Clip-on door locks
4. Film cutter (on some magazines)

12.11b Capacity
122m (400 ft)

12.11c Lids
Two. Located at each side of magazine, which is divided longitudinally. Lip and clip-on locked. Right side only is hinged at front of feed chamber.

12.11d Feed
Right side. (Magazine pressure plate should be at the loader's right, the gate access door *UP*). Film (wound emulsion in) pulls off spindle counter-clockwise.

NOTE: Forward of the feed lid is a gate access door.

Gate Access Door: Hinged at front of feed chamber. Held closed by magnet.
    To Open Gate Access. Grasp top and bottom of door with thumb and index finger; lift door *up* to clear edge of door from gate, feed sprocket, and loop formers.

NOTE: Feed sprocket is accessible without opening door.

    To Remove Gate. Grasp edge of gate assembly, and lift straight *UP* until clear of magazine.

NOTE: Lower loop-former is attached and will come with it.

Figure 12–17b. Cinema Products GSMO 120m (400-ft) magazine take-up side. Courtesy of Cinema Products.

1. Film keeper
2. Take-up sprocket
3. White roller
4. Light trap

5. Mid-rip scribe mark
6. Light-trap roller
7. Flange

To Clean Pressure-Plate. (1) Remove gate assembly from magazine. (2) Lift pressure-plate retaining-spring. Plate will slide out.

To Replace Pressure Plate. Lift pressure-plate retaining-spring; slide pressure-plate into guide-tracks. Make certain that pin on pressure-plate engages matching notch in retaining-spring.

To Clean Curved Swinging Gate. (1) Remove pressure plate from gate. (2) Pull spring-loaded curved gate back from frame; insert swab and clean.

WARNING: Pulling the curved gate more than 6–9.5mm (1/4–3/4″) from frame can result in weakening of holding spring.

To Hold Spring-Loaded Curved Gate Back from Frame. Insert a swab stick into pivot point of arm where it is riveted to frame.

To Replace Gate. Align gate to spring levers in magazine guide slot. Slightly tilt side that is *UP* toward back of camera. Slide gate down over spring levers. Make sure that gate is seated by pushing plate *toward* magazine compartment and *down*.

Figure 12–17c. Cinema Products GSMO 120m (400-ft) magazine loop detail. Courtesy of Cinema Products.

1. Guide catch
2. Gate-access door
3. Feed sprocket
4. Upper-loop former
5. Upper pressure-plate assembly guide track
6. Engagement pins
7. Aperture
8. Magazine-lock catch
9. Lower pressure-plate assembly guide track
10. Pressure-plate retaining spring
11. Magnet
12. Lower-loop former

12.11e Take-up

Left side. Film winds onto spindle clockwise, emulsion always in.

12.11f Loading

(1) Open gate access door; press upper loop-former *down.*

NOTE: The upper loop-former remains down *during and after* loading. It is automatically released when magazine is put *on the camera.*

Open feed lid. (2) In darkness, remove film roll from can and bag. Insert film end into cutter at bottom of magazine door, and cut film end by depressing cutter. Remove cut-off piece of film and discard.

NOTE: Not all magazines have a film cutter installed.

(3) Place roll onto spindle; insert film over feed roller and into light-trap slot until film touches feed sprocket in gate access door. Continue to push film until sprocket starts to rotate. Rotate feed sprocket counterclockwise, and feed film through.

CAUTION: When loading single-perforated (B-wind) film, perforations must be toward lid on feed side, away from lid on take-up side.

(4) Close feed-side lid, and push down firmly. Rotate latches on lid clockwise one-quarter turn until latches remain *down*. (5) Open gate access door (see Fig. 12.17c, detail).

NOTE: Gate access door threading and take-up loading may be done in light.

Ascertain that upper loop-former is *down*. Rotate feed sprocket counter-clockwise, and feed film through gate. Push film with finger as it passes aperture to keep it in the race. Close access door, and turn magazine over; remove take-up lid. (6) Rotate take-up sprocket clockwise. Film end will take a natural spiral within lower loop former. Make sure that edge of loop emerging rides *under* white roller. Continue rotating take-up sprocket until film end touches scribe mark on midrib. (7) Grasp film end; insert into take-up sprocket's. This will lift film away from lower loop-former into a natural nontouching spiral loop. Rotate take-up sprocket clockwise, and feed film end through. (8) Bring film end down light-trap roller, and wind onto core clockwise. Feed film end through and *under* light-trap roller, and wind onto core clockwise.

NOTE: Take-up sprocket's film keeper may be opened if loop adjustment is required. (Pull out and turn spring-loaded keeper to left, to open. Turn and push in, to close.)

To Load Daylight Spools. Depress button in core spindles, and remove core holders and take-up flange. Place spools onto driver pins of spindles.

12.11g Unloading
In darkness, open magazine take-up side lid. Place index finger on core-spindle button, thumb on edge of roll. Turn magazine over, and press core spindle. Let film drop into hand. Push core holder out of core. Place exposed roll into bag and can.

12.11h Footage Counter
Subtractive indicator is on feed lid instead of counter. Must be manually operated by rotating knob on lid. In quarterly increments only: 3/4, 1/2, 1/4. Indicates film remaining.

12.12 CINEMA PRODUCTS GSMO 61M (not shown) AND 30.48M MAGAZINE (Fig. 12–18)

12.12a Type
Coaxial.

12.12b Capacity
61m (200 ft) spool load only. 30.48m (100 ft) spool load only.

12.12c Lids
Two. Located at each side of magazine which is divided longitudinally. Clip-on locked.

12.12d Feed
Right side. (Magazine pressure-plate should be at the loader's right, the magazine guide catch *up*.) Film (wound emulsion in) pulls off spindle counterclockwise.

NOTE: With lid removed the gate can be removed from the magazine.

Figure 12–18. 30.48m (100-ft) spool load magazine. Courtesy of Cinema Products.

1. One-piece lid

To Remove Gate. Grasp edge of gate and lift straight *up* until clear of magazine.

NOTE: The lower loop-former is attached and will come with it.

To Clean Pressure Plate. (1) Remove gate from magazine. (2) Lift pressure-plate retaining-spring. Plate will slide out.

To Replace Pressure-Plate. Lift pressure-plate retaining-spring, slide pressure-plate into guide tracks. Make certain pin on pressure-plate engages matching notch in retaining-spring.

To Clean Curved Swinging Gate. (1) Remove pressure-plate from gate. (2) Pull spring-loaded curved gate back from frame, insert swab, and clean.

WARNING: Pulling the curved gate more than 6–9.5mm (1/4–3/8″) from frame can result in weakening of holding spring.

To Hold Spring-Loaded Curved Gate Back from Frame. Insert a swab stick into the pivot-point of arm where is it riveted to frame.

To Replace Gate. Align gate to spring levers in magazine-guide slot. Slightly tilt side that is *up* toward back of camera. Slide gate down over spring levers. Make sure that gate is seated by pushing plate toward magazine compartment and *down.*

12.12e Take-up

Left side. Film winds onto spindle clockwise, emulsion always in.

12.12f Loading

(1) Remove feed lid; press top loop-former *down.*

NOTE: Top loop-former remains down *during and after* loading. It is automatically released when magazine is put *on the camera.*

(2) In subdued light, remove film spool from can. If magazine has a film-cutter, insert film end into cutter at bottom of magazine, and cut film end by depressing cutter. Remove cut-off piece of film, and discard.

NOTE: Not all magazines have a film cutter installed.

(3) Place spool onto spindle; insert film over feed roller and into feed sprocket. Rotate feed sprocket counterclockwise, and engage film perforations.

CAUTION: When loading single-perforated (B-wind) film, perforations must be toward lid on feed side, away from lid on take-up side.

(4) Ascertain that upper loop-former is *down.* Rotate feed sprocket counterclockwise, and feed film through gate. Push film with finger as it passes aperture to keep it in the race. (5) Replace feed-side lid. Rotate thumb-actuated latches on lid clockwise one-quarter turn until latches remain *down.*

WARNING: Check lid to see whether bright band on each latch can be seen. If band is visible, latch is *not* secure. Tighten.

(6) Turn magazine over; remove take-up lid. Rotate take-up sprocket clockwise. Film end will take a natural spiral within lower loop-former. Make sure that edge of loop emerging rides *under* the loop edge roller. Continue rotating take-up sprocket until film touches scribe mark on midrib. (7) Grasp film end; insert into take-up sprocket. This will lift film away from loop-former into a natural nontouching spiral loop. Rotate take-up sprocket clockwise, and feed film end through.

NOTE: Take-up sprocket film keeper may be opened if a loop adjustment is required. (Pull out and turn spring-loaded keeper to left, to open. Turn and push in, to close.)

(8a) *For magazines with serial numbers up to 599:* Bring film end down and under spool roller and wind onto spool clockwise. Place spool on driver pin of spindle. (8b) *For magazines with serial numbers 600 and up:* Bring film end laterally and wind into spool clockwise. Place spool on drive pin of spindle.

12.12g Unloading

In subdued light, open magazine lid. Place index finger on spindle, thumb on edge of spool. Turn magazine over. Let film spool drop into hand. Place exposed film in can.

12.12h Footage Counter

None.

chapter 13

Eclair Cameras, Magazines, and Blimp

13.1 35mm ECLAIR CAMEFLEX CAMERAS* (Figs. 13–1a and 13–1b)

NOTE: All directions are from the Operator's point of view.

13.1a Base

Base includes camera body and turret. Attached to bottom is a flat male dovetail (Fig. 13–1a) fitted with a 3/8"-16 and/or 1/4"-20 tapped hole to accommodate tripod-lockdown screw. Otherwise, the wedge-shaped dovetail is inserted into a female adapter on an Eclair tripod.

To Mount on Eclair Tripod. Slide camera dovetail into female adapter until lock pin snaps into hole in bottom of dovetail.

To Remove from Tripod. Lift pressure cam at front of female adapter; pull lock pin down; remove camera from female adapter.

13.1b Motors

To Mount. Tilt motor base 45° toward rear. Insert motor-drive dog into female fitting. Tilt forward. Secure by tightening spring-loaded motor-locking screw. Rotate magazine drive gear (at right of pulldown claw—see Fig. 13–1b) to check engagement of motor.

Variable-Speed-Motor Regulator. Squeeze pressure catch (at top front of motor) to disengage it from rheostat. Turn motor rheostat (clockwise to increase speed, counterclockwise to decrease speed), and check fps on tachometer. Re-engage pressure catch to hold motor at desired speed.

NOTE: A minimum of 8 volts is required to run camera with a 12.2m (400-ft) load.

Motors Available for Eclair 35mm Cameflex.
Variable-Speed Motor. 6/8V DC; 24V DC.
Governor-Controlled (constant-speed) Motor. 12V DC (24 fps); 12V DC (25 fps).
Synchronous Motor. 110V AC 60 Hz (24 fps) single phase; 110V AC 50 Hz (25 fps) single phase; 220V AC 60 Hz (24 fps) single and three-phase; 220 V AC 50 Hz (25 fps) single and three-phase.
Animation/Stop-Motion Motor. 24V DC (with magnetic brake).

13.1c Powerline

Square two-pin Eclair biplug (one male, one female contact) is inserted into base of motor. Rotating the screw at bottom of plug will spread the slotted male pin and lock the plug to motor.

---

*In the United States, the Cameflex is also known as the Camerette or CM3.

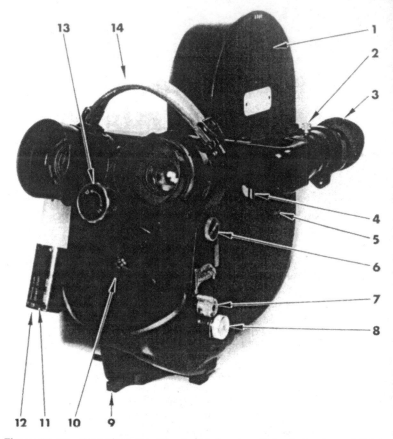

Figure 13–1a Eclair Cameflex Standard (without matte box). Courtesy of Eclair International Diffusion

1. Magazine
2. Dioptrics lock
3. Eyepiece
4. Magazine lock bar
5. Magazine footage counter
6. Groundglass-cleaning plug
7. Shutter-setting knob
8. Inching knob
9. Male dovetail
10. Taking lens
11. ON/OFF switch
12. Power plug (not visible)
13. Turret lock
14. Carrying handle

CAUTION: Be sure that power switch is off ("ARRET") before plugging in power line.

Three-position *ON/OFF switch* is in base of motor (see Fig. 13–1a). Positions are (1) ARRET (stop); (2) DEPART (start); and (3) MARCHE (run). DEPART (start) is an interim position used only to bring up motor to speed; switch is then to be moved immediately to MARCHE (run) for normal filming.

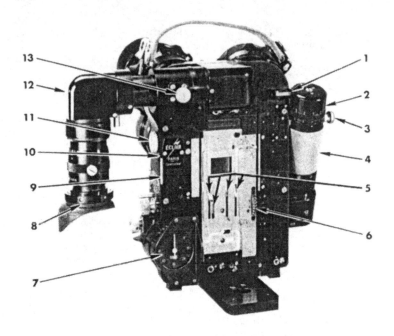

Figure 13–1b Eclair 16/35mm Cameflex (rear view, without magazine). Courtesy of Eclair International Diffusion

1. Protector-unit bracket
2. Motor rheostat regulator
3. Motor-locking screw
4. Variable-speed motor
5. 16/35mm pulldown claws
6. Magazine drive gear
7. Tachometer
8. Eyepiece latch
9. Filter holder
10. Filter holder safety catch
11. Groundglass cleaning plug
12. Prism housing
13. Eyepiece lockdown screw

CAUTION: Never leave switch in DEPART position. This position is only for turning on power.

13.1d Turret

Three-position; 21° divergence. Lowest port is the taking lens (see Fig. 13–1a).

To Rotate. Turn central turret lock knob clockwise toward "D" (*desserer:* unlock). Pull knob outward, and swivel the turret counterclockwise until desired lens is in taking position. Push turret in until seated.

To Secure. Turn lock knob counterclockwise to "S" (*serrer:* lock).

13.1e Lenses

To Mount. Insert bayonet base of lens into turret port, and turn counterclockwise until secure.

To Remove. Grasp milled ring on lens, turn clockwise, and withdraw lens slowly.

NOTE: Lenses used in a blimp must be fitted with geared rings in order to mesh with blimp external controls. (See Secs. 13.6b and 13.6d).

Eyepiece. Moves in and out. Adjusts to achieve focus on groundglass. Dioptrics lock holds eyepiece at individual's focus.

To Lock Eyepiece Open. Turn eyepiece latch clockwise around eyepiece plate. Rotate counterclockwise to close.

13.1f Viewfinder

Reflex. Image magnified 6 1/2 ×.

To Align Reflex Mirror for Viewing. Depress and rotate counterclockwise the inching knob (Fig. 13–1a) at lower left side of camera (marked "REFLEX").

To View through Eyepiece. Press eye against eyecup to open automatic eyepiece-closure device.

Groundglass (not shown). Installed above the aperture with the smooth side up. Nonremovable.

To Clean Smooth Side. Remove groundglass-cleaning plug (the screw securing the gelatine-holder safety catch) (see Fig. 13–1a) completely from camera. Insert Eclair groundglass cleaning brush through tapped hole.

To Clean Grainy Side. Remove taking lens, and insert Eclair groundglass cleaning brush through lens port.

Right- or Left-Eye Viewing. Loosen eyepiece lockdown screw (see Fig. 13–1b) counterclockwise (at camera housing) one turn. Pull prism housing laterally in its restricted slot. To remove completely, rotate screw counterclockwise all the way. Slide prism housing out of keyed slot.

To Alter Finder Position for Viewing. Rotate prism housing in desired direction (it will rotate 360°). Four-position "recess lock" halts finder in up, down, forward, back position, but finder will stay at any in-between position.

13.1g Sunshade/Matte Box (not shown)

Bellows sunshade/matte box mounts onto two rods that fit into the Eclair female adapter (not shown). To use the sunshade/matte box on any tripod other than an Eclair, the detachable female adapter must be taken off tripod and fitted to the male dovetail on camera. Unit is adjustable left and right, in and out.

Individual Masks. Correspond to focal length of lens in use; mask slides into front of sunshade.

To Verify Clearance. Sight through eyepiece, and run forefinger around inner edge of mask. If tip of finger is visible, move entire unit toward lens. Repeat check until matte box is clear of lens.

13.1h Filters

76.2 × 76.2mm (Two 3 × 3 in.) glass holders are housed in matte box. Rear holder revolves. A circular ring at back measures 48mm for polascreen.

Gelatine. Filter slot is located at camera left side. Holder is held in place by a safety catch. Bent portion of holder (used as a finger grip) should *always* face Operator.

CAUTION: Filter holder must *always* be inserted into camera to avoid fogging of film—whether or not gelatine filter is used.

NOTE: The manufacturer emphasizes extreme care and inspection of gelatine filters. Dirt or lint on gelatine may register on film when lens is stopped down. Manufacturer recommends that filter be removed after each take and inspected.

To Remove Holder. (1.) Loosen groundglass-cleaning plug and lift filter-holder safety catch. (2.) Slide holder out.

13.1i Door
None.

13.1j Footage Counter.
None.

13.1k Magazines
122m (400 ft) (shown) 61m (200 ft) and 30.48m (100 ft).

To Mount. (1) Clean plate and gate. Pull film from face of magazine; set loops (see Sec. 13.3f, no. 16). (2) Grasp front of camera with one hand. Slide magazine forward to meet plate until it locks (use bottom of eyepiece mounting and side of tachometer as guides). (3) Make certain that magazine catch (at top front of magazine) is *up* (locked). Gently try to move magazine sideways to make sure that it is properly secured.

To Remove. Press magazine catch down, pull magazine back.

13.1l Tachometer
Located at left side of camera near base (see Fig. 13–2). Registers 0–40 fps in increments of 8 frames per second.

13.1m Shutter
Variable; 35–200°.

To adjust: (1) Remove taking lens. Depress spring-loaded REFLEX (inching) knob, and turn until leading edge of mirror reaches upper left corner of aperture—i.e., edge closest to inching knob. (2) Loosen slotted shutter-plate locking screw (located below aperture, not visible) inside lens port. (3) Push in spring-loaded knob marked OBTURATEUR (shutter) located above REFLEX (inching) knob (see Fig. 13–1a). Turn clockwise until desired shutter setting appears on scale along edge of mirror. (4) Tighten shutter-plate locking screw, and replace lens.

WARNING: Check shutter setting often.

13.1n Lubrication (Fig. 13–2)
Manufacturer recommends frequent oiling of all moving parts with a small quantity of oil. Oil holes are usually marked in red (older cameras may not have color coding).

Claw-Slide Guide. Two holes (one at each side of plate).

Claw-Slide Drive Bearing. Two holes in plate.

Drive Mechanism. Depress antidust covers (ball bearings at right side of plate) with point of oil can.

13.1o Cleaning
Optics: Use soft camel's hair brush or bulb syringe.

Use *only* a bulb syringe on reflex mirror because the silver on the mirror is delicate and lifts easily.

Manufacturer recommends the following maintenance *each time film is changed:* (1) Remove emulsion buildup with orangewood stick. (2) Wipe plates with chamois or soft cotton handkerchief (not linen). (3) Clean pulldown claws with soft brush. Avoid entering slot.

13.1p Weight
(With 122m [400 ft] load), 8.6 kg (19 lb).

Figure 13–2 Eclair Cameflex lubrication. Courtesy of Eclair International Diffusion

1. 35mm pulldown-claw register slots
2. Shaft for accessory-drive mechanism
3. Claw-slide guide
4. Claw-slide drive bearing
5. Claw-slide guide

13.1q Troubleshooting

Trouble	Probable Cause
Camera does not start	Dead battery; power line faulty
Camera "hunts"	Motor cold; power terminals dirty; magazine threaded improperly
Camera stops while filming	Magazine jam—loops set improperly
Perforation tear; accordion pleat in film	Dirty pressure plate; loop uneven
Intermittent grind	Magazine not mounted properly

13.2 16/35mm ECLAIR CAMEFLEX CAMERA (see Fig. 13–1b)

The 16/35 Cameflex camera is distinguished from the 35mm standard camera only by its aperture plate. The 16/35 aperture plate has three pulldown claws—one for 16mm and two for 35mm. When 35mm film is running through the camera, the 16mm pulldown claw misses the 35mm emulsion by 0.005 in. The camera can be converted by inserting a 16mm *gate* into the 35mm aperture plate and using 16mm Cameflex magazines.

13.2a To Convert 35mm to 16mm

(1) Loosen groundglass-cleaning plug and lift filter-holder safety catch.
(2) Remove gelatine-filter holder. (3) Insert 16mm gate into 35mm plate.

NOTE: The long *narrow arm* on the 16mm gate (not shown) fits to the *left* side when the gate is inserted into the 35mm plate. The short lateral pressure guide fits to the right. On older cameras, the *narrow arm* is the same length as the lateral pressure guide. The unit is inserted the same way as the long-narrow-arm type.

(4) Insert the 16mm *gate holder* (not shown) into gelatine-filter slot (unit looks similar to gelatine-filter holder but is open at the end that is inserted into camera). Secure safety catch on holder. Secure groundglass-cleaning plug. (5) Check to see that the 16mm gate is being held in place by gate holder (pull gently on the 16mm gate).

CAUTION: The 16mm gate on any one camera is *not* interchangeable with gates of other cameras—each gate must be factory adjusted to the specific camera.

13.2b To Convert from 16mm to 35mm
Reverse the procedure in Section 13.2a.

WARNING: Be sure to insert the 35mm gelatine-filter holder into the camera to avoid fogging the film!

13.2c Protector Unit (not shown)
Purpose of unit is to store and protect the 16mm gate and gate holder so that camera can be converted from 35mm to 16mm at any time. Horizontal slot in protector unit accepts the bent portion of the gate holder. Gate holder is stored within protector unit in a vertical position, with gate below it. When protector unit is inserted under protector bracket at top right of camera and secured by a screw into a tapped hole at base of camera (see Fig. 13–1b), the unit also acts as a right-side magazine guide.

13.3 ECLAIR 35mm CAMEFLEX MAGAZINE (Figs. 13–3a, 13–3b, 13–3c)

13.3a Type
Displacement (over and under).

13.3b Capacity
122m (400 ft) (shown).

13.3c Lid
One. Dog-locked.
    To Open. Rotate lock bar counterclockwise.

13.3d Feed
Top. Film (wound emulsion in) pulls off of spindle clockwise. Film (wound emulsion out) pulls off spindle counterclockwise.

NOTE: Film (wound emulsion in) should be loaded as pictured. (The magazine interior is usually scribed with emulsion-out guide lines.)

13.3e Take-up
Bottom. Film winds onto spindle counterclockwise, emulsion always out.

13.3f Loading (Fig. 13–3b)
(1) Remove magazine lid. (2) Pull, then slide, the upper guide roller toward top of magazine to free upper pressure rollers from sprocket.

Figure 13–3a Eclair Cameflex magazine (threaded emulsion in). Courtesy of Eclair International Diffusion

1. Magazine catch

(3) Pull, then slide, the lower guide roller toward bottom of magazine to free the lower pressure rollers from sprocket. (4) Lift *up,* and rotate spring-loaded upper-side pressure plate counterclockwise and lower-side pressure plate clockwise. (5) In darkness, remove film roll from can and bag. Place roll of film onto feed spindle, and pull off clockwise. (6) Depress upper light trap below pivot pin, causing shoe of trap to move away from pressure pads. Push film through upper curved slot (approximately 76.2m (2 1/2 ft)). Release upper light trap. (7) Place film *over* the middle guide roller, then *between* the upper pressure rollers and sprocket, then *back* (i.e., to right) of upper guide roller. (8) Push the upper guide roller down to engage film between upper pressure rollers and sprocket. (9) Depress the lower light trap above the pivot pin. Push film through the lower curved slot. (10) *To prepare the proper size loop* (Fig. 13–3c): (a) place left hand against pressure pads and behind film; (b) slide left hand along pressure pads upward to top of magazine just below magazine catch,

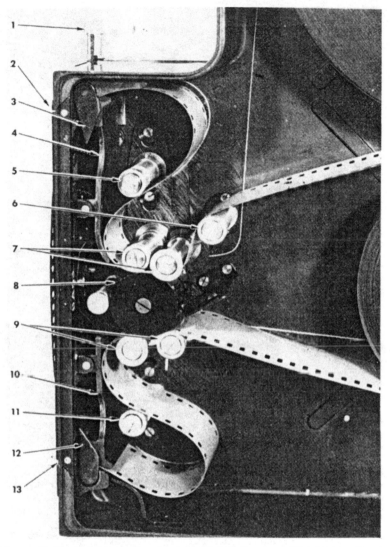

Figure 13–3b Eclair Cameflex magazine (detail). Courtesy of Eclair International Diffusion

1. Magazine catch
2. Upper curved slot
3. Upper side pressure plate
4. Upper light trap
5. Upper guide roller
6. Middle guide roller
7. Upper pressure rollers

8. Sprocket
9. Lower pressure rollers
10. Lower light trap
11. Lower guide roller
12. Lower side pressure plate
13. Lower curved slot

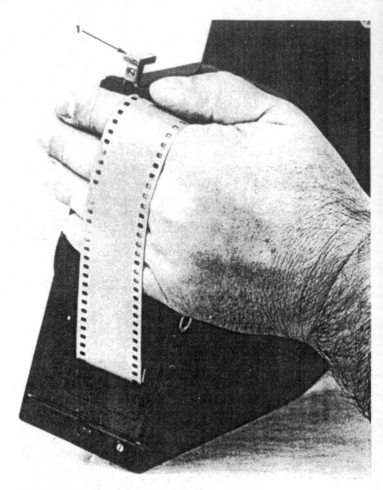

Figure 13–3c Cameflex magazine setting the loop. Courtesy of Eclair International Diffusion

1. Magazine catch

thus pulling up enough film for internal loops, which will be set later. (11) Holding film with left hand, pull surplus film into magazine with right hand. (12) Thread film in *back* (i.e., to right) of lower guide roller, then *between* lower pressure rollers and sprocket. Push lower guide roller *up* to engage film. (13) Rotate and depress the spring-loaded side pressure plates (top and bottom). (14) Wind excess film inside magazine counterclockwise onto take-up core. Pull taut by turning external lower spindle wheel clockwise. To remove slack from feed roll, rotate external top spindle wheel clockwise. (15) Replace lid.

CAUTION: If lid does not fit easily, check seating of guide rollers, pressure rollers, and side pressure plates.

(16) To Set Loops.   In light, the film outside the magazine is pulled away from pressure pads to form an arc extending from the upper curved slot to the lower curved slot. With forefinger, press center of arc against the magazine to form two equal halves, which, when individually pushed into the magazine, form the upper and lower internal loops.

NOTE: (a) It is recommended that loops always be reset just before fitting magazine to camera. (b) Most magazines have protective covers, which snap over pressure pads and film after being loaded. Covers are released from magazine by depressing magazine catch. (See Figs. 13–3a, b, and c). (c) Magazines are released from camera by depressing magazine catch and pulling magazine back.

13.3g Unloading
In darkness, remove lid. Place index finger on core, thumb on edge of roll. Turn magazine over, remove film roll, and place exposed roll in black bag and can.

13.3h Lubrication
Remove screws on feed, take-up, and main sprocket spindles. Insert four drops of oil in each. Replace screws. Lubricate often.

13.3i Footage Counter
In lid. Subtractive in increments of 3m (10 ft).

13.4 ECLAIR 16mm CAMEFLEX MAGAZINE (not shown)
Feeds, loads, takes up, and unloads the same as the 35mm magazine (see Sec. 13.3). Feed and take-up spindles are removable to accommodate spools. Footage counter on lid is subtractive in increments of 3m (10 ft). An additional counter on back is additive up to 61m (200-ft), in increments of 3m (10 ft).

13.5 ECLAIR 35mm MAGAZINE FOR AQUAFLEX (low silhouette) (not shown)

Magazine is designed for use in low-clearance areas (underwater blimp, airplane wing, auto interiors, etc.)

13.5a Type
Displacement

WARNING: Unlike standard magazines (over-and-under feed and take-up), the feed and take-up rolls are in *tandem*. Feed spindle is at right side (farthest from magazine pressure plates), take-up spindle is at left.

13.5b Capacity
122m (400 ft).

13.5c Lid
One. Dog-locked.

13.5d Feed
Right side. Film (wound emulsion in) pulls off spindle clockwise. Film (wound emulsion out) pulls off spindle counterclockwise.

13.5e Take-up
Left side. Film winds onto spindle counterclockwise, emulsion always out.

13.5f Loading

Same as standard magazines (see Sec. 13.3) except for placement of feed and take-up spindles (as noted) and two additional rollers (see following note).

NOTE: Two extra film-guide rollers, located at top of magazine, aid in transport of film from feed (right) side *over* take-up roll and down to middle guide roller, where magazine is threaded in conventional manner and then wound onto take-up (left) side.

13.5g Unloading

Same as standard magazine.

13.5h Footage Counter

In lid. Subtractive in increments of 3m (10 ft).

13.6 ECLAIR CAMEFLEX BLIMP (Figs. 13–4a and 13–4b)

NOTE: All directions are from Operator's point of view.

13.6a Base

Bottom of blimp may be fitted with a male dovetail adapter plate (see Fig. 13–4b), which fits to an Eclair tripod/dolly.

NOTE: Removal of blimp adapter plate reveals that blimp bottom has two 3/8"-16 tapped holes to accommodate a standard tripod-lockdown screw.

Figure 13–4a Cameflex blimp (right side). Courtesy of Eclair International Diffusion

1. Accessory units
2. Two-stage filter holder
3. Carrying handle
4. Filter-holder dovetail

5. Extended sunshade
6. Internal baseplate
7. Access catch

Figure 13–4b Cameflex blimp (left side). Courtesy of Eclair International Diffusion

1. Viewfinder
2. Internal light switch
3. Footage-counter viewing port
4. Red warning light
5. Tachometer viewing port
6. Inching knob
7. ON/OFF switch
8. Adapter plate
9. Aperture-setting arm
10. Sunshade head screw
11. Aperture lock knobs
12. Power plug
13. Focus knob
14. Marking disc
15. Lens viewing port

Adapter Plate (see Fig. 13–4*b*): Unit is secured to blimp by ten screws. It is fitted with three $\frac{3}{8}$"-16 tapped holes to accommodate a standard tripod-lockdown screw.

Two sockets at rear of adapter plate have lock levers that accept an Eclair tripod handle. The flat bar between the two sockets is a release handle.

To Mount Blimp. Slide adapter plate at bottom of blimp into the female Eclair tripod plate until a loud click is heard, indicating that plate is locked.

To Remove Blimp. Pull flat-bar release handle (not shown) at rear of plate. Slide blimp back.

13.6b Camera Preparation

Lenses. Remove two top lenses from turret. Place lens-port plugs into empty ports.

NOTE: When used in a blimp, camera requires CICCA lenses (Eclair designation for mounts fitted with geared footage and aperture rings).

Figure 13–4c Eclair Cameflex blimp (coupling detail). Courtesy of Eclair International Diffusion

1. CICCA lens
2. Focus gear
3. Aperture gear
4. Aperture coupling
5. Focus coupling
6. Lens-gear lock
7. Inching-knob intermediate

Inching Knob. Slide ⅛-in. intermediate (extension) piece (see Fig. 13–4c) over camera inching knob. Secure jaw by rotating milled nut. Extension will engage arm rotated by exterior inching knob when camera is inserted into blimp.

Eyepiece. Remove from camera.

Eyepiece Adapter. (Unit measures 1 3/8″ long and contains a compensation lens.) Insert long part of barrel into camera. Knurled ring acts as a shoulder stop. Unit is slotted to accept lockdown screw in eyepiece holder.

Magazine can be on camera and threaded when inserted into blimp.

13.6c Access
To interior. Release catch at top of blimp. Right side of blimp is hinged, drops 90°.

13.6d Camera Insertion (see Fig. 13–4c)
(1) Release spring-loaded catches on internal base plate (push outward), and drop double-hinged rails 90°. Pull base from blimp interior along rails. (2) Pull knurled screw on spring-loaded camera lock at rear of base. (3) Unlock scalloped lens gear lock at front of gear box. Push it away from lens. (4) *Insert camera* into dovetail on base, making certain to slide the geared aperture ring on lens into the aperture gear at bottom front of base. (5) Rotate and release the spring-loaded camera lock at back of base, to secure camera. (6) Push teeth of scalloped lens gear lock toward lens focus ring. Secure lens gear lock. (7) Slide base into blimp; raise rails; close side of blimp.

13.6e Powerline
External. Eight-pin Jaeger plug located at left side below inching knob.
ON/OFF switch: At left side. (MARCHE = on, *down:* ARRET = stop, *up.*) Red warning light glows when camera runs.

Internal. Extension from camera inserts into eight-pin Jaeger plug at right side of blimp interior.

13.6f Sunshade
To mount. Insert rods into sunshade (flanges out). Rotate tapped rods into screws below front lens glass. Insert top of bellows over retaining screws. Align slots on bottom of sunshade over retaining screws. Slide rear of sunshade down. Move sunshade in and out by releasing knurled head screw (below rods).

NOTE: Rods are in three sections; they can be shortened if the wide-angle lens "sees" ends of rods.

13.6g External Controls
At left side of blimp.

Internal-Light Switch. Exterior pushbutton at left side. (Dry cell for power inserts inside housing near internal eight-pin plug.)

Inching Knob. Rotates counterclockwise. Engages intermediate piece attached to camera (see Sec. 13.6b, Fig. 13–4c).

Focus Knob. Rotates in either direction. Engages drive gear in base. Set lens at infinity, and mark removable plastic marking discs with infinity (∞) and other footage marks. Removable marking discs can be made for each lens in use.

(1) Set each lens to infinity. (2) Align infinity mark on corresponding disc to the footage-indicator pointer.

Aperture. Unlock the aperture-setting arm (which is locked by two small knurled knobs in a restricted slot), below focus knob. Move lever forward or back to set lens diaphragm. Lock the two knurled knobs to maintain desired aperture.

13.6h Ports
Left-front window above focus knob permits the viewing of footage and aperture settings on lens. Left-rear window at back allows the viewing of magazine footage counter. Window below eyepiece allows the viewing of tachometer.

13.6i Filters
Two-stage filter-holder bracket slides into dovetail located at right side of internal base, and it locks with a knurled nut. Two 7.62 × 7.62 (3 × 3 in.) glass filters insert into holder from top.

13.6j Viewfinder
Reflex. Eyepiece adjusts as camera eyepiece. Dioptrics lock holds eyepiece at individual's focus. It adjusts to achieve focus on grain of groundglass.

13.6k Cams
None.

13.6l Camera Removal
Open blimp side. Drop double-hinged rails; pull internal base plate from blimp along rails. Pull camera lock at back of base. Push the knob in the restricted slot at right front of base forward. Push camera back and out of dovetail.

13.6m Blimp Top
Scalloped knob and two tapped holes at top of blimp are for accessory light units.

13.6n Weight
(less camera) 50kg (110 lb).

13.7 ECLAIR NPR 16 CAMERA* (Figs. 13–5a and 13–5b)

NOTE: All directions are from Operator's point of view.

13.7a Base
None. An *angled cradle* (not shown) with a flat bottom fitted with a $\frac{3}{8}$"-16 tapped hole to accommodate a tripod-lockdown screw is used whenever camera is to be mounted on a tripod. Camera motor inserts into felt-lined cradle up to its hubs, which are located at each side of motor ON/OFF switch. Camera is secured to cradle by a lock screw located at bottom of cradle.

---

*Manufacturer states that the designation "NPR" stands for Noiseless Portable Reflex.

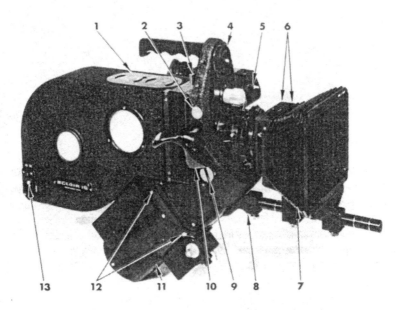

Figure 13–5a   Eclair NPR with standard lens and matte box (right side). Courtesy of Eclair International Diffusion

1. Magazine footage counters
2. Magazine-lock button
3. Magazine-lock cam
4. Turret
5. Viewfinder position lock
6. Matte-box filter holders
7. Sunshade
8. Matte box rod socket
9. Variable-shutter control
10. Thumbgrip (optional accessory)
11. Governor-controlled (constant-speed) motor
12. Motor lock blades
13. Magazine-lid lock

13.7b   Motors

To Mount.   Insert motor drive shaft into female receptacle located at bottom of camera body. Swing lock blades inward to secure motor.

To Remove.   Hold hand under motor. Swing four lock blades away from motor. Motor will drop free.

Governor-Controlled (constant-speed) Motor (shown).   Pilot light at top left side indicates motor running at 24 fps when lit. There is *no* inching knob on motor.

Variable-Speed Motor (not shown).   Has a built-in electronic tachometer. Tachometer registers 0–40 fps in increments of 5 fps. A high-speed/low-speed selector switch is located at left side of motor. For 0–25 fps, set selector for low; for 20–40 fps, set selector for high.

A speed-control knob is located below the high/low switch. Rotate clockwise for fast, counterclockwise for slow.

No reverse; *no* inching knob on motor.

NOTE: A minimum of 12V DC is required to run camera with a 122 mm (400-ft) load.

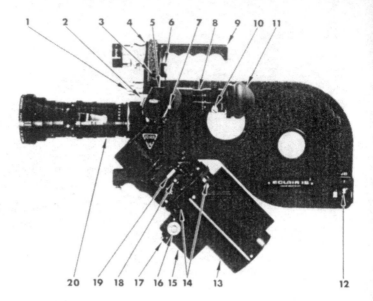

Figure 13–5b Eclair NPR with varifocal lens (left side). Courtesy of Eclair International Diffusion

1. Turret lock knob
2. Viewfinder-position lock
3. Automatic clapper
4. Auxiliary lens mount
5. Prism box
6. Magazine-locking cam
7. Eyepiece locking screw
8. Viewfinder
9. Carrying handle
10. Dioptrics lock
11. Eyecup
12. Magazine-lid lock
13. Governor-controlled (constant-speed) motor
14. Motor-lock blades
15. Powerline receptacle
16. Cradlehub
17. ON/OFF switch
18. Shutter-control lever
19. Inching knob
20. Taking-lens position

CAUTION: Application of more than 14V DC or any AC will damage a governor-controlled or variable-speed DC motor.

Motors Available for Eclair NPR.
Variable-Speed Motor. 8/12V DC (set at 8V: 0–25 fps; set at 12V: 20–40 fps).
Governor-Controlled (constant-speed) Motor. 12V DC (24 fps): 12V DC (25 fps).
Synchronous Motor. 120V AC 60 Hz (24 fps); 120V AC 50 Hz (25 fps); 220V AC 60 Hz (24 fps); 220 V AC 50 Hz (25 fps).
Crystal-Controlled Motor. (For cordless double-system sound recording): 12V DC (60 Hz signal to tape recorder); 12V DC (50 Hz signal to tape recorder).

NOTE: The 12V DC crystal-controlled motor can be used as follows: (1) cord-type sync operation (cable from camera to recorder); (2) cordless-type sync operation (crystal generated reference frequency to camera and recorder); (3) mains reference sync (camera motor follows *frequency* of local house power—the "mains"—via an intermediate transformer) (motor is *not* powered by house voltage); (4) playback (camera motor will follow frequency of a prerecorded sync pulse on tape); (5) multiple camera sync operation (more than one camera in sync with only one recorder in use); (6) with an additional accessory attached, it becomes an 8–40 fps variable-speed motor.

13.7c Powerline
Input to camera (see Fig. 13–5b) inserts into a four-pin receptacle below the ON/OFF button at front of motor; pin 1, ground (minus); pins 2 and 3, synchronous pulse; pin 4, plus.

Lock holds ON/OFF button down. To release, push up on lock.

13.7d Turret
Two-position. Lowest lens port is the taking lens.

To rotate. Turn central turret-lock knob toward "D" (*desserer:* unlock). Pull outward, and swivel turret 180°. Push in until seated. Turn lock knob toward "S" (*serrer:* lock) to secure. Pull knob to check seating.

13.7e Lenses
To mount. Insert bayonet base of lens into taking-lens port, with split flange of bayonet facing the turret lock *(up)*. Turn in port counterclockwise until secure.

CAUTION: Snug lens only! Do *not* tighten!

13.7f Viewfinder
Reflex. Image magnified 10×. Views more than full aperture. Area within scribe denotes full aperture. Some models may have a TV scribe (pumpkin) within the aperture.

To View through Lens. Press eye against eyecup to open diaphragm.

To Lock Eyecup Diaphragm Open. Press firmly on eyecup.

To Close Eyecup Diaphragm. Push eyecup to side.

To Align Reflex Mirror for Viewing. Turn shutter-control lever (at left side of camera housing) to "REFLEX" (Fig. 13–5b), then rotate milled inching knob (forward of lever) until shutter clears the eyepiece. Return the lever to "MOTEUR" (motor).

To Alter Finder Position for Viewing. Loosen viewfinder-position lock (lever at left of knurled coupling ring). Rotate eyepiece parallel to camera in desired direction (eyepiece will rotate 360° and lock in any position).

To Swivel Eyepiece at Right Angles to Camera (to set it for the left or right eye). Loosen eyepiece-locking screw on left behind the prism box (Fig. 13–5b).

To Focus. Remove the taking lens, or unlock turret, and set it in a horizontal position. Loosen dioptrics lock. Focus on scribe of groundglass aperture.

To Detach Eyepiece. Loosen viewfinder coupling (knurled nut next to camera body). Pull eyepiece out of housing.

Groundglass. Located inside camera housing, above aperture. Nonremovable.

13.7g Sunshade/Matte Box (Fig. 13–5a)
Bellows sunshade slides on a single rod, which inserts into a socket below the taking lens. On some models, a cradle mounted on a rod, which is

inserted into the socket, supports a zoom lens when a sunshade is not used.

13.7h Filters
Double holder in matte box houses two 50.8mm × 50.8mm (2 × 2 in.) glass holders. The rear holder rotates.

No filter slot for gelatines in camera body.

13.7i Door
None.

13.7j Footage Counter
None.

13.7k Magazine
122m (400-ft.)

To Mount. (1) Pull film from face of magazine, and set loops (see Sec. 13.8f and Fig. 13–6c). (2) Set lower front of magazine into notches at bottom of gate plate. Press circular magazine-lock button (Fig. 13–10) at top right of turret housing. Tilt magazine up and forward until it is flush with camera plate. (3) Release the magazine-lock button, and check magazine for proper seating. If lock button is not quite flush with side of camera and magazine is tight, it is secure. (4) Push the locking cam at top of camera toward eyepiece (to the left), and force the wedge into top of magazine recess.

To Remove. (1) Push locking cam away from eyepiece (to the right) to unlock the wedge. (2) Hold magazine. Depress the circular magazine-lock button. (3) Lower the back of magazine. Remove.

13.7l Tachometer
None. Correct fps rate is determined on governor-controlled (constant-speed) motor by observing the glowing pilot lamp on left side of motor. When lamp flickers or goes out, motor is out of synchronism (see Sec. 13.7b).

13.7m Shutter
Variable; 5–180°.

To Change Shutter Opening. (1) Either remove taking lens or unlock turret, and set it in a horizontal position. (2) Turn shutter-control lever to "REFLEX." (3) Rotate the inching knob until leading edge of shutter reaches left side of aperture (nearest the eyepiece). (4) Turn the shutter-control lever down to "REGLAGE OBTURATEUR" (shutter adjustment), and hold. (5) Push the raised variable-shutter-control knob *in,* and turn it until desired shutter setting appears on scale along edge of mirror. (6) Release the shutter-control knob, and return the lever back to "MOTEUR" (motor). (7) Check the adjustment often.

13.7n Lubrication
None. All bearings and gears are permanently lubricated.

13.7o Cleaning
Optics: Clean with bulb syringe or camel's hair brush.

CAUTION: Use *only* the bulb syringe on the reflex mirror, as the silver is delicate and lifts easily.

Manufacturer recommends the following maintenance *each time magazine is changed:* 1. Remove emulsion buildup with orangewood stick.

2. Wipe plates with chamois or soft cotton (not linen) handkerchief. 3. Clean single pulldown claw spring with soft brush. Avoid entering into slot.

CAUTION: The spring can be knocked out when cleaning it. Repair is a factory job.

13.7p Weight
(With 122m (400-ft) load) 9.5 kg (21 lb).

13.7q Troubleshooting

Trouble	*Probable Cause*
High-speed whirr	REFLEX lever not set to "MOTEUR" (motor)
Knocking noise	Film jam or lost loop
Pilot light out while camera is running	Low battery or battery cold
Bloop light stays on in eyepiece	Low battery
Pilot light remains on after camera is turned off	Relay not pulling; low battery
Camera will not start	Dead battery; powerline faulty
Camera stops while filming	Film jam
Perforation tear, accordion pleat	Dirty pressure plate; loop uneven
Motor runs at excess speed	Transistors burned out by overload of battery voltage
Motor smells of "burning"	Wrong polarity of plugs
Magazine "chatter"	Lost loop
Noisy camera "grind"	Shrunken film stock; loose magazine
Clutch "chatter"	Magazine jam

13.8 ECLAIR NPR 16 MAGAZINE (Figs. 13–6a and 13–6b)

13.8a Type
Coaxial.

13.8b Capacity
122m (400-ft).

13.8c Lids
Two. Located at each side of magazine, which is divided longitudinally. Both lids are lip- and dog-locked.
   To remove. Slide safety lock toward rear of magazine. Push lock button down. Lift rear of magazine up and off.

13.8d Feed
Right half. (Magazine pressure plate should be at Loader's right, the magazine drive shaft toward Loader, and the footage counters away from Loader.) Film (wound emulsion in) pulls off of spindle counterclockwise. Film (wound emulsion out) pulls off of spindle clockwise.

NOTE: Feed interior is scribed with both emulsion-in and emulsion-out guide lines. Film wound emulsion-in should be loaded as pictured.

13.8e Take-up
Left half. (Magazine pressure plate should be at Loader's left, the magazine drive shaft toward Loader, and the footage counters away from Loader.) Film winds onto spindle counterclockwise, emulsion always out.

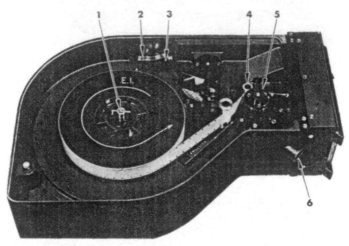

Figure 13–6a Eclair NPR magazine (feed side). Courtesy of Eclair International Diffusion

1. Spindle lock
2. Spring-arm holder
3. Footage-counter arm

4. Feed sprocket-guide roller
5. Feed-sprocket wheel
6. Magazine drive shaft

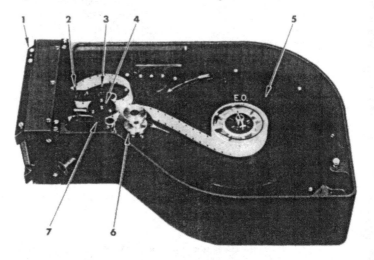

Figure 13–6b Eclair NPR magazine (take-up side). Courtesy of Eclair International Diffusion

1. Pressure plate
2. Film-guide opening pin
3. Upper take-up sprocket guide
4. Sprocket

5. Flange
6. Guide roller
7. Lower take-up sprocket guide

(1) (Fig. 13–6a) Remove feed lid. Swing footage-counter arm toward top of magazine and lock it into spring-arm holder. (2) In darkness, remove film roll from can and bag. Place film, emulsion in, onto supporting flange (which rides the feed spindle), and pull film off of roll counterclockwise.

CAUTION: When loading single-perforated (B-wind) film, perforations must be toward lid on feed side, away from lid on take-up side.

(3) Lift sprocket-guide roller, and push the guide *up* toward top of magazine. Place a few inches of film *between* the sprocket wheel and sprocket-guide roller. Depress guide to engage film on sprocket. (4) Replace feed-side lid. Slide the right-hand side of lid under the magazine lip, and push down firmly. Cover will depress the pin on spring-arm holder and release the footage-counter arm, which will drop onto roll. Check lock by attempting to lift lid with fingernails. (5) Flip magazine over, and remove take-up lid.

NOTE: Take-up loading may be done in light.

(6) (Fig. 13–6b) Rotate take-up spindle counterclockwise to transport film through upper channel. Wind sufficient film through, and follow scribed film guide lines. (7) Lift upper take-up sprocket guide. Push guide *up* (toward top of magazine). Insert film *between* sprocket and upper take-up sprocket guide. Push guide down to engage film on sprocket. (8) Push top of pressure plate in. Rotate take-up spindle counterclockwise until approximately 76.2 cm (2½ ft) of film exits the magazine take-up side, above pressure plate.

CAUTION: It is very important that film be taut between sprocket and top pressure-plate exit.

(9) Release top of pressure plate. Push bottom of pressure plate *in*. Place two fingers over the pressure pads (forefinger against the pads). Insert film end below the pressure plate, and draw film into magazine take-up side again. Hold film taut against the index finger (the two fingers provide a rough guide for setting the 12- to 13-frame loop). (10) Keeping fingers in place, lift lower sprocket guide, and push guide toward bottom of magazine; insert film *between* sprocket and lower sprocket guide. Push the guide *up* to engage film in sprocket. (11) Remove the two fingers from between film and pressure plate. An arc of 12–13 frames should be outside of magazine; if not, adjust. (12) Place any excess film that may be *inside* the magazine *over* the guide roller (follow scribed line). Wind film counterclockwise (emulsion out) onto take-up core. Insert core onto spindle, allowing little or no slack. (13) To check threading, rotate magazine drive shaft clockwise. (14) Slide left hand of lid under magazine lip; push down firmly and engage. Slide safety lock on lid toward pressure plate.

NOTE: On older magazine with the tension knob in the door, rotate the tension knob counterclockwise to remove slack.

(15) *To set loops* (Fig. 13–6c): Press the forefinger into center of the 12- to 13-frame arc to form two equal halves, which—when pushed back into the magazine—will form the upper and lower internal loops. (There should be six frames for top loop, six to seven frames for bottom loop.)

Figure 13–6c Eclair NPR—dividing the loop. Courtesy of Eclair International Diffusion

NOTE: (a) Flanges in newer magazines are held in place by a spindle lock (Fig. 13–6a) that fits horizontally across top of spindle. Older magazines merely hold the cores by pressure fit. Flanges are removed from magazine when daylight spools are loaded into magazine. (b) Older magazines are equipped with flange-ejector buttons in feed and take-up sides. Newer magazines do *not* have ejectors.

13.8g Unloading

In darkness, remove lid. Place index finger on core, thumb on edge of roll. Turn magazine over, remove film roll, and place exposed roll into black bag and can.

13.8h Footage Counters

Two sets. Located at top of magazine. Subtractive in both feet and meters, in increments of 5 ft and 2 m. One set of counters, marked "ROULEAU," registers the amount of film on a darkroom-core load. The other counter, marked "BOBINE METAL," registers the amount of film on a daylight spool.

13.9 16mm ECLAIR ACL* CAMERA (Figs. 13–7a and 13–7b)

NOTE: All directions are from the Operator's point of view.

13.9a Base

Bottom fitted with a 3/8"-16 tapped hole to accommodate a tripod-lockdown screw.

NOTE: An accessory handgrip, adjustable to a number of positions, fits to tapped hole in base, as well as tapped hole at top of camera. Some (but not all) handgrips are slotted to accommodate two filter holders.

---

*Manufacturer states that the designation "ACL" stands for Anston Coma/Jacques Lecoeur, after the designers of the camera.

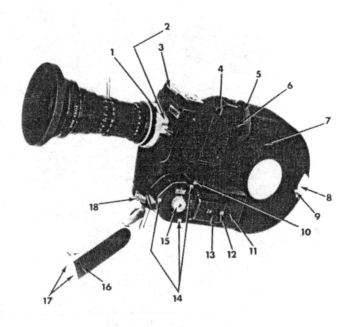

Figure 13-7a Eclair ACL (with 200-ft magazine). Courtesy of Eclair International Diffusion

1. Special adapter
2. Lens flange
3. Filter holder
4. Viewfinder
5. Eyecup
6. Eyecup lock
7. 61mm (200-ft) magazine
8. Magazine-lock latch
9. Magazine-release button
10. Pilot light
11. Motor
12. Crystal cover screw
13. Motor crystal
14. Motor screws
15. Inching knob
16. Accessory handgrip
17. Filter holders
18. ON/OFF switch

Base also contains Cannon plug for motor (see Sec. 13.9b), input to camera; ON/OFF switch; accessory plug; bloop light switch (see Sec. 13–9c); also a rheostat for a semiautomatic light-meter accessory not yet available.

13.9b Motor

Brushless Crystal Control (shown). *Pilot light* at top illuminates when battery is low and camera is not running up to speed.

Interchangeable Crystal Frequency. Motor can be converted to 24 fps or 25 fps by simple change of crystal.
To Change Crystal. Loosen crystal cover screw at side of motor. Remove cover. Slide crystal toward Operator, disconnect unwanted crystal, and replace with desired crystal.

NOTE: The fps speed is engraved on cover of crystal unit.

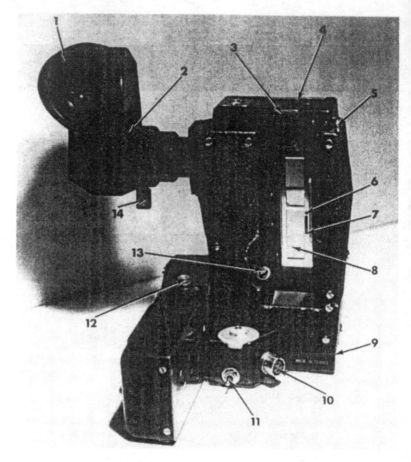

Figure 13–7b Eclair ACL (magazine removed). Courtesy of Eclair International Diffusion

1. Eyecup
2. Viewfinder
3. Lock-release lever
4. Filter holder
5. Safety-lock catch
6. Bloop marker
7. Pulldown claw
8. Aperture plate
9. Accessory plug (not visible)
10. Power plug
11. Bloop switch
12. Pilot light
13. Magazine take-off shaft
14. Viewfinder position lock

To Mount Motor to Camera.   Rotate the magazine take-off shaft until the two holes in the rubber drive block located at left side of camera are vertical. Align the two drive pins and the plastic Cannon plug on motor to the corresponding holes on camera. Snug motor to camera. Tighten three screws on the motor. Rotate inching knob to ascertain engagement of motor to camera.

To Remove.   Hold motor; loosen three screws on motor. Pull motor away from camera along drive shaft axis.

CAUTION: Do not twist motor up or down before motor clears plastic Cannon plug!

NOTE: A minimum of 12V DC is required to run camera with a 61m (200-ft) or 122m (400-ft) load.

WARNING: Application of more than 14V DC or any AC will damage the motor.

13.9c Powerline

Input to Camera. Four-pin Jaeger plug located at right side of camera base. Facing the plug and counting clockwise from they key, pin 1 is ground (minus), pin 2 is bloop signal, pin 3 is 12V (motor), pin 4 is 12V (plus).

ON/OFF Switch. Located at front of camera base. *To start camera,* push knurled switch in and toward eyepiece (left). *Short burst button* is located in center of switch.

Accessory Plug. Nine-pin Cannon plug located at right side of base accommodates accessory units (see below). Facing the plug and reading left to right, top to bottom, pin 1 is ground (minus), pin 2, 12V for test circuit, pin 3 is 12V, remote control, pin 4 is 12V, pin 5 is 1 MHz signal, pin 6 is 1 KHz signal, pin 7 is bloop, pins 8 and 9 are blank.

Sync-Pulse Module. Inserts into aforementioned nine-pin accessory plug and delivers reference pulse to recorder through a sync cable.

Motor Switch Module. Inserts into aforementioned accessory plug and bypasses ON/OFF switch at front of base. Switch also accommodates a handgrip, permitting Operator to hold camera and start/stop camera with thumb.

NOTE: Both the sync-pulse module and the motor-switch module require removal of the two short screws located above and below the accessory plug. Two longer screws must be used to secure the modules to the camera.

Bloop Switch. Toggle located at rear of base. In *center* position, *NO* signal is delivered. Operator has option of (a) placing switch to left or right *prior* to filming so that signal *automatically* registers on film when camera and recorder are started, or (b) placing switch to left or right to register signal *manually after* the camera and recorder have been started.

NOTE: Activating the switch illuminates a lamp at round hole at side of aperture to record a visual sync mark on film and at the same time to register an audio signal at recorder. To transmit a signal to the recorder, of course, requires that a sync-pulse module with cable (described previously) to recorder be plugged into camera, and that recorder be fitted with 400- or 1000-cycle oscillator (for putting an audible signal on tape).

To Change Bloop Lamp. Invert camera. Loosen three screws in base; lift base straight *up gently.* Lamp is in socket at end of wiring extending from base. Pull gently until lamp exits camera body. Replace lamp (available only from manufacturer). Reinsert lamp into camera body, lower base, and secure to camera body.

Motor Plug. Plastic nine-pin Cannon plug at left side of base accepts matching plug of motor. On the base, reading from top, left to right, pin 1 is 1 Mhz; pin 2 is ground (minus); pin 3 is +5V; pin 4 is +5V; pin 5 is 1 KHz; pin 6 is +12V; pin 7 is ground; pin 8 is ground; pin 9 is +12V.

13.9d Turret

None. Camera is fitted with a single C-mount lens port. A flange encircling the C-mount takes a *special adapter* that accepts either Eclair or Arriflex mounts.

WARNING: The type of mount of the special adapter should be ascertained before ordering lenses for camera.

To mount special adapter. Align the locating pin on adapter to the slot in flange. Snug adapter to flange. Rotate the knurled retaining ring on adapter counterclockwise *tightly,* to lock adapter to flange.

WARNING: Make sure that retaining ring on special adapter is *tight* on the flange.

13.9e Lenses

To mount. C-Mount. Align threads of lens to port, rotate counterclockwise. Snug.

Other Mounts. Require a special adapter (see Sec. 13.9d).

NOTE: See respective camera sections, titled "Lenses: To mount:" for instructions regarding mounting the particular manufacturer's lens to the special adapter.

13.9f Viewfinder

Reflex. Image magnified $10\times$.

Views more than full aperture. Area within scribe denotes full aperture. Most models might have a TV scribe (pumpkin), but this is not standard.

To View through Lens. Press eye against eyecup.

To Lock Eyecup Diaphragm Open. Turn knurled ring forward of eyecup counterclockwise.

To Close Eyecup Diaphragm. Turn knurled ring clockwise.

To Align Reflex Mirror for Viewing. Rotate inching knob located at left front of motor until oscillating mirror aligns to groundglass.

To Alter Finder Position for Viewing. Loosen viewfinder position lock (knob at bottom of eyepiece). Rotate eyepiece parallel to camera in desired direction. (Eyepiece will rotate 360° and lock in any position.)

To Focus Eyepiece. Loosen knurled knob on front of eyepiece; with lens on turret stopped down, slide eyepiece toward or away from camera body until grain on groundglass becomes sharp; lock knurled knob.

Groundglass. Located inside camera housing at side of aperture. Nonremovable.

13.9g Sunshade/Matte Box

None.

13.9h Filters

Gelatine. Filter slot located at top of camera. *Always* insert holder with chamfered side forward.

NOTE: The ACL filter holder will *NOT* accept a sandwich—i.e., two or more filters.

CAUTION: Filter holder must *always* be inserted into camera to avoid fogging of film—whether or not gelatine filter is used.

NOTE: The manufacturer emphasizes extreme care and inspection of gelatine filters. Dirt or lint on gelatine may register on film when lens is stopped down. It is recommended that filter be removed after each take and inspected.

To Remove Holder. Pull holder straight up until clear of camera. Depress top catch to insert gelatine in holder.

13.9i Door
None.

13.9j Footage Counter
None.

13.9k Magazine
61m (200 ft) and 122m (400 ft.)

To Mount. (1) Pull film from face of magazine, and set loops. (See Sec. 13.10*f* and Fig. 13–6*c*) (2) Push magazine-lock safety catch to right. Place lower front of magazine at bottom of aperture plate. (3) Tilt magazine up and forward until a loud click indicates that magazine is flush with camera plate. (4) Push magazine-lock safety catch to left (inward) to secure.

To Remove. (1) Slide the magazine-lock safety catch to right (outward). (2) Hold magazine. Depress lock-release lever. (3) Lower the back of magazine. Remove.

13.9l Tachometer
None. Correct fps rate is determined by inserting correct crystal in motor (see Sec. 13.9b) and by observing extinguished pilot lamp on top of crystal motor. If lamp lights, motor is out of sync.

13.9m Shutter
Nonadjustable. 175°.

13.9n Lubrication
None. All bearings and gears are permanently lubricated.

13.9o Cleaning
Optics: Clean with bulb syringe or camel's hair brush.

CAUTION: Use *only* the bulb syringe on the oscillating mirror, as the silver is delicate and lifts easily.

Manufacturer recommends the following maintenance *each time magazine is changed:* 1. Remove emulsion buildup with orangewood stick. 2. Wipe plates with chamois or soft cotton (not linen) handkerchief. 3. Clean single pulldown-claw spring with soft brush. Avoid entering into slot.

CAUTION: The spring can be knocked out when cleaning it. Repair is a factory job.

13.9p Weight

(With 61m (200-ft) load) 3.6 kg (8 lb), (with 122m (400-ft load) 4.5 kg (10 lb)

13.9q Troubleshooting

Trouble	*Probable Cause*
Knocking noise	Film jam or lost loop
Pilot light on while camera is running	Low battery voltage; motor out of sync
Camera will not start	Dead battery; powerline faulty
Camera stops while filming	Film jam
Perforation tear; accordion pleat	Dirty pressure plate; loop uneven; dirty side pressure rail
Motor runs at excess speed	Transistors burned out by overload of battery voltage
Motor smells of "burning"	Wrong polarity of plugs
Soft focus on lens mounted in special adapter	Special adapter not tight on flange
Magazine or clutch "chatter"	Magazine jam; lost loop
Noisy camera "grind"	Shrunken film stock; loose magazine

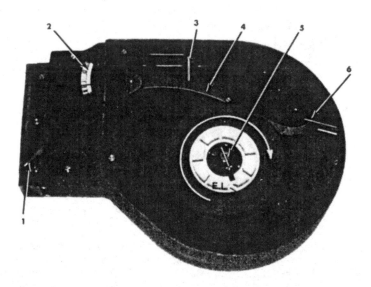

Figure 13–8a Eclair ACL 61m (200-ft) magazine, feed side. Courtesy of Eclair International Diffusion

1. Magazine drive shaft
2. Footage counter
3. Counter-arm holder
4. Footage-counter arm
5. Spindle lock
6. Feed rollers (not visible)

13.10 ECLAIR ACL 61m (200-FT) (16mm) MAGAZINE (Figs. 13–8a and 13–8b)

13.10a Type

Coaxial

13.10b Capacity

61m (200 ft)

13.10c Lids

Two. Located at each side of magazine, which is divided longitudinally. Both lids are lip and dog locked.

To Remove. Depress magazine-release button, and rotate magazine-lock latch counterclockwise. Lift rear of lid *up;* slide toward rear.

13.10d Feed

Left half. (Magazine pressure plate should be at Loader's left, magazine drive shaft toward Loader, footage counter *up.*) Film (wound emulsion in)

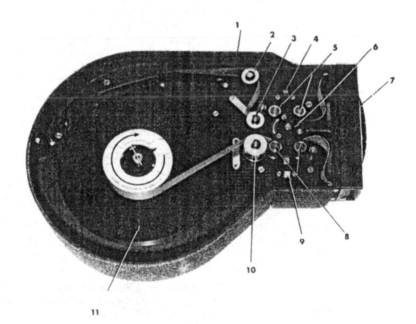

Figure 13–8b Eclair ACL 61m (200-ft) magazine, take-up side. Courtesy of Eclair International Diffusion

1. Small upper feed roller
2. Large upper feed roller
3. Entry roller
4. Upper guide-roller catch
5. Upper guide rollers
6. Sprocket
7. Pressure plate
8. Lower guide rollers
9. Lower guide-roller catch
10. Exit roller
11. Flange

pulls off of spindle clockwise. Film (wound emulsion out) pulls off of spindle counterclockwise.

NOTE: Film wound emulsion in should be loaded as pictured.

13.10e Take-up

Right half. (Magazine pressure plate should be at Loader's right, magazine drive shaft and footage counter *down*.) Film winds onto spindle clockwise, emulsion always out.

13.10f Loading

(1) Remove feed lid. Swing footage-counter arm toward top of magazine, and lock into holder. (2) In darkness, remove film roll from can and bag. Pull film off of roll clockwise. (3) Insert film end between the two feed rollers (emulsion toward exterior of magazine), and push approximately 6 in. into the take-up light trap. (4) Place film roll, emulsion in, on supporting flange (which rides the feed spindle).

CAUTION: When loading single-perforated (B-wind) film, perforations must be away from lid on feed side, toward lid on take-up side.

(5) Replace feed-side lid. (Slide left side of lid under magazine lip, push down firmly, and rotate the lid lock clockwise to secure.) Cover will depress the pin on holder and release the footage-counter arm, which will drop onto edge of roll. Check lock by attempting to lift lid with fingernails. (6) Flip magazine over, and remove take-up lid.

NOTE: Take-up loading may be done in light.

(7) Insert film *between* the small and large upper feed rollers. Push top of pressure plate *in* and insert film end into upper film guide; pull until approximately 18 in. of film exits the magazine take-up side above the pressure plate. (8) Release top of pressure plate, and draw film into magazine take-up side again. (9) Place forefinger on upper guide roller catch and thumb on lower guide roller catch. Squeeze thumb and forefinger together. Spring-loaded upper and lower guide rollers will move away from sprocket. (10) Place film to left of sprocket-entry roller and between sprocket and upper guide rollers. Push upper guide rollers *down* to engage film in sprocket. (11) Place forefinger against pressure plate, slide forefinger toward magazine locking tongues at top of magazine. Loop excess film around forefinger and into the lower part of magazine (Fig. 13–8c). (12) Insert film *between* the sprocket and lower guide rollers, and *over* the sprocket exit roller. Push the lower guide rollers *up* to engage film in sprocket.

NOTE: Manufacturer recommends a 12- to 14-frame loop outside the magazine. Forming the loop as described usually results in 14 frames. (See "To Set Loops").

(13) Wind any excess film inside magazine clockwise (emulsion out) onto take-up core. Insert core onto spindle, allowing no slack. (14) Replace take-up side lid (slide right side of lid under the magazine lip, push down firmly, and rotate the lid lock clockwise to secure).

To Set Loops. Manufacturer recommends that loader pull film outside the magazine, away from pressure plate, then press forefinger into center of arc to form two equal halves, which—when pushed into magazine—will form the upper and lower internal loops.

Figure 13–8c Setting the ACL loop. Courtesy of Eclair International Diffusion

1. Magazine locking tongues

NOTE: In some instances, excess frames in the loops have caused magazine jams. Field experience has brought about the following recommendation: Pull film away from pressure plate to form arc, press forefinger against film at top of pressure plate, slide fingertip down to center of pressure plate, keeping film flat against pressure plate. Press on film, and slide *two frames only* back into top of magazine. Push excess film into bottom of magazine so that internal lower loop will be larger than internal upper loop.

Daylight Spools. Slide spindle lock horizontally in its slot, then raise to vertical position; lift and remove flange. Place daylight spool onto spindle. Secure in place by turning spindle lock to horizontal position.

13.10g Unloading
In darkness, remove lid. Place index finger on edge of film roll, thumb on core. Turn magazine over, remove film roll, and place exposed roll in black bag and can.

13.10h Footage Counter
One. On feed side of magazine. Does not measure footage by numerals but is marked in increments of quarter-loads and scribed at "1" (one) for full "1/2" for 100 ft; unnumbered scribe for zero on darkroom loads.

Red segment of footage counter is for daylight spools and is marked in quarter-load segments of "0" (zero) for empty spool.

13.11 ECLAIR ACL 122m (400-FT) (16 mm) MAGAZINE

13.11a Type
Coaxial

13.11b Capacity
122m (400 ft)

13.11c Lids
Two. Located at each side of magazine, which is divided longitudinally. Both lids are lip and dog-locked.

To Remove. Depress spring-loaded release button in milled edge of lid knob, and rotate knob counterclockwise. Lift rear of lip up, and slide toward rear.

13.11d Feed
Left half. (Magazine pressure plate should be at Loader's left, the magazine drive shaft toward Loader, the footage counter *UP*.) Film—wound emulsion in—pulls off of spindle clockwise. Film—wound emulsion out—pulls off of spindle counterclockwise.

NOTE: Film wound emulsion in should be loaded as pictured.

13.11e Take-up
Right half. (Magazine pressure plate should be at Loader's right, the magazine drive shaft and footage counter *DOWN*.) Film winds onto spindle counterclockwise, emulsion always in.

13.11f Loading
(1) Remove feed lid.

NOTE: There is *NO* film-guide arm on feed side.

(2) In darkness, remove film roll from can and bag. Pull film off of roll clockwise. (3) Insert film end between the two feed rollers at left top of magazine (emulsion toward exterior of magazine), and push approximately 6 in. into take-up light trap. (4) Place film roll, emulsion in, on the supporting flange (which rides the feed spindle).

CAUTION: When loading single-perforated (B-wind) film, perforations must be away from lid on feed side, toward lid on take-up side.

(5) Replace feed-side lid. (Slide left side of lid under the magazine lip, push down firmly, and rotate the lid knob clockwise until a definite click is heard.) (6) Check by attempting to lift lid with fingernails. Flip magazine over, and remove take-up lid. Push film-guide arm *DOWN* until it locks into place.

NOTE: Take-up loading may be done in the light.

(7) Place film over large roller at top of magazine. Push top of pressure plate *in,* and insert film end into upper film guide; pull until approximately 18 in. of film exits the magazine take-up side above the pressure plate. (8) Release top of pressure plate, and draw film into magazine take-up side again. (9) Place forefinger on upper guide-roller catch and thumb on lower guide-roller catch. Squeeze thumb and forefinger together. Spring-loaded upper and lower guide rollers will move away from sprocket. (10) Place film to right of sprocket-entry roller, then between sprocket and upper guide rollers. Push upper guide rollers *down* to engage film in

sprocket. (11) Place forefinger against pressure plate, slide forefinger toward magazine locking tongues at top of magazine, and loop excess film around forefinger. (12) Pull excess film into lower part of magazine, and insert film between sprocket and lower guide rollers, over center roller, and between large and small tensioning rollers. Push lower guide rollers *UP* to engage film in sprocket.

NOTE: Manufacturer recommends a minimum of 14 frames be outside the camera.

(13) Wind any excess film that may be inside the magazine counterclockwise (emulsion in) onto take-up core. Insert core onto spindle, allowing no slack. (14) Place thumb on film-guide-release knob. Depress and rotate knob counterclockwise. Film-guide arm will swing up and rest against edge of film roll.

CAUTION: Do *NOT* attempt to move film-guide arm manually. Use the release knob!

(15) Replace take-up side lid (slide right side of lid under the magazine lip, push down firmly, and rotate lid knob clockwise until a definite click is heard.) Check by attempting to lift lid with fingernails.

To Set Loops. Manufacturer recommends that Loader pull film outside the magazine, away from pressure plate, then press forefinger into center of arc to form two equal halves, which—when pushed into magazine—will form upper and lower internal loops.

Daylight Spools. Slide spindle lock horizontally in its slot, then raise to vertical position; lift and remove flange. Place daylight spool on spindle. Secure in place by turning spindle lock to horizontal position.

13.11g Unloading

In darkness, remove lid. Place index finger on edge of film roll, thumb on core. Turn magazine over, remove film roll, and place exposed roll in black bag and can.

13.11h Footage Counter

One. Additive. On feed side of magazine. Counter registers each foot of film transported through magazine up to 999m/ft then reverts to 0. *NO* frame counter.

To Zero the Counter. Depress spring-loaded reset button at right side of counter.

chapter 14

Mitchell Cameras, Magazines, Blimps, and Accessories

Since the initial publication of this handbook, many Mitchell cameras have been "reflexed," thereby rendering the rackover aspect of the camera almost obsolete. Nonetheless, because many rackover cameras are still in use, the sections on Mitchell cameras remain as previously written.

The manufacturer, while maintaining the basic configuration, has reflexed the camera in one of two ways:

1. A mirror-shutter is at an angle of 45° (the image transmitted through the focusing tube via prisms to a larger-diameter eyepiece at back of camera); a light-trap is located on the tube, to avoid kickback from stray light; a windowed-snoot housing encloses the lenses (conventional and zoom sizes); sunshade is fitted with a glass front; extra sheet rubber and leaded foam rubber isolate camera noise. Filter slot is retained. With the exception of the elimination of the Academy-matte and effects-matte slots in the focus tube, and the rackover handle and gibs and gears, the camera is the same. There is virtually no light loss through the reflex-mirror system, and shutter flicker is visible, or

2. The area directly behind the taking lens is milled out (thereby eliminating the gelatine filter slot), and a *pellicle* (i.e., a thin transparent membrane) is inserted at a 45° angle to the lens, to split the image so that it is simultaneously transmitted to the film and, via the prism optics in the focusing tube, to the eyepiece. While providing a flickerless viewing (because it is placed forward of the shutter) it necessitates an increase in lens opening to compensate for the loss of light transmission through the pellicle. The Academy- and effects-matte slots in the focus tube, and the rackover handle and gibs and gears are eliminated; a light-trap, snoot, sunshade, and rubber insulation are added.

Any Mitchell camera that has been converted to reflex, or manufactured as a reflex, has had the letter "R" added to its initial designation.

14.1 MITCHELL 35mm STANDARD/HIGH-SPEED CAMERA* (Fig. 14–1)

NOTE: All directions are from Operator's point of view.

14.1a Base

Bottom fitted with 3/8″-16 tapped hole to accommodate tripod-lockdown screw. Base is L-shaped, includes turret (see Fig. 14–1a). Flat section of base is fitted with dovetail tracks (gibs), allowing camera to slide (rack over) horizontally to align the focusing tube with the taking lens.

Figure 14–1a Mitchell Standard/High-Speed with variable motor attached, and matte box in place (front view). Courtesy of Mitchell Camera Corp.

1. Motor-door latch
2. Four-way matte knob
3. Extension shade screw
4. Sunshade/matte box
5. Taking lens (not visible)
6. Turret-setting knob
7. L-shaped matte-box bracket
8. Matte-box rods
9. Turret-locating pin
10. Base and turret
11. Power plug
12. Crank shaft
13. Motor-lockdown screws
14. Manual motor-turning knob
15. Variable-speed motor (compare motor position to NC)
16. 1000-ft magazine

---

*The manufacturer no longer uses the designation "Standard"; however, it is included here because there are so many "Standard" cameras still in use. While basically the same design, the immediately apparent differences between the Standard and High-Speed are as follows: The Standard has two buttons at back of camera, which actuate an automatic dissolve (see Sec. 14.1q); High-Speed has *no* automatic dissolve. Interior of a High-Speed camera has a lower-loop roller and a stabilizing roller (see Sec. 14.1m, Fig. 14–3), both of which steady the film in its rapid progress from feed to take-up side; the Standard does not have these two rollers.

Figure 14–1b Mitchell Standard/High-Speed with high-speed motor attached (rear view). Courtesy of Mitchell Camera Corp.

1. Manual motor-turning knob
2. High-speed motor
3. Rheostat
4. Rheostat knob
5. Tachometer
6. Motor twistlock male extension plug
7. Powerline extension
8. Powerline plug
9. Rackover handle
10. Dial counter
11. Footage and frame counters
12. Counter reset knob
13. Offset viewfinder
14. Focusing-tube eyepiece
15. Shutter handle
16. Magazine-lockdown knob
17. Take-up belt
18. 400-ft magazine

A dovetailed viewfinder bracket, into which an offset viewfinder is inserted, is also fitted with a filter slot, and is an integral part of the upright section of base (see Fig. 14–29 for detail).

Four-way mattes: Used when a split-screen effect is to be achieved "in the camera." Adjustments permit any given size of "framing" or division of the screen. Two double knobs (see also Fig. 14–6a, NC) control the mattes, which are located behind the taking lens. The knobs rotate clockwise to move mattes into the aperture. One double knob is located above the turret. Top half of this knob controls the bottom matte. Lower section of this knob controls the upper matte. The other double knob is located below the viewfinder bracket. Smaller half of this knob controls the right-side matte. The larger half of this knob controls the left-side matte.

WARNING: Because mattes can slip or be pushed and loosened, it is important to check the matte positions, prior to shooting and at each hair check, to make certain that they have not moved into the aperture and thus cut out a portion of film frame.

14.1b Rackover

Camera box must be racked over (i.e., moved laterally on gibs until focusing tube is directly behind taking lens) to sight through the taking lens.

To Rack Over. (1) Grasp handle at rear of camera (see Fig. 14–1*b*), and depress button to release locating plunger. (2) Start to rotate handle clockwise, and *release the button immediately,* so that the locating plunger can engage the camera box.

CAUTION: Some cameras are *not* equipped with stops to prevent excessive lateral movement of the camera box. Therefore, unless the button is released immediately, the camera can be racked completely off its base.

(3) Rotate the handle only, counterclockwise, to make sure that plunger has engaged and that the focusing tube is aligned with the taking lens.

CAUTION: Because the camera will run racked over unless fitted with an automatic cutout switch, it must be racked back *before* shooting commences.

To Rack Back. (1) Depress button, and start to rotate handle counterclockwise. *Release the button immediately* so that the locating plunger can engage the camera box. (2) Rotate handle clockwise to make sure that the locating plunger has engaged the camera box and that the aperture is aligned with the taking lens.

14.1c Focusing Tube

Located in camera-box door (see Fig. 14–29).

To Change or Clean Groundglass. (1) Slide access door (at side of focusing tube) toward Operator, open camera door, and insert eraser end of pencil into forward opening of tube. (2) Slide groundglass sideways; grasp glass by edges, and remove; clean and reinsert; close access door.

NOTE: *Always* insert groundglass with smooth surface toward rear of tube.

Matte Slot. Located forward of groundglass. Academy matte is inserted with bent portion (used as a finger grip) pointed toward Operator.

Effects Matte. A frame of film cut with Mitchell Matte Cutter (see Sec. 14.11d).

To Insert Effects Matte. Remove Academy matte from focusing tube. Slide frame into matte slot upside down, perforations toward access door.

Magnification. Push magnification knob (located below focusing tube) forward to magnify image $10 \times$. Push back for normal image.

Contrast Filter. Two. Knurled knob at top rear flips green filter into view for orthochromatic film. Bottom-rear knob flips pan filter into view for panchromatic film.

Eyepiece. Rotates; moves in and out; adjusts to achieve focus on groundglass. Locking screw holds eyepiece at desired focus.

14.1d Motors (Fig. 14–2)

Before mounting motor to camera, make sure a motor door is mounted on right side of camera (see Fig. 14–1a).

To Mount Motor Door. Insert door in bottom retaining lip of camera. Depress recessed latch in motor door; press door to camera. Release latch.

NOTE: (a) The upper left drive shaft in the door accepts the motor drive shaft and operates the camera at one frame per turn. (b) Center drive shaft in door is for hand cranking or rewinding film manually and operates

Figure 14–2 Mitchell variable-speed (wild) motor. Courtesy of Mitchell Camera Corp.

1. FWD/REV switch
2. Manual motor-turning knob
3. Side motor-lockdown screw knob
4. FPS scribe
5. Rheostat
6. Tachometer
7. Powerline extension plug

377

camera at eight frames per turn. (Three turns per second equals sound speed—i.e., 24 fps.)

To Mount Variable-Speed Motor (Figs. 14–1*a* and 14–2). (1) Align drive shafts of both door and motor. Lift top motor-lockdown screw *up* to slide motor against camera easily. (Manual motor-turning knob is at side of motor.) (2) Secure top and side motor lockdown screws to camera. (3) Insert six-pin Cannon plug of powerline into motor-door receptacle. (4) Loop the wire, and insert three-pin Cannon plug extension of powerline into the motor. (ON/OFF switch is in cable.) (5) Turn top of motor clockwise for "forward," counterclockwise for "reverse." (6) Adjust camera speed by turning rheostat at bottom of motor.

NOTE: (a) Frame-per-second scribes (8–24 fps) on the rheostat are approximate. Correct speed is obtained by observing the tachometer and adjusting the rheostat. (b) Tachometer registers 0–32 fps in increments of 2 fps and 0–120 ft/minute in increments of 2 ft per minute.

To Reverse Variable-Speed Motor. Turn top of motor to "REV"; transfer belt from take-up to feed spindle wheel. Loop belt into a figure-8, to cause feed to act as take-up; adjust motor speed.

CAUTION: Cover lens or close shutter when running film back to beginning of scene intended for double exposure.

To Mount High-Speed Motor (Fig. 14–1*b*). (1) Align drive shafts of both camera door and motor. Lift the top motor lockdown screw *up* to slide motor against camera easily. (Manual motor-turning knob is at top of motor.) (2) Secure top and side motor lockdown screws to camera. (3) Slide inverted V-slots of rheostat bracket over the motor rheostat mounting pins on the motor bracket. Rheostat knob should always face Operator. (4) Insert six-pin Cannon plug of powerline into motor-door receptacle. (5) Insert both the female twistlock extension of powerline and the male twistlock extension of motor into mating receptacles located at bottom of the rheostat. Set rheostat knob to 0.

To Adjust Motor Speed. Turn rheostat knob clockwise while observing tachometer.

CAUTION: Never start a camera at any speed faster than 24 fps. Starting at a higher speed will tear the film perforations. Best method is to start camera with rheostat knob at 0 and crank it up *slowly!*

WARNING: Rheostat must be zeroed—i.e., turned counterclockwise, to slow down camera before turning powerline switch OFF. Slowing down the camera via the rheostat acts as a brake on the film roll. If the camera is stopped abruptly, centrifugal force will cause a film roll to continue unraveling and pile up inside the camera.

CAUTION: A magazine brake should be installed on the feed spindle wheel to slow down and prevent the film roll in the feed compartment from unraveling and piling up inside the *magazine*.

NOTE: High-speed motor tachometer registers 0–144 fps in increments of 24 fps. Digits on face of tachometer numbered 1–6 indicate "times normal" speed (e.g., 24 fps = normal, or "1" on the tachometer; 48 fps = "2" on the tachometer; 72 fps = "3" on the tachometer, etc.).

Motors Available for the Mitchell Standard/High Speed.
Variable-Speed Motor. 12V DC; 110V AC/DC (60 Hz); 110V AC/DC (50 Hz).
Slow-Motion Motor. 110V AC/DC (60 Hz) (24–128 fps); 110V AC/DC (50 Hz) (24–128 fps).
Synchronous Motor. 110V AC (60 Hz) (single phase); 110V AC (50 Hz) (single phase); 220V AC (60 Hz) (3-phase); 220V AC (50 Hz) (3-phase); 220V AC interlock (3-phase).
Multi-duty Motor. 220V AC (60 Hz) (3-phase), 96V DC.

NOTE: Multi-duty motor is only synchronous at 220V AC (60 Hz).

Animation Motor. 110V AC (60 Hz); 110V AC (50 Hz).

14.1e Power Line
Inserts into motor door and motor on variable-speed motor (see Fig. 14–1a). On high-speed motor, insert powerline into motor door, then insert extensions of power line and motor into rheostat (see Fig. 14–1b). ON/OFF switch of both units is in cable.

14.1f Turret
Four-position (see also Fig. 14–6a).
  To Rotate. Pull out turret locating pin (lower right side), turn turret until desired lens is in position at right of viewfinder bracket. Release locating pin to lock turret.

NOTE: (a) Center turret-locking knob may be tightened to hold a heavy telephoto lens. Ideal tension on turret for normal operation is obtained by tightening the knob by hand and then backing it off a quarter-turn. (b) Longest lens on turret should be mounted opposite the shortest lens. (c) On some models, one port is fitted with *quick-set locks* (not shown—i.e., clamps that grasp the lens-mount shoulder. These clamps are placed above and below the lens port and are loosened with a screwdriver. Quick-set locks permit efficient mounting and dismounting of a variety of lenses.

An Easy Method for Mounting a Lens Using Quick-set Locks. (1) Rotate turret until quick-set locks are at top. Slide clamps aside horizontally, insert new lens mount (cut-off portion of lens-mount shoulder aligns with perimeter of turret). (2) Slide clamps back over shoulder of mount, and tighten. (3) Rotate turret to place lens in taking position.

NOTE: Lens *can* be mounted without rotating the turret. However, the upper quick-set lock drops down behind the lens-mount shoulder in this position, making it more difficult to slide mount into port. Safety of the lens must always be considered: Possibility of dropping the lens while fighting the top lock is increased if turret is not rotated.

Turret Setting Knob. Adjacent to and below the turret locating pin. For normal operation, scribe line on turret-setting-knob bracket must be aligned with zero scribe line on base. Turret setting knob is used to minimize distortion while photographing architecture at an angle. To achieve a rising and falling effect, as with a view camera (equivalent to a 15° tilt of a tripod), loosen the turret setting knob, and rotate turret clockwise to lower front, counterclockwise to raise front. Tighten the setting knob, and check focusing tube for any possible aperture cut-in on lens.

NOTE: Rising- and falling-front effects are limited to static shots. Effect is limited to lenses 35mm or longer.

CAUTION: Realign the scribe line on turret-setting-knob bracket with zero scribe line on base, immediately (see Fig. 14–6a) on completion of shot. Tighten the turret setting knob with a wrench, to prevent slippage.

14.1g Lenses

To Fit Lens to Turret. (1) Unscrew lens barrel from threaded Mitchell mount. Align screw holes of mount with tapped holes in turret, and secure with screws. (2) Insert lens barrel into threaded mount.

NOTE: (a) Rear elements of 18.5mm, 25mm, and 30mm lenses extend into camera aperture when seated: therefore, these lenses must be backed off to clear the aperture prior to rotating the turret. (b) Each mount is fitted with a focus-lockdown screw.

14.1h Viewfinder

Offset (see Fig. 14–28). Fits and locks into dovetailed bracket (see Fig. 14–29) at left side of camera base.

Ribbon-Matte-Adjusting Knobs. Located at top and left side of finder; scribed to indicate various focal-length settings: *wide-angle lenses* (25mm, 30mm, and 35mm) are scribed in red; *normal and long lenses* (40–100mm) are scribed in black; *152mm lens* scribed in red *and* black.

Knobs may be set to two different indicators; projector or TV. Top knob adjusts vertical ribbon mattes (frame sides). Side knob adjusts horizontal ribbon mattes (frame top and bottom).

When using a wide-angle lens, remove the threaded circular sunshade at front of finder, and replace it with a reducer lens.

When using an 18.5mm lens, the fields of focusing tube and of viewfinder with a reducer lens attached must be compared visually, to set top and bottom frame lines in viewfinder. Side lines will not match (viewfinder cannot "see" as wide as lens can). Camera Operator must make allowance for viewfinder cut-in and frame the scene accordingly.

Without the reducer lens, the full field of viewfinder approximates 35mm.

When using the 152mm red scribe, remove the circular sunshade at front of finder, and replace it with an *enlarging lens*. The 152mm black scribe on the knob denotes the field without the enlarging lens.

NOTE: Some viewfinders are fitted with a slot in the left viewfinder wall to accommodate plastic mattes for other than standard aspect ratios (see Sec. 14.11f).

Parallax Adjustment.

To Prepare Viewfinder. (1) Screw the worm-gear-bushing bracket into bottom of finder. (2) Fit bushing into catch at side of the camera base (pressure latch holds the bushing in place).

To Align Vertical Cross Hair. Rotate worm-gear knob in bushing bracket until vertical cross hair in viewfinder matches reference point of cross hair in focusing tube. To hold the finder in place, secure the parallax lock knob, which is located between the focus lock knob and parallax throw-out lock knob at top front of finder (it rides in a restricted slot). This knob must be loosened each time parallax is to be corrected.

NOTE: A follow-focus unit with parallax-correction cams is also available (see Sec. 14.11b).

To Align Horizontal Cross Hair (in finder—with horizontal cross hair in focusing tube). (1) Verify that viewfinder dovetail is properly seated in camera base bracket before making *any* adjustments. Sight viewfinder cross hair on a horizontal reference point. Lock the camera down. (2) Loosen the turret setting knob (see Sec. 14.1f), and with Operator's help, tilt turret until horizontal cross hair in focusing tube aligns with horizontal reference point in viewfinder. Compare top, bottom, and side clearances in finder and focusing tube. If satisfactory, tighten setting knob with wrench. If alignment is *not* possible, return the turret setting knob to 0. Operator will then have to make horizontal parallax correction when composing a scene.

Focus Knob. Large knurled knob at left side of finder behind the prism causes the prism box to slide in and out on a shaft. Prism box is secured at desired focus by a lock knob, directly above shaft.

Pivot Point. Viewfinder swings horizontally, full 90° for access to camera door. To pivot finder, loosen the parallax throw-out lock knob (at top front of finder and closest to dovetail bracket), and release the worm-gear bushing from its pressure catch at camera base. Push rear of finder away from camera body.

14.1i Matte-box/Sunshade

Bellows-type sunshade/matte box mounts on two rods that fit into an L-shaped bracket. Bracket is independent of camera. A slotted female dovetail in the bracket slides on a dovetail mount at side of camera base. Bracket tightens with a screw. Front of bracket is secured to bottom front of base with a knurled screw.

The sunshade/matte box is adjustable up and down; left and right; in and out. Top of matte box is fitted with an extension-shade screw.

To Verify Clearance. Sight through the focusing tube, run forefinger around inner edge of matte-box opening—if tip of finger is visible, move entire unit toward lens. Repeat check until matte box is clear of lens.

A standard matte box allows for use of the 35mm lens if its bellows is fully collapsed; a wide-angle matte box is necessary for 25mm and 30mm lenses. Matte box must be removed entirely to use a lens wider than 25mm.

Lenses 50mm or longer may have to be removed from turret in order to slide a wide-angle matte box back far enough to clear a wide-angle lens.

14.1j Filters

Gauze frames, matte holders, and a 76.2mm × 76.2mm (3 × 3″) filter holder are housed in matte box. A polascreen holder and a 50.8mm × 50.8mm (2 × 2 in.) filter holder are housed in bellows. A wide-angle matte box houses three 76.2mm × 76.2mm (3 × 3″) filter holders and has no bellows.

Gelatine: Slot for internal filter is located in viewfinder bracket (see Fig. 14–29). When inserting filter holder, bent portion of holder (used as a fingergrip) *ALWAYS* points toward Operator. To check filter after insertion of holder, rack camera over, open camera door, and expose aperture opening in upright section of base. Determine visually that gelatine "covers" the aperture.

14.1k Door

Hinged at bottom.

To Open. Depress catch in door; pull out and down.

To Close. Lift up until flush with camera; pull focusing tube to verify that door is secure.

14.1l Magazines

120m (400-ft) and 304.8m (1000-ft) (see Sec. 14.2, Fig. 14–5).

To Mount. (1) Pull a loop from magazine feed side. (2) Insert magazine toe into magazine guide groove (at top of camera). Draw film loop into camera body. (3) Slide magazine forward and down until tapped hole in magazine heel aligns with magazine-lockdown screw (below the magazine plate). Rotate the magazine-lockdown knob clockwise to tighten magazine to camera. Thread camera (see Sec. 14.1m).

To Remove. Unthread film and break it. Place two fingers under the belt, pull laterally away from magazine, rotate fingers clockwise, and lift belt from spindle-wheel groove. Disengage magazine by rotating the lockdown knob counterclockwise, and lift magazine clear of camera.

14.1m Threading (Fig. 14–3)

(1) Press buckle-trip apron down and back to avoid accidental starting of camera during threading procedures (see Sec. 14.1n). Rotate upper and lower sprocket-guide rollers counterclockwise away from sprocket (on early models, rotate the sprocket-guide rollers clockwise). (2) Rotate manual turning knob on motor (see Fig. 14–2) until scribe on movement cam aligns to arrow (or zero line) on shuttle cam shaft—this retracts registration pins from aperture plate. (3) Loosen knurled and notched thumb screw located below the pulldown claw. Push pulldown-claw arm down and back, to clear claw from aperture plate. Rotate and lock the thumb screw, to hold claw in retracted position. (4) Raise the upper and lower aperture-plate locks. Remove aperture plate by pulling *gently*. If plate does not slide easily, check to see whether pulldown claw and or registration pins are clear of plate. (5) Clean plate. Make a special check of pulldown claw and registration-pin holes for emulsion buildup or film chips. Replace plate. Depress aperture-plate locks to secure. (6) Swing pressure-plate-spring arm clockwise, and remove pressure plate from register plate. Clean, making sure rollers revolve freely. Replace pressure plate and spring arm. (7) Pull film from magazine feed side. Extend loop to lower front corner of camera (a rough guide for amount of film needed for threading).

Starting Clockwise from the Magazine Take-up Side, Insert Film (a) under buckle-trip roller and over stabilizing roller at right of lower sprocket-guide rollers, if the particular model has one; (b) between sprocket and lower sprocket-guide rollers and under the thumb screw, and under the lower-loop roller (located below pulldown claw), if the model has one; if not, proceed. *Starting Counterclockwise from Magazine Feed Side, Insert Film* (a) under the feed roller (directly below the magazine feed rollers); between sprocket and upper sprocket-guide rollers; over lower-right and under upper-left twin rollers; (b) in groove (the race) between the removable aperture plate and stationary register plate. (8) Hold film in race; loosen thumb screw. Pulldown claw will spring forward. If claw touches film, raise or lower film in race until claw drops into perforation holes. Tighten thumb screw finger-tight. (9) Adjust lower loop so that when lower sprocket-guide rollers close, loop will clear bottom of camera interior by 3.175mm–6.35mm ($\frac{1}{8}$–$\frac{1}{4}$ in.) at lowest arc of loop. Adjust upper loop so that when upper sprocket-guide

Figure 14-3 Mitchell Standard/High-Speed threading detail. Courtesy of Mitchell Camera Corp.

1. Upper aperture-plate lock
2. Matte slot
3. Pressure-plate lock
4. Twin rollers
5. Upper sprocket-guide rollers
6. Feed roller
7. Buckle-trip roller
8. Buckle-trip reset knob
9. Buckle-trip apron
10. Stabilizing roller (some models missing this roller)
11. Lower sprocket-guide rollers
12. Notched thumbscrew
13. Pulldown claw arm
14. Lower loop roller (some models missing this roller)
15. Registration pin (one of two)
16. Lower aperture-plate lock
17. Aperture plate

rollers close, arc of loop aligns with top of movement plate. (10) Rotate the magazine take-up spindle wheel clockwise to take up the film slack. Place uncrossed belt at bottom of take-up spindle wheel and, in a clockwise direction, slip belt into wheel groove (this follows rotation of take-up wheel and subjects belt to a minimum of stretching). (11) Rotate manual motor-turning knob and observe film being transported in camera. If satisfactory, proceed. (12) Pull buckle-trip reset knob (inside camera, below buckle-trip apron); hold pins on upper and lower sprocket-guide rollers with thumb and forefinger.

CAUTION: Keep the knuckles of the hand clear of the movement!

Apply power in short bursts, and observe action of film. If satisfactory, stop camera, close door, and reset footage counter.

14.1n Buckle-trip

Apron (a curved metal plate, see Fig. 14–3) is located behind and below take-up side of sprocket. Apron cuts out power automatically if film fails to take up when camera is running. Power should be deliberately cut out prior to threading (by tripping apron toward rear of camera), to prevent accidental starting of camera.

To Reset. Pull buckle-trip reset knob below apron until unit snaps forward.

14.1o Footage and Frame Counters

Located at rear of camera, above bubble level (see Fig. 14–1b). Additive. Non-metric.

Footage Counter. Registers each foot of film transported through camera, up to 999 ft, then reverts to 0 and counts forward again. May be reset to 0 each time magazine is changed; reset knob is located at left-rear side near camera door.

Frame Counter. Additive in increments of 1 frame up to 16 frames, then back to 1. Does not reset.

Dial Counter. At rear of camera. Additive in increments of 20 ft, up to 1000 ft, then reverts to 0. Reset in center of dial.

NOTE: Dial counter provides information regarding total footage exposed on a roll of film when footage counter is reset to 0 before all film in magazine is expended. This may occur when a specific length of a scene is needed (such as double exposure, special effects, etc.).

14.1p Tachometer

None on camera.

14.1q Shutter

Variable; 0–170°. Calibrations and external control at back of camera (Fig. 14–1b).

To Change Shutter Opening. (1) Pull out and turn locking-pin knob in handle to move arm. When desired shutter opening appears at slot in shutter handle, proceed to step 2. (2) Rotate knob until positive locking pin drops into place. Agitate handle to test engagement of pin.

To Clear the Shutter From the Lens. Remove lens from lens mount. Observe shutter through lens port. Rotate manual motor turning knob until shutter clears camera aperture.

NOTE: Standard models may be fitted with automatic dissolve; high-speed models do not have this feature.

Automatic Dissolve (not shown): Depress either of two buttons located at left of shutter-arm lever to provide a 4-ft fade-in or fade-out while camera is running. Depress OUT button (closes the shutter) to fade-out a scene. Depress IN button (opens the shutter) to fade-in a scene.

14.1r **Lubrication** (Fig. 14–4)

Manufacturer recommends lubricating the following parts every 304.8m (1000 ft) of normal operation with one or two drops of camera oil:

• *Eccentric (movement):* shuttle cam shaft, registration-pin pads, registration-pin arm (both sides of bracket); pulldown-claw arm (both sides of bracket), and pulldown-arm bearing oil hole.

CAUTION: At high-speed operation, these parts should be oiled *before every run.*

Figure 14–4 Mitchell Standard/High-Speed lubrication. Courtesy of Mitchell Camera Corp.

1. Registration-pin arm (plunger arm)
2. Pulldown-arm bearing oil hole
3. Pulldown-claw arm (swivel bearing)
4. Registration-pin pads (oilers)
5. Pressure-plate rollers
6. Shuttle cam shaft

- *Rollers.* Every 10,000 ft, normal and high-speed.
- *Pressure-Plate rollers.* Every 10,000 ft, normal speed; every 1000 ft, high-speed.

NOTE: After oiling, run camera to eliminate excess oil and wipe camera interior.

14.1s Cleaning

Optics: Clean with bulb syringe or soft camel's hair brush. Manufacturer recommends the following maintenance *each time film is changed:* (1) Remove aperture and pressure plates. (2) Remove emulsion buildup with orangewood stick. (3) Wipe plates with soft cotton (not linen) handkerchief. (4) Use bulb syringe on camera interior to remove dust, dirt, etc.

14.1t Weight

With 304.8m (1000-ft) load 70 ½ lb (32 kg).

14.1u Troubleshooting

Trouble	*Probable Cause*
Camera will not start	Buckle-trip not reset; camera racked over; powerline connection faulty; low temperature; FWD/REV switch at top of variable-speed motor in neutral position
Camera "hunts"	Camera not warmed up; voltage variation in powerline
Camera door will not close	Sprocket-guide-rollers not seated properly; interior thumb screw not tightened; film chips or dirt in door
Film jam	Improper threading; take-up belt not on; magazine cover not relieved on "dished" roll
Lens will not focus	Lens not screwed all the way into mount; mount not seated properly; turret not seated properly; lens damaged
Viewfinder does not match focusing-tube cross hair	Camera not completely racked over; viewfinder not properly seated in dovetailed bracket; viewfinder parallax not set; turret not seated properly; wrong lens on front of viewfinder
Film will not slide into race	Registration pin or pulldown claw not retracted; emulsion or film chip in race
Torn or punctured film	Improper threading
Film scratches	Dirt or emulsion buildup on aperture plate, sprocket-guide rollers, pressure plate, registration pins, or magazine rollers
Focusing tube blurred	Magnification knob seated between magnifying position (forward) and normal position (back)
No take-up, or sporadic take-up	Belt slipping, or belt too loose

| Cut-in on focusing tube | Internal filter holder not seated in filter slot; matte box extended; matte in focusing tube not seated; four-way mattes not wide open |

14.2 MITCHELL 35mm NC, BNC, STANDARD/HIGH-SPEED, AND S35R MARK II MAGAZINES (Fig 14–5)

14.2a Type
Double compartment.

14.2b Capacity
120m (400-ft) and 304.8m (1000-ft) (shown)

14.2c Lids
Two. Threaded.
To Remove. Rotate counterclockwise.

14.2d Feed
Left side. Film (wound emulsion in) pulls off of spindle clockwise.

14.2e Take-up
Right side. Film winds onto spindle counterclockwise, emulsion always out.

14.2f Loading
(1) Unscrew feed lid. (2) In darkness, remove film roll from can and bag. Insert film end between feed-idler roller and magazine-compartment wall (emulsion faces idler roller). (3) Push film through the feed-side light-trap

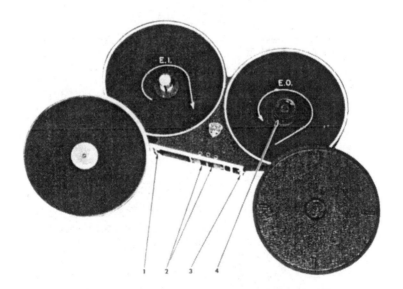

Figure 14–5 Mitchell NC, BNC, Standard/High-Speed, S35R 1000-ft magazine. Courtesy of Mitchell Camera Corp.

1. Magazine toe
2. Light traps
3. Magazine heel
4. Metal core

rollers. (4) Place film roll on feed spindle. Rotate feed spindle until spindle pin engages the core keyway. (5) Replace feed lid. (6) Unscrew take-up lid in the light. (7) Insert film end through take-up-side light-trap rollers; push film end between take-up-idler roller (emulsion faces roller) and magazine-compartment wall. (8a) When magazine has a *plastic core,* hold core on spindle pin; rotate take-up spindle wheel until spindle pin engages the core key-way. (8b) When magazine has a *metal core* (shown), hold core in hand; insert film end into core slot, and pull center of core *up,* squeezing slot against film. (9a) When magazine has a *plastic core,* insert film end into core slot and wind film onto take-up spindle counterclockwise (emulsion side out). Replace take-up lid. (9b) When magazine has a *metal core,* seat metal core in the "horns" of grooved take-up spindle. Wind film onto take-up spindle counterclockwise (emulsion out). Replace lid.

14.2g Unloading

In darkness, unscrew take-up lid.

When Magazine Has a Plastic Core. Place index finger on core, thumb on edge of film roll. Turn magazine over, remove film roll, and place exposed roll in black bag and can.

When Magazine Has a Metal Core. Push center of metal core down, release film in core slot. Turn magazine over, remove film roll, and push core out.

CAUTION: *Metal core stays with magazine!* Do not ship core with exposed film. Core is intended for reuse with each loading of magazine.

Place exposed roll in black bag and can.

14.2h Miscellaneous

NOTE: The NC and BNC 122m (400-ft) magazines and the NC, BNC, and Mark II/S35R 304.8m (1000-ft) magazines are interchangeable 60.3mm ($2\frac{3}{16}$ in. wide). The inverted Mark II/S35R 122m (400-ft) magazine is not interchangeable because it is gear driven. A magazine shim (called a "tuning fork" because of its shape) is required when using a standard/high-speed 122m (400-ft) or 304.8m (1000-ft) magazine 33.3mm (1 5/16″ wide) on the NC, BNC, or Mark II/S35R. A *magazine shim* consists of two 3.2mm × 3.2mm (1/8 × 1/8″) metal bars joined by a thin flat bar at one end. The shim slides, flat bar *up,* into camera-magazine guide groove, with flat bar of shim under magazine toe catch. Open end of shim must face Operator.

CAUTION: Mitchell magazine light-trap rollers are velvet covered, which necessitates constant checking for lint or dust.

CAUTION: While spring tension on the outer rollers helps to keep the magazine lighttight, a light trap should be taped or covered with a black bag after each loading.

NOTE: Relieving the lid a quarter-turn eliminates drag and/or the scraping noise of a roll, which may have "dished" in loading.

14.2i Footage Counter

None on magazine.

14.3 MITCHELL 35mm NC CAMERA* (Fig. 14–6)

NOTE: All directions are from Operator's point of view.

14.3a Base

Bottom fitted with 3/8″-16 tapped hole to accommodate tripod-lockdown screw. The base is L-shaped; includes turret (see Fig. 14–7). Flat section of base is fitted with dovetail tracks (gibs), allowing camera to slide (rack over) horizontally to align focusing tube with taking lens.

A dovetailed viewfinder bracket, into which offset viewfinder is inserted, is also fitted with a filter slot and is an integral part of the upright section of base (see Fig. 14–29 for detail).

Four-way mattes (see Fig. 14–6a): Used when a split-screen effect is to be achieved "in the camera." Adjustments permit any given size division of the screen. Two double knobs (see Fig. 14–6a) control mattes, which are located behind the taking lens. Knobs rotate clockwise to move mattes into aperture. One double knob is located above the turret. Top half of this knob controls the bottom matte. Lower section of this knob controls the upper matte. Other double knob is located below the viewfinder bracket. Smaller half of this knob controls the right-side matte. Larger half of this knob controls the left-side matte.

WARNING: Because mattes can slip or be pushed and loosened, it is important to check the matte position prior to shooting, and at each "hair check" to make certain that they have not moved into the aperture, thus cutting out a portion of film frame.

14.3b Rackover

Camera box must be racked over (i.e., moved laterally on gibs until focusing tube is directly behind taking lens) to sight through the taking lens.

To Rack Over. (1) Grasp handle at rear of camera (see Fig. 14–6b) and depress button to release the locating plunger. (2) Start to rotate handle clockwise and *release button immediately* so that the locating-plunger can engage the camera box.

CAUTION: Some cameras are *not* equipped with stops to prevent excessive lateral movement of the camera box. Therefore, unless the button is released immediately, the camera can be racked completely off its base.

(3) Rotate handle only counterclockwise to check that plunger has engaged the camera box and that the focusing tube is aligned with the taking lens.

CAUTION: Because camera will run racked over unless fitted with an automatic cutout switch, the camera must be racked back *before* shooting commences.

To Rack Back. (1) Depress button, and start to rotate handle counterclockwise. *Release button immediately* so that the locating plunger can engage the camera box. (2) Rotate handle clockwise to check that the locating plunger has engaged the camera box and that aperture is aligned with taking lens.

---

*Manufacturer states that the designation NC stands for "Newsreel Camera."

Figure 14–6a Mitchell NC with variable-speed motor; matte box removed (front view). Courtesy of Mitchell Camera Corp.

1. Horizontal bottom-matte knob (of 4-way matte)
2. Horizontal top-matte knob (of 4-way matte)
3. Turret-lock knob
4. Taking lens
5. Viewfinder bracket
6. Right vertical matte knob (of 4-way matte)
7. Left vertical matte knob (of 4-way matte)

8. Turret-setting knob bracket
9. Turret-setting scribe lines
10. Rising/falling front adjust knob
11. Turret-locating pin
12. Base and turret
13. Top motor lockdown screw
14. Variable-speed motor (compare position of motor on NC door to standard/high-speed motor)
15. Manual motor-turning knob
16. Side motor-lockdown screw

14.3c Focusing Tube

Located in camera-box door (see Fig. 14–29).

To Change or Clean Groundglass. (1) Slide access door (at side of focusing tube) toward Operator, open camera door, and insert eraser end of pencil into forward opening of tube. (2) Slide groundglass sideways; grasp glass by edges, and remove; clean and reinsert; close access door.

Figure 14–6b Mitchell NC (sync motor attached; rear view). Courtesy of Mitchell Camera Corp.

1. Offset viewfinder
2. Focusing-tube eyepiece
3. Eyepiece-locking screw
4. Magazine-lockdown knob
5. Shutter handle knob
6. Motor mounting screws
7. Manual motor-turning knob
8. Sync motor
9. Powerline
10. Rackover handle
11. Dial counter
12. Bubble level
13. Frame counter
14. Footage counter
15. Counter-reset knob
16. Worm gear and bracket

NOTE: *Always* insert groundglass with smooth surface toward rear of tube.

Matte Slot. Located forward of groundglass. Academy matte is inserted with bent portion (used as a fingergrip) pointed toward Operator.

Effects Matte. A frame of film cut with the Mitchell Matte Cutter (see Sec. 14.11d).

To Insert Effects Matte. Remove the Academy matte from focusing tube. Slide frame into matte slot upside down, perforations toward access door.

Magnification. Push magnification knob (located below focusing tube) forward to magnify 10 × ; push back for normal image.

Contrast Filters. Two. Knurled knob at top rear flips green filter into view for orthochromatic film. Bottom-rear knob flips pan filter into view for panchromatic film.

Eyepiece. Rotates; moves in and out; adjusts to achieve focus on ground-glass. Locking screw holds eyepiece at desired focus.

14.3d Motors

To Mount Synchronous Motor (Fig. 14–6b). (1) Rotate manual-turning knob (at rear of motor) until drive coupling aligns with movement drive shaft in camera. Press motor up against camera body. (2) Slide motor-door latch at bottom, toward rear of camera. Secure the two knurled screws on motor to tapped holes in camera.

NOTE: The NC and BNC synchronous motors are *not* interchangeable. An NC has a manual motor turning *knob* at rear of motor (Fig. 14–8); a BNC has a manual motor turning *gear* (not shown) at rear of motor. This motor gear accommodates teeth of internal gear within the BNC motor housing (see Sec. 14.4a and Sec. 14.4e). Also, a BNC motor is fitted with a six-pin Cannon plug in motor, which fits to a receptacle in camera. The NC has *no* Cannon plug in motor or receptacle in camera.

To Mount Variable-Speed Motor (Figs. 14–2 and 14–6a). Requires that NC motor door be mounted to right side of camera before mounting motor. (1) Fit motor door to camera, slide latch at bottom of camera toward rear. Secure the two knurled screws to tapped holes. (2) Align drive shafts of both door and variable-speed motor at the protruding motor-drive housing. (Lift the top motor-lockdown screw to slide motor easily onto housing.) Manual motor-turning knob is at side of motor. (3) Secure top and side motor-lockdown screws to motor-door housing. (4) Insert six-pin Cannon plug of powerline into motor-door receptacle. (5) Loop the wire, and insert three-pin Cannon-plug extension of powerline into motor. ON/OFF switch is in cable. (6) Turn top of motor clockwise for forward, counterclockwise for reverse. (7) Adjust motor speed by turning rheostat at bottom of motor.

NOTE: (a) The fps scribes (8–24 fps) on the rheostat are approximate. Correct speed is obtained by observing tachometer and adjusting the rheostat. (b) Tachometer registers from 0 to 32 fps in increments of 2 fps and 0–120 ft/minute in increments of 2 ft/minute.

To Reverse Variable-Speed Motor. Turn top of motor to "REV"; transfer belt from take-up to feed spindle wheel. Loop belt into a figure 8, to cause feed to act as take-up; adjust motor speed.

CAUTION: Cover lens or close shutter when running film back to beginning of scene intended for double exposure.

Motors Available for Mitchell NC.
Variable-Speed Motor.   12V DC; 110V AC/DC (60 Hz); 110V AC/DC (50 Hz).
Slow-Motion Motor.   110V AC/DC (60 Hz) 24–128 fps; 110V AC/DC (50 Hz) 24–128 fps.

NOTE: Variable-speed and slow-motion motors used on an NC require a special motor door (see To mount variable-speed motor, this section).

Synchronous Motor.   110V AC (60 Hz) (single phase); 110V AC (50 Hz) (single phase); 220V AC (60 Hz) (3-phase); 220V AC (50 Hz) (3-phase); 220V AC interlock (3-phase).
Multi-duty Motor.   220V AC (60 Hz) (3-phase)/96V DC.

NOTE: Multi-duty motor is only synchronous at 220V AC (60 Hz).

Animation Motor.   110V AC (60 Hz); 110V AC (50 Hz).

14.3e Powerline
Wired directly into sync motor (Fig. 14–6*b*); ON/OFF switch in cable. Powerline inserts into motor door and motor on variable-speed motor (Fig. 14–6*a*).

14.3f Turret
Four-position (see Fig. 14–6*a*).
   To Rotate.   Pull out turret locating pin (lower right side), turn turret until desired lens is in position at right of viewfinder bracket. Release locating pin to lock turret.

NOTE: (a) Center turret-locking knob may be tightened to hold a heavy telephoto lens. Ideal tension on turret for normal operation is obtained by tightening the knob by hand and backing it off a quarter-turn. (b) Longest lens on turret should be mounted opposite the shortest lens. (c) On some models, one port is fitted with *quick-set locks* (not shown)—i.e., clamps that grasp the lens mount shoulder. These clamps are placed above and below the lens port and are loosened with a screwdriver. Quick-set locks permit efficient mounting and dismounting of a variety of lenses.

An Easy Method for Mounting a Lens, Using Quick-set Locks.   (1) Rotate the turret until quick-set locks are at the top; slide clamps aside horizontally, insert new lens mount (cutoff portion of lens mount shoulder aligns with perimeter of turret). (2) Slide clamps back over the shoulder of the mount, and tighten. (3) Rotate turret to place lens in taking position.

NOTE: The lens *can* be mounted without rotating the turret. However, the upper quick-set lock drops down behind the lens-mount shoulder in this position, making it more difficult to slide the mount into the port. Safety of lens must always be considered; the possibility of dropping the lens while fighting the top lock is increased if turret is not rotated.

Turret Setting Knob.   Adjacent to and below the turret locating pin. For normal operation, scribe line on turret-setting-knob bracket must be aligned with zero scribe line on base. Turret setting knob is used to minimize distortion while photographing architecture at an angle. To achieve a rising and falling effect, as with a view camera (equivalent to a 15° tilt of the tripod), loosen turret setting knob, and rotate the turret clockwise to lower the front, counterclockwise to raise the front. Tighten the setting knob, and check focusing tube for any possible aperture cut-in on lens.

NOTE: Rising- and falling-front effects are limited to static shots. Effect is limited to lenses 35mm or longer.

CAUTION: Realign the scribe line on turret-setting-knob bracket with zero scribe line on base immediately (see Fig. 14–6a) upon completion of shot. Tighten the turret setting knob with a wrench to prevent slippage.

14.3g Lenses

To Fit Lens to Turret. (1) Unscrew lens barrel from threaded Mitchell mount. Align screw holes of mount with tapped holes in turret, and secure with screws. (2) Insert lens barrel into threaded mount.

NOTE: Rear elements of 18.5mm, 25mm, and 30mm lenses extend into camera aperture when seated; therefore these lenses must be backed off to clear the aperture prior to rotating the turret.

NOTE: Each mount is fitted with a focus-lockdown screw.

14.3h Viewfinder

Offset (see Fig. 14–28). Fits and locks into dovetailed bracket at left side of camera base (see Fig.14–29).

Ribbon-Matte Adjusting Knobs. Located at top and left side of finder; scribed to indicate various focal-length settings: *Wide-angle lenses* (25mm, 30mm, and 35mm) are scribed in red; *normal and long lenses* (40–100mm) are scribed in black; *152mm lens* scribed in red *and* black.

Knobs may be set to two different indicators: projector or TV. Top knob adjusts vertical ribbon mattes (frame sides). Side knob adjusts horizontal ribbon mattes (frame top and bottom).

When using a wide-angle lens, remove the threaded circular sunshade at front of finder, and replace it with a *reducer lens*.

When using an 18.5mm lens, the fields of the focusing tube and of the viewfinder with a reducer lens attached must be compared visually, to set the top and bottom frame lines in viewfinder. Side lines will not match (viewfinder cannot "see" as wide as lens). Camera Operator must make allowance for viewfinder cut-in and must frame the scene accordingly.

Without reducer lens, the full field of viewfinder approximates 35mm.

When using the 152mm red scribe, remove the circular sunshade at front of finder, and replace it with an *enlarging lens*. The 152mm black scribe on the knob denotes the field without the enlarging lens.

NOTE: Some viewfinders are fitted with a slot in the left (or top) finder wall to accommodate plastic mattes for other than standard aspect ratios, but these are modifications of the manufacturer's product. (See Sec. 14.11f.)

Parallax Adjustment.
To Prepare Viewfinder. (1) Screw the worm-gear-bushing bracket into bottom of finder. (2) Fit bushing into catch at side of camera base (pressure latch holds bushing in place).

To Align Vertical Cross Hair. Rotate worm-gear knob in bushing bracket until vertical cross hair in viewfinder matches reference point of cross hair in focusing tube. To hold the finder in place, secure the parallax lock knob, which is positioned in horizontal restricted slot between focus lock knob and parallax throw-out lock knob at top front of finder (it rides in a restricted slot). This knob must be loosened each time parallax is to be corrected.

NOTE: A follow-focus unit with parallax correction cams is also available. (See Sec. 14.11b.)

To Align Horizontal Cross Hair (in finder—with horizontal cross hair in focusing tube). 1. Verify that viewfinder dovetail is properly seated in camera base bracket before making *any* adjustments. Sight viewfinder cross hair on a horizontal reference point. Lock the camera down. 2. Loosen the turret setting knob (see Sec. 14.3f), and with Operator's help, tilt turret until horizontal cross hair in focusing tube aligns with horizontal reference point in viewfinder. Compare top, bottom, and side clearances in finder and focusing tube. If satisfactory, tighten setting knob with wrench. If alignment is *not* possible, return the turret setting knob to zero. Operator will then have to make horizontal parallax corrections while composing scenes.

Focus Knob. Large knurled knob at left side of finder behind prism box causes the prism box to slide in and out on a shaft. Prism box is secured at desired focus by a lock knob, directly above shaft.

Pivot Point. Viewfinder swings horizontally, full 90°, for access to camera door. To pivot the finder, loosen the parallax throw-out lock knob (at top front of finder and closest to dovetail bracket), and release the worm-gear bushing from its pressure catch at camera base. Push rear of finder away from camera body.

14.3i Matte-box/Sunshade (Fig. 14–1a)
Bellows-type sunshade/matte box mounts on two rods that fit into an L-shaped bracket. Bracket is independent of camera. A slotted female dovetail in bracket slides on a dovetailed mount at side of camera base. Bracket tightens with a screw. Front of bracket secures to bottom front of base with a knurled screw.

Matte/Sunshade box is adjustable up and down; left and right; in and out. Top of matte box is fitted with an extension shade screw.

To Verify Clearance. Sight through the focusing tube, run forefinger around inner edge of matte box opening—if tip of finger is visible, move entire unit toward lens. Repeat check until matte box is clear of lens.

A standard matte box allows use of the 35mm lens if its bellows is fully collapsed; a wide-angle matte box is necessary for 25mm and 30mm lenses. The matte box must be removed entirely to use a lens wider than 25mm.

Lenses 50mm or longer may have to be removed from turret in order to slide a wide-angle matte box back far enough to clear a wide-angle lens.

14.3j Filters
Gauze frames, matte holders, and a 76.2mm × 76.2mm (3 × 3 in.) filter holder are housed in the matte box. A polascreen holder and a 50.8mm × 50.8mm (2 × 2 in.) filter holder are housed in the bellows. A wide-angle matte box houses three 76.2mm × 76.2mm (3 × 3 in.) filter holders and has no bellows.

Gelatine: Slot for internal filter is located in viewfinder bracket (see Fig. 14–29). When inserting filter holder, bent portion of holder (used as a fingergrip) *ALWAYS* points toward Operator. To check filter after insertion of holder, rack camera over, open camera door, and expose aperture opening in upright section of base. Determine visually that gelatine "covers" the aperture.

14.3k Door

Hinged at bottom.

To Open. Depress catch in door; pull out and down.

To Close. Lift up until flush with camera; pull focusing tube to verify that door is secure.

14.3l Magazines

122m (400 ft) and 304.8m (1000 ft) (see Fig. 14–5)

To Mount. (1) Pull a loop from the feed side. (2) Insert the magazine toe into the magazine guide groove (at top of camera). Draw film loop into camera body. (3) Slide magazine forward and down until tapped hole in heel aligns with magazine lockdown screw. Rotate the magazine lockdown knob clockwise to tighten magazine to camera. Thread camera (see Sec. 14.3m).

To Remove Magazine. Unthread film, and break it. Place two fingers under the belt, pull laterally away from magazine, rotate fingers clockwise, and lift belt from spindle-wheel grooves. Disengage the magazine by rotating the lockdown knob counterclockwise, and lift magazine clear of camera.

14.3m Threading (Fig. 14–7)

(1) Press buckle-trip apron toward rear of camera to avoid accidental starting of camera during threading procedures (see Sec. 14.3n). Rotate upper and lower sprocket-guide rollers counterclockwise away from the sprocket (on early models, rotate the sprocket-guide rollers clockwise). (2) Rotate manual turning knob on motor (see Figs. 14–6*a* and 14–6*b*) until pulldown claw retracts from register plate (a back and upward stroke). Pull the registration-pin throw-out knob, and move it toward rear of camera. (3) Raise upper and lower aperture-plate locks, remove aperture plate by pulling *gently*. If plate does not slide easily, check to see that pulldown claw and/or registration pins are clear of plate. (4) Clean plate. Make a special check of pulldown claw and registration-pin holes for emulsion buildup or film chips; replace plate. Depress aperture-plate locks to secure. (5) Swing pressure-plate spring arm clockwise. Remove pressure plate from register plate. Clean and make sure rollers revolve freely. Replace pressure plate and spring arm. (6) Pull film from magazine feed side. Extend loop to lower front corner of camera (a rough guide for amount of film needed for threading).

Starting clockwise from the magazine take-up side, insert film (a) under large take-up film roller nearest to magazine take-up rollers, then to right of buckle-trip roller, then to left of small roller, and between lower sprocket-guide rollers and sprocket; (b) *under* small lower roller at left of sprocket-guide rollers, and *over* small roller below pulldown claw eccentric. *Starting counterclockwise from the magazine feed side, insert film* (a) between upper sprocket-guide rollers, and *under* small roller above registration-pin throw-out knob; (b) then in groove (the race) between the removable aperture plate and stationary register plate.

(7) Hold film in race, pull registration-pin throw-out knob, and move it toward the aperture plate *gently,* to determine whether registration pins are entering the film perforations. If pins touch film, raise or lower the film in the race, while moving the throw-out knob back and forth until pins engage the perforations. (8a) Adjust lower loop so that when the lower sprocket-guide roller closes, loop will clear bottom of camera interior by 3.175mm–6.35mm (1/8–1/4″) at lowest arc of loop. (8b) Adjust upper loop

Figure 14–7   NC threading. Courtesy of Mitchell Camera Corp.

1. Aperture plate
2. Upper aperture-plate lock
3. Register plate
4. Roller
5. Registration-pin throw-out knob
6. Upper sprocket-guide rollers
7. Take-up roller
8. Buckle-trip roller
9. Buckle-trip apron
10. Buckle-trip reset knob
11. Lower sprocket-guide rollers
12. Rollers
13. Pulldown claw
14. Pressure plate
15. Matte slot
16. Lower aperture-plate lock

so that when upper sprocket-guide roller closes, top of loop aligns with top of movement plate. (9) Rotate the magazine take-up spindle wheel clockwise to take up film slack. Place uncrossed belt at bottom of take-up spindle wheel and, in a clockwise direction, slip belt into wheel groove (this follows the rotation of take-up wheel and subjects belt to a minimum of stretching). (10) Rotate manual motor-turning knob, and observe film being transported in camera. If satisfactory, proceed. (11) Pull buckle-trip reset knob (inside camera below buckle-trip apron); hold pins on upper and lower sprocket-guide rollers with thumb and forefinger.

CAUTION: Keep the knuckles of the hand clear of the movement!

Apply power in short bursts, and observe action of film. If satisfactory, stop camera, close door, and reset footage counter.

14.3n Buckle-trip

Apron (a curved metal plate) is located behind take-up side of the sprocket (see Fig. 14–7). The apron cuts out power automatically if film fails to take up when camera is running. Power should be deliberately cut

397

out prior to threading (by tripping apron toward rear of camera), to prevent accidental starting of camera.

To Reset. Pull buckle-trip reset knob below apron until unit snaps forward.

14.3o Footage and Frame Counters

Located at back of camera above bubble level (see Fig. 14–6*b*). Non-metric.

Footage Counter. Additive. Registers each foot of film transported through camera up to 999 ft, then reverts to 0 and counts forward again. May be reset to 0 each time magazine is changed; reset knob is located at left-rear side near camera door.

Frame Counter. Additive in increments of 1 frame up to 16 frames, then back to 1. Does not reset.

Dial Counter. At rear of camera below miniature shutter. Additive in increments of 20 ft up to 1000 ft, then reverts to 0. Reset knob in center of dial.

NOTE: Dial counter provides total footage count exposed on a roll of film when footage counter is reset to zero before all film in magazine is expended. This occurs when a specific length of a scene is needed (such as double exposure, special effect, etc.).

14.3p Tachometer

None on camera.

14.3q Shutter

Variable; 0–175°. Calibrations and external control at back of camera (Fig 14–16*b*).

To Change Shutter Opening. (1) Pull out and turn locking-pin knob in handle to move arm. When desired shutter opening appears at slot in shutter handle, proceed to step 2. (2) Rotate knob until positive locking pin drops into place. Agitate handle to test engagement of pin.

Miniature Shutter. At rear of camera. Circular dial is scribed with a miniature aperture, which provides an easy visual check of shutter opening and its position in relation to camera aperture. Black area of dial conforms to adjustments made to camera shutter. White area of dial denotes degrees of shutter opening. Miniature shutter rotates in synchronization with camera shutter.

To Clear the Shutter from the Lens. Rotate manual motor-turning knob (see Fig. 14–6) until white area of miniature shutter fills miniature-aperture scribe.

14.3r Lubrication (Fig. 14–8)

Manufacturer recommends lubricating the following parts every 2000 ft with one or two drops of camera oil:

- *Eccentric (movement).* Registration-pin pads, plunger arm, and bracket (both sides), sliding block, rear bearing, sliding-block bearing of pulldown claw, eccentric-arm bearing, and timing-block unit.

- *Rollers.* Every 10,000 ft, except for the large take-up roller and buckle-trip roller, which should be lubricated every 3000 ft.

- *Pressure-Plate Rollers.* Every 10,000 ft.

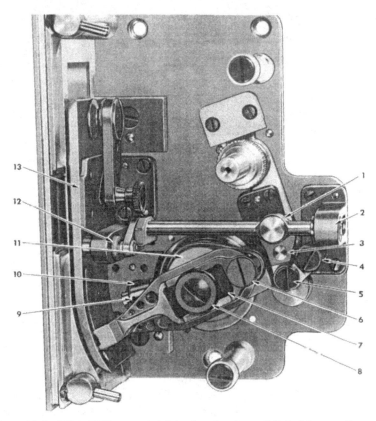

Figure 14–8 Mitchell NC eccentric lubrication. Courtesy of Mitchell Camera Corp.

1. Swivel block
2. Plunger-arm bracket
3. Pivot-arm bearing
4. Toggle-arm rear bearing
5. Toggle-arm rear bearing
6. Pull-down claw rear bearing
7. Sliding block

8. Sliding-block bearing
9. Eccentric-arm bearing
10. Timing-block unit
11. Eccentric-arm bearing
12. Registration-pin pads (oilers)
13. Pressure-plate rollers (not visible)

NOTE: After oiling, run camera to eliminate excess oil and wipe interior.

14.3s Cleaning

Optics: Clean with bulb syringe or soft camel's hair brush.

Manufacturer recommends the following maintenance *each time film is changed.* (1) Remove aperture and pressure plates. (2) Remove emulsion buildup with orangewood stick. (3) Wipe plates with soft cotton (not linen) handkerchief. (4) Use bulb syringe on camera interior to remove dust, dirt, etc.

14.3t Weight

(With 304.8m (1000-ft) load) 32kg (70 1/2 lb).

14.3u Troubleshooting

Trouble	Probable Cause
Camera will not start	Buckle-trip not reset; camera racked over; Powerline connection faulty; low temperature; when using variable-speed motor, FWD/REV switch at top of motor in neutral position
Camera "hunts"	Camera not warmed up; voltage variation in powerline
Camera door will not close	Sprocket-guide rollers not seated properly; registration-pin throw-out knob not forward; film chip or dirt in door
Film jam	Improper threading; take-up belt not on; magazine cover not relieved on "dished" roll
Lens will not focus	Lens not screwed all the way into mount; mount not seated properly; turret not seated properly; lens damaged
Viewfinder does not match focusing-tube cross hair	Camera not completely racked over; viewfinder not properly seated in dovetail bracket; viewfinder parallax not set; turret not seated properly; wrong lens on front of viewfinder
Film will not slide into race	Registration pin or pulldown claw not retracted; emulsion or film chip in race
Torn or punctured film	Improper threading
Film scratches	Dirt or emulsion buildup on aperture plate, sprocket-guide rollers, pressure plate, registration pins, or magazine rollers
Focusing tube blurred	Magnification knob seated between magnifying position (forward) and normal position (back)
No take-up or sporadic take-up	Belt slipping or belt too loose
Cut-in on focusing tube	Internal filter holder not seated in filter slot; matte box extended; matte in focusing tube not seated; four-way mattes not wide open

14.3v NC Magazine-Loading Instructions

See Section 14.2.

14.4 MITCHELL 35mm BNC CAMERA* (Fig. 14–9)

NOTE: All directions are from Operator's point of view.

14.4a Outer case

Consists of three sound-insulated sections: (1) main housing, (2) motor housing, (3) magazine housing.

Main Housing. Fitted with $\frac{3}{8}''$-16 tapped hole on bottom. A modified NC camera and base are permanently installed within the main housing.

---

*Manufacturer states that the designation BNC stands for "Blimped Newsreel Camera."

Figure 14–9a Mitchell BNC (left front). Courtesy of Mitchell Camera Corp.

1. Magazine-access door
2. Camera-access door
3. Bayonet-type-lens lock
4. Ribbon-matte adjusting knobs
5. Offset viewfinder
6. Focus lock knob
7. Vernier focus knob
8. Follow-focus knob
9. Marking dial
10. Follow-focus bracket
11. Follow-focus bracket lock lever
12. Phenolic gear
13. Matte box (in open position)
14. Lens light
15. Eye-light bracket
16. Magazine housing

Access to camera: Squeeze main housing door handles together, pull out and down.

Motor Housing. Attaches to right side of main housing and covers the motor.

NOTE: A manual motor-turning wheel is at back of housing (see Fig. 14–12). This spring-loaded wheel is connected by a shaft to a gear inside the housing and is used for engaging the manual motor-turning gear of BNC synchronous motor (see Sec. 14.4e).

To Install. Slide bottom lip of motor housing into two upright supports in base of main housing. Secure the two knurled screws at top of motor housing to tapped holes in main housing.

To Engage Manual Motor-Turning Gear on Motor. Push in the spring-loaded wheel at rear of motor housing (see Fig. 14–9b).

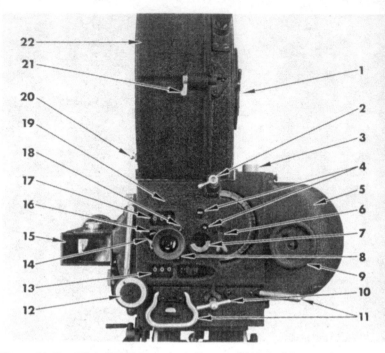

Figure 14–9b   Mitchell BNC (rear view). Courtesy of Mitchell Camera Corp.

1. Viewing ports
2. Magazine-housing lock handle
3. Powerline plug
4. Automatic dissolve control
5. Motor housing
6. Hand dissolve lever
7. Miniature shutter
8. Pan contrast filter
9. Manual motor-turning wheel
10. Rackover handle
11. Carrying handles
12. Vernier focus knob
13. Footage and frame counter
14. Focusing-tube magnification lever
15. Viewfinder
16. Ortho contrast filter
17. Footage totalizer
18. Eyepiece locking screw
19. Main housing
20. Magazine-door stud
21. Magazine-access door lock
22. Magazine housing

Magazine Housing.   Must be mounted on main housing *before* magazine is installed on camera.

To Install.   (1) Slide locating flange (the toe) of magazine housing under the front hold-down bar (lip) of main housing. (2) Insert rear magazine-housing lock into hold-down bracket on main housing. To lock, turn handle.

Access to Magazine.   Push access door lock (at rear) *up.* Swing magazine-access door forward, and engage door stud into catch at front of housing.

NOTE: Some catches may be worn and may fail to hold the door. Tilting the camera down slightly will prevent the door from closing and thus facilitate the loading operation.

Latched viewing ports at right side provide access to magazine spindle wheels and belt. Front porthole can be fitted with a "tattletale": a bent paper clip that engages the magazine feed spindle and makes a pinging noise if the camera is run in the racked over position. This is not a standard installation, but a device most crews will install themselves.

NOTE: Some BNCs may have a microswitch (not shown) installed in camera to prevent operation when camera is in rackover position, but which provides no warning sound.

14.4b Base

Inside main housing, base is L-shaped but has *no* turret. Instead, a single bayonet-base lens is mounted through the main housing and locked into place by rotating the lens lock clockwise (see Sec. 14.4h).

Flat section of base is fitted with dovetail tracks (gibs), allowing camera to slide (rack over) horizontally to align focusing tube with taking lens.

A filter slot is in upright section of base.

Four-way mattes (see Fig. 14–10): Used when a split-screen effect is to be achieved "in the camera." Adjustments permit any given size division of the screen. Two double knobs (see Fig. 14–10, threading) control the mattes, which are located behind the taking lens. The knobs rotate clockwise to move mattes into the aperture. One double knob is located above the lens port. Top half of this knob controls bottom matte. Lower section controls upper matte.

The other double knob is located below the internal filter slot. Smaller half of this knob controls right-side matte, larger half controls left-side matte.

WARNING: Because mattes can slip or be pushed and loosened, it is important to check matte positions prior to shooting and at each "hair check," to make certain that they have not moved into the aperture thus cutting out a portion of film frame.

14.4c Rack Over

Camera box must be *racked over* (i.e., moved laterally on gibs until focusing tube is directly behind taking lens) to sight through the taking lens.

To Rack Over. (1) Grasp handle at rear of camera (see Fig. 14–9b), and depress button to release locating plunger. (2) Start to rotate handle clockwise and *release button immediately* so that the locating plunger can engage the camera box.

CAUTION: Some cameras are *not* equipped with stops to prevent excessive lateral movement of camera box. Therefore, unless button is released immediately, camera can be racked completely off base.

(3) Rotate handle only counterclockwise to check that the plunger has engaged the camera box and that the focusing tube is aligned with the taking lens.

CAUTION: Because camera will run racked over unless fitted with an automatic cutout switch, camera must be racked back *before* shooting commences.

To Rack Back. (1) Depress button, and start to rotate handle counterclockwise. *Release button immediately* so that the locating plunger can engage the camera box. (2) Rotate handle clockwise to check that the locating plunger has engaged the camera box, and that the aperture is aligned with the taking lens.

14.4d Focusing Tube

Located in camera box door (see Fig. 14–29).

To Change or Clean Groundglass. (1) Slide access door (at side of focusing tube) toward Operator, open camera door, and insert eraser end of pencil into forward opening of tube. (2) Slide groundglass sideways; grasp glass by edges, and remove; clean and reinsert; close access door.

NOTE: *Always* insert groundglass with smooth surface toward rear of tube.

Matte Slot. Located forward of groundglass. Insert Academy matte with bent portion (used as a finger grip) pointed toward Operator.

Effects Matte. A frame of film cut with the Mitchell matte cutter (see Sec. 14.11d).

To Insert Effects Matte. Remove Academy matte from focusing tube. Slide frame into matte slot upside down, perforations toward access door.

Magnification. Push spring-loaded magnification lever at rear of main housing (left side of eyepiece) (see Fig. 14–9b) to engage notched adjusting knob on camera. Depress lever to magnify tube $10 \times$; push lever up for normal image.

Contrast Filters. Two (see Fig. 14–9b). Push spring-loaded button above eyepiece to engage rod, which flips green filter into view for orthochromatic film. Push spring-loaded button below eyepiece to engage rod, which flips pan filter into view for panchromatic film.

Eyepiece (see Fig. 14–9b). Rotates; moves in and out; adjusts to achieve focus on groundglass. Locking screw holds eyepiece at desired focus.

14.4e Motors

To Mount Synchronous Motor. (1) Rotate the manual turning gear (at rear of motor) until the drive coupling and the six-pin Cannon plug in motor align with drive shaft and receptacle in camera; press motor against camera to a snug fit. (2) Slide the motor door latch at bottom toward rear of camera. Secure the two knurled screws on motor to the tapped holes in camera. (3) Mount motor housing onto main housing (see Sec. 14.4a). Push wheel in (at rear of motor housing) to engage teeth of manual motor-turning gear.

NOTE: The BNC and NC synchronous motors are *not* interchangeable. A BNC has a manual motor-turning *gear* (not shown) at the rear of the motor. This turning gear accommodates the teeth of the internal gear within the BNC Motor Housing (see Sec. 14.4a). An NC has a manual motor-turning *knob* at the rear of motor (see Fig. 14–6b). Also, a BNC motor is fitted with a six-pin Cannon plug in motor, which fits to a receptacle in camera. The NC has *no* Cannon plug in its motor or receptacle in camera.

Variable-speed motors (Fig. 14–2) *are* interchangeable and are mounted to BNC, as on the NC (see Sec. 14.3d, and Fig. 14–6a). However, the vertical configuration of a variable-speed motor prohibits use of BNC motor housing (see Sec. 14.4a and Fig. 14–9b). The resultant motor noise, of course, makes filming with sound impractical.

Motors Available for the Mitchell BNC.

Variable-Speed Motor.   12V DC; 110V AC/DC (60 Hz); 110V AC/DC (50 Hz).

NOTE: A variable-speed motor used on a BNC requires a special motor door.

Synchronous Motor.   110V AC (60 Hz) (single phase); 110V AC (50 Hz) (single phase); 220V AC (60 Hz) (3-phase); 220V AC (50 Hz) (3-phase); 220V AC interlock (3-phase).

Multi-duty Motor.   220V AC (60 Hz) (3-phase)/96V DC.

NOTE: Multi-duty motor is only synchronous at 220V AC (60 Hz).

Animation Motor.   110V AC (60 Hz); 110V AC (50 Hz).

14.4f Powerline

Insert six-pin Cannon-plug extension of powerline into receptacle at top right rear of main housing (see Fig. 14–9b). ON/OFF switch is in the cable. Motor housing may be fitted with an ON/OFF switch holder (not shown) but this is not standard equipment.

14.4g Turret

None (see Sec. 14.4b).

14.4h Lenses

To Fit Bayonet-base Lens to Camera Through Main Housing.   (1) Lower and lock the follow-focus knob bracket (see Sec. 14.4i). (2) Rotate the lens lock on main housing clockwise as far as it will go. (3) Align hole in lens flange with the positioning stud located in upper left of lens port. Insert the lens flange flush with camera, making certain that stud engages the lens-flange hole. (4) Rotate the lens lock counterclockwise to secure. (5) Align lens gear and phenolic gear. *Witness mark*—i.e., a white arrow on the lens gear—denotes proper alignment with white tooth on phenolic gear (see Sec. 14.4i).

14.4i Focus and Parallax Controls

On main housing (see Fig. 14–9a).

To Change Focus and Provide Automatic Parallax Correction of Viewfinder.   Rotate either of two follow-focus knobs located at both ends of bracket (at front of camera).

Vernier (fine) Focus Knobs.   3:1 ratio, located within follow-focus knobs and at rear of camera (left of the bubble level) for Operator's use.

A white circular marking disc in back of the follow-focus knob provides an area for penciling follow-focus marks.

To Lock the Focus Unit.   Rotate the focus lock knob (below buckle-trip reset plunger) clockwise in the worm gear.

To Align Phenolic and Lens Gears.   (1) Rotate the follow-focus knobs until cam roller on worm gear is at extreme rear of travel. (2) Release follow-focus bracket lock lever. Depress right side of follow-focus bracket, and secure it by rotating the follow-focus bracket lock lever counterclockwise. (3) Insert lens into camera (see Sec. 14.4h). (4) Rotate witness mark on lens gear so that it faces the phenolic gear. (5) Align white scribed tooth on phenolic gear with witness mark of lens gear. (6) Release follow-focus bracket lock lever, and engage phenolic scribed tooth with lens witness mark; secure follow-focus bracket lock lever. (7) Rotate the follow-focus knob to check tension and meshing of gears. If tension is too great, camera noise will transmit through lens; if too loose, phenolic gear will vibrate in sympathy with motor.

To Mesh Gears Properly. (1) Loosen nut on hex-head screw above follow-focus bracket lock lever. (2) Rotate hex-head screw until gears just mesh with no air space between them. (3) Back the hex-head screw off until phenolic gear drops away from lens gear (approximately one half-turn). A slight air space should be discernible. (4) Run camera. If noise persists, back the hex screw off more. (5) Secure locknut on hex-head screw.

14.4j Viewfinder

Offset (see Fig. 14–9*a*). Fits and locks into dovetail bracket in door of main housing.

Cams. 35mm, 40mm, 50mm, 75mm, and 100mm cams (not shown) are attached underneath finder and fold under when not in use. The cam corresponding to focal length of lens being used is flipped out so that it will ride the cam roller and provide automatic parallax correction to finder.

The 100mm cam is slotted and punched with alignment holes to accept auxiliary (wide-angle) cams (18.5mm, 25mm, and 30mm).

To Mount Auxiliary Cams. (1) Flip 100mm cam out. Insert auxiliary cam pins from bottom into slot and holes of 100mm cam. (2) Slide lock on 100mm cam forward to secure auxiliary cam.

NOTE: Auxiliary cams must be removed in order to use normal complement of cams.

Ribbon-Matte-Adjusting Knobs. Located at top and left side of finder, scribed to indicate various focal-length settings. *Wide-angle lenses* (25mm, 30mm, and 35mm) are scribed in red. *Normal and long lenses* (40–100mm only) are scribed in black. Knobs may be set to two different indicators: projector or TV. Top knob adjusts vertical ribbon mattes (frame sides). Side knob adjusts horizontal ribbon mattes (frame top and bottom).

When using a wide-angle lens, remove threaded circular sunshade at front of finder, and replace it with a *reducer lens.*

When using an 18.5mm lens, the fields of the focusing tube and of the viewfinder with a reducer lens attached must be compared visually, to set the top and bottom frame lines in the viewfinder. Side lines will not match (viewfinder cannot "see" as wide as lens). Camera Operator must make allowance for viewfinder cut-in and must frame the scene accordingly.

Without the reducer lens, the full field of viewfinder approximates 35mm.

Parallax Adjustment. Automatic. A viewfinder return spring next to the dovetail locking lever exerts tension against finder. This forces the finder cam against the cam roller on the worm gear, which in turn regulates parallax and focus of finder.

NOTE: To insert finder easily into dovetail bracket, place forefinger of right hand between the circular prism box and the viewing assembly. Fold cams under, insert finder dovetail into dovetail bracket on door, release finder, and secure the finder dovetail locking lever forward.

Horizontal Cross-hair Adjustment. *None.* Finder is factory adjusted. Misalignment would be due to (1) improper riding of cam on roller or (2) improper insertion of finder in dovetail bracket.

Focus Knob. None on finder. Focus is automatic.

Pivot Point. None. Finder locks into bracket in door of main housing, drops down with door for access to camera interior.

14.4k Sunshade/Matte Box (Fig. 14–9a)

Bellows sunshade/matte box mounts on two rods, one above the other, which fit into a vertical bracket pivot attached to front of main housing. Matte box swings aside for access to lens mount (see Fig. 14–9a). The sunshade/matte box moves in and out only on the rods. Top of matte box is fitted with an extension-shade screw.

To Verify Clearance. Sight through focusing tube, run forefinger around inner edge of matte-box opening. If tip of finger is visible, move entire unit toward lens. Repeat checking until matte box is clear of lens. A BNC standard matte box allows use of a 35mm lens if its bellows is fully collapsed; a BNC wide-angle matte box is necessary to use a 25mm or 30mm lens. The matte box must be removed entirely to use a lens wider than 25mm.

14.4l Filters

Gauze frames and mattes are housed in matte box. Three 76.2mm × 76.2mm (3 × 3 in.) filter holders are housed at rear of bellows. A wide-angle matte box houses three 101.6mm × 101.6mm (4 × 4 in.) filter holders and has no bellows.

Gelatine. Slot for internal filter is located in upright section of base (see Fig. 14–10). When inserting filter holder, bent portion of holder (used as a fingergrip) should be pointed *AWAY* from Operator (opposite from all other Mitchell cameras), to avoid possibility of excess rackback of camera box catching bent portion of holder. Excess rackback can pull the gelatine holder out of its slot just enough to cause it to cover a portion of the aperture, and a partially exposed frame will result.

To Check Filter after Insertion of Holder. Rack camera over, open camera door, and expose aperture opening in upright section of base. Determine visually that gelatine "covers" the aperture.

14.4m Door

Hinged at bottom.

To Open. Depress catch in door; pull out and down.

To Close. Lift up until flush with camera; pull focusing tube to verify that door is secure.

14.4n Magazines

400 ft and 1000 ft (see Fig. 14–5).

To Mount. (1) Pull magazine belt through rear port of magazine housing, and close port window on belt to hold it out of the way. (2) Pull a film loop from magazine feed side. (3) Insert the magazine toe into magazine guide groove (at top of camera). Draw film loop into camera body. (4) Slide magazine forward and down until tapped hole in heel aligns with magazine lockdown screw. Rotate the magazine lockdown knob at left side of camera clockwise to tighten magazine to camera. Thread camera (see Sec. 14.4o).

To Remove Magazine. Unthread film, and break it. Place two fingers under belt; pull laterally away from magazine. Rotate fingers clockwise, and lift the belt from spindle-wheel grooves. Disengage magazine by rotating the lockdown knob counterclockwise, and lift magazine clear of camera and out of housing.

14.4o Threading (Fig. 14–10)

1. Press buckle-trip apron toward rear of camera to avoid accidental starting of camera during threading procedures (see Sec. 14.4p). Rotate upper and lower sprocket-guide rollers counterclockwise away from sprocket (on early models, rotate sprocket-guide rollers clockwise).

2. Depress and rotate manual turning wheel on motor housing (see Fig. 14–9*b*) until pulldown claw retracts from register plate (a back and upward stroke). Pull the registration-pin throw-out knob, and move it toward rear of camera.

3. Raise upper and lower aperture-plate locks, and remove aperture plate by pulling *gently*. If plate does not slide easily, check to see that pulldown claw and/or registration pins are clear of plate.

4. Clean plate. Make a special check of pulldown claw and registration-pin holes for emulsion buildup or film chips; replace plate. Depress aperture-plate locks to secure.

5. Swing pressure-plate spring arm clockwise. Remove pressure plate from register plate. Clean, making sure rollers revolve freely. Replace pressure plate and spring arm.

6. Pull film from magazine feed side. Extend loop to lower front corner of camera (a rough guide for amount of film needed for threading).

Starting clockwise from magazine take-up side, insert film (a) under large take-up film roller nearest to magazine take-up rollers, then to right of buckle-trip roller, then to left of small roller, and between lower sprocket-guide rollers and sprocket; (b) *under* small lower roller at left of sprocket-guide rollers, and *over* small roller below pulldown claw eccentric.

Starting counterclockwise from magazine feed side, insert film (a) between upper sprocket-guide rollers, and *under* small roller above registration-pin throw-out knob; (b) then in groove (the race) between the removable aperture plate and stationary register plate.

7. Hold film in race, pull registration-pin throw-out knob, and move it toward aperture plate *gently,* to determine whether registration pins are entering the film perforations. If pins touch film, raise or lower the film in the race while moving the throw-out knob back and forth until pins engage the perforations.

8. (a) Adjust lower loop so that when lower sprocket-guide roller closes, loop will clear the bottom of camera interior by 3.175mm × 6.35mm ($\frac{1}{8}$–$\frac{1}{4}$ in.) at lowest arc of loop. (b) Adjust upper loop so that when upper sprocket-guide roller closes, the top of loop aligns with top of movement plate.

9. Rotate the magazine take-up spindle wheel clockwise to take up film slack. Place uncrossed belt at bottom of take-up spindle wheel, and, in a clockwise direction, slip belt into wheel groove (this follows rotation of take-up wheel and subjects belt to a minimum of stretching).

10. Rotate manual motor-turning knob, and observe film being transported in camera. If satisfactory, proceed.

Figure 14–10 Mitchell BNC threading detail. Courtesy of Mitchell Camera Corp.

1. Horizontal top matte knob (of 4-way matte)
2. Horizontal bottom matte knob (of 4-way matte)
3. Aperture plate
4. Upper aperture-plate lock
5. Register plate
6. Roller
7. Registration-pin throw-out knob
8. Upper sprocket-guide rollers
9. Take-up roller
10. Buckle-trip roller
11. Buckle-trip apron
12. Magazine lockdown knob
13. Buckle-trip reset knob
14. Roller
15. Lower sprocket-guide rollers
16. Rollers
17. Pulldown claw
18. Matte slot
19. Lower aperture-plate lock
20. Filter slot
21. Left vertical matte knob (of 4-way matte)
22. Right vertical matte knob (of 4-way matte)

11. Pull buckle-trip reset knob (inside camera, below buckle-trip apron); hold pins on upper and lower sprocket-guide rollers with thumb and forefinger.

CAUTION: Keep the knuckles of the hand clear of the movement!

Apply power in short bursts, and observe action of film. If satisfactory, stop camera, close door, and reset footage counter.

14.4p Buckle-trip

Apron (a curved metal plate) located behind take-up side of the sprocket (see Fig. 14–13). Apron cuts out power automatically if film fails to take up when camera is running. Power should be deliberately cut out prior to threading (by tripping apron toward rear of camera), to prevent accidental starting of camera.

To Reset. (1) pull buckle-trip reset knob below apron until unit snaps forward, or (2) push reset plunger (not shown) (at lower left edge of main housing door, below rear of viewfinder).

14.4q Footage and Frame Counters

Viewed through lower window at rear of main housing, above the bubble level (see Fig. 14–9*b*). Non-metric.

Footage Counter. Additive. Registers each foot of film transported through camera, up to 999 ft, then reverts back to 0 and counts forward again. May be reset to 0 each time magazine is changed; reset knob is located at left rear near camera door, inside main housing.

Frame Counter. Additive in increments of 1 frame up to 16 frames, then back to 1. Does not reset.

Footage Totalizer (see Fig. 14–9*b*). Viewed through upper window at rear of camera above eyepiece. Additive. Registers each foot up to 999 ft, then reverts back to 0 and counts forward again. Has no frame counter. The totalizer provides total footage count exposed on a roll when footage counter is reset to 0 before all film in magazine is expended. This occurs when a specific length of a scene is needed (e.g., double exposure, special effect). Reset knob is located at left side of camera, above eyepiece, inside main housing.

NOTE: Most camera crews cover the totalizer window with black masking tape when it is not being used, to avoid confusion between the two counters and/or to eliminate having to zero both counters at every magazine change.

14.4r Tachometer

None on camera.

14.4s Shutter

Variable; 0–175°. Calibrations and pointer can be viewed through semicircular window at rear of main housing. External control lever is at back of main housing (Fig. 14–9*b*).

To Change Shutter Opening. (1) Align shutter-arm lever with pointer. (2) Push shutter-arm lever in until spring-loaded lever engages notched shutter knob. (3) Rotate pointer to desired shutter opening, and release lever.

Automatic Dissolve. Depress either of two buttons located at left of shutter-arm lever to provide a 4-ft fade-in or fade-out while camera is running. Top (OUT) button closes shutter to fade-out scene. Lower (IN) button opens shutter to fade-in scene.

Miniature Shutter. At rear of camera below automatic dissolve buttons. Circular dial is scribed with a miniature aperture. Miniature aperture provides an easy visual check of shutter opening and of its position in relation to camera aperture. Black area of dial conforms to adjustments made to the camera shutter. White area of dial denotes the degrees of shutter opening. Miniature shutter rotates in synchronization with camera shutter.

To Clear the Shutter from the Lens. Depress and rotate manual motor-turning wheel on motor housing (see Fig. 14–9*b*) until white area of miniature shutter fills miniature-aperture scribe.

14.4t Lubrication (Fig. 14–11)

Manufacturer recommends lubrication with one or two drops of camera oil of the following parts every 2000 ft:

- *Eccentric (movement),* registration-pin pads, plunger arm and bracket (both sides), sliding block, rear bearing, sliding-block bearing of pulldown claw, eccentric-arm bearing, timing-block unit.
- *Rollers.* Every 10,000 ft, except for large take-up roller and buckle-trip roller, which should be lubricated every 3000 ft.
- *Pressure-Plate Rollers.* Every 10,000 ft.

NOTE: After oiling, run camera to eliminate excess oil and wipe interior.

14.4u Cleaning

Optics. Clean with bulb syringe or soft camel's hair brush.

Manufacturer recommends the following maintenance *each time film is changed:* (1) Remove aperture and pressure plates. (2) Remove emulsion buildup with orangewood stick. (3) Wipe plates with soft cotton (not linen) handkerchief. (4) Use bulb syringe on camera interior to remove dust, dirt, etc.

14.4v Weight

(With 304.8m (1000-ft) load) 55.3kg (122 lb)

14.4w Troubleshooting

Trouble	Probable Cause
Camera will not start	Buckle-trip not reset; camera racked over; powerline connection faulty; low temperature
Camera "hunts"	Camera not warmed up; voltage variation in powerline
Camera door will not close	Sprocket-guide rollers not seated properly; registration-pin throw-out knob not forward; film chip or dirt in door
Film jam	Improper threading; take-up belt not on; magazine cover not relieved on "dished" roll

Figure 14–11 Mitchell BNC eccentric lubrication. Courtesy of Mitchell Camera Corp.

1. Swivel block
2. Plunger-arm bracket
3. Pivot-arm bearing
4. Toggle arm
5. Toggle arm
6. Rear bearing
7. Sliding block
8. Sliding-back bearing
9. Eccentric-arm bearing
10. Timing-block unit
11. Eccentric-arm bearing
12. Registration-pin pads (oilers)
13. Pressure-plate rollers

Lens will not focus	Mount not seated properly; lens damaged
Viewfinder does not match focusing-tube cross hair	Wrong cam "up" on finder; camera not completely racked over; viewfinder not properly seated in dovetail bracket; wrong lens on front of viewfinder
Focusing tube blurred	Magnification knob seated between magnifying position (forward) and normal position (back)
Cut-in on focusing tube	Internal filter holder not seated; matte in tube not seated; matte box extended; four-way mattes not wide open

Torn or punctured film	Improper threading
Film will not slide into race	Registration pin or pulldown claw not re-tracted; emulsion or film chip in race
Film scratches	Dirt or emulsion buildup on aperture plate, sprocket-guide rollers, pressure plate, registration pins, or magazine rollers
No take-up, or sporadic take-up	Belt slipping, or belt too loose

14.4x BNC Magazine-Loading Instructions
See Sec. 14.2.

14.5 MITCHELL 35mm S35R/MARK II CAMERA (Figs. 14–12a and 14–12b)

NOTE: All directions are from Operator's point of view.

NOTE: In 1965, the manufacturer redesigned the Reflex "Mark II" to incorporate additional features. The redesigned camera is now identified as the Mitchell Reflex "S35R"; the Mark II camera is no longer manufactured. Because of similarities in basic design, appearance and utilization of the same accessories, the S35R camera is often referred to as

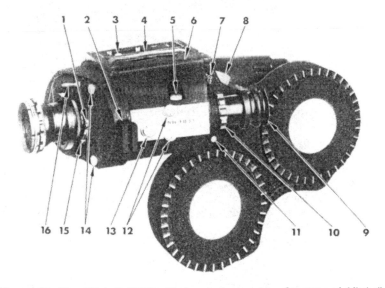

Figure 14–12a Mitchell S35R with inverted magazine. Courtesy of Mitchell Camera Corp.

1. Turret-holddown screw
2. Dovetail (offset-viewfinder) bracket
3. Shutter control knob
4. Carrying handle
5. Light-trap knob
6. Top-cover plate (shoe removed)
7. Footage-counter reset knob
8. Inverted magazine lockdown knob

9. Eyepiece
10. Eyepiece locking ring
11. Short-burst button
12. Contrast-filter knobs
13. Hi/Lo magnification knob
14. Turret locks
15. Lens-mount lock
16. Turret-release lever

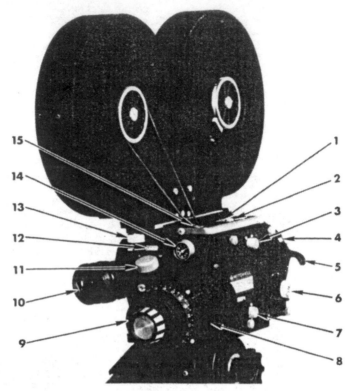

Figure 14-12b Mitchell S35R with top load (rear view). Courtesy of Mitchell Camera Corp.

1. Shutter-scale calibrations
2. Shutter control
3. Remote connector
4. Turret ON/OFF switch
5. Thumb grip
6. Manual motor-turning knob
7. Powerline plug
8. Variable-speed motor
9. Motor rheostat
10. Eyepiece
11. Dust coverplate holddown knob/ inverted magazine lockdown knob
12. Footage counter
13. Magazine-lockdown knob
14. Tachometer
15. Bulls-eye level

the Mark II, R35, or Mitchell Reflex. The standard Mark II, however, has two mounting positions for the film magazines—slant load and inverted, while the S35R has three mounting positions—slant load, inverted, and top load. (There are many Mark II cameras in use, which have been mechanically converted for top loading by someone other than the Mitchell Camera Corp. These cameras should not be confused with the standard S35R.) Additional features in the S35R are removable, repositioned drive belt for top and slant load magazines; double buckle-trip system; improved slant-magazine adapter; improved shutter-control mechanism permitting use of camera with the S35R sound blimp; less weight and more quiet operation; improved internal mechanical features;

and groundglass that is removable through the lens port without removing the turret.

This section describes both the Mark II and the S35R cameras. Directions apply to both unless otherwise noted.

14.5a Base

Bottom fitted with two 3/8"-16 tapped holes to accommodate tripod-lockdown screw and/or adapter-plate screw. The forward tapped hole is utilized to secure the camera when it is placed on a Mark II/S35R hi-hat, or as a locating receptacle when camera is placed on an adapter plate.

The Mark II/S35R does *not* have an L-shaped base; it has *no* rackover and *no* four-way mattes.

14.5b Hi-hat

Required when a camera with a 122m (400 ft) inverted magazine is to be mounted on a tripod (not shown). Base of hi hat is fitted with a 3/8"-16 tapped hole to accommodate a tripod-lockdown screw. A handle at right side rotates a 3/8"-16 camera-lockdown screw at top of hi-hat. The unit is secured to the forward tapped hole in the camera base, so that the take-up compartment of the 400-ft inverted magazine conforms to curvature of hi-hat.

14.5c Adapter Plate (not shown)

Required when a sunshade matte box, a follow-focus unit, or a zoom-lens cradle is used with camera. Top of plate is fitted with a forward locating pin, which is inserted into forward tapped hole of camera base. A large knob located between top and base of plate has a 3/8"-16 threaded screw, which is inserted in the back tapped hole of camera base.

Bottom of plate is fitted with four 3/8"-16 tapped holes for variety of placement on a tripod or geared head.

Insert matte-box rods into lower front of plate, and secure with retaining screws.

Upper left front of adapter plate has tapped holes for attaching a follow-focus unit.

To Mount Zoom Lens Cradle. (1) Mount matte-box rods in adapter; slide inverted U-bracket onto rods. (2) Insert short cradle rods into inverted U-bracket; slide adjustable cradle on short rods. Adjust rods and brackets to zoom lens. Secure all retaining screws.

14.5d Viewfinder/Focusing Tube

Reflex (see Fig. 14–12a).

There is also a dovetail bracket into which an offset viewfinder may be inserted. Three types of offset viewfinders are available for use with this camera: (1) BNC-type, with captive cams and automatic focus (see Sec. 14.4j); (2) NC-type (Fig. 14–28), with manual focus (see Sec. 14.3h); (3) frame-type (tracking finder) (not shown), with transparent colored mattes for change of field size.

Focusing Tube. In camera-box door, as an integral part of reflex system.

To Align Reflex Mirror for Viewing. Rotate manual motor-turning knob (see Fig. 14–12b).

Groundglass. Located behind turret. Views more than full aperture. Groundglass may be scribed with full aperture, Academy, or TV aperture fields.

To Change or Clean Groundglass. On Mark II, remove turret (see Sec. 14.5g); grasp groundglass by edges, pull forward. Clean and reinsert with smooth surface facing eyepiece, granulated surface toward reflex shutter. Replace turret. *On S35R,* remove lens from turret. Wrap forefinger with lens tissue, reach forefinger through lens port, and slide groundglass toward opening. Clean and reinsert into camera with smooth surface facing eyepiece, granulated surface toward reflex shutter.

WARNING: On both cameras, it is extremely important to reach through the lens port and push the groundglass into its stop each time the camera is set up.

Matte Slot. Located forward of groundglass (toward reflex shutter). Academy matte is inserted with the portion (used as a finger grip) pointed toward Operator.

Effects Matte. A frame of film cut with the Mitchell book-type matte cutter (see Sec. 14.11d).

To Insert Effects Matte. Remove Academy matte from matte slot. Slide frame into matte slot upside down, perforations toward lens port.

Magnification. Rotate large knob in door counterclockwise ("HI") to magnify $10 \times$; clockwise ("LO") for normal viewing to magnify $5 \times$.

Contrast Filters. Two. Knob at top flips filter (Eastman negative viewing filter, minus blue, 10% white-light transmission) into view for color film. Knob at bottom flips pan filter (No. 74U on the Spectro Wedge; Wratten 90G; Harrison and Harrison YL-9) into view for black-and-white film.

Eyepiece. Slides in and out; adjusts to achieve focus on groundglass. Knurled locking ring holds eyepiece at individual's focus.

Light Trap. Horizontal knob (in door recess) rotates to close the viewing system. It should be closed when an offset viewfinder is used in place of reflex system.

14.5e Motors

Synchronous Motors (not shown). Have a manual turning knob at back, which extends at a right angle to camera when mounted. Therefore, Operator reaches to side of camera to rotate the sync motor-turning knob.

Variable-Speed Motors (shown). Have a manual turning knob at side, speed-control rheostat at the back, and a FWD/REV switch at side.

To Mount Synchronous or Variable-Speed Motor. Rotate manual motor-turning knob until drive coupling aligns with camera drive shaft and five-pin Cannon plug aligns with receptacle in camera. Press motor to camera for snug fit. Secure four knurled screws on motor to tapped holes in camera.

To Reverse Variable-Speed Motor. Turn motor switch to REV. Transfer the belt from take-up to feed spindle wheel. Loop the belt into a "figure 8" to cause feed to act as "take-up"; adjust motor speed.

CAUTION: Cover lens or close shutter when running film back to beginning of a scene intended for double exposure.

Motors Available for the Mitchell S35R.
Variable-Speed Motor. 24V DC; 110V AC/DC (60 Hz); 110V AC/DC (50 Hz).

Slow-Motion Motor. 110V AC/DC (60 Hz) (36–128 fps); 110V AC/DC (50 Hz) (36–128 fps).

Synchronous Motor. 110V AC (60 Hz) (single phase); 110V AC (50 Hz) (single phase); 220V AC (60 Hz) (3-phase); 220V AC (50 Hz) (3-phase).

Animation Motor. 115V (50/60 Hz) AC.

14.5f Powerline

Elbowed three-pin Cannon plug is inserted into motor. ON/OFF switch is in cable.

NOTE: A thumb-actuated ON/OFF switch is at top right of turret-housing cover, above handgrip. This switch should be taped to hold it in forward position when using the ON/OFF switch in the cable.

Remote connector plug on motor accommodates an extension cable when a pistol-grip accessory is used.

A short-burst button is at lower rear of door.

A synchronous-generator Cannon-plug connection is located at back of camera, below the tachometer. Pins read clockwise starting from key: A and B, midshutter pulse (an optional feature when indication of shutter position is required); C–F, dual timing lights (another optional feature that marks film outside perforation holes, to indicate beginning and end of scenes or segments of scenes); G and H, camera synchronous generator that provides a frequency signal to the sound recorder.

14.5g Turret

Single-lens turret is standard equipment; three-lens turret is optional.

To Rotate Three-Lens Turret. Depress turret-release lever (upper right); turn turret to bring desired lens into position, then release lever, which locks turret.

To Remove Turret. (1) Remove slotted screw from knurled holddown screw in center of turret; remove holddown screw. (2a) *Single-lens turret:* Rotate turret locks clockwise at top and bottom; depress turret-release lever; pull turret from housing. (2b) *Three-lens turret:* Depress turret-release lever, pull turret from housing.

To Replace Turret. (1) Depress turret-release lever, slide turret into housing; rotate turret until release lever snaps into *up* position. (2) Install knurled holddown screw, and hand-tighten until screw touches the turret locating face; back the screw off $\frac{1}{16}$ of a turn. (3) Depress the release lever, and rotate the turret. Feel for slight drag on holddown screw. If satisfactory, allow turret-release lever to snap into *up* position, and insert the slotted screw into the knurled holddown screw, and tighten. (4) Try to rotate the turret in both directions. If rigid, turret is properly seated. If unit moves, remove turret, and begin again. (5) *On single-lens turret only,* rotate turret locks (at top and bottom) counterclockwise after rigidity of turret is found satisfactory.

14.5h Lenses

Bayonet base. Three protrusions (bayonets) on base are spaced so that lens can be inserted into turret one way only. One bayonet is usually marked with a dot that aligns with a similar dot on the turret. On lenses without this feature, the lens focus and/or T-stop arrow is to be placed at "6 o'clock" and the lens abutted to the lens port then rotated until bayonets on base slide into bayonet guides on turret.

To Mount. (1) Hold lens by forward scalloped ring, align the lens (as just described), and insert into turret. (2) Rotate lens counterclockwise until lens-mount lock below the lens secures the mount to the turret. (3) Try to rotate the lens clockwise to determine that lens is seated and locked.

To Remove. Hold lens by forward scalloped ring, and depress lens-mount lock below the lens. Rotate lens clockwise, then withdraw slowly.

NOTE: (a) When used with a follow-focus unit or in a blimp, the scalloped focus ring is replaced by a geared ring. (b) Each mount is fitted with a focus lockdown ring. (c) Each mount is fitted with a screw-out filter-retaining ring.

14.5i Sunshade/Matte box (not shown)

Bellows sunshade/matte box mounts onto two rods that fit into adapter plate. Camera must be mounted on adapter plate to utilize sunshade/matte box.

Sunshade/matte box is adjustable in and out. It accommodates all lenses—wide-angle (20mm) to telephoto (152mm), and zoom lens. Left side of matte box is hinged to permit field clearance when offset viewfinder is used on camera. Bellows can be detached from matte box.

To Verify Clearance. Sight through reflex system; run forefinger around inner edge of matte-box opening—if tip of finger is visible, move entire unit toward lens.

14.5j Filters

Polascreen and 127mm × 127mm (5 × 5 in.) glass filters can be housed in the sunshade/matte-box bellows.

Each Super Baltar lens (standard equipment) can accommodate a circular glass filter in its retaining ring (20mm and 25mm, 4 in. in diameter; 35mm, Series 7; 50mm, 75mm, 100mm, and 152mm, Series 8).

Gelatine: Filter slot located in aperture plate (see Fig. 14–13*a*). Bent portion of holder (used as a fingergrip) should be pointed toward Operator.

CAUTION: The raised nibs in the holder (intended for pressure-tight retention of holder in plate) have a tendency to stop the holder before it is fully inserted. Therefore, after insertion of holder into plate, remove plate from camera, and inspect, to determine that gelatine fully "covers" all of aperture-plate opening.

CAUTION: Manufacturer emphasizes frequent inspection of filter. Dirt or lint on gelatine may register on film when lens is stopped down. Manufacturer recommends that gelatine filter be removed and inspected after each "take." Many Cinematographers refuse to use the internal filter.

14.5k Door

Hinged at top.

To Open. Raise catch in door, lift up.

To Close. Lift door to clear hinge catch, then lower until flush with camera. Grasp viewing tube and pull to verify that door is secure.

14.5l Magazines

122m (400 ft) and 304.8 (1000 ft)

NOTE: On the S35R, 122m (400-ft) magazines may be mounted one of three ways: inverted, slant load, or top load. A 304.8m (1000-ft) magazine may be slant- or top-mounted only.

Inverted Magazine (see Figs. 14–12*a* and 14–13*b*).

To Mount. (1) Rotate inverted-magazine lockdown knob (below footage counter) counterclockwise, and remove dust-cover plate from rear of camera. Pull film loop from magazine feed slide. (2) Insert loop carefully into camera. Slide magazine into camera-body guide grooves until tapped hole in magazine aligns with magazine-lockdown screw. (3) Make sure that camera and magazine-drive gears are properly meshed. Rotate inverted magazine-lockdown knob clockwise to tighten magazine to camera. Thread camera (see Sec. 14.5m).

To Remove. Unthread film, and break it; rotate inverted magazine-lockdown knob counterclockwise, and pull magazine away.

Slant-Load Magazine (not shown).

To Place a Slant-Load Adapter on a Top-Load Camera. (1) Remove screws that secure the top-load magazine-guide groove (the shoe) to top of camera. (2) Insert a top-cover plate in the depressed cut in camera top (to provide a lighttight cover). Secure top-cover plate with aforementioned screws. (3) Rotate inverted-magazine-lockdown knob (below footage counter), and remove dust-cover plate from rear of camera. (4) Align adapter with inverted-magazine-lockdown screw extending from rear of camera, and slide adapter into camera-body guide grooves until gears mesh. Rotate inverted-magazine-lockdown knob clockwise to secure the adapter to the camera body.

NOTE: Mark II slant-load adapter has a top-lockdown screw located in front of slant-load magazine-guide groove. This screw inserts into camera body in a tapped hole above footage counter. S35R adapter is provided with an upper hold-down lip instead of a screw.

(5) Rotate manual motor turning knob (see Fig. 14–12*b*) to verify that gears are properly meshed.

To Mount a Slant-Load Magazine. (1) Remove adapter door at left side of adapter throat. Insert magazine toe into magazine guide groove (the shoe). Draw film loop through adapter throat (feed side under top roller, take-up side under lower roller) and into camera body. (2) Slide magazine forward and down until tapped hole in magazine heel aligns with magazine-lockdown screw in adapter. Rotate the adapter magazine-lockdown knob at bottom of rear plate clockwise to tighten magazine to adapter. Thread camera (see Sec. 14.5m).

WARNING, CAUTION, NOTE: Replace the adapter door!

To Remove. Unthread film, and break it. Remove adapter door. Place two fingers under magazine belt, pull laterally away from magazine; rotate fingers clockwise, and lift belt from spindle-wheel grooves. Rotate adapter magazine-lockdown knob counterclockwise. Lift magazine.

Top-Load Magazine (S35R and modified Mark II—see Figs. 14–12*b* and 14–13*a*).

To Mount. (1) Pull film loop from magazine feed side. (2) Insert magazine toe into magazine guide groove (the shoe); draw the film loop into camera body. (3) Slide magazine forward and down until tapped hole in magazine heel aligns with top-load magazine-lockdown screw. Rotate screw knob clockwise to tighten magazine. Thread camera (see Sec. 14.5m).

To Remove. Unthread film and break it. Place two fingers under magazine belt, pull laterally away from magazine; rotate fingers clockwise, and lift belt from spindle-wheel grooves. Rotate top-load magazine-lockdown knob counterclockwise. Lift magazine.

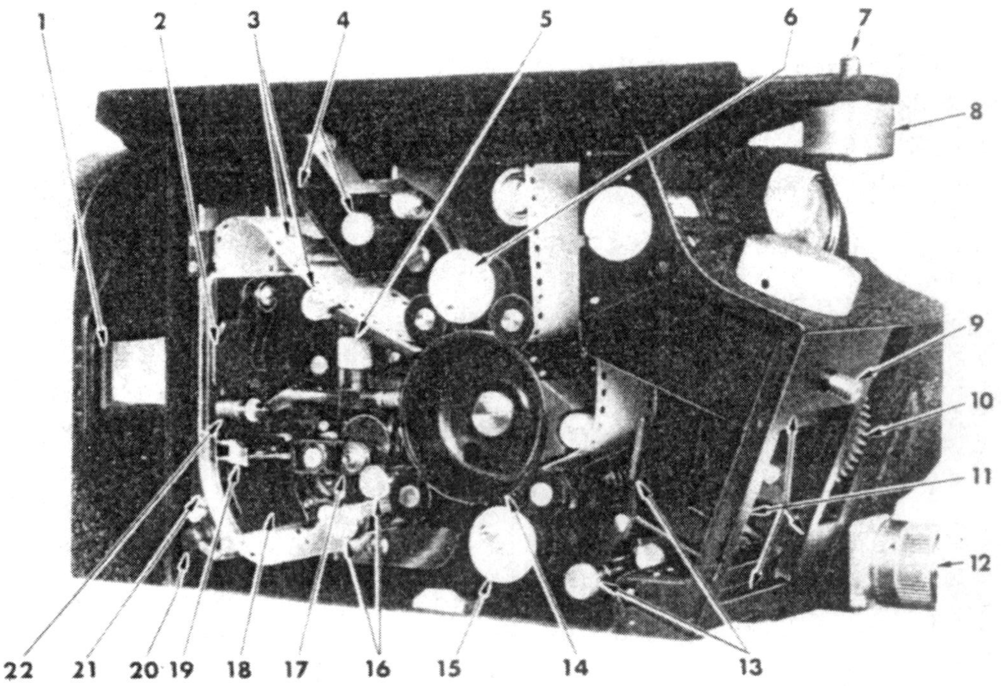

Figure 14–13a Mitchell S35R threading detail (for top-mounted magazine). Courtesy of Mitchell Camera Corp.

1. Filter holder
2. Pressure plate
3. Upper twin rollers
4. Upper buckle-trip apron and reset knob
5. Registration-pin throw-out knob
6. Upper film-guide eccentric
7. Top-load magazine lockdown screw
8. Top-load magazine lockdown knob
9. Inverted magazine and coverplate-lockdown screw (coverplate removed for illustration)
10. Camera drive gear for inverted magazine
11. Camera-body guide grooves for inverted magazine
12. Sync-generator connection
13. Lower buckle-trip apron and reset knob
14. Sprocket
15. Lower film-guide eccentric
16. Lower twin rollers
17. Sliding block
18. Register plate
19. Pulldown claw
20. Aperture-plate locks
21. Aperture plate
22. Registration pins

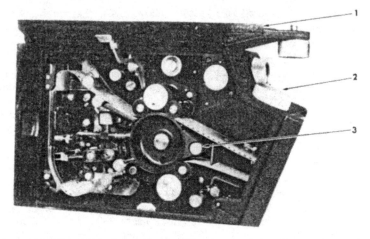

Figure 14–13b Mitchell threading detail for slant-loaded and inverted magazines. Courtesy of Mitchell Camera Corp.

1. Top-load magazine guide-groove (shoe)
2. Inverted magazine lockdown knob
3. Buckle-trip roller

14.5m Threading (Fig. 14–13)

(1) Depress buckle-trip apron toward rear of camera prior to threading, to avoid accidental starting of camera (see Sec. 14.5n). *On S35R and some modified top loading Mark II's,* a second upper buckle-trip located above the upper twin rollers should be pushed *up.* Rotate upper and lower film-guide eccentrics away from sprockets. (2) Rotate the manual motor-turning knob until pulldown claw retracts from register plate (a back, upward stroke). Lift registration-pin throw-out knob *up,* to retract pins from aperture plate. (3) Raise aperture-plate lock; remove aperture plate by pulling *gently.* If plate does not slide easily, check that pulldown claw and/or registration pins are clear of plate. (4) Clean the plate, and make a special check of pulldown claw and registration-pin holes for emulsion buildup or film chips; replace plate. Depress aperture-plate lock to secure. (5) Swing pressure-plate spring-arm clockwise. Remove pressure plate from register plate; clean. Replace pressure plate and spring arm. (6) Pull film from magazine feed side. Extend loop to lower corner of camera (a rough guide for amount of film needed for threading).

NOTE: S35R Mark II interiors are very compact. Film pulled from magazine to form loop may contact the camera interior, scraping emulsion from raw-stock edges. Care should be exercised to prevent emulsion from dropping into camera movement.

For Inverted and Slant-Load Magazines. (7) *Starting clockwise from the magazine take-up side, insert film* (a) *under* the buckle-trip roller and between lower film-guide eccentric and sprocket, (b) between lower twin rollers (*under* top small roller and *over* lower small roller) located below pulldown arm. (8) *Starting counterclockwise from magazine feed side, insert film* (a) *over* the buckle-trip roller and between upper film-guide eccentric and sprocket; (b) between upper twin rollers (*over* lower small roller and *under* top small roller) located above registration-pin throw-out knob; (c) in groove (the race) between the removable aperture plate and stationary register plate.

For Top-Load Magazines. (9) *Insert film clockwise from magazine take-up side* (a) to the right of buckle-trip roller, then between lower film-guide eccentric and sprocket; (b) between lower twin rollers (*under* top small roller and *over* lower small roller). (10) Starting counterclockwise from magazine feed side, insert film (a) between upper film-guide eccentric and sprocket; (b) between upper twin rollers (*below* top small roller and *under* lower small roller) located above registration-pin throw-out knob; (c) in groove (race) between removable aperture plate and stationary register plate. (11) Hold film in race. Rotate manual motor-turning knob (see Fig. 14–12*b*) gently in reverse until pulldown claw engages perforations. Registration pin will drop in automatically with one full *forward rotation* of the manual motor-turning knob. (12a) Adjust lower loop so that when lower film-guide eccentric closes, loop will clear bottom of box by 3.175mm × 6.35mm (1/16–1/8″) at lowest arc of loop. (12b) Adjust upper loop so that when upper film-guide eccentric closes, arc of loop bisects second screw from top of aperture-plate guide-rail bracket. (13) Rotate magazine take-up spindle wheel clockwise to take up film slack. Place uncrossed belt at bottom of take-up spindle wheel, and, in a clockwise direction, slip belt into wheel groove (this follows the rotation of the take-up wheel and subjects the belt to a minimum of stretching). (14) Rotate manual motor-turning knob and observe film being transported in camera. If satisfactory, proceed. (15) Pull lower buckle-trip reset knob (below the buckle-trip apron). For top-load magazine, also pull top buckle-trip knob located above upper twin rollers. Hold pins on upper and lower film-guide eccentrics with thumb and forefinger.

CAUTION: Keep the knuckles of the hand clear of the movement! Apply power in short bursts and observe action of film. If satisfactory, stop camera, close door, and reset footage counter.

14.5n Buckle-trip

Apron (a curved metal plate), in camera behind take-up side of sprocket, cuts out power automatically if film fails to take up. *On S35R and modified top-load Mark II,* a second buckle-trip is located above the upper twin rollers. Power should be cut out prior to threading by tripping the apron toward rear of camera to prevent accidental starting of camera.

To Reset. Pull reset knob below apron until unit snaps forward. For top-load magazines, also pull reset knob above top apron until unit snaps into place.

14.5o Footage and Frame Counters

Located at back of camera above the magazine-lockdown knob (see Fig. 14–12*b*).

Footage Counter. Additive. Registers each foot of film transported through camera up to 999 ft, then reverts to 0 and counts forward again. May be reset to 0 each time magazine is changed. Reset knob is located at top left rear of camera door, above eyepiece. Push in to engage and change numbers.

Frame Counter. Additive in increments of 1 up to 16 frames, then reverts to 1. Frame counter *does* go back to 0 when footage counter is zeroed. This is unlike any other Mitchell footage counter.

14.5p Tachometer

At top rear of camera. Registers speed from 0 to 128 fps in increments of 4 fps.

14.5q Shutter

Variable; 0–170°. Calibrations and external shutter control (see Fig. 14–12*b*) are at top of camera (right side), forward of the bull's-eye bubble level.

To Change Shutter Opening.   (1) Loosen the two slotted knurled stops (one at each side) of the external control knob. (2) Depress control knob and move indicator to desired shutter opening; release. (3) Turn control knob clockwise to lock. As a safety precaution, slide the knurled stops against the front and rear of the control-knob block. Tighten both stops with a screwdriver. (4) *On the S35R only,* the control knob can be turned an additional quarter of a turn counterclockwise to completely release the shutter control when installing camera in a sound blimp (see Sec. 14.6).

14.5r Lubrication (Fig. 14–14)

Manufacturer recommends lubrication of the following parts every 20,000 ft with one or two drops of high-speed-camera oil when operating at 24 fps, or before every high-speed run:

- *Movement:* registration-pin bearing; spring-loaded registration-pin bearing and ball bearing, which is at back of registration-pin throw-out knob; rear bearing on pulldown-claw arm, registration-pin cam; cam bearing; top and lower sides of sliding block; pressure-plate retainer arm.
- *Rollers:* every 50,000 ft, or before every high-speed run.

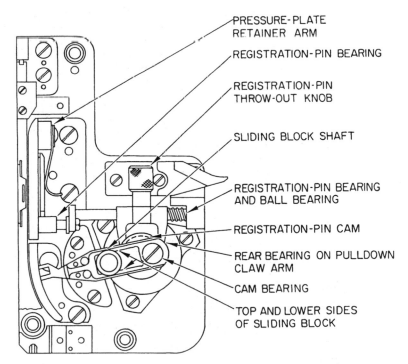

Figure 14–14 Mitchell S35R movement lubrication points. Courtesy of Mitchell Camera Corp.

NOTE: After oiling, run camera to eliminate excess oil, and wipe clean.

14.5s Cleaning

Optics: Clean with bulb syringe or soft camel's-hair brush.

Manufacturer recommends the following maintenance *each time film is changed:* (1) Remove aperture and pressure plates. (2) Remove emulsion buildup with orangewood stick. (3) Wipe plates with soft cotton (not linen) handkerchief. (4) Use bulb syringe on camera interior.

14.5t Weight

With 122m (400 ft) load, 17.7kg (39 lb) with 304.8m (1000 ft) load, 19.5kg (43 lb)

14.5u Troubleshooting

Trouble	*Probable Cause*
Camera will not start	Buckle-trip not set; powerline connection faulty; low temperature; thumb switch on turret not forward
Camera "hunts"	Camera not warmed up; voltage variation in powerline
Camera door will not close	Film-guide eccentrics not seated properly; film chip or dirt in door
Film jam	Improper threading; magazine covers not relieved on "dished" roll; take-up belt not on
Lens will not focus	Mount not seated properly; turret not seated properly; lens damaged
Cammed or noncammed offset viewfinder does not match reflex-tube cross hair	Turret not seated properly; offset-viewfinder parallax not set; offset viewfinder not seated in dovetail bracket; wrong cam on finder; wrong lens on front of viewfinder
Film will not slide into race	Registration pin or pulldown claw not retracted; emulsion or film chip in the race
Torn or punctured film	Improper threading
Film scratches	Dirt or emulsion buildup in aperture or pressure plates, film-guide eccentrics, registration pins, or magazine rollers
Reflex viewing tube blurred	Magnification knob seated between magnifying position (HI) and normal position (LO)
No take-up or sporadic take-up	Belt either slipping or too loose
Cut-in on reflex tube	Shutter not clear of reflex mirror; turret not seated; matte box extended; internal filter holder not seated; matte forward of groundglass not seated
Light trap will not close	Eyepiece inserted too far into focusing tube

14.5v S35R/Mark II Magazine-Loading Instructions

See Sec. 14.2.

14.6 MITCHELL S35R BLIMP (Figs. 14–15*a* and 14–15*b*)

NOTE: All directions are from Operator's point of view.

NOTE: Blimp requires a special S35R riser (not shown) when used on a geared head.

Blimp only accepts an S35R camera with a top-load magazine.

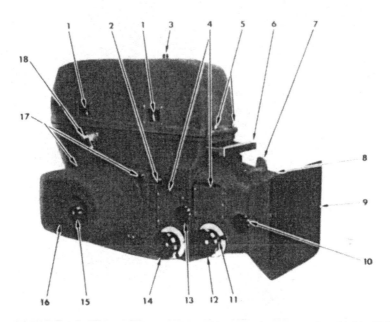

Figure 14–15a Mitchell S35R blimp with zoom lens extension (right side). Courtesy of Mitchell Camera Corp.

1. Magazine spindle-wheel viewing ports
2. Internal light switch
3. Tally light
4. Lens viewing-window covers
5. Hood-hinge pin knobs
6. Carrying handle
7. Lightshade bracket
8. Zoom housing (snout) front door assembly (optional)
9. Matte box
10. Front door lock knob
11. Focus-lock knob
12. Zoom focus knob
13. Lens access or zoom door lock knob
14. Standard follow-focus knob or zoom focal length drive
15. Manual motor-turning knob
16. Motor-cover housing
17. Motor-cover housing attaching screws
18. Shutter dissolve control handle

14.6a Base

Bottom fitted with one 3/8″-16 tapped hole to accommodate tripod-lockdown screw.

14.6b Blimp Hood

Mounts *before* magazine is installed on blimped camera. When blimp hood (magazine-housing cover) is separated from blimp,

To Mount. (1) Squeeze retractable hood hinge-pin knobs at front of blimp hood (shown), and insert hood-hinge knuckle into hinge leaves; release hinge pins to secure hood to blimp; (2) raise rear of hood; remove keyed pin from yoke (not shown) in blimp hood, and insert shock-absorber arm into yoke (not shown); insert keyed pin onto yoke through shock-absorber arm. To lock, rotate keyed pin.

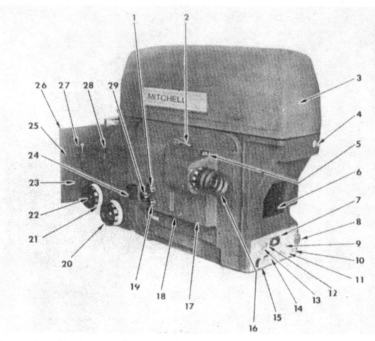

Figure 14–15b Mitchell S35R blimp with zoom lens extension (left side). Courtesy of Mitchell Camera Corp.

1. Color filter knob
2. Focus tube door latch
3. Blimp hood
4. Hood latch button
5. Light trap knob
6. Tachometer/counter port
7. Spirit level
8. Remote console plug (optional)
9. Control panel
10. Powerline plug
11. Power-selection toggle switch
12. Phone jack
13. Zoom-control Cannon plug accessory
14. ON/OFF switch
15. Fuse
16. Eyepiece
17. Focus tube door
18. Bracket for worm gear fits here
19. Black-and-white filter knob
20. Standard lens follow-focus knob or zoom focal-length knob
21. Marking disc
22. Adjusting knob
23. Cutout cover plate
24. Offset-viewfinder bracket
25. Thumb-lock pins
26. Front door assembly
27. Zoom housing brackets
28. Blimp brackets
29. Hi/Lo magnification knob

CAUTION: Pin is inserted into yoke only one way. It must be seated and rotated to lock. Once rotated, pull pin to be sure it is secure. When properly installed, shock absorber will prevent hood from dropping unexpectedly and will allow hood to remain in any desired open position.

14.6c Front Door

Unit is inserted between blimp brackets. Two slotted holding pins, threaded at shoulder of shanks, screw into the top and bottom brackets to secure door to the blimp.

NOTE: When using an offset viewfinder on blimp, unscrew thumblock pins (see Fig. 14–15b) and remove cutout cover plate on left side of matte box to obtain clearance for viewfinder optics.

Varifocal-lens (zoom-lens) extension housing (see Fig. 14–15).

To Mount. Insert housing between blimp brackets. Insert straight front-door hinge pins into mounting holes.

To Remove. Depress button on front-door hinge pin, pull up to remove top pin; pull down to remove bottom pin.

NOTE: (a) Pins can be pulled out but remain "captive" until a button in the head of the pin is depressed, which causes safety catches to recede into pin shank. (b) Front door (see Fig. 14–15a) mounts onto zoom extension housing the same as it does on blimp. (c) When extension is mounted, the front-door lock becomes the zoom-door lock. (d) Focus-lock knob on the scalloped zoom focus knob (Fig. 14–15a) locks the mechanical stops on the follow-focus shaft. (e) Front-door glass has a multilayer antireflectance coating. (An optical flat glass is no substitute because it is not coated.)

14.6d Motor Cover

Attaches to right side of blimp. Cover is mounted *after* camera is inserted into blimp.

To Mount. Slide bottom lip of cover into two upright supports; secure two knurled attaching screws at cover top into tapped holes in blimp.

14.6e Camera Preparation

Magazine. Remove from camera.

Eyepiece. Remove by loosening the four screws holding the eyepiece to the door. Replace with blimp eyepiece adapter, found in blimp accessory case.

Lenses. When used in a blimp, camera requires lenses fitted with focus-lens-gear rings. (T stops are set manually.)

Motor. Removal is optional before insertion of camera into blimp.

CAUTION: Voltage and phase of motor must be checked for agreement with voltage switch on panel at back of blimp (120V single-phase; 208–220V single- or three-phase). When switch has been set, tape switch down so that it cannot be changed accidentally.

Shutter. Rotate the camera-shutter-control knob counterclockwise until it stops; depress knob, and rotate counterclockwise one more quarter-turn.

CAUTION: Shutter opening on camera must be checked after installation for agreement with shutter-control setting on blimp. (See "Shutter" in Sec. 14.6j.)

14.6f Access

To Magazine. Depress hood-latch button at back of blimp (see Fig. 14–15b) (top right). The hood, hinged at front, lifts up and away from Operator.

To Lenses. Rotate small lens-access knob above follow-focus knob (Fig. 14–15*a*) (at right side) counterclockwise. Open door, and swing it to left.

To Motor. Rotate the two knurled screws on motor cover (Fig. 14–15*a*) counterclockwise. Lift cover from holding lugs.

To Camera. Turn latch on blimp focus-tube door (Fig. 14–15*b*) counterclockwise, and allow blimp door to hinge downward.

14.6g Camera Insertion

(1) Unscrew gear-location knob (see Fig. 14–15*c*) inside lens-access door. Push knob *up* to move coupling gear away from lens-gear area. Tighten gear-location knob. (2) Slide camera through blimp focus-tube door. Place the front $\frac{3}{8}''$-16 tapped hole of camera on the locating stud in the blimp base plate. Place rear of camera in trough that accommodates camera body. Slide camera until spring-loaded lockdown screw in base plate inserts into rear tapped hole. (3) Rotate offset knob at rear of plate until the $\frac{3}{8}''$-16 lockdown screw locks camera to plate.

14.6h Powerline

External. A four-pin Cannon plug (at lower right of panel at back of blimp) accepts the powerline.

Power Panel. Located at back of blimp (see Fig. 14–15*b*).

Top Row, Left to Right. Zoom-control Cannon-plug receptacle (the FWD, REV, and speed-control box attaches to left top of blimp); phone jack; spirit level; 20-pin Cannon remote-console plug, which is used in conjunction with a multiple-camera setup or a vidicon system and remote television console (i.e., Operator views through a TV monitor instead of a standard Mitchell viewfinder).

NOTE: A blimp intended strictly for single-camera filming will not have a 20-pin Cannon plug.

Bottom Row, Left to Right. Fuse (illuminates when it blows out and remains illuminated until replaced); motor ON/OFF switch (glows white to indicate that there is power to camera, glows red when motor is running); power-selection toggle switch (*up* for 208–220V, single- to three-phase; *down* for 110V, single-phase—this switch must correspond to voltage and phase of motor being used on camera); camera powerline Cannon plug.

Internal. Single three-pin Cannon plug (not shown), located at back below tachometer viewing port, is inserted into camera-motor receptacle. Sync-pulse plug (not shown), located at back below tachometer viewing port, is inserted into camera sync-pulse receptacle.

14.6i Internal Lights

Toggle switch for internal lights (see Fig. 14–15*a*) is located at right side of blimp exterior, above focus knob. Switch activates all lights and works off AC line, not a battery, as found on other blimps. Two adjustable lens lights inside blimp (Fig. 14–15*c*) illuminate the taking-lens barrel.

An adjustable rear light (not shown) illuminates tachometer and footage counter.

NOTE: (a) Manufacturer states that lamps can be left burning during filming because lamps are shielded. However, lamps (especially the rear light) should be checked to make certain that light does not hit the rear of the front-door glass. Although the glass is coated, and skip light does not reflect, if the rear lightbulb is accidentally aimed at the glass, the direct beam could cause a flare and "kick back" into the lens. (b) *When using a zoom-extension housing,* the Cannon plug that provides AC to the two zoom-lens lights (which are permanently affixed inside extension housing) must be coupled to the four-pin female Cannon-plug receptacle (located directly above coupling gear) to illuminate the taking-lens barrel. (This receptacle is not used when standard lenses are mounted in blimp.) (c) Tally light (red light at top of blimp hood) is illuminated only when camera is running. It must be coupled internally with the four-pin Cannon plug located above and opposite the lens-coupling gear. (d) On both the zoom-extension-light plug (located directly above coupling gear) and the tally-light plug (located opposite the zoom-extension plug): clockwise from each plug key, pins 1 and 2 are AC lines.

14.6j Coupling Alignment (Fig. 14–15c)

Standard Lens. (1) Rotate lens access (or zoom-door) lock knob (at right side of blimp; see Fig. 14–15a), and swing front door open. (2) Unscrew knurled gear-location knob (see Fig. 14–15c) counterclockwise, and push knob down to move coupling gear away from lens gear; insert lens into port. (3) Rotate scalloped standard lens follow-focus knob (located at both sides, lower front of blimp, Figs. 14–15a and 14–15b) counterclockwise until it is as far back (toward Operator) as it will go. On units with a worm gear mounted below the focus-tube door, rotate knob counterclockwise until cam roller is as far back as it will go. (4) Set lens at infinity, or slightly beyond if gear teeth of lens will not mesh with coupling gear precisely at infinity. (5) Push gear-location knob up, and engage coupling gear into teeth of lens gear; tighten clockwise the knurled gear-location knob. (6) Make a penciled infinity mark (∞) on white disc behind follow-focus knob for a constant reference. (7) Set T stop manually; close front door. If using an offset viewfinder (see Sec. 14.6l), place cam that corresponds to the taking lens on the viewfinder.

Varifocal (zoom) Lens (also see Sec. 14.6c). Place zoom-extension housing on front of blimp (see Figs. 14–15a and 14–15b).

  To Align Manual Zoom. (1) Open (lens access or) zoom-door lock knob (see Fig. 14–15a), and swing extension housing away from blimp. Rotate counterclockwise the knurled gear-location knob inside blimp; push knob down, and move coupling gear away from lens gear. (2) Align the horizontal-support arm (see Fig. 14–15d) (an accessory) with front of camera base plate, inside blimp. Two locating pins at each side of the single thumb screw on the support arm insert into mating register holes and a single tapped hole in base plate (see Fig. 14–15c); secure. Adjust horizontal support knob until support arm is level to camera base. (3) Insert zoom lens into turret port (see Sec. 14.5h for proper method of lens insertion). (4) Place vertical-support arm (zoom-lens cradle) under lens. Align pilot hole at base of vertical arm with tapped hole at end of horizontal-support arm. Secure with vertical-arm lock knob. Adjust bottom circular clamp-support ring to lens. (5) Fasten zoom lens to vertical bracket by securing the top circular clamp-support ring to the bottom support ring. (6) Set lens at longest focal length. Push gear-location knob up, and engage coupling gear into teeth of geared focal-length ring. Tighten gear-location knob. Pencil in all

Figure 14–15c Mitchell S35R blimp (lens coupling detail). Courtesy of Mitchell Camera Corp.

1. Tally light and/or zoom motor plug
2. Adjustable lens lights
3. Camera base plate
4. Register holes for horizontal support arm (see Fig. 16–23)
5. S35R geared lens
6. Geared lens ring
7. Turret lock
8. Coupling gear
9. Zoom-extension light plug
10. Gear-location knob
11. Tapped holes

Figure 14–15d Mitchell motorized zoom and bracket detail. Courtesy of Mitchell Camera Corp.

1. Zoom-motor drive gear
2. Geared focal-length ring (manual)
3. Single thumb screw
4. Geared focal-length ring (motor)
5. Horizontal support arm
6. Motor bracket
7. Bottom clamp support ring
8. Horizontal-support knob
9. Vertical-support arm
10. Vertical-arm-lock knob
11. Zoom motor
12. Zoom lens

focal lengths of lens scale onto white disc behind the zoom focal-length knob. (7) Set zoom lens to infinity (∞) (or slightly beyond if gear teeth will not mesh precisely at infinity).

WARNING: *Before closing zoom-extension housing, ALWAYS* screw in the adjusting knob located in left zoom focal-length knob (see Fig. 14–15*b*) of zoom-extension housing. Close zoom-extension housing, and lock it.

(8) Rotate front-door lock knob on right side of zoom-extension housing (see Fig. 14–15*a*), and swing the front door open. (9) Release adjusting knob, and ascertain that spiral teeth of zoom-focus knob gear properly engages teeth of focus ring on lens.

WARNING: *Before opening zoom-extension housing, ALWAYS* set lens focus at infinity, and screw in the adjusting knob to clear spiral-zoom-focus-knob gear from geared focus ring on lens.

Make a penciled infinity mark (∞) on white disc behind zoom focus knob for a constant reference.
   Set T stops and *f*/stops manually.
   Close front door, and lock it.

Zoom Lens: Motorized. Follow steps 1–4 as described for varifocal lens, then (5) Loosen gear-location knob; push knob down to disengage coupling gear from focal-length geared ring on lens. Tighten the gear-location knob. Set lens at its longest focal length. (6) Engage zoom-motor gears to focal-length gear ring by securing the top circular clamp-support ring and its motor bracket to the bottom ring.

NOTE: Focal-length ring is fitted with adjustable stops to limit zoom travel within a preselected range.

(7) Insert the zoom-motor-extension Cannon plug into upper right female Cannon receptacle (tally-light receptacle) (see Fig. 14–15*c*). (8) Insert the zoom remote-control extension into power panel at rear of blimp (see "Power Panel" in Sec. 14.6h and Fig. 14–15*b*). Zoom remote-control unit is fitted with FWD/REV buttons and a speed-control rheostat.

Shutter
   To Align Blimp Shutter-Control-Arm Knob to Camera Shutter. (1) Make certain that adjustable shutter-control knob on *camera* (see Figs. 14–12*a* and 14–12*b*) is rotated counterclockwise until it stops; then depress and rotate knob, counterclockwise one more quarter-turn. Shutter should slide free in its restricted slot without interference. Set shutter indicator *on camera* to 170°. (2) Pull lock pin on shutter-control handle (at right side of blimp above motor cover) (see Fig. 14–15*a*), and set shutter indicator on blimp at 170°. (3) Align screw on shutter arm (which is internally coupled to external handle) (not shown) with top of camera shutter knob. (4) Hold knurled shutter knob on camera to prevent it from rotating and locking down the shutter. Insert the screw on the internal shutter arm into tapped hole on top of knurled shutter knob; secure. (5) Pull lock pin, and move shutter-control handle (Fig. 14–15*a*) to verify that shutter opens and closes.

CAUTION: Check all shutter settings on camera scale (see Fig. 14–12*b*) for agreement with shutter settings on blimp scale (at the shutter-control handle, see Fig. 14–15*a*).

When Blimp and Camera Shutter Settings Do Not Agree. (1) Leave shutter screw-on-arm extension (not shown) coupled to knurled shutter knob on camera. (2) Loosen set screws holding shutter dissolve bracket (not shown) to shutter arm; loosen bracket. (3) Set blimp shutter-control handle (Fig. 14–15*a*) at 170°. Set camera-shutter (Figs. 14–12*a* and 14–12*b*) indicator at 170°. (4) Tighten the set screws securely. Place blimp shutter-control handle at various shutter settings, and compare camera-shutter indicator for agreement.

14.6k Filters

To Mount Internal Holder. (1) Align filter horizontal-support arm with front of camera base plate. Two locating pins—one at each side of a single thumb screw on the support arm—insert into two mating register holes and tapped hole in base plate; secure. (2) Adjustable U-shaped bracket accommodates glass filters in sizes 76.2mm × 76.2mm (3 × 3 in.) to 127mm × 127mm (5 × 5 in.) Filter unit fits to horizontal-support arm, which slides in and out.

To Mount Filter. Insert square glass filter into U-bracket. Slide filter toward lens. Verify that filter covers *all* of lens; secure in place.

Circular glass filters can be inserted into lenses, or gelatine can be inserted into filter slot of camera (see Sec. 14.5j).

14.6l Viewfinder/Focus Tube

Reflex. In blimp door (see Fig. 14–15*b*.)

To Align Reflex Mirror for Viewing. Depress manual motor-turning knob on motor cover (right side of blimp—Fig. 14–15*b*), and rotate.

Eyepiece. Slides in and out; adjusts to achieve focus on groundglass. Knurled ring locks eyepiece at individual's focus.

Light-Trap Control. Horizontal knob above eyepiece. Depress and rotate to close viewing system. Should be closed when offset viewfinder is used in place of reflex system.

Magnification Control. Center knob closest to offset-viewfinder bracket. Depress and rotate counterclockwise (HI) to magnify image 10×; rotate clockwise (LO) for normal viewing to magnify image 5×.

Contrast Filters. Two. Control is vertically positioned behind magnification knob. Depress upper knob, and rotate to flip filter into view for color film. Depress lower knob, and rotate to flip pan filter into view for black-and-white film.

Offset Viewfinder. Unit is inserted into bracket located forward of magnification and contrast-filter knobs. Three types of offset viewfinders are available: (1) BNC-type with cams and automatic focus capability (see Sec. 14.4j).

NOTE: An S35R blimp must be fitted with a cam bracket and worm gear for use with a BNC-type viewfinder.

(2) NC-type with manual setting of focus and parallax (see Sec. 14.3h). (3) Frame-type (tracking finder, not shown) with transparent colored mattes for change of field size.

CAUTION: The tracking finder is only usable with lenses 50mm or longer.

14.6m Ports

Window at back of blimp allows viewing of tachometer and footage counter. Lens-viewing windows are located at each side of blimp front and/or zoom-extension housing; each lens-viewing window is fitted with vertical sliding covers to prevent stray light from striking interior of blimp lens area.

Windows in hood allow viewing of magazine take-up and feed spindle wheels.

14.6n Weight

Camera 42.2kg (93 lb)

14.7 MITCHELL 16 PRO AND HS CAMERAS* (Fig. 14–16)

NOTE: All directions are from Operator's point of view.

Figure 14–16a Mitchell 16 with matte box removed (right front view). Courtesy of Mitchell Camera Corp.

1. Carrying handle
2. Forward motor screw
3. Lens-focus lockdown screw
4. Turret-locking knob (partially obscured)
5. Taking lens position
6. Turret-release lever

7. Sunshade-bracket holes
8. Rackover stop
9. Motor-door latch
10. Base and turret
11. Synchronous motor
12. Powerline plug

---

*The Mitchell 16 PRO (Professional) and the Mitchell 15 HS (High Speed) cameras are basically the same design. The immediately apparent difference between the PRO and the HS is in the shutter (see Sec. 14.7q) and, in some instances, in the turret (see Sec. 14.7f).

Figure 14–16b Mitchell 16 (rear view). Courtesy of Mitchell Camera Corp.

1. Horizontal matte-adjusting knob (not visible, see Fig. 16–41)
2. Focusing tube eyepiece (with chamois eye-guard)
3. Viewfinder matte-adjusting knob
4. Viewfinder parallax-locking screw
5. Magazine lockdown knob
6. Powerline plug
7. Shutter handle
8. Manual motor-turning knob
9. 110V sync motor
10. Parallax-adjustment screw (accessory)
11. Offset viewfinder
12. Counter reset knob
13. Buckle-trip reset button
14. Footage and frame counter
15. Tachometer
16. Bubble level
17. Rackover handle
18. Motor-door latch

14.7a Base

Bottom fitted with ⅜"-16 tapped hole to accommodate tripod-lockdown screw. The L-shaped base includes turret (see Fig. 14–16a). Flat section of base is fitted with dovetail tracks (gibs), which allow camera to slide (rackover) horizontally to align focusing tube with taking lens. A dovetailed viewfinder bracket, into which offset viewfinder is inserted, is an integral part of upright section of base.

Mitchell 16 does *not* have four-way mattes.

14.7b Rackover

Camera box must be *racked over* (i.e., moved laterally on gibs until focusing tube is directly behind taking lens) to sight through the taking lens.

To Rack Over. (1) Grasp handle at rear of camera (see Fig. 14–16b), and depress button to release locating plunger. (2) Start to rotate handle clockwise, and *release button immediately* so that the locating plunger can engage the camera box.

CAUTION: Some cameras are *not* equipped with stops in prevent excessive lateral movement of camera box. Therefore, unless button is released immediately, camera can be racked completely off base.

(3) Rotate handle only counterclockwise to check that plunger has engaged camera box and that focusing tube is aligned with taking lens.

NOTE: A microswitch cuts off power when the camera is racked over; camera will not run until it is racked back to shooting position.

To Rack Back. (1) Depress button, and start to rotate handle counterclockwise. *Release button immediately* so that the locating plunger can engage the camera box. (2) Rotate handle clockwise only, to check that locating plunger has engaged the camera box and that the aperture is aligned with the taking lens.

14.7c Focusing Tube

Located in camera-box door (see Fig. 14–29).

To Change or Clean Groundglass. (1) Slide access door (at side of focusing tube) (see Fig. 14–29) toward Operator, open camera door, and insert eraser end of pencil into forward opening of tube. (2) Slide groundglass sideways; grasp glass by edges, and remove; clean and reinsert; close access door.

NOTE: *ALWAYS* insert groundglass with smooth surface toward rear of tube.

Matte Slot. None.

Effects Matte. No provision.

Magnification. Push magnification knob (located below focusing tube) forward to magnify 10 ×; push back for normal image.

Contrast Filters (see Fig. 14–29). Two. Knurled knob at top rear flips green filter into view for orthochromatic film. Bottom-rear knob flips pan filter into view for panchromatic film.

Eyepiece (see Figs. 14–16b and 14–28). Rotates; moves in and out; adjusts to achieve focus on groundglass. Locking screw holds eyepiece at desired focus.

14.7d Motors

NOTE: *Synchronous motors* (see Fig. 14–16a) have manual turning knob (see Fig. 14–25) located at back.

Variable-speed motors (not shown) have manual turning knob at right side, speed-control rheostat at back, and FWD/REV switch at right side.

High-speed motors (not shown) have manual turning knob at right side, speed-control rheostat at back, and high-speed tachometer at top. Some models may have a FWD/REV switch, but it is not standard.

To Mount Synchronous, Variable-Speed, or High-Speed Motor. (1) Make certain that motor-door latch, at right side of camera base, is pushed all the way forward. (2) Rotate manual motor-turning knob until drive coupling aligns with movement drive shaft in camera, and four-pin Cannon-motor plug aligns with camera receptacle. Fit motor against camera. (3) Slide motor-door latch, at base, toward rear of camera. Secure two knurled screws on motor to tapped holes in camera.

To Reverse Variable-Speed Motor. (Also high-speed motor if fitted with reverse switch). (1) Turn motor switch to "REV." (2) Transfer belt from take-up to feed spindle wheel. Loop belt in a "figure-8"; this will cause feed to act as "take-up"; adjust motor speed.

CAUTION: Cover lens, or close shutter when running film back to beginning of scene intended for double exposure.

Motors Available for the Mitchell 16 PRO and HS.
Variable-Speed Motor.   12V DC; 110V AC/DC (60 Hz); 110V AC/DC (50 Hz).
Slow-Motion Motor.   24V DC (16–64 fps); 110V AC/DC (60 Hz) (48–128 fps); 110V AC/DC (50 Hz) (48–128 fps).
High-Speed Motor.   115V AC (60 Hz) (12–400 fps); 115V AC (50 Hz) (12–400 fps).
Synchronous Motor.   110V AC (60 Hz) (single phase); 110V AC (50 Hz) (single phase); 220V AC (60 Hz) (3-phase); 220V AC (50 Hz) (3-phase).
Multi-duty Motor.   220V AC (60 Hz) (3-phase)/96V DC.

NOTE: Multi-duty motor is only synchronous at 220V AC (60 Hz).

CAUTION: *Never* run a Mitchell 16 PRO at a speed greater than 128 fps! The Mitchell 16 HS may be run at speeds up to 400 fps.

14.7e Powerline

Insert powerline plug (see Figs. 14–16a and 14–16b) into four-pin receptacle at top rear of camera.

Variable-speed and/or high-speed motors have ON/OFF switch in cable. A 110V synchronous motor requires a capacitor box in the cable. ON/OFF switch is in capacitor box.

14.7f Turret

Four-position (see Fig. 14–16a).

To Rotate. (Some, but not all, HS cameras are fitted with only a single lens, nonrotating turret.) Depress turret-release lever (lower right side), turn turret until desired lens is in position at right of viewfinder bracket. Release lever to lock turret.

NOTE: (a) Center turret-locking knob may be tightened to hold a heavy telephoto lens. Ideal tension for normal operation is obtained by tightening the knob by hand and backing it off a quarter-turn. (b) The longest lens on the turret should be mounted opposite the shortest lens. (c) On some models, one port is fitted with *quick-set locks* (not shown), i.e., clamps that grasp the lens-mount shoulder. These clamps are placed above and below the lens port and are loosened with a screwdriver. Quick-set locks permit efficient mounting and dismounting of a variety of lenses.

An Easy Method for Mounting a Lens Using Quick-set Locks. (1) Rotate turret until quick-set locks are at top. Slide clamps aside horizontally; insert new lens mount (cutoff portion of lens-mount shoulder aligns with perimeter of turret). (2) Slide clamps back over shoulder of mount, and tighten. (3) Rotate turret to place lens in taking position.

NOTE: Lens *can* be mounted without rotating the turret. However, the upper quick-set lock drops down behind the lens-mount shoulder in this position, making it more difficult to slide mount into port. Safety of lens must always be considered. The possibility of dropping the lens while "fighting" the top lock is increased if the turret is not rotated.

There is *no* turret-setting knob on the Mitchell 16.

14.7g Lenses

To Fit Lens to Turret. (1) Unscrew lens barrel from threaded Mitchell mount. Align screw holes of mount with tapped holes in turret, and secure with screws. (2) Insert lens barrel into threaded mount.

NOTE: (a) Rear element of 15mm lens extends into camera aperture when seated; therefore, this lens must be backed off prior to rotating the turret. (b) Each mount is fitted with a focus-lockdown screw.

14.7h Viewfinder

Offset (see Sec. 14.11b, Fig. 14–24). Fits and locks into dovetailed bracket at left side of camera base (see Fig. 14–29).

Ribbon-Matte-Adjusting Knobs. Located at top and left side of finder, scribed to indicate various focal-length settings: *Wide-angle lens* (15mm) is scribed in red. *Normal and long lenses* are scribed in black.

Knobs may be set to two different indicators—projector or TV—but TV indicators are not standard equipment on Mitchell 16.

Top knob adjusts vertical ribbon mattes (frame side). Side knob adjusts horizontal ribbon mattes (frame top and bottom).

When using a 15mm lens, remove the circular sunshade at front of finder, and replace it with a *reducer lens* to correct the image size.

Without the reducer lens, the full field of the viewfinder approximates 17.5mm.

Parallax Adjustment.

To Align Vertical Cross Hair. (1) Loosen parallax lock knob (see Sec. 14.11b, Fig. 14–24), which is positioned in the horizontal restricted slot between focus lock knob and dovetailed bracket at top front of finder. (2) Move rear of finder horizontally until vertical cross hair in finder matches reference point of cross hair in focusing tube. Secure parallax lock knob.

NOTE: A follow-focus unit with parallax-correction cams is also available. (See Sec. 14.11b.)

To Align Horizontal Cross Hair (in finder—with horizontal cross hair in focusing tube). (1) Verify that viewfinder dovetail is properly seated in viewfinder bracket before making *any* adjustments. Sight cross hair on horizontal reference point through focusing tube. Lock camera down. (2) Loosen locknut of vertical-adjustment screw (see Sec. 14.11b, Fig. 14–24), which is located on pivot point near dovetailed bracket. Turn the hex-head adjustment screw clockwise to move finder cross hair *up,* counterclockwise to move finder cross hair *down.* (3) Align the horizontal cross hair in viewfinder with horizontal reference point in focusing tube.

Focus Knob (see Sec. 14.11b, Fig. 14–24): The large knurled knob at left side of finder behind prism box causes the prism box to slide in and out on a shaft. The prism box is secured at desired focus by a lock knob above the shaft.

Pivot Point (see Sec. 14.11b, Fig. 14–24): Viewfinder swings vertically for access to camera door. To pivot the finder, loosen the knurled finder tilt lock located in the restricted slot, forward of dovetail lock.

14.7i Sunshade/Matte Box (not shown)

Bellows-type sunshade/matte box mounts onto two rods that fit into a bracket. Bracket is independent of camera and has two locating pins and one screw that insert in mating holes in bottom front of base.

Sunshade/matte box is adjustable up and down, left and right, in and out. Top of matte box is fitted with an extension-shade screw.

To Verify Clearance. Sight through focusing tube, then run forefinger around inner edge of matte-box opening—if tip of finger is visible, move entire unit toward lens. Repeat until sure that matte box is clear of lens.

A standard matte box allows use of the 15mm lens if bellows is fully collapsed. Mitchell 16 has *no* wide-angle matte box. Standard matte box must be removed entirely to use a lens wider than 15mm.

The 100mm lens must be removed from turret in order to slide matte box far enough toward camera to clear the other lenses.

14.7j Filters

Gauze holders and matte frames are housed in matte box. A polascreen, one 50.8mm × 50.8mm (2 × 2 in.) glass filter holder, and one 76.2mm × 76.2mm (3 × 3 in.) glass filter holder are housed in the bellows.

Gelatine: Filter slot for internal filter is located in aperture plate (*inside* camera—see Fig. 14–17). Camera door must be opened each time a filter holder is inserted (or removed). When inserting filter holder, bent portion of holder (used as a fingergrip) should be pointed toward Operator. To check filter after insertion in aperture plate, remove taking lens to expose aperture opening in upright section of base. Determine visually that gelatine "covers" the aperture.

14.7k Door

Hinged at bottom.

To Open. Depress catch in door; pull out and down.

To Close. Lift until flush with camera; pull focusing tube to verify that door is secure.

14.7l Magazines

122m (400 ft) (shown in Fig. 14–18) and 366m (1200 ft)

To Mount. (1) Pull a loop from magazine feed side. (2) Insert magazine toe into magazine guide groove (at top of camera). Draw film loop into camera body. (3) Slide magazine forward and down until tapped hole in magazine heel aligns with magazine lockdown screw. Rotate magazine lockdown knob clockwise (located at top left rear of camera) to tighten magazine to camera. Thread camera (see Sec. 14.7m).

To Remove. Unthread film, and break it. Place two fingers under the belt, pull laterally away from magazine, rotate the fingers clockwise, and lift belt from spindle wheel groove. Disengage the magazine by rotating the lockdown screw counterclockwise, and lift the magazine clear of the camera.

14.7m Threading (Fig. 14–17)

1. Press buckle-trip toward rear of camera to avoid accidental starting of camera during threading procedures (see Sec. 14.7n). Rotate upper and lower sprocket-guide rollers counterclockwise away from sprocket.

2. Rotate manual turning knob on motor (see Fig. 14–16*b*) until pulldown claw aligns with scribe mark on register plate (this indicates claw is retracted from aperture plate). Rotate registration-pin throw-out knob counterclockwise.

3. Raise aperture-plate lock; remove aperture plate by pulling *gently.* If plate does not slide easily, check to see whether pulldown claw and/or registration pins are clear of plate.

4. Clean plate. Make a special check of registration pin and pulldown claw holes for emulsion buildup or film chips. Replace the plate. Depress aperture-plate lock to secure.

5. Swing pressure-plate spring arm clockwise. Remove pressure plate from register plate; clean. Replace pressure plate and spring arm.

6. Pull film from magazine feed side. Extend loop to lower front corner of camera (a rough guide for amount of film needed for threading). Starting clockwise from magazine take-up side, insert film (a) between lower sprocket-guide rollers and sprocket, (b) between lower twin rollers.

7. Starting counterclockwise from the magazine feed side, insert film (a) between upper sprocket-guide rollers and sprocket, (b) over middle idler roller, (c) under the upper idler roller, (d) in groove (the race) between the removable aperture plate and stationary register plate.

8. Place forefinger and little finger above and below the register plate to hold film straight in the race. Align perforation hole in film with index mark inscribed in lower part of register plate. *Gently* rotate registration-pin throw-out knob clockwise to determine whether registration pins are entering film perforations. If pins touch film, raise or lower the film in the race while rotating the pins back and forth until they drop into the perforations.

9. (a) Adjust lower loop so that when lower sprocket-guide roller closes, loop will clear bottom of box by 3.175mm–6.35mm (1/8–1/4 in.) at lowest arc of loop. (b) Adjust upper loop so that when upper sprocket-guide roller closes, arc of loop aligns with top of movement plate.

10. Rotate the magazine take-up spindle wheel clockwise to take up the film slack. Place uncrossed belt at bottom of take-up spindle wheel, and, in a clockwise direction, slip belt into wheel groove (this follows the rotation of the take-up wheel and subjects the belt to a minimum of stretching).

11. Rotate manual motor-turning knob, and observe film being transported in camera. If satisfactory, proceed.

12. Push buckle-trip reset button at back of camera above counter (see Fig. 14–16*b*); hold pins on upper and lower sprocket-guide rollers with thumb and forefinger.

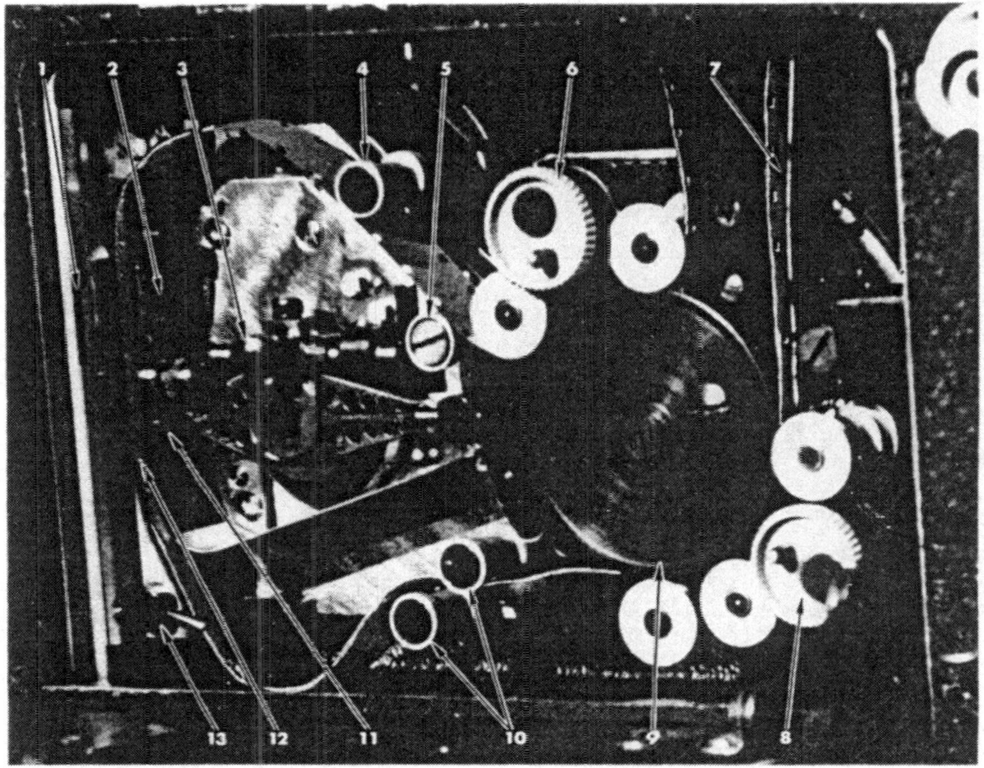

Figure 14–17 Mitchell 16 threading. Courtesy of Mitchell Camera Corp.

1. Filter slot
2. Pressure plate
3. Registration-pin throw-out knob
4. Upper idler roller
5. Middle idler roller
6. Upper sprocket-guide roller
7. Buckle-trip
8. Lower sprocket-guide roller
9. Sprocket
10. Lower twin rollers
11. Pulldown claw
12. Register-plate scribe mark
13. Aperture-plate lock

CAUTION: Keep the knuckles of the hand clear of the movement!

Apply power in short bursts, and observe action of film. If satisfactory, stop camera, close door, and reset footage counter.

14.7n Buckle-trip (see Fig. 14–17)
Apron (a vertical metal strip) located behind take-up side of sprocket cuts out power automatically if film fails to take up when camera is running. Power should be deliberately cut out prior to threading (by tripping apron toward rear of camera), to prevent accidental starting of camera.

To Reset. Push reset button located above footage counter (see Fig. 14–16*b*).

14.7o Footage and Frame Counters
Located at back of camera above bubble level (see Fig. 14–16*b*).

Footage Counter. Additive. Registers each foot of film transported through camera up to 999 ft, then reverts to 0 and counts forward again. May be reset to 0 each time magazine is changed; reset knob is located at left rear side near camera door.

Frame Counter. Additive in increments of 2 frames up to 40 frames, then reverts to 0 and counts forward again. Does not reset.

14.7p Tachometer
Located at back of camera (see Fig. 14–16*b*). Registers speeds from 12 to 36 fps in increments of 1 fps. When speed exceeds 36 fps camera tachometer is superseded by tachometer on a wild (variable-speed) or high-speed motor.

14.7q Shutter
Variable; Professional: 0–235° (Fig. 14–16*b*). (Cameras previous to serial no. 227 (not shown), have a variable shutter of 0–175° only.)

HS (high-speed camera) (not shown).   0–140° only, regardless of serial number. Calibrations and external control at back of camera.

To Change Shutter Opening. (1) Pull out and turn locking-pin knob in handle to move arm. When desired shutter opening appears at slot in shutter handle, proceed to step 2. (2) Rotate knob until positive locking pin drops into place. Agitate handle to test engagement of pin.

To Clear the Shutter from the Lens. Remove lens from lens mount. Observe shutter through lens port. Rotate manual motor-turning knob (see Fig. 14–16*b*) until shutter clears camera aperture.

14.7r Lubrication (Fig. 14–18)
Manufacturer recommends lubricating the following parts every 1000 ft with one or two drops of oil: registration-pin pads (oilers), register shaft (both sides of bracket), pulldown-claw cam at upper corners, plunger arm, pressure-plate rollers.

NOTE: After oiling, run camera to eliminate excess oil, and wipe interior.

14.7s Cleaning
Optics: Clean with bulb syringe or soft camel's-hair brush.

Manufacturer recommends the following maintenance *each time film is changed:* (1) Remove aperture and pressure plates. (2) Remove emulsion buildup with orangewood stick. (3) Wipe plates with soft cotton (not

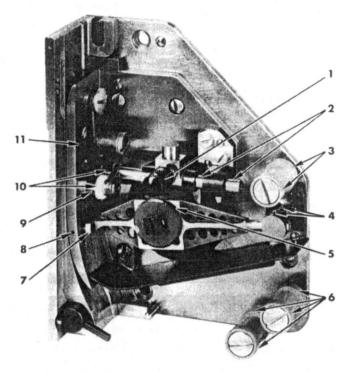

Figure 14–18 Mitchell 16, lubrication points. Courtesy of Mitchell Camera Corp.

1. Registration-pin throw-out knob
2. Registration shaft
3. Idler rollers
4. Plunger-arm oil holes
5. Pulldown-claw cam
6. Idler rollers
7. Pulldown claw (not lubed)
8. Register-plate scribe mark (not lubed)
9. Registration pin (one of two)
10. Oilers
11. Pressure-plate rollers (not visible)

linen) handkerchief. (4) Use bulb syringe on camera interior to remove dust, dirt, etc.

14.7t Weight

With 122m (400-ft) load, 19.1kg (42 lb.)

14.7u Troubleshooting

Trouble	*Probable Cause*
Camera will not start	Buckle trip not reset; camera racked over; powerline connection faulty; low temperature
Camera door will not close	Sprocket-guide rollers not seated properly; registration-pin throw-out knob not forward; film chip or dirt in door

Camera "hunts"	Camera not warmed up; voltage variation in powerline
Film jam	Improper threading; take-up belt not on; magazine cover not relieved on dished roll
Lens will not focus	Lens not screwed all the way into mount; mount not seated properly; turret not seated properly; lens damaged
Viewfinder does not match focus-tube cross hair	Camera not completely racked over; viewfinder not properly seated in dovetail bracket; viewfinder parallax not set; turret not seated properly; wrong lens on front of viewfinder
Film will not slide into race	Registration pin or pulldown claw not retracted; emulsion or film chip in race
Torn on punctured film	Improper threading
Film scratches	Dirt or emulsion buildup on aperture plate, sprocket-guide rollers, pressure plate, registration pins, or magazine rollers
Focusing tube blurred	Magnification knob seated between magnifying position (forward) and normal position (back)
No take-up, or sporadic take-up	Belt slipping, or belt too loose
Cut-in on focusing tube	Internal filter holder not seated in filter slot; turret not seated; matte box extended

14.8 MITCHELL 16 AND R-16 MAGAZINES (Fig. 14–19)

14.8a Type
Double-compartment.

14.8b Capacity
122m (400-ft) (shown) and 366m (1200-ft)

14.8c Lids
Two. Threaded.
To remove. Rotate counterclockwise.

14.8d Feed
Left side. Film (wound emulsion in) pulls off spindle clockwise.

14.8e Take-up
Right side. Film winds on spindle counterclockwise, emulsion always out.

14.8f Loading
(1) Unscrew feed lid. (2) In darkness, remove film roll from can and bag. Pull film off roll clockwise. (3) Insert film end between feed-idler roller and magazine-compartment wall (emulsion faces idler roller). Push film through the feed light-trap rollers. (4) Place roll on the feed spindle. Rotate the feed spindle wheel until the spindle pin engages the core keyway. (5) Replace the feed lid. (6) Unscrew the take-up lid in the light. Insert film end into take-up light trap. Push film between magazine-compartment wall and take-up idler roller (emulsion faces the roller). (7) Hold core. Rotate take-up spindle wheel until the spindle pin engages the core keyway. (8) Insert film into core slot, and wind on take-up spindle counterclockwise (emulsion side *out*). (9) Replace take-up lid.

Figure 14–19 Mitchell 16; R-16 magazine.
Courtesy of Mitchell Camera Corp.

1. Magazine toe
2. Feed light trap
3. Take-up light trap
4. Lockdown screw hole
5. Magazine heel

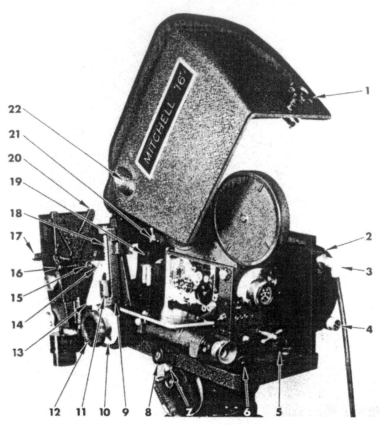

Figure 14–20a Mitchell 16 blimp (open). Courtesy of Mitchell Camera Corp.

1. Scalloped access knob
2. Camera motor cover
3. External powerline
4. Internal motor connection (optional)
5. Camera support plate
6. Offset camera-lockdown knob in plate
7. Vertical bracket height-screw adjustment
8. Follow-focus-bracket lockdown knob
9. Follow-focus bracket
10. Marking disc
11. Cam holder
12. Follow-focus knob
13. Cam
14. Cam roller
15. Cam adjusting screw-lock
16. Adjusting screw
17. Upper-section viewfinder harness
18. Worm gear
19. Filter holders
20. Lower-section viewfinder harness
21. Internal lens light
22. Magnifying window

NOTE: (a) Relieving a lid one-half turn eliminates drag and/or noise of roll that may have "dished" in loading. (b) Mitchell light-trap rollers are velvet covered and require constant checking for lint and dust. While spring tension on outer rollers helps keep the magazine lighttight, the light trap should be taped or covered with a black bag after loading.

WARNING: (a) When using the 366m (1200-ft) Mitchell 16 magazine, a camera-belt change is necessary. (b) When using the 366m 1200-ft DSR magazine, *no* camera-belt change is necessary. The DSR magazine is fitted with an intermediate (double) spindle wheel. The standard 122m (400-ft) camera belt attaches to the outside wheel. A permanent belt is attached from the inside wheel to the take-up spindle wheel. (c) Mitchell 16 and R-16 magazines are interchangeable.

14.8g Unloading
In darkness, take up all slack; unscrew take-up lid; place middle finger on core and thumb on edge of roll. Turn magazine over, remove film roll, and place exposed roll into black bag and can.

14.8h Footage Counter
None.

14.9 MITCHELL 16 BLIMP (Fig. 14–20)

NOTE: All directions are from Operator's point of view.

14.9a Base
Bottom fitted with a 3/8"-16 tapped hole to accommodate tripod-lockdown screw.

Figure 14–20b Mitchell 16 blimp (closed); follow-focus bracket in shooting position. Courtesy of Mitchell Camera Corp.

1. Viewfinder harness screws
2. Offset viewfinder
3. Cam
4. Worm gear
5. Cam holder
6. Follow-focus bracket lockdown knob
7. Follow-focus knob
8. Marking disc
9. Lens access knob
10. Hood latch
11. Internal light toggle switch
12. Sunshade/blimp hood
13. Lens magnifying window

CAUTION: When blimp is mounted on a Worrall Geared Head, a riser (see Sec. 9.5) is required to clear the blimp front door from the geared head's upper rails.

14.9b Camera Preparation

Remove offset viewfinder from camera (see Fig. 14–28). Magazine may be on camera and threaded. Remove matte-box bracket and rods from camera.

14.9c Access

To Blimp Interior. Rotate scalloped access knob (see Fig. 14–20*a*) at back of blimp counterclockwise to open. Top, hinged at front, lifts up and away from Operator. (Some blimps may have a button in the handle that is depressed to open.)

CAUTION: On older blimps, place a small wooden wedge at hinge, to prevent the blimp top from accidentally dropping shut.

To Lenses (see Fig. 14–20*b*). Rotate lens-access knob on front door counterclockwise; open door, and swing it to the right.

To Motor. Rotate counterclockwise the two knurled screws on the motor cover (see Fig. 14–20*a*). Lift cover from holding lugs.

14.9d Camera Insertion

(1) Swing front door open. Loosen lens-coupling-arm lock (not shown), and move the coupling-arm gear (not shown) toward left side of blimp. (2) Raise blimp hood. Slide camera onto internal plate (see Fig.14–20*a*) until front and right sides of camera base fit against stops. Rotate offset camera-lockdown knob at rear of plate until $\frac{3}{8}$"-16 screw in center locks camera to plate. Camera may be placed in blimp with motor and magazine in place.

14.9e Powerline

External (see Fig. 14–20*a*). Uses standard camera line. Cannon plug inserts into fitting on motor cover.

Internal. Extension (in motor cover) fits into camera body. Line must follow contour of cover, or it may prevent camera from racking over properly.

NOTE: Motor cover on right side of blimp might be fitted with an ON/OFF switch holder, but this is a luxury, not standard equipment.

14.9f Sunshade/Blimp Hood (Fig. 14–20*b*)

Slides into recess on front door.

To Lock. Slide hood latch (on outside of front door) *down*.

To Soundproof. Insert optical flat glass (inside door) into recess. To lock in place, turn small knurled latch (not shown) clockwise.

14.9g Internal Light

Toggle Switch (see Fig. 14–20*b*). Located at left side of blimp exterior below the lens magnifying window. Light is inside blimp front and illuminates the taking-lens barrel (see Fig. 14–20*a*). The combination of magnifying lens and internal light provides an easy visual check of lens and footage settings. Internal battery-powered bulb in a flexible socket may be moved to various positions around the top of the camera turret.

To Change Batteries. (1) Open the lens-access door. Reach in and unlock internal-spring holder (above lens-access door). (2) Lower the holder, remove cap; insert new batteries, replace holder above lens-access door.

CAUTION: Lamp must be turned "OFF" while shooting so that optical flat in the door will not reflect light into the lens.

14.9h Coupling Alignment
Lenses: (1) Rotate lens-access knob (see Fig. 14–20*b*) below matte box, and swing front door open. (2) Loosen coupling-arm lock (not shown), and move coupling-arm gear away from taking lens. (3) Rotate follow-focus knob (see Fig. 14–20*b*) counterclockwise until cam holder on worm gear is as far *forward* as it will go. (4) Set lens at infinity, or slightly beyond if teeth will not mesh precisely at infinity. (5) Set coupling-arm gear into teeth of geared ring on lens; tighten coupling-arm lock. (6) Set *f*/stop manually; close front door. (7) Place cam (of the same focal length as taking lens) onto follow-focus cam holder (see Fig. 14–20*a*).

14.9i Filters
Two 50.8mm × 50.8mm (2 × 2 in.) glass filter holders (on a single bracket arm) (see Fig. 14–20*a*) slide on short rods attached to plate inside blimp.

14.9j Viewfinder (Figs. 14–20*a*, 14–20*b*, and 14–28)
Same as the one used on the camera. It slides into dovetail on blimp follow-focus bracket (see Fig. 14–20*a*).
    To Use. Install two-piece harness at rear of finder (see Fig. 14–20*a*).
Harness
Upper Section (piece 1) (see Figs. 14–20*a* and 14–20*b*): Consists of a straight flat bar containing two long knurled screws.
Lower Section (piece 2) (see Fig. 14–20*a*): Consists of a Y-shaped bracket with heavy base. The base includes (a) a cam roller (steel bushing that rides against cam), (b) cam-adjusting screw (to make fine adjustment of *vertical* finder cross hair to match cross hair in focusing tube),

NOTE: To align *horizontal* cross hair, see Sec. 14.9k.

(c) cam-adjusting-screw lock (frees and secures cam-adjusting screw), (d) two tapped holes (to receive knurled screws from upper section).
    The Y-shaped bracket includes (a) 90° raised edges at the end of each arm, (b) a finder-return spring (hook on spring attaches to blimp follow-focus unit, causing viewfinder to ride on cam).
    To Install Harness. (1) Hook the 90° raised edges of the Y-shaped bracket to bottom rear of finder (see Fig. 14–20*a*). (2) Rest upper flat bar across top of viewfinder, and secure screws into tapped holes in lower section. (See Sec. 14.11b, Fig. 14–24.)

CAUTION: Hand-tighten only!

NOTE: Harness for blimp differs from harness of a standard follow-focus attachment (see Sec. 14.11b), in that the blimp cam roller is an integral part of the harness, and *cams* ride on the blimp follow-focus worm-gear unit. In a standard follow-focus attachment, the cams fit to the harness, and the cam *roller* rides on the worm gear.

14.9k Follow-Focus Bracket

Left side. Bracket consists of a follow-focus knob attached to a worm gear, which moves the cam holder. (See Figs. 14–20*a* and 14–20*b*.)

To Clear Viewfinder from Side of Blimp. Loosen follow-focus bracket lockdown knob, swing follow-focus bracket and viewfinder vertically.

NOTE: The follow-focus bracket is held horizontally along the axis of the lens by securing the follow-focus-bracket lockdown knob, and is adjustable up and down.

To Align Horizontal Cross Hair. In viewfinder, with cross hair in focusing tube: (1) Loosen locknut (beneath bracket lockdown knob). (2) Adjust vertical-bracket height screw up or down until horizontal cross hair in viewfinder matches horizontal cross hair reference point in focusing tube. Tighten locknut.

NOTE: The 16mm blimp follow-focus bracket differs from the standard follow-focus attachment, which fits directly to camera. (See Sec. 14.11b.)

14.9l Cams (Figs. 14–20*a* and 14–20*b*)

Cam holder must be as far forward on the follow-focus bracket as possible, prior to mounting a cam on it.

To Mount. (1) Loosen cam-lockdown screw (not shown) in cam holder, and place cam on rear pilot pin (with hypotenuse of cam facing left and rear). (2) Pivot cam forward, and slide it under the cam-lockdown screw until notches in the cam abut the cam-lockdown screw and the forward pilot pin. Lock into place.

NOTE: When cams are not slotted, remove the cam-lockdown screw, place cam on pilot pins (not shown) of cam holder, and replace the cam-lockdown screw.

Finder-Return Spring. Must be attached in order for the finder to ride the cam.

Parallax Check. Should be made at every change of lens and cam, to verify alignment of viewfinder and focusing-tube cross hairs.

NOTE: Cams fitted to a blimp are placed on the holder differently than cams fitted to a standard follow-focus attachment. (See Sec. 14.11b, Fig. 14–24.)

14.9m Ports

Window at back of blimp permits viewing of tachometer, footage counter, and bubble level. (Some blimps do not have a back window—blimp must be opened to check tachometer, footage counter, etc.) Magnifying window at left front above focusing knob permits viewing of footage and aperture setting on lens.

14.9n Weight

(without camera) 20.4kg (45 lb)

14.10 MITCHELL R16 (SS AND DS) CAMERAS (Fig. 14–21)

NOTE: All directions are from Operator's point of view.

NOTE: Manufacturer states that the model SS-R16 (single system) reflex and the model DS-R16 (double system) reflex cameras are physically and optically the same in all respects, except that the Model DS-R16 is not equipped with an integral sound-recording capability. The DS-R16 film

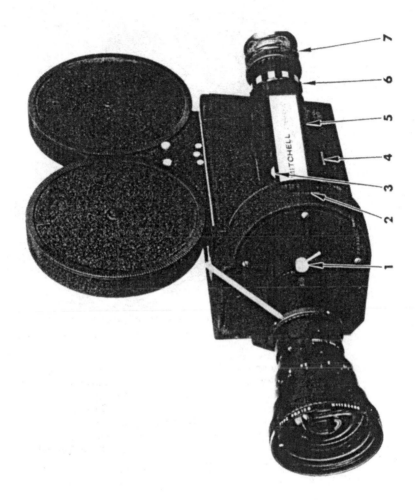

Figure 14-21a Mitchell SS-R16 and DS-R16 (front view). Courtesy of Mitchell Camera Corp.

1. Lens lock
2. Offset-viewfinder bracket mount
3. Light-trap wheel
4. Door latch
5. Focusing tube
6. Eyepiece locking ring
7. Eyepiece

Figure 14–21b Mitchell SS-R16 and DS-R16 (rear view). Courtesy of Mitchell Camera Corp.

1. Carrying handle
2. Magazine lockdown knob
3. Camera power plug
4. Rear-motor latch
5. 12-volt DC governor-controlled (constant-speed motor)
6. Manual motor-turning knob
7. Adapter plate (base section)
8. Adapter plate (top section)
9. Sound connector plug
10. Tachometer
11. ON/OFF switch
12. Eyepiece
13. Footage counter
14. Buckle-trip reset button

movement is provided with an optional single- or dual-pin registration. Also, the DS-R16 uses only two film drive sprockets instead of three, as found on the SS-R16.

14.10a Base

Bottom is fitted with two $\frac{3}{8}$"-16 and one $\frac{1}{4}$"-20 tapped holes to accommodate tripod-lockdown screw. The Mitchell R16 does *not* have an L-shaped base as do other Mitchell cameras; there are *no* four-way mattes, and there is *no* rackover device.

14.10b Adapter Plate (see Fig. 14–21b)

The unit is optional, thus not used with every camera. It is utilized as a quick disconnect from shoulder-pod to tripod (and vice versa) and is in two sections. Top section of plate is wedge-shaped and fitted with one $\frac{3}{8}$"-16 threaded screw, which attaches it to bottom of camera. Wedge inserts into base of adapter. Bottom of adapter base is fitted with one $\frac{3}{8}$"-16 tapped hole for placement on a tripod head.

To Release Wedge. Pull spring-loaded lock pin at left side of base; slide camera back and away.

14.10c Viewfinder/Focusing Tube (see Fig. 14–21a)

Reflex. Magnifies $10 \times$. Views more than full aperture area.

NOTE: An offset-viewfinder bracket (not shown) is not standard but might be mounted on turret housing.

Focusing Tube. In camera door as an integral part of reflex system.

To Align Reflex Mirror for Viewing. Rotate manual motor-turning knob at side of motor.

To Change or Clean Groundglass. (1) Remove taking lens. Reach through lens port with fingers, grasp edges of groundglass, and pull. (2) Reinsert into camera, making certain that chamfered edges are "in" and the V-notch *up*.

NOTE: The Mitchell R16 does *not* have a matte slot, nor does it take an effects matte.

CAUTION: It is extremely important to reach through the lens port and push the groundglass into its stop each time the camera is set up.

Eyepiece (see Figs. 14–21a and 14–21b). Slides in and out; adjusts to achieve focus on groundglass. Scalloped ring locks eyepiece at desired focus.

Light trap. Rotate knurled light-trap wheel (in forward part of focusing tube) (see Fig. 14–21a) forward (counterclockwise) to close the viewing system. Light trap should be closed when an offset viewfinder is used instead of the reflex system, so that stray light cannot strike mirror and kick back onto film.

14.10d Motors (see Fig. 14–21b)

Fitted to right side of camera box.

NOTE: *Synchronous motors* (not shown) and governor-controlled (constant-speed, shown) motors have manual motor-turning knob located at side. *Variable-speed motors* (not shown) have manual motor-turning knob at the right side, the speed-control rheostat at the back.

To Mount Synchronous, Governor-Controlled (constant-speed), or Variable-Speed Motor. (1) Rotate manual motor-turning knob until drive coupling and five-pin Cannon plug aligns with drive shaft and receptacle in camera. (2) Snug motor against camera. Rotate the motor latches on camera body (forward latch clockwise, rear latch counterclockwise) until they are vertical.

To Reverse Variable-Speed Motor. (1) Turn motor switch to "REV." (2) Transfer belt from take-up to feed spindle wheel. Loop the belt into a figure-8; this will cause feed to act as take-up; adjust motor speed.

CAUTION: Cover lens when running film back to beginning of scene intended for double exposure.

Motors Available for the Mitchell SS and DS-R16.
Variable-Speed Motor. 110V AC/DC (60 Hz) (12–36 fps; 24–64 fps); 110V AC/DC (50 Hz) (12–36 fps; 24–64 fps).
Governor-Controlled (Constant-Speed) Motor. 12V DC (24 fps); 12V DC (25 fps).

Synchronous Motor. 110V AC (60 Hz) (single phase); 110V AC (50 Hz) (single phase).

Animation Motor. None.

14.10e Powerline

Input to Camera. Insert into recessed five-pin male Cannon receptacle at back of camera. Pins read clockwise, starting from keyway: pin 1 is ON/OFF switch to camera; pins 2 and 3 are buckle-trip switch; pin 4 is synchronous generator; pin 5 is ground for 12V DC.

For 115V AC, pins 1 and 3 are AC power.

Sound-Connector plug. Pins 1 and 2 are reproduce head; pin 3 is shielded ground; pins 4 and 5 are record head.

ON/OFF rocker-type *switch* is at back of camera.

14.10f Turret

Newer Models (see Fig. 14–21*a*). Single-lens turret port accommodates varifocal (zoom) lens. Lens-lock lever is in *center* of turret. Turret does *not* rotate.

Older Models (not shown). Three position; 20° divergence. Unlike any other Mitchell camera, the position of the taking lens is *above the turret-release lever.*

To Rotate Three-Lens Turret. Depress turret-release lever at lower right of turret. Grasp turret grips (there are three), and turn turret to bring desired lens into position. Release turret-release lever to lock turret.

14.10g Lenses

The base of the R16 lens mount is similar in appearance to an Arriflex mount—i.e., it has a lens channel that inserts into a turret port key, and base has a circular groove that is grasped by blades located within turret.

To Fit Lens to Turret

Newer Models. Align the channel at rear of varifocal lens to the guide key (inside port). Rotate clockwise the lens-lock lever at center of turret to clear blades in port. Insert the lens. Rotate lens lock counterclockwise to engage blades in lens groove. Give snug fit to lens lock—do not tighten!

Older Models. Grasp lens by knurled footage ring. Align channel (at rear of mount) with the guide key (inside port). Squeeze locking levers at each side of lens port on turret, and insert lens into port. Release locking levers. Pull lens gently to ascertain mount is locked into port.

To Remove Lens

Newer Models. Rotate center lens-lock lever clockwise; grasp lens, and pull gently out of port.

Older Models. Grasp knurled footage ring. Squeeze locking levers at each side of lens port, and pull lens away.

CAUTION: On a three-lens turret, always plug an empty port(s) when using fewer than three lenses, to prevent a light leak.

14.10h Sunshade/Matte Box

None.

14.10i Filters

Each lens accommodates a circular glass filter in retaining ring.

Gelatine: Filter slot for internal filter is located in aperture plate (*inside* the camera—see Figs. 14–22*a* and 14–22*b*). The camera door must be opened each time a filter holder is inserted (or removed). When inserting filter holder, bent portion of holder (used as a fingergrip) should be pointed toward Operator. To check filter after insertion in aperture plate, remove the taking lens to expose aperture opening. Determine visually that gelatine "covers" the aperture.

CAUTION: Manufacturer emphasizes frequent inspection of the filter. Dirt or lint on gelatine may register on film when lens is stopped down. Manufacturer recommends that gelatine filter be removed after each take and inspected. Many Camera Professionals refuse to use the internal filter.

14.10j Door
Hinged at top.
To Open. Lift hatch below viewfinder, pull out and up.
To Close. Lift door to relieve hinge catch. Lower the door so that it is flush with camera; pull focusing tube to verify that door is secure.

14.10k Magazines
122m (400-ft) 366m (1200-ft)
To Mount. (1) Pull a loop from magazine feed side. (2) Insert magazine toe into magazine guide groove (at top of camera). Draw film loop into camera body. (3) Slide magazine forward and down until tapped hole in magazine heel aligns with magazine-lockdown screw. Rotate magazine-lockdown knob (at top right, rear of motor mount) clockwise to tighten magazine to camera. Thread camera (see Sec. 14.10l).
To Remove. Unthread film, and break it. Place two fingers under the belt, pull laterally away from magazine, rotate fingers clockwise, and lift belt from spindle-wheel groove. Disengage the magazine by rotating the lockdown knob counterclockwise; lift magazine clear of camera.

14.10l Threading

Model SS-R16 (Single System) (Fig. 14-22a).

1. Press buckle-trip toward rear of camera to avoid accidental starting of camera during threading procedure, then (a) pull pin and move the sprocket-guide 1 (located at upper-left front) *down;* (b) pull pin, and move sprocket-guide 2 (center bottom) toward back of camera; (c) pull pin, and move sprocket-guide 3 roller (at the upper-right rear) toward back of camera.
2. Rotate manual motor-turning knob (see Fig. 14–21b) until single pulldown claw (at the bottom of its stroke) retracts from aperture plate. Rotate registration-pin throw-out knob counterclockwise.
3. Raise aperture-plate lock, remove aperture plate by pulling *gently.* If plate does not slide easily, check to see whether pulldown claw and/or registration pin is clear of plate.
4. Clean plate. Make a special check of registration-pin and pulldown-claw holes for emulsion buildup or film chips. Replace the plate. Depress aperture-plate lock to secure.
5. Rotate pressure-plate spring arm clockwise. Remove pressure plate from register plate. Clean. Replace pressure plate and spring arm.
6. Pull film from magazine feed side. Extend loop to front corner of camera (a rough guide for amount of film needed for threading). Starting from magazine feed side, insert film (a) in groove (the race) between removable aperture plate and stationary register plate; (b) to right of feed-side throat roller; (c) over upper film-guide roller and between

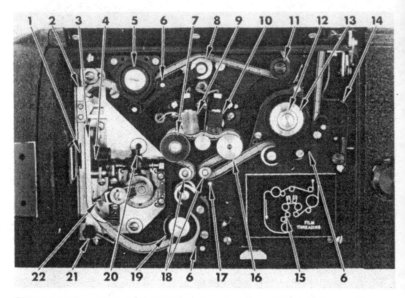

Figure 14–22a Mitchell SS-R16 threading. Courtesy of Mitchell Camera Corp.

1. Filter slot
2. Aperture plate
3. Register plate
4. Pressure plate
5. Sprocket 1
6. Sprocket guides
7. Sound roller
8. Upper film-guide roller
9. Record head
10. Reproduce head
11. Throat roller

12. Sprocket-adjusting knob
13. Sprocket 3
14. Buckle-trip apron
15. Threading diagram
16. Sound drum
17. Tension-roller alignment dot
18. Adjustable tension rollers
19. Sprocket 2
20. Registration-pin throw-out knob
21. Aperture-plate lock
22. Pulldown claw

sprocket guide and (upper-left) sprocket 1; (d) between (center-bottom) sprocket 2 and sprocket guide; (e) to right of left tension roller; (f) to left of the sound roller; (g) below record and reproduce heads; (h) to right of sound drum; (i) to left of right tension roller; (j) between (upper rear) sprocket 3 and sprocket guide.

7. Align one film perforation hole to film-positioning pin at base of aperture plate, and press film onto pin. Use forefinger and little finger to hold film above and below the register plate. Rotate the manual motor-turning knob counterclockwise until pulldown claw engages film perforation. Registration pin will drop in automatically with one full rotation of manual motor-turning knob.

8. Set pulldown claw at bottom of its stroke: (a) Adjust upper loop so that when sprocket guide 1 closes, arc of loop aligns with top of aperture plate. (b) Adjust lower loop so that when sprocket guide 2 closes, arc of loop clears bottom of camera by 3.175mm × 6.35mm (1/8–1/4".)

9. Close sprocket guide 3. Pull out geared knob on sprocket 3 to disengage camera drive. Rotate knob until tension on film threaded through camera aligns the center of the left-hand tension roller with the red dot on the mechanism plate and aligns the center of the right-hand tension roller with the white dot on the mechanism plate. Depress the geared knob on sprocket 3 to engage camera drive.

10. Rotate magazine take-up spindle wheel clockwise to eliminate film slack. Place uncrossed belt at bottom of take-up spindle wheel and, in a clockwise direction, slip belt into wheel groove (this follows the rotation of the take-up wheel and subjects belt to a minimum of stretching).

11. Rotate manual motor-turning knob, and observe film being transported in camera. If satisfactory, proceed.

12. Press buckle-trip reset button (at back of camera above footage counter—see Fig. 14–21b). Apply power in short bursts, and observe action of film. If satisfactory, stop camera and close door. Reset footage counter.

NOTE: *When using silent film in single-system camera,* after threading sprocket 2, bypass the sound heads and tension rollers by inserting the film below the right tension roller and into sprocket 3 (follow dotted line in diagram).

Model DS-R16 (Double-System) (see Fig. 14–22b)

1. Move buckle-trip toward rear of camera to avoid accidental starting of camera during threading procedure, then (a) pull pin, and move sprocket guide 1 (located at upper-left front) *down;* (b) pull pin and move sprocket guide 2 (at the upper-right rear) toward back of camera.

2. Rotate manual motor-turning knob (see Fig. 14–21b) until pulldown claw (at the top of its stroke) retracts from aperture plate. Rotate registration-pin throw-out knob counterclockwise.

3. Raise aperture-plate lock, remove aperture plate by pulling *gently.* If plate does not slide easily, check to see whether pulldown claw and/or registration pin is clear of plate.

4. Clean plate. Make a special check of registration-pin and pulldown-claw holes for emulsion buildup or film chips. Replace the plate. Depress aperture-plate lock to secure.

5. Rotate pressure-plate spring arm clockwise. Remove pressure plate from register plate; clean. Replace pressure plate and spring arm.

6. Pull film from magazine feed side. Extend loop to front corner of camera (a rough guide for amount of film needed for threading). Starting from the magazine feed side, insert film (a) in groove (the race) between the removable aperture plate and the stationary register plate; (b) to right of feed-side throat roller; (c) over upper film-guide roller and between sprocket guide and sprocket 1 (upper left); (d) over lower (small) idler roller; (e) under upper (large) idler roller; (f) between sprocket 2 (upper rear) and sprocket guide.

7. Align one film perforation hole with film-positioning pin at base of aperture plate, and press film onto pin. Use forefinger and little finger to hold film above and below the register plate. Rotate the manual motor-turning knob (see Fig. 14–21b) counterclockwise until pulldown

Figure 14–22b Mitchell DS-R16 threading. Courtesy of Mitchell Camera Corp.

1. Filter slot
2. Pressure plate
3. Sprocket 1
4. Upper film-guide roller
5. Throat roller
6. Sprocket-adjusting knob
7. Sprocket 2
8. Buckle-trip apron
9. Upper idler roller
10. Lower idler roller
11. Registration-pin throw-out knob
12. Varistroke adjustment
13. Aperture-plate lock
14. Pulldown claw

claw engages film perforation. Registration pin will drop in automatically with one full rotation of the manual motor-turning knob.

8. Set pulldown claw at bottom of its stroke, and adjust upper loop so that when sprocket guide 1 closes, arc of loop aligns with top of aperture plate.

9. Close sprocket guide 2. Pull out geared knob on sprocket 2 to disengage camera drive. Rotate knob until lower loop clears bottom of camera by 1/8–1/4 in. at lowest arc of loop. Depress geared knob on sprocket 2 to engage camera drive.

10. Rotate magazine take-up spindle wheel clockwise to eliminate film slack. Place uncrossed belt at bottom of take-up spindle wheel and, in a clockwise direction, slip belt into wheel groove (this follows rotation of take-up wheel and subjects belt to a minimum of stretching).

11. Rotate the manual motor-turning knob, and observe film being transported in camera. If satisfactory, proceed.

12. Press buckle-trip reset button (at back of camera above footage counter—see Fig. 14–21b). Apply power in short bursts, and observe action of film. If satisfactory, stop camera and close door. Reset footage counter.

NOTE: Because the Model DS-R16 movement is provided with optional single- or dual-pin registration, it is important to verify the type of movement in the camera before ordering film stock. When in doubt, order double-perforated film for the DS-R16.

14.10m Buckle-trip
Apron (a curved metal plate), located behind geared sprocket (sprocket 3 on the Model SS-R16 behind sprocket 2 on the Model DS-R16), cuts out power automatically if film fails to take up. Power should be cut out prior to threading by tripping the apron, to avoid accidental starting of the camera.

To Reset, push button located above footage counter at back of camera.

14.10n Footage Counter (see Fig. 14–21b).
Located at back of camera above tachometer. Additive. Non-metric. Registers each foot of film transported through camera up to 9999 ft, then reverts to 0 and counts forward again. May be reset to 0 each time magazine is changed.

Reset knob: Located at left rear near door.

No frame counter.

14.10o Tachometer (Fig. 14–21b)
Located at back of camera. Registers speed from 8 to 28 fps in increments of 2 fps. When speed exceeds 28 fps, camera tachometer is superseded by tachometer on a wild (variable-speed) or high-speed motor.

14.10p Shutter
Nonadjustable; 175°.

14.10q Lubrication (Fig. 14–23)
Manufacturer recommends lubricating the following parts every 304.8 meters (1000 ft) with one or two drops of camera oil: registration-pin pads ("oilers"); eccentric shaft and register-pin shaft surfaces; pulldown-claw cam-plunger arm; eccentric (through lube holes).

NOTE: After oiling, run camera to eliminate excess oil, and wipe interior.

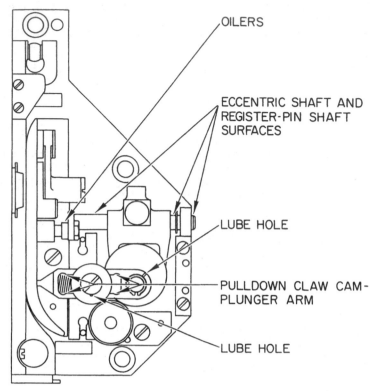

OILERS

ECCENTRIC SHAFT AND
REGISTER-PIN SHAFT
SURFACES

LUBE HOLE

PULLDOWN CLAW CAM-
PLUNGER ARM

LUBE HOLE

Figure 14–23 Mitchell SS-R16 and DS-R16 lubrication. Courtesy of Mitchell Camera Corp.

14.10r Cleaning

Optics: Clean with bulb syringe or soft camel's-hair brush.

Manufacturer recommends the following maintenance *each time film is changed:* (1) Remove aperture and pressure plates. (2) Remove emulsion buildup with orangewood stick. (3) Wipe plates with soft cotton (not linen) handkerchief. (4) Use bulb syringe on camera interior to remove dust, dirt, etc.

14.10s Weight

With 122m (400-ft) load: Model SS-R16, 11.1kg (24 $\frac{1}{2}$ lb); Model DS-R16, 10.4kg (23 lb). With 366m (1200-ft) load: Model SS-R16, 16kg (35 lb); Model DS-R16, 15.2kg (33 1/2 lb.)

14.10t Troubleshooting

Trouble	*Probable Cause*
Camera will not start	Buckle-trip not reset; powerline connection faulty; low temperature
Camera door will not close	Sprocket-guide rollers not seated; registration-pin throw-out knob not forward; film chip or dirt in door

Camera "hunts"	Camera not warmed up; voltage variation in line
Film jam	Improper threading; take-up belt not on; camera drive not engaged on sprocket 2 on DS or on sprocket 3 on SS; magazine cover not relieved on dished roll
Lens will not focus	Lens not seated in turret; turret not seated properly; lens damaged
Film will not slide into race	Registration-pin or pulldown claw not retracted; emulsion or film chip in race
Torn or punctured film	Improper threading
Film scratches	Dirt or emulsion buildup in aperture plate, sprocket-guide rollers, pressure plate, registration-pin or magazine rollers
Cut-in on viewing tube	Shutter not clear of reflex mirror; turret not seated properly
"Wow" or "flutter" on sound phones	Tension rollers not aligned to red and white marks on camera mechanism
No take-up or sporadic take-up	Belt slipping, or belt too loose; film off take-up core; loose power connection; take-up clutch too loose or too tight.*

14.10u R16 Magazine-Loading Instructions
See Section 14.8.

14.11 MITCHELL ACCESSORIES

14.11a Mitchell Camera Belt

All Model Belts (except S35R)

To Replace Old Belt. (1) Detach *one* end of old belt from hook, and attach one end of *new* belt to that hook (so that it appears to be a continuation of the old belt). (2) Pull old belt out of camera, automatically bringing new belt into place in camera. (3) When new belt is in place, detach old belt; insert hook through end of new belt, squeezing the hook into belt with pliers.

NOTE: New belt lengths may not have an eyelet for the hook; a jeweler's punch is ideal for punching a new eyelet. Care should be taken to place eyelet properly, leaving no space between belt ends because this would place unnecessary strain on both hook and ends.

To Clean. Soak stretched or greasy belts in a capped jar of alcohol for a few days.

To adjust take-up clutch: (1) Before making *any* adjustment, ascertain that belt is not greasy or has not stretched. (2) Remove motor. (3) Locate the clutch-adjustment screw (at upper left between flywheel and female five-pin motor receptacle). (4) Insert screwdriver into clutch-adjustment screw (on the Model SS, it is in center of motor side of sprocket-gear shaft 3, on Model DS, it is in center of motor side of sprocket-gear shaft 2. (5) Rotate screw in or out so that film magazine takes up immediately upon starting of camera. (6) Replace motor.

CAUTION: Adjust carefully in quarter-turns of the screw. Too tight an adjustment will render the clutch inoperative. Too loose an adjustment will cause film to buckle or take up loosely on core.

WARNING: Always use in a well-ventilated room.

Treat cleaned belts by pulling belt through cotton dipped in neat's-foot oil.

S35R Belt

To Change Top-Load Type. Pull belt retainer slide *up* (located at point where belt enters camera body); remove belt from grooved drive wheel by pushing belt down and away from wheel. Loop new belt, and insert into slot under drive wheel. Replace belt retainer slide.

To Change Slant-Load-Adapter Type. Remove knurled screw at right of adapter; unhook belt; attach new belt, and pull through.

14.11b Mitchell Follow-Focus Attachment (Fig. 14–24)

The Mitchell follow-focus attachment is an L-shaped unit consisting of matte-box rods, lens-focusing gear, worm gear with cam roller, dovetail pivot bracket, finder harness, and cams.

Matte-Box Rods. The short rod inserts into left hole at front of bracket. The long rod inserts into right hole. Secure both with extension-tube retaining screws.

Focusing Knob. A scalloped knob attached to a worm gear, which moves the cam roller. The circular plastic marking plate behind it is used to scribe the focus changes.

Lens-Focusing Gear. Meshes with a geared ring on lens.

NOTE: The lens-focusing gear on the 35mm follow-focus attachment (not shown) is in *two sections:* Front section may be pulled away from rear section to permit pressing the matte box closer to a wide-angle lens. (Pull pin at front of gear to separate sections.)

One tooth of both sections is painted white with a witness mark, which is aligned with one tooth of the gear ring on the lens similarly marked.

When both sections are locked together, witness mark on front focusing gear must be aligned to witness mark on back focusing gear (rotate front section until front gear pin locks into rear gear).

The 16mm follow-focus attachment (see Fig. 14–24) has only *one* lens-focusing gear with witness mark and does not separate.

Cam Roller. Rides on worm gear. Roller must be as far to rear (infinity) as possible before meshing the lens-focus gear to geared ring of a lens set at infinity. Spring-loaded locknut below the roller pulls out; cam roller drops forward in a restricted slot so that camera door may open all the way.

Dovetail Pivot Bracket. Inserts into camera dovetail so that viewfinder may be tilted up and forward to gain access to camera interior.

Finder Harness. Two-piece.

Upper Section. Consists of a straight flat bar containing two long knurled screws.

Lower Section. Consists of Y-shaped bracket with heavy base. Base consists of (a) cam holder (two pins and lockdown screw); (b) cam-adjusting screw (to make fine adjustments of *vertical* finder cross hair in focusing tube);

NOTE: To adjust *horizontal* cross hair, turn hex screw in dovetail pivot bracket.

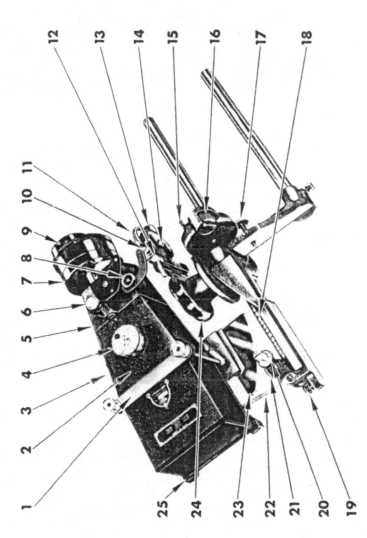

1. Finder harness: upper section
2. 16mm offset viewfinder
3. Vertical matte-adjusting knob (partially obscured)
4. Horizontal matte-adjusting knob
5. Focus knob
6. Focus-lock knob
7. Prison box
8. Parallax lock knob
9. Circular sunshade
10. Vertical-adjustment screw
11. Finder-tilt lock (not visible)
12. Dovetail lock
13. Dovetail pivot bracket
14. Pivot point
15. Focus-gear engaging lever
16. Lens-focus gear
17. Front-attaching thumbscrew
18. Worm gear
19. Side-attaching thumbscrew
20. Cam roller
21. Cam-roller-release knob
22. Finder-return spring
23. Cam
24. Focus knob
25. Finder harness: lower section

Figure 14–24 16mm Mitchell follow-focus attachment. Compare 16mm offset viewfinder with Figure 14–28.

NOTE: Focus knob is often factory removed when finder is used on follow-focus attachment. Courtesy of Mitchell Camera Corp.

(c) two tapped holes (to receive knurled screws from upper section). Y-shaped bracket consists of (a) 90° raised bracket at end of each arm; (b) a finder-return spring (hook on spring attaches to screw at rear of cam roller, causing cam to ride on roller).

To Install Finder Harness. (1) Hook 90° brackets of Y to bottom rear of finder; (2) Rest upper flat bar across top of finder, and secure the screws into tapped holes in lower section.

CAUTION: Hand-tighten only.

NOTE: Harness for viewfinder differs from harness on Mitchell 16 Blimp (see Sec. 14.9j), in that the *cams* fit to the harness and cam *roller* rides on the worm gear. On the 16mm blimp, cams fit to the worm gear and roller, which are an integral part of the harness.

To Mount Follow-Focus Attachment on Camera. (1) Loosen lens-focusing-gear engaging lever; move lens-focusing gear toward follow-focus knob; lock. (2) Rotate follow-focus knob until cam roller is at extreme rear of bracket (infinity). (3) Insert the two bracket-locating pins (one at each side of front attaching thumb screw) into mating tapped hole and register holes at front base of camera; tighten thumb screw. Secure side-attaching thumb screw (rear of cam roller) into camera. (4) Set lens to infinity; make certain that cam roller is in upright position; loosen focusing-gear engaging lever; engage lens-focusing gear and geared ring on lens; lock focusing-gear engaging lever. (5) Place dovetail pivot/bracket into camera dovetail; secure. (6) Place harness on finder; slide finger into dovetail pivot bracket. (7) Place cam that corresponds to lens in taking position on finder-cam bracket (hypotenuse of cam faces right and toward rear); engage finder-return spring.

14.11c Mitchell Variable-Diffusion Assembly (Fig. 14–25)

Used for special diffusion effects. Two glass graduated diffusers in holders are on rack-and-pinion gears. The optically flat glass of the forward diffuser overlays the optically flat glass of the rear diffuser. When the operating knob is rotated to change the scale from "1" to "12," the holders simultaneously traverse the camera lens in opposite directions, gradually increasing the diffusion to the capacity of the two diffusers. Shoulder of the numbered scale limits lateral movement of holders. The scale scribed 1–12 is for reference only, as to the amount of diffusion desired.

When a scene calls for a movement from a long shot to a close-up and requires diffusion on the close-up only, the amount of diffusion used on the close subject is determined visually by the Director of Photography. Reference number on scale is noted and marked by the Camera Assistant. As movement is made, the operating knob is rotated from 1 (clear) to the reference number for the desired amount of diffusion.

A 89mm × 101.6mm (3 1/2 × 4 in.) filter may be mounted in a holder forward of the diffuser holders.

To Mount. Slide wide-angle matte box forward on rods. Lift matte-box filter-holder assembly at rear of matte box *up,* and remove. With operating knob at Camera Operator's left, insert variable-diffusion assembly on filter-holder assembly grooves; push down to its limit.

NOTE: (a) The variable diffusion assembly is manufactured for 16mm or 35mm cameras, and the camera size and desired diffusers should be noted when including the assembly as an accessory. (b) Diffusion glass is rated alphabetically: A = slight, B = moderate, C = heavy, and D = very heavy.

Figure 14–25 Mitchell diffusion holder. Courtesy of Mitchell Camera Corp.

1. Forward diffusion holder (not visible)   3. Operating knob
2. Reference scale   4. Rear diffusion holder

14.11d Mitchell Matte Cutters
Used when a film-frame effects matte is desired. The frame is cut and inserted into the focusing tube, to align an object in a previously filmed scene with an object to be photographed, in order to create as perfect a match dissolve as possible (e.g., art work to live action).

There are two types of matte cutters: block and book.

NC, BNC, Standard/High-Speed (block-type) Matte Cutter (Fig. 14–26a).   Two blocks of hard steel: *Lower block* contains a matte die; four registration pins; four guide posts. *Upper block* contains a matte punch; four bushings; Mitchell emblem. Upper block is attached to lower block by two spring-loaded screws secured through holes in lower block to the bar below the matte die. Guide posts of lower block ride in four bushings of the upper block, to assure alignment of the punch and die.

To Use.   (1) Mark two frames: the one in front of and the one in back of the frame intended for use. (2) Hold the cutter with the emblem right-side up. Insert the film vertically between the upper and lower blocks.

NOTE: Negative: film *emulsion* should face the user. Print: film *base* should face the user.

(3) Align the *top* of second sprocket perforation of the first marked frame with the top edge of the lower block. Align *bottom* of second perforation of the last marked frame with bottom edge of lower block. Place film on

Figure 14–26a Mitchell matte cutter, block type.

NOTE: Matte die and matte punch not visible. See book-type matte cutter for detail.

Courtesy of Mitchell Camera Corp.

1. Registration pins (2 of 4 visible)   3. Lower block
2. Guide post   4. Spring-loaded screw

registration pins. (4) Place index and second fingers of both hands at back of lower block. Place thumbs on spring-loaded screws. Press thumbs firmly until registration pins touch the top block—matte has then been cut. Release the spring-loaded screws, and shake the matte out. (5) Insert matte, upside down, into focusing-tube matte slot, with perforations toward access door.

S35R (book-type) Matte Cutter (Fig. 14–26b). Two pieces of hinged steel: *Lower block* contains a matte die and two registration pins. *Top block* contains the matte punch.

To Use.   (1) Mark two frames: the one in front of and the one in back of the frame intended for use. (2) Place hinge at left. Open the cutter, and insert the film vertically onto the lower block.

NOTE: Negative: Film emulsion should face user. Print: base should face user.

(3) Align the *top* of the second sprocket perforation of the leading frame with the top edge of the lower block. Align the *bottom* of the second perforation of the trailing frame with the bottom edge of the lower block. Place the film on the registration pins. (4) Close top block until the punch

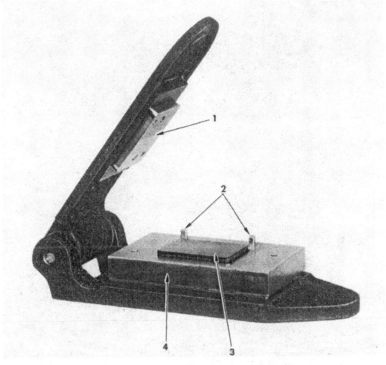

Figure 14–26b Mitchell matte cutter, book type. Courtesy of Mitchell Camera Corp.

1. Matte punch
2. Registration pins
3. Matte die
4. Lower block

hits the stop—the matte has then been cut. Open top block, and remove the matte. (5) Insert matte, upside down, into the slot in front of groundglass, with perforations toward the turret face.

14.11e Mitchell Varistroke Adjustment (Fig. 14–27)

The varistroke is an adjustment built into the camera movement to allow compensation for film-pitch variations and shrinkage.

By rotating the stroke adjustment knob, an eccentric shifts the claw-pivot block in relation to the registration pins and shortens or lengthens this dimension, in an effort to eliminate the "picking" noise.

The stroke-adjustment knob rotates clockwise ("plus") or counterclockwise ("minus"). Direction of rotation of the adjustment knob may differ on each roll because of variations in raw stock.

Correct plus or minus stroke is determined by listening while threaded film stock is run through camera with door open. Starting with the adjustment knob at zero, knob may be rotated in either direction until film noise diminishes to its lowest level.

If in doubt as to noise level, leave the adjustment knob at zero (center).

NOTE: The Varistroke unit is not installed in each Mitchell camera movement. It is generally found on sound models (BNC, SS-R16, etc.) or a silent model that can be blimped.

Figure 14–27 Mitchell varistroke adjustment. Circled area varistroke adjustment. Courtesy of Mitchell Camera Corp.

14.11f Plastic Mattes for Modified Mitchell Viewfinders

Plastic mattes for modified Mitchell viewfinders are rectangular slides with an aperture cut out in the center. The cutout area of the matte defines the correct top-and-bottom and side-to-side frame lines for Camera Operator.

Size of cutout of each matte is determined by a combination of two dimensions: a specific aspect ratio and a particular focal length (e.g., 1:85 to 1, 50mm; 1:85 to 1, 25mm; or 1:75 to 1, 100mm; 1:75 to 1, 30mm).

A number of mattes are kept together on a shower-curtain hook, in "sandwich" fashion. The desired matte is swiveled out from the "sandwich" (not removed from ring) and inserted into a slot in the left side

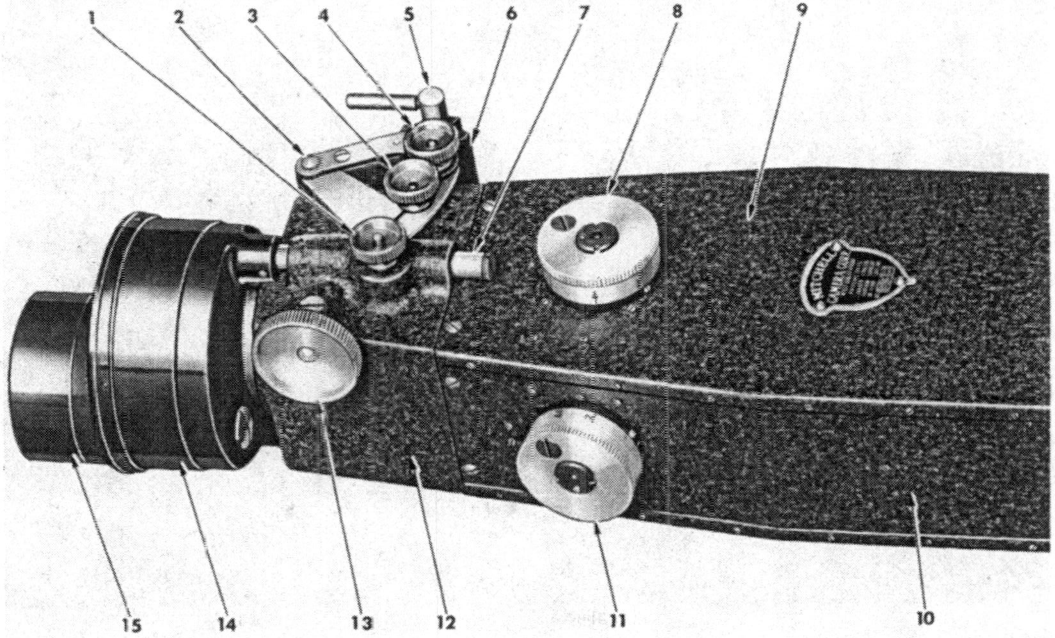

Figure 14-28 Mitchell offset-viewfinder for standard/high-speed, NC, and S35R models. Courtesy of Mitchell Camera Corp.

1. Focus lock knob
2. Pivot point
3. Parallax lock knob
4. Parallax throwout knob
5. Dovetail lock
6. Dovetail
7. Focus shaft
8. Vertical ribbon-matte adjusting knob
9. Top viewfinder plate
10. Left viewfinder wall
11. Horizontal ribbon-matte adjusting knob
12. Viewfinder nose piece
13. Focus knob
14. Prism box
15. Circular sunshade

469

Figure 14–29 Mitchell focusing tube (camera racked over). Courtesy of Mitchell Camera Corp.

1. Viewfinder dovetail
2. Filter slot
3. Academy and effects matte slot
4. Groundglass
5. Focusing-tube lens
6. Groundglass access door (open)
7. Magnification knob
8. Contrast filters
9. Eyepiece locking screws
10. Eyepiece

(occasionally, slot is in top of viewfinder). The matter, of course, must correspond to the taking lens.

The focal length *engraved* on each matte is inserted upright and toward Camera Operator.

Remaining mattes on the shower-curtain hook dangle from the matte that has been inserted into the viewfinder.

NOTE: Slotted viewfinders that accommodate mattes are *not* a standard Mitchell item; they have been modified.

Plastic mattes are used when a specific aspect ratio is preferred in the viewfinder (for composition purposes), while a full aperture negative is desired in the camera (e.g., filming for theatrical release at 1:85 to 1 ratio, with intentions of printing from the same negative for TV at a later date).

14.11g Mitchell Offset Viewfinder (Fig. 14–28)

14.11h Mitchell Focusing Tube Detail (Fig. 14–29)

chapter 15

MOVIECAM COMPACT
Camera, Magazines, and
Accessories

15.1 MOVIECAM COMPACT CAMERA (Figs. 15–1a, 15–1b, 15–1c)

NOTE: All directions are from the Operator's point of view.

15.1a Base

Fitted with two rows of 3/8"-16 tapped holes for mounting camera to either MOVIECAM Base Plate (See Sec. 15.3a) or Arriflex Base Plate, to a tripod, or to a geared head.

Row of two tapped holes (nearest viewfinder) are for mounting camera to a MOVIECAM Base Plate (see Accessories 15.3a, Base Plate).

Row of three tapped holes (nearest long accessory plug) are for mounting camera to the Arriflex Base Plate and/or Geared Head (see Chapter 9, Sec. 9.2a, Arriflex Geared Head, Sliding Base Plate), and/or Arriflex Bridge Plate (see Chapter 11, Sec. 11.11), or Arriflex Shoulder Support (see Arriflex Accessories, Chapter 11, Sec. 11.3k).

A velcro® adhesive strip (nearest Operator) is for mounting a MOVIECAM shoulder rest (see Sec. 15.3k, Shoulder Rest).

15.1b Motors

Built-in 24v DC Crystal-controlled. Nonremovable.
Can be set to run from 12 to 32 fps forward in one-frame increments.

NOTE: The camera can run at lesser or greater speeds and/or in reverse, but it requires the addition of a special accessory (see Super Speed Control Box, Sec. 15.3d), which allows for fps selection of from 2 to 50 fps forward, and 12 to 32 fps in reverse.

To Run Motor at Desired Speed. Frame Speed Selector located at right rear of camera Control Board Panel (see Sec. 15.1c, Powerline, below). Reset slots over and under two digits labeled PRESET, permit end of 2mm probe to be inserted and depress microbuttons that change the numbers. Top two slots subtract; lower two slots add.

NOTE: Speed set on digits does not appear on the fps LED display windows until the camera runs. With camera Off, the Control Board Panel (see Sec. 15.1c) window and the Footage Counters (see Sec. 15.1m) show 0 (zero) plus remaining footage in magazine. However, if speed selected is below 12 fps or higher than 32 fps, the panel window and the

473

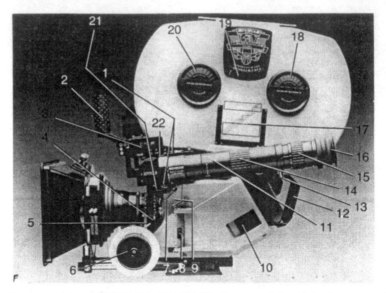

Figure 15–1a MOVIECAM COMPACT Camera (left side). Courtesy of MOVIECAM F.G. Bauer GmbH.

1. Prism adjusting screws
2. Carry handle
3. Ffs/footage readout
4. Lens lock
5. Lens-gear bracket
6. Focus knob
7. Dust check knob
8. On/Off button
9. 24-volt connectors
10. Door latch
11. Magnifier indicator

12. Topload adapter
13. Leveler-rod bracket
14. Magnifier zoom ring
15. Diopter-setting ring
16. Eyecup
17. Camera report holder
18. Take-up tightening wheel
19. Manual footage indicator
20. Feed tightening wheel
21. Eyepiece tension brake
22. Eyepiece release slider

footage counters will flash 12 or 32, to indicate that the setting is beyond the camera's capability.

15.1c Powerline

Input to camera. Four-pin XLR plug of 24 volt battery inserts into matching plug at rear of camera below magazine rail.

Counterclockwise from key, pin 1 is - (ground); pins 2 and 4 are 24v; pin 3 is blank.

On/Off Switch. Red button located at left side of camera between camera door hinges. Also on Control Board Panel (see next).

Control Board Panel (Fig. 15–2). Located at upper right rear of camera body.

On/Off Button. Uppermost large button.

fps Display window. Shows:

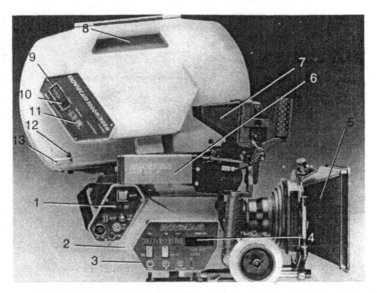

Figure 15–1b MOVIECAM COMPACT Camera (right side). Courtesy of MOVIECAM F.G. Bauer GmbH.

1. Control panel
2. Power connector (not visible)
3. Fuse access (not visible)
4. Super Speed Control Accessory
5. Matte-box
6. Color CCD accessory
7. Video monitor accessory

8. Magazine carry handle
9. Magazine footage/meter entry data buttons
10. Preset (read) button
11. Display window
12. Safety catch button (1 of 2)
13. Magazine lock latch (1 of 2)

   0   (zero) with camera in stand-by mode (not running)

   B   (buckle) if film jam occurs or buckle is tripped (see also 15.1k Buckle-trip, below)

  12   when camera runs at 12 fps. Otherwise flashes 12 when camera speed selection is set at less than 12 fps

  24   when camera runs at 24 fps

  32   when camera runs at 32 fps. Otherwise flashes 32 when camera speed selection is set at more than 32 fps

 DC   when electronic inching knob (see Sec. 15.1f, Viewfinder) and aperture is open

With a Super Speed Control Box on the camera, the display also shows the following warnings:

MSP   Flashes when speed selected on the speed box is either too high or too low.

   2   Camera running at 2 fps, but when flashing indicates that an invalid lower speed has been selected.

 50   Camera running at 50 fps, but when flashing indicates that an invalid higher speed has been selected.

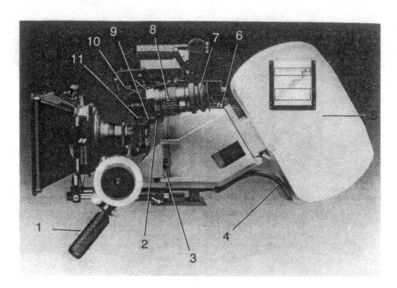

Figure 15–1c MOVIECAM COMPACT Camera hand-held configuration. Courtesy of MOVIECAM F.G. Bauer GmbH.

1. Balance handle
2. Dust check knob
3. On/Off button
4. Shoulder rest
5. 122m (400′) magazine
6. Rear mount adapter

7. Short eyepiece eyecup
8. Diopter-setting ring
9. Prism
10. Eyepiece release slider
11. Eyepiece tension brake

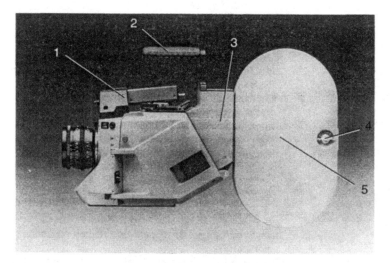

Figure 15–1d MOVIECAM COMPACT Camera Steadicam configuration. Courtesy of MOVIECAM F.G. Bauer GmbH.

1. Lightweight video camera
2. Carry handle
3. Adapter throat

4. Magazine lock
5. 122m (400′) plastic magazine

Figure 15–2 MOVIECAM COMPACT control panel detail. Courtesy of MOVIECAM F.G. Bauer GmbH.

1. On/Off button
2. Fps display
3. Fps setting
4. Acoustic beeper
5. Acoustic volume control knob
6. Sync connector
7. Take-up/TV bar button

- 12   Camera running in reverse at 12 fps, but when flashing indicates that an invalid lower reverse speed has been selected.
- 24   Camera running in reverse at 24 fps.
- 32   Camera running in reverse at 32 fps, but when flashing indicates that an invalid lower reverse speed has been selected.
SFR   Shows when the shutter remains in the shooting position (approximately 4 seconds) when the Single Frame Connector (see below) is connected.

NOTE: All data in display window also appears in the Footage Counters (see Sec. 15.1m) and the Remote Control Box (see Sec. 15.3j).

Preset Digits. For entering fps speeds (see Sec. 15.1b Motors, To Run Motor at Desired Speed, above).

T.UP Bar. Take-up/TV bar button forward of Preset digits. Used to synchronize the camera with a video or computer screen when filming at 25fps—50Hz, or 30fps—60Hz.

To Electronically Shift Image Bar. Depress T.UP Bar button and hold until the frameline on the monitor moves down to the bottom of the screen (see also, Sec. 15.3c Accessories, Video Cameras)

CAUTION: Although it can be done without it, a Moviecam Syncobox (see Sec. 15.3f, Accessories), is recommended when filming monitors so as to avoid having to reset the bar each take.

Sync Out Plug. Female five-pin Fischer outlet to an audio tape recorder. From the keyway, pin 1 is blank for 50 Hz, ground for 60 Hz; pin 2 is clapper for Nagra; pin 3 is TRP/1.7m SEC; pin 4 is Pilotone (5v AC, peak to peak), and selectable 24 fps 50Hz or 24 fps 60 Hz; pin 5 is ground return for the pilotone.

Signal Volume Control. An acoustic signal sounds when the camera starts up, or is switched off, or if the camera's speed differs from the setting on the programmed preset digits (see above). Left of the volume control is the signal speaker.

To Adjust Signal Volume. Rotate the lowest knurled knob on the Control Panel.

Four Accessory Female Fisher Plugs. Two are located below the Dust Check button at left front of camera and two located at front of camera (one at lower right and the other just below the right side accessory bracket). Plugs are used for a Handgrip, (see below, this section), Zoom Drive (see Sec. 15.1e, Lenses; Sec. 15.1f, Assistant's Worklight and Sec. 15.3l, Accessories).

Fuse. A 5 × 20mm (3/8 in. × 25/32 in.) 6.8 ampere fuse is located below the 24 volt input-to-camera plug. The fuse cuts power to the internal circuit board's electronics if and when unit becomes overloaded.

NOTE: If an external short occurs on any unit plugged into one or more of the four female Fischer plugs, a circuit breaker cuts power to the outlets.

To Restore Power to the Connectors. Remove faulty unit, disconnect camera power plug for at least 30 seconds, re-insert.

On/Off Handgrip. Used when camera is in hand-held mode. Handgrip contains a small ON/OFF button to run/stop camera.

To Mount. Align latched handgrip screw to rosette on lower right front of camera, tighten clockwise. Insert plug on handgrip's cable into lower-right 24 volt Fischer plug at front of camera.

NOTE: A right handgrip-extension is available when follow-focus unit is attached to the hand-held camera. An adjustable nonpowered left handgrip is also available but requires iris rods to be mounted on camera baseplate (see Sec. 15.3a, Base Plate).

Heater. Built-in. Heaters automatically start when ambient temperature falls to +5° Celsius (41° Farenheit).

15.1d Turret
None. Single port accepts lenses fitted with PL (positive lock), and/or BNCR mounts.

15.1e Lenses
To Fit Lens to Camera. (1) Rotate lens lock clockwise as far as it will go. (2) Align guide groove in lens flange with locating pin in the upper left of lens port. Insert the lens flange flush with the camera, making certain the stud engages the lens-flange hole. (3) Rotate lens lock counterclockwise to secure.

To Remove Lens. (1) Grasp lens firmly. (2) Rotate lens lock clockwise as far as it will go. (3) Slide lens out from the port.

To Support Long Lenses.   Requires Lens Support (see Sec. 15.3b).

15.1f Viewfinder

Reflex. Image magnified 6.1 × .

Three types available: (1) *Standard* (optics with accessories); (2) *Video* (same standard optics with accessories, but with video camera and accessories attached (see Sec. 15.3h, Video Assist Systems), and, (3) Lightweight B&W Video (no optics, video camera, for Steadicam mode) (see Sec. 15.3h, Video Assist Systems).

Standard Viewfinder.   Mounts to top-front of camera.

To Mount.   Remove cap covering optics at top of camera and bottom of viewfinder. Align guide-pins on the viewfinder and three captive screws to matching holes on the camera and secure with an M5 Allen (a 5mm ballpoint hex socket) screwdriver.

NOTE: Top of Standard Viewfinder has an accessory connector plate (removable with an M5 Allen screwdriver), when attaching the dual unit that the manufacturer calls a READOUT ACCESSORY (see Sec. 15.1m Footage Counters).

To Open/Close/Insert 60 ND into Viewing System.   Rotate horizontal knob at top-front of viewfinder to OPEN or FILTER or CLOSED positions.

Eyepieces.   Four interchangeable bayonet-mount extension tubes *are* the camera's eyepieces: (1) Short symmetrical-lens eyepiece, for hand-held mode, (2) Long symmetrical-lens eyepiece with built-in 2.4 × magnifier for studio mode. (3) Short anamorphic-lens eyepiece for hand-held wide-screen mode, and (4) Long anamorphic-lens eyepiece with built-in 2.4 × image magnifier and built-in correction lens (de-anamorphoser) for studio wide-screen mode.

NOTE: A Right Eyepiece (for viewing a scene while Operator is filming) is also available (see Sec. 15.3i)

Eyecup.   Rubber cushionable eyecup is fitted with a 31.5mm diameter ring that will accept a diopter correction lens or a filter, if desired.

To Remove.   Pull eyecup straight out.

To View Through Lens.   Place eye to eyecup.

NOTE: Camera stops with mirror shutter in viewing position except when shutter has been inched by hand.

To Align Mirror if Shutter Has Been Inched by Hand.   Depress electronic inching button (manufacturer calls it a "Dust-Check" and labels it DC on camera) at upper left-front of camera.

NOTE: Whenever the electronic inching button is depressed the Control Board Panel Display (see Sec. 15.1c) and the Footage Counters (see Sec. 15.1m) flash the initials DC to indicate the viewing optics are obscured and the aperture open.

To Focus.   Rotate knurled rubber ring nearest eyecup until groundglass grains and crosshair are sharp.

NOTE: A reference scale forward of the focus ring (+ 5 to − 5) can be used to mark eyepiece focus for various users of the camera (Director, Director of Photography, Camera Operator, etc.).

To Change or Clean Groundglass.   (1) Disconnect camera from its power source. (2) Remove lens (see Sec. 15.1e). (3) Open camera door and rotate the inching knob to clear the mirror shutter and reveal the groundglass in its metal frame at the top of the port. Screw the combitool into the upper left threaded hole in the groundglass holder until snug. (4) Pull the groundglass *gently* and clean with brush or vacuum cleaner.

WARNING: Manufacturer cautions against moistening, wiping, or touching the groundglass.

To Insert Groundglass.   (1) Using the combitool, *gently* slide the groundglass atop the mirror shutter with the dull side UP until snug. (2) Unscrew the combitool and remove. (3) Connect camera to a power source, depress DC button at left front of camera, or apply a short burst to camera to bring the mirror shutter into viewing position.

To Alter Eyepiece for Viewing.   (1) Loosen the Eyepiece Tension Knob located below the viewfinder's left side. (2) Rotate eyepiece to desired viewing position (it is rotatable 360°). (3) Tighten Tension Knob.

NOTE: The tension knob *can* hold the weight of the long eyepiece, but the manufacturer recommends that a leveling rod be attached when using the long eyepiece.

To Attach Leveling Rod to Long Eyepiece.   Place leveling rod collar forward of the eyepiece's diopter scale—the collar stud, with its BNC type pins, down. Align and rotate leveling-rod catch onto pins. Clamp base of leveling rod to tripod or geared head.

WARNING: With leveling rod attached, ALWAYS loosen the Tension Knob!

To Critical-Focus Image in Long Eyepiece.   Rotate the Magnifying Ring forward of the leveling rod collar to check focus.

WARNING: ALWAYS return the Magnifying Ring to the regular image-size scribe on the tube.

To Detach Eyepiece.   (1) Slide Locking Button, located at left front of viewfinder elbow, forward. (2) Hold Locking Button forward, turn eyepiece counterclockwise, and remove from viewfinder.

To Attach Eyepiece.   (1) Align red dots (one in viewfinder elbow, and one in eyepiece). (2) Insert eyepiece and turn clockwise until eyepiece clicks into position.

NOTE: When exchanging long and short eyepieces, the image always appears inverted due to the different optical systems in each eyepiece.

To Orient the Image, Regardless of Eyepiece.   (1) Loosen the Prism Locking Screw at the bottom front of the eyepiece. (2) Rotate small knurled Prism Rotating Knob at the top front of the eyepiece counterclockwise until the image is correct when looking through the eyepiece (lower right of groundglass reads aspect ratio).

NOTE: Prism can be felt to drop into different orientation detentes as it rotates.

(3) Tighten Prism Locking Screw.

Eyepiece Heater. Prevents fogging of back element of eyepiece when filming in low temperatures. Insert the short cable plug into the outlet on eyepiece and the other end into one of the two plugs below the DC (dust check) button.

NOTE: Heater only works if there is power to the camera.

Movielite Module. Superimposes illuminated aspect ratios on the groundglass. Two types of modules are available: Standard 35mm and Super 35.

CAUTION: Both modules are similar in appearance. The Super 35 module is engraved with a small S next to the unit's serial number.

Standard framelines are: TV; 1:1.375; 1:1.66; 1:1.85; 1:2.35 (anamorphic). Super 35 framelines are: TV:1:33 (full aperture) 1:1.85 S; 1:2.35 S (anamorphic).

To Mount Either Module. (1) Disconnect camera from its power source. (2) Rotate eyepiece forward until vertical. Lock. (3) Align pin on module to matching hole on viewfinder behind optic barrel, taking care to see that the electronic connectors match and are properly seated. (4) Secure module to viewfinder with single captive M5 Allen screw. (5) Connect power to camera.

NOTE: LEDs labeled Format 1 and Format 2 (at side of module) display aspect ratios illuminated in viewfinder.

Aspect Ratios. In addition to the frame inscribed on the groundglass, two illuminated aspect ratio format outlines and/or crosshair can be superimposed in the viewfinder.

To Add Illuminated Aspect Ratios. Use one or more of the three buttons at back of unit. Depress center button labeled SELECT 1 to superimpose a frame on the groundglass. Release. Depress again until desired illuminated aspect ratio appears on groundglass.

NOTE: The selected aspect ratio entered in SELECT 1 will appear in the LED labeled FORMAT 1.

To Extinguish Selected Aspect Ratio. Depress SELECT 1 until the aspect ratio cycle disappears from the groundglass and the LED labeled FORMAT 1.

To Add a Second Illuminated Format. Depress lowest button labeled SELECT 2 to superimpose a frame over the one showing on the groundglass. Continue depressing until second desired illuminated aspect ratio appears.

NOTE: The selected aspect ratio entered in SELECT 2 will appear in the LED labeled FORMAT 2.

To Extinguish Selected Aspect Ratio. Continue depressing SELECT 2 until the aspect ratio cycle disappears from the groundglass and LED labeled FORMAT 2.

To Illuminate/Extinguish the Crosshair. Depress the uppermost button.

Format LEDs. Identify the aspect ratios superimposed in the viewfinder.

To Adjust Frameline Brightness. Rotate *Movielite Intensity Knob* located at top rear of module to desired intensity.

15.1g Sunshade/Matte-Box

Top of each matte-box is fitted with *lockdown knobs* to hold a sunshade or French flags (not shown).

To Mount the Matte-Box. (1) Insert two long *43cm (17-in.) rods* into a Base Plate (see Section 15.3a) and secure. Slide *L-bracket* onto long rods.

NOTE: Long rods may also be fitted with a lens support (see Section 15.3b) or a Follow-Focus unit (see Section 15.3c).

(2) Insert short 15.24cm (6-in.) *eccentric (rotatable off-center)* rod into top channel of bracket, its knob facing the Operator; loosen the knob's adjusting screw. Insert short 15.24cm (6 in.) *geared (serrated) rod* into lower channel and secure. (3) Align lower matte-box channel to geared rod, rotate upper eccentric knob, and align to fit to upper matte-box channel. (4) Loosen bracket locking lever and rotate bracket knob SLOWLY; allow internal teeth in bracket to grasp ridges of lower rod and bring matte-box onto rods. Adjust matte-box to lens; rotate *bracket locking lever* to secure.

To Insert/Remove Filter Holder into Matte-Box. Pull appropriate knurled *holder lock* at side of *filter stage.* Insert/remove *filter holder* from top.

To Rotate Either Stage. Unscrew *rotating stage lock* (top knurled knob) in desired stage, rotate.

To Rotate Round Filter in Matte-Box. Unscrew knurled *round filter lock*, rotate.

To Raise/Lower Geared Filter Holder. Rotate *filter gear knob.*

NOTE: Rotatable knob on rear filter stage accepts a "hand wheel" which fits over the filter gear knob for ease of movement of the graduated filter.

Access to Lens. Lift lever at top right side of matte box hinge; opens laterally.

15.1h Filters

Matte-box accepts two 167.6mm × 167.6mm (6.6″ × 6.6″) filter stages. Each stage holds two filters. Front stage is rotatable; second stage has fixed, top sliding holders.

The rear of each filter stage has an attachment for either a 152mm (6 in.), 138mm (5.4 in.), or 114mm (4.5 in.) filter ring, and/or an item the manufacturer calls a reflex prevention ring (a circular piece of metal intended to prevent light rays from striking the back of a filter and reflecting into the lens) and an additional 101.6mm × 101.6mm (4 × 4 in.) filter.

There is NO internal filter holder.

15.1i Door

Hinged at front.

WARNING: To prevent door from hitting eyepiece, tilt the viewing system up and forward approximately 10° to 15°

To Open Door. Lift door-latch at rear of door and swing door forward.
To Close Door. Swing door flush to camera, push door latch into door

15.1j Magazines

304.8m (1000 ft), 152.4m (500 ft) and 122m (400 ft).

Magazines fit on camera at either the top (studio mode), or rear (hand-held mode and/or Steadicam mode).

NOTE: Before magazine can be mounted in either mode, a magazine adapter must be fitted to the camera.

To Mount Top Load Adapter. Grasp adapter by its handle. Insert bottom of adapter into Magazine Mounting Rail at back of camera. Tilt adapter forward and carefully lower it to the camera, making certain the adapter's electronic connector aligns and inserts into the matching connector on the camera body. Depress gently and align two captive screws in adapter to the camera. Secure adapter with an M5 Allen screwdriver.

To Mount Back Load Adapter. With the unit's safety latch at the top, align the four captive screws in the adapter to the matching holes on the camera. Secure the rear two screws, then the top screws, with an M5 Allen screwdriver.

To Mount Magazine to Top Load Adapter. Depress the safety button and push the sliding latch lock (at left top of adapter) toward the Operator. Pull approximately 10cm (4 in.) of film from the magazine throat. Place heel of magazine in rail at back of adapter, guide film loop into camera body. Lower gently until nose of magazine engages the adapter latch. Push the sliding latch forward until the safety button snaps up and secures the magazine to the adapter.

To Remove. Depress the safety button, push the sliding latch toward the Operator. Lift the sliding latch UP to clear magazine nose and pull magazine away.

To Mount Magazine to Rear Load Adapter. Depress the adapter's safety button and turn its latch mechanism counterclockwise to hold the button down. Pull approximately 10cm (4 in.) of film from the magazine throat. Place heel of magazine in rail at back of camera, guide film loop into camera body. Tilt magazine forward gently until nose of magazine engages the adapter latch. Rotate the latch mechanism clockwise until the safety button snaps up and secures the magazine to the adapter.

To Remove. Hold magazine. Depress the adapter's safety button and turn its latch mechanism counterclockwise to hold the button down. Lift the sliding latch UP to clear magazine nose and pull magazine away.

NOTE: Many lightweight Steadicam magazines are fitted with a carry handle that should be removed before mounting on a Steadicam rig (see Sec. 15.1t, Miscellaneous).

15.1k Buckle-Trip

Three. Main switch (red) located at the back of the sprocket-guide block cuts out power to camera if film piles up. Two microswitches located above and below each sprocket guide cut power to the camera if either loop is too large.

To Reset Main Trip. Turn main (red) switch so that it points fore and aft (parallel to bottom of camera). Microswitches re-set when pressure against them is relieved.

15.1l Threading (Fig. 15–3a, 15–3b)

Before Mounting Magazine. (1) Flip red buckle-trip UP or DOWN to cut power to camera.

CAUTION: Failure to flip the buckle-trip will leave power to the magazine, which will take up film once the magazine and camera connectors engage, and result in loss of the loop.

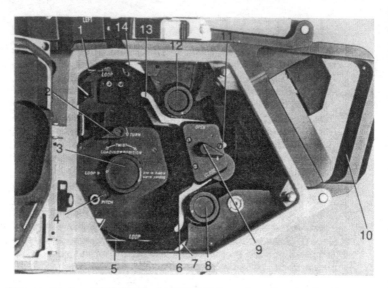

Figure 15–3a MOVIECAM COMPACT threading (top load). Courtesy of MOVIECAM F.G. Bauer GmbH.

1. Upper loop line
2. Movement lever
3. Inching knob
4. Pitch control slot
5. Lower loop line
6. Lower film guide
7. Lower buckle-trip

8. Lower sprocket
9. Sprocket-guide lever
10. Topload magazine adapter
11. Threading buckle-trip
12. Upper sprocket
13. Upper film guide
14. Upper buckle-trip

(2) Slide movement block back away from gate by rotating the Movement Lever clockwise toward the rear of the camera. (3) Lift the Sprocket Guide Lever UP to clear guides from sprocket. (4) Remove and clean dual aperture plate and pressure plate (see Sec. 15.1q, Cleaning). Re-insert. Mount magazine (see Sec. 15.1j, Magazines). (5) Pull film from feed side. Extend loop to lower corner of camera (a rough guide for amount of film needed for threading). (6) Insert film between the upper and lower sprockets and guides, then between the aperture plates and movement block. (7) Lower the Sprocket Guide Lever and engage film perforations on sprockets. (8) *Gently* rotate the Movement Lever counterclockwise toward the aperture while rotating the inching knob back and forth between the arrow labeled TWIST, and engage the pulldown claws in the film perforations. (9) Once engaged, rotate the Movement Lever further until it locks in its front position.

To Adjust Loop Size. (10) Rotate dot on inching knob and align to the word LOOP on movement. (11) Depress and turn the upper sprocket knob until the upper film loop is at, or slightly below, the upper line in the camera interior marked LOOP. (12) Depress and turn the lower sprocket knob until the lower film loop is at, or slightly above, the lower line in the camera interior marked LOOP. (13) Turn the main buckle-trip to its horizontal position. (14) Rotate inching knob and observe movement of

484

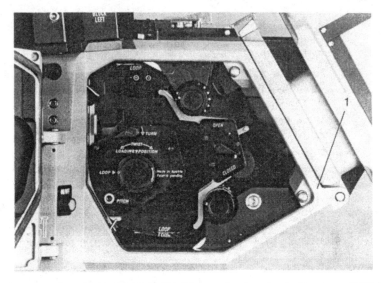

Figure 15–3b MOVIECAM COMPACT threading (rear load). Courtesy of MOVIECAM F.G. Bauer GmbH.

1. Rear load adapter

film. Apply power in a short burst and observe the action of film. If satisfactory, reset footage counters, close door.

15.1m Footage Counter

None on camera. To read footage remaining requires removal of an accessory connector plate at the top of the Standard Viewfinder (see Sec. 15.1f), and placement of a unit manufacturer calls a READOUT ACCESSORY, which does more than note footage.

Readout Accessory. Fits to top of Viewfinder. Dimmable digital displays at both sides of camera read fps and footage. Diodes denote battery condition and out-of-sync running. Top of each readout is fitted with a bracket for additional accessories.

To Install. (1) Disconnect the camera. (2) Remove the accessory connector plate at top of Standard Viewfinder with an M5 Allen screwdriver. (3) Align and insert accessory *gently* into connector. (4) Secure accessory to viewfinder with single M5 Allen screw. (5) Reconnect camera.

Right Display Unit. Upper LED reads fps when camera runs, otherwise registers 0 (zero) when camera is in stand-by. Lower LED shows footage remaining. Red diode labeled BAT lights only if battery power falls below 21 volts, otherwise is out. Red diode labeled SYNC lights only if camera speed differs from that set on the camera (see 15.1c, Powerline, Control Panel). A dimmer, facing forward, adjusts brightness of both left and right displays.

Left Display Unit. Upper LED reads fps when camera runs, otherwise registers 0 (zero) when camera is in stand-by. Lower LED shows footage remaining. Red diode labeled BAT illuminates only if battery power falls below 21 volts, otherwise is out. Red diode labeled SYNC illuminates only if camera speed differs from that set on the camera (see 15.1c, Powerline, Control Panel). A reset button, facing forward, zeros footage count in both left and right displays.

NOTE: If not zeroed, when the camera is disconnected, the readout "memory" will retain and display the last footage amount registered on the counter.

Metric Readout Accessory. Available from the manufacturer. Feet/meters canNOT be changed in the field. A factory service job.

15.1n Tachometer
An LED fps display is on the camera (see Sec. 15.1c, Powerline, Control Panel). Registers from 12 to 32 fps in increments of one frame. Also shows on Readout Accessory displays (see Sec. 15.1m, Footage Counter), if attached.

To Run at Other fps Frame Rates. Requires Accessory Super Speed Control Box (see Sec. 15.3d).

15.1o Shutter
Variable. Adjustable in six positive stops: 45°, 90°, 120°, 144°, 172.8°, and 180°.

NOTE: Shutter can be set at angles between the positive stops but settings can only be guesses since the shutter is not scribed. The possibility of shutter creep exists when a shutter is not in detentes.

To Set Shutter Opening. (1) Disconnect the camera. (2) Remove lens (see Sec. 15.1e, Lenses). (3) Open camera door, grasp inching knob, and rotate until shutter angle mark and the access shaft in the shutter are both visible. (4) Insert MOVIECAM COMBITOOL into access shaft and turn it slowly until the desired shutter angle appears on the scale. (5) Remove COMBITOOL from the shaft. (6) Reconnect the camera, and either depress the Dust Cover (DC) button or run camera to return shutter to viewing position.

15.1p Lubrication
None in the field. Manufacturer recommends camera be lubricated by a camera service technician.

15.1q Cleaning

Optics. Clean with blower bulb syringe.
Manufacturer recommends the following maintenance each time film is changed:

Remove and Clean Aperture and Pressure Plates.
To Remove Aperture Plate. (1) Flip red buckle-trip UP or DOWN to cut power to camera. (2) Slide movement block back away from gate by rotating the Movement Lever clockwise toward the rear of the camera.

NOTE: The aperture plate is in two sections: Upper Plate and Lower Plate, separated by a rail.

(3) Lift small spring-loaded upper aperture plate lock lever, grasp handle of upper plate and pull back and out. (4) Press down on spring-loaded lower aperture plate lock lever; grasp base of lower aperture plate; pull back and remove. (5) Clean upper and lower aperture plates with air or a

soft cotton handkerchief (not linen), making certain that grooves at top and bottom of plates are meticulously clean of dirt. Remove emulsion build-up with an orangewood stick.

NOTE: Manufacturer cautions against lubricating the plates!

To Replace Upper Aperture Plate. Insert upper plate into camera parallel to, and above, the rail separating the upper and lower plates. Rest the lower grooves in the upper plate on the rail. Lift the upper spring-loaded aperture plate lock lever and push the upper plate forward *gently* until flush. Release the upper aperture lock lever and secure the plate.

To Replace Lower Aperture Plate. Insert lower plate into camera parallel to, and below, the rail separating the upper and lower plates. Slide the upper grooves in the lower plate up, toward the rail. Depress the lower spring-loaded aperture plate lock lever and *gently* push the lower part of the plate inward until flush. Release the upper aperture lock lever and secure the plate.

To Remove/Replace Pressure Plate. (1) Slide pressure plate block backward to retract its spring-loaded pin from the recess at the back of the aperture plate. (2) Lift and remove the pressure plate. Clean pressure plate with a cotton handkerchief (not linen) and the dimple at back of plate with orangewood stick. (3) Re-insert the pressure plate. Tap the pressure plate lightly to drive the spring-loaded pin forward and into the recess at the back of the plate.

CAUTION: ALWAYS make certain the pin is in place.

Use bulb syringe on camera interior to remove dust, dirt, etc. When done, reset buckle-trip.

15.1r Weight

With 304.8m (1000 ft) load	29.76 kg	(65.6 lbs)
With 152.4m (500 ft) load	14.8 kg	(32.6 lbs)
With 122m (400 ft) load	12.2 kg	(26.9 lbs)

15.1s Troubleshooting

Trouble	Probable Cause
Camera will not start	Powerline connector faulty; buckle-trip not set; dead battery; circuit board malfunction; cover plate not firmly attached to large terminal strip
Intermittent start and stop	Battery connections loose; broken connection in powerline
Torn perforations	Improper threading
Door will not close	Movement block not seated forward; dirt or film chips in door
Viewing system blocked out	Shutter closed; eyepiece magnification knob in closed position; viewfinder knob closed
Lens will not focus	Lens not seated properly; camera too close for minimal focusing; lens element damaged
Cut-in on groundglass	Matte-box or sunshade extended; shutter not full open

Super 35mm Conversion. The COMPACT camera is available with a three-perforation movement that exposes film at 20.57m per minute (67.5 ft per minute), as well as the standard four-perforation movement that exposes film at 27.43m per minute (90 ft per minute). The Super 35 movement canNOT be changed in the field.

The centers and axes of Standard 35mm and Super 35mm format are 1.2mm apart. A conversion requires changing the film gate, adapting the viewfinder system, lens mount, lens support, and matte-box brackets. (See also Base Plate, Sec. 15.3a, for field changes that can be made.)

Carry Handles. Numerous handles are made for convenience of carrying the camera and its magazines.

Upper Carry Handle. For use when magazine is mounted at rear. Attaches to the camera right side with two M5 Allen screws and the camera top with one M5 Allen screw.

Auxiliary Handle. As an aid for easier camera handling. Mounts to various other carry handles: to the Upper Carry handle (described above) with one M5 Allen screw; to the Side Handle.

Side Handle. When a magazine is mounted to the camera top. Slides onto the dovetail bracket at camera right side. It secures to the bracket with (a) a knurled screw, and (b) a lower latched-screw that inserts into the rosette at the lower right camera body. Side handle has threaded sockets for placement of Auxiliary Handle.

Rear Carrying Handle. Mounts to camera instead of a magazine. Attaches same as a rear-load magazine adapter.

122m (400 ft) Magazine Carrying Handle. For ease of handling Steadicam magazine. Mounts to lightweight magazine with two M5 Allen wrenches.

15.2 MOVIECAM COMPACT MAGAZINES (Fig. 15–4)

15.2a Type
Displacement.

15.2b Capacity
304.8m (1000 ft), 152.4m (500 ft), 122m (400 ft)

15.2c Lid
One. Dog-locked.

NOTE: There are two locks on the 304.8m (1000 ft) and the 152.4m (500 ft) but only one lock on the 122m (400 ft) magazine.

To Remove Lid. (1) Place the magazine with its lid UP.
304.8m (1000 ft) and 152.4m (500 ft) Magazine. (2a) Reach under and depress the two black safety-catch buttons that secure the magazine lock latches (located at the lower-left and lower-right backside of the magazine). Then rotate the lock-latches toward each other.
122m (400 ft) Magazine. (2b) Depress single black button above magazine throat and rotate lock latch counterclockwise.
(3) Lift hinged lid up and back.

15.2d Feed
Left side. Film (wound emulsion in) pulls off of spindle clockwise.

15.2e Take-up
Right side. Film winds onto spindle clockwise, emulsion always in.

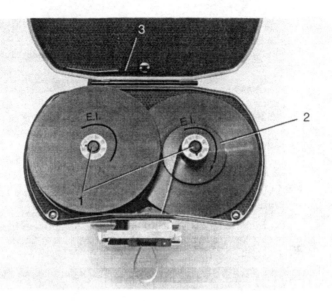

Figure 15-4 MOVIECAM COMPACT 304.8m (1000 ft) magazine. Courtesy of MOVIECAM F.G. Bauer GmbH.

1. Feed spindle
2. Plate

3. Internal mechanical footage/ meters indicator

15.2f Loading

(1) Raise lid. Depress center of feed spindle to retract its three core locks. (2) In darkness, remove film from can and bag. Insert film end between the left feed idler rollers and push through until film end emerges from the feed side of the magazine.

NOTE: Film end must take a small turn in feeding through the rollers; therefore it may require more than one attempt to push end through.

(3) Lower film roll on spindle and film plate until the core locks expand and "grab" the core. (4) Insert film end through the take-up side light trap rollers. (5) Place core on take-up spindle and rotate until the spindle pin engages the core keyway and core locks expand and "grab" the core. (6) Insert film end into take-up core slot and wind onto core clockwise. (7) Replace lid and rotate lock levers to secure.

15.2g Unloading

In darkness, unlock hinged lid, lift up and back.

(1) Depress center of take-up spindle to retract its core locks. (2) Place your index finger on the core, your thumb on the edge of roll. (3) Carefully lift film roll from take-up spindle and place exposed roll into black bag and can.

15.2h Footage Counter.

Digital. Subtractive. At back of magazines.

To Enter Digital Footage. (1) Depress three buttons on "PRESET" panel to match the amount of footage loaded in camera (top row subtracts; bottom row adds). (2) Depress "SET" button to enter data into the magazine's electronic counter. Display window at right of buttons reads amount of footage or meters entered into "PRESET" in subtractive feet or meters (999–0, then reverts to 999 and counts down again).

NOTE: A small dash (—) in display indicates if magazine is reading in feet or meters.

Spring-Loaded Mechanical Footage/Metric Indicator. In the lid of the 304.8 (1000 ft) magazine only. Internal arm reads amount of rawstock remaining in magazine. Subtracts in increments of 100 ft except for next-to-last scribe of 50 ft.

To Read Amount of Rawstock Remaining on the Feed Roll. (1) Turn camera OFF.

CAUTION: Using the indicator arm to determine amount of rawstock while the camera is running could jam the film!

(2) Slide external knob of the spring-loaded mechanical indicator arm toward the rear of the magazine. (3) Read. (4) Guide indicator arm back to center.

CAUTION: Letting the arm snap back could bend the arm and result in false readings!

15.2i Manual Tightening Wheels
Built into lid of 304.8 (1000 ft) magazine only. The 152.4m (500 ft) and the 122m (400 ft) magazines do not have this feature.

To Take Slack Out of Rawstock and/or Exposed Roll. Depress either spring-loaded tightening wheel to engage its internal friction plate with the core and rotate (toward lens on feed side, toward Operator on take-up side).

15.3 MOVIECAM ACCESSORIES
15.3a Base Plate (Fig. 15–5)
MOVIECAM Base Plate is a small riser fitted with two 3/8–16″ lockdown screws and two locating studs at its top to secure it to the camera.

NOTE: The Base Plate is affixed to the right tapped holes at the bottom of the camera (near long accessory plug) if Arriflex accessories are to be used. It is affixed to the left tapped holes at the bottom of the camera (near viewfinder) if MOVIECAM COMPACT accessories are to be used on the camera.

Base of the plate is fitted with two 3/8–16″ tapped holes that accept a tripod or gear head lockdown screw.

CAUTION: A 3/8″-16 screw longer than 7mm (9/32-in) might damage the camera.

Front of the Base Plate is fitted with two Locking Slider pins flanked by two iris rod holders with Adjustable Rings.

NOTE: Adjustable Rings allow Base Plate accessories to be aligned for standard 35mm or Super 35mm formats.

CAUTION: ALWAYS determine placement of the rings in relation to the format being used: white dots face the center in the Standard 35mm format; red dots face the center in the Super 35 format.

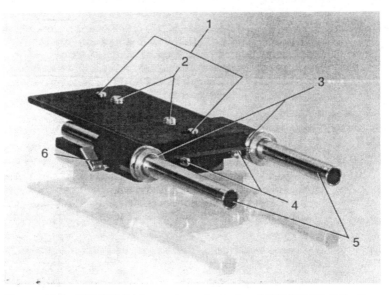

Figure 15–5 MOVIECAM base plate. Courtesy of MOVIECAM F.G. Bauer GmbH.

1. Locating pin studs
2. 3/8″-16 lockdown screws
3. Adjustable rings
4. Locking slider-pins
5. Iris rods
6. Iris rod lock lever (1 of 2)

To Adjust Iris Rod Rings. (1) Squeeze locking slider pins toward each other. (2) Rotate rings so that same color dots face each other. (3) Release slider pins making certain they engage and lock in place.

Iris Rods. Two sizes available: 22cm (8 1/2 in.) and 44cm (17 in.). They fit into holders and are secured by an Iris Rod Lock Lever.

15.3b Lens Support
Used on iris rods to support telephoto or zoom lenses. Consists of a Lens Mount Base and adjustable Lens Support Ring.

Lens Mount Base.
To Mount. Push Lock Lever in base UP to relieve locks in rod cutouts. Place cutouts on iris rods with Lock Lever at Operator's right. Secure to rods by depressing the Lock Lever.

Lens Support Ring. Might require adjustment to shift its central axis to the center of a manufacturer's accessories. The forward facing engraving on the lens ring, MC (MOVIECAM COMPACT) or ARRI (Arriflex) *must* match the accessories (follow-focus, matte-box, etc.) in use on the camera.

To Adjust Ring if Its Central Axis Must Be Shifted. (1) Determine which engraving is facing forward. (2) If engraving differs from the type of accessories you are using, loosen the two M4 Allen screws in the asymetrically mounted bottom half of the ring and lift UP. (3) Turn ring 180° until the proper engraving faces forward, rest the bottom half on the pin in the base. (4) Secure bottom half to lens mount.

To Insert Long Lens in Mount. (1) Loosen and remove the two M4 Allen screws in top half of Lens Support Ring and remove. (2) Cradle lens in lower half of Lens Support Ring. (3) Loosen lock on Lens Mount and slide lens into port (see Sec. 15.1d and 15.1e). (4) Replace top half of Lens Support Ring and secure with M4 Allen screws. (5) Lock Lens Mount to iris rods.

15.3c Follow-Focus

Two types available: Studio and Lightweight.

Studio. Slides on iris rods. Dual focus knobs allow for focusing from either side of camera (right knob is detachable). Center of focus knobs are fitted with insets that accept a lever and/or 15cm (6 in.) extension knob, for focusing at short distances from camera.

Magnetic circular discs in back of the focus knob provide an area for penciling in follow-focus marks for marking.

NOTE: When adding a disc to the focus knob, the slot on the disc must engage the locating pin.

A small Knob Lock, on the perimeter of the marking disc, provides "drag" on the knob or secures it in one position, if so desired.

To Change Gear Ratio. Depress small button in focus knob and rotate the knob until detente is engaged.

To Engage Lens. Loosen Driver Arm Locking Lever (behind the left focus knob) and push the Driver Arm forward to engage teeth in gear on lens.

NOTE: The gear on the Driver Arm can be changed to accommodate ratio of geared rings on various manufacturers' lenses.

To Change a Driver Arm Gear. Grasp gear on Driver Arm and pull. Re-insert new gear into gear receptacle.

Lightweight Follow-Focus. Used in hand-held mode.

To Mount. (1) Slide female dovetailed bracket on the square support rod onto the matching male dovetail bracket at the upper right front side of the camera and secure with its knurled knob. (2) Attach the Lightweight Follow-Focus to the support rod and slide the unit on the bar until the gear on the driver arm aligns with the lens gear. Rotate its screw and secure. (3) Loosen the Driver Arm Lever at the back of the unit and engage the lens gear. Tighten the Driver Arm Lever.

To Focus. Center of drive knobs are fitted with insets that accept a lever and/or 15cm (6-in.) extension knob, for focusing at short distances from camera.

15.3d Super Speed Control Box (Speedbox) (Fig. 15–6)

The Super Speed Control Box (Speedbox) permits filming forward in speeds from 2 to 50 fps and in reverse from 12 to 32 fps. Also allows for programming change of speeds while filming.

Fits to right side of camera and consists of the following buttons, displays, and outlets.

Fps 1. Five-digit Frame Speed Selector located at right-rear of Speedbox. Buttons over and under digits are depressed to insert starting frame speeds with accuracy of .001 fps. Top buttons subtract; lower buttons add. The first two digits are the fps; the next three are the thousandths of a frame

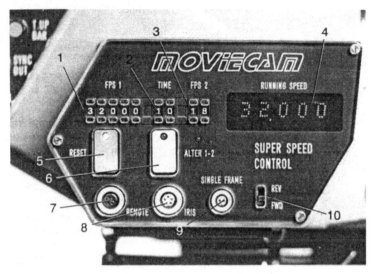

Figure 15–6 MOVIECAM Super Speed Control. Courtesy of MOVIECAM F.G. Bauer GmbH.

1. Starting fps selector
2. Time selector
3. Ending fps selector
4. LED display
5. Reset (to fps-1) button
6. Alter (go from FPS 1 to FPS 2) button
7. Remote control connector
8. Automatic iris control connector
9. Single frame connector
10. Fwd/Rev switch

desired (e.g., 29.970). If thousands or hundredths are not desired, zero last three digits.

NOTE: Start speed that is set on digits does not appear in display windows until camera runs. With camera Off, the Control Board Panel (see Sec. 15.1c, Viewfinder) window and the Footage Counters (see Sec. 15.1m, Footage Counters, Readout) and the Display window on the Speedbox (see below) show 0 (zero).

Time. Two-digit Time Selector (forward of fps buttons). Buttons over and under digits are depressed to program a speed change ranging from 1 to 99 seconds. Top buttons subtract, lower buttons add.

NOTE: Time set on digits does NOT appear on displays.

Minimum input time that can be set on selector is 01 second. If set at 00, camera will NOT change speed.

NOTE: It is not possible to program time change from FPS 2 to FPS 1 unless the Remote Control is used (see below).

FPS 2. Two-digit Frame Speed Selector (forward of Time Selector). Buttons over and under digits are depressed to insert desired ending frame speeds, from 2 to 50 fps forward or 12 to 32 fps in reverse. Top buttons subtract; lower buttons add. Thousandths of a frame are not displayed as in FPS 1.

Running Speed. LED display forward of speed selector buttons. Five digits display actual speed of camera when it runs.

Reset. Red diode in button illuminates when camera runs at speed set in five-digit speed selector. After speed change to FPS 2, depressing RESET button returns camera speed to the frame rate set in FPS 1.

Alter 1–2. Switches camera frame rate from FPS 1 to the frame rate set on the FPS 2 buttons. Red diode in button illuminates only during the speed change. Diode next to button illuminates when FPS 2 speed is attained.

NOTE: Camera will run at frame rate set in FPS 1 until the ALTER 1–2 button is depressed, *then* will change speed within the time rate set on the TIME buttons.

Remote. Accepts cable plug from the Speedbox Remote Control unit (see Sec. 15.3e). When connected, the programmable time control is de-activated.

Iris. Accepts socket of plug on lenses fitted with automatic iris controls.

Single Frame Connector. Accepts various controls (e.g., single frame system, timer, etc.). When using a single frame connector, the camera requires an external shutter to compensate (open and close) for the time the camera shutter is open (approximately four seconds).

REV/FWD. Switch slides to desired reverse or forward mode.

NOTE: When reversing film, the magazine does not have to be altered, although rawstock should be placed on take-up instead of feed side. If running film back for double exposure, place cap on lens.

To Mount Speedbox to Camera. (1) Disconnect the camera. (2) Remove long accessory connecter cover at lower right side of camera and let it hang down. (3) Insert the latch on the back of the Speedbox into the MOVIECAM nameplate at camera right side, lower the box, and align the Speedbox connector to the camera connector. Push bottom of Speedbox toward the camera and insert connector. (4) Reconnect the camera.

15.3e Speedbox Remote Control

Circular hand-holdable unit is fitted with two marks on its perimeter labeled FPS 1 and FPS 2, and a handwheel in its center. All programs require input of data into the Speedbox as noted above. However, when the plug of the Remote Control cable is inserted into the Remote socket on the Speedbox, the Speedbox's timer is inactivated. The time change from FPS 1 to FPS 2 and back is determined by manually rotating the remote control handwheel from one mark to another.

CAUTION: Before starting the camera, make certain the handwheel is at FPS 1!

15.3f Synco Box (Fig. 15–7)

The Synco Box permits exact and repeatable synchronization of the camera with video and computer images, generators, "master" or "slave" cameras, front and rear projectors, etc.

Figure 15–7 MOVIECAM Syncobox. Courtesy of MOVIECAM F.G. Bauer GmbH.

1. Fps digits
2. Red (int) diode
3. Int/ext toggle switch
4. Green (ext) diode
5. Sync connector
6. Sync/video toggle switch

7. Video Connector
8. 90°/0° toggle switch
9. Manual/automatic phase switch
10. Rotary phase knob
11. LED display
12. HZ/fps stick-in module

NOTE: When the SYNCOBOX is mounted to the camera, the frame speed input at the Control Board Panel (see Sec. 15.1, Powerline Control Panel) and the camera's crystal control are bypassed.

Fits to right side of camera and consists of the following buttons, displays, and outlets:

Fps Digits. Five-digit Frame Speed Selector located at right-rear of Syncobox. Buttons over and under digits are depressed to insert frame speeds with accuracy of .001 fps. Top buttons subtract; lower buttons add. The first two digits are the fps; the next three are the thousandths of a frame desired (e.g., 29.970). If thousands or hundredths are not desired, zero the last three digits.

NOTE: Speed that is set on digits does not appear in display windows until camera runs. With camera Off, the Control Board Panel (see Sec. 15.1c, Viewfinder) window, the Footage Counters (see Sec. 15.1m, Footage Counters, Readout) and the Running Speed window on the Speedbox (see above) show 0 (zero).

Running Speed. LED display forward of speed selector buttons. Five digits display actual speed of camera when it runs.

INT. Red diode illuminates to indicate there is internal crystal control to the camera.

EXT. Green diode illuminates to indicate there is an external SYNC signal to the camera.

Unmarked Toggle Switch. Between the red and green diodes. When flipped toward Operator (red diode illuminates), unit changes from external crystal control to internal crystal control. When flipped forward (green diode illuminates), unit changes from internal crystal control to external crystal control. It is important that this toggle be turned toward the type of control (internal/external) being input or sync can be lost.

SYNC. Connector accepts external synchronization devices (when used as a "master/slave" camera, projector/camera sync, Mains Sync Adapter [see below], etc.).

Video. Connector accepts external video-sync signal.

Unmarked Toggle Switch. Between the SYNC and VIDEO connectors. When flipped toward Operator, unit accepts external sync signal. When flipped forward, unit accepts video-sync signal. It is important that this toggle be turned toward the type of signal being input or sync can be lost.

0°/90°. Switch turns the phase 90°.

Man/Auto. Used to choose between manual or automatic phase setting when filming a monitor or syncing with a projector, etc.

PHASE. Rotary knob that manually synchronizes the phase position of the shutter with an external phase (e.g., fine-tuning a camera/projector).

Stick-in Module. Located at the top of the Syncobox. The interchangeable module, inserted into the Syncobox with two M 2.5 screws, allows the unit to be used with a variety of Hertz (depending on the mains or generator encountered) and fps frame rates. The types of modules available are:

24 Hz—24 fps	25 Hz—25 fps	30 Hz—30 fps
48 Hz—24 fps	50 Hz—25 fps	60 Hz—30 fps
60 Hz—24 fps	75 Hz—25 fps	
72 Hz—24 fps		

WARNING: Always make certain the Syncobox in use has a module with the correct Hertz and fps frame rate.

To Mount Syncobox to Camera. (1) Disconnect the camera. (2) Remove long accessory connector cover at lower right side of camera and let it hang down. (3) Insert the latch on the back of the Syncobox into the MOVIECAM nameplate at camera right side, lower the box, and align the Syncobox connector to the camera connector. Push bottom of Syncobox toward the camera and insert connector. (4) Reconnect the camera.

CAUTION: If not connected properly, the digits 1.0 will appear on the camera display.

NOTE: It is not necessary for the camera to be threaded when "setting up" and entering data into the Syncobox. Unlike some cameras, input is not altered due to "drag" after the camera is threaded and filming commences.

Using the Syncobox

To Synchronize Camera Shutter with TV Monitor or Computer Screen Using a Connecting Cable. (1) Follow instructions regarding mounting the Syncobox. (2) Set toggle switch to EXT (green diode will illuminate). (3) Connect coaxial cable from video outlet on video recorder (or monitor or computer) to the VIDEO outlet. (4) Set unmarked toggle switch (located between SYNC and VIDEO outlets) away from the Operator (VIDEO).

CAUTION: If a sync out connector from the video player instead of a video out connector is used (or a Magnetic Pickup Unit is used), then attach a sync cable to the SYNC outlet and set the unmarked toggle switch (located between SYNC and VIDEO outlets) toward the Operator (SYNC).

(5) Flip 0°/90° switch *down* to 0°. (6) Flip MAN/AUTO switch *down* to AUTO.

CAUTION: AUTO can only be used if the fps rate corresponds to one-half the sync frequency, i.e., if filming on a frequency of 48 Hz, the camera can be run at 24 fps. At 50 Hz, the camera can be run at 25 fps. At 60 Hz, the camera can be run at 30 fps. The SYNCOBOX must be fitted with a compatible Stick-in Module (see above). If the Hertz to fps ratio is 2 to 1, then when the switch is set to AUTO, the video image frameline bar on the monitor will automatically drop to the bottom of the viewfinder corner and remain there when the camera is reconnected. If frameline does NOT drop, or alternately "clips" the viewfinder frame corner, then see no. 8 CAUTION, (below).

(7) Align camera lens to the monitor screen. (8) Enter the same fps engraved on the Stick-in Module into the five-digit Frame Speed Selector located at right-rear of SYNCOBOX. (9) Turn camera on and observe monitor.

CAUTION: If the Stick-in Module is: (1) other than a 2 to 1 Hertz to fps ratio (e.g., 60 Hertz–24 fps), or (2) it *is* a 2 to 1 ratio, but the frameline does not automatically drop, then:

(10) Set the 0°/90° switch *up* to 90°. (11) Flip the MAN/AUTO switch *up* to MAN. (12) Rotate the PHASE shift knob until the lower edge of the frameline is in the center of the viewfinder crosshair. (13) Flip the 0°/90° switch *down* to 0°. The bar will drop to the bottom of the viewfinder.

NOTE: It is possible to synchronize a camera shutter and TV monitor without a Syncobox, but the procedure has its limitations.

To Synchronize Camera Shutter with TV Monitor or Computer Screen without a Syncobox. (1) Make certain that the long accessory plug cover is in place at lower right of camera. (2) Determine the Hertz of the monitor or computer. (3) Align camera lens to the monitor screen and enter into the five-digit Frame Speed Selector on camera, one-half or one-third of the video frequency. (4) Turn camera on and observe monitor. (5) Continue to enter fps rate until the video frameline bar stops.

NOTE: Camera speed can be entered in thousandths of a frame. If frameline bar changes direction, leave the first two digits alone and concentrate on the latter three until frameline bar is halted.

(6) Press the T./UP button on the Control Panel (see Sec. 15.1c, Powerline Control Panel) and move the bar toward the lower corner of the view-finder.

NOTE: This procedure will have to be repeated each take.

To Synchronize Camera Shutter with Front or Rear Projector Using Connecting Cables. Two Methods available: Mains and Sync Pulses.

Mains: Plug projector into an AC wall outlet. Plug *Mains Sync Adapter* (see below) into the same outlet to provide camera with same frequency as the projector. (1) Follow instructions regarding mounting the Syncobox. (2) Insert cable-end (four-pin Fischer connector) of Mains Sync Adapter (see below) into SYNC outlet on Syncobox. (3) Set unmarked toggle switch (located between SYNC and VIDEO outlets) toward the Operator (SYNC). (4) Set toggle switch to EXT (green diode will illuminate). (5) Set MAN/AUTO switch *up* to MAN. (6) Align camera lens to the projector screen. (7) Enter the same fps engraved on the Stick-in Module into the five-digit Frame Speed Selector located at right-rear of Syncobox. (8) Turn camera and projector on and observe screen. (9) Rotate PHASE shift knob until projected image appears darkest.

NOTE: Once darkest image is achieved, flip 0°/90° toggle switch up or down to see if image can be darkened more. Set switch at deepest rendition.

NOTE: With mains, sync does NOT stay stored when camera and/or projector is turned on or off. It must be reset each take.

Sync Pulses: Only possible when projector is fitted with either (1) a pulse generator and the camera has contacts at the shutter, or (2) a photo cell is inserted into the projected beam and the light pulses are used as sync signals.

(1) Follow instructions regarding mounting the Syncobox. (2) Insert the four-pin Fischer connector of the projector "sync cable" into the SYNC outlet on Syncobox. (3) Set unmarked toggle switch (located between SYNC and VIDEO outlets) toward the Operator (SYNC). (4) Set toggle switch to EXT (green diode will illuminate). (5) Set MAN/AUTO switch *up* to MAN. (6) Align camera lens to the projector screen. (7) Enter the same fps engraved on the Stick-in Module into the five-digit Frame Speed Selector located at right-rear of Syncobox. (8) Turn camera and projector on and observe screen. (9) Rotate PHASE shift knob until projected image appears darkest.

NOTE: Once darkest image is achieved, flip 0°/90° toggle switch up or down to see if image can be darkened more. Set switch at deepest rendition.

NOTE: With pulses, the entered data stays stored regardless of how many times the camera and projector are turned on or off and does NOT have to be reset.

NOTE: It is possible to synchronize a camera shutter and projector without a Syncobox, but the procedure has its limitations.

To Synchronize Camera Shutter and Projector without a Syncobox. (1) Make certain that the long accessory plug cover is in place at lower right of camera. (2) Set camera speed to match that of the projector (e.g., 24 fps). (3) Turn camera and projector on and observe screen. (4) Press the T./UP button on the Control Panel (see section 15.1c, Powerline Control Panel) and hold until the projected picture appears in the viewfinder at its darkest.

NOTE: This procedure will have to be repeated each take.

Mains Sync Adapter
Small unit with a connecting cable, can be connected to either a 110v AC or a 220v AC outlet (wall or AC generator). Its pulses scan the frequency and are used for synchronizing only, NOT for running the camera at sync speed. To run the camera, requires power from mains or battery.

To Use Mains Sync Adapter. (1) Insert cable end of Mains Sync Adapter (four-pin Fischer connector) into SYNC outlet on Syncobox. (2) Set toggle switch to EXT (green diode will illuminate). (3) Flip MAN/AUTO switch down to AUTO. (4) Set unmarked toggle switch (located between SYNC and VIDEO outlets) toward the Operator (SYNC). (5) Plug Mains Sync Adapter, with its connected cable, into wall outlet or AC generator. Maintains sync no matter how many times camera is turned on/off.

CAUTION: Always be certain that the Stick-in Module on the Syncobox agrees with the Hertz emanating from the mains or AC generator, and that the fps is the frame rate desired.

Video Assist Systems
Four Video Assists Systems available: (1) a B&W Video Camera with a B&W Video Assist Monitor; (2) a Color Video Camera with a Color Video Assist Monitor; (3) a Video Viewfinder; (4) a Lightweight B&W Video Viewfinder (for use when film camera is rigged for Steadicam shots).

B&W Video Camera. Mounts to the right side of the Standard Viewfinder. Top of camera is fitted with a monitor *On/Off* toggle. Front of camera (facing forward) is fitted with a *Video Out* Fischer connector and, below that, an *Iris Knob,* which when rotated adjusts the brightness of the monitor image. At rear of camera is a *BNC Video Outlet,* for connecting external monitors, recorders, transmitters, etc.

To Mount. (1) Disconnect film camera. (2) Remove cover from right side of Standard Viewfinder with an M5 Allen screwdriver and reveal optics. (3) Ascertain that optics in viewfinder and camera are clean. (4) Align video camera connector and its two captive screws with matching connector and tapped holes on film camera. (5) Attach B&W camera to viewfinder with M5 Allen screwdriver. (6) Reconnect film camera.

B&W Monitor.
To mount: (1) Slide rotatable arm of monitor into shoe on top of B&W camera. (2) Insert attached monitor cable plug into Fischer connector at front of B&W camera. (3) Turn toggle on camera to on. (4) Adjust viewfinder brightness by rotating Iris Knob on video camera.

CAUTION: Adjust monitor brightness only after the lens aperture on the film camera has been set.

(5) Loosen *Sunshade Screw* at top of monitor and slide the *Monitor Sunshade* in its restricted slot back to shade the monitor screen.

Trim Potentiometers: Recessed 2mm slotted screws at left side of monitor are for finite adjustments of brightness and contrast, but these should be changed only if necessary and by a video technician.

Color Video Camera. Mounts to the right side of the Standard Viewfinder. Top front of camera is fitted with a monitor *On/Off* toggle, and a three-position toggle that can be set to *AUTO. 3200K or 5600K.*

NOTE: The three-position switch adjusts the video camera's white balance. Set to AUTO, the camera achieves a "neutral" color reproduction. It is set to 3200 when filming under incandescents or when a correction filter is on the camera lens. It is set to 5600 when filming in daylight.

Front of camera (facing forward) is fitted with a *Video Out* Fischer connector and, below that, an *Iris Knob,* which when rotated adjusts the brightness of the viewfinder image. At rear of camera is a *BNC Video Outlet,* for connecting external monitors, recorders, transmitters, etc.

To Mount. (1) Disconnect film camera. (2) Remove cover from right side of Standard Viewfinder with an M5 Allen screwdriver and reveal optics. (3) Ascertain that optics in viewfinder and camera are clean. (4) Align video camera connector and its two captive screws with matching connector and tapped holes on film camera. (5) Attach color camera to viewfinder with M5 Allen screwdriver. (6) Reconnect film camera.

Color Monitor. *To mount:* (1) Slide rotatable arm of monitor into shoe on top of color camera; secure with locking screw.

NOTE: The monitor is mounted on a ball joint (which allows for tilting the monitor at any desired angle), attached to the rotatable arm.

(2) Insert attached monitor cable plug into Fischer connector at front of color camera. (3) Slide On/Off switch at upper right side of monitor to On. (4) Adjust monitor brightness by rotating Iris Knob at front of video camera.

CAUTION: Adjust monitor brightness only after the lens aperture on the film camera has been set.

(5) Depress bracket of removeable sunshade and unfold the sides until they lock in place. Attach the sunshade with a rubber band to monitor.

Brightness and color intensity: Set on monitor left side with two small knobs.

Video Viewfinder. Replaces the standard viewfinder. Uses a video camera and its monitor, although the Right Eyepiece (see Sec. 15.3i) can be mounted in place of a video camera. The Video Viewfinder has NO filter wheel, NO beamsplitter (provides 100% light transmission to a camera or Right Eyepiece as a result), and canNOT be fitted with Readouts (see Sec. 15.1m, Footage Counter) or a Movielite (see Sec. 15.1f, Standard Viewfinder). A Remote Control Box (see Sec. 15.3j below) can be connected to the top of the Video Viewfinder.

To Mount Video Viewfinder to Camera. (1) Disconnect film camera. (2) Remove Standard Viewfinder (see Sec. 15.1f). (3) Align Video Viewfinder optics to camera optics and attach with three captive M5 Allen screws. (4) Remove cover from right side of Video Viewfinder with an M5 Allen screwdriver and reveal optics. (5) Ascertain that optics in viewfinder and camera are clean. (6) Align B&W or color video camera connector and its two captive screws with matching connector and tapped holes on film camera. (7) Attach camera to viewfinder with M5 Allen screwdriver. (8) Mount and connect monitors as noted for B&W and/or color monitors (above). (9) Reconnect film camera.

To Install Remote Control Box to Video Viewfinder. (1) Disconnect the camera. (2) Remove the accessory connector plate at top of Video Viewfinder with an M5 Allen screwdriver. (3) Align and insert small connector on the Remote Control Box cable *gently* into connector. (4)

Secure Remote Control Box cable connector to Video Viewfinder with single M5 Allen screw. (5) Reconnect camera.

Lightweight B&W Video Viewfinder. Attached when camera is prepared for Steadicam Mode. (See also Chapter 18, Steadicam.) Viewfinder is equipped with an On/Off switch at the front, a BNC video outlet at the right side, and Iris Control Knob at the left side above a Fischer outlet that connects to the cable plug of a B&W Video Monitor (see above). The monitor is secured in the shoe at the top of the viewfinder.

To Mount Lightweight B&W Video Viewfinder to Camera. (1) Disconnect film camera. (2) Remove Standard Viewfinder (see Sec. 15.1f). (3) Align Lightweight B&W Video Viewfinder optics to camera optics and attach with two captive M5 Allen screws (unlike other viewfinders that attach with three screws). (4) Secure monitor in viewfinder shoe. (5) Insert attached monitor cable plug into Fischer connector at front of camera. (6) Reconnect film camera. (7) Flip On/Off switch at right side of monitor to On. (8) Adjust monitor brightness by rotating Iris Knob at front of video camera.

CAUTION: Adjust monitor brightness only after the lens aperture on the film camera has been set.

15.3i Right Eyepiece
Fits to right side of viewfinder. Can be used by Director to view action, or Director of Photography to check lighting while Operator is filming.

To Mount. (1) Remove cover from right side of Standard Viewfinder with an M5 Allen screwdriver to reveal optics. (2) Attach Right Eyepiece with single M5 Allen screw.

NOTE: Right Eyepiece can also be fitted to the Video Viewfinder (see Sec. 15.3c)

Eyecup. Cushionable eyecup is fitted with a 31.5mm diameter ring that will accept a diopter correction lens or a filter, if desired.
To Remove. Pull eyecup straight out.
To View through Lens. Place eye to eyecup.

WARNING: The image in the right eyepiece is darker than that in the left eyepiece due to the beamsplitter in the viewfinder optics, NOT the glass in the eyepiece.

To Orient the Image. Rotate knurled barrel of eyepiece until image is correct when looking through the eyepiece (lower right of groundglass reads aspect ratio).
To Focus. Rotate knurled rubber ring nearest eyecup until groundglass grains and crosshair are sharp.

NOTE: A reference scale forward of the focus ring (+5 to −5) can be used to mark eyepiece focus for various users of the camera (Director, Director of Photography, etc.).

Eyepiece Heater. Prevents fogging of back element of eyepiece when filming in low temperatures. Insert short cable plug into outlet on eyepiece and other end into plug at right front of camera.

NOTE: Heater only works if there is power to the camera.

NOTE: When the eyepiece is on the camera, no video assist can be used.

Remote Control Box (Fig. 15–8)

Controls camera from as far away as 10m (32 ½ ft). Used as a distant On/Off switch and readout. Not to be confused with the Speedbox Remote Control (see Section 15.3b). Remote Control Box is fitted with *On/Off* button, LED *fps* display that only lights when camera runs, a *check* button to recall and show (in the fps display) camera's Control Board preset fps rate, a *footage counter* that is illuminated and readable as long as the unit is connected to the camera, a *reset* button to set the counter back to zero when desired, a red battery condition diode labeled BAT that lights when the battery voltage drops to 20 volts or less, a red diode labeled SYNC that illuminates only if camera speed differs from that set on the camera and/or when camera is coming up to speed or slowing down to stop. Attached cable with connector installs on Standard Viewfinder.

To Install. (1) Disconnect the camera. (2) Remove the accessory connector plate at top of Standard Viewfinder with an M5 Allen screwdriver. (3) Align and inset small connector on the Remote Control

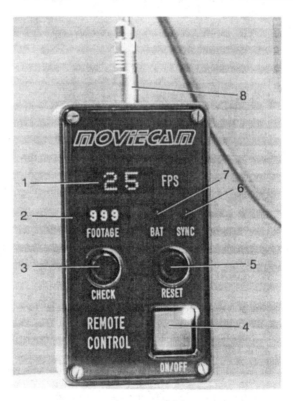

Figure 15–8 MOVIECAM Remote Control Box. Courtesy of MOVIECAM F.G. Bauer GmbH.

1. Fps display
2. Footage/meter counter
3. Check (recall) button
4. On/Off button

5. Counter reset button
6. Out-of-sync (red) diode
7. Low battery (red) diode
8. Cable connector to camera

Box cable *gently* into connector. (4) Secure Remote Control Box cable connector to viewfinder with single M5 Allen screw. (5) Reconnect camera.

NOTE: To use the Remote Control requires removing the Readouts (see Sec. 15.1m, Footage Counters, Readouts). They canNOT be used at the same time.

15.3k Shoulder Rest

Curved unit is padded on under side and fitted with a velcro adhesive strip on its crown, which adheres to the velcro pad affixed to the underside of the camera (see 15.1, Base).

15.3l Assistant Cameraman's Light

Small 24v/4w work light is mounted on a shoe atop the Movielite (see Sec. 15.1.f, Viewfinder), or on a shoe atop the Readout (see Sec. 15.1m, Footage Counter).

To Mount AC's Light. Slide base of light into shoe and tighten mounting screw.

Disconnect camera. Insert the worklight's attached coiled cable into one of the two connectors below the DC (dust check) button. Reconnect camera. Turn lamp on/off by rotating its cap.

chapter 16

Panavision Panaflex 35mm Cameras and Magazines

16.1 PANAVISION PANAFLEX* 35mm CAMERA SYSTEMS

Golden Panaflex/Golden Panaflex II (G2) (Figs. 16–1a, 16-1b), Platinum Panaflex (Figs. 16-2a, 16-2b, 16-2c), and Panaflex-X (Fig. 16-3a, 16-3b) Cameras.

NOTE: All directions are from Operator's point of view.

The Golden Panaflex, Golden Panaflex II (G2), Platinum Panaflex, and Panaflex-X are basically the same camera. Their differences are noted as follows:

The Golden Panaflex has (a) groundglass (aspect ratio) markings that can be clearly defined in low-light-level situations by illuminating the outline of the field (manufacturer calls this feature "Panaglow"); (b) viewfinder controls (ratio selector, magnification knob, contrast filters) located on the optics housing that extends vertically and forward of the lens mount; (c) a removable eyepiece; (d) a detachable viewing extension tube that contains an additional sliding magnifying control; (e) a rotatable (360°) eyepiece coupling; and (f) the ability to be converted from studio mode to hand-held mode quickly.

The Golden Panaflex GII (G2) has, in addition to (a) through (f) cited for the Golden Panaflex, (g) brighter viewfinder optics, and (h) a drive system that reduces its noise level by 35 percent of the Golden Panaflex and Panaflex-X cameras.

The Platinum Panaflex has, in addition to (a) through (f) cited for the Golden Panaflex, (g) a total crystal-controlled drive system (1/10th frame stages) that is quieter than the Golden Panaflex II (G2); (h) a brighter viewfinder; (i) an internal microprocessor control that monitors all the camera's functions (e.g., battery level, crystal frame rate deviation, illegal frame rate [i.e., if camera is running at other than a programmed frame rate, or if running faster than 36fps]) alerts Operator if camera jams, and displays a warning when approximately 15.2 meters (50ft) of film remains in magazine and/or when it is out of film (but only if a platinum magazine [see Sec. 16.2e] is used on the camera); (j) a shutter angle adjustment measurable to within 1/10th of a degree (as opposed to shutter adjustments of only 10° in the other cameras); (k) an LCD digital status/warning

---

*Manufacturer states the designation PANAFLEX stands for "PANAvision ReFLEX"; Panaflex-X stands for "PANAvision ReFLEX with modified door and viewing system."

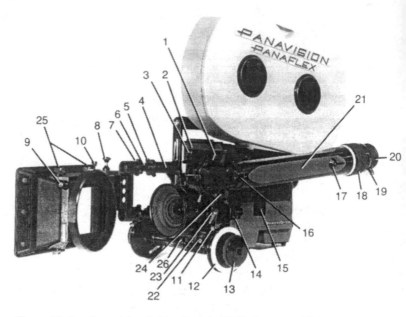

Figure 16–1a Panavision Golden Panaflex (G2). Courtesy of Panavision, Inc.

1. Brake ring handle
2. "O" button
3. "X" button
4. Iris rod bracket
5. Bracket scalloped knob
6. Iris rod
7. Matte-box scalloped knob
8. Swing-away release knob
9. Filter holder retaining dowel knob
10. Retaining lock screw
11. Follow-focus limiter
12. Follow-focus scale plate
13. Follow-focus knob
14. Panaglow switch
15. Door latch
16. Extension tube locking ring
17. Eyepiece magnifier
18. Eyepiece focus ring
19. Panaclear connector
20. Eyepiece
21. Extension viewing tube
22. Follow-focus locking knob
23. Lens port lock
24. ND filter switch
25. Sunshade lock knob
26. Modular follow-focus extension lock

display of fps, footage/meters, and shutter angle; (l) inching and run buttons inside the camera; (m) automatic shut-off when the magazine has only 1.52m (5ft) of film remaining; (o) an additional ON/OFF switch located below the Panaglow switch.

The Panaflex-X has (a) a non-removable eyepiece; (b) viewing controls (ratio selector, open/close knob, and contrast filters) located on the horizontal optics housing; (c) a viewing system that, as an integral part of the camera door precludes the camera from being converted to a hand-held mode; (d) NO "Panaglow" and; (e) NO magnification knob.

The Panaflex-X is often used when a hand-held camera is not necessary to a production, and/or as a second camera.

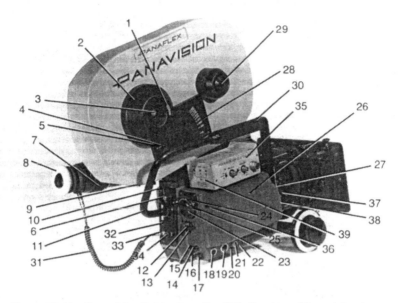

Figure 16–1b Panavision Golden Panaflex (G2). Courtesy of Panavision, Inc.

1. Magazine spiral marking
2. Spindle wheel housing
3. Take-up spindle wheel
4. Internal roller lever
5. Heater light
6. Magazine port lock
7. Focus ring
8. Eyepiece (with cover)
9. Viewing tube bracket
10. Magazine lock button
11. Auxiliary carry handle
12. Inching knob
13. Inching knob lock
14. Variable speed safety lock
15. Sync/vary switch
16. Variable speed knob
17. On/Off switch
18. 10-pin LEMO accessory plug
19. 3-pin LEMO power plug
20. Amber light

21. 2-pin LEMO plug
22. Green/red light
23. External shutter control latch
24. Shutter
25. Shutter safety locks
26. Motor cover
27. 2-pin zoom LEMO (not visible)
28. Magazine footage indicator
29. Feed spindle
30. Auxiliary carry handle
31. Panaclear cable
32. Panaclear on/off switch
33. Panaclear receptacle plug
34. Panaclear fuse
35. Super CCD video tap
36. Eyeglass holder
37. Iris rod bracket lock
38. Iris rod bracket
39. Super CCD control panel

Except where specifically noted, information herein applies to all four cameras.

16.1a Base

Camera is fitted with female dovetail at front catch-lock at rear so as to conform to manufacturer's geared head (see Sec. 9.6, Panahead). Manufacturer calls the center indented portion of the camera base the "cave." A

Figure 16–2a Panavision Platinum Panaflex, studio configuration. Courtesy of Panavision, Inc.

1. Dual digital display
2. Annunciator Panel
3. On/Off switch
4. Panaglow Switch
5. Erector Lock
6. Door latch

bracket in the cave accommodates an accessory shoulder rest and a zoom control holder.

Sliding Base Plate (Fig. 16–4). Required in order to use camera on a non-Panavision tripod or geared head. Unit consists of two parts

1. *Base:* Fitted with multiple 3/8″-16 tapped holes to accommodate tripod or geared-head lockdown screw (series of tapped holes permits better balance of camera on head when various-weight lenses are used.) Bubble-level on base always faces Operator.

NOTE: Newer units do not have a bubble-level.

2. *Dovetail Carriage:* Slides on base for ease of balance of camera on tripod.
   To Lock. In older units, push lever on sliding block forward. In newer units, rotate side knob toward Operator.
   To Release. In older units, push lever toward Operator. In newer units, rotate side knob away from Operator.
   To Mount Camera to Dovetail Carriage or Panahead. Match female dovetail at front of camera base to male dovetail in carriage. Slide camera forward until it secures to carriage with audible click. Rotate *Lock Shoe* at rear of carriage until it secures rear of camera.
   To Remove Camera. Grasp camera securely. Undo lock screw at rear of carriage. Pull spring-loaded *quick-release catch* at side of dovetail. Slide camera back and up.

Figure 16–2b   Panavision Platinum Panaflex. Courtesy of Panavision, Inc.

1. Fps selector switch
2. Fwd/rev Switch
3. On/Off switch
4. Velcro strap cable holder

5. Lens light/right-hand grip shoe
6. Indicator lights (red/amber)
7. Tape hook
8. Exterior motor cover screws

16.1b Motor
Built-in crystal sync/variable. 24v DC

Golden Panaflex, Golden Panaflex II (G2), and Panaflex-X Only.   Motor does NOT reverse.

Platinum Panaflex.   Motor will reverse.

WARNING: To reverse film in a Platinum Panaflex, it is necessary to use a Platinum Reversing Magazine. (See Sec. 16.2e. Platinum Magazine).

NOTE: On all cameras, change of motors is a factory job.

Golden Panaflex, Golden Panaflex II (G2), and Panaflex-X.
To Preset 24/25 fps Speed of Crystal Motor.   Invert camera; insert thin-bladed screwdriver into slot in cover of fps switch (not shown) located in side wall of cave; slide switch toward desired fps.

NOTE: The "24" setting is always 24fps. The "25" setting is either 25, 29.97, or 30fps (see below and Sec. 16.1c. Power Panel).

CAUTION: *Always* ascertain the fps section of this switch.

To Set the Motor to Alternate 25 fps or 29.97 fps or 30 fps Crystal-Sync Speed.   Unplug camera; remove motor cover (see Sec. 16.1c. Power Panel), and change the position of the switch at the top of the second circuit board from camera front to desired fps speed.

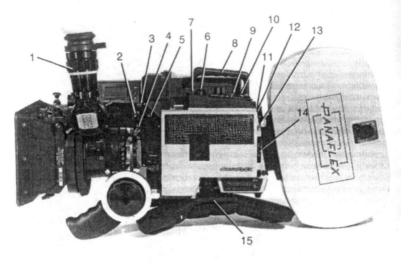

Figure 16–2c Panavision Platinum Panaflex, hand-held configuration. Courtesy of Panavision, Inc.

1. Short eyepiece
2. Selector lever
3. Anamorphic setting
4. Closed setting
5. Spherical lens setting
6. Top magazine latch
7. Top magazine safety catch
8. Carry handle

9. Panaclear switch
10. Panaclear connector
11. Rear magazine port latch
12. Rear magazine port latch
13. Long eyepiece resting post
14. Door release
15. Shoulder pad

To Run Motor in Crystal Sync.   Set SYNC/VARY selector switch at rear of camera to SYNC.

To Run Motor at Variable Speed.   Raise variable-speed safety lock; slide selector switch to VARY. Run camera. Observe fps counter and rotate Variable Speed Knob located below selector switch until desired fps appears.

NOTE: Camera will run from 4 to 34 fps only.

Platinum Camera Only.

To Preset Normal (24 fps)/29.97 fps Speed of Crystal Motor.   Invert camera; insert thin-bladed screwdriver into slot in cover of fps switch (not shown) located in side wall of cave; slide switch toward desired fps.

To Run Motor in Crystal Sync.   Set crystal control speed at back of camera.

To Set Forward/Reverse on Camera.   Insert thin-bladed screwdriver into slot in cover of switch on rear side wall of camera that faces the ON/OFF switch. Slide to desired position (FWD or REV).

WARNING: The Platinum will NOT run if switched to REV and the camera is mounted with a magazine other than one capable of reversing (see Sec. 16.2e).

Figure 16–3a Panavision Panaflex-X, left front. Courtesy of Panavision, Inc.

1. Lens lock
2. Digital display
3. Door latch
4. ND switch
5. Focus ring

6. Eyepiece
7. Open/close lever (not visible)
8. Ratio selector
9. Follow Focus knob
10. 009.0m (2000-ft) magazine

16.1c Power Panel (Fig. 16–5).
At lower right side on all cameras.

Powerline. Three-pin LEMO plug of 24v battery cable inserts into matching center of plug.

NOTE: When facing the three-pin LEMO, with the single male pin down, the right female pin is no. 1 (positive), the left female pin is no. 2 (ground, or minus). The male pin is used by Panavision technicians.

Heater. Two-pin LEMO accepts a battery-powered connector. To heat the camera in cold weather conditions, Panavision recommends the use of a separate battery.

NOTE: On the two-pin LEMO plug, the female is no. 1 (positive [+]), the male no. 2 (negative [−]), or ground).

Amber Light. Indicates heater is on; will extinguish when camera heat is normal (21°C [70°F]).

Green/red Battery Condition Light. Green indicates battery is connected and will turn red when power to camera drops below 21 volts.

NOTE: There is NO green condition light on the Platinum as on the other cameras (See Fig. 16–6).

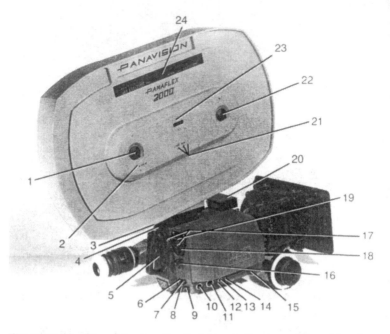

Figure 16–3b Panavision Panaflex-X, right-rear. Courtesy of Panavision, Inc.

1. Manual take-up knob
2. Take-up indicator light
3. Magazine lock button
4. Magazine lock lever
5. Carry handle
6. Sync-vary switch
7. Variable speed safety lock
8. Variable speed knob
9. On/Off switch
10. 10-pin LEMO auxiliary plug
11. 3-pin LEMO power plug
12. Amber light

13. 2-pin LEMO heater plug
14. Green/red light
15. Tape hook
16. Inching knob
17. Shutter safety locks
18. External shutter control latch
19. Shutter
20. Digital display
21. Fast/Slow/Clear buttons
22. Manual feed knob
23. LCD elapsed footage display
24. Footage remaining indicator

Ten-pin LEMO Accessory Plug. Accepts connector on remote ON/OFF switch and fps read-out.

NOTE: Extension cables up to 12.2m (40 ft) are available for controlling the camera remotely.

Also accepts connector on the following Synch Box Control Units:

1. *Time-Lapse Synchronizer,* which will run camera at speeds of 0.25 to 640 seconds per frame.

CAUTION: It is *seconds per frame,* NOT frames per second.

2. *Phasable Synchronizer,* which synchronizes camera with a foreground or background projector or video playback (accommodates 24/24,

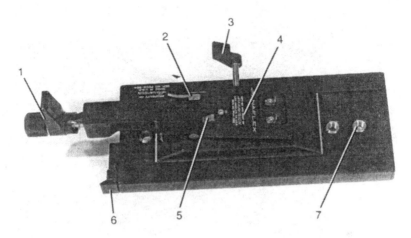

Figure 16–4 Panavision sliding base plate. Courtesy of Panavision, Inc.

1. Shoelock
2. Camera mount release
3. Base plate lock
4. Sliding baseplate dovetail

5. Camera locking pin
6. Sliding base plate safety lock
7. ⅜-16" tapped hole (1 of 9)

24/30, 25/25, 30/30 film/video fps rates and allows for adjustable phase selection on both video and projector synch),

3. *Field-to-Frame Synchronizer,* which synchronizes the camera to a video playback (accommodates 24/24, 24/30, 25/25, 30/30 film/video fps rates).

NOTE: The above cited Sync Boxes control the speed of the camera. When synchronized to NTSC video, 24 fps is actually 23.976 fps, and 30 fps is actually 29.97 fps. An audio output on each box is a one volt [1v] peak to peak pilot tone available for audio sync purposes.

WARNING: Shutter setting is crucial for video playback. When using one of the aforementioned synchronizers to shoot 30-fps video with a 24-fps camera, set shutter to 144°. At other film/video speeds (i.e., 24/24, 25/25, 30/30) set shutter to 180°.

ON/OFF Switch—Golden Panaflex, Golden Panaflex II (G2), and Panaflex-X. Located at lower rear of camera, right of variable-speed knob of camera.

ON/OFF Switch—Platinum Camera. Located at right of speed selector fps door. A secondary ON/OFF Switch is located at the camera left side below the Panaglow Switch.

CAUTION: The camera must be turned ON or OFF by this switch ONLY (or an accessory Handgrip or Remote Control—through the accessory port [see following references]) in order to properly follow a sequence of circuitry and optical/mechanical alignment.

Never apply or interrupt power to the camera by using an in-line switch in a cable, or by disconnecting/connecting the power plug from/to the battery!

Figure 16–5 Panavision Golden Panaflex, G2, and Panaflex-X Circuit Boards. Courtesy of Panavision, Inc.

1. Power supply board
2. Drive board
3. Crystal tachometer board
4. Catch-all board
5. Retaining knobs
6. Lens light/handgrip switch dovetail
7. Crystal speed selection switch
8. 10-pin LEMO accessory plug
9. 3-pin LEMO power plug
10. Amber light
11. 2-pin LEMO heater plug
12. Red/green light

Platinum Camera only: A secondary ON/OFF Switch is located at the camera left side below the Panaglow Switch.

ON/OFF Handgrip Accessory (not visible). Overrides ON/OFF Switch at back of camera.

To Mount Handgrip. Slide bracket into dovetail at right front of camera; rotate locking lever away from Operator to secure. Grip contains a pressure switch that starts camera when depressed, stops camera when released. Second thumb-actuated switch starts camera when pushed UP, stops camera when pushed DOWN.

Remote Control. A separate unit that inserts into right front dovetail in place of handgrip. Contains a 2m (6 ft) or longer length of cable with ON/OFF switch attached so that camera can be run/stopped from a distance.

NOTE: This remote control, often referred to as a "Tacho" (Tachometer) unit, plugs into the ten-pin accessory connector. The unit displays camera footage, fps speed, and allows On/Off switching of camera from up to 12.2m [40 ft] away.

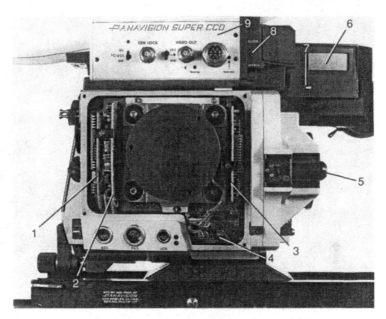

Figure 16–6 Panavision Platinum Panaflex Circuit Boards. Courtesy of Panavision, Inc.

1. Warning board	4. Accessory power	7. Display mode switch
2. Drive board	fuse (5 amps)	8. CCD filter selector
3. Master Board	5. 2-pin LEMO (– 24v)	9. CCD video tap
	6. Digital display	

Front Power Plug. Small two-pin LEMO 24-volt outlet at front of camera. A multipurpose plug. When a short pigtail cable, fitted with LEMO plugs at each end, is used, power is provided to: (1) a zoom lens motor; (2) an accessory lens light; or (3) any accessory that requires + 24 volts.

WARNING: Do NOT use this outlet as a heater to the camera. Manufacturer recommends that a separate battery be used for a heater.

CAUTION: While this outlet is intended to supply power to the zoom lens or lens light from the same 24v source that supplies power to the camera, the use of one battery for two purposes (e.g., camera and zoom motor, camera and lens light, etc.) can drain the battery if the motor is used constantly or often.

Interchangeable Circuit Boards. Boards contain major electronic systems of camera.

NOTE: The Golden Panaflex, Golden Panaflex II (G2), and Panaflex-X contain four boards (Fig. 16–6), the Panaflex Platinum contains three boards (Fig. 16–7). Access to boards requires removal of motor cover at right side of either camera.

    To Remove Motor Cover. Golden Panaflex, Golden Panaflex II (G2), and Panaflex-X: Open camera door; reach over camera, grasp motor cover. With 6.4mm (¼ in.) hex-nut driver (provided by Panavision in the

Figure 16–7 Panavision Platinum display panel. Courtesy of Panavision, Inc.

1. Left side display panel
2. Mode button
3. Counter set/reset/clear button
4. Ratio selector knob

5. Prism lock
6. Eyepiece brake
7. Eyepiece lock release
8. Eyepiece locking ring

camera's accessory case, rotate forward screw located in camera wall behind movement and through interior upholstery, one-quarter turn counterclockwise. Rotate rear screw located in camera wall behind buckle-trip apron one-quarter turn counterclockwise.

NOTE: Buckle-trip apron is shaped to allow for hex-nut driver.

Push motor cover UP; swing bottom of cover away from camera; lift entire cover away from camera to reveal four boards.

Function of Boards (Fig. 6–6).

Power Supply Board: Board nearest Operator. Contains circuitry for reduction of 24v system to 9v circuitry in camera; also battery condition circuit (green and red light digital display).

Drive Board: Second Board from Operator, nearest motor. Contains circuitry that supplies information to motor (crystal phase, speed, start, stop, etc.).

Crystal-Tachometer Board: Third board from Operator, near motor. Contains the crystal standards (24 fps, 25 fps, 29.97 fps, 30 fps) that maintain the speed of the camera, as well as the dividing networks that maintain the counter and tachometer.

Catch-All Board: Farthest Board from Operator near motor. Contains circuitry for other functions, such as mirror-search speed (quickness of clearing shutter from viewfinder), heater conditions light, shutter pulse buffer, main on/off relay, etc.

NOTE: Other circuitry, within the camera body cannot be changed except by Panavision technicians.

To Change Boards.

NOTE: There is a tendency to assume that the moment a problem develops in the camera it is in the circuit boards. While boards have been known to malfunction, it is recommended that all other measures be explored before changing the boards. (It takes less time in the final analysis.)

To Remove Boards. First, remove the power plug from the camera. Double-check that there is NO power to the camera. Ascertain that ALL power to the camera is disconnected.

WARNING: Removing boards while there is power to the camera can destroy *all* its circuitry if done wrong. Pull the power plug and all other power connections! With NO power to the camera, removing boards is a simple, safe procedure.

Pull horizontal spring-loaded retaining knob at side of boards, rotate until vertical, and release. Pull board straight out, parallel to connectors.

To Insert New Board. First, make certain that power plug is removed from camera. Check to see that there is NO power to the camera. Ascertain that ALL power is disconnected.

WARNING: Inserting boards while there is power to the camera can destroy *all* its circuitry if done wrong. Pull the power plug and all other power connections! With NO power to the camera, inserting boards is a simple, safe procedure.

Ascertain that correct board is to be inserted into proper connector. Hold board parallel to connectors and push straight in. When all boards have been inserted, rotate spring-loaded retaining knobs to a horizontal position, with board edges fitting in retainer groove. Replace motor cover.

Panaflex Platinum only.

To Remove Motor Cover. Use a 2.38mm (3/32 in.) Allen wrench to loosen four screws on outside corners of motor cover. When screws are loose, gently lift motor cover UP and away from camera to reveal three boards.

Function of Boards (Fig. 16–7).

Boon Board (nearest Operator). Contains circuitry for detecting low and out-of-film; reads out-of-film reset signal; notes illegal speed; reads film jam, low battery, and 29.97 function; generates the counter reset signal; displays reverse signal; notes when filter is in.

Drive Board (second from Operator). Contains circuitry for mirror stopping position; shutter pulse, ON/OFF signal, speed selection, external enable, external clock, FET (Field Effec Transistor) drive signal, Magazine FET, inching switch, and the FET kill.

Master CPU (Central Processing Unit) Board (near lens). Contains circuitry that measures the camera speed; detects illegal speeds above 40 fps, counts footage, measures shutter degrees, controls serial bus.

NOTE: Other circuit boards are within the camera body and cannot be changed except by Panavision technicians. These are: *Digital display board*—which shows feet/meters, speed and shutter degrees; shows when camera runs at 29.97fps; displays when filter is in the camera; and holds the camera footage in memory. *Bottom board*—controls motor power, time code, ON/OFF switch, reverse switch and drive, power to all boards, and other miscellaneous circuits.

To Remove Platinum Boards. (1) Remove the power plug from the camera. (2) Make certain that there is NO power to the camera. (3) Ascertain that ALL power to the camera is disconnected.

WARNING: Removing boards while there is power to the camera can destroy *all* its circuitry if done wrong. Pull the power plug and all other power connections! With NO power to the camera, removing boards is a simple, safe procedure.

(4) Pull horizontal spring-loaded retaining knob at side of boards, rotate until vertical, and release. (5) Pull board straight out, parallel to connectors.

To Insert New Board. (1) Make certain that power plug is removed from camera. (2) Check to see that there is NO power to the camera. (3) Check that ALL power is disconnected.

WARNING: Inserting boards while there is power to the camera can destroy *all* its circuitry if done wrong. Pull the power plug and all other power connections. With NO power to the camera, changing boards is a simple, safe procedure.

(4) Ascertain that correct board will be inserted into proper connector. (5) Hold board parallel to connectors; push straight in. (6) When all boards have been inserted, rotate spring-loaded retaining knobs to a horizontal position, with board edges fitting in retainer groove; replace motor cover.

Batteries. 24-v power supply. Battery serial numbers denote voltage, type, ampere hour, and the order of manufacture (e.g., 24/NC/12/123 would be a 24-volt, nickel cadmium, 12-ampere hour battery, the 123rd unit to be manufactured). Sometimes the last number is a letter.

Battery types available: Block: 24v/NC (nickel cadmium)/12AH, 15AH, or 16AH (ampere hours); 24v/LA (lead acid)/10AH or 17 AH; 24v/GC (gel cel)/17 AH; *Purse* (shoulder-slung unit with built-in charger & voltage/amperage meter): 24v/NC/10AH; 24v/LA/10AH; *Belt:* 24v/NC/ 4AH, 6AH, or 10 AH.

NOTE: All block and newer purse-type batteries are fitted with two three-pin Cannon XLR connectors.

16.1d Turret
None. Single lens mount accepts Panavision mount lenses only, spherical or anamorphic.

16.1e Lenses
Must be fitted with Panavision lens mounts.

To Fit Lens to Camera. Rotate lens lock clockwise as far as it will go. Align pin on lens flange of matching hole in lower center of lens port. Insert lens flange flush to camera, making certain that pin engages the lens-port hole. Rotate the lens lock counterclockwise to secure.

16.1f Viewfinder
Reflex. Image 1:1.

Views more than full aperture. Numerous groundglass aspect ratios are available.

To View through Lens. Place eye to eyepiece.

To Focus Eyepiece. Rotate knurled ring of eyepiece until the center crosshair on groundglass is sharp.

NOTE: A reference ring forward of the focus ring can be used to mark eyepiece focus for various users of the camera (Director, Director of Photography, Camera Operator, etc.).

To Change or Clean Groundglass. Remove lens. First, unplug power to the camera to avoid accidental starting while working in lens port. Use *inching knob* to clear reflex mirror from groundglass. Wrap forefinger with lens tissue, reach forefinger through lens port, and slide groundglass toward opening. Clean and re-insert into camera with frosted (dull) side toward mirror, chamfered edges toward lens-port opening.

Matte Slot. Located forward of groundglass. *Hard Matte* is inserted with the bent portion (used as a fingergrip) pointing toward mirror. *Soft matte*—i.e., frame of film cut with Panavision or comparable matte cutter (see Fig. 14–25, Sec. 14.11d, Mitchell Matte Cutters)—slides into matte slot forward of the groundglass and upside down.

NOTE: Only certain groundglass holders (marked with an "M") can accept a matte.

To Clear Reflex Mirror from Groundglass. Push *inching knob safety lock* from under inching knob at back of camera. Depress and rotate inching knob.

CAUTION: *Always* return safety lock under inching knob to prevent possible damage to camera if the inching knob is accidentally depressed when camera is running.

NOTE: Camera stops with shutter in viewing position except when utilizing variable-speed mode or when shutter has been inched by hand (e.g., when threading or clearing mirror from the groundglass).

To Re-align Mirror for Viewing. Depress and rotate inching knob or turn camera on, run a few seconds, stop camera.

Golden Panaflex, Golden Panaflex II (G2), and Platinum Panaflex Eyepieces. Three available: *Long 48cm (19 in.) extension* (21) for studio mode; *Short 14cm (5.5 in.) eyepiece* for hand-held mode; *Intermediate 38cm* (15 in.) extension (not shown) for close-quarter filming. All three eyepieces fit to a rotatable (360°) coupling fitted with an eyepiece lock on the optics housing.

Eyepiece Brake. A metal disc with protruding *brake handle* at the viewfinder-rotation joint is used to lock the eyepiece into position.

To Lock. Rotate brake handle counterclockwise.

To Unlock. Rotate brake handle clockwise.

To Remove Eyepiece from Camera. Disengage eyepiece leveler and Panaclear from eyepiece, if attached. Hold eyepiece firmly. Loosen the eyepiece brake and rotate the eyepiece up and forward (the eyepiece housing "elbow" will swivel) until the eyepiece is vertical. Depress the *eyepiece locking ring button* and rotate the outside of the eyepiece locking ring until its white reference mark aligns to the matching reference mark on the eyepiece. Holding optics housing firmly, *gently* move eyepiece back and forth while lifting UP and away.

To Place Eyepiece on Camera. Make certain that optics housing elbow is UP. Align the slot on the eyepiece to pin in the optics housing. Hold the optics housing and gently slide in eyepiece until it seats. Rotate the locking ring past the button's audible click and until the ring is snug. Loosen the eyepiece brake and bring eyepiece down into desired position; rotate brake to secure.

WARNING: Each time an eyepiece is changed, the optics in the long, intermediate, and short eyepieces will invert the image. The optics should be erected while the short eyepiece is on the camera—*before* changing to the long eyepiece.

To Erect the Viewfinder Image. First, loosen the eyepiece brake. Depress the *Erector Lock* (located next to the brake) with right thumb in direction of inscribed arrow, and rotate eyepiece counterclockwise until it points down (180° from UP). Release Erector Lock and rotate eyepiece clockwise until an audible click is heard. Continue rotating eyepiece to viewing position; set eyepiece brake.

NOTE: When the short eyepiece is mounted (hand-held mode), it is not necessary to set the eyepiece brake.

Eyepiece Support Bracket (not shown). A foldable bracket placed at the right rear of the eyepiece fits to a locating pin (above hinge of door) to steady the eyepiece when shipping or storing the camera.

Eyepiece Leveler Accessory (not shown). Maintains long eyepiece at Operator's eye level, regardless of degree of tilt of camera.

To Fit Eyepiece Leveler. Fold in *Eyepiece Support Bracket* at rear of eyepiece and screw one end of the leveler to the thread on the left side of the Panahead. At other end, depress silver tab at back of leveler with thumb and fit hole to peg on support bracket. Release tab.

CAUTION: *Always* loosen the eyepiece brake when using the eyepiece leveler accessory. Failure to do so will damage the brake.

To Illuminate Aperture Field on Groundglass. Slide *"Panaglow" switch* at bottom of optic housing *forward.*

To Extinguish. Slide "Panaglow" switch toward Operator.

NOTE: *To adjust brightness of Panaglow on the Platinum,* simply rotate the *Panaglow Adjustment Knob* above the lens.

To Adjust Brightness of Panaglow on the Gold, Gold II, and the Panaflex-X requires removing the screw directly above the lens mount, inserting a jeweler's screwdriver into a slot, and rotating it.

Ratio Selectors. For use with anamorphic or spherical lenses. The handle on the vertical optic tube *ratio selector lever* (behind the lens) aligns to one of three ratio scribes on the optic housing. With *anamorphic lens* in mount, align lever UP to anamorphic scribe. With *spherical lens* in mount, position lever to CENTER to full aperture scribe.

To close. viewing system, align turn DOWN to square X-marked box.

Magnification Knob Lever. On long eyepiece, located near focus ring.

To Magnify Image 2×. Push lever down. For normal viewing, set lever horizontal.

Contrast Filters. Two. Spring-loaded lever below tachometer on optic housing. Push counterclockwise (DOWN) to view through .60 ND; push clockwise (UP) to view through .90 ND.

520

NOTE: Manufacturer will install a .30 ND if so desired.

Panaflex-X Only. Viewing system is an integral part of the camera door. Eyepiece is non-removable.

Ratio Selector: For use with anamorphic or spherical lenses. Lever at front of viewing tube. With *anamorphic lens* in mount, push lever *away* from camera and align to anamorphic scribe. With *spherical lens* in mount, push lever *forward* and align to full aperture scribe.

Contrast Filters. Two. Spring-loaded lever forward of eyepiece. Push lever *toward* camera to view through .60 ND; push lever *away* from camera to view through .90 ND.

NOTE: Manufacturer will install a .30 ND if so desired.

NOTE: There is no magnification knob on the Panaflex-X.

Open/Close Lever. On bottom of tube near door hinge; closes eyepiece so that stray light cannot enter tube and fog film.

16.1g Sunshade/Matte-box

Two types of mounting brackets are available: one accepts short matte-box rods; the other accepts mid-size and long matte-box rods. The *short rod bracket* is used when filming with wide angle lenses, when shooting in the hand-held mode, or when filming with lenses shorter than 100mm; the *long-rod bracket* is used when filming with a zoom lens, a lens longer than 100mm, or any type requiring support, such as an anamorphic lens.

NOTE: Rods are three sizes: 12.7cm (5 in.), 17.78cm (7 in.), and 22.86cm (9 in.). Size of the rods used depends on the lens that is "up."

To Mount Bracket for Short Matte-Box Rods. Slide bracket over two-pin LEMO plug at right front of camera. Insert short rods in bracket (one above the other).

NOTE: The lower rod must be inserted into the bracket *before* tightening the lever that secures the bracket to the camera.

Rotate scalloped knob on bracket counterclockwise to secure the upper rod.

To Mount Bracket for Long Matte-Box rods. Slide bracket over two-pin LEMO plug at right front of camera; push lock-lever down to secure. Insert rods into bracket; rotate scalloped knobs on bracket to secure rods.

To Mount Matte-Box on Rods. Slide matte-box onto rods, rotate scalloped knobs on matte-box clockwise to secure.

To Clear Matte-Box from Lens. Pull spring-loaded knob at top right of matte-box UP; swing matte-box to right.

NOTE: The following wide-angle and telephoto lenses cannot be used with a matte-box on the camera:

Spherical

9.8mm	T2.3	(uses 138mm retaining ring)
10mm	T1.9	Primo
14mm	T1.9	(uses 138mm retaining ring)
15mm	T4	(uses 101.6 × 127mm [4 × 5 in.] rectangular holder)
16mm	T2.8	(uses 114.3mm [4 ½ in.] retaining ring)
300mm	T2.8	

400mm	T4
500mm	T4
1000mm	T6.3

Anamorphic

28mm	T2.3	E-series
800mm	T5.6	
1000mm	T5.6	
2000mm	T9	

The standard matte-box will accommodate all other Panavision lenses, but be aware that:

- 10mm T1.9 Primo spherical lens has its own filter holder.
- 28mm T2.3 anamorphic lens has its own matte-box.
- 35mm T2 (all E-series) anamorphic lenses use a *one-stage filter matte-box.*

The tops of all matte-boxes are fitted with two knurled knobs that hold an extension shade.

16.1h Filters

Standard Matte-Box. Holds two 101.6 × 143.5mm (4 × 5.65 in.) filter holders. Its retaining rings contain a 108mm (4 ¼ in.) round filter holder and a 138mm (5.43 in.) polarizing circular filter holder.

One-Stage Filter Matte-Box. Has one 101.6 × 143.5mm (4 × 5.65 in.) rectangular holder, one 151.4mm (5.960 in.) diameter retaining ring, and one 138mm (5.43 in.) filter-retaining ring.

NOTE: A filter retaining ring with reducer to 114.3mm (4 ½ in.), for use with spherical prime lenses, is available.

To Remove Filter Holders from Matte-Box. Pull spring-loaded knob at left top of matte-box until retaining dowel clears holder; lift holder.

To Remove Retaining Ring from Matte-Box. Loosen lock screw.

Gelatine. Slot for curved *internal filter* is located behind door below prism of viewfinder tube.

To Insert Filter. Slide filter slot access cover aside. Place chamfer of filter holder into slot with bent portion of holder pointing forward (away from Operator). Push holder into camera body. Holder will follow curve of slot until bent portion of holder is flush. Slide filter access cover closed.

To Check Filter after Insertion of Holder. Remove lens. Rotate inching knob to clear reflex mirror from aperture. Determine visually that gelatine "covers" the aperture.

NOTE: Manufacturer also has filter holders that fit to rear housing of some lenses. A filter cutter is also available.

Platinum Panaflex Only. When a filter is inserted in the camera body, the Footage/Frame Counters (see Sec. 16.1p, Subsection 6) displays the letters FIL in the lower left corner.

16.1i Focus Controls

Four types available for these cameras: Panaflex Follow Focus (PFF); Super Follow Focus (SFF), Modular (MOD), and Remote Focus & T-Stop (RF&T).

It is not necessary to remove or clear any follow-focus unit when mounting or removing a lens from the lens port.

Generally, the PFF is used when camera is rigged for the hand-held mode, the other units used when camera is rigged for studio mode. All units fit to the *follow-focus pivot shaft* at front of camera below lens mount.

To Mount. Hold unit at 45° angle to shaft with left focus knob down, slide onto shaft, then pivot unit UP until it snaps into spring-loaded follow-focus locking pin.

To Remove. Hold follow-focus unit, pull knob on follow-focus locking pin, pivot unit down and away.

PFF. *Golden Panaflex, Golden Panaflex II (G2), & Panaflex-X:* Single follow-focus knob on left side. Does NOT have a marking disc.

PFF-P. *Platinum:* Same as the PFF (above) but has a marking disc.

SFF. Double-scalloped follow-focus knobs (on each side of camera). Knobs have smaller knobs inset in the larger knobs, but they are not vernier (fine-focus) type. Also inset in the knobs are circular halved marking discs that are magnetic, removable. Can be marked with grease or lead pencil for focus marks. To remove and clean discs, insert fingernail under disc-half and pry away from knob.

NOTE: The right side of the SFF is detachable, making it the same length as the PFF, but with a marking disc.

Modular. Requires a separate mounting plate. Plates vary, depending on type of camera in use.

To Mount. Slide Modular gear box into matching dovetail in either mounting plate. Rotate follow-focus lock-knob to secure to plate. Single-speed focus knob with removable disc fits to left side of gear box. Secure to gear box with second lock-knob. Fit extension tube to right side of gear box to clear motor housing. Secure with *its* lock-knob. Two-speed focus knob fits to either side of the gear box, secures with a lock-knob.

To Change from Close Focus to Infinity. On single-speed requires three revolutions of the focus knob.

To Change from Close Focus to Infinity. On two-speed setting requires one revolution of the focus knob.

NOTE: Shaft on the focus knob can be used to thumb-focus.

RF (Remote Focus). Wireless focus system. Requires Modular follow-focus unit on camera.

To Use. Mount gear box. Plug remote motor into gear box. Focus from remote panel.

NOTE: The wireless system will work up to 0.8km ($\frac{1}{2}$ mi.) The unit can remote focus, but will NOT control T-stops.

RF&T. A wireless focus system that has a separate gear box to control focus *and* T-stops.

NOTE: Both the RF and RF&T follow focus units consist of motors, gear box(es), cables, receivers, and senders.

All follow-focus knobs contain a 1.27cm ($\frac{1}{2}$ in.) square receptacle that accept a flexible follow-focus extension and/or a lever-type handle. Extension alone is 40.64cm (16 in.); with handle inserted in extension, 45.72cm (18 in.) in length.

All left focus knobs have *limiters,* i.e., two lockdown screws that can be rotated around the knob and screwed tight to restrict the amount of turn (focus) of the knob (lens).

16.1j Door

Hinged at back.

Golden Panaflex, Golden Panaflex II.

To Open.   Lift latch in door recess, twist counterclockwise, pull door.

NOTE: Microswitch at bottom rear of door recess automatically cuts out power to camera when door opens.

To Run Camera when Door Is Open.   Turn ON/OFF Switch to ON. Depress microswitch.

To Close.   Push door flush to camera, rotate latch clockwise, fold latch into door recess.

WARNING: *Always* turn the ON/OFF switch to OFF before closing the camera door. (The person threading the camera often forgets this step.) Once the door is closed, film being transported through the camera CANNOT be heard and CAN run out.

NOTE: Door will not close if the movement registration-pin is out or the sprocket keepers are open.

A locating pin at top of hinge of door accepts the pilot hole of the foldable support-arm bracket, which is fitted to the long eyepiece.

Platinum Panaflex.

To Open.   Lift latch in door recess, twist counterclockwise, pull door.

NOTE: The Platinum has NO microswitch inside the door. Instead, inside the camera are electronic RUN and INCH buttons.

To Run Camera when Door Is Open.   Turn camera ON/OFF Switch to ON. Depress RUN button.

To Inch Film when Door Is Open.   Depress INCH button or inch manually using inching knob at rear of camera.

To Close Door.   Push door flush to camera, rotate latch clockwise, fold latch into door recess.

WARNING: *Always* turn the ON/OFF switch to OFF before closing the camera door. (The person threading the camera often forgets this step.) Once the door is closed, film being transported through the camera CANNOT be heard and CAN run out.

NOTE: The locating pin at top of hinge of door accepts the pilot hole of the foldable support-arm bracket, which is fitted to the long eyepiece.

Panaflex-X.

To Open.   Lower the latch in door recess, twist clockwise, pull door.

NOTE: Microswitch at bottom of door recess automatically cuts out power to camera when door opens.

To Run Camera when Door Is Open.   Turn camera ON/OFF Switch to ON. Depress microswitch.

To Inch Film When Door Is Open. Use manual inching knob at rear of camera.

To Close Door. Push door flush to camera, rotate latch counterclockwise, push latch up into door recess.

WARNING: *Always* turn the ON/OFF switch to OFF before closing the camera door. (This step has often been forgotten after threading the camera.) Once the door is closed, film being transported through the camera CANNOT be heard and CAN run out.

NOTE: The viewing tube is an integral part of the door.

16.1k Buckle-Trip

Apron (a metal plate) located behind take-up side of sprocket cuts out power automatically if film jams when camera is running. It *automatically resets* when film jam is cleared.

16.1l Magazines

609.6m (2000 ft); 304.8m (1000 ft); 152.4m (500 ft); 76.2m (250 ft).

Mount on top of camera for studio mode; at back of camera for hand-hold mode or low-profile mode.

CAUTION: The 609.6m (2000 ft) magazine fits to the top port only on *all* the cameras. (It will break loose if fitted to back of camera.)

To Remove Cover at Top of Camera. Depress magazine lock forward of handle/cover; pull lock lever toward camera door. Lift handle/cover away.

To Remove Cover at Back of Camera. Depress magazine lock above back cover; rotate the lock lever toward camera door and down.

NOTE: A *Panaclear handle*, fitted with a LEMO receptacle is available for those cameras fitted with a *heater eyepiece*. The handle is usually placed at the back when in the studio mode, at the top when in the hand-hold mode. A short connecting cable inserts into both the handle and a matching LEMO receptacle on the heater-eyepiece. The generated heat eliminates condensation on the glass when the eye is pressed to it.

NOTE: The heater eyepiece is only found on a few retrofitted Panaflex-X cameras.

Magazine Guide Groove Contacts. Upon removal of the covers, gold contacts (pins), varying in number, depending on the camera model, are revealed as follows:

Panaflex Golden, Panaflex Golden II, and Panaflex-X. Five contacts (pins). Looking down at the top contacts and/or looking at the back contacts from the Operator's point of view:

Top left pin is the heater; top right pin is shutter pulse; center pin is +24 volts; lower left pin is (−) ground; lower right pin is to the torque motor on the magazine.

NOTE: Cameras and magazines are being constantly modified as they are updated. Some older units might not yet be fitted with shutter pulse circuitry.

Panaflex Platinum. Nine contacts (pins). Looking down at the top contacts and/or looking at the back contacts from the Operator's point of view: topmost pin is blank; upper left pin is +24 volts; upper right pin is shutter pulse; center-left pin is magazine tachometer; center pin is +24 volts;

Figure 16–8a Panavision threading detail (all cameras) top load. Courtesy of Panavision, Inc.

1. Registration-pin throwout knob
2. Peg
3. Upper small rollers
4. Spring-loaded dog screw
5. Perforation alignment pin
6. Pressure-plate spring-arm
7. Pressure-plate
8. Matte slot
9. Race
10. Aperture plate lock
11. Pitch control knob
12. Cylindrical pin-bushing
13. Lower small rollers
14. Lower sprocket-guide lock knob
15. Inching button
16. Run button
17. Buckle-trip
18. Lower back roller
19. Center back roller
20. Top roller
21. Upper feed roller
22. Upper sprocket-guide roller
23. Upper sprocket-guide lock knob

center-right pin is feet/meters counter; lower-left pin is (−) ground; lower-right pin is to the torque motor on the magazine; lowest pin is reverse relay.

NOTE: Cameras and magazines are being constantly modified as they are updated. Some older units might not yet be fitted with shutter pulse circuitry.

To Mount Magazine to Camera. (1) Pull loop of film from magazine feed side. (2) Insert loop in magazine guide groove, twist film to clear sprocket, and pull through. (3) Place magazine heel into guide groove, making certain that film does not catch between magazine and camera body, then lower (or push) magazine toe into guide groove. (4) Depress magazine lock and rotate lever to secure magazine.

To Remove Magazine. Unthread film and break it. Disengage magazine by depressing magazine lock and rotating lock lever—at top, toward camera door; at back, toward camera door and down.

NOTE: When replacing top cover, the handle *always* points forward for better carrying balance.

16.1m Threading (Figs. 16–8*a* and 16–8*b*)
(1) Depress inching knob at back of camera and rotate until pulldown claw retracts from gate, moves up, and starts to enter gate again. Pull registration-pin throw-out knob and move it toward the rear of the camera. (2) Remove, clean, and replace aperture plate and pressure plate (see Cleaning, Sec. 16.1t, for details). (3) Pull upper sprocket-guide lock knob and rotate upward; pull lower sprocket-guide lock knob and rotate

Figure 16–8*b* Panavision threading detail (all cameras) back load. Courtesy of Panavision, Inc.

1. Registration-pin throwout knob
2. Peg
3. Upper small rollers
4. Spring-loaded dog screw
5. Perforation alignment pin
6. Pressure-plate spring-arm
7. Pressure-plate
8. Matte slot
9. Race
10. Aperture plate lock
11. Pitch control knob
12. Cylindrical pin-bushing
13. Lower small rollers
14. Lower sprocket-guide lock knob
15. Inching button
16. Run button
17. Buckle-trip
18. Lower back roller
19. Center back roller
20. Top roller
21. Upper feed roller
22. Upper sprocket-guide roller
23. Upper sprocket-guide lock knob

downward. (4) Pull film from feed side. Extend loop to lower front corner of camera (a rough guide for amount of film needed for threading).

Top Load (Fig. 16–8a). Starting clockwise from the magazine take-up side, insert film:

(a) to the left of the top back roller, then to right of center back roller; (b) over lower back roller and then between the lower sprocket guide rollers and sprocket; (c) *under* small roller at left of sprocket-guide rollers and *over* small roller below pulldown claw eccentric.

Starting counterclockwise from the magazine feed side, insert film:

(d) *to the right* of the upper feed roller; (e) between the upper sprocket-guide rollers and sprocket; (f) over the small roller above the registration-pin throw-out knob; (g) under the small peg in the camera wall; (h) under the small roller above the movement block.

Back Load (Fig. 16–8b). Starting clockwise from the magazine take-up side, insert film:

(a) *over* lower back roller, then between the lower sprocket-guide rollers and sprocket; (b) *under* small roller at left of sprocket-guide rollers; and (c) *over* small roller below pulldown claw eccentric.

Starting counterclockwise from the magazine feed side; insert film: (d) *under* the center back roller; (e) between the upper sprocket-guide rollers and sprocket; (f) over the small roller above the registration-pin throw-out knob; (g) under the small peg in the camera wall; (h) under the small roller above the movement block.

(5) Insert film into groove (the race) between the movable aperture plate and stationary register plate. Place film on perforation alignment pin above aperture plate. (6a) Adjust the lower loop so that when the lower sprocket-guide roller closes, the loop will clear the bottom of camera interior by 1.6mm ($\frac{1}{16}$ in) at lowest arc of loop. (6b) Reach toward back of registration-pin throw-out knob with little finger of right hand and nudge the cylindrical pin-bushing *forward*.

NOTE: The registration-pin knob is NOT used to determine if registration-pins are entering perforations, as is done with other cameras with a similar type of movement.

(7) Disengage film from perforation-alignment pin above aperture plate. Adjust so that there is 0.8mm ($\frac{1}{32}$ in) clearance of film from the perforation-alignment pin when the upper sprocket-guide rollers are closed. (8) Depress inching knob to remove slack on the take-up side; recheck loops.

NOTE: Depressing the inching knob puts 9 volts of power on the take-up motor in the magazine (see Sec. 16.2), which pulls slack into the magazine. This tension precludes the pulling of film from the take-up side if the lower loop needs readjusting.

If lower loop is too short: Insert forefinger behind center back roller and against the film and depress the inching knob. This will advance film into the camera but not into the magazine take-up chamber. Release inching knob; readjust lower loop to proper size.

(9) Rotate inching knob and observe film being transported in camera. If satisfactory, then on the:

Golden Panaflex, Golden Panaflex II (G2), and Panaflex-X. (a) Turn ON/OFF switch at back of camera to ON; depress microswitch in door. Apply power in short bursts and observe action of film. If satisfactory, turn ON/OFF switch at back of camera to OFF. Release microswitch, close door, and reset footage counter.

Platinum Panaflex. Turn ON/OFF switch at back of camera to ON; depress RUN button inside camera. Apply power in short bursts and observe action of film. If satisfactory, turn ON/OFF switch at back of camera to OFF. Release RUN button, close door, and reset footage counter.

CAUTION: REMEMBER to turn the ON/OFF switch to OFF before closing the camera door. (The person threading the camera often forgets this step.) Once the door is closed, film being transported through the camera CANNOT be heard.

Pitch Control Knob. Located below eccentric block on all cameras. Built-in to minimize noise of movement. Correct setting on the pitch control might differ on each roll because of variations in rawstock perforation pitch and/or film shrinkage. Optimum setting of control is determined by ear while adjusting the claw pivot point until the eccentric (movement) runs at its quietest. To adjust for a minus pitch rotate knob toward lens; to adjust for a plus pitch rotate knob toward Operator.

16.1n Footage Counter

Golden Panaflex, Golden Panaflex II (G2). Located forward on the optic housing near the viewfinder brake lock.

Panaflex-X. Located above the lens port.
Additive. LED counter registers each foot of film transported through the camera up to 999 ft, then reverts to zero and counts forward again. Displays footage expended whenever camera runs.

To Read Footage with Camera OFF. Depress tiny "O" *readout button* at top of counter.

NOTE: Until and unless the digital counter reset button is depressed and counter is zeroed, the LED footage counter will "remember" the footage used and will continue to add, although power has been disconnected and camera stored overnight, a week, a month, etc. Reset footage counter to zero after each magazine change.

To Reset Counter. Depress tiny "X" *readout button* at left side of counter AND the readout button marked "O" at the top of the counter *at the same time.*

NOTE: Battery condition lights are located between the footage counter and fps display. (See Sec. 16.1c, Power Panel, Green/Red Battery Condition Light. This secondary light allows the Operator to view the battery condition.)

Platinum Panaflex. Located in Dual Display and Annunciator panels (see Sec. 16.1p, for details).

16.1o Tachometer

Golden Panaflex and Golden Panaflex II (G2). Located on optic housing above lens port. LED tachometer reads in frames and tenths of frames when camera is ON. Registers 24.0 fps or 25.0/30 fps in sync mode, depending on position of fps switch located in side wall of cave, and the setting on the circuit board underneath the motor cover. (see Motor, Sec. 16.1b.) Displays from 4.0 to 36.0 fps in variable-speed mode.

NOTE: 29.97 fps will display as 30 fps because that is the closest 1/10th frame it can show.

To Replace Malfunctioning Tachometer and/or Footage Counter. Remove two 4-40 screws at top of camera above lens and the single 2-56 hold-down screw at front of unit (behind the footage counter). Lift. Align new unit to camera plug. Replace screws.

CAUTION: If a camera is fitted with a permanently installed SCCD (Super Charged Coupled Device) video tap, the tachometer and/or counter are NOT field replaceable.

Panaflex-X Only. Located below footage counter and above lens port. LED tachometer reads in frames and tenths of frames when camera is ON. Registers 24.0 fps or 25.0/30 fps in sync mode, depending on position of fps switch located in side wall of cave and the setting on the circuit board underneath the motor cover (see Sec. 16.1b, Motor). Displays from 4.0 to 36.0 fps in variable-speed mode.

NOTE: 29.97 fps will display as 30 fps because that is the closest tenth of a frame it can show.

To Replace Malfunctioning Tachometer and/or Footage Counter. Remove two 4-40 screws at top of camera above lens. Lift. Align new unit to camera plug. Replace screws.

Platinum Panaflex. Located in Dual Display and Annunciator panels (see Sec. 18.1p, for details).

16.1p **Dual Display and Annunciator Panels** (Fig. 16–9)

Platinum Panaflex Only.

Dual Display Panels. Located on both sides of the camera. Each panel has six display modes:

1. *Footage and FPS:* Additive footage up to 9999 ft then reverts to zero. Registers 24.0 fps or 25.0/29.97/30 fps in sync mode, depending on position of fps switch located in side wall of cave and the setting on the circuit board underneath the motor cover (see Sec. 16.1b, Motor). Displays from 4.0 to 36.0 fps in crystal-speed mode.

NOTE: When the Platinum is set to 29.97 fps, the LCD will flash "29.9."

2. *Meters and FPS:* Additive metric measurement up to 999.9m then reverts to zero. Registers 24.0 fps or 25.0/29.9/30 fps in sync mode, depending on position of fps switch located in side wall of cave and the setting on the circuit board underneath the motor cover. (See Sec. 16.1b, Motor.) Displays from 4.0 to 36.0 fps in crystal-speed mode.

NOTE: When the Platimnum is set to 29.97 fps, the LCD will flash "29.9" even when camera is turned to OFF.

3. *Shutter Angle and FPS:* Displays shutter angle (within 1/10th degree) and fps at which shutter revolves.

4. *Time Code:* Shows time code hours, minutes, seconds, and frames only on cameras fitted with Aaton Code, otherwise reads all zeroes.

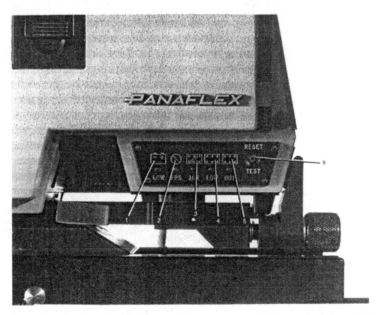

Figure 16–9 Panavision Panaflex annunciator panel. Courtesy of Panavision, Inc.

1. Low battery
2. Fps
3. Film jam
4. Low film
5. Out of film
6. RESET button

5. *Time Code User Bits:* Shows date the Time Code was entered, otherwise reads all zeroes.

6. *FIL:* Appears only when a gelatine behind-the-lens filter is inserted into camera, otherwise is blank.

To Change Display Mode. Depress the MODE button on either of the two displays.

To Zero Footage/Meters Counters. Depress the scribed UP and DOWN arrows simultaneously.

NOTE: Although both displays have a MODE button, only the left-side display has UP and DOWN arrows.

To Increase Footage/Meters on Counter. Depress the UP arrow.

To Decrease Footage/Meters on Counter. Depress the DOWN arrow.

NOTE: When either arrow is depressed continuously, the footage/metric count will increment/decrement faster.

NOTE: When any of the LEDs on the Annunciator Panel (see below) illuminate to warn of a problem, flashing small letters will appear at the top of the display.

Annunciator Panel. (Fig. 16–10). Located left-rear side below camera door. Five red LEDs above graphic icons illuminated to indicate camera problems:

Figure 16–10 Panavision hand-held shoulder rest (disassembled). Courtesy of Panavision, Inc.

1. Mounting bracket retainer   3. Shoulder rest
2. Camera mounting bracket   4. Shoulder pad

1. *Low Battery:* indicates that the battery supplying power to the camera is less than 21 volts (±0.5v) and should be changed at end of take.

2. *Illegal FPS:* indicates a speed outside of the range of 4-36 fps has been selected on the fps setting at the rear of the camera.

NOTE: The camera will NOT run until the fps speed has been changed.

3. *Film Jam:* Indicates interior buckle-trip has shut camera OFF.

4. *Low Film:* Indicates that there are 15m/50-ft less of film left in the magazine.

NOTE: This LED is triggered by revolutions of the spindle in the magazine, NOT by the footage/metric counters which might display any total other than the correct amount of film in the magazine.

5. *Out of Film:* Indicates there is only 1.5m/5-ft of film in camera. Shuts camera off, to prevent film-end from passing through the movement.

WARNING: If any LED's illuminate, the Annunciator Panel MUST be reset before reloading.

To Reset Annunciator Panel. Turn camera OFF. Depress Reset Button at right of Panel to extinguish/reactivate LEDs.

16.1q Shutter

Variable: 50–200°. On all cameras, calibrations and external control are located at top rear of camera.

NOTE: Shutter settings can be changed even while filming.

Golden Panaflex, Golden Panaflex II (G2), and Panaflex-X. Shutter detentes adjust in increments of 10°.

To Change Shutter Opening. (1) Pull safety locks at side of External Control Knob and move them aside. (2) Pull out external control latch and move indicator to desired shutter opening; close latch; make certain that pin is engaged. (3) Move each safety lock against each side of the external control knob to prevent accidental opening or closing of the shutter.

NOTE: Each safety lock can be set to a different degree mark to set the extremes of an in-shot shutter adjustment.

Platinum Panaflex. Shutter adjusts in increments of 0.1° (see also Section 16.1o, Dual Display, no. 3).

To Change Shutter Opening. (1) Open camera door. Grasp primary shutter lock, located above the movement, and rotate in opposite direction of arrow to unlock. (2) At top-rear of camera, pull safety locks at side of External Control Knob, and move them aside. (3) Pull out external control latch and move indicator to desired shutter opening; close latch; make certain that pin in engaged. (4) Move each safety lock against each side of the external control knob to prevent accidental opening of the shutter.

NOTE: Each safety lock can be set to a different degree mark to set the extremes of an in-shot shutter adjustment.

Accessory 144° Shutter Vernier. Used when filming TV screens. Fits to shutter block.

To Fit to Camera. (1) Remove upper right 4-40 screw in shutter block with 2.4mm (3/32″) hex wrench. (2) Hold the shutter Vernier, pull spring-loaded locking knob on Vernier, and rotate clockwise to draw pin into Vernier. (3) Insert 4-40 screw into recess on Vernier and attach Vernier to shutter block. (4) Rotate shutter knob to 144° scribe. (5) Rotate spring-loaded locking knob on Vernier counterclockwise until pin of the locking knob snaps into Vernier and against the shutter knob. (6) Loosen screws on the Vernier and then snug *lightly* (do *not* tighten). (7) Align camera to telecasting TV screen so that screen fills full frame. (8) Open camera door; swing pressure-plate spring arm clockwise; remove pressure-plate; then rotate pressure-plate spring arm toward camera wall. (9) Insert Aperture-Mirror TV Gauge (provided by manufacturer) in place of pressure-plate. Bring pressure-plate spring-arm back to retain gauge. (10) Turn ON/OFF switch to ON; push microswitch and observe shutter attachment until shutter bar running across TV screen is a very thin line. Tighten the two Vernier screws. (11) Remove Aperture Mirror TV Gauge from pressure-plate, replace pressure-plate, and thread camera.

NOTE: When finished with 144° Vernier, pull spring-loaded locking knob on Vernier knob at side of attachment—rotate clockwise to draw pin from shutter block. Return shutter to 200° setting. It is NOT necessary to remove Vernier from the shutter when finished.

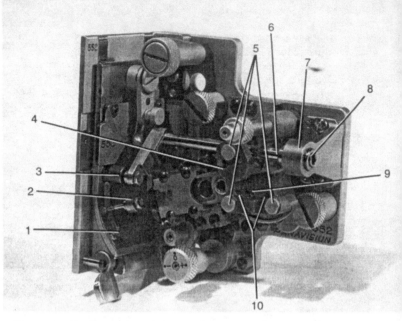

Figure 16–11   Panavision lubrication (all cameras). Courtesy of Panavision, Inc.

1. Pulldown pad
2. Pulldown arm
3. Register-pin shaft bearing
4. Register-pin rocker block
5. Register-pin linkage

6. Eccentric shaft
7. Register-pin bushing
8. Pulldown pivot pin
9. Bearing block
10. Rocker pivot bearing

16.1r   Hand-Held Mode (Fig. 16–2c)
The Panaflex-X can*not* be hand-held.

Golden Panaflex, Golden Panaflex II (G2), and Platinum Panaflex Only.
Standard Accessories Necessary for Conversion.   Short eyepiece, right-hand grip, left-hand grip, shoulder rest.

NOTE: Hand-held mode might also require a follow-focus whip, battery belt, and 152m (500 ft) magazine that fits to the back magazine port.

To Convert from Studio to Hand-Held Mode.   Complete the two steps per Section 16.1f; that is: (1) Remove the extension eyepiece. (2) Place short eyepiece on camera and invert the viewfinder image. Then: (3) Mount right-hand grip.

NOTE: The grip can be attached with the camera still on geared head. Unit contains a momentary index-finger switch that starts camera when depressed, stops camera when released. Second thumb-activated switch starts camera when pushed UP, stops camera when pushed DOWN.

To Mount Right-Hand Grip.   Slide onto dovetail bracket at right-front of camera. Tighten knob on grip.

WARNING: Camera may run intermittently if right-hand grip is not seated properly.

(4) Mount left-hand grip. Secondary grip has no switch for power but is used to balance the camera.

To Mount Left-Hand Grip. Remove camera from tripod head and rest it on its motor side. Slide handgrip bracket back into bottom dovetail until it secures to camera with an audible click. Later, adjust handgrip so that when camera is held, the left thumb can reach the follow-focus knob.

To Release Left-Hand Grip. Pull down on latch in bracket; pull handgrip forward.

(5) Mount shoulder-rest to camera.

NOTE: The shoulder-rest consists the three basic parts (Fig. 16–11):
1. Camera-mounting bracket.
2. Shoulder-rest attached to the bracket.
3. Shoulder-pad, adjustable to the shoulder-rest with Velcro® strips.

To Mount Shoulder-Rest to Camera. (1) Squeeze sides of mounting-bracket retainer and insert into matching grooves in bottom of camera (the cave). (2) Push bracket all the way until it locks in place with an audible click. (3) Place a Velcro® pad on the bracket for shoulder comfort.

To Remove Shoulder-Rest from Camera. Squeeze sides of mounting-bracket retainer and pull away from camera body.

16.1s Lubrication (Fig. 16–12)
Manufacturer states that all rollers are maintenance-free.

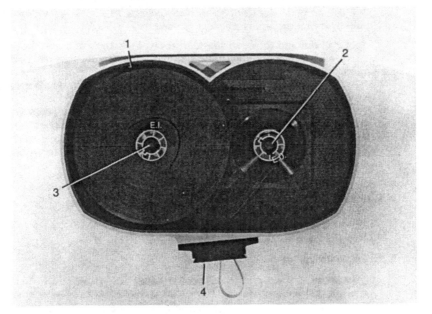

Figure 16–12 Panavision 304.8m (1000 ft) magazine (all cameras). Courtesy of Panavision, Inc.

1. Internal roller
2. Core lock
3. Core lock
4. Current pins (not visible)

To Lubricate Eccentric (movement). Clean and—only if needed—lubricate at the end of each shooting day.

NOTE: Manufacturer states that it is no longer necessary to remove movement for cleaning and lubrication as in earlier cameras.

1. Remove aperture plate (see Sec. 16.1t, Cleaning). Apply one drop of silicone on each pulldown pad at bottom of pulldown claw slots in the register plate.

CAUTION: Do not spill silicone on any other part of the movement; this could cause seizure of other mechanical parts in the movement.

2. Apply one drop of oil in each well of the pulldown arm, pulldown arm pivot, eccentric shaft, two wells of the bearing block, rocker pivot bearing, three wells of the register-pin linkage, register-pin bushing, register-pin shaft bearing, and the register-pin rocker block.

16.1t Cleaning

Optics. Clean with bulb syringe or soft camel's-hair brush.
Manufacturer recommends the following *each time film is changed:* (1) Remove aperture and pressure-plates.
To Remove. (1a) Depress inching knob at back of camera and rotate until pulldown claw retracts from gate, moves up, and starts to enter gate again. Pull registration-pin throw-out knob and move it toward the rear of the camera. (1b) Rotate spring-loaded dog-lock knob clockwise; rotate lower aperture-plate lock counterclockwise; pull gently on aperture plate.

NOTE: If plate does not slide easily, check to see that pulldown claw and/or registration-pins are clear of plate.

(1c) Pull out and rotate spring-loaded dog-lock knob to secure bottom of plate. (1d) Swing pressure-plate spring arm clockwise. Remove pressure-plate from back plate.
(2) Remove emulsion build-up with orangewood stick. (3) Wipe plates with soft cotton (not linen) handkerchief.
To Replace. Insert pressure plate in back plate; swing pressure-plate spring arm counterclockwise to secure pressure plate. Insert aperture plate into camera. Pull out and rotate spring-loaded dog-lock knob counterclockwise to secure top of plate; depress lower aperture plate lock knob to secure bottom of plate.
(4) Use bulb syringe on camera interior to remove dust, dirt, etc.

16.1u Weight
With 304.8m (1,000 ft) load: 18.6 kg (41 lb)
With 122m (400 ft) load: 15.4 kg (34 lb)
With 60.1m (200 ft) load: 13.4 kg (29.5 lb)

16.1v Troubleshooting

Trouble	*Probable Cause*
Camera will not start	Door switch not actuated; battery disconnected or low battery; bad power cable; one or more circuit boards malfunctioning; buckle-trip triggered
	Platinum only: Check Annunciator Panel

Camera hunts	Camera too cold; low battery
Camera door will not close	Sprocket keepers not seated properly or registration pin pulled back
Film jam	Improper threading; magazine contacts dirty
Viewfinder dark/cut-in viewing tube	Mirror out of position; light shut-off lever in; groundglass not inserted fully; matte-box too far from lens; lens cap on; magnification knob improperly seated.
Eye focus off	Groundglass inserted with frosty side pointing away from mirror
Torn or punctured film	Improper threading
Film will not slide in or out of gate	Registration-pin or pull-down claw not retracted; emulsion or film chip in gate
Nonexistent or sporadic	No power to magazine motor; magazine take-up contacts dirty; magazine drive electronics malfunctioning (a factory job)
Film scratches	Dirt or emulsion build-up on aperture plate, sprocket wheel, sprocket keeper, rollers, pressure-plate, registration-pins, magazine rollers
Erratic fps speeds at crystal setting	Circuit Board malfunctioning
Camera does not stop with mirror in viewing position	Circuit Board malfunctioning
LEDs not working	Circuit Board not functioning

16.2 PANAVISION 35mm PANAFLEX MAGAZINES (Figs. 16–13, 16–14, 16–15)

16.2a Type
Displacement.

16.2b Capacity

Panaflex Golden, Panaflex Golden II, and Panaflex-X.

- 609.6m (2000 ft)
- 304.8m (1000 ft)
- 152.4m (500 ft)
- 76.2m (250 ft)

Panaflex Platinum. Two 304.8m (1000 ft) types: Standard and Reversing.

- 152.4m (500 ft)
- 76.2m (250 ft)

NOTE: 152.4m (500 ft) and 76.2m (250 ft) magazines are generally used when operating hand-held.

16.2c Lid
One. Dog-locked.

NOTE: There are two locks on the 609.6m (2000 ft) and 304.8m (1000 ft) magazines, but only one lock on the 152.4m (500 ft) and 76.2m (250 ft) magazines.

To Remove. Lift door latch, rotate counterclockwise. Lift lid.
To Replace. Seat lid on magazine. Turn lock(s) clockwise.

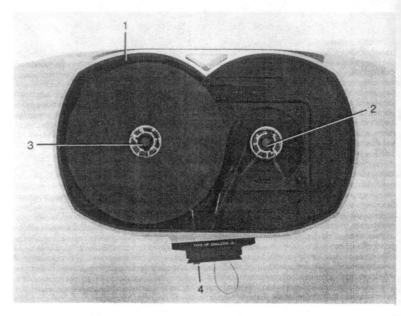

Figure 16–13 Panavision 304.8m (1000 ft) Platinum Panaflex reversing magazine. Courtesy of Panavision, Inc.

1. Internal roller
2. Core lock

3. Core lock
4. Current pins (not visible)

16.2d Feed
Left side. Film (wound emulsion in) pulls off of spindle clockwise.

16.2e Take-up
Right side. Film winds onto spindle counterclockwise, emulsion out, except for Platinum reversing magazine.

Platinum Reversing Magazine. Film winds onto spindle clockwise, emulsion in (Fig. 16–14).

16.2f Loading
(1) Remove lid. Ascertain that manual core lock on feed spindle is pressed into spindle recess. (2) In darkness, remove film from can and bag. Insert film end between the left feed-idler rollers and push through until film end emerges from the feed side of the magazine.

NOTE: Film end must take a small turn in feeding through the rollers; therefore, it may require more than one attempt to push the end through.

(3) Place film roll on feed spindle. Rotate feed spindle until spindle pin engages the core keyway. Push manual core lock on spindle outward to engage feed core. (4) Ascertain that manual core lock on take-up spindle is pressed into spindle recess. (5) Insert film end through the take-up side light-trap rollers. (6) Insert film end into core slot and wind film onto take-up spindle counterclockwise (emulsion side out), except for the reversing magazine where the film is wound onto the take-up spindle

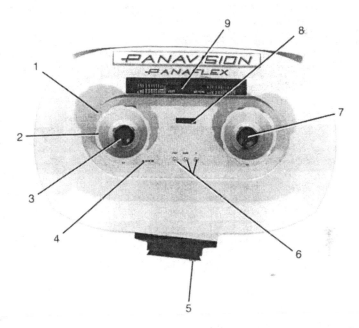

Figure 16–14 Platinum Panaflex magazine back. Courtesy of Panavision, Inc.

1. Motor housing
2. Hand grip
3. Manual take-up knob
4. Take-up indicator light
5. Current pins
6. Reset buttons
7. Manual feed knob
8. LED counter
9. Mechanical counter

clockwise (emulsion in). Push manual core lock on spindle outward to engage take-up core. Replace lid and turn locks clockwise to secure.

NOTE: *To lengthen loop,* pull film out from feed side. *To shorten loop,* depress and turn either of the external spindle wheels at the back of the magazine clockwise.

16.2g Unloading

(1) In darkness, remove lid. (2) Push manual core lock on spindle into spindle recess. (3) Place index finger on core, thumb on edge of film roll. Turn magazine over, remove film roll, and place exposed roll in black bag and can.

16.2h Spindle-Wheel Housings

Located at back of magazine.

Golden Panaflex, Golden Panaflex II (G2), and Panaflex-X. The feed spindle wheel housing contains a constant-torque clutch to prevent film from unwinding on the feed side. It also contains a *manual-feed knob* to tighten film on core—if needed—and to rotate the spindle wheel when loading.

The take-up spindle-wheel housing contains a take-up motor to wind film on the take-up core. Center of take-up spindle contains a spring-

loaded manual take-up knob to rotate the spindle wheel when loading.
Between the housings are:

- *External amber light* on magazine, which indicates when the internal magazine heater is working.
- A *magazine window,* which also reveals a *spiral marker* when the camera is running.
- A footage counter (see Sec. 16.2i).

Platinum Panaflex. The *feed spindle wheel housing* and the *take-up spindle-wheel housing* is a single unit. It contains a constant-torque clutch to prevent film from unwinding on the feed side, a *manual-feed knob* to tighten film on core—if needed—and to rotate the spindle wheel when loading, as well as the take-up motor to wind film on the take-up core. Center of the take-up spindle contains a spring-loaded manual take-up knob to rotate the spindle wheel when loading.

Between the take-up knobs are: three reset buttons and an LED additive footage counter (see Sec. 16.2i).

Above it, is a subtractive mechanical footage/meter counter (see Sec. 16.2i).

Magazine Running Light. A red light, located below the take-up spindle, which blinks to indicate magazine is running.

Magazine Heater Light. None. Heater automatically works when camera is turned ON.

16.2i Footage/Meter Counter

NOTE: The 76.2m (250 ft) magazine does not have a counter.

Golden Panaflex, Golden Panaflex II (G2), and Panaflex-X. Fitted with subtractive mechanical counter located on back of magazine. Scale reads in increments of 15.24m (50 ft).

NOTE: Counter is not automatic.

To Measure Remaining Footage in Magazine. Depress lever below magazine motor until internal roller touches film roll. Read scale.

Platinum Panaflex. Fitted with two counters located on back of magazine—a subtractive mechanical counter, which is used to determine amount of film remaining, and an additive LED counter.

NOTE: Mechanical counter is not automatic.

To Measure Remaining Footage/Meters in Magazine Mechanically. Slide lever on horizontal scale above magazine motor until internal roller touches film roll. Scale reads in increments of 15.24m (50 ft).

To Determine Expended Footage/Meters in Magazine. Read LED counter directly. LED reads in increments of 1.5cm or 1 ft.

To Reset all of LED Numbers at Once. Depress small white button on magazine motor farthest from Operator marked "c" (clear).

To Quickly Increment (add) LED Numbers. Depress small white button on motor nearest Operator marked "FAST."

To Slowly Increment (add) LED Numbers. Depress center small white button on motor marked "SLOW."

NOTE: The additive counter is powered by an internal battery. This enables the magazine to "remember" and display on the LED the last footage/meters registered, even when not on the camera.

Golden Panaflex, Golden Panaflex II (G2), and Panaflex-X. Current to the take-up motor and heater comes into the magazine through five pins on the magazine throat which match the five pins on the magazine guide groove at top and back of camera (except Panaflex-X) (see Sec. 16.1l and below).

Platinum Panaflex. Current to the take-up motor, heater, and reversing motor comes into the magazine through nine pins on the magazine guide groove at top and back of camera (see Section 18.1l).

16.3 PANAVISION PANAFLEX-16 (PFX16) CAMERA (Figs. 16–15a, 16–15b)
The Panaflex-16 shares many of the design elements of the 35mm Panaflex, but it is not the same camera and has many unique features not found on the 35mm camera. Many of the accessories are exclusive to the Panaflex-16, but it will accept some of the accessories from the 35mm camera system.

NOTE: All directions are from Operator's point of view.

16.3a Base
Fitted with a female dovetail at front, catch lock at rear, to conform to dovetail carriage on Panavision's geared head or a sliding baseplate. Manufacturer calls the center indented portion of the base the "cave." A bracket in the cave accommodates the accessory shoulder rest.

Sliding Base Plate (not shown). Required in order to use camera on non-Panavision tripod head or geared head. Unit consists of two parts: (1) *Base*—fitted with a series of 3/8"-16 tapped holes to accommodate tripod or geared-head lockdown screw. (Series of tapped holes permits better balance of camera on head when lenses of various weights are used.) Bubble-level on base *always* faces Operator. (2) *Dovetail carriage*—slides on base for ease of balance of camera on tripod.
    To Lock. Turn lever on sliding block clockwise, toward rear of camera.
    To Release. Turn lever counterclockwise, toward lens.
    To Mount Camera to Dovetail Carriage or Panahead. (1) Match dovetail at front of camera base to dovetail plate. (2) Slide camera forward until it secures to plate with audible click. (3) Rotate and tighten *tail lock* to secure rear of camera.
    To Remove Camera. (1) Grasp camera handle securely. (2) Unto tail lock at rear of camera. (3) Pull spring-loaded *quick-release catch* at side of dovetail, slide camera back, release catch, and lift camera off carriage.

Secondary Handgrip. Inserts into front camera base dovetail when camera is used in hand-held mode.
    To Mount Secondary Handgrip. (1) Slide handgrip bracket into camera dovetail until it secures to camera with an audible click. (2) Adjust handgrip so that when camera is held, left thumb can reach the follow-focus knob.
    To Release Handgrip. (1) Pull down on latch in bracket. (2) Pull handgrip forward.

16.3b Motor
Built in crystal-controlled sync/variable 24-volt DC.

NOTE: Every speed of the camera is crystal controlled.

Figure 16–15a Panavision Panaflex-16 (PFX-16) camera (left front view). Courtesy of Panavision, Inc.

1. Red/green light
2. Amber heater light
3. "O" button
4. "X" button
5. Lens lock
6. 2-pin LEMO plug
7. Door latch

8. Contrast filter lever
9. Eyepiece
10. Focus ring
11. Open/close lever (not visible)
12. Footage counter
13. Tachometer

Speed Selection. (1) Located to left of ON/OFF switch at rear of camera. (2) Speed setting can be selected in 1/10 frame increments (e.g., 24.1).

To Change the Speed. (1) Lift the small window covering the digits. (2) Push the small buttons above or below the digit to be changed. (3) Replace the small window covering the digits.

Forward/Reverse Selection. Camera will run from 4 to 50 fps in reverse when fitted with a 400 ft reversing magazine.

To Change Forward/Reverse Selection. (1) Insert thin-bladed screwdriver into slot in cover of switch on rear side wall of camera, facing the ON/OFF switch. (2) Slide the switch to desired position (FWD or REV).

16.3c Power Panel

Power panel on the lower right side of camera below the motor housing contains three LEMO plugs, labeled "PWR" (power), "HTR" (heater), and "ACC" (accessory).

Power Line. The two-pin LEMO plug of 24 volt battery cable inserts into matching PWR LEMO plug on camera.

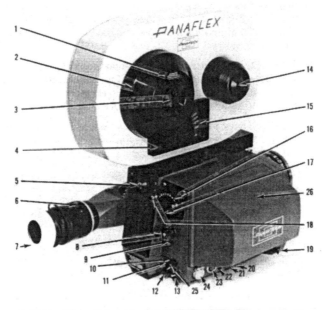

Figure 16–15b Panavision Panaflex-16 (PFX-16) camera (right rear view). Courtesy of Panavision, Inc.

1. Spiral marking
2. Spindle wheel housing
3. Take-up spindle wheel
4. Internal roller lever
5. Magazine lock lever
6. Focus ring
7. Eyepiece
8. Inching knob
9. Inching knob safety lock
10. Variable speed safety lock
11. Sync/vary switch
12. Variable speed knob
13. On/off switch

14. Feed spindle
15. Magazine footage indicator
16. Shutter
17. Shutter control latch
18. Shutter safety locks
19. Tape hook
20. Green/red light (not visible)
21. 2-pin LEMO plug (not visible)
22. Amber light
23. 3-pin LEMO plug
24. 10-pin LEMO plug
25. Red running light
26. Motor cover

Heater. Supplies 24 volts to power the internal camera heater. Heater activates when temperature drops below 20°C, (68° F.)

Indicator Lights. An *amber* light indicates heater is on. A *green* battery-condition light indicates power in *on*.

WARNING: Green light will turn *red* when power to heater drops below 21 volts.

Accessory Plug. A 10-pin LEMO connection for attaching various Panavision accessories to the camera, including the following.
Remote Switch. Provides remote ON/OFF switch with digital display of film speed and film footage.

Phasable Synchronizer. Will synchronize camera with a foreground or background projector, or video playback. Accommodates 24/24, 24/30, 25/25, 30/30 film/video fps rates. Adjustable-phase selection on both video and projector sync.

WARNING: Shutter setting is crucial for video playback. When using the phasable synchronizer to shoot 30 fps video with a 24 fps camera, set the shutter to 144°. In all other cases (film/video 24/24, 25/25, 30/30), set shutter to 180°.

NOTE: Sync box controls the camera speed. When synchronized to NTSC video, 24 fps is actually 23.976 fps, and 30 fps is actually 29.97 fps. An audio output is provided for Nagra sound recorders.

24-Volt Batteries. Available: block, purse, and belt type.
Block. Nickel Cadmium 12, 15, or 16 amp hour and Lead Acid 17-amp hour.
Purse. Nickel Cadmium and Lead Acid 10 amp hour with built-in charger and amp/volt meter.
Belt. Nickel Cadmium 4, 6, or 10 amp hour.

NOTE: Most block, purse, and belt batteries are fitted with three-pin XLR connectors but some have two-pin XLR connectors.

ON/OFF Switch. Located at bottom rear of camera. A small red light in the switch housing indicates that camera is running.

ON/OFF Right Handgrip Accessory. Contains a momentary *pressure switch* that starts the camera when depressed and stops the camera when released and a *thumb-activated switch* that starts the camera when pushed *up* and stops the camera when pushed *down*. Both finger-switches override the ON/OFF switch at back of camera.
   To Mount Handgrip. (1) Slide handgrip into the dovetail slot located on right front of camera. (2) Rotate locking lever clockwise to secure.
   To Remove Handgrip. (1) Rotate locking lever counterclockwise. (2) Slide handgrip out from dovetail slot.

Remote ON/OFF Switch. Optional switch, inserts into right-front dovetail in place of the handgrip. Contains 2m (6 ft) or longer length of cable with an ON/OFF switch attached, so that camera can be started/stopped from a distance.
   Another type of remote switch is available with a LEMO connector, which attaches to the ACC plug at right side of camera, under motor housing.

Zoom/Panalens light Power Plug. Two-pin LEMO, at front of camera. Accepts pigtail from zoom lens motor or Panalens light.

CAUTION: While this outlet is intended to supply power to the zoom lens or lens light from the same 24-volt source that supplies power to camera, the use of one battery for two purposes (e.g., camera and zoom motor) can cause a considerable drain on the battery if the zoom is used very much. Where practicable, it is recommended that a separate battery be used for the zoom-lens motor.

Changeable Fuse for Electronics. Camera contains one 6.35mm ($\frac{1}{4}$ in.) × 9.5mm (3/8″) including leads, 5 ampere Littleman Microfuse fuse for the electronics. Access to fuse requires removal of motor cover.

NOTE: If camera is equipped with a video-assist unit, it must be removed before attempting to remove the motor cover.

To Remove Motor Cover. (1) Using a 2.38mm (3/32 in.) hex-head wrench, remove four screws, one each located on the four corners of the motor cover. (2) Pull motor cover away from camera, exposing motor and fuse panel.

To Change Fuse. (1) Pull old fuse leads out from motor connection. (2) Insert new fuse leads in place of old fuse.

NOTE: There are NO interchangeable boards as in the 35mm cameras.

16.3d Turret
None. Single lens mount accepts Panavision PFX-16 mount lenses only.

16.3e Lenses
Must be fitted with Panavision PFX-16 lens mounts.

To Fit Lens to Camera. (1) Rotate lens locking ring clockwise as far as it will go. (2) Align pin on lens to match slot at 12 o'clock position on lens port. (3) Hold lens lock in place while inserting lens into lens-port opening. (4) Rotate lens lock counterclockwise to secure lens in place.

To Remove the Lens. (1) Grasp lens, and turn lens locking ring clockwise as far as it will go. (2) Pull lens straight out and away from camera.

16.3f Viewfinder
Reflex. Image magnified 6 ×.

Views more than full aperture. Two interchangeable viewfinders are available: (1) Short magnifying viewfinder for hand-held shots or for shooting in confined spaces, (2) long magnifying viewfinder for use when shooting from a tripod or gear head. Long eyepiece may be moved out from camera approximately 15° for ease of left- or right-eye viewing.

To View through the Lens. Place eye to eyepiece.

To Align Mirror for Viewing. (1) Rotate inching knob safety lock counterclockwise. (2) Depress and rotate inching knob, located on rear of camera.

To Focus Eyepiece. Rotate knurled ring on the eyepiece until the center crosshair on groundglass is sharp. The white ring just forward of the black knurled ring on the eyepiece can be used to mark the eyepiece focus marks for the various users of the camera (Director, Director of Photography, Camera Operator, Camera Assistant, etc.).

Groundglass. Available in various aspect ratios. Located inside camera lens opening at top, above mirrored shutter. (Visible with lens removed and shutter in viewing position).

To Change or Clean Groundglass. (1) Remove lens. (2) Inch reflex mirror away from groundglass. (3) Wrap index finger with lens tissue, reach forefinger through lens-port opening, and slide groundglass out. (4) Clean; reinsert into camera with frosted side toward mirror, tapered edges toward lens-port opening.

To Clear Reflex Mirror from Groundglass. (1) Rotate safety lock from under inching knob counterclockwise. (2) Depress and rotate the inching knob.

CAUTION: *Always* return safety lock under inching knob to prevent possible damage to camera if the inching knob is accidentally depressed when camera is running.

NOTE: Camera stops with shutter in viewing position except when utilizing variable-speed mode, or when shutter has been inched by hand (e.g., when threading or clearing mirror from groundglass).

To Position Eyepiece for Viewing. (1) Release locking ring, located at eyepiece-rotation joint, by turning the two metal rods in the opposite direction of arrow. (2) Position eyepiece at proper position for viewing. (3) Secure eyepiece into position by turning the two metal rods of locking ring in the direction of the arrow.

To Swing Eyepiece out from Camera. (1) Release locking lever, located on underside of rotation joint, by turning it counterclockwise. (2) Gently swing eyepiece away from camera. (3) Lock eyepiece into place by turning the locking lever clockwise.

WARNING: Eyepiece will only swing away from camera approximately 15°. Attempting to move it past its stopping point will damage the eyepiece and its mount.

Eyepiece Support Bracket. Folding support bracket at right rear of eyepiece fits to the locating pin above hinge on door, to steady the eyepiece.

NOTE: Eyepiece should be supported on the locating pin when camera is stored in its case.

Eyepiece Leveler. Used to maintain the eyepiece at the Operator's eye level, regardless of camera tilt.

To Attach Eyepiece Leveler. (1) Fold in eyepiece-support bracket. (2) Screw one end of eyepiece leveler to thread on left side of Panahead. (3) On the other end of eyepiece leveler, hold the silver tab in with thumb, and fit hole to peg on support bracket. (4) Release silver tab.

CAUTION: Loosen the eyepiece lock when using eyepiece leveler. Failure to do this may cause damage to eyepiece lock.

Critical Focus Magnification Lever. At left side of eyepiece. Magnifies image to 10×.

To Critical Focus. Push lever down.

To Return to Standard Viewing. Push lever up.

Viewfinder Open/Close Switch. Located just above small striped button on eyepiece coupling. Closes eyepiece so that stray light cannot strike mirror and kick back onto film.

To Close Viewfinder. Push switch toward camera door.

To Open Viewfinder. Push switch away from camera door.

Contrast Viewing Filters. Spring-loaded lever above the Panaglow switch on left side of camera. Push forward (toward lens) on lever to view through 0.60 ND and backward (toward Operator) on lever to view through 0.90 ND.

Panaglow Switch. Illuminates frame lines on the groundglass when shooting in low-light situations. Located forward of camera door.

To Illuminate Frame Lines. Slide switch forward.

To Turn off. Slide switch toward rear of camera.

To Detach Eyepiece. (1) Loosen eyepiece lock, rotate eyepiece to vertical position, and lock into place. (2) Depress small striped button on side of eyepiece coupling. (3) While depressing small striped button, rotate locking ring of eyepiece counterclockwise until line inscribed on locking ring matches line inscribed on eyepiece. (4) Gently pull eyepiece up and off of coupling.

To Attach Eyepiece. (1) Hold eyepiece firmly in hand. (2) Align the inscribed line on eyepiece with the inscribed line on eyepiece coupling. (3) Push eyepiece into position. (4) Rotate the locking ring clockwise in the direction of the arrow until eyepiece locks into position with an audible click.

NOTE: When switching from the long eyepiece to the short eyepiece, remember to invert the viewfinder so that the image will appear in the correct upright position.

Invert Viewfinder Image. Because of the optics of the viewfinder, the coupling where the eyepiece attaches must be rotated when exchanging the eyepieces.

To Invert Eyepiece. (1) Loosen eyepiece lock. (2) Press thumb control, on the inner side of the eyepiece lock, in the direction of the inscribed arrow. (3) While rotating the eyepiece counterclockwise, release the thumb control, and continue to rotate eyepiece until click is heard. Tighten eyepiece lock.

Eyepiece Heaters. The long eyepiece contains an integrated heater element. Used when shooting in extreme cold weather situations to prevent the elements of the eyepiece from fogging.

To Activate Eyepiece Heater. (1) Plug one end of short coiled cord, containing a two-pin LEMO plug, into receptacle on outside ring of eyepiece. (2) Plug other end of cord into LEMO plug on auxiliary handle that mounts to rear of camera in place of rear magazine cover, marked "Panaclear."

NOTE: As long as there is power to the camera, the eyepiece heater will work whenever it is plugged in.

16.3g Sunshade/Matte-Box

Two types of mounting brackets are available: one accepts short-iris rods; the other accepts long-iris rods. The short-rod bracket is used when filming with lenses shorter than 100mm; the long-rod bracket is used when filming with a zoom lens or a lens longer than 100mm.

To Mount Short-Iris-Rod Bracket. (1) Slide bracket over two-pin LEMO power plug at right front of camera. (2) Insert short rods into bracket (one above the other).

NOTE: The lower rod *must* be inserted into the bracket *before* tightening the lever that secures the bracket to the camera.

(3) Rotate scalloped knob on bracket to secure the upper rod.

To Mount Long-Iris-Rod Bracket. (1) Slide bracket over two-pin LEMO power plug at right front of camera. (2) Push lock lever down to secure bracket. (3) Insert long rods into bracket. (4) Rotate scalloped knobs on bracket to secure rods.

To Mount Matte-Box on Rods. (1) Slide matte-box onto rods and position according to the lens. (2) Rotate scalloped knobs on matte-box clockwise to secure.

To Clear Matte-Box from Lens. (1) Pull spring-loaded knob at top right of matte-box *up.* (2) Swing matte-box to right and away from lens.

The tops of all matte-boxes are fitted with two knurled knobs that hold the sunshade.

To Attach Sunshade. (1) Loosen the two knurled knobs at top of matte box. (2) Place sunshade on matte box so that slots of shade line up under the knobs. (3) Tighten knobs to secure sunshade in place.

16.3h Filters

Standard Matte Box. Holds two 101.6 × 143.5mm (4 in. × 5.65 in.) filter holders. Also included with the matte-box are one circular 138mm diameter filter retaining ring and one circular 114.3mm (4 ½-in. reducing ring.

To Remove Filter Holders from the Matte-Box. (1) Pull spring-loaded knob at top left of matte-box until retaining dowel clears filter holder. (2) Lift holder from matte-box.

To Remove Retaining Rings from Matte Box. (1) Loosen lock screw at top rear of matte-box. (2) Pull retaining ring out from rear of matte-box.

16.3i Focus Controls

Follow-focus unit knob fits to the *follow-focus pivot shaft* at left front of camera below lens. Knob and end of shaft each contain a 12.7mm (½-in.) square receptacle that accepts a flexible follow-focus extension and/or a lever-type handle. Knob does *not* have a marking disc.

To Mount. (1) Hold unit at 45° angle to shaft, with focus knob down. (2) Slide unit onto shaft. (3) Pivot unit *up* until it snaps into spring-loaded follow-focus locking pin.

To Remove. (1) Hold follow-focus unit. (2) Pull knob on follow-focus locking pin; pivot unit down and away.

NOTE: A 35mm follow-focus unit will not fit the 16mm camera.

16.3j Door

Hinged at back.

To Open. (1) Lift latch in door recess. (2) Twist counterclockwise and pull door open.

NOTE: Microswitch at bottom rear of door recess automatically cuts out power to camera when door opens.

To Run Camera When Door is Open. (1) Turn ON/OFF switch to ON. (2) Depress microswitch.

To Close Door. (1) Push door flush to camera. (2) Rotate latch clockwise. (3) Fold latch into door recess.

WARNING: Always turn the ON/OFF switch to OFF before closing the camera door. This step has often been forgotten by those threading the camera. Once the door is closed, film being transported through the camera *cannot* be heard.

NOTE: The locating pin at the top hinge of door accepts the pilot hole of the support-arm bracket, which is fitted to the long eyepiece viewfinder.

To Remove Door. (1) Open door. (2) Rotate the safety lock between the two hinges away from camera. (3) Lift door off of hinge pins.

16.3k Buckle-Trip

Apron (a metal plate), located behind take-up side of sprocket, cuts out power automatically if film jams when camera is running. Automatically resets when film jam is cleared.

16.3l Magazines

122m (400 ft) and 365.8m (1200 ft) displacement type. 122m (400 ft) reversing, displacement type.

Magazines mount on top of camera for studio mode and at back of camera for hand-held or low-profile mode.

To Remove Handle/Cover from Top of Camera. (1) Depress magazine lock forward of handle/cover. (2) Pull lock lever toward camera door. (3) Lift handle/cover up and away.

NOTE: When replacing top cover/handle, the handle *always* points forward for better carrying balance.

To Remove Cover at Back of Camera. (1) Depress magazine lock above back cover. (2) Rotate lock lever toward camera door and down. (3) Pull cover away from camera.

To Mount Magazine to Camera. (1) Pull loop of film from magazine feed side. (2) Insert loop in magazine guide groove, twist film to clear sprocket, and pull through. (3) Place magazine heel into guide groove, making certain that the film does not catch between the magazine and the camera body. (4) Lower (or push) magazine toe into guide groove. (5) Depress magazine lock, and rotate the lever to secure magazine. (6) Thread camera.

To Remove Magazine. (1) Unthread film, and break it. (2) Depress magazine lock forward of magazine, and pull lock lever toward camera door. (3) Lift magazine up and or away from camera.

16.3m Threading (Fig. 16–16)

(1) Depress inching knob at back of camera and rotate until pulldown claw retracts from register plate, moves up, and starts to enter plate again. (2) Pull registration-pin throw-out knob and move it toward rear of camera. (3) Rotate spring-loaded lock knob clockwise. (4) Rotate the lower aperture-plate lock counterclockwise. (5) Remove aperture plate by *gently* pulling it out away from camera. If plate does not slide out easily, check to see that the single pulldown claw and/or double registration pins are clear of plate. (6) Clean aperture plate. Make a special check of the pulldown claw and registration-pin holes for emulsion buildup or film chips; replace plate. (7) Pull out and rotate the spring-loaded lock knob counterclockwise to secure top of plate. (8) Depress lower aperture lock knob to secure bottom of plate. (9) Swing pressure-plate spring arm clockwise. (10) Remove pressure plate and clean. (11) Replace pressure plate and spring arm. (12) Pull upper sprocket-guide lock knob, and rotate upward. (13) Pull lower sprocket-guide lock knob, and rotate downward. (14) Pull film from magazine feed side, and extend loop to lower front corner of camera (a rough guide for the amount of film needed for threading).

Starting clockwise from the magazine take-up side, insert film.

Top Load. (a) To left of top back roller, then to right of center back roller, (b) between the lower sprocket-guide rollers and the sprocket, (c) *under* small roller at left of sprocket guide rollers and *over* small roller below pulldown claw eccentric.

Back Load. (a) Between the lower sprocket-guide rollers and the sprocket, (b) *under* small roller at left of sprocket guide rollers and *over* small roller below pulldown claw eccentric.

Starting counterclockwise from the magazine feed side, insert film.

Figure 16–16 PFX-16 Threading. Courtesy of Panavision, Inc.

1. Upper small rollers
2. Perforation alignment pin
3. Register plate
4. Pressure-plate swing arm
5. Pressure-plate
6. Pulldown claw
7. Pitch control knob
8. Aperture plate lock
9. Lock lever
10. Magazine lock
11. Registration-pin throw-out knob

12. Peg
13. Upper sprocket-guide lock knob
14. Upper center roller
15. Top back roller
16. Center back roller
17. Buckle-trip
18. Lower small rollers
19. Lower sprocket-guide lock knob
20. fps switch (not visible)
21. Cave area
22. Microswitch

Top Load. (d) To the right of upper center roller, (e) between upper sprocket-guide rollers and sprocket, (f) *over* the small roller to left of sprocket-guide rollers and *under* the small roller above the movement block.

Back Load. (c) Under the center back roller, (d) between upper sprocket-guide rollers and sprocket, (e) *over* the small roller to left of sprocket-guide rollers and *under* the small roller above the movement block.

Both Top and Back Load. (15) Insert film into groove (the race) between the movable aperture plate and stationary register plate. (16) Align film to perforation-alignment pin above aperture plate. (17) Adjust lower loop so that when the lower sprocket-guide roller closes, loop will clear bottom of camera interior by 1.6mm (1/16″) at lowest arc of loop. (18) Reach toward back of registration-pin throw-out knob with little finger of right hand, and nudge the cylindrical-pin bushing *forward*.

NOTE: The registration-pin knob is not used to determine whether the registration pins are entering the perforations, as is done with other cameras with a similar type of movement.

(19) Disengage film from the perforation-alignment pin above the aperture plate. (20) Adjust the upper loop so that there is 0.8mm (1/32") clearance of film from perforation-alignment pin when upper sprocket-guide rollers are closed. (21) Depress inching knob to remove slack on take-up side. (22) Recheck loops.

NOTE: Depressing the inching knob puts 9 volts of power on take-up motor in magazine, which pulls slack film into magazine. This tension precludes the pulling of the film from the take-up side if lower loop needs to be readjusted.

If lower loop is too short, insert forefinger behind center back roller and against the film. Depress the inching knob. This will advance film into camera but not into magazine take-up chamber. Release inching knob; readjust lower loop to proper size.

(23) Rotate inching knob, and observe film being transported in the camera. (24) If satisfactory, turn ON/OFF switch at back of camera to ON. (25) Depress microswitch in door. (26) Apply power in short bursts, and observe action of film. (27) If satisfactory, release microswitch, turn ON/OFF switch at back of camera to OFF. (28) Close door, and reset footage counter.

CAUTION: Remember to turn ON/OFF switch to OFF before closing the camera door. (This step has often been forgotten by those threading the camera.) Once door is closed, film being transported through camera *cannot* be heard.

Pitch-Control Knob. Located below eccentric block. Built in to minimize noise of movement. Correct setting of the pitch control may differ on each roll because of variations in raw-stock perforation pitch and/or film shrinkage. Optimum setting of control is determined by ear, while threaded film stock is run through camera with the door open, and by adjusting the claw pivot point until the eccentric (movement) runs at its quietest. To adjust for a minus pitch, rotate knob toward lens; to adjust for a plus pitch, rotate knob toward Operator.

16.3n Footage Counter

Located forward on optic housing near the viewfinder brake lock. Additive type. LED counter registers each foot of film transported through camera, up to 1999 ft, then reverts to 0 (zero) and counts forward again.

NOTE: First digit will often turn into a dash (—) until counter is reset.

Displays footage expended when camera runs. Contains three buttons on top of counter, labeled, "RCL" (recall), "FAST," "SLOW." One button—labeled "C"—is located at right side of counter.
To Read Footage with Camera off. Depress tiny button on top of camera, marked "RCL."

NOTE: Until and unless the digital-counter reset button is depressed and the counter zeroed, the LED footage counter will "remember" the footage used and will continue to add even though power has been disconnected and camera stored overnight, a week, a month, etc. Reset footage counter to zero after each magazine change.

To Reset Counter. Simultaneously depress tiny button marked "C" at right side of counter *and* the readout button marked "RCL" at top of counter.

To Advance Footage Counter Forward. (1) Depress the button marked "SLOW" to advance footage counter 1 ft at a time. (2) Depress button marked "FAST" to advance the footage counter rapidly.

16.3o Tachometer

LED counter located to right of footage counter. Reads in frames and tenths of frames when camera is running. Registers from 4.0 to 50.0 fps in variable-speed mode, 24.0 fps in sync mode.

NOTE: In cold weather, until heater reaches temperature, the tachometer may vary 0.2 to 0.5 fps (+ or −).

To Replace Malfunctioning Tachometer and/or Footage Counter. (1) Remove two 4-40 screws at top of camera above lens. (2) Lift unit. (3) Align new unit to camera plug. (4) Replace screws.

16.3p Annunciator Panel

Located at camera left, below door. Panel has a series of red or yellow LEDs above graphic icons, which alert user to possible problems:

LOW (Low Battery). Lights when batteries should be changed after the current shot.

FPS. Lights when a speed outside the range of 4–50 fps has been selected on the FPS setting at rear of camera. Camera will not run until FPS has been changed.

JAM (Film Jam). Triggered by buckle-trip switch within camera. Shuts camera off.

LOW (Low Film). Triggered by revolutions per fps in the magazine (*not* by the footage counter). Indicates that 20 ft or less are left in camera.

OUT (Out of Film). Triggered by the magazine when 5 ft is left in camera. Shuts camera off, to prevent film end from passing through movement.

WARNING: Reset annunciator panel before reloading.

To Reset Annunciator Panel. (1) Turn camera off. (2) Depress RESET/ TEST switch to extinguish LEDs.

16.3q Shutter

Variable: 50–200°, in increments of 10°. Calibrations and external shutter control are located at top rear of camera.

To Change Shutter Opening. (1) Release shutter lock, located inside camera body just above top small roller, by turning it counterclockwise toward front of camera. (2) Pull shutter safety locks at side of external shutter knob, and move aside. (3) Pull out shutter control latch, and move shutter to desired opening. (4) Push in latch release, making certain that pin is engaged. (5) Move both safety locks against each side of shutter knob to prevent accidental opening of shutter. (6) Return shutter lock inside camera body to the locked position by turning it clockwise, toward rear of camera.

NOTE: Each safety lock can be set to different degree marks if it is desirable to vary the shutter while filming.

NOTE: Critical shutter settings—such as 144°, 172.8°, and 180°—are observable by removing the aperture plate and looking at the shutter from the camera interior.

16.3r Video Assist
Unit is part of the film camera. Video unit slides onto camera at right side, top of camera.

Video unit switches are:

- POWER—Turns power to the unit on or off.
- IRIS—Allows switching between automatic and manual iris control.
- BLC—Backlight control switch allows compensation for hard or soft backlight.
- GAIN—Two-stop gain switch allows adjustment between normal gain and high gain for low-light shooting situations.

To Attach Video Assist Unit to Camera. (1) Lift small black door at top right side of camera above motor cover to reveal small terminal strip.

NOTE: Video unit contains a connection, which engages a terminal strip.

(2) Hold up the small black door while sliding until video unit locks with an audible "click."

To Remove Video Assist Unit from Camera. (1) Pull small silver pin forward of where the video unit attaches. (2) While holding silver pin out, slide video assist unit off. (3) Small black door is spring-loaded and will snap back into place to cover the terminal strip.

An optional CCD unit slides onto camera in the same place as the regular video unit. CCD unit switches are:

- VIDEO—Allows selection of either local or remote video signal.
- IRIS—Allows selection of either manual or auto iris adjustment. When using the manual iris adjustment, there are two buttons, which allow either opening or closing of iris, as needed.
- POWER—Turns power to the video unit on or off.

16.3s Hand-held Mode
Standard accessories necessary for conversion: short eyepiece, right-hand grip, left-hand grip, shoulder rest. Hand-held mode may also require follow-focus whip, battery belt, and 122m (400-ft) magazine fitted to back magazine port.

To Convert from Studio Mode to Hand-Held Mode. (1) Remove the long eyepiece (see Sec. 16.3f). (2) Place short eyepiece on camera and invert the viewfinder image so that it is erect (see Sec. 16.3f). (3) Mount right-hand grip (can be attached with camera still on head see Sec. 16.3a). (4) Mount left-hand grip. This has no switch for power but helps to balance the camera (see Sec. 16.3a). (5) Insert shoulder rest. The shoulder rest unit consists of three basic parts: a bracket, the rest itself, and a pad. Bracket fits into the cave in the camera's underside and accommodates the rest of the unit. Shoulder rest pad is attached to the rest by Velcro™.

To Insert Bracket. (1) Pinch sides on bracket locking mechanism. (2) Insert bracket into grooves in the cave. (3) Push bracket all the way in until it locks into place.

16.3t Lubrication (Fig. 16–17)

NOTE: Manufacturer provides two plastic containers as a standard maintenance kit. One contains silicone liquid to lubricate the pulldown pads. The other contains oil for applying to the various oiling points in movement.

Manufacturer recommends that the movement be oiled at the start of each shooting day and every 10,000 feet.

Manufacturer states that all rollers are maintenance free.

Eccentric (movement). Clean and—only if needed—lubricate at the end of each shooting day.

NOTE: Manufacturer states that it is not necessary to remove movement for cleaning and lubrication. Manufacturer warns that removing and replacing the movement might affect the flange focal distance and states that if the movement is removed, the flange focal distance should be checked before camera is used again. Usually, a service center job.

Lubricate as Follows. (1) Remove aperture plate and apply one drop of silicone on pulldown pad at bottom of pulldown-claw slot in the register plate.

CAUTION: Do not spill silicone on any other part of the movement; this may cause camera seizure.

(2) Apply one drop of oil "in each well of pulldown arm, pulldown-arm pivot, eccentric shaft, bearing block (two wells), rocker pivot bearing,

Figure 16–17 PFX-16 Lubrication. Courtesy of Panavision, Inc.

1. Spring-loaded dog-lock screw
2. Registration-pin bushings
3. Pivot eccentric arm
4. Registration-pin eccentric arm
5. Pivot drive link
6. Registration-pin rocker
7. Pulldown arm link
8. Registration-pin shaft bushing
9. Registration-pin rocker block
10. Registration-pin rocker bearing
11. Bearing block
12. Pulldown arm pivot

registration-pin linkage (three wells), registration-pin bushing, registration-pin shaft bearing; registration-pin rocker block.

NOTE: If oil wells look moist, do *not* lubricate!

CAUTION: Manufacturer states that only the lubrication material furnished by the company should be used.

16.3u Cleaning

Optics. Clean with blower bulb syringe or compressed air.

Manufacturer recommends the following maintenance *each time film is changed:* (1) Remove aperture plate and pressure plate. (2) Remove emulsion buildup with orangewood stick. (3) Wipe plates with soft cotton (not linen) handkerchief. (4) Use bulb syringe or compressed air on camera interior to remove dirt, dust, etc.

16.3v Weight
With 365.8m (1200 ft) magazine 17.2 kg (38 lb)

16.3w Troubleshooting

Trouble	*Probable Cause*
Camera will not start	Power switch OFF; powerline faulty; battery disconnected; low battery; blown fuse; check annunciator panel
Camera "hunts"	Camera too cold; voltage variation; low battery.
Camera is noisy	Pull-down pads need lubrication; movement needs oiling.
Camera door will not close	Sprocket-guide rollers not seated properly; registration-pin throw-out knob not forward; obstruction in door channel (dirt, dust, etc).
Film jam	Improper threading
Viewfinder not clear/cut-in on viewing tube	Shutter closed; groundglass inserted incorrectly; matte box incorrectly extended; eyepiece cutoff switch not open; magnification knob improperly seated.
Eye focus off	Groundglass inserted incorrectly; eyepiece focus adjustment set for another person; lens not seated properly.
Torn or punctured film	Improper threading
Film will not slide in or out of gate	Registration pin or pulldown claw not retracted; emulsion or film chip in gate
Nonexistent or sporadic take-up	No power to magazine motor; magazine contacts dirty; magazine drive's electronics malfunctioning (a factory job)
Film scratches	Dirt or emulsion build up on the following: aperture plate, sprocket-guide rollers, pressure plate, registration pin, magazine rollers
Footage counter or tachometer erratic	Electronics malfunctioning (factory job)
Blown 5-amp fuse	Improper threading—if continuous, check threading procedure

16.4 PANAVISION PANAFLEX-16 MAGAZINE (Fig. 16–18)

16.4a Type
Displacement.

16.4b Capacity
122m (400 ft), 366m (1200 ft) forward running magazines.
122m (400 ft) reversing magazine.

16.4c Lid
One. Dog-locked.
To Remove. Lift door latch, rotate counterclockwise. Lift lid up and off from magazine.
To Replace. Place lid on magazine. Rotate door latch clockwise to lock door to magazine.

16.4d Feed

Forward-Running Magazine. Left side. Film (wound emulsion in) pulls off of spindle clockwise.

Reversing Magazine. Right side. Film (wound emulsion in) pulls off of spindle counterclockwise.

Figure 16–18 Panavision Panaflex-16 152.4m (500 ft) Magazine. Courtesy of Panavision, Inc.

1. Feed adapter (not visible)
2. Core lock
3. Retaining flange
4. Internal roller
5. Core lock
6. Take-up adapter
7. Retaining flange

Forward-Running Magazine. Right side. Film winds onto spindle counterclockwise, emulsion always out.

Reversing Magazine. Left side. Film winds onto spindle counterclockwise, emulsion always in.

16.4f Loading

Forward-Running Magazine. (1) Remove lid. Ascertain that the manual core lock on feed spindle is pressed into the spindle recess. (2) In darkness, remove film from can and bag. (3) Insert the film between the left feed-idler rollers, and push through until film end emerges from feed side of magazine.

NOTE: Film-end must take a small turn in feeding through the rollers; therefore, it may require more than one attempt to push the end through.

(4) Place film on feed spindle. (5) Rotate feed spindle until spindle pin engages the core keyway. (6) Push manual core lock on spindle outward to engage the feed core. (7) Place empty plastic core on take-up spindle.

NOTE: When using 366m (1200 ft) magazines, always use a 3-in. core on the take-up side.

(8) Ascertain that manual core lock on take-up spindle is pressed into spindle recess. (9) Insert film-end through the take-up side's light-trap rollers. (10) Insert film-end into core slot, and wind film onto take-up spindle counterclockwise (emulsion out). (11) Push manual core lock on spindle outward to engage take-up core. (12) Replace lid.

NOTE: Reversing magazine may be loaded the same as the forward-running magazine, but doing this requires the film to be run through the camera first before shooting any shots in reverse. It is suggested that film be loaded the opposite way from the forward-running magazines as follows.

Reversing Magazine.

WARNING: Feed side is now on the right and take-up side is now on the left.

(1) Remove lid. Ascertain that the manual core lock on feed spindle is pressed into the spindle recess. (2) In darkness, remove film from can and bag. (3) Insert the film between the right feed-idler rollers, and push through until the film-end emerges from magazine.

NOTE: Film-end must take a small turn in feeding through the rollers; therefore, it may require more than one attempt to push the end through.

(4) Place film on feed spindle. (5) Rotate feed spindle until spindle pin engages the core keyway. (6) Push manual core lock on spindle outward to engage feed core. (7) Place empty plastic core on take-up spindle. (8) Ascertain that manual core lock on take-up spindle is pressed into spindle recess. (9) Insert film-end through the take-up side light-trap rollers. (10) Insert film-end into core slot and wind film onto take-up spindle counterclockwise (emulsion in). (11) Push manual core lock on spindle outward to engage take-up core. (12) Replace lid. (13) Reset electronic footage counter.

16.4g Unloading

In darkness, remove lid. (1) Push manual core lock on spindle into spindle recess. (2) Place index finger on core, thumb on edge of film roll. (3) Turn magazine over, remove film roll, and place exposed film into black bag and can.

16.4h Footage Counter

Two: subtractive mechanical counter, additive LCD counter.

To Read Footage Remaining in Magazine. Slide lever above magazine motor until internal roller touches film roll.

To Reset Electronic Footage Display. Press small white button labeled "C" (clear).

To Rapidly Advance Electronic Footage Display. Press small white button labeled "FAST."

To Slowly Advance Electronic Footage Display. Press small white button labeled "SLOW."

NOTE: Counter is powered by a long-life internal battery, so LCD "remembers" footage even when magazine is not on camera.

16.4i Spindle-Wheel Housings

Feed Spindle-Wheel Housing. Contains a constant-torque clutch to prevent film from unwinding on feed side. Also contains a *manual feed knob*, to tighten film on core if needed, and to rotate spindle wheel when loading.

Take-up Spindle-Wheel Housing. Contains a *take-up motor* to wind film on take-up core. Center of take-up spindle contains a *manual take-up knob*, to rotate spindle wheel when loading. Take-up motor can only rotate in a counterclockwise direction.

To Turn Manual Feed and Take-up Knobs. Depress knob, and turn in direction of film winding onto core.

chapter 17

ULTRACAM Camera, Magazines, and Accessories

17.1 35mm ULTRACAM CAMERA* (Figs. 17–1a, 17–1b, and 17–1c)

NOTE: All directions are from the Operator's point of view.

17.1a Base

Sliding Balance Plate. Used in order to provide the camera with a "quick-release" system on a tripod or geared head.

Unit consists of three parts: (1) A dovetailed *wedge plate* (with a 3/8–16″ screw and two locating pins), that is attached to the bottom of the camera.

(2) A dovetailed *mount* that accommodates the wedge plate at its top and, in turn, fits onto the dovetail of the base (lower) plate. It slides on the base for ease of balance of the camera on the tripod.

NOTE: The upper plate can slide back and forth but will not slide off because of the front-, center-, or back-mounted 1/4–20 × 12.7mm (1/2″) bolts fitted in one of three tandem tapped holes in the bottom of the mount.

NOTE: The front of the mount accommodates two 12.7 mm (1/2″) iris rods and ALWAYS faces forward (see Sec. 17.1h, for mounting rods).

(3) A *base plate* (Fig. 17–2) with a dovetail at its top that accommodates the dovetail on the bottom of the mount. Also at the base plate's top is a restricted slot to accommodate bolts on the bottom of the mount and allow the mount to slide back and forth on the base.

Base plate also contains a lock release lever and a locking pin knob.

Bottom of the base plate has multiple 9.1mm (3/8″)-16 tapped holes to accommodate tripod or geared-head lockdown screw(s).

To Mount Plates and Camera. (1) Attach the wedge plate securely to bottom of the camera. (2) Place the baseplate on a tripod or geared head and secure. (3) Pull out upper plate locking lever at left side of base plate until it stops (approximately 80°). Pull lock release lever at back of base plate until locking lever springs further away from base. (4) Align and slide upper plate into dovetail of base. (5) Push in on the baseplate locking lever to secure the upper plate. (6) Slide the camera wedge plate into the top of the upper plate until the spring-loaded upper safety locking pin "clicks" behind the wedge.

---

*Manufacturer states the designation ULTRACAM stands for "Ultra Camera."

Figure 17–1a ULTRACAM camera (left front view). Courtesy of Leonetti ULTRA-CAM.

1. Zoom lens focus linkage
2. Lens lock
3. Base plate
4. Focus knob
5. Battery condition lights & LCD
6. On/Off switch
7. ND selector
8. Door latch
9. Rear magazine lock lever
10. Top magazine lock lever
11. Viewfinder scalloped knob
12. Long extension eyepiece
13. Viewfinder-leveler bracket
14. Eyecup
15. Magazine cover latch
16. Eyepiece lock
17. Prism release pin
18. Eyepiece focus knob
19. Magnification lever
20. Video tap cover
21. Zoom motor bracket
22. Studio matte-box

To Balance Camera on Tripod. Pull out locking lever at left side of base plate until it stops (approximately 80°). Slide mount in dovetail of base until desired balance is attained. Push upper plate locking lever toward base to secure camera.

To Remove Camera from Upper Plate. Grasp camera securely. Pull out base locking lever to first position. Pull on locking pin knob at left-rear of mount. Slide camera back and up.

17.1b Motor

Built-in 28v DC crystal control. Nonremovable in the field. Does NOT reverse.

To operate camera at sync or variable speeds. Set Motor Speed Selector Switch (labeled F.P.S. on Control Panel, see 17.1c) to desired fps.

Hertz Output. At 24 fps–60 Hz; at 25 fps–50 Hz.

17.1c Powerline

Control Panel. At rear of camera (Fig. 17–3).
Power Input to Camera. 2-pin LEMO plug at lower right-rear of panel.

Figure 17–1b ULTRACAM camera (right rear view). Courtesy of Leonetti ULTRACAM.

1. Rear magazine lock
2. Rear magazine cover
3. Power panel (see detail)
4. Pistol grip dovetail
5. Beeper
6. Feed core lock

7. Mechanical footage scale
8. Mechanical footage counter lever
9. Motor housing
10. Take-up core lock
11. Eyecup

Remote Input. 2-pin LEMO plug at lower left of panel. Used to run camera by Pistol Grip, or from another camera when "slaved."

NOTE: The LEMO plug on the remote cable is a different size than that of the power cable. They are NOT interchangeable.

Volume Control. Above input to camera. Adjusts sound level of out-of-sync warning signal.

Indicator Lights at Center-Rear of Panel. Green and red. *Green light* indicates camera speed is in crystal speed frame rates of 8 fps, 20 fps, 24 fps, 25 fps, or 30 fps sync mode. *Red light* flashes when camera is in a variable (non-crystal speed mode) (12, 16, 18, 28, 32, fps or EX).

NOTE: Green and red indicator lights at the left-front of the camera serve a different purpose (see below).

Run/Stop Switch. At left center of panel.

NOTE: A second Run/Stop switch is located at the left-front of the camera above the tachometer.

Sync Pulse Four-Pin Input/Output LEMO Plug. At right of Run/Stop switch. Dual purpose receptacle can be used to input and drive the camera from a

Figure 17–1c ULTRACAM camera (hand-held configuration). Courtesy of Leonetti ULTRACAM.

1. Pistol-grip triggers
2. Hand-held cradle
3. Pistolgrip adjustment knob
4. Battery light (red)
5. Battery light (green)
6. Lens focus knob
7. Shoulder pad
8. Frame rate LCD
9. Baseplate dovetail release
10. Door latch
11. Magazine cover latch
12. Magazine lock
13. ND filter selector
14. Eyepiece lock
15. Prism release pin
16. Pechan prism
17. Video tap cover
18. Hand-held sunshade
19. On/Off switch
20. Lens lock

video sync signal, or a Precision Speed Control unit, (see 17.3, Accessories) or to output a sync signal (60 Hz at 24 fps; 50 Hz at 25 fps) to an audio recorder.

NOTE: Counterclockwise from the bottom, pin no. 1—1440 Hz 10 v peak to peak input; pin no. 2—1 pulse-per-frame output; pin no. 3—ground; pin no. 4—60 Hz .2v output.

Heater Switch. At top right. Flips up to heat movement, motor, shutter, and sub-assembly in cold weather. A tiny *red heater light* at the heater's right illuminates when the switch is in ON position.

Motor Speed Selector Switch (labeled F.P.S.). Knob located at top left of panel.

To Operate Camera at Sync Sound Speed. Set Motor Speed Selector switch to 24 or 25.

To Run Motor at Other Speeds. Set Motor Speed Selector switch to desired fps rate. Variable setable speeds are 8, 12, 16, 18, 20, 30, 32, and EX.

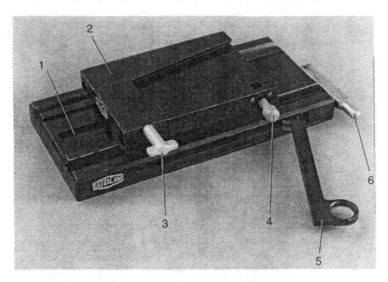

Figure 17–2   Base plate. Courtesy of Leonetti ULTRACAM.

1. Base plate
2. Dovetailed mount
3. Iris rod lock

4. Spring-loaded wedge-locking pin
5. Upper plate locking lever
6. Lock release lever

NOTE: A mechanical safety stop prevents the switch from being turned from 24 to EX (or vice-versa) in one step. The switch must be rotated through all the numbers to reach EX, or 25.

EX Setting.   The Speed Selector Switch is set to EX when syncing with another film camera or a TV camera, or while using a Precision Speed Control, or when the film camera is a "slave" to another camera, etc.

NOTE: When operated as a "slave," if the camera speed exceeds 32 fps the "slave" will automatically shut off. *To reset,* unplug power cable on "slave" camera and re-insert.

Indicator Lights at the Left-Front of the Camera.   Green and red. *Green light* indicates battery has ample voltage to run camera. *Red light* indicates battery is low.

11-pin Fischer Accessory Plugs.   Two. At front of camera. Supply 12v power to zoom motor, lens lights, splitter box, etc.

Pistol Grip.   In hand-held mode, the trigger on the pistol grip functions as the camera's On/Off switch.

To Mount Pistol Grip on Camera.   Rotate large scalloped knob on pistol grip counterclockwise. Align notched dovetail of pistol grip to either the upper or lower dovetailed bracket behind the matte-box mount dovetail at the right front of the camera; slide forward until notch in the pistol grip dovetail engages the pin in the camera bracket. Rotate the large scalloped knob clockwise to secure. Loosen outer grip knob to adjust handle to desired angle.

Figure 17–3 Control panel. Courtesy of Leonetti ULTRACAM.

1. Motor speed switch
2. On/Off switch
3. Bubble level
4. Red light
5. Remote plug

6. Green light
7. Power connector
8. Volume knob
9. Sync pulse plug
10. Heater toggle

NOTE: Extension cables are not necessary when pistol grips are mounted to the camera (electrical connection is made).

To Remove Pistol Grip from Camera.   Rotate large scalloped knob on grip counterclockwise; slide back and away from camera.

Pistol Grip as Remote Trigger.   Remove pistol grip from the camera. Plug one end of a two-pin LEMO cable into the "Remote" input on the control panel. Insert other end of the cable into the pistol grip. Use On/Off trigger to start/stop camera.

NOTE: The LEMO plug on the remote cable is a different size than that of the power cable. They are NOT interchangeable.

NOTE: A hand-held cradle that mounts on the front rods is available. It requires a cable from the pistol grip to the "Remote" input on the camera.

17.1d Turret

None. Single lens mount accepts Ultranon Lenses and/or BNCR mount lenses.

NOTE: Ultranon lenses will NOT fit on any other cameras that have BNC lens mounts.

WARNING: While lens mount will hold all Ultranon and BNCR spherical lenses without support, ALL anamorphic or zooms and telephotos require an ULTRACAM Lens Support Bracket and/or an Ultracam Follow-Focus Unit.

17.1e Lenses

To Fit Lens to Camera. (1) Rotate lens lock clockwise as far as it will go. (2) Align hole in lens flange with positioning stud located in the upper left of lens port. Ascertain that gear ring on lens meshes with the follow-focus gear on the camera. Insert the lens flange flush with the camera, making certain the stud engages the lens-flange hole. (3) Rotate lens lock counterclockwise to secure.

To Remove Lens. (1) Grasp lens firmly. (2) Rotate lens lock clockwise as far as it will go. (3) Slide lens from the port.

17.1f Focus Controls

Built-in mounts, located on both sides of the camera, are fitted with detachable 50mm (2 in.) knobs. Also available are 22.8cm (9 in.) extensions and 38cm (15 in.) "whips" for focusing at short distances from camera.

To Attach Focus Knob. (1) Align guide pins on shaft of focus knob with slots in camera focus mount. (2) Hold large focus knob; rotate small inner scalloped knob clockwise to secure.

To Detach Focus Knob. Hold large focus knob; rotate small inner scalloped knob counterclockwise. Remove.

17.1g Viewfinder

Reflex Telescopic image magnifies 6–9×. Rotates 360°; maintains upright position at any angle.

To Focus Eyepiece. Rotate knob numbered 0–9 at top of camera optics housing until groundglass lines are sharp.

NOTE: No. 5 on the knob is considered 20/20 vision, but this may vary + or − 1/2 diopter.

To Change or Clean Groundglass. Remove lens. Use inching knob to clear mirror from groundglass.

NOTE: There are two types of groundglass: Cameras with numbers 251–256 are fitted with the "old style" groundglass; cameras with numbers 257 and up are fitted with the "new style" groundglass.

"Old Style" Groundglass. T-shaped (or with "wings"). To remove, grasp "wings" on front edge of the groundglass and gently pull straight out. To insert, hold groundglass by its "wings" and gently slide into slot with frosted side toward the mirror shutter.

"New style" Groundglass. Straight (no "wings"). To remove, grasp forward edge of the groundglass and gently pull straight out. To insert, hold groundglass by the end that has the most space between the format scribe and the groundglass edge and gently slide into slot with frosted side toward the mirror shutter.

To Align Reflex Mirror for Viewing. Open camera door; rotate inching knob on the movement until image appears in the viewfinder.

NOTE: Camera stops with shutter in viewing position except when inched by hand (e.g., when threading).

Short Eyepiece and Long Extension.

NOTE: Short eyepiece is used with camera in hand-held mode. Long extension is used with camera in production mode.

To Attach Long Extension. (1) Rotate scalloped ring on rear of eyepiece elbow counterclockwise to loosen. Remove short eyepiece that is on camera. (2) Tighten Eyepiece Brake (knob forward of counters). Pull Eyepiece Mode Pin on eyepiece elbow. Rotate elbow until the pulled pin aligns to the letter "L" (long) on the center of the elbow. Mode pin will "click" into place. Loosen eyepiece brake. Push Eyepiece Mode Pin IN and ascertain that pin is seated. (3) Align notch on Long Extension flange to pin in eyepiece elbow. Push extension *gently* into elbow. Rotate knurled locking ring clockwise to secure. (4) Align Short Eyepiece to pin in Long Extension. Push short eyepiece gently into Long Extension to the flanges. Rotate knurled ring clockwise to secure.

Long Eyepiece Support Rod. Top fits to collar on rear of Eyepiece Extension. Bottom is affixed to tripod or geared head.

To Remove Long Extension. (1) Rotate scalloped ring forward of short eyepiece counterclockwise to loosen. Remove short eyepiece from long extension. (2) Rotate scalloped ring on rear of eyepiece elbow counterclockwise to loosen; remove long extension. (3) Pull Eyepiece Mode Pin on eyepiece elbow. Rotate elbow until the pulled pin aligns to the letter "S" (short) on the center of the elbow. Mode pin will "click" into place. Push Eyepiece Mode Pin IN and ascertain that pin is seated. (4) Align notch on short eyepiece flange to pin in eyepiece elbow. Push short eyepiece *gently* into elbow to the flanges. Rotate knurled locking ring clockwise to secure.

To Alter Viewfinder Position for Viewing. Loosen Eyepiece Brake counterclockwise. Grasp finder; rotate perpendicular to camera body. Viewfinder will rotate 360°.

To Secure in Desired Position. Tighten Eyepiece Brake.

Magnification. Rotate Magnifier Lever on top of the camera clockwise (toward rear of camera) to magnify image $9 \times$.

Contrast Filters. Knurled knobs at left front of camera. Rotate to insert ND filters into viewing system. Spring-loaded small center knob is .30 ND. Spring-loaded large outer knob is .60 ND. Rotated together, value is .90 ND.

NOTE: ND filters insert into the viewing system only; they have no effect on the film.

Anamorphic Correction Element. Lever at left front of camera next to the lens port. Flips up (horizontally) to insert an element into the viewing system for an unsqueezed viewing of anamorphic images. For spherical lenses, lever is flipped vertically.

Video Assist. CCD camera attaches via a bayonet mount to the top of the camera.

To Attach CCD Camera. Rotate scalloped knob at top right of camera counterclockwise and lift cover. Align locating hole on video tap lens with locating pin in mount. Insert lens and turn scalloped knob clockwise to secure. Connect Herosa plug on CCD camera to 11-pin Fischer plug at camera front.

17.1h Sunshade/Matte-Box and Filters

Three types available: (1) Three-stage unit accepts 127 × 152mm (5 × 6 in.) fixed filters.

(2) Five-stage unit accepts three 127 × 152mm (5 × 6 in.) fixed filters, and two 167 × 167mm (6.6 × 6.6 in.) square rotatable filters. Unit also has a circular 138mm diameter filter at its rear.

(3) Hand-held matte-box is a circular rubber shade with a 114mm (4.5 in.) circular filter ring at its rear.

To Insert Filters in Three- or Five-Stage Matte-Box. Place filter into holder. Pull back one end of velcro strap and slide holder into matte-box slots from the top. Replace velcro strap to hold filter in place.

NOTE: There is no internal filter slot.

NOTE: Gelatin filter holders fit to back of Ultranon lenses (two on each lens except for 18mm which accepts only one holder).

Iris Rods for Matte-Box. Mount on Balance Plate.

NOTE: Standard rods for the ULTRACAM are 28cm (11 in.). Other length rods available are: 33cm (13 in.) (for zoom lens); 20 cm (8 in.); 10cm (4 in.).

With camera mounted on a balance plate (see Section 17.1a), front of base plate accommodates two 12.7mm (1/2 in.) diameter iris rods.

To Mount Standard Matte-Box to Balance Plate. Slide L-shaped mounting bracket onto iris rods. Secure by turning Matte-Box Lock Knob on left side of mounting bracket.

For Access to Lens Mount. Depress catch-lever at left-front of L-shaped bracket. Swing matte-box aside.

17.1i Door

Hinged on the bottom.

To Open. Lift catch in door; rotate counterclockwise; pull out and down.

NOTE: A microswitch located above the sprocket will cut power to the camera when the door is open.

To Close. Push door up until flush with camera; rotate latch clockwise; depress until flush with door.

WARNING: *Always* turn the Run/Stop switch to OFF before closing the camera door. (The person threading the camera often forgets this step.) Once the door is closed, film being transported through the camera CANNOT be heard. It is possible to roll all the film through the camera unknowingly. (It has been done.)

17.1j Buckle-Trip

Two.

Buckle-Trip. Apron (long thin plate) below sprocket cuts out power to camera automatically if film jams; resets automatically when jam is cleared.

Film Run-Out Switch. Roller above pitch control knob rides on film edge and cuts power to camera automatically to prevent film-end from going through movement race. The roller is raised and locked UP when threading, automatically drops when door is closed or the cut-out switch is depressed.

17.1k Magazines

152.4 (500 ft) and 304.8m (1000 ft).

Mounts at top or back of camera.

To Mount. (1) Depress safety lock pin above magazine lever; rotate lever counterclockwise as far as it will go and magazine toe-lock raises from camera body; remove camera cover. (2) Pull a film loop from the magazine feed side. (3) Insert heel of magazine into the magazine guide groove. Draw film loop into camera. (4) Slide magazine back and down into grooves until flush to camera. (5) Rotate lock lever clockwise until safety lock pin secures lever. Thread camera (see Sec. 17.1l).

Figure 17–4a   Threading detail (top-load). Courtesy of Leonetti ULTRACAM.

1. Sprocket	9. Aperture plate lock
2. Upper sprocket-guide roller	10. Pulldown claw
3. Registration-pin retractor lever	11. Inching knob
4. Center roller	12. Take-up tension roller
5. Film run-out switch roller	13. Lower center rollers
6. Stroke-adjustment knob	14. Buckle-trip
7. Upper roller	15. Lower sprocket-guide roller
8. Race	16. Take-up tension roller

To Remove. (1) Unthread film. Hand-wind film into take-up side of magazine. (2) Disengage the magazine by depressing the safety lock above the magazine lever; rotate lever counterclockwise as far as it will go and clear magazine toe-lock from magazine. (3) Grasp magazine and rock it back on its heel to clear the magazine toe-lock; *then* lift the magazine up and away.

NOTE: Three pins in the magazine guide groove match contacts in the magazine. Reading from door side to right: pin no. 1 is positive (powers magazine brake and LED readouts); pin no. 2 is negative (ground); pin no. 3 is positive (powers magazine motors).

17.1I   Threading (Figs. 17–4a, 17–4b)

Before Placing Magazine on Camera. (1) Push film run-out switch UP and engage in catch. (2) Rotate inching knob and clear single pulldown claw from register plate. (3) Press registration-pin retractor lever DOWN to clear dual registration pins from register plate. (4) Pull out Upper Sprocket Guide Knob and rotate upper sprocket-guide roller counterclockwise; pull out Lower Sprocket Guide Knob and rotate lower sprocket-guide roller clockwise. (5) Pull out and rotate Aperture Plate Lock clockwise; pull out and rotate lower Aperture Plate Lock counterclockwise, then *gently* pull Aperture Plate away.

NOTE: If Aperture Plate does not slide out easily, check to see if pulldown claw and/or registration pin is clear of register plate.

Figure 17–4b   Threading detail (back-load). Courtesy of Leonetti ULTRACAM.

1. Top rear roller   2. Lower rear roller

(6) Clean plate. Make a special check of the pulldown claw and registration-pin holes for emulsion or film chips; replace plate. Depress and secure aperture plate locks. (7) Swivel pressure plate and cam clockwise. Remove pressure plate; clean and re-install. (8) Place magazine on camera (see Section 17.1k). Pull film from magazine feed side; extend loop to lower front corner of camera (a rough guide for amount of film needed for threading).

Top Load. (9) Starting counterclockwise from the feed side, insert film: (a) between sprocket and upper sprocket-guide roller, (b) over center roller, (c) under upper roller. (10) Starting clockwise from the take-up side, insert film: (a) under the take-up tension roller, (b) between the two lower center rollers, (c) between the two lower center rollers, (d) over the front roller below the registration-pins.

Back-Load. (9) Starting counterclockwise from the feed side, insert film: (a) under the rear top roller, (b) between the sprocket and upper sprocket-guide roller, (c) over the center roller, (d) under the upper roller. (10) Starting clockwise from the take-up side, insert film: (a) over the lower rear roller, (b) under the take-up tension roller, (c) between the sprocket and lower sprocket-guide roller, (d) between the two lower center rollers, (e) over the front roller below the registration pin. (11) Insert film into groove (the race) between the removable aperture plate and the stationary register plate. (12) Slide film up and down in the race until a perforation engages a spring-loaded pin in the register plate.

NOTE: This pin is not visible when loading. Engagement of the perforation in the pin is by "feel." The pin is only visible when the movement is removed (see Sec. 17.1p, Lubrication). It is located below the right registration-pin.

(13) Push Registration-Pin Retractor Lever UP to engage perforations. (14) Rotate inching knob to engage pulldown claw and advance film. Observe that film moves freely through the race. (15) Set pulldown claw at bottom of movement just before it disengages the film perforation. (16) Set the lower loop so that when the lower sprocket-guide closes the loop clears the bottom of the camera interior by 3.2–6.4mm (1/8–1/4 in.). (17) Set upper loop so that when the upper sprocket-guide is closed, the top of the loop aligns with the top of the movement plate. (18) Rotate inching knob and observe film being transported through the camera. If satisfactory, proceed. (19) Depress cut-out switch in door. Apply power in short bursts and observe action of film. If satisfactory, set Pitch Adjustment (see below), stop camera, close door, and reset footage counter.

Pitch Adjustment. Knob located above inching knob. Built-in to minimize noise of movement. Correct setting of the adjustment knob may differ on each roll because of variations in rawstock perforation pitch and/or film shrinkage. Optimum setting is determined by ear while threaded film stock is run through camera with door open and by adjusting the claw pivot point until the eccentric (movement) runs at its quietest. To adjust for a minus stroke, rotate knob toward lens; to adjust for a plus stroke, rotate knob toward Operator.

17.1m Footage Counter
Located atop camera behind eyepiece elbow. LED counter registers each foot of film transported through the camera up to 999 feet, then reverts to

zero and counts forward again. Displays footage expended whenever camera runs.

NOTE: Counter can also be set to read in meters.

To Change Counter to Read in Feet/Meters. Open camera door. Loosen 4.8mm (3/16 in.) Allen head screws at top and bottom of movement (at rear of registration-pin cam). Remove motor cover at right side of camera. Remove motor. Flip feet/meter switch on circuit board to desired selection.

To Read Footage with Camera Off. Press READ button at top of Counter.

To Preset Footage on Counter. Press RESET button on side of footage counter until desired footage count is reached.

NOTE: Preset will not work unless power is supplied to camera.

To Clear Counter. Depress READ and RESET simultaneously.
There is *no* frame counter.

Counter "Memory." A 9v internal battery retains counter memory although camera might be disconnected. Counter will dim as battery loses voltage.

To Replace Footage Counter Battery. Loosen slotted screw and remove square plate at top of camera, forward of the top magazine mount. Unplug bad battery and change. Replace plate.

17.1n Tachometer
LED tachometer is located at left front side of camera. Registers fps as set on Speed Selector Switch on Control Panel (see Sec. 17.1c, Powerline Control Panel)

17.1o Shutter
Fixed. Equivalent to 175°.

17.1p Lubrication (Fig. 17-5)
Manufacturer recommends lubrication of the following parts only when needed: registration-pin cam, pulldown claw shaft guide, toggle arm bearings. Use liquid silicone (NOT oil) on chamois pad at bottom of claw raceway every 1524m (5000 ft).

17.1q Cleaning

Optics. Clean with bulb syringe or soft camel's-hair brush.

Manufacturer recommends the following maintenance *each time film is changed:* (1) Remove aperture and pressure plates. (2) Remove emulsion build-up with orangewood stick. (3) Wipe plates with soft cotton handkerchief (not linen). (4) Use bulb syringe on camera interior to remove dust, dirt, etc.

To Remove Movement for Cleaning. With 7.1mm (9/32 in.) 12-point socket screwdriver, loosen two captive screws holding movement in camera body; slide movement out.

CAUTION: A fibre connecting-gear fits between the gear on the movement and the gear in the camera body. It is possible that it will come out with the removal of the movement. DON'T LOSE IT!

Figure 17–5 Ultracam movement Lubrication. Courtesy of Leonetti ULTRACAM.

1. Registration-pin block
2. Pulldown claw shaft
3. Chamois pad
4. Toggle-arm bearings
5. Registration-pin cam

WARNING: *Never* lubricate the fibre gear.

To Insert Movement into Camera Body. (1) Make sure fibre gear is properly mounted on camera gear.

WARNING: The fibre connecting-gear must be in place or the camera will be excessively noisy.

(2) Align guide hole on movement gear to match guide pin on camera gear. (3) Slide movement block into camera until flush.

NOTE: There are two guide pins on the camera wall that align with the guide holes in the movement block.

(4) Rotate inching knob to ascertain that it is moving freely before tightening the captive screws.

NOTE: Timing of the camera is not necessary.

17.1r Miscellaneous

The ULTRACAM is available with a three-perforation movement that exposes film at 20.57m per minute (67.5 ft per minute), as well as the standard four-perforation movement that exposes film at 27.43m per minute (90 ft per minute). Changing to a three-perforation movement is a qualified service technician's job.

17.1s Weight

With 152.4m (500 ft.) load: 14kg (31 lbs).
With 304.8m (1000 ft.) load: 18kg (40 lbs).

17.1t Troubleshooting

Trouble	*Probable Cause*
Camera will not start	Power cable connection faulty; Runout Switch tripped; camera door not closed; buckle-trip engaged
Camera door will not close	Film chip or dirt in door; door latch not opened
Film jam	Improper threading
Footage Counter does not read or hold memory	9v battery needs replacement
Film snaps when camera starts	Film loop not under take-up tension roller
Brake on magazine does not hold	Dirty contact on magazine; damaged contact on camera; electronics out
Red light next to tachometer on	Battery low
Torn or punctured film	Improper threading; sprocket-guide rollers not properly set
Film scratches	Improper threading, or dirt or emulsion build-up on the following: aperture plate, sprocket guide rollers, pressure plate, registration plate, magazine rollers
Sporadic or no take-up	Dirty or damaged contacts on magazine or camera; electronics malfunctioning; door not closed
Camera loses loop	Sprocket guide rollers not locked down; dirt or heavy emulsion build-up in race
Viewfinder image upside down	Pechan prism not oriented to eyepiece being used
Viewing system blocked	Mirror not in viewing position; cap on lens; de-anamorphoser partially in
Mirror/shutter does not stop in viewing position	Movement and/or mirror/shutter timing off
Follow focus loose on zoom lens	Allen screws on universal joints of follow-focus shaft loose
Noisy magazine	Film cores not properly locked; dirt on magazine rollers; film spooled against side of magazine interior (dished)
Noisy movement	Pitch not adjusted; film perforation pitch bad; dirt in race; aperture plate or registration plate dirty; pad at bottom of registration plate needs silicone; improper threading; rollers need cleaning (do NOT lubricate)
Camera beeps when camera is off	Overspeed protection electronics warning is over-riding OFF switch (unplug camera and plug back in)

17.2 35mm ULTRACAM MAGAZINE (Fig. 17–6)

17.2a Type
Displacement.

17.2b Capacity
152.4m (500 ft) and 304.8m (1000 ft)

17.2c Lid
Dog-locked.
To Remove. Lift latch in lid; rotate latch counterclockwise; lift lid.

17.2d Feed
Left side. Film (emulsion in) pulls off spindle clockwise.

17.2e Take-up
Right side. Film winds on spindle clockwise, emulsion in.

17.2f Loading
(1) Remove lid.

WARNING: Ascertain that spindle locks are retracted!

To Retract Spindle Locks. Rotate feed-side scalloped knob on back of magazine counterclockwise. Rotate take-up scalloped knob clockwise.
(2) In darkness, remove film roll from can and bag. Insert the film-end into feed-side light-trap rollers and push approximately 30cm (12 in.) through. (3) Place film roll on feed spindle and rotate until spindle-pin engages the core. (4) Reach to back of magazine; rotate scalloped knob of feed spindle clockwise until spindle locks expand and secure the core. (5) Insert film-end into take-up side light-trap rollers. (6) Rotate core on take-up spindle counterclockwise until spindle engages core keyway; hold core,

Figure 17–6 Ultracam magazine. Courtesy of Leonetti ULTRACAM.

1. Feed spindle lock
2. Take-up spindle lock

reach to back of magazine, and rotate scalloped knob of take-up spindle clockwise until spindle locks expand and secure core. (7) Insert film-end into core slot and wind film onto take-up spindle clockwise (emulsion always in). (8) Replace lid.

17.2g Unloading
(1) In darkness, remove lid. Place index finger on core, thumb on edge of film roll. Turn magazine over. (2) Reach to back of magazine, rotate scalloped take-up knob clockwise until spindle locks retract and film roll drops into hand.

17.2h Footage Counter
Manual. Subtractive. Measures in increments of 15.24m (50 ft).
To Determine Footage Remaining in Magazine. Depress latch above torque motor housing; read indicator.

17.2i Miscellaneous
The feed spindle assembly at the back of the magazine contains a built-in brake which keeps the feed roll from unraveling in the magazine. The brake releases automatically when camera is turned ON and is activated when camera is turned OFF.

The take-up spindle assembly contains a torque motor for film take-up when the camera is activated.

17.3 ULTRACAM ACCESSORIES

17.3a Ultra Crystal Speed Control (UCSC) (Fig. 17–7)
An external unit for crystal speed setting on camera.

Unit consists of a two-pin LEMO plug, a Phase Button, a Toggle Switch, and a five digit counter flanked by two rows of selector buttons.

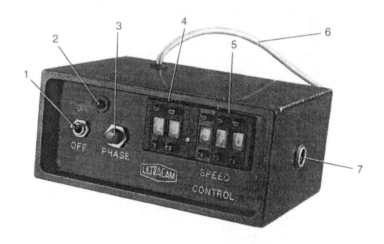

Figure 17–7 Ultracrystal speed control (UCSC). Courtesy of Leonetti ULTRACAM.

1. On/off switch
2. Power indicator light
3. Phase shift-button
4. Frame digit indicator
5. Frame fraction indicator
6. Power cable
7. Two-pin LEMO Sync cable connector

The − (minus) row subtracts the counter; the + (plus) row increases the counter.

NOTE: Although five digits are available, only the first two digits are used to input the desired number of crystal fps.

WARNING: The camera cannot exceed 32 fps.

To Mount. (1) Align USCS unit's dovetail to the large dovetail on right side of the camera and slide toward Operator. (2) Insert the two-pin LEMO plug on the connector cable into the unit and the four-pin LEMO plug on the cable into the SYNC plug on the camera Control Panel.

To Use UCSC. (1) Set camera F.P.S. Selector Switch on Control Panel to EX. (2) Plug in box and flip toggle switch to ON.

NOTE: The toggle switch activates the unit's internal 9-volt battery only, NOT the camera.

(3) Set desired speed on box; wait for red LED to extinguish. (4) Turn camera on.

To Remove a Scan Line if Filming a Monitor. Depress Phase button until scan line disappears.

17.3b Variable Speed Control (VSC)

An external unit for variable (non-sync) speed setting on camera.

Unit consists of an attached cable with a four-pin LEMO plug and a Speed Control Knob.

To Mount Unit to Camera. (1) Remove rear magazine cover (see 17.1k, Magazines). (2) Insert VSC into rear magazine opening and lock.

To Run Camera from 1 to 32 fps. (1) Insert four-in LEMO plug on unit's attached cable into Sync plug on Control Panel. (2) Set F.P.S. Switch on Control panel to EX. (3) Turn beeper volume down. (4) Turn camera ON. (5) Observe Footage Counter on camera and adjust circular Speed Control Knob on VSC to desired speed.

NOTE: Scale on the circular knob does NOT designate fps. Scale is from 0 to 8.3 in increments of five scribe intervals per number (e.g., 0||||1||||2||||3|||, etc., up to and including 8|||). Knob is purposely set to rotate only to 8.3 on scale to avoid exceeding 32 fps. A setting of 7.5 on knob is approximately 24 fps but may vary from unit to unit.

WARNING: Always turn knob to 0 (zero), OFF, at end of each take to avoid wearing down internal 9-volt battery and rendering VSC inoperable.

chapter 18

Cinema Products Steadicam Film/Video Camera Stabilizing System Model 3A

Model 3A is a camera-mounting and stabilizing system for use with 16mm and 35mm film and video cameras. The System consists of a Stabilizer-Support Arm attached at one end to the Operator's Vest and to a Camera Mounting Assembly at the other.

18.1 SYSTEM COMPONENTS (Fig. 18–1)

18.1a Operator's Vest

Transfers and distributes weight of Steadicam system (including camera and lens) across Operator's shoulders, back, and hips.

18.1b Stabilizer Support Arm

Adjustable arm counteracts camera weight with calibrated spring force. Has articulated elbow hinge, which frees arm to move 360° horizontally from elbow. One end of arm attaches to vest frontplate. Gimbal connects Arm to Camera Mounting Assembly.

18.1c Camera Mounting Assembly

Utilizes central Telescoping Balance Post, around which individual components rotate as needed. One end of post supports Mounting Platform; other end terminates on Electronics Module. Battery housing piggybacks on Electronics Module. Compact video monitor attached to pivoting bracket slides up, down, or around post.

Steadicam Telescoping/Balance Post. Expands to maximum length of 23.5 in. or contracts to 14 in., allowing greater adjustment to camera's point of view. At one end of post is standard fore/aft camera control and Side-to-Side Camera Balance Plate for lateral movement of Camera Mounting Platform. Other end features Fore/Aft/Rotating Balance-Control Knob for balance at Electronics Module.

Video Viewfinder System. Video monitor for viewing what camera sees. If using a film camera, it must be equipped with video assist. Electronic level and frame lines which can be adjusted to any aspect ratio, visible on CRT viewing screen.

18.1d Power Supplies

Power for Steadicam viewfinder system and camera (optional) provided by 12–15 volt, 3.5 ampere/hour (nickel-cadmium) battery pack, Model

Figure 18–1. Steadicam system components. Courtesy of Cinema Products.

1. Camera Operator's Vest
2. Parachute-Type Quick-Release System
3. Removable Vest Pads
4. Adjustable Support Arm
5. Reversible Frontplate
6. Fore/Aft Rotating Balance Control
7. 12V 3.5 Amp NiCd Battery
8. Battery Housing
9. Camera Mounting Assembly
10. Electronics Module
11. Five-Amp External Fuse Holder Kit
12. High Intensity Video Monitor
13. Telescoping/Balance Post
14. Free-Floating Gimbal
15. JB-3 Junction Box
16. Side-to-Side Camera Balance Plate
17. Side-to-Side Knob.
18. Camera Mounting Platform

NC-12, which plugs into lower portion of Camera Mounting Assembly. (Two battery packs and two overnight chargers supplied). Optional External Power Adapter, to power from other 12-volt sources, such as 12-volt NiCd battery belt, heavy-duty 12-volt, 30-ampere/hour lead-acid battery, or directly from alternating current line-operated power supply. Optional quick-charger, Model NCQC-12 charges two standard batteries in 35 minutes.

18.2 PREPARATION FOR USE

18.2a Camera Mounting Assembly

(1) Remove Camera Mounting Assembly from case and stand vertically. (2) Slip Steadicam battery into housing, socket down. Attach battery strap. (3) Rotate video monitor 180° so it is parallel to lens; to unwind two cables to monitor. Pivot monitor so that screen faces upward toward Operator. Attach Monitor Hood, as needed. (4) Loosen thumb screw on monitor bracket, and lower monitor down Telescoping/Balance Post. Tighten thumb screw. (5) Tighten Telescoping Post Lock Knob on right top of Electronics Module. (6) Attach Junction Box to Camera Mounting Platform via two thumb screws on front of platform. Face four-pin Cannon connector on Junction Box to front. (7) Insert Junction Box Cable 10-pin connector into mate on front of electronics module.

NOTE: Prior to installing camera, set Film PGM switch on rear control panel of Electronics Module. Switch should be in up position for film cameras (provides power to Sync Generator) and down for video cameras.

18.2b Installing the Camera

NOTE: Most cameras require a Camera Mounting Plate, which interfaces specific cameras with clamp plate. Arri IIC and three cameras with CP flat bases mount directly onto standard clamp plate with no camera mounting plate. Arri 35BL utilizes special clamp plate and does not require Camera Mounting Plate.

Installing Cameras with a Camera Mounting Plate. (1) Remove clamp plate and two fillister-head screws from Steadicam Camera Mounting Platform. Obtain specific Camera Mounting Plate and mounting screws for camera. (2) Attach adapter plate to bottom of camera. (3) Attach clamp plate to adapter plate with two fillister-head screws in center holes. Make sure that rack is on left outside of clamp plate.

NOTE: Clamp-plate screws may be moved to outer holes if necessary to balance cameras fitted with special accessories.

(4) Put camera behind the Camera Mounting Platform and the dovetail to clamp plate. (5) Turn knurled rack-control knob on side of Camera Mounting Platform to move camera forward over center of platform. (6) Tighten clamp screw under platform to hold camera in position. (7) Tighten safety screw to prevent camera from slipping when clamp is loose. (8) Attach camera power cable to four-pin Cannon connector on front of Junction Box, if necessary.

CP/Arri 35 2C and 35-3 Installation.

NOTE: These cameras require special CP-modified magazine or Steadi-mag.

(1) Take clamp plate and two fillister-head screws from Steadicam Camera mounting platform. (2) Attach clamp plate to camera bottom with two screws in center holes. Leave outside of mounting plate.

NOTE: Mounting screws may be moved to outer holes to balance cameras fitted with special accessories.

(3) Put camera behind Camera Mounting Platform and dovetail to clamp plate. (4) Turn knurled rack control knob on side of Camera Mounting Platform to move camera forward over center of platform. (5) Tighten safety screw to prevent camera from slipping backward off platform if clamp is loose. (6) Tighten clamp screw under Camera mounting platform to hold camera. (7) Connect video cable from video assist to seven-pin DIN plug on front of electronics module. Plug ground from video assist to camera body. (8) Connect ground cable from camera flat base to single-pin connector on front of junction box. (9) Connect power cable from camera motor drive to connector on junction box front. (10) Load camera magazine with a full roll of film, and install lens.

18.2c Adjusting the Center of Gravity from Side to Side
(1) Rotate monitor horizontally until unit balances. (2) Loosen monitor-support screw and rotate Monitor-Support Arm around Telescoping Support Post until unit balances. (3) Loosen locking knob on right top side of Electronics Module. Rotate module around Telescoping Support Post to balance. (4) Move camera side-to-side at camera support plate. Usually not necessary to rotate Electronics Module more than 15°. If so, remove camera from mounting plate and reattach by adjacent set of holes until it balances.

18.2d Adjusting the Center of Gravity: Top to Bottom

NOTE: Changing to a heavier or lighter camera requires adjustment of gimbal position to return to optimum balance. Optimum balance occurs with center of gravity slightly below gimbal.

Locate two stainless-steel screws on either side of gimbal. One screw will become pivot point to check out balance of Camera Mounting Platform with the camera. Place Steadicam so that pivot point (one of stainless-steel screws) is supported by a fixture (any object that is a few inches high and will support 50 lb). It should balance. If not, establish new center of gravity by loosening 10/32 socket head screw on gimbal to free it to move along post until balanced. Tighten socket head screw.

18.2e Adjustment of Camera Operator's Vest
(1) Unfasten clasps 1, 2, and 3 as shown in Figure 18.2a and 18.2b. (2) Loosen Velcro® straps 1, 2, 3, and 4. (3) Pass head and right arm through vest top with spar to front. (4) Fasten clasps 1, 2, and 3 so that vest fits loosely. (5) To adjust length, loosen T-nut screws 1 and 2. Properly adjusted vest wraps around hips yet clears thigh when leg is lifted. Expand or contract spar to desired length. If spar is completely contracted and vest is too long, loosen the two T-nut screws (3 and 4) on vest frontplate for more contraction. When length is correct, tighten T-nut screws. (6) Tighten Velcro straps 1, 2, 3, and 4 evenly and securely, keeping spar centered. (7) Leave quick-release strap intact. It should remain slack.

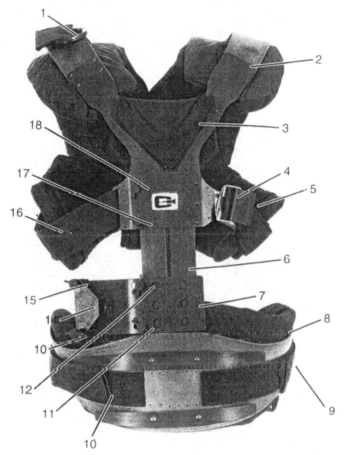

Figure 18–2a. Steadicam Camera Operator's Vest (front view). Courtesy of Cinema Products.

1. Quick-Release Handle
2. Clasp 1
3. Chest Pad
4. Clasp 2
5. Velcro™ Strap 2
6. Spar
7. Reversible Frontplate
8. Waist Pad
9. Velcro™ Strap 4
10. Velcro™ Strap 3
11. T-Nut 4
12. T-Nut 3
13. T-Nut 6
14. Arm Socket
15. T-Nut 5
16. Velcro™ Strap 1
17. T-Nut 2
18. T-Nut 1

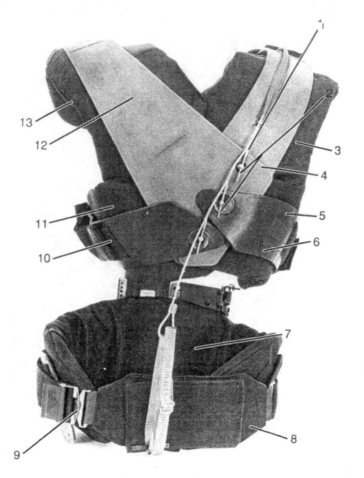

Figure 18–2b. Steadicam Camera Operator's Vest (back view). Courtesy of Cinema Products.

1. Ripcord
2. Pins and Cones
3. R-1 Pad
4. R-1 Strap
5. R-2 Pad
6. R-2 Strap
7. Pad Release Strap

8. R Hip Pad
9. Clasp 3
10. L-2 Strap
11. L-2 Pad
12. L-1 Strap
13. L-1 Pad

18.2f Quick-Release of Universal Model 3A Vest

Quick-release feature of vest operates by a parachute-type pin-and-cone release system. To release, tug quick-release handle.

18.2g Reassembly of Vest

(1) Place L-1 strap over R-1 strap, carefully lining up holes over cones. (2) Place R-2 strap hole over middle cone. (3) Place L-2 strap hole over

bottom cone. (4) Insert three pins on ripcord through the three cones, in sequence. (5) Reattach left hip pad to release pad.

18.2h Vest Front Plate

Provides two functions: (1) *Mounting Stabilizer Support Arm*—partially loosen two T-nut thumb screws (5 and 6), on mounting socket; insert arm plug into socket; tighten T-nuts. (2) *Mounting Arm on right or left side*—loosen (do not remove) T-nuts 3 and 4 (adjacent to socket) until frontplate easily comes off. Rotate 180°, and reattach to spar in desired position.

18.2i Connecting Camera Mounting Assembly to Stabilizer Arm

(1) Insert Telescoping/Balance Post into Docking Bracket. Gimbal should be *above* Docking Bracket. If Docking Bracket not available, raise Camera Mounting Assembly up to be loaded onto Arm.

WARNING: *Do not press Arm down.*

(2) Operator should lower body and bend over until able to grasp gimbal yoke with one hand and insert mounting post with other hand. (3) Rotate gimbal yoke approximately 45°, clearing hand. (4) Lower Camera Mounting Assembly slowly, allowing Arm to take up its weight.

NOTE: If rear section of Arm will not drop when taking up camera weight, place heel of hand on top spring cover near elbow joint, and push down firmly.

Check for secure fastening of support-plate lock and safety screws.

NOTE: *Height of arm,*—Camera system should be sufficiently heavy that Steadicam arm floats camera slightly below its midposition.

NOTE: If camera pulls to either side, use ¼-in. hex wrench in either socket screw to adjust. Screws operate independently of each other.

(6) For finer adjustment, rotate Electronics Module around Telescoping/Balance Post by loosening the Telescoping Post Locking Knob. Check side-to-side adjustment at Camera Mounting Platform and/or fore and aft adjustment at Electronics Module.

18.2j Adjusting Weight Load Capacity on Steadicam Adjustable Arm

Steadicam Adjustable Arm permits approximately a 15-lb range of Steadicam weight load capacity. To adjust: (1) Locate Allen screws at end of both fore Arm and upper Arm. (2) With Allen wrench, turn screws until marker reads approximate weight desired. Each section must be adjusted separately to achieve elevation desired. All four screws must be adjusted to same mark.

18.3 OPERATION

18.3a Activating Steadicam Power

(1) Make sure that NC-12 battery is firmly connected in battery housing. Check battery status meter to verify power. (2) Push in two circuit breakers on Electronics Module. (3) Move three-position toggle switch on control panel to "Standby." Wait 15 seconds for warm-up, and turn toggle switch ON.

18.3b Adjusting Electronic Level on CRT

Properly aligned level forms a grid pattern in lower center of CRT. To form grid: (1) Stand Camera Mounting Assembly/Camera on level surface, and turn ON. (2) Locate Electronic Sensor Orientation Knob on side of Junction Box, which vertically positions level's electronic sensor. White line points upward at all times. When changing to low mode, rotate knob 180° (white line must point UP). (3) Check High/Low slide switch on back of Junction Box, to make sure it is in position for desired mode. (4) For true level, place mechanical level on top of Electronics Module, and conform. Loosen Level-Adjustment Knob on Junction Box back. Observing monitor, move knob until *cursor* (horizontal stripes) and *target* (vertical stripes) overlap. Tighten down knob.

NOTE: Monitor must be receiving a signal from camera (or other video source) in order to see electronic level and frame lines.

18.3c Adjustment of Video Monitor
(1) Depress circuit breaker marked "MONITOR," and place ON/STANDBY/OFF switch in STANDBY position. (2) After 20 to 30 seconds, turn to ON position. Picture should appear on monitor. If no picture, check to see whether one of the following is the cause: (a) Lens cap not removed; (b) camera shutter not in viewing position—if so, either turn inching knob or run camera a few seconds to place mirror in viewing position; (c) for CP/Arri 35-IIC, which has 45° mirror in extended eyepiece, depress small stainless-steel video viewing button on mirror housing. (3) Adjust brightness and contrast with knobs located below monitor: (a) Turn Brightness Knob until screen just brightens; (b) turn Contrast Knob to optimum image. (4) Adjust video monitor swivel mount as convenient. Rebalance.

18.3d Operation with Portable Video Cameras
(1) Connect co-axial cable from monitor output to Junction Box (BNC Connector). (2) Depress ACC circuit breaker and MONITOR circuit breaker. (3) Set Steadicam ON/STANDBY/OFF switch to STANDBY. (4) Wait 30 seconds; set switch to ON. (5) On rear control panel of Electronics Module, slide Film PGR Switch OFF. (6) Adjust Steadicam monitor for BRIGHTNESS and CONTRAST.

18.3e Low-Mode Operation for Most Cameras
To operate Steadicam with camera on bottom and Electronics Module on top, follow procedure to use Steadicam in Low Mode with all cameras except Arri 35 BL: (1) Mount camera in Cinema Products optional Low-Mode Cage accessory. (2) Attach standard clamp-plate assembly to top of Low-Mode Cage with ¼-20 screws supplied. (3) Dovetail Cage/Camera Assembly to inverted Camera Mounting Platform. (4) Invert monitor to suit new configuration by removing 10-32 × 5/8" socket head screw on Monitor-Support Arm. Remove monitor and 78-5118 Swivel Post. Rotate Monitor, and reinsert screw to install. (5) Optional J-bracket provides flexibility of lens height. Remove mounting post from Steadicam Arm, and replace with longer end of J-bracket. (6) With entire rig in upside-down position, readjust fore-and-aft and side-to-side trim of camera. (7) Install Camera Mounting Assembly on Arm. (8) Clamp must be removed to move monitor below clamp or higher on tube. (9) Readjust height of gimbal by loosening clamp screw and positioning so that center of balance falls about 1 in. below gimbal.

18.3f Low-Mode Operation for Arri 35 BL

(1) Remove top handle and two viewfinder screws from Arri 35 BL. (2) In place of top handle, install special Low-Mode Bracket for Arri 35 BL and reinstall viewfinder screws. (3) Attach CP Steadicam Dovetail Assembly to top of Low-Mode Bracket. (4) Follow remaining steps 4–7 listed in Section 18.3e.

18.3g Conversion from 50 Hz to 60 Hz Systems

(1) Open access cover in front of Electronics Module. (2) Adjust vertical hold control R69 to stop picture from rolling. (3) Adjust standard vertical hold control R66 for a picture height that just fills tube face from top to bottom, with VERTICAL HEIGHT switch in STD position. (4) Set VERTICAL HEIGHT switch to 2:1 position and adjust R67 so that picture height is one-half screen height or as required for compatibility with lens.

18.4 TROUBLESHOOTING

See Operations Manual supplied with camera.

chapter 19

Lenses

19.1 LENS CASES

The best lens container is a unit in which lenses "float" on sponge rubber or a similar shock-absorbent substance. When using "nonfloating" felt-lined cases (fitted with holes or compartments to accommodate the lens barrels) tissue paper must be stuffed around the lens barrel, especially if the case is to be shipped. If a lens case is not available, place an unmounted lens in a black raw-stock bag and wrap enough paper around it to absorb shock.

Even when the lens is stored in a case, the front and rear lens elements must have caps for protection against dust and fingerprint smudges.

19.2 TURRET LENSES

Lenses mounted on a camera turret (except the one in use, of course) remain capped at all times. If windy or dusty conditions prevail, the front element of the "taking" lens must be protected by an optical flat or filter. (A dirt-pitted flat or filter is easier—and cheaper—to replace than a lens.)

When a lens is removed from a turret, the port must be capped or taped to keep dirt and dust from the inner turret surface.

19.3 CLEANING

To clean a lens properly, first, remove it from the turret. Angle the element to be cleaned downward. Rotate the *lens* (not the brush) so that dirt particles are shaken loose and fall down and out, rather than just being moved around as happens when the element is facing up. Use the sides of the lens brush bristles to clean the metal on the inside of the barrel and the *tip* of the brush to clean the element.

19.3a Lens tissue

To avoid scratching the fluoride coating, use lens tissue *after* the element has been *brushed* free of dirt and dust particles. *Never* put a dry tissue to a lens. The most widely used and safest cleaner is the moisture from the human breath. Liquid lens cleaner should be used sparingly (excess liquid cleaner can destroy lens-element cement).

CAUTION: Never use silicone-impregnated lens tissue (such as eyeglass-cleaning tissue)! Silicone discolors the fluoride coating.

Figure 19–1 illustrates a method of using lens tissue. (1) and (2) Roll up a sheet of lens tissue. (3) Tear into two sections. (4) Join, with shredded ends all facing one way. Squeeze one drop *only* of liquid cleaner on the end of the bundle. Use a circular motion applied with very light pressure, and

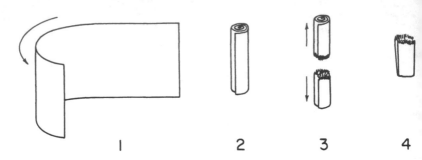

Figure 19–1   A method for using lens tissue.

check the element often for cleanliness, so that as few strokes as possible are made against the lens surface.

19.4   APERTURE
Check lens diaphragm often to determine that its leaves are in working order.

19.4a   f/Stops and T Stops
Most older lenses are calibrated in f/stops, most newer lenses in T stops. Lenses calibrated in both f/stops and T stops are inscribed with markings— *white* to indicate f/stops and *colored* (red, yellow, etc.) to indicate T stops.

When setting the diaphragm on a doubly marked lens, use the T stop markings.

19.4b   To Set a Lens Stop
(1) Set the lens to its widest opening. (2) Close down to the desired stop.

For example: When an aperture of T 5.6 is called for on a T 2.3 lens, which has been stopped down to T 8: first, open the lens to its maximum setting of T 2.3, then close down to T 5.6. Do not merely move the setting from T 8 to T 5.6.

This method compensates for inherent backlash in the diaphragm leaves, provides more accurate settings, and is consistent with the method used to determine the f/stop of T stop settings when the lens was manufactured.

19.5   WIDE-ANGLE LENSES
These short lenses must constantly be checked for flare and matte-box clearance. Rear element of a wide-angle lens should always be checked for shutter clearance by slowly rotating the manual motor-turning knob on offset viewfinder cameras (inching knob on reflex cameras) several times after lens has been inserted into turret. This is especially important on 16mm and 35mm cameras that have interchangeable lenses.

Never place a gelatine filter on the rear element of a wide-angle lens. Filters have been lifted off rear element by the shutter and ground up in the camera mechanism, resulting in ruined footage and major repairs.

It is better to place a filter at the front element of a wide-angle lens, because a filter placed in a filter slot *behind* the lens, being closer to the focal plane, will register dust and dirt more readily, especially if stopped down smaller than f/8. If the filter is taped in place, make certain that tape holding the gelatine or glass filter is clear of front element.

The 2 × 2 in. glass filter used in extreme-wide-angle lenses (5.7mm, 9.8mm) should have *rounded corners*. Filters with squared corners have no leeway and may crack or shatter from pressure exerted by filter lock when secured, or if camera is jarred.

Neutral-density filters—most commonly used are 0.30 (one stop), 0.60 (two stops), 0.90 (3 stops)—should be part of a lens kit because most wide-angle lenses will vignette if stopped down smaller than $f/8$.

19.6 TELEPHOTO LENSES

Lenses 125–2000mm require a supporting cradle when mounted to a camera.

Filters for telephoto lenses should always be placed at, or as close as possible to, the rear element. Make certain that a tape holding a gelatine filter in place is clear of rear element.

On lenses fitted with filter holders, a gelatine filter is better than a glass—there is less aberration, due to the thinner material.

Skylight or ultraviolet (UV) filters (most commonly used are skylight: 1A, 2A; and UV: 15, 16) should be part of a lens kit because telephoto lenses suffer image deterioration due to haze, heat waves, etc.

Temperature changes cause expansion or contraction of lens components; therefore, check focus just prior to filming.

Tripod and camera must be rigidly secured with a tie-down chain, to avoid sway or vibration. Vibration can only be detected by sighting through the lens with the viewing tube set at maximum magnification and with *camera motor running*.

19.7 FOCUS

Always remove the lens to focus the camera eyepiece. Aim the empty lens port at a medium-bright area. Adjust eyepiece until cross hair or granular surface of groundglass is sharp.

If a tape measurement varies from a groundglass measurement, rely on the groundglass focus (providing that eyepiece has been adjusted as described herein, not with lens in place). If in doubt, shoot a few feet of film focused at both measurements, and conduct a hand test (see Sec. 3.11).

Where focus change is extremely critical (especially with long focal-length or telephoto lenses), select a number of intermediate reference points between a beginning and an end focus. Measure off each intermediate focus point, and transcribe each measurement to either a strip of tape over the footage indicator on the lens or the follow-focus disc. As subject moves to each reference point, match respective distance on lens (or disc). If subject is stationary but the camera moves, place intermediate reference points on floor. While this procedure is time-consuming, the greater accuracy of focus is worth it. Where possible, hook a tape measure to subject, and let a Second Assistant call off footage as the tape is reeled in or out.

When a new lens is brought up on the turret, always set focus at the approximate camera-to-subject distance, so that Operator and/or Director of Photography can see a reasonably sharp scene and concentrate on composition and lighting.

A word of caution regarding matte boxes (or filter holders as found in some blimps): When a focus change from a *far* subject to a close subject is necessary, it is well to remember that the shorter the distance from film plane to subject, the longer the lens barrel extends from the mount.

Therefore, the matte box (or filter holder) must be positioned on the rods when the lens is at its longest extension, *i.e.,* focused on the close subject. Otherwise, the *f*/stop ring on the end of the lens barrel will come into contact with matte box (or glass filter) and be moved inadvertently as lens rotates from far to near focus, resulting in an underexposed shot.

19.7a Split Focus

While depth of field varies greatly, depending on focal length, aperture, and focus setting, a rule of thumb is that depth of field extends approximately one third from plane of focus to its nearest limit and two thirds from plane of focus to its farthest limit. Therefore, instead of splitting the focus equidistant between two subjects, pull focus closer to (but still beyond) the near subject, so as to carry both subjects in sharp focus.

19.7b Extreme Close-up with Normal Lens

To use a lens closer than its normal minimum focal point (on a reflex camera, or a camera fitted with a focusing tube), the lens is released from its mount and extended toward the subject.

Extension of a C-mount Lens. Accomplished by unscrewing the lens from the port far enough to achieve the desired focus, but not far enough to remove the lens entirely. This extension procedure is limited by the number of threads on the lens.

Extension of a Bayonet Base Lens. Accomplished by releasing the lens from the turret and extending it from the port to achieve the desired focus. To maintain stability and focus, scrap film is broken into small pieces, and these film "chips" are wedged between turret and shoulder of bayonet base.

Extension of a Mitchell Baltar Lens. Accomplished by unscrewing the lens from the mount; if additional extension is needed, the mount itself can be extended to the length of the screws holding the mount to the turret. When extension is achieved, film "chips" are wedged in the top area first, then "filled in" at bottom area, between the shoulder of the mount and the turret, to give the lens stability and to maintain focus.

NOTE: When a lens is extended from the normal position and held by hand to determine focus, it is said to be "at air rest." When a lens is wedged in place with film, it is said to be "at chip rest."

CAUTION: When extending a lens from its normal position on the turret, always sling a net or blanket below the turret, to catch a dropped lens.

19.8 VARIFOCAL (ZOOM) LENSES

Never mount a zoom lens without a support.

There are two types of lens supports: (1) the boom (overhang), and (2) the cradle.

Boom. A one-piece assembly that clamps the lens from above and mounts to the camera matte-box shoe or matte-box mounting pin. Located above the turret, it is nonadjustable.

Cradle. An adjustable unit that mounts on matte-box rods located below the turret. The cradle provides a solid rest *beneath* the lens barrel and allows the lens to be adjusted in any direction (left, right, up, or down).

NOTE: Although the lens lock on the Mitchell BNC is sufficient to keep the Som Berthiot 38–154mm zoom lens rigid without additional support, the 24–240mm and the 25–250mm Angenieux zoom lenses require support at all times to alleviate strain on the lens mount at the turret port, as well as on the entire optical system.

19.8a Mounting Zoom Lenses

Assemble the cradle and attach to the camera, then sit down, holding the camera in your lap (when feasible), turret *up*. Mate the lens to the turret port, letting the lens seat itself in the mount. Adjust the cradle to the lens. Only then is the camera mounted to the tripod head.

This method has two advantages: (1) The lens rests properly against the turret port face, and (2) the cradle support is adjusted to the lens with no strain on the turret.

With cameras employing top-mounted boom supports (e.g., Arriflex), this method must be used so that the support can be secured with the lens in a vertical position. This prevents *sag*, which would warp the turret and cause damage to the camera. Lens sag also throws the lens out of alignment with the film plane and results in loss of definition in the wide-angle aspect of the zoom move.

When this "lap method" is not possible because of the size of the camera, insert lens into turret port, and press lens against turret-port face. Never let the lens rest in the turret unsupported! While still maintaining pressure with one hand against the port face, adjust the cradle with the other hand, or get help from another crew member to secure the lens.

NOTE: It is important to remember that no matter which method is employed, the various adjusting screws and knobs of the support cradle are always loosened before mounting the lens. The cradle or support is then made to conform to the lens, never vice versa.

It is extremely important that the zoom lens be securely attached to the camera when making angled-down shots because the weight of the lens can pull against the turret and throw the shot out of focus.

After the assembled lens and camera are placed on the tripod, the various steps necessary to align the internal tracking of the lens begins.

NOTE: A zoom lens may be adjusted internally by certain expert optical or camera-repair firms to track perfectly for a particular camera. On rented equipment, of course, this is not always possible, although it may be requested of the rental agency. Time and expense must be allowed for this adjustment.

19.8b Tracking

Varifocal lenses have an inherent side drift when zoomed. This can be minimized by mounting the lens on an adjustable cradle. Each time the lens is mounted, the same procedure must be followed. After mounting, set the lens at its longest focal length, footage scale at infinity, and aperture at its widest opening. Align the cross hairs (horizontal and vertical) with an object at infinity through the camera optical system (reflex or focusing-tube). Slowly zoom to the shortest focal length. Correct any shift of the cross hair from the object by moving the adjustable barrel rest in the opposite direction of the shift. For example, if, on its longest focal length, the horizontal cross hair corresponds to a horizontal object at infinity but shifts below the object when zoomed to its shortest focal length, elevate the adjustable lens rest half the distance of the cross-hair shift. Zoom in, realign the cross hair with the object, and repeat the procedure until minimum shift remains. If the horizontal cross hair rises above the object, lower the adjustable lens rest half the distance, readjust the cross hair, etc.

If the vertical cross hair corresponds to a vertical object at infinity but shifts to the left when zoomed back, slide the barrel rest to the right, half the distance of the shift. If it shifts to the right, slide the barrel rest to the left, half the distance; realign, etc.

Until cross-hair shift is minimized, small adjustments and frequent zooms to check progress are better than large adjustments.

Care must be taken that the entire framing is in sharp focus: too much adjustment can throw one side of the frame out of focus.

19.8c Focus Shift

If a lens that is in sharp focus on a long focal length softens when zoomed to a short focal length (or vice versa), remove the lens and reseat the unit in another turret port. Sometimes, a slight rotation of the lens in the port will eliminate a focus problem due to faulty seating. A slight cradle adjustment (left, right, up, or down) may seat the lens better.

If a series of corrective attempts fail to eliminate the problem, retire the lens until it can be bench-checked.

19.8d Offset-Viewing-Tube Mismatch

On 35mm nonreflex zoom lenses, it is not uncommon to discover that the offset-viewing-tube cross hair and field scribe do not match the cross hair and field scribe as viewed through the racked-over camera. This could be due to improper seating of the groundglass. More likely, however, it is the result of improper locking of the viewing tube on the lens. Loosen the tube, and retighten.

If this fails to correct the problem, zoom the lens to its longest focal length; set the footage scale to infinity and the aperture at its widest opening. Align the cross hair, as viewed through the racked-over camera, on an object at infinity. Compare the offset viewing-tube cross hair to the camera cross hair. Remove the cover plate in the viewing-tube elbow.

CAUTION: The five cover screws are tiny and can be easily lost!

Reveal the prism held in place by one prism lock (a small piece of brass wedged in recessed slots, with a center screw holding the prism in place). Relieve the screw on the lock slightly; compare cross hairs of the camera and viewing-tube optics once more before adjustment.

Align the vertical cross hair by a very slight shift of the prism, left or right; align the field scribe by rotating the prism on its axis to match the viewing-tube field with the camera field. Alignment complete, tighten the locks firmly, and compare the cross hairs and field again. (Tightening the screw can shift the prism out of alignment, and the procedure must be repeated with allowances for prism shift with the renewed adjustments.)

Adjustments of the horizontal cross hair that cannot be taken up in the elevation or depression by wedging with strips of paper require an optical bench correction.

Replace the elbow cover.

NOTE: Adjustment of the prism is a delicate and critical procedure requiring time, patience, and persistence. It is best done on an optical bench by a technician, preferably before the camera is sent to the photographic site.

To ascertain the alignment of an offset-viewing-tube 16mm zoom lens in a nonreflex camera, zoom the lens to its longest focal length; set the footage scale to infinity and the aperture at its widest opening. Align the viewing-tube field with an object at infinity. Remove the offset viewing tube. Open the camera door. Open the camera gate, insert a focusing prism into the gate, and sight through the camera aperture. Check the side lines, top, bottom, and center, to verify their positions. Compare the alignment; slowly zoom out; check the framing; replace the offset viewing tube, and compare the side lines—top, bottom, and center.

With the exception of ascertaining that the offset-viewing tube on the lens is properly seated, nothing can be done on the job to correct the variance of a 16mm offset-viewing tube except to ask Operator to compensate for it. Correction is a bench job.

19.8e Hand Zooming

On nonmotorized varifocal lenses, the Assistant is required to zoom and change focus by hand. Smooth moves, proper focusing, and correct image sizes may be enhanced by applying the following methods.

Smooth Moves. The zoom-dampening lever may have a tendency to "hang up" or "slip" momentarily, creating a "jump" in the field as the image changes. With very slow, almost imperceptible, zooms, the lever can be grasped with both hands, and while one hand moves the lever in the direction of the zoom, the other hand resists, thereby passing smoothly over the hang-up or slip. If a focus change is required at the same time, however, the attachment of a rubber band, one end looped around the lever, the other end looped around some part of the cradle, provides resistance to the direction of the zoom. Proper tension of the band (by doubling or tripling it, depending on the elasticity and amount of tension desired) depends on the desired speed of the zoom.

CAUTION: Do not release the lever at the end of the zoom until the shot is completed, or the resistance of the rubber band will return the focal-length setting to its starting point and spoil the shot.

Zooming. Covering the entire focal range (long to short, or vice versa) by hand affords little problem when doing the zooming, but stopping short at a desired focal length demands greater accuracy. In a situation where a zoom and focus change are rapid or differ in speed, coming to a halt on the exact setting desired is not as simple as it sounds. The problem of an over- or undersized field can be eliminated by using a piece of camera tape as a stop. On a radial (rotating barrel) lens, set the desired *final* focal setting to the barrel witness mark. Wrap one end of a length of camera tape around the focal-length ring and the other end (called the "anchor" of the tape) around the cradle. Set the lens to the *starting* focal length, and allow the excess tape to hang loose between the lens and cradle. When the lens is zoomed to the desired final focal length, the tape becomes taut and stops the rotation of the focal-length ring. Thus, the person zooming can concentrate on smoothness of movement and focus and not miss the end of the zoom.

On a linear (push–pull type of lever) lens, the camera tape is wound around the focal-length *lever,* anchored to the cradle, and the same procedure followed.

For extremely fast zooms, set the starting focal length, grasp the ends of a length of camera tape in both hands, and apply the adhesive side to the focal-length ring. Be sure that the tape forms a sideways U around the ring. On cue, quickly rotate the ring by pulling the tape until the final focal length is reached.

For extremely slow zooms, secure a dowel or metal rod with camera tape or Gaffer's tape to the focal-length lever, and apply light pressure to the end of the dowel or rod. The longer the lever extension, the slower and smoother the zoom will be.

19.9 ZOOM-LENS ACCESSORIES

19.9a Zoom Motors

Zoom-motor types and their manufacturers are far too numerous to list. Basically, a unit consists of three components: (1) motor drive, (2) rheostat, and (3) power pack.

Motor Drive. Size varies according to the lens for which it is intended. Depending on the manufacturer, it may be positioned on lens at the top, bottom, or side of the barrel. Bidirectional. A slip clutch ensures smooth starts and stops.

Two adjustable stop rings allow specific zoom ranges to be preset.

On a radial zoom lens, a geared ring is usually pressure-fitted over the focal-length barrel or is clamped with hex screws. The motor-drive shaft is geared. To check the unit, set the focal-length indicator on the barrel at its maximum (longest) focal length, and the drive-selector switch at optimum "in" position. Fit the geared end of the drive shaft to the geared ring on the barrel, and lock it in place. Operate the drive to determine whether the full focal range can be reached. If it cannot, the drive was not set at maximum in and the unit must be readjusted.

NOTE: Some 16mm zooms use a plastic pressure band coupled to the motor instead of a geared ring around the barrel.

On a linear zoom lens, the motor drive is usually side-slung. The focal-length lever fits between two projecting rods connected to the drive shaft with a slip clutch. To check the unit, set the focal length at its maximum (longest), and the drive at the optimum in position. Focal range is checked out as described previously.

NOTE: If the drive motor operates but does not change the focal length, the drive unit is either at the wrong position (out instead of in), or it is clamped too tightly to the geared ring or focal-length lever.

If, during a zoom movement, the ring slips or the image hangs up or jumps momentarily, the drive unit is too loose and requires tightening. A prerequisite for smooth zooms is fine adjustment of all movable parts and a rheostat in good condition.

Rheostat. Depending on the manufacturer, this unit may be attached to the motor drive or housed in a separate unit, or it may have a forward–reverse switch attached or housed in a separate unit, connected with cables. Turning the speed-selector switch clockwise increases the rate of zoom speed; turning it counterclockwise decreases it. Duration of a zoom must be determined by a stopwatch. The speed selector may be numbered, but numbering is not standard. Numbers are only good for reference in setting of zoom speeds; they are not consistent because speeds may vary, depending on the state of the power pack.

Power Pack. Battery power. Size varies, depending on motor drive (from single flashlight cell up to 28 volts). Improper voltage, either high or low, can burn out a motor drive, so it is imperative that proper voltage be determined and maintained.

19.9b Zoom-Lens Retaining Rings

Used to mount circular glass filters or diopters (see Sec. 19.9d) to the front element of a zoom lens.

To Remove. Because zoom-lens retaining rings are very large and extremely thin-walled, grasping them around the circumference with the fingers exerts pressure, which deforms the rings in the threads, thereby further affecting the rings. Merely *pinching* the ring with thumb and forefinger *at only one point* on the edge of the ring, *then* rotating the fingers, can generally free the impacted ring.

NOTE: Extremely tight rings may need a few drops of solvent in the thread channels to loosen. In the absence of solvent, a popular cola soft drink may be used. The soft drink has also been found useful for removing rusted and paint-frozen screws on equipment.

CAUTION: The cola will remove paint from camera surface unless removed immediately!

19.9c Zoom-Lens Filters and Sizes (Table 19-1)

Table 19–1   Zoom Lens List Filter Size*

Manufacturer	35mm	16mm	Focal Range	Front Filter Size
Angenieux				
(Spherical)				
	X		17–102mm	168mm square (6.6 in. sq.)
	X		20–120mm	140mm (5.5 in.)
	X		25–250mm	119mm
		X	9.5–57mm	65mm (step-up to Series 9)
		X	9.5–95mm	103.5mm
		X	10–150mm	72mm (step-up to Series 9)
		X	12–120mm	Series 9
		X	12–240mm	107mm
		X	12.5–75mm	Series 8
		X	17–68mm	Series 7
		X	17.5–70mm	Series 7

(Table 19–1 continued)

Manufacturer	35mm	16mm	Focal Range	Front Filter Size
Canon				
(Spherical)	X		25–120mm	114mm (4.5 in.)
		X	25–100mm	Series 8
	X		150–600mm	none
Century Precision Optics	X		23–460mm	114mm (4.5 in.)
Clairmont**				
(Spherical)				
Clairmont/Angenieux	X		50–500mm	122.5mm
Clairmont/Canon	X		150–600mm	none
(Anamorphic)				
Clairmont/Cooke	X		28–140mm	168mm square (6.6 in. sq.)
	X		36–200mm	138mm
	X		40–120mm	114mm (4.5 in.)
	X		40–200mm	138mm
	X		50–500mm	122.5mm
	X		300–1200mm	none
Kern-Paillard				
(Spherical)		X	17–85mm	Series 5.5
		X	18–88mm	Series 8
Panavision				
(Spherical)				
Primo 4-1	X		17.5–75mm	138mm
Panavision/Cooke	X		20–60mm	114mm (4.5 in.)
Panavision/Cooke	X		20–100mm	138mm
Panavision/Angenieux	X		20–120mm	140mm (5.5 in.)
Ultra	X		20–125mm	152mm (6 in.)
Panavision/Angenieux	X		23–460mm	114mm (4.5 in.)
Primo 11:1†	X		24–275mm	152mm (6 in.)
Panavision/Cooke	X		25–250mm	114mm (4.5 sin.)
Panavision/Angenieux	X		25–250mm	119mm
Panavision/Angenieux	X		35–140mm	Series 8
Primo 3-1‡	X		148–420mm	152mm (6 in.)
Panavision/Cooke		X	9–50mm	83mm
Panavision/Zeiss		X	10–100mm	Series 9
Panavision Super 16		X	10.4–52mm	83mm
(Anamorphic)				

(Table 19–1 continued)

Manufacturer	35mm	16mm	Focal Range	Front Filter Size
Panavision/Cooke		X	40–200mm	122.5mm
PV Cooke/Angenieux		X	50–500mm	122.5mm
Rank Taylor				
Hobson (Cooke)				
(Spherical)	X		14–70mm	168mm square
	X		18–100m§	138mm
	X		20–60mm	114mm (4.5 in.)
	X		20–100mm	138mm
	X		25–250mm Mk 2	114mm (4.5 in.)
		X	9–50mm	83mm
		X	10.4–52mm (Super 16)	83mm
		X	12–120mm (hunting)	Series 8
		X	12–120mm (studio)	Series 9
		X	13–100mm	Series 9
		X	16–160mm	Series 9
		X	17–85mm (f/3.8)	Series 7
		X	17–85mm (f/2)	Series 8
		X	17–130mm	Series 9
(Anamorphic)	X		40–200mm	122.5mm
	X		50–500mm	122.5mm
Schneider				
(Spherical)		X	10–100mm	Series 9
		X	16–60mm	Series 8
		X	16–80mm	Series 8
Zeiss				
(Spherical)		X	10–100mm	Series 9
		X	12.5–75mm	Series 9

*Front filter size is also the size of the diopter lens for extreme close-up photography.

**Many rental companies have rebuilt an original manufacturer's lens by retrofitting the housing and gearing, usually to match their respective rental cameras while retaining the original optics. Companies that have done so are listed with a / (slash) after their names, followed by that of the optics manufacturer. E.g., Clairmont/Canon is a Clairmont retrofitted housing using Canon optics; Panavision/Cooke is a Panavision retrofitted housing using Cooke optics, etc, etc.

†Primo 11:1 contains a rear Tiffen clear gel 40.5mm in diameter. The lens is ALWAYS calibrated with the clear gel in position. Do not remove, unless replacing with a B&W/color/ND gelatine filter! Remember to replace the clear gel when done using other type of filters!

‡Primo 3-1 lens has a rear element housing that can hold three gelatine filters 40.5mm in diameter.

§Filter holder in rear unit of Cooke lens accepts up to three gelatine filters plus a glass holder that accommodates two 30.5mm filters.

19.9d Zoom Diopter Lenses (Table 19–2)

Supplemental meniscus-lenses permit close-up cinematography by allowing the zoom lens to be used at a distance shorter than the minimum footage incorporated in the original design. Thus, while most varifocal lenses cannot be focused at less than 5 or 6 ft, the addition of a diopter lens or lenses enables the zoom lens to be focused as close as 4 in. without the need for extension tubes.

Table 19–2 Zoom Diopter-Lens Ranges

Diopter	Range (inches)
$+\frac{1}{2}$	39–79
$+1$	20–39
$+2$	13–20
$+3$	10–13
$+4$ ($+3$ and $+1$)	8–10
$+5$ ($+3$ and $+2$)	$6\frac{1}{2}$–8
$+6$ ($+3$ and $+3$)	$5\frac{1}{2}$–$6\frac{1}{2}$
$+7$	5–$5\frac{1}{2}$
$+8$	$4\frac{1}{2}$–5
$+9$	4–$4\frac{1}{2}$
$+10$	4 inches only

With a diopter lens attached, the footage indicator on the zoom lens must be converted. While tables are given for mathematical computation of subject distance to lens, lens manufacturers caution that such data are approximate. Therefore, a groundglass focus (which is also quicker) is more accurate than the tables.

Most diopters are fitted with metal rims in which an etched arrow points toward the subject. Lenses without the arrow should be mounted with the bulge of the lens toward the subject.

When mounting lenses in combination, place the more powerful lens closest to the camera lens.

No exposure compensation is necessary when the lens or lenses are added.

When a particular diopter lens is called for, Table 19–2 will provide a rough rule of thumb as to the distances a camera can be set from the subject and maintain focus. Conversely, if the camera must remain in one position, the table indicates which supplementary lens will provide the focus desired.

Once focus is within the diopter range, a slight focus adjustment or movement of the camera will determine the exact measurement.

Glossary

BNC: (Camera). A Blimped Newsreel Camera.

BNC: (Electronics). A Bayonet Neil-Councilman plug.

Boom: An extension piece used to support a matte box or, on some cameras, to support a lens from above the turret.

Buckle-trip: A spring-actuated circuit breaker that cuts power to the camera.

Cam: (Camera. (See *eccentric*)

Cam: (Viewfinder). A flat metal piece used to guide a roller so that the viewfinder parallax always coincides with the focus of the camera lens.

Cannon plug: A tubular-shaped, multiple-contact connector, fitted with a guide-key to ensure correct mating of contacts, and equipped with either a spring-lock on the receptacle or a threaded nut and collar on the plug shaft to hold the plug securely to the receptacle.

CCD: Charged Coupling Device. A silicon chip etched with circuitry and coated with photoconductive material that converts light into electrons.

Connector: A coupling device, consisting of a plug and a receptacle, that provides an electrical junction between two cables, or between a cable and a camera, etc. (See also *plug* and *receptacle*.)

Cradle: A device used to support the weight of a heavy lens and to relieve the turret of that extra weight.

Dog: A gripping device consisting of a rod or bar attached to the magazine lid lock or door lock. When the magazine lid (or door) lock is turned to *close*, the "fang" at the end of the rod or bar engages the lug of the magazine or camera body and secures it to the larger unit. (See also *lug*.)

Eccentric: A mechanical device consisting of a disc having its axis of revolution located elsewhere than at the geometrical center, which, when rotated causes an attached registration pin and/or pulldown claw to obtain a reciprocating motion from a circular one.

Flange: A projecting rim, or rib, which gives a unit additional strength.

Gib: A wedge-shaped piece of metal that holds the camera box to the base, yet permits the camera to slide laterally.

Governor: An attachment for controlling a motor so that it runs at a constant rate of speed.

Handgrip: An integral piece of the equipment grasped by the hand when carrying or filming with a unit.

Hex-head: A screw or bolt with a hexagonal (six-sided) head.

Holddown: A screw that secures in place any integral part of the camera that may have to be frequently removed (such as a magazine, which is secured to a camera by a holddown screw). As opposed to *lockdown* screw (although the terms are used interchangeably).

Housing: An enclosure on a camera or part thereof, which soundproofs, or protects the user from, the moving parts.

Intermittent movement: The assembly consisting of the cams, gears, pins, claws, and shutter, which work in concert to control the movement of film.

Jack: A female socket into which a plug is inserted. As opposed to a *receptacle*, a jack usually accepts a single pin and is DC, while a receptacle is usually multipin and AC. (See also *receptacle*.)

Knurled: Covered with small rough protuberances, to facilitate a better grip by the fingers (as opposed to *milled*).

LEMO: A particular type of plug manufactured by LEMO, Inc.

Lockdown: A screw that secures an integral part of the camera is not frequently moved. As opposed to *holddown*, although the terms are used interchangeably.

Locknut: A secondary nut used with a primary nut on a screw or bolt, to prevent the primary nut from turning.

Locating pin: A short rod or stud projecting from an accessory, which, when aligned with the camera pilot holes places the accessory in the proper position for mounting. As opposed to *positioning stud*, although the terms are interchangeable.

Lug: A short flange that engages a dog "fang," to secure a magazine lid or camera door.

Milled: Even ridges or corrugations on the edge of a screw head (as opposed to *knurled*).

Phenolic gear: A toothed wheel molded of plastic with a phenol resin base. It is of high mechanical strength and high electrical resistance and water and acid resistant.

Phillips head: A screw head with a cross ("×") slot; requires a special screwdriver.

Pilot hole: An opening that accepts a locating pin or positioning stud.

Plug: The movable half of a connector that is attached to a cable and is inserted into a receptacle.

Polarity: The correct negative and/or positive terminal of two opposing directions of current flow.

Positioning stud: A short rod fixed in and projecting from a camera (as opposed to a *locating pin*, which is on an accessory). Used as an assist in the alignment of another piece of equipment being mounted.

Rack: A bar with teeth on one edge, positioned on the bottom of the camera box. The teeth engage a gear in the camera base. When the gear is rotated (by a rackover handle) the camera box moves to one side.

Receptacle: The stationary half of a multipin connector, which is mounted on a camera (or powerpack). (See also *jack*, for comparison.)

Registration pin: A shaft that holds a film frame in position behind the aperture as the frame is being exposed.

Rheostat: A variable resistor.

Ring: A hoop of metal.

Rocker switch: A type of switch that is pivoted in the middle so that is "rocks" when turned to "ON" or "OFF" position.

Scribed: Etched (usually in glass).

Snug fit: The closest fit that can be assembled by the fingers.

Spindle: A slender rod on which a core holder or a wheel turns.

Swivel: A pin and collar, which permits circular motion of a component (e.g., the turret).

Tapped holes: A hole that has internal screw threads.

Toe: The pointed extremity of a magazine.

Toggle switch: A type of switch having a small projecting lever.

Travel: The restricted distance and/or course that a part can be moved.

Tuchel connector: A miniature connector in which the plug half is fitted with : sleeve that acts as a coupling nut to secure the plug to the receptacle.

Vernier: A small auxiliary focusing knob used with a larger focus knob, to obtai fine adjustment.

CPSIA information can be obtained at www.ICGtesting.com
Printed in the USA
BVOW021034160812

297838BV00006B/1/P